ADEA | THE VOICE OF DENTAL EDUCATION

OFFICIAL GUIDE TO
Dental Schools

2015–2016

For Students Entering Fall 2016 or Fall 2017

American Dental Education Association

655 K Street, NW, Suite 800
Washington, DC 20001

Phone: 202-289-7201
Fax: 202-289-7204

publications@adea.org
adea.org

ADEA | THE VOICE OF DENTAL EDUCATION

Disclaimer
ADEA has made every effort to ensure that the information in this publication is correct, but makes no warranty, either express or implied, of its accuracy or completeness. ADEA intends the reader to use this publication as a guide only and does not intend that the reader rely on the information herein as a basis for advice for personal or financial decisions. The school-specific information was supplied to ADEA by each dental school in the summer and fall of 2014; however, ADEA reminds the reader that authoritative, up-to-date information about a school's admissions policies and practices is issued directly by the school itself.

Managing Editor: Nancy Lang
Contributor: Paul Garrard

Photo Credits:
The following photos are used with permission:

Cover.	Herman Ostrow School of Dentistry of the University of Southern California—photography by Phil Channing.
Page 3.	Fourth-year East Carolina University dental student Sheena Neil.
Page 6.	Fourth-year dental student Jessica Baron.
Page 10.	Fourth-year dental student Charlene Brown.
Page 18.	Fourth-year dental student Braxton M. Henderson.
Page 21	Fourth-year dental student William Allan Jacobson.
Page 22.	Fourth-year dental student Derrick C. Nelson.
Page 56.	Second-year dental student Julissa Guerra Percolla.
Page 59.	Second-year dental student Erica Recker.
Page 62.	Second-year dental student Gilbert Tapia.
Page 64.	Fourth-year dental student Andrew Welles.
Page 83.	Fourth-year East Carolina University dental student Alex Crisp.

To the Readers of This Book,

As you explore the pages of the *ADEA Official Guide to Dental Schools*, you will learn more about an exciting and rewarding profession, one that *U.S. News and World Report* ranked number one again in 2015 based on work-life balance, salary and expected employment growth. As a wonderful and key next step to a career in dentistry, a dental education will prove to be a sound investment in the future.

If you are a student considering a career in the dental profession, I share with you my personal experience that the practice of dentistry has stimulated my scientific and intellectual curiosity, and fulfilled my desire to give back to others. As a former dental school faculty member, I can also affirm that dental students' inherent discipline and inquisitiveness can take them far beyond their academic expectations and into new research interests and projects that help improve oral health. I can also assure you that, after graduation, new dentists have many options to consider and can enter into their professional lives with confidence.

If you are advising students interested in the health professions, this resource can be invaluable. Dental school can be a transformative experience and knowing as much as possible about how to get there and what to expect is critical both for you and your advisees. This guide will help you provide reliable information on the many career paths in dentistry, stimulate important questions and help you offer sound advice on financing a dental education. Thank you for making dentistry a viable option for the talented and diverse students who value your guidance.

And finally, **whether you are a student or an advisor**, know that ADEA membership is open—at no charge—to students at U.S. and Canadian dental schools. The ADEA community, over 20,000 strong, offers members enhanced networking opportunities and up-to-date print and electronic resources available nowhere else. I urge you to join ADEA as an entering dental student so that you can take full advantage of all that ADEA has to offer you during and after your formal education.

On behalf of the 76 dental schools we represent in North America, we look forward with enthusiasm to assisting each entering class through the *ADEA Official Guide to Dental Schools* and all of our resources.

I wish you the best!

Richard W. Valachovic, D.M.D., M.P.H.
President and CEO
American Dental Education Association

ORDERS

Orders for this book should be addressed to:
Publications Department
American Dental Education Association
655 K Street, NW, Suite 800
Washington, DC 20001
adea.org
publications@adea.org
202-289-7201

CONTENTS

LIST OF TABLES

INTRODUCTION

Welcome to the *ADEA Official Guide to Dental Schools!* Whether you're seeking specific information about becoming a dentist or just beginning to wonder if dental school might be a career path for you, this book will be of value. And if you're in a position to advise and mentor students considering and preparing for the dental profession, this book will help you give them the information they need.

The *ADEA Official Guide to Dental Schools* is the only authoritative guide to dental education on the market. This comprehensive resource—updated annually—has been edited and published for more than five decades by the American Dental Education Association (ADEA). Indeed, since 1923, ADEA has worked to promote the value and improve the quality of dental education, as well as to expand the role of dentistry among other health professions. The Voice of Dental Education, ADEA is the only national organization dedicated to serving the needs of the dental education community. As such, ADEA is perfectly positioned to provide you with both the most up-to-date information about dental schools in the United States and Canada and the most useful insights into how to prepare for, apply to, and finance your dental education.

The *ADEA Official Guide to Dental Schools* has two parts:

Part I, BECOMING A DENTIST, contains five chapters that will familiarize you with the dental profession and guide you through all the steps toward becoming a dental student.

Chapter 1, Exploring a World of Opportunities, explains the wide range of careers in dentistry.

Chapter 2, Applying to Dental School, describes the academic preparation generally necessary for admission to dental school and prepares you for the application process.

Chapter 3, Deciding Where to Apply, defines important factors to help you decide which schools are the best match for your educational, professional and personal goals.

Chapter 4, Financing a Dental Education, is an in-depth look at financing options for dental school.

Chapter 5, Getting More Information, lists additional resources about topics covered in the previous chapters.

Part I also contains tables of information about dental schools and dental students across a wide range of categories. These data were collected from ADEA, the American Dental Association (ADA) and the dental schools.

Part II, LEARNING ABOUT DENTAL SCHOOLS, introduces each of the U.S. and Canadian dental schools. The information on each school is designed to help you decide which will best suit your academic and personal needs.

The entry for each school includes the following:

- General information

- Admissions requirements

- Application and selection factors

- A timetable for submitting application materials

- Degrees granted and characteristics of the dental program

- Estimated costs

- Information about financial aid

- Special programs and services

- Websites, addresses, and telephone numbers for further information

The *ADEA Official Guide to Dental Schools* gives you everything you need to increase the likelihood of success in planning for and entering both dental school and the dental profession.

We wish you well!

PART I

BECOMING A DENTIST

CHAPTER 1
EXPLORING A WORLD OF OPPORTUNITIES

A career in dentistry attracts students who are:

- Motivated, scientifically curious, ambitious and socially conscious.
- Interested in doing work that makes a difference.
- From diverse cultures and backgrounds.
- Interested in serving diverse communities.

Perhaps this Dr. Seuss quote explains why dentistry is considered one of the top careers to pursue:

"Teeth are always in style."

Indeed, because teeth never go out of style, dentistry remains a dynamic and vital health profession, and the demand for dental care will continue to grow in the future. In addition to enjoying job satisfaction, stability and security, the men and women who pursue dentistry will be financially successful, highly respected members of their communities.

This chapter's four sections, which provide an overview of dentistry, will help students evaluate the possibilities:

- An Introduction to Dentistry outlines dentistry and dentists' responsibilities
- Opportunities in Dentistry illustrates the growing demand for dentists
- Rewards of Practicing Dentistry describes the satisfactions of practicing dentistry
- Career Options surveys dentistry's fields and practice options

> *Dentistry— in all of its forms—serves as a vital link within the health care delivery system.*

AN INTRODUCTION TO DENTISTRY

Readers consulting this book probably already know that dentists do far more than simply "fill teeth." As highly trained health professionals, dentists prevent:

- Tooth decay.
- Periodontal (gum or gum-related) disease.
- Malocclusion (misaligned bite).
- Oral-facial irregularities.

The above problems can cause significant pain, improper chewing or digestion, dry mouth, abnormal speech and altered facial appearance.

Dentists serve additional vital functions:

1. They save lives by detecting oral cancer and systemic conditions (conditions affecting the whole body), the symptoms of which can show up in or around the mouth.

2. They follow the latest developments in cosmetic and aesthetic practices to help their patients feel more comfortable with their appearance.

Dentistry—in all of its forms—serves as a vital link within the health care delivery system, which promotes social and economic change and individual well-being. Members of the dental profession influence health care reform, educate the public and policy makers about the importance of oral health, and ensure that dental care is available to everyone.

Playing an especially critical role, dental faculty influence the entire field and contribute to shaping the profession in the United States and Canada, as well as around the world. They bring new discoveries into the classroom, stimulating students' intellect and helping determine the future of oral health.

OPPORTUNITIES IN DENTISTRY

The combination of the following two trends translates into a growing need for new dentists over the coming decades: (1) Between 2010 and 2014, the U.S. resident population grew by about 10.4 million people; (2) Dentists born during the baby boom and educated in the 1960s and '70s are beginning to retire.

The need for preventive and geriatric dental care, as well as for cosmetic treatments, contributes to the demand for dental care.

Not necessarily interested in being a dentist who treats patients directly?

In addition to clinicians (practicing dentists), the profession of dentistry includes professors, researchers, public health professionals, policy makers and international health workers.

STUDENT PROFILE

JESSICA BARON

CHARLESTON, SC
FOURTH-YEAR DENTAL STUDENT
MEDICAL UNIVERSITY OF SOUTH CAROLINA
JAMES B. EDWARDS COLLEGE OF DENTAL MEDICINE

Why did you choose dentistry as your career path?
I have always known that I wanted to help others but was unsure how or to what extent. Growing up in a health care household (both of my parents are physicians), I was interested in health care but was not interested in medical school. When I was living in Scotland, I was pondering different career paths on my way home from a photography class and walked by the Glasgow School of Dentistry. I thought, "What about dentistry?" I started researching the profession and shadowed some local dentists, and I quickly knew that it was the perfect fit for me. Dentistry allows me to make a difference, and I can apply my public policy background in organized dentistry. Dentistry also serves as the perfect outlet for my artistic and creative side.

What classes, externships or experiences (including clinical) are you involved in now?
I am involved in a plethora of activities. For starters, I am currently enrolled in an elective on orofacial pain, which is utterly fascinating. I am also the president of our student chapter for the Academy of General Dentistry, tasked with planning a multitude of continuing education-style lectures. Recently, I arranged for a small group of students to visit a local dentist to learn how to make sports mouth guards. I also spent a summer working at the American Dental Education Association (ADEA) as a legislative liaison. I externed for two weeks with the Indian Health Services in White Earth, MN, and participated in a service trip to Pisac, Peru. All of my experiences have contributed to my education in various ways. It is important to immerse yourself in extracurricular activities.

What are your short- and long-term goals?
My goal as a dentist is to provide the best comprehensive care to my patients. I plan on attending numerous continuing education courses, ranging from the Academy of General Dentistry to courses at a leading institution, such as The Pankey Institute or Kois Center. I also want to give back in a meaningful way through organized dentistry, educational outreach and volunteering my time at a dental school.

As an applicant, how did you prepare for dental school? For example, did you participate in summer programs, shadowing, research or activities to improve your manual dexterity?
I shadowed a wide variety of dentists to gain different perspectives on the profession. It is important to see how different providers practice and constantly ask yourself, "Is this the field for me?" I really wish that I had worked in a dental lab before dental school—it would have made waxing a whole lot easier!

What advice would you like to share with applicants or those considering dental school?
Research, research, research. Talk to dentists (both experienced and recent graduates) and really try to visualize yourself in the profession. It is truly a fantastic career path, but you have to love it or else you will be miserable.

Did you move to a new city to attend dental school? If so, what factors helped you make the transition?
I did not move to a new city to attend school. I have really enjoyed living in my hometown while attending dental school.

Have you taken advantage of scholarships or loans? Do you plan to take advantage of loan repayment programs? What advice would you give applicants about financial aid and dental education financing?
Most dental schools are very expensive. Therefore, choosing which school you attend is an important decision. Even though my school is very expensive, I have been very satisfied with the education that I have received. My professors are truly outstanding and make time to help students one-on-one. When taking out loans to finance your education, it is important to take out only what is necessary. Do not spend frivolously. Remember, $1 you borrow is really $1 + 6.9% interest.

Simply put: We must have more dentists, and because we serve people from all cultures and walks of life, dental schools are strengthening their efforts to recruit and retain highly qualified women and men from diverse backgrounds.

REWARDS OF PRACTICING DENTISTRY

In addition to the job satisfaction resulting from helping patients every day, dentists often provide community consultations and services.

Although incomes vary, on the whole, dentists are well-compensated.

- In 2013, the average take-home salary for an independent private general practitioner who owned all or part of his or her practice was $192,400.
  Source: American Dental Association, Health Policy Institute, 2014 *Survey of Dental Practice*

- During the same period, the average take-home salary for a dental specialist was $302,500.
  Source: American Dental Association, Health Policy Institute, 2014 *Survey of Dental Practice*

Our need and respect for dentists continue to grow as we recognize that optimal oral health contributes to our overall health and well-being.

CAREER OPTIONS

A career in dentistry has two key aspects:

1. The dentist's specialization or field

2. The type of practice he or she works in

Making decisions about these components will help you build a career that suits your professional interests and fits your lifestyle. To help you make decisions about your dental career, this section describes both clinical fields and professional and research opportunities.

Dentistry has many clinical fields. While most dentists active in private practice are general practitioners, others are specialists in one particular field.

■ Clinical Fields

Most of the clinical fields indicated below—except for General Dentistry—require advanced dental education. Keep in mind, however, that a General Practice Residency or an Advanced Education in General Dentistry Residency can expand the general dentist's career options and practice scope.

Table 1-1 lists available advanced dental education programs, their average length and the number of first-year enrollees.

General Dentistry

- Dentists use preventive, diagnostic, surgical and rehabilitative skills to restore patients' damaged or missing tooth structures and to treat diseases of the bone and soft tissue in and around the mouth.

Dental Public Health

- Dental public health professionals help develop policies and programs that affect the community at large.

Practicing Dentists...

- In 2013, across the United States as a whole, there were 191,347 practicing dentists, or about 60 dentists for every 100,000 individuals.

- Considered regionally, the dentist-to-population ratio varies significantly: from roughly 43 to 89 dentists per 100,000 in population.

Source: American Dental Association (ADA), Health Policy Institute analysis of ADA masterfile, 2015

Why consider a dental career?

- Dentistry is a dynamic field offering a variety of professional opportunities.
- Employment of general dentists and specialists is projected to grow 16% through 2022, according to the *Occupational Outlook Handbook*, 2014–15, published by Bureau of Labor Statistics, U.S. Department of Labor.
- General dentistry graduates can typically enter practice directly after completing their four years of dental school.
- The lifestyle of a private practice dentist tends to be predictable and self-determined.
- Dentists enjoy unusual patient loyalty.
- The relationship between oral health and systemic (overall) health has been recognized.
- Dentistry offers a wide range of clinical, research and academic opportunities to recent graduates and practicing dentists at any stage of their careers.

Most of the clinical fields—except for General Dentistry—require advanced dental education. It is important to note, however, that General Practice Residencies and Advanced Education in General Dentistry residencies are available and can expand the general dentist's career options and scope of practice.

■ Students can choose a certificate, a master's (M.P.H.) or a doctoral (D.P.H.) degree program.

Endodontics

■ Endodontists diagnose and treat diseases and injuries affecting dental nerves, pulp (the matter inside the tooth) and tissues that maintain tooth health.

Oral and Maxillofacial Pathology

■ Oral pathologists study and research the causes, processes and effects of diseases with symptoms that affect the mouth and oral cavity. These diseases may also affect other parts of the body.

■ Most oral pathologists provide critical diagnostic and consultative biopsy services to dentists and physicians in the treatment of their patients.

Oral and Maxillofacial Radiology

■ Oral radiologists have experience in radiation physics, biology, safety and hygiene related to taking and interpreting conventional and digital images, Computed Tomography (CT) and Magnetic Resonance Imaging (MRI) scans, and other images of oral-facial structures and disease.

Oral and Maxillofacial Surgery

■ Oral and maxillofacial surgeons provide a broad range of diagnostic services and treatments for diseases, injuries and defects of the neck, head, jaw and associated structures.

■ Some programs offer certificates; others award M.D. degrees within residency programs.

Orthodontics and Dentofacial Orthopedics

■ Orthodontists treat problems related to irregular dental development, missing teeth and other abnormalities.

■ Beyond "straightening teeth," orthodontists establish normal functioning and appearance for their patients.

Pediatric Dentistry

■ Pediatric dentists specialize in treating children from birth to adolescence.

■ They also treat patients with disabilities beyond the age of adolescence.

Periodontics

■ Periodontists diagnose and treat diseases of the gingival tissue and bone supporting the teeth. (Gingival tissue includes the gums, the oral mucous membranes and other tissue that surrounds and supports the teeth.)

Prosthodontics

■ Prosthodontists replace missing natural teeth with fixed or removable appliances, such as dentures, bridges and implants.

TABLE 1-1. ADVANCED DENTAL EDUCATION AND SPECIALTY EDUCATION PROGRAMS

Program Type	No. of Programs	Average Length in Months	First-Year Enrollment
General Dentistry			
General Practice Residencies	185	12	1,070
Advanced Education in General Dentistry	88	13	709
Specialties			
Dental Public Health	13	15	24
Endodontics	56	26	209
Oral and Maxillofacial Pathology	15	36	18
Oral and Maxillofacial Radiology	7	31	18
Oral and Maxillofacial Surgery	101	54	251
Orthodontics and Dentofacial Orthopedics	66	31	369
Pediatric Dentistry	77	24	429
Periodontics	55	35	184
Prosthodontics	47	33	157

Source: American Dental Association, Health Policy Resources Center, 2013–14 *Survey of Advanced Dental Education*

■ Practice Options and Other Professional Opportunities

Depending on your interests and preferred lifestyle, you can choose from among several professional opportunities:

Self-Employment in Private Practice

If you prefer self-employment, you could choose, as do many dentists, between two types of private practice:

1. Sole practitioner

2. Partnered with other dentists

Most practitioners provide care by:

1. Using a fee schedule.

2. Participating in a preferred provider (insurance) plan.

3. Accepting some combination of the above two options.

According to the ADA Health Policy Institute's 2014 *Survey of Dental Practice*, 4.8% of patients treated by owner dentists in private practice in 2013 were covered by government programs.

Salaried Employment

If you are not self-employed, you might want to work for:

■ A private-practice dentist as a salaried employee or associate.

■ A corporation that provides dental care.

■ A managed health care organization, such as an HMO.

Academic Dentistry and Dental Education

You can start your career in private practice and then choose to move into academic dentistry. Each year, the vast majority of new dental faculty—both full- and part-time—enter academic dentistry after time spent in private practice.

Many dental educators say they benefit greatly from the stimulation of working with outstanding colleagues and bright students. They also thrive on a variety of activities:

■ Teaching in classroom, clinical and laboratory settings

■ Caring for patients in a clinic or a faculty practice

■ Designing and conducting research and writing for journals

■ Exploring new technologies and materials

■ Assuming administrative responsibilities

Many dental school faculty members combine their love for teaching and research with private practice.

ADEA has excellent information on careers in academic dentistry at adea.org and at adea.org/godental.

Dental Research

As a dental researcher, you could contribute significantly to improving health care in the United States and abroad. Many researchers are university faculty members. Others work in federal facilities, such as the National Institute of Dental and Craniofacial Research, which is part of the National Institutes of Health. Still others work in the private sector.

> *Self-Employment . . .*
>
> In 2013, 84% of active private-practice dentists owned their own practices, either as sole proprietors (70%) or as partners (14%).
>
> *Source:* American Dental Association, Health Policy Institute, 2014 *Survey of Dental Practice*

> *Take advantage of dental school to learn about the opportunities that are open to dentists who choose careers in dental education.*

As a dental student or practitioner interested in benefiting from a research experience, you could apply for advanced dental fellowships and research opportunities—sponsored by public and private organizations—in a variety of areas.

The American Association for Dental Research, www.aadronline.org, can provide more information.

Service in the Federal Government

If you joined the federal government as a dentist, you could serve in varied capacities or pursue research opportunities as described briefly above. Enlisted dentists serve the oral health needs of military personnel and their families. Dentists in the U.S. Public Health Service care for the underserved, and dentists in the Indian Health Service provide dental care for American Indians and Alaska Natives.

STUDENT PROFILE

CHARLENE BROWN

KENNER, LA
FOURTH-YEAR DENTAL STUDENT
LOUISIANA STATE UNIVERSITY HEALTH NEW ORLEANS
SCHOOL OF DENTISTRY

Why did you choose dentistry as your career path?

As a nontraditional dental student candidate, I chose to leave business management consulting to pursue a career that I found more fulfilling while also allowing me to leverage my business knowledge. Through the culmination of my life experiences, passion for working with my hands and desire to serve others, I have found the perfect harmony in seeking dentistry as a profession. Since leaving corporate America, I haven't looked back.

What classes, externships or experiences (including clinical) are you involved in now?

I am involved in the Leonard J. Chabert Medical Center extraction clinic, Special Olympics Special Smiles dental screening, National Dental Association, Amercian Dental Association Mission of Mercy and Diversity in Dentistry (in Georgia). I also serve as the Making Impressions volunteer group co-lead.

What are your short- and long-term goals?

Upon graduation in May 2015, I plan to relocate to Atlanta, GA, to practice. After completing the Central Regional Dental Testing Service board examination, I intend to pursue a postgraduate program or an opportunity within a public health or private practice, which would enhance my dental skill set. My long-term goal is to continue practicing dentistry in Atlanta and become a cornerstone in Georgia's dental community.

As an applicant, how did you prepare for dental school? For example, did you participate in summer programs, shadowing, research or activities to improve your manual dexterity?

To prepare myself for dental school, I shadowed various dentists at two dental clinics in Atlanta: Good Samaritan Health Center and The Ben Massell Dental Clinic. Through my volunteer experiences at both of these clinics, combined with serving as the vice president of Georgia State University's American Undergraduate Dental Association, I completed over 100 hours of dental-related community service. My time spent volunteering exposed me to terminology, procedures and patient circumstances that prepared me for my current experiences in dental school with my own patients. I also took a Kaplan prep class to prepare for the Dental Admission Test (DAT). I found that the online exams were very helpful in providing a realistic example of the test. "Crack the DAT" online was very useful as well.

What advice would you like to share with applicants or those considering dental school?

I assumed that all of my classmates would be geniuses because everyone talks about how competitive it is to get into the dental program and that only the best of the best are accepted. Most students entering dental school don't realize that people who earned Cs in organic chemistry—as well as people who majored in meteorology or psychology—will be sitting next to them in class. There is a wide array of students in dental school; a science major does not matter and is not required.

Also, a lot of what it means to become a dentist was really one big question mark for me. I had no idea that a dentist did this much. Had I known the depth and complexities of all the technical aspects of dentistry, I might not have pursued it as a career because it seemed so intimidating! Practicing dentists make it all look easy when you're shadowing them. But I'm glad that all of my questions weren't answered prior to starting school because then I might not have this awesome career ahead of me.

Overall, it's going to be overwhelming at first, and you're going to have questions and be unsure about everything. Don't worry. All dental students feel this way! You may come in feeling unprepared, but the professors are invested in your success and take a lot of time to make sure that you're confident and competent by the time you graduate.

Did you move to a new city to attend dental school? If so, what factors helped you make the transition?

Yes. I am originally from New Orleans, LA, and moved back here to attend dental school because I wanted to be close to my father. Having grown up here, New Orleans is home and a place that I am familiar with, so I knew I would feel comfortable enough here to stay for four years. One of the most important factors in selecting a dental school was the city life. Now that I am in my final year of school, I have more free time to enjoy all that New Orleans has to offer, and the city's motto of "Laissez les bon temps rouler" (Let the good times roll!) never lets you down.

Have you taken advantage of scholarships or loans? Do you plan to take advantage of loan repayment programs? What advice would you give applicants about financial aid and dental education financing?

As an out-of-state student, loans were a must for me. I plan to take advantage of a loan repayment program for a couple years after graduation. I think that is a great option for those who can find a position that allows them to do so. My advice for dental education financing is to live within your means while in dental school. Stick to a very strict budget. You will have plenty of opportunities to splurge once you're working in the real world.

Would you like to share whether you are married, partnered or single and if you have any children?

I am single with no children.

Public Health Care Policy

As a dentist/public policy expert, you could work at universities or in government entities, such as the U.S. Department of Health and Human Services and state departments of health. Or, you could choose to work for professional associations, such as the ADA and ADEA, or for elected officials to help develop laws dealing with health care issues.

International Health Care

If you wanted to expand your horizons beyond the United States, you could engage in international health care and serve developing populations. You would work for agencies such as the World Health Organization or for other global public health organizations. The International Federation of Dental Educators and Associations, www.ifdea.org, offers numerous resources for those interested in international oral health.

Final Thoughts

The above list of practice options is not exhaustive: Dentistry's horizons continue to expand. Some dentists work in private practice, alone or with partners, and are self-employed; others are salaried employees in group practices. Dental researchers serve as university faculty members or work for the federal government or private industry. New areas in dental service are being created with opportunities for dental health care providers in practice, industry, government, dental societies, national scientific organizations and educational institutions.

Be sure to check out Chapter 5 of this guide for additional resources.

Life in academia: becoming a faculty member

Would you like to help shape the future of the dental profession and dental education? An academic career would enable you to achieve that goal while offering you these benefits:

- Working in an intellectually stimulating environment with engaged colleagues and bright students.
- Participating in a variety of activities, including:
  —Research and publishing scholarly articles.
  —Teaching in laboratory and classroom settings.
  —Treating patients in school clinics.
  —Assuming administrative responsibilities.
  —Exploring new technologies and materials.
- Discovering professional development opportunities at national and international conferences.
- Taking advantage of employer-sponsored benefits, including retirement.
- Avoiding the additional financial responsibilities of starting and managing a private practice.

And, did you know the following?

- With more than 250 vacant teaching positions (of which nearly 200 are full-time) in 2012–13, dental educators are in demand.
- Federal and state loan forgiveness programs are available for young faculty.
- You can get started as a dental student by talking with professors about academic life, shadowing instructors and looking into additional training and research opportunities.
- Our website, adea.org, provides more information on becoming a faculty member and the future of academic dentistry.

CHAPTER 2
APPLYING TO DENTAL SCHOOL

This chapter is divided into the following four sections:

1. THE DENTAL SCHOOL PROGRAM summarizes the basic curriculum.

2. QUALIFYING FOR DENTAL SCHOOL reviews applicant and enrollee statistics and general admission requirements.

3. THE APPLICATION PROCESS describes the steps needed to apply to dental school.

4. SPECIAL ADMISSIONS TOPICS addresses advanced standing and transferring, combined degree programs and international student admissions.

These sections are designed to guide predental students—whether they are getting ready to apply to dental school or seeking information.

DENTAL SCHOOLS

Dental schools have a three-part goal, which is to graduate students who are:

- Competent in the basic biological and clinical sciences.

- Capable of providing quality dental care to diverse populations.

- Committed to high moral and professional standards in their service to the public.

■ Years One and Two

During their first two years, dental students generally study the biological sciences to learn about the structure and function of the human body and the diseases that affect it. More specifically, students learn about the following:

- Basic sciences, such as human anatomy, physiology, biochemistry, microbiology and pharmacology

- Clinical sciences, such as oral anatomy, oral pathology, and oral histology

The students also learn the basic principles of oral diagnosis and treatment and begin mastering dental treatment procedures by practicing on models of the mouth and teeth. While completing courses in the basic and clinical sciences, they might begin interacting with patients and providing basic dental care. In many schools, first- and second-year students also learn about providing health care to diverse populations.

■ Years Three and Four

The final two years of dental school generally concentrate on clinical study. Broad clinical training instills the competence to prevent, diagnose and treat oral diseases and disorders.

Through treating patients, students learn to:

- Apply basic principles and techniques in

    —Oral diagnosis.

    —Treatment planning.

    —Restorative dentistry.

    —Periodontics.

    —Oral surgery.

    —Orthodontics.

    —Pediatric dentistry.

    —Prosthodontics.

    —Endodontics.

    —Other types of treatment.

- Treat chronically ill, disabled, special needs and geriatric patients, as well as children.

Students also learn about:

- Practice management.

- Working effectively with allied dental personnel, including dental hygienists and dental assistants.

During these two years, supervised by clinical instructors, students may rotate through various clinics to treat patients. They may also acquire additional clinical experience in hospitals and other off-campus, community settings. Through these experiences working with other health professionals and students, they gain an appreciation for team-based health care delivery or interprofessional practice.

Clinical training now emphasizes comprehensive patient care, a training method that permits each student—within his or her existing competence level—to meet patients' needs. Depending on the school, students might also have access to community service opportunities and research activities.

QUALIFYING FOR DENTAL SCHOOL

At least sixty-five U.S. and 10 Canadian dental schools will be accepting applications for the first year of their Doctor of Dental Medicine (D.M.D.) or Doctor of Dental Surgery (D.D.S.) programs in 2015–16. Equivalent degrees, the D.M.D. and D.D.S. are awarded to students upon successful completion of dental school.

■ Applicant and Enrollee Numbers

In fall 2013, 5,769 first-time, first-year students enrolled in D.M.D. and D.D.S. programs in the United States. Of the 12,162 total applicants in 2013, 47.4% enrolled. Women comprised 47.4% of the applicants. Black or African Americans, Hispanic/Latinos, American Indian or Alaska Natives, and Native Hawaiian or Pacific Islanders comprised 13.4% of the applicants and 13% of the enrollees in 2013. Table 2-1 compares the number of dental school applicants to the number enrolled for the 2013–14 academic year.

■ General Admission Requirements

Dental schools consider many factors when deciding which applicants to accept. Using "holistic" application review, admissions committees assess biographical and academic information provided both by applicants and by their undergraduate and graduate schools. Typically, these committees also assess each applicant's Dental Admission Test

The D.M.D. and the D.D.S. are equivalent degrees that are awarded to dental students upon completion of the same types of programs.

(DAT) results, grade point average (GPA), application, secondary information submitted in the application process, letters of evaluation and interviews.

All U.S. dental schools require students to take the DAT. Canadian dental schools, with the exception of McGill University, require students to take the Canadian DAT. Other admission requirements vary from school to school. Differences may exist in the areas of undergraduate courses required, interview policies and state residency requirements. Part II of this guide specifies each school's requirements.

Although most dental schools require a minimum of two years (60 semester hours) or three years (90 semester hours) of undergraduate (also called "predental") education, the majority of students admitted will have earned bachelor's degrees prior to starting dental school. Of all U.S. students entering dental schools in 2013, 97% have completed four or more years of college and 13% have graduate training.

Taking certain science courses is advisable, but applicants do not have to be science majors to be accepted by a dental school and successfully complete the program. Table 2-2 shows that although most dental students were science majors as undergraduates, many majored in nonscience fields.

■ ADEA Admissions Guidelines

As The Voice of Dental Education, the American Dental Education Association (ADEA) has developed guidelines addressing dental school admission. Although adhering to the guidelines is voluntary, member institutions—which include all U.S. and Canadian dental schools—are encouraged to follow these guidelines as they consider and accept applicants to their schools. These are the guidelines:

■ ADEA encourages dental schools to accept students from all walks of life who, on the basis of past and predicted performance, appear qualified to become competent dental professionals.

■ ADEA further encourages dental schools to use, whenever possible as part of the admissions process, a consistently applied assessment of an applicant's nonacademic attributes.

■ ADEA urges dental schools to grant final acceptance only to students who have completed at least two years of postsecondary education and have taken the DAT.

> ## More on holistic review . . .
>
> Holistic review—a flexible, individualized applicant assessment tool—provides admissions committees a balanced means of considering candidates' personal experiences, attributes and academic credentials, along with qualities and characteristics that would prove valuable in both dental school and the oral health profession.
>
> Grounded in each institution's mission, holistic review uses multiple criteria to assess applicant qualifications. These criteria—both traditional and nontraditional—include, among others, the following:
>
> - ■ Traditional criteria: —Standardized test scores and
>   —Grade point average.
> - ■ Nontraditional criteria: —Linguistic or cultural experience (or both),
>   —Demonstrated commitment to community service,
>   —Specific career interests, such as plans to practice in underserved communities and
>   —Life experiences, such as personal, familial or other challenges overcome.

TABLE 2-1. CLASS ENTERING FALL 2013: TOTAL U.S. DENTAL SCHOOL APPLICANTS AND FIRST-YEAR ENROLLEES

Status	Total	M	W	Gender Unknown	Hispanic/ Latino[1]	American Indian or Alaska Native	Asian	Black or African American	Native Hawaiian or Other Pacific Islander	White	Two or More Races	Race/ Ethnicity Unknown	International
Applicants	12,162	6,235	5,770	157	946	36	2,916	635	7	6,022	353	544	703
Enrollees	5,769	3,045	2,660	64	467	10	1,325	268	3	3,034	174	248	240

Source: American Dental Education Association, U.S. Dental School Applicants and Enrollees, 2013 Entering Class
[1]Hispanic/Latino of any race

TABLE 2-2. UNDERGRADUATE MAJORS OF DENTAL SCHOOL APPLICANTS AND ENROLLEES, 2013

Predental Major	Percent of Applicants	Percent of First-Time First-Year Enrollees	Percent Rate of Enrollment
Biological and Biomedical Science	58.9	60.5	48.7
Physical Sciences	5.1	5.0	46.9
Psychology	4.0	4.0	47.0
Health Professions and Related Programs	3.5	2.9	39.0
Dental Support Services and Allied Professions	*0.9*	*0.7*	*40.4*
Dental, Medical or Health Preparatory Programs	*1.3*	*1.3*	*41.9*
Health Professions and Related Programs, Others	*1.3*	*0.9*	*41.1*
Business, Management, Marketing and Related Support Services	2.6	2.8	51.6
Social Sciences	2.4	2.4	48.3
Parks, Recreation, Leisure and Fitness Studies	2.3	2.4	48.4
Engineering and Engineering-Related Fields	1.6	1.9	57.8
Family and Consumer Sciences or Human Sciences	1.3	1.5	51.2
Other	14.8	13.7	43.4

Source: American Dental Education Association (ADEA), U.S. Dental School Applicants and Enrollees, 2013 Entering Class

Note: ADEA follows Classification of Instructional Programs (CIP) to report undergraduate fields of study.

■ ADEA suggests that dental schools encourage applicants to earn baccalaureate degrees before entering dental school.

The recommendation for at least two years of postsecondary education may be waived for students accepted at a dental school under an early selection program. Under these programs, a dental school and an undergraduate institution have a formal, published agreement that gives a student, prior to completing the predental curriculum, guaranteed admission to the dental school. Admission depends upon successful completion of the dental school's entrance requirements and normal application procedures.

■ ADEA recommends that dental schools notify applicants, either orally or in writing, of provisional or final acceptance on or after December 1 of the academic year prior to the academic year of matriculation.

■ ADEA further recommends that:

—Applicants accepted on or after December 1 be given at least 30 days to reply to the offer.

—Applicants accepted on or after February 1 be given a response period of 15 days.

—Applicants accepted on or after May 15 may have the response period lifted.

■ ADEA suggests that applicants consult schools' websites for any updates, as response periods are subject to change.

■ Finally, ADEA recommends that dental schools encourage a close working relationship between their admissions and financial aid staff in order to counsel dental students early and effectively on financial obligations.

THE APPLICATION PROCESS

This section explains how the application process works. Once you have a basic framework, you will find it easier to adapt to these variations.

The application process has three main steps:

1. Taking the DAT or, for Canadian schools, taking the Canadian DAT

2. For U.S. schools and for Dalhousie University Faculty of Dentistry, submitting an online application through the ADEA Associated American Dental Schools Application Service (ADEA AADSAS℠)

3. Acquiring and submitting institution-specific materials

A brief description of each step follows. This section concludes with advice on effectively managing the timing of the application process, which may vary for individual schools. Part II of this guide outlines specific school requirements.

■ Taking the DAT

As mentioned above, all U.S. dental schools—and most Canadian dental schools—require applicants to take the DAT, which is designed to measure general academic ability, comprehension of scientific information and perceptual ability. Although in general, the DAT is one of many candidate-evaluation factors, individual dental schools weigh various parts of the exam differently.

The U.S. DAT, which is conducted by the American Dental Association (ADA), consists of multiple-choice test items in English and takes about four and a half hours to complete. The exam covers natural sciences, perceptual ability, reading comprehension and quantitative reasoning.

For more information about preparing for and taking the U.S. DAT, visit the ADA's Dental Admission Test website: www.ada.org/en/education-careers/dental-admission-test/.

The Canadian Dental Association (l'Association dentaire canadienne) and the Association of Canadian Faculties of Dentistry (l'Association des facultés dentaires du Canada) have developed the Dental Aptitude Test (DAT) for applicants to Canadian dental schools. Most Canadian dental schools require the Canadian DAT, and some accept the U.S. DAT.

For more information, contact the Dental Aptitude Test Program of the Canadian Dental Association (l'Association dentaire canadienne) by email at dat@cda-adc.ca (or, in French, at taed@cda-adc.ca) or visit www.cda-adc.ca.

■ Submitting an ADEA AADSAS Application

ADEA AADSAS (pronounced "add-sass," the acronym for the Associated American Dental Schools Application Service) is a centralized application service—sponsored and administered by ADEA—that enables students to submit only one application to several dental schools.

ADEA AADSAS, which serves as an information clearinghouse only, does not influence any school's evaluation or selection of applicants, nor does ADEA recommend applicants to dental schools or vice versa.

Not sure what to write about in your essay? Consider these ideas:

The ADEA AADSAS application requires a personal essay describing your reasons for pursuing a dental education.

Before starting your essay, consider how admissions committee members might evaluate you.

- Remember that they are seeking motivated, academically prepared, articulate, and socially conscious men and women who are knowledgeable about the profession.
- What can you tell admissions committees about yourself that will make you stand out?

These ideas might help you:

- How did you become interested in studying dentistry? Be honest. If you knew you wanted to be a dentist from the age of six, that's fine, but if you didn't, that's all right, too. Explain how you discovered dentistry as a career possibility and what you have done to research the profession. Show how well-thought-out your career plans are.

- How have you explored your interest in dentistry? Have you observed or worked in dental offices? Talked to practicing dentists? How good is your understanding of general dental practice? How do you envision yourself using your dental degree?
- Describe the ways you have demonstrated your commitment to helping others.
- Include any special talents or leadership skills that could be transferable to the practice of dentistry.
- Relate any special experiences, such as participating in research or internships.
- If you had to work while in school, explain how that experience affected you.
- If you had to overcome hardships or obstacles to get where you are today, indicate how these experiences influenced your motivation for dental education.

Important notes for U.S. DAT takers . . .

✓ DAT candidates should have completed prerequisite courses in biology, general chemistry and organic chemistry.

✓ Most applicants complete two or more years of college before taking the exam.

✓ ADEA strongly encourages applicants to prepare for the DAT by reviewing both the exam's content and basic biology and chemistry (both general and organic) principles, and by taking practice tests.

✓ You can find the DAT Program Guide, the online tutorial, and the application and preparation materials at www.ada.org/en/education-careers/dental-admission-test/.

✓ The ADA suggests that applicants take the DAT well in advance of their intended dental school enrollment and at least one year prior to the date they hope to enter dental school.

A note on DAT scores and timing

See Tables 3-3 and 3-4 in Chapter 3 of this guide for the following:

- An overview of individual schools' DAT requirements
- Mean (average) DAT scores and DAT score ranges for entering class 2014

Individual school profiles in Part II of this guide provide information on most recent and oldest DAT scores that are accepted.

The Application

The ADEA AADSAS application is available online at adea.org. The online ADEA AADSAS application requires students to submit the following information:

- A DENTPIN®, for which students are prompted to register when they create their applications (if they did not obtain one when they took the DAT)

- Biographical information

- Colleges or universities attended, as well as coursework completed and planned prior to enrollment in dental school

- DAT scores—reported electronically to the dental schools that each student selects on his or her DAT application

- Personal statement—an essay in which students present themselves and their reasons for wanting to attend dental school

- Background information—information about personal history, including experiences related to the dental profession; extracurricular, volunteer and community-service experiences; honors, awards and scholarships; work and shadowing; and academic enrichment programs and research experiences

- Dental school designations—the section where students select which dental schools they want to receive their application

- Official transcripts—submission to ADEA AADSAS of an official transcript from each college or university students have attended

Since many schools have a rolling admissions process and begin to admit highly qualified applicants as early as December 1, applicants are encouraged to submit their applications early.

STUDENT PROFILE

BRAXTON M. HENDERSON

MEMPHIS, TN
FOURTH-YEAR DENTAL STUDENT
UNIVERSITY OF PITTSBURGH
SCHOOL OF DENTAL MEDICINE

Why did you choose dentistry as your career path?

Dentistry was actually not my first choice as a career. I was introduced to dentistry in my junior year at the University of Pittsburgh. As a premedical student, I participated in a visit to the university's School of Dental Medicine with a premedical student organization that I was a member of. During my visit, I was able to take a different look at dentistry. We were given the opportunity to make impressions of each other's teeth, as well as perform cavity preparations on plastic teeth. At that time, I was known as the campus barber, and, given my experience in barbering, I took a particular interest in the artistic detail of dentistry. After shadowing several dentists, I realized that dentistry was a career I wanted to pursue. I realized that dentistry, like barbering, would give me the opportunity to make people look and feel good.

What classes, externships or experiences (including clinical) are you involved in now?

In my last year of dental school, my focus has been on immersing myself within the field of dental anesthesiology. Last summer, I was fortunate to extern with three different programs: University of Pittsburgh, Ohio State University and Stony Brook University. I am also currently enrolled in the dental anesthesiology clinical selective course, which provides me the opportunity to get great hands-on and educational experience.

What are your short- and long-term goals?

My short-term goals are to matriculate into a dental anesthesiology residency program and be successful on all of my dental licensure exams. One of my long-term goals is to establish a dental anesthesiology program or develop a dental anesthesiology component within an oral and maxillofacial surgery and/or pediatric dentistry department at a historically Black dental school, such as Meharry Medical College School of Dentistry or Howard University College of Dentistry.

As an applicant, how did you prepare for dental school? For example, did you participate in summer programs, shadowing, research or activities to improve your manual dexterity?

As a premedical student, I was exposed to service and leadership opportunities on campus, which included mentoring, tutoring and participating in student organizations. As a barber, I was very fortunate to have a high level of manual dexterity prior to dental school. When I decided to pursue dental school, I researched a number of programs to determine which would be the best fit for me. In preparation for dental school, I spent countless hours shadowing dentists with careers in various sectors of dentistry, such as academia, private practice and public health dentistry.

What advice would you like to share with applicants or those considering dental school?

One piece of advice that I always like to give prospective applicants is that there is no such thing as a dumb question. Many people are unable to get a behind-the-scenes look into the dental profession and what it entails, and therefore it is paramount to educate yourself about dentistry and dental schools in order to make the best decision for your future.

Did you move to a new city to attend dental school? If so, what factors helped you make the transition?

I attended the University of Pittsburgh for my bachelor's degree, and I had such a good experience at the university and spending time visiting the dental school that I decided to stay.

Have you taken advantage of scholarships or loans? Do you plan to take advantage of loan repayment programs? What advice would you give applicants about financial aid and dental education financing?

I have been fortunate to have the bulk of my tuition covered by scholarships and the remainder covered by federal student loans. I advise applicants to apply to those outside scholarships. Many people think that their chances of obtaining these scholarships are slim, and therefore many people don't end up applying. There are a lot of resources out there, such as military scholarships and loan repayment programs. Definitely do your research and take advantage of all financial support that is available to you.

- Letters of evaluation—ADEA AADSAS accepts and distributes these with each student's application.

Submission Deadlines

Applicants may complete and submit the ADEA AADSAS application any time after it becomes available online in early June. Schools' individual application deadlines are noted in the ADEA AADSAS application and in the profiles in Part II of this guide.

- Because deadlines are subject to change:

—Consult each dental school's website for up-to-date information.

—Check the ADEA AADSAS application deadlines listed for the schools to which you plan to apply.

Since many schools have a rolling admissions process and begin to admit highly qualified applicants as early as December 1, applicants are encouraged to submit their applications early.

Application Fees

Check ADEA AADSAS (at adea.org) for complete information about application fees. All fees must be paid in U.S. currency drawn on a U.S. bank or the U.S. Postal Service. ADEA AADSAS offers a Fee Assistance Program for applicants with demonstrated financial hardship. Look for details on the ADEA AADSAS website.

ADEA AADSAS Schools

Consult Table 2-3 of this guide to see which dental schools use ADEA AADSAS. If you are applying only to schools that do not participate in AADSAS, you should apply directly to those schools. Texas residents applying to Texas dental schools must use the Texas Medical & Dental Schools Application Service, www.tmdsas.com.

> *Looking ahead to the acceptance phase . . .*
>
> Some schools require a background check. If students receive admissions offers from any of these schools, Certiphi® or a similar organization will contact them. They will be required to sign a release for the background check to take place.

Submitting the ADEA AADSAS Application: Words of Advice

Before beginning the application process

- Read all of the ADEA AADSAS instructions before completing the application.
- Meet with a health professions advisor to discuss the ADEA AADSAS application process, including the timing of the application submission.
- Consider the timing of taking the Dental Admissions Test (DAT). Applicants may submit an ADEA AADSAS application before taking the DAT, but they should know that many schools consider an application only after receiving official DAT scores.
- Collect copies of all transcripts and have them available for reference.
- Confirm individuals who will be providing letters of evaluation. The ADEA AADSAS application asks applicants to indicate the names and email addresses of individuals who will be providing these letters.

- Note the opening date of the ADEA AADSAS application cycle, which is in early June each year. Visit the ADEA website for this year's start date.
- Determine if you qualify as a re-applicant. For further information, visit the ADEA AADSAS instructions at adea.org.

While completing the ADEA AADSAS application

- Review the Fee Assistance Program (FAP), which is available for applicants who demonstrate extreme need for financial assistance. It is important to read the FAP policies carefully before completing the ADEA AADSAS application.
- Submit the application early; ADEA AADSAS recommends applying well in advance of any deadlines set by the designated schools.
- Print the Transcript Request Form from the application for each college and university attended. The Transcript Request Form must be attached to the official transcript and mailed by the registrar to ADEA AADSAS. Applications are not pro-

cessed until all official undergraduate transcripts are received.

- Ensure the application, fee payment and official transcripts from every college and university attended are received by ADEA AADSAS. Once these documents are received, it generally takes about four to six weeks to process an application.

After submitting the ADEA AADSAS application

- Check with the designated dental schools (and review their individual entries in this guide) to find out what supplemental materials or fees are required. These materials must be submitted directly to the dental school, not to ADEA AADSAS.
- Monitor the status of the application while it is being processed and after it has been sent to the dental schools.
- Update contact information in the application during the application process, even after the application has been sent to the designated dental schools.

International dental school graduates (i.e., graduates of non-ADA accredited dental schools) may be eligible for admission into advanced placement programs offered by many dental schools. International dental graduates may want to refer to the ADEA Centralized Application for Advanced Placement for International Dentists (ADEA CAAPID), located on the ADEA website (adea.org) for more information.

■ Acquiring and Submitting Institution-Specific Materials

Each school has its own policy regarding a supplemental application fee and additional application materials, which may include the following:

- A completed institution-specific supplemental (secondary) application form

- Official academic transcripts

TABLE 2-3. DENTAL SCHOOLS PARTICIPATING IN ADEA AADSAS (AS OF JANUARY 1, 2015)

State	School
Alabama	University of Alabama at Birmingham School of Dentistry
Arizona	Arizona School of Dentistry & Oral Health
	Midwestern University College of Dental Medicine-Arizona
California	Loma Linda University School of Dentistry
	Herman Ostrow School of Dentistry of the University of Southern California
	University of California, Los Angeles, School of Dentistry
	University of California, San Francisco, School of Dentistry
	University of the Pacific, Arthur A. Dugoni School of Dentistry
	Western University of Health Sciences College of Dental Medicine
Colorado	The University of Colorado School of Dental Medicine
Connecticut	University of Connecticut School of Dental Medicine
District of Columbia	Howard University College of Dentistry
Florida	Lake Erie College of Osteopathic Medicine School of Dental Medicine
	Nova Southeastern University College of Dental Medicine
	University of Florida College of Dentistry
Georgia	Georgia Regents University College of Dental Medicine
Illinois	Midwestern University College of Dental Medicine-Illinois
	Southern Illinois University School of Dental Medicine
	University of Illinois at Chicago College of Dentistry
Indiana	Indiana University School of Dentistry
Iowa	The University of Iowa College of Dentistry & Dental Clinics
Kentucky	University of Kentucky College of Dentistry
	University of Louisville School of Dentistry
Louisiana	Louisiana State University Health New Orleans School of Dentistry
Maine	University of New England College of Dental Medicine
Maryland	University of Maryland School of Dentistry
Massachusetts	Boston University Henry M. Goldman School of Dental Medicine
	Harvard School of Dental Medicine
	Tufts University School of Dental Medicine
Michigan	University of Detroit Mercy School of Dentistry
	University of Michigan School of Dentistry
Minnesota	University of Minnesota School of Dentistry
Mississippi	University of Mississippi Medical Center School of Dentistry
Missouri	Missouri School of Dentistry & Oral Health
	University of Missouri - Kansas City School of Dentistry
Nebraska	Creighton University School of Dentistry
	University of Nebraska Medical Center College of Dentistry
Nevada	University of Nevada, Las Vegas, School of Dental Medicine
New Jersey	Rutgers, The State University of New Jersey, School of Dental Medicine
New York	Columbia University College of Dental Medicine
	New York University College of Dentistry
	Stony Brook University School of Dental Medicine
	Touro College of Dental Medicine at New York Medical College (pending as of this guide's publication date)
	University at Buffalo School of Dental Medicine
North Carolina	East Carolina University School of Dental Medicine
	University of North Carolina at Chapel Hill School of Dentistry
Ohio	Case Western Reserve University School of Dental Medicine
	The Ohio State University College of Dentistry
Oklahoma	University of Oklahoma College of Dentistry
Oregon	Oregon Health & Science University School of Dentistry
Pennsylvania	The Maurice H. Kornberg School of Dentistry, Temple University
	University of Pennsylvania School of Dental Medicine
	University of Pittsburgh School of Dental Medicine
Puerto Rico	University of Puerto Rico School of Dental Medicine
South Carolina	Medical University of South Carolina James B. Edwards College of Dental Medicine
Tennessee	Meharry Medical College School of Dentistry
	University of Tennessee Health Science Center College of Dentistry
Texas	Texas A&M University Baylor College of Dentistry
	University of Texas Health Science Center at San Antonio School of Dentistry
	The University of Texas School of Dentistry at Houston
Utah	Roseman University of Health Sciences College of Dental Medicine – South Jordan, Utah
	University of Utah School of Dentistry
Virginia	Virginia Commonwealth University School of Dentistry
Washington	University of Washington School of Dentistry
West Virginia	West Virginia University School of Dentistry
Wisconsin	Marquette University School of Dentistry
Nova Scotia	Dalhousie University Faculty of Dentistry

Visit portal.aadsasweb.org for an up-to-date list of ADEA AADSAS participating dental schools.

In addition to this guide's summary (see Part II) of each dental school's application requirements, the ADEA AADSAS application website (portal.aadsasweb.org) includes a chart that identifies participating schools' supplemental requirements. This information is subject to change; always double check dental schools' websites for up-to-date requirements.

After receiving your materials, the dental schools considering you for admission will contact you for a campus visit. This visit likely will include an interview with the admissions committee, a tour of the campus and facilities, meetings with faculty and students, and other activities.

■ Manage the Timing of the Application Process

Do not procrastinate! Most dental schools will fill a large percentage of their 2016 entering classes by December 2015. Even though schools have deadlines ranging from September 2015 to February 2016 for completing all the application requirements, you should not wait until the last minute to take the DAT, submit the ADEA AADSAS application, or complete any required supplemental materials.

Each school profile in Part II includes an admissions timetable for its entering class. Make sure you follow the specific timetables for the schools to which you are applying so that you complete the requirements on time.

When you visit a dental school, remember these two points:

1. The admissions committee is evaluating you as a prospective student.
2. The visit represents your opportunity to assess whether the dental school program and environment are a good fit for you.

STUDENT PROFILE

WILLIAM ALLAN JACOBSON

SAN DIEGO, CA
FOURTH-YEAR DENTAL STUDENT
CASE WESTERN RESERVE UNIVERSITY
SCHOOL OF DENTAL MEDICINE

Why did you choose dentistry as your career path?

My interest in becoming a dentist started when I had traditional braces in middle school. I had a good relationship with my orthodontist and saw that he was very happy with his career choice. Various aspects of the field interested me, such as being able to work with my hands, esthetics, the social aspect of working with patients and helping others as a health care provider. The idea of developing a skill was also very important to me—a concept passed on to me by my wise parents.

What classes, externships or experiences (including clinical) are you involved in now?

Currently, I am taking two elective courses, Invisalign and computer-aided design/computer-aided manufacturing (CAD/CAM), both offered at our school! During junior and senior year, we have didactic classes in the morning (8–10 a.m.) and clinic until the end of the day (5 p.m.). I also completed a Master of Public Health (M.P.H.) program in one year (between my second and third years of dental school) through the dual-degree M.P.H./D.M.D. program offered here at Case Western Reserve University.

What are your short- and long-term goals?

My short-term goal is to complete a one-year residency to gain more clinical training in dentistry. My long-term goals are to become a more competent clinician by continuing to learn every day from every experience and to one day become a preceptor to teach dental students.

As an applicant, how did you prepare for dental school? For example, did you participate in summer programs, shadowing, research or activities to improve your manual dexterity?

As an undergraduate, I made a timeline of the steps that I believed were necessary to help me get from undergrad to dental school. This included planning how I would complete the prerequisites, preparing for the Dental Admission Test, shadowing dentists, the application process, etc.

As a fine arts major, I spent many hours in the art studio drawing, painting and sculpting, which helped me develop my manual dexterity. I also spent part of my summer break shadowing local dentists. I shadowed a general dentist as well as various specialists, such as an orthodontist, to get a better idea of the many facets of dentistry.

What advice would you like to share with applicants or those considering dental school?

Make sure dentistry is truly the career you see yourself in. Dentistry can be very rewarding, but it takes a lot of work to become a dentist, along with humility and an open attitude of wanting to be a lifelong learner and learning from every experience.

Drive, discipline and determination are important, along with organizational skills. Do not burn yourself out on the road toward getting into dental school because the race does not end there. Dental school is very demanding, and so are the prerequisites, but do not be discouraged.

Did you move to a new city to attend dental school? If so, what factors helped you make the transition?

Yes, I moved from Southern California to Cleveland, OH—new city, new state. The people make the place. Being open to new friendships helped my transition. Our school offers problem-based learning, so working with my classmates in small groups really facilitated communication among all my classmates, and friendships flourished from there!

Have you taken advantage of scholarships or loans? Do you plan to take advantage of loan repayment programs? What advice would you give applicants about financial aid and dental education financing?

Yes, my M.P.H., which I completed through my school's M.P.H./D.M.D. dual-degree program, was funded by a scholarship through the Health Resources and Services Administration. Dental school is expensive, and it is typical to take out loans for dental education. However, it is an investment. Talking to your financial aid advisor in dental school can help you come up with a plan to pay back your loans.

SPECIAL ADMISSIONS TOPICS

This section briefly addresses advanced standing and transferring, combined degree programs and international student admission. Part II of this guide provides some additional information, but you should contact the dental schools you are considering for more details.

■ Advanced Standing and Transfers

Students with advanced standing are exempted from certain courses or are accepted as second- or third-year students.

- Students who receive advanced standing at the time of admission have mastered some of the dental school curriculum due to previous training.

  —Someone with a Ph.D. in a basic science, such as physiology, for example, may be exempted from taking that course.

- Some schools grant advanced standing to transfer students from other U.S. or Canadian dental schools or to graduates from international dental schools.

Part II will provide information on each dental school's policy on advanced standing and transfer students.

Take into consideration that...

Most students do not obtain advanced standing, and very few students transfer from one school to another.

STUDENT PROFILE

DERRICK C. NELSON

PHILLIPSBURG, NJ
FOURTH-YEAR DENTAL STUDENT
LOMA LINDA UNIVERSITY SCHOOL OF DENTISTRY

Why did you choose dentistry as your career path?

At age 16, I became a Christian, and I knew I wanted to live a life where I could be a part of the health care profession and serve those in need, both locally and internationally. Dentistry offers many opportunities for providers to reach out to their communities. Also, dentistry is a field where your impact on a patient can be simultaneously immediate and long-term.

What classes, externships or experiences (including clinical) are you involved in now?

I'm taking a course in advanced removable prosthodontics, which provides an advanced clinical understanding and also reiterates concepts we've learned in previous years. Now that we have a clinical base to build on, these classes are far more enjoyable.

I've also had the opportunity to do a couple of molar root canals and implant crown workups in conjunction with several of our residency programs, as well as delivering the final restorations. I've been blessed to be a part of the orthodontics honors program, and I've also spent several hours with the residents in oral surgery. I've completed an externship in oral surgery and was able to see a variety of procedures, ranging from impacted third molar extractions, biopsies and Botox treatment to dental implant placements.

I've been given the opportunity to present small lectures to second-year students on some of my preprosthetic surgery and removable prosthodontics cases. These lectures have been a major help in my development, as I've learned a lot from my successes and failures!

What are your short- and long-term goals?

My short-term goal is to finish dental school with an increased drive for learning. You can start to feel a little tarnished toward the end, but I've made it my challenge to learn as much as I can over the next couple months. After graduation, I will be working in a low-income clinic.

My long-term goals include returning in four years to become a resident in oral and maxillofacial surgery. I also plan on working relatively close to a dental school so I can help educate and mentor predoctoral students. Outside of dentistry, I aim to author several books, mentor youth in the urban community and travel at least once a year to participate in mission and outreach trips internationally.

As an applicant, how did you prepare for dental school? For example, did you participate in summer programs, shadowing, research or activities to improve your manual dexterity?

In high school, I was exposed to a summer program for minority students that allowed students to visit Loma Linda University (LLU) for three weeks and learn what it truly means to study at this level. Once I attended college, I was privileged enough to have the LLU School of Dentistry visit our institution twice a year. I made sure that every year I met with the Dean of Admissions to go over which areas I needed to improve in order to become a dental student. I also surrounded myself with a good support group that recognized and shared an appreciation for my goals. I also spent numerous hours at a community dental office observing the day-to-day role of a dentist.

As for manual dexterity, I did not do anything in particular to strengthen this area. However, my father is a contractor, so I grew up in the construction field, which helped me in comprehending some of the concepts I've come across in school.

What advice would you like to share with applicants or those considering dental school?

Be proactive. Doing only what is required of you will make you just another applicant, and there are already too many of those. Also, set both short- and long-term goals periodically to keep you focused. And finally, priority is everything: Never sacrifice things like family and faith.

Did you move to a new city to attend dental school? If so, what factors helped you make the transition?

I moved to Southern California from New Jersey. The main adjustment was the environment. The Northeast is very fast-paced, and SoCal is just on a different pace. I really enjoy that I can go to the beach or the mountains whenever I want—or as much as traffic permits.

Have you taken advantage of scholarships or loans? Do you plan to take advantage of loan repayment programs? What advice would you give applicants about financial aid and dental education financing?

I was selected for the National Health Service Corps (NHSC) Scholarship Program. Being selected as an NHSC scholar means that the government program pays my tuition and fees directly to my dental school and gives me a monthly stipend. After I complete dental school, I will work for the NHSC, year-for-year, until the contract is complete. I received a four-year scholarship, so my contract will terminate after four years of work. I will come out of school with no debt because I do not have a loan repayment; the program actually pays my tuition while I'm in school. I highly recommend this option.

Would you like to share whether you are married, partnered or single and if you have any children?

Yes, I am married, and we have one 10-month-old boy. My family is the highlight of my life. My wife has been an amazing support, both in sharing my goals and providing encouragement.

■ Combined Degree Programs

Many dental schools in the United States and Canada offer combined degree programs that enable students to obtain other degrees, such as those noted below, along with their D.D.S. or D.M.D.:

- A baccalaureate degree (B.A. or B.S.)

- A master's degree (M.A., M.S., M.B.A., or M.P.H.)

- A doctoral degree (Ph.D., M.D., or D.O.)

Numerous dental schools have formal **combined baccalaureate and dental degree programs,** which expand career options, especially for those interested in dental education, administration and research.

- Specific agreements between a dental school and its parent institution may shorten the length of training.

- The undergraduate and dental school portions of some combined degree programs take place at the same university, while other combined programs are arranged between a dental school and other undergraduate institutions.

- Sometimes colleges independently grant baccalaureate degrees to students who attended and did not finish their undergraduate education but did successfully complete some of their dental training.

Many dental schools sponsor **combined graduate and dental degree** programs.

- These programs, which usually take six to seven years to complete, are offered at the master's or doctoral level in subjects that include the basic sciences (biology, physiology, chemistry), public policy, medicine and other areas.

See Table 3-6 in Chapter 3 for a list of dental schools with combined degree programs, and for more information, contact the schools directly.

Preparing for Dental School : A Guide for High School and College Students

Maybe you already know that you have a strong interest in dentistry but don't know where to start. It's never too early to begin preparing. Below are a few guidelines to help you plan your coursework and get in touch with mentors and other professionals who can help you along the way.

This guide offers a general timeline for preparation. Many successful dental students have been nonscience majors or pursued other careers before deciding dentistry was right for them. In fact, the guide can be used at any point in your academic or professional career. If you are not completely sure that dentistry is where you want to focus your energy, the guide can help you decide if attending dental school is a commitment you want to make.

FOR HIGH SCHOOL STUDENTS

- Take science and math classes, including chemistry, biology and algebra. If available, take Advanced Placement courses.
- Talk to people in the field. Call local dentists or contact the dental society in your city or town to find people who can help answer your questions. You can locate your local dental society through the American Dental Association (ADA) website at:

  ebusiness.ada.org/mystate.aspx

  Information on the ADA's mentoring program can also be found at:

  www.ada.org/en/education-careers/careers-in-dentistry/be-a-dentist/career-mentoring

- Check out ExploreHealthCareers.org and go to

  explorehealthcareers.org/en/Field/3/Dentistry

  to visit "Dentistry Overiew."

FOR FIRST-YEAR COLLEGE STUDENTS

Fall semester

- Meet with your prehealth advisor and plan coursework.
- If your school doesn't have a prehealth advisor, look into obtaining the latest edition of the *ADEA Official Guide to Dental Schools* to review the admission requirements. Although most schools require a minimum of one year of biology, general and inorganic chemistry, organic chemistry and physics, specific requirements vary from school to school.

Spring semester

- Think about summer volunteer or employment opportunities in dentistry, such as shadowing a dentist or volunteering in a community health clinic.
- Research prehealth enrichment programs at: www.explorehealthcareers.org. Look into the Summer Medical and Dental Education Program for college freshmen and sophomores at http://explorehealthcareers.org/en/careers/programs or at www.smdep.org. Prehealth enrichment programs can help you decide if a career in dentistry is a good fit and help you prepare for the application process.

Summer

- Complete an internship or volunteer program.
- Attend summer school if necessary.

FOR SECOND-YEAR COLLEGE STUDENTS

Fall semester

- Schedule a time to meet with your prehealth advisor.
- Attend prehealth activities.
- Join your school's predental society if one is available.
- Explore community service opportunities through your school (they don't necessarily need to be health-related). If possible, continue activities throughout your undergraduate career.

Spring semester

- Look into paid or volunteer dental-related research opportunities.

Summer

- Complete a summer research or volunteer dental-related program.
- Attend summer school if necessary.
- Prepare for the Dental Admission Test (DAT).

FOR THIRD-YEAR COLLEGE STUDENTS

Fall semester

- Meet with your prehealth advisor to make sure you are on track to complete prerequisite coursework for dental school by the end of your senior year.
- Visit ADEA's website at adea.org to learn about applying to dental schools.
- Place your order for the *ADEA Official Guide to Dental Schools.*
- Research schools.

Spring semester

- Review each dental school's required documents early in the semester.
- Identify individuals to write letters of recommendation.
- Take the DAT during late spring or early summer.
- Prepare to submit the ADEA AADSAS application. Applications become available in early June.
- Schedule a volunteer or paid dental-related activity.

Summer

- Take the DAT if you have not done so already.
- Prepare for school interviews in the fall.
- Budget time and finances appropriately to attend interviews.
- Participate in a volunteer or paid opportunity.
- Attend summer school if necessary.

FOR FOURTH-YEAR COLLEGE STUDENTS

Fall semester

- Meet with your prehealth advisor.
- Attend interviews with schools.
- Notification of acceptances begins December 1.

Spring semester

- Apply for federal financial aid.

Summer

- Relax and get ready for the first semester of dental school!
- Attend school's open houses and/or other events.
- Prepare to relocate if necessary.

■ Admission for International Students

The category "international student" refers to a native of another country who plans to study in the United States or Canada on a student visa. Students who have permanent residency status in the United States or Canada are not considered international students; they have the same rights, responsibilities and options as U.S. and Canadian citizens applying for admission to dental school.

■ International applicants who are not graduates of international dental schools are considered for admission by most U.S. and Canadian dental schools.

—Each dental school has its own policies on admission requirements for international students.

—Most dental schools require international students to complete all the application materials mandated for U.S. citizens and permanent residents.

—Dental schools may ask international students to take the Test of English as a Foreign Language or demonstrate English language proficiency.

—International students should expect to finance the entire cost of their dental education.

■ The ADEA AADSAS application contains details for international applicants.

—Applicants who have completed coursework outside the United States or Canada (except through study abroad) should supply a copy of their transcripts, translated into English, plus a course-by-course evaluation of all transcripts.

■ International Dental Graduates

Graduates of international (non-ADA accredited) dental schools may be eligible for admission into an advanced placement program. These programs enable dentists educated outside the United States and Canada to obtain an accredited degree recognized by state and province licensing officials.

ADEA CAAPID provides an online portal for applicants to submit materials, which are directed to multiple institutions. Look for information about International Dental Graduate programs, their admissions requirements and the application process on adea.org/caapidapp.

CHAPTER 3
DECIDING WHERE TO APPLY

Selecting the dental schools to which you want to apply is a very personal decision. Every applicant is looking for different characteristics in an educational experience. Your individual decision depends on many factors, such as career goals, personal interests, geographical preference and family circumstances. For these reasons, dental school rankings may not reflect your priorities and can be misleading. The education provided by U.S. and Canadian dental schools is of a high quality overall. This chapter offers a framework from which you can tailor a list of potential dental schools to match your interests and needs. The chapter covers fundamental issues that will help you both decide the kind of educational experience you are looking for and begin to identify the schools most likely to offer it.

The general information in Chapter 2 provides a broad introduction to the dental school program. However, dental school variations can be important when you make your decision about where to apply. If you have a commitment to providing community-based care, for example, you may prefer to attend a dental school that offers a public health focus and varied opportunities for gaining experience in community clinics. Similarly, if you are interested in ultimately focusing on oral health research, you may want to look for a dental school with a strong research focus and student research opportunities. Academic dental institutions also offer a range of curriculum options. Some schools offer innovative problem-based curricula, and some organize their curricula along more integrative rather than discipline-based lines, while others follow a more traditional discipline-based, classroom-instruction-followed-by-clinical-training structure. You should therefore consider what type of educational environment makes you feel most comfortable and best prepares you for the kind of career you may choose.

The same approach holds true as you consider dental schools in different areas of the country. You may want to determine whether you are more comfortable in a particular geographical or physical location—a rural versus a big city setting, for example—or if you prefer to attend a school near where you grew up or one in a new area where you may want to remain after graduation. The composition of the student body also varies. Some schools have student bodies made up of individuals from all over the country (and some include students from around the world); some (primarily those affiliated with state universities) give preference to students from their home states; and some have partnership agreements with states that do not have dental schools, allowing students from those states to attend for the in-state tuition fee.

The key is to define your needs and preferences and then identify dental schools that correspond to your selections. To help you do that, here are some questions that can help you think through what you are looking for in a dental school:

Dental School Rankings

Dental school applicants should be aware that there are proprietary publications available that purport to rank dental schools according to the quality of their programs.

The American Dental Education Association (ADEA) and the American Dental Association (ADA) advise applicants to view these rankings with caution. The bases for these rankings are questionable, and even those individuals most knowledgeable about dental education would admit to the difficulty of establishing criteria for, and achieving consensus on, such rankings. The accrediting organization for all U.S. dental schools is the ADA's Commission on Dental Accreditation (CODA). Applicants interested in the current accreditation status of any U.S. dental school should contact CODA at 800-621-8099. All schools have their relative strengths. A dental school ideally suited for one applicant might not be appropriate for another. ADEA and the ADA recommend that applicants investigate on their own the relative merits of the dental schools they wish to attend.

What is the focus of the dental school's training, and does it match my interests and needs?

You might say, for example:

- I want to become a general practitioner, either in my own practice or in a group practice environment.
- My dream is to become a professor, so I'd like opportunities to prepare for an academic career while I'm in dental school. I want to prepare myself for eventual specialty training. I hope to obtain a combined degree.
- I have a strong interest in scientific research regarding oral health.
- I am undecided about the type of dentistry I would like to practice, so I want to be in a school where I have a range of options from which to choose.

What is the structure of the curriculum in terms of what is taught and when?

You might say, for example:

- I would like to start getting hands-on clinical experience as soon as possible.
- I would like the opportunity to participate in research while in dental school.
- I am very interested in externships, especially the opportunity to participate in short-term service programs in other countries.
- I am devoted to helping the underserved. I want to make sure there are plenty of opportunities for community service.
- I plan to return to my home community as a general practitioner, so I want to focus on the training I need for that.
- I learn best in active learning situations. I want to find a curriculum that focuses on that style of education.

What academic resources are available?

You might say, for example:

- I want to gain experience working with the most state-of-the-art technologies in dentistry.
- I am very interested in having easy access to modern clinical facilities and a large number of patients.
- I would like to get as much experience as possible working in a community setting.
- I would like to get as much experience as possible in a hospital setting.
- I want to have the opportunity to earn a Ph.D. as well as a dental degree.

What services are available to students?

You might say, for example:

- I need to feel comfortable seeking academic help if I need it.
- I would like to be active in student government.
- I want to attend a school that provides a supportive atmosphere for women and people of diverse backgrounds.
- I want to attend a school in which the faculty and administration are sensitive to the stresses dental students experience.
- I want to be able to live on campus or to obtain inexpensive housing near campus.

Where is the school located?

You might say, for example:

- My family situation requires me to attend dental school close to home.
- I prefer attending dental school in an urban setting.
- I need to attend a school where I can benefit from in-state tuition.
- I would like to attend a dental school in an area where outdoor recreation is easily available.

Your answers to all these questions—and others that you may think of as well—should help you conduct an initial analysis of the information you can find on individual schools in Part II of this book. You can then expand your research by asking for more information directly from each school that you consider a prospect.

To get you started, the tables in this chapter provide an at-a-glance, cumulative comparison of a number of aspects of the individual dental schools.

Table 3-1 presents the number of applicants and enrollees at each school, broken down by gender, race and ethnicity.

Table 3-2 shows the number of applicants (including the number interviewed and the number accepted) and enrollees at each school, broken down by in-state/in-province and out-of-state/out-of-province categories.

Table 3-3 summarizes specific admissions requirements for each school.

Table 3-4 provides characteristics of the entering class of each school.

Table 3-5 shows the geographic breakdown of each school's entering class.

Table 3-6 provides information on the combined degree programs at each school.

Table 3-7 offers a national perspective on admissions trends.

The tables present the information alphabetically by state, territory and province. Although ADEA has made every effort to ensure that the information in the tables is correct, the Association makes no warranty, either express or implied, of its accuracy or completeness. The school-specific information is supplied annually to ADEA by each dental school.

For more information and detailed admissions requirements for each school, consult the individual school profiles in Part II of this book. **As you determine where you plan to send applications, you should contact those dental schools directly for the most complete information about admission requirements. The telephone numbers, addresses and websites of each school are included in the profiles.**

TABLE 3-1. DENTAL SCHOOL APPLICANTS AND ENROLLEES BY GENDER, RACE AND ETHNICITY—CLASS ENTERING FALL 2014

STATE, TERRITORY OR PROVINCE	DENTAL SCHOOL	APPLICANTS TOTAL	M	W	GENDER UNKNOWN	AMERICAN INDIAN OR ALASKA NATIVE	ASIAN	BLACK OR AFRICAN AMERICAN	HISPANIC OR LATINO	NATIVE HAWAIIAN OR PACIFIC ISLANDER	WHITE	TWO OR MORE RACES	RACE AND ETHNICITY UNKNOWN	ENROLLEES TOTAL	M	W	GENDER UNKNOWN	AMERICAN INDIAN OR ALASKA NATIVE	ASIAN	BLACK OR AFRICAN AMERICAN	HISPANIC OR LATINO	NATIVE HAWAIIAN OR PACIFIC ISLANDER	WHITE	TWO OR MORE RACES	RACE AND ETHNICITY UNKNOWN
ALABAMA	University of Alabama at Birmingham School of Dentistry	764	394	360	10	2	149	37	42	2	484	24	16	60	30	30	0	0	8	5	1	0	45	1	0
ARIZONA	Arizona School of Dentistry & Oral Health	3,263	1,841	1,394	28	13	966	86	240	9	1,606	156	98	76	41	34	1	2	13	1	7	0	50	1	1
ARIZONA	Midwestern University College of Dental Medicine-Arizona	2,872	1,702	1,170	0	9	234	59	58	1	1,417	922	81	140	89	51	0	2	23	2	10	0	91	10	1
CALIFORNIA	Herman Ostrow School of Dentistry of the University of Southern California*	3,329	1,851	1,432	46	5	1,273	72	254	2	1,171	109	89	144	75	69	0	1	58	7	11	2	62	3	0
CALIFORNIA	Loma Linda University School of Dentistry	1,678	1,113	819	34	3	650	60	165	0	782	51	51	93	61	30	2	0	33	6	14	0	23	9	34
CALIFORNIA	University of California, Los Angeles, School of Dentistry	1,711	905	785	21	1	683	43	151	3	597	63	62	87	46	40	1	0	51	1	4	0	25	3	2
CALIFORNIA	University of California, San Francisco, School of Dentistry	1,968	1,005	945	18	3	806	37	152	4	715	56	58	87	35	52	0	0	38	5	7	0	30	4	1
CALIFORNIA	University of the Pacific, Arthur A. Dugoni School of Dentistry	2,787	1,523	1,237	27	7	1,042	46	180	6	1,013	84	73	139	76	61	2	0	56	0	10	1	56	5	5
CALIFORNIA	Western University of Health Sciences College of Dental Medicine	2,699	1,469	1,192	8	3	991	41	205	3	1,037	155	86	69	37	32	0	0	23	0	11	0	26	5	3
COLORADO	The University of Colorado School of Dental Medicine	1,607	895	703	9	9	301	30	126	6	999	51	47	80	45	34	1	0	14	0	7	0	55	1	2
CONNECTICUT	University of Connecticut School of Dental Medicine	1,246	618	614	14	1	345	43	81	0	605	33	57	46	21	25	0	0	3	3	5	0	31	1	2
WASHINGTON, D.C.	Howard University College of Dentistry	2,076	969	1,072	31	4	687	342	204	6	506	66	54	72	29	44	0	0	19	23	6	0	12	5	1
FLORIDA	Lake Erie College of Osteopathic Medicine School of Dental Medicine	3,157	1,618	1,495	44	5	1,069	129	309	3	1,451	95	96	100	59	39	2	1	19	2	7	0	66	1	4
FLORIDA	Nova Southeastern University College of Dental Medicine*	2,901	1,461	1,440	0	5	980	101	311	0	1,460	0	44	120	68	52	0	1	40	2	25	0	51	0	1
FLORIDA	University of Florida College of Dentistry	1,343	637	691	15	0	318	60	214	0	638	43	43	93	34	59	0	0	23	2	18	0	46	2	2
GEORGIA	Georgia Regents University College of Dental Medicine	881	436	443	2	1	223	63	8	0	515	32	39	85	47	38	0	0	10	8	5	0	55	6	1
ILLINOIS	Midwestern University College of Dental Medicine-Illinois	2,938	1,555	1,349	34	4	850	48	144	3	1,253	90	439	130	70	60	0	1	40	0	5	1	80	2	0
ILLINOIS	Southern Illinois University School of Dental Medicine	827	408	406	13	4	227	44	49	1	419	19	23	50	27	23	0	0	7	1	3	0	36	2	1

State	School																							
ILLINOIS	University of Illinois at Chicago College of Dentistry	458	225	233	0	1	133	25	34	0	0	265	0	0	50	26	24	0	15	2	7	0	26	0	0
INDIANA	Indiana University School of Dentistry	1,431	874	686	0	4	401	41	21	38	0	815	0	0	104	62	47	0	4	5	4	0	90	1	0
IOWA	The University of Iowa College of Dentistry & Dental Clinics	930	506	424	0	4	132	36	57	24	22	604	1	0	80	45	35	1	10	2	1	0	66	0	0
KENTUCKY	University of Kentucky College of Dentistry	1,801	947	838	16	5	384	59	113	44	39	1,084	2	0	66	29	37	1	9	3	3	0	45	5	0
KENTUCKY	University of Louisville School of Dentistry	3,116	1,736	1,348	32	9	654	116	184	90	76	1,845	4	1	119	76	42	0	13	3	9	0	89	3	1
LOUISIANA	Louisiana State University Health New Orleans School of Dentistry	659	338	318	3	4	143	39	43	16	12	397	0	1	65	32	33	1	7	3	6	0	45	1	2
MAINE	University of New England College of Dental Medicine	1,228	657	558	13	0	390	23	70	35	39	605	2	0	130	63	67	0	25	21	7	0	66	5	2
MARYLAND	University of Maryland School of Dentistry	2,620	1,315	1,278	27	1	826	135	155	62	110	1,202	2	0	64	33	31	0	6	0	1	0	49	3	4
MASSACHUSETTS	Boston University Henry M. Goldman School of Dental Medicine	4,115	2,061	2,004	50	3	1,358	85	278	107	116	1,657	4	0	101	56	45	0	28	2	8	0	45	4	1
MASSACHUSETTS	Harvard School of Dental Medicine	1,012	513	488	11	1	288	27	65	26	44	421	0	0	35	16	19	0	7	1	7	0	15	3	1
MASSACHUSETTS	Tufts University School of Dental Medicine	3,679	1,921	1,720	38	4	1,358	110	279	117	129	1,654	3	0	195	84	111	0	66	9	19	0	85	8	5
MICHIGAN	University of Detroit Mercy School of Dentistry	1,631	894	717	20	2	467	66	76	30	42	622	1	0	144	78	66	0	28	5	5	0	60	4	2
MICHIGAN	University of Michigan School of Dentistry	1,961	1,042	909	10	3	563	55	99	42	49	984	1	0	108	54	54	0	14	2	6	0	77	1	0
MINNESOTA	University of Minnesota School of Dentistry*	1,184	637	537	10	15	352	34	48	0	0	449	0	1	98	58	40	1	19	1	4	0	68	10	3
MISSISSIPPI	University of Mississippi Medical Center School of Dentistry	119	65	54	0	0	18	11	5	4	4	77	0	0	35	19	16	0	3	4	2	0	24	1	1
MISSOURI	Missouri School of Dentistry & Oral Health	1,029	594	426	9	6	276	33	57	58	41	557	1	0	42	17	25	1	5	0	2	0	31	1	2
MISSOURI	University of Missouri - Kansas City School of Dentistry	859	446	366	10	5	195	21	41	27	20	501	1	1	109	63	45	1	7	1	8	0	87	4	1
NEBRASKA	Creighton University School of Dentistry	2,206	1,283	906	17	11	521	51	123	58	56	1,236	6	0	52	26	26	0	5	9	3	0	35	0	0
NEBRASKA	University of Nebraska Medical Center College of Dentistry	690	369	314	7	2	122	20	45	24	15	414	2	0	48	31	17	0	1	0	1	0	43	2	0
NEVADA	University of Nevada, Las Vegas, School of Dental Medicine	1,977	1,185	768	24	4	674	36	149	70	52	883	4	0	81	49	32	0	33	2	2	0	34	8	1
NEW JERSEY	Rutgers, The State University of New Jersey, School of Dental Medicine	1,842	864	954	24	1	647	72	151	45	90	734	1	0	91	41	50	0	26	9	19	0	32	0	4

(continued)

31

TABLE 3-1. DENTAL SCHOOL APPLICANTS AND ENROLLEES BY GENDER, RACE AND ETHNICITY—CLASS ENTERING FALL 2014 (CONTINUED)

STATE, TERRITORY OR PROVINCE	DENTAL SCHOOL	APPLICANTS TOTAL	M	W	GENDER UNKNOWN	AMERICAN INDIAN OR ALASKA NATIVE	ASIAN	BLACK OR AFRICAN AMERICAN	HISPANIC OR LATINO	NATIVE HAWAIIAN OR PACIFIC ISLANDER	WHITE	TWO OR MORE RACES	RACE AND ETHNICITY UNKNOWN	ENROLLEES TOTAL	M	W	GENDER UNKNOWN	AMERICAN INDIAN OR ALASKA NATIVE	ASIAN	BLACK OR AFRICAN AMERICAN	HISPANIC OR LATINO	NATIVE HAWAIIAN OR PACIFIC ISLANDER	WHITE	TWO OR MORE RACES	RACE AND ETHNICITY UNKNOWN
NEW YORK	Columbia University College of Dental Medicine	2,056	992	1,038	26	2	703	88	154	3	732	52	87	80	44	36	0	0	23	5	5	0	37	3	3
NEW YORK	New York University College of Dentistry	4,595	2,323	2,213	49	4	2,041	150	349	3	1,822	121	139	384	195	189	0	0	183	6	18	0	148	4	25
NEW YORK	Stony Brook University School of Dental Medicine	1,106	505	591	10	2	332	32	79	0	504	28	47	80	43	36	0	0	23	5	5	0	37	3	3
NEW YORK	Touro College of Dental Medicine at New York Medical College	NA	NA	NA	NA	NA	NA	NA	NA	NA	NA	NA	NA	NA	NA	NA	NA	NA	NA	NA	NA	NA	NA	NA	NA
NEW YORK	University at Buffalo School of Dental Medicine	1,760	906	830	24	3	527	36	91	1	724	39	64	42	19	23	0	0	14	2	1	0	22	0	3
NORTH CAROLINA	East Carolina University School of Dental Medicine*	392	212	175	7	2	72	47	19	0	228	7	11	52	26	26	0	0	5	9	3	0	35	0	0
NORTH CAROLINA	University of North Carolina at Chapel Hill School of Dentistry	1,700	853	831	16	9	377	106	99	0	1,007	4	26	90	42	48	0	0	22	1	5	0	50	5	5
OHIO	Case Western Reserve University School of Dental Medicine	2,719	1,484	1,204	31	4	792	67	140	3	1,179	66	79	74	39	35	0	0	17	0	2	0	39	0	2
OHIO	The Ohio State University College of Dentistry	1,003	543	460	0	3	231	23	13	0	621	62	31	110	65	45	0	0	13	6	2	0	77	10	2
OKLAHOMA	University of Oklahoma College of Dentistry	694	397	291	6	11	148	18	36	0	392	36	19	56	33	23	0	3	5	1	3	0	37	5	1
OREGON	Oregon Health & Science University School of Dentistry*	1,235	720	498	17	1	301	20	86	1	688	46	41	75	47	27	1	0	14	0	3	0	55	1	2
PENNSYLVANIA	The Maurice H. Kornberg School of Dentistry, Temple University	3,374	1,762	1,569	43	3	1,103	121	213	6	1,405	97	106	139	78	59	2	0	39	4	8	0	75	3	5
PENNSYLVANIA	University of Pennsylvania School of Dental Medicine	2,233	1,120	1,096	17	4	863	55	128	4	986	54	34	118	52	66	0	1	39	3	5	0	48	5	0
PENNSYLVANIA	University of Pittsburgh School of Dental Medicine*	2,149	1,189	960	0	11	700	46	34	1	982	0	0	80	44	36	0	0	23	2	4	0	54	0	0
PUERTO RICO	University of Puerto Rico School of Dental Medicine*	396	180	207	9	3	75	21	147	0	132	2	16	40	11	29	0	0	0	0	39	0	1	0	0
SOUTH CAROLINA	Medical University of South Carolina James B. Edwards College of Dental Medicine	1,014	509	502	3	4	179	41	69	1	647	30	22	75	31	44	0	1	8	3	3	0	57	1	2
TENNESSEE	Meharry Medical College School of Dentistry*	1,721	817	882	22	7	496	344	169	0	522	56	30	60	26	34	0	0	4	38	9	0	7	0	0
TENNESSEE	University of Tennessee Health Science Center College of Dentistry	1,202	655	534	13	2	258	43	74	1	754	31	25	90	50	40	0	0	12	4	1	0	70	2	1

TEXAS	Texas A&M University Baylor College of Dentistry	1,611	824	787	0	20	495	87	176	0	751	24	53	104	54	50	0	2	18	12	20	0	49	0	3
TEXAS	University of Texas Health Science Center at San Antonio School of Dentistry	1,429	751	673	5	2	425	58	179	2	647	34	38	104	53	51	0	0	20	4	25	0	49	0	6
TEXAS	The University of Texas School of Dentistry at Houston	1,413	725	681	7	14	187	77	168	0	507	23	388	100	46	54	0	0	13	3	24	0	55	2	3
UTAH	Roseman University of Health Sciences College of Dental Medicine – South Jordan, Utah	1,816	1,130	660	26	5	628	25	106	5	803	45	51	82	40	40	2	25	25	0	2	0	47	0	4
UTAH	University of Utah School of Dentistry	690	476	205	9	4	169	5	40	3	407	18	19	23	17	6	0	0	0	0	4	0	18	0	1
VIRGINIA	Virginia Commonwealth University School of Dentistry	2,146	1,122	998	26	2	618	100	120	3	1,060	56	59	95	52	41	2	25	25	0	2	0	56	3	3
WASHINGTON	University of Washington School of Dentistry	1,046	564	473	9	9	359	22	69	3	515	43	26	63	34	29	0	17	17	0	5	0	39	2	0
WEST VIRGINIA	West Virginia University School of Dentistry	1,145	619	516	10	2	271	36	50	2	613	28	31	57	27	30	0	10	10	1	2	0	39	1	1
WISCONSIN	Marquette University School of Dentistry	2,396	1,310	1,058	28	5	538	72	145	6	1,358	54	72	100	49	51	0	13	13	4	7	0	71	3	1
ALBERTA	University of Alberta School of Dentistry	431	216	215	0	NA	NA	NA	NA	NA	NA	NA	431	32	20	12	NA	NA	NA	4	NA	NA	NA	NA	NA
BRITISH COLUMBIA	University of British Columbia Faculty of Dentistry*	NR	NR	NR	NR	NA	NA	NA	NA	NA	NA	NA	NA	NR	NR	NR	NR	NA	NA	NA	NA	NA	NA	NA	NA
MANITOBA	University of Manitoba College of Dentistry	227	106	121	0	NA	NA	NA	NA	NA	NA	NA	NA	29	11	18	0	NA	NA	0	NA	NA	NA	NA	NA
NOVA SCOTIA	Dalhousie University Faculty of Dentistry*	NR	NR	NR	NR	NA	NA	NA	NA	NA	NA	NA	NA	NR	NR	NR	0	NA	NA	0	NA	NA	NA	NA	NA
ONTARIO	University of Toronto Faculty of Dentistry	540	247	293	0	NA	NA	NA	NA	NA	NA	NA	NA	96	42	54	0	NA	NA	0	NA	NA	NA	NA	NA
ONTARIO	Western University Schulich School of Medicine & Dentistry	585	275	310	0	NA	NA	NA	NA	NA	NA	NA	NA	54	31	23	0	NA	NA	0	NA	NA	NA	NA	NA
QUEBEC	McGill University Faculty of Dentistry	413	290	NR	413	NA	NA	NA	NA	NA	NA	NA	NA	38	10	28	0	NA	NA	0	NA	NA	NA	NA	NA
QUEBEC	Université de Montréal Faculté de Médecine Dentaire	762	290	472	0	NA	NA	NA	NA	NA	NA	NA	NA	89	26	63	0	NA	NA	0	NA	NA	NA	NA	NA
QUEBEC	Université Laval Faculté de Médecine Dentaire	631	225	406	0	NA	NA	NA	NA	NA	NA	NA	NA	48	13	35	0	NA	NA	0	NA	NA	NA	NA	NA
SASKATCHEWAN	University of Saskatchewan College of Dentistry	400	181	219	0	NA	NA	NA	NA	NA	NA	NA	NA	29	17	12	0	NA	NA	0	NA	NA	NA	NA	NA

SOURCES: ADEA and dental schools.

NOTES: Information for schools with an asterisk (*) dates from the *2014 ADEA Official Guide to Dental Schools.*

The numbers mentioned above may not match those listed by the individual schools in their profiles (in Part II) because of different reporting procedures. Additionally, separate statistics for international students, while not included on this table, may be reflected in totals.

Separate statistics for international students are included in individual school profiles. Neither the numbers above nor those in the school profiles are intended to provide exact statistics, but rather, a sense of the applicant and enrollee profiles of each school.

NA: Not Applicable

NR: Not Reported

TABLE 3-2. DOMESTIC DENTAL SCHOOL APPLICANTS AND ENROLLEES, IN-STATE OR -PROVINCE VS. OUT-OF-STATE OR -PROVINCE— CLASS ENTERING FALL 2014

| STATE, TERRITORY OR PROVINCE | DENTAL SCHOOL | APPLICANTS | | | | | | ENROLLEES | | | |
| | | IN-STATE OR -PROVINCE | | | OUT-OF-STATE OR -PROVINCE | | | IN-STATE OR -PROVINCE | | OUT-OF-STATE OR -PROVINCE | |
		TOTAL	NUMBER INTERVIEWED	NUMBER ACCEPTED	TOTAL	NUMBER INTERVIEWED	NUMBER ACCEPTED	TOTAL	% OF TOTAL ENROLLEES	TOTAL	% OF TOTAL ENROLLEES
ALABAMA	University of Alabama at Birmingham School of Dentistry	110	66	50	646	63	35	47	78%	13	22%
ARIZONA	Arizona School of Dentistry & Oral Health	163	77	29	3,011	299	98	22	29%	53	70%
ARIZONA	Midwestern University College of Dental Medicine-Arizona	169	72	52	2,612	448	254	37	26%	102	73%
CALIFORNIA	Herman Ostrow School of Dentistry of the University of Southern California*	1,128	316	165	2,201	292	114	89	62%	55	38%
CALIFORNIA	Loma Linda University School of Dentistry*	1,125	166	46	842	245	47	46	49%	47	51%
CALIFORNIA	University of California, Los Angeles, School of Dentistry	934	129	117	669	12	12	78	90%	8	9%
CALIFORNIA	University of California, San Francisco, School of Dentistry	887	162	75	944	87	38	65	75%	20	23%
CALIFORNIA	University of the Pacific, Arthur A. Dugoni School of Dentistry	1,081	188	159	1,370	59	53	110	79%	23	17%
CALIFORNIA	Western University of Health Sciences College of Dental Medicine	1,003	216	NR	1,518	201	NR	35	51%	33	48%
COLORADO	The University of Colorado School of Dental Medicine	126	90	51	1,443	162	29	51	64%	29	36%
CONNECTICUT	University of Connecticut School of Dental Medicine	78	35	25	1,086	128	60	21	46%	24	52%
WASHINGTON, D.C.	Howard University College of Dentistry	4	3	2	1,865	137	117	0	0%	66	90%
FLORIDA	Lake Erie College of Osteopathic Medicine School of Dental Medicine	491	133	82	2,666	453	200	34	34%	66	66%
FLORIDA	Nova Southeastern University College of Dental Medicine*	612	329	67	746	29	53	67	56%	53	44%
FLORIDA	University of Florida College of Dentistry	537	253	87	806	54	6	87	94%	6	7%
GEORGIA	Georgia Regents University College of Dental Medicine	337	167	90	544	53	18	77	91%	8	9%
ILLINOIS	Midwestern University College of Dental Medicine-Illinois	350	109	86	2,481	256	191	48	37%	81	63%
ILLINOIS	Southern Illinois University School of Dental Medicine	357	112	86	429	4	4	48	96%	2	4%
ILLINOIS	University of Illinois at Chicago College of Dentistry	458	138	80	0	0	0	50	100%	0	0%
INDIANA	Indiana University School of Dentistry	201	130	70	1,230	137	34	70	67%	34	33%
IOWA	The University of Iowa College of Dentistry & Dental Clinics	106	73	60	824	151	78	57	71%	23	29%
KENTUCKY	University of Kentucky College of Dentistry	152	93	57	1,578	119	72	37	56%	29	44%
KENTUCKY	University of Louisville School of Dentistry	154	102	65	2,824	332	204	42	35%	76	64%
LOUISIANA	Louisiana State University Health New Orleans School of Dentistry	180	93	58	474	40	15	58	89%	7	11%
MAINE	University of New England College of Dental Medicine	35	34	23	1,129	244	105	15	23%	48	75%
MARYLAND	University of Maryland School of Dentistry	253	152	84	2,240	333	222	70	54%	56	43%
MASSACHUSETTS	Boston University Henry M. Goldman School of Dental Medicine	155	57	61	3,453	160	182	29	29%	59	58%

TABLE 3-2. DOMESTIC DENTAL SCHOOL APPLICANTS AND ENROLLEES, IN-STATE OR -PROVINCE VS. OUT-OF-STATE OR -PROVINCE—
CLASS ENTERING FALL 2014 (CONTINUED)

| STATE, TERRITORY OR PROVINCE | DENTAL SCHOOL | APPLICANTS | | | | | | ENROLLEES | | | |
| | | IN-STATE OR -PROVINCE | | | OUT-OF-STATE OR -PROVINCE | | | IN-STATE OR -PROVINCE | | OUT-OF-STATE OR -PROVINCE | |
		TOTAL	NUMBER INTERVIEWED	NUMBER ACCEPTED	TOTAL	NUMBER INTERVIEWED	NUMBER ACCEPTED	TOTAL	% OF TOTAL ENROLLEES	TOTAL	% OF TOTAL ENROLLEES
MASSACHUSETTS	Harvard School of Dental Medicine	68	2	0	804	108	34	0	0%	34	97%
MASSACHUSETTS	Tufts University School of Dental Medicine	161	72	58	3,493	427	344	49	25%	143	73%
MICHIGAN	University of Detroit Mercy School of Dentistry	357	156	129	965	238	138	72	50%	32	22%
MICHIGAN	University of Michigan School of Dentistry	299	95	75	1,497	226	94	65	60%	43	40%
MINNESOTA	University of Minnesota School of Dentistry*	192	89	62	1,006	212	126	59	60%	39	40%
MISSISSIPPI	University of Mississippi Medical Center School of Dentistry	119	89	35	0	0	0	35	100%	0	0%
MISSOURI	Missouri School of Dentistry & Oral Health	107	28	16	922	86	49	12	29%	30	71%
MISSOURI	University of Missouri - Kansas City School of Dentistry	168	76	58	660	61	48	76	69%	33	30%
NEBRASKA	Creighton University School of Dentistry	66	13	12	1,996	233	139	10	12%	74	88%
NEBRASKA	University of Nebraska Medical Center College of Dentistry	86	56	36	558	49	14	35	73%	12	25%
NEVADA	University of Nevada, Las Vegas, School of Dental Medicine	70	56	43	1,802	290	37	43	53%	37	46%
NEW JERSEY	Rutgers, The State University of New Jersey, School of Dental Medicine	326	155	61	1,415	157	30	61	67%	30	33%
NEW YORK	Columbia University College of Dental Medicine	369	67	37	1,452	190	113	34	43%	42	53%
NEW YORK	New York University College of Dentistry	571	NR	NR	1,670	NR	NR	111	29%	192	50%
NEW YORK	Stony Brook University School of Dental Medicine	453	NR	39	571	NR	3	39	93%	3	7%
NEW YORK	Touro College of Dental Medicine at New York Medical College	NA	NA	NA	NA	NA	NA	NA	NA	NA	NA
NEW YORK	University at Buffalo School of Dental Medicine	488	150	110	1,029	99	52	72	80%	16	18%
NORTH CAROLINA	East Carolina University School of Dental Medicine*	361	249	52	31	1	0	52	100%	0	0%
NORTH CAROLINA	University of North Carolina at Chapel Hill School of Dentistry	345	174	69	1,283	82	24	69	84%	13	16%
OHIO	Case Western Reserve University School of Dental Medicine	174	41	38	2,156	225	208	21	28%	39	53%
OHIO	The Ohio State University College of Dentistry	218	117	100	766	101	63	91	83%	19	17%
OKLAHOMA	University of Oklahoma College of Dentistry	123	86	46	537	74	23	44	79%	11	20%
OREGON	Oregon Health & Science University School of Dentistry	110	58	57	1,218	57	55	52	68%	24	32%
PENNSYLVANIA	The Maurice H. Kornberg School of Dentistry, Temple University	273	132	111	2,781	268	214	61	44%	73	53%
PENNSYLVANIA	University of Pennsylvania School of Dental Medicine	149	34	NR	1,979	219	NR	17	14%	84	71%
PENNSYLVANIA	University of Pittsburgh School of Dental Medicine	199	82	NR	1,692	317	NR	40	50%	40	50%

(continued)

TABLE 3-2. DOMESTIC DENTAL SCHOOL APPLICANTS AND ENROLLEES, IN-STATE OR -PROVINCE VS. OUT-OF-STATE OR -PROVINCE—
CLASS ENTERING FALL 2014 (CONTINUED)

| STATE, TERRITORY OR PROVINCE | DENTAL SCHOOL | APPLICANTS | | | | | | ENROLLEES | | | |
| | | IN-STATE OR -PROVINCE | | | OUT-OF-STATE OR -PROVINCE | | | IN-STATE OR -PROVINCE | | OUT-OF-STATE OR -PROVINCE | |
		TOTAL	NUMBER INTERVIEWED	NUMBER ACCEPTED	TOTAL	NUMBER INTERVIEWED	NUMBER ACCEPTED	TOTAL	% OF TOTAL ENROLLEES	TOTAL	% OF TOTAL ENROLLEES
PUERTO RICO	University of Puerto Rico School of Dental Medicine*	77	58	38	319	9	2	38	95%	2	5%
SOUTH CAROLINA	Medical University of South Carolina James B. Edwards College of Dental Medicine	141	93	50	852	109	36	50	67%	25	33%
TENNESSEE	Meharry Medical College School of Dentistry*	92	24	15	1,629	201	115	9	15%	51	85%
TENNESSEE	University of Tennessee Health Science Center College of Dentistry	163	94	55	1,025	150	113	46	51%	44	49%
TEXAS	Texas A&M University Baylor College of Dentistry	898	210	130	708	30	15	94	90%	10	10%
TEXAS	University of Texas Health Science Center at San Antonio School of Dentistry	883	296	202	502	29	17	NR	NR	NR	NR
TEXAS	The University of Texas School of Dentistry at Houston	902	280	100	462	1	0	100	100%	0	0%
UTAH	Roseman University of Health Sciences College of Dental Medicine – South Jordan, Utah	151	63	42	1,517	370	132	20	24%	58	71%
UTAH	University of Utah School of Dentistry	144	45	21	521	6	2	21	91%	2	9%
VIRGINIA	Virginia Commonwealth University School of Dentistry	325	124	81	1,690	160	130	60	63%	29	30%
WASHINGTON	University of Washington School of Dentistry	254	113	55	792	48	30	49	78%	14	22%
WEST VIRGINIA	West Virginia University School of Dentistry	49	48	29	988	95	61	26	46%	28	49%
WISCONSIN	Marquette University School of Dentistry	187	112	56	2,063	220	102	50	50%	49	49%
ALBERTA	University of Alberta School of Dentistry	271	85	29	155	20	3	29	91%	3	9%
BRITISH COLUMBIA	University of British Columbia Faculty of Dentistry*	261	101	44	130	19	4	44	92%	4	8%
MANITOBA	University of Manitoba College of Dentistry	105	67	28	122	6	1	28	97%	1	3%
NOVA SCOTIA	Dalhousie University Faculty of Dentistry*	114	60	NR	238	30	NR	28	74%	10	26%
ONTARIO	University of Toronto Faculty of Dentistry	428	153	111	110	19	16	86	90%	9	9%
ONTARIO	Western University Schulich School of Medicine & Dentistry	442	167	47	143	22	7	47	87%	7	13%
QUEBEC	McGill University Faculty of Dentistry	144	42	21	223	30	7	31	82%	7	18%
QUEBEC	Université de Montréal Faculté de Médecine Dentaire	711	NR	85	51	NR	5	84	94%	5	6%
QUEBEC	Université Laval Faculté de Médecine Dentaire	600	207	83	26	2	0	48	100%	0	0%
SASKATCHEWAN	University of Saskatchewan College of Dentistry	113	56	21	287	23	8	21	72%	8	28%

SOURCES: ADEA and dental schools

NOTES: Information for schools with an asterisk (*) dates from the *2014 ADEA Official Guide to Dental Schools*. In the 2014 edition, the out-of-state/-province statistics include internationals.

The numbers mentioned above may not match those listed by the individual schools in their profiles (in Part II) because of different reporting procedures. Additionally, separate statistics for international students, while not included on this table, may be reflected in totals. Separate statistics for international students are included in individual school profiles. Neither the numbers above nor those in the school profiles are intended to provide exact statistics, but rather, a sense of the applicant and enrollee profiles of each school.

NA: Not Applicable

NR: Not Reported

TABLE 3-3. ADMISSIONS REQUIREMENTS BY DENTAL SCHOOL

STATE, TERRITORY OR PROVINCE	DENTAL SCHOOL	ACADEMIC AND INTERVIEW REQUIREMENTS					RESIDENCY REQUIREMENTS		
		NUMBER OF YEARS OF PREDENTAL EDUCATION REQUIRED	DAT?	GPA?	INTERVIEW MANDATORY?	DISTINGUISH IN-STATE/-PROV. VS. OUT-OF-STATE/-PROV.?	PREFERENCE GIVEN TO?	ACCEPT INTER-NATIONAL?
ALABAMA	University of Alabama at Birmingham School of Dentistry	Formal minimum 3 years	Mandatory	3.3 or above recommended	Yes	Yes	AL	Yes
ARIZONA	Arizona School of Dentistry & Oral Health	Minimum 3 years	Mandatory	Minimum 2.5; 3.0 or above recommended	Yes	No	None	Yes
ARIZONA	Midwestern University College of Dental Medicine–Arizona	Minimum 3 years; bachelor's degree recommended	Mandatory	3.0 or above recommended	Yes	No	None	Yes
CALIFORNIA	Herman Ostrow School of Dentistry of the University of Southern California	Minimum 2 years	Mandatory	NA	Yes	No	None	Yes
CALIFORNIA	Loma Linda University School of Dentistry	Preference given to those with a B.S./B.A.	Mandatory	Minimum of 2.7; above 3.0 recommended	Yes	No	None	Yes
CALIFORNIA	University of California, Los Angeles, School of Dentistry	Minimum 3 years	Mandatory	NA	Yes	Yes	AK, AZ, CA, HI, MT, NM, ND, WY	Yes
CALIFORNIA	University of California, San Francisco, School of Dentistry	Minimum 3 years	Mandatory	2.7 in science and total GPA (CA residents); 3.0 in science and total GPA (all others)	Yes	No	None	Yes
CALIFORNIA	University of the Pacific, Arthur A. Dugoni School of Dentistry	Minimum 3 years	Mandatory	Assessed	Yes	No	None	Yes
CALIFORNIA	Western University of Health Sciences College of Dental Medicine	Minimum 90 semester hours	Mandatory	Assessed	Yes	No	None	Yes
COLORADO	The University of Colorado School of Dental Medicine	Minimum 3 years; bachelor's degree recommended	Mandatory	NA	Yes	Yes	CO	Yes
CONNECTICUT	University of Connecticut School of Dental Medicine	Minimum 3 years; bachelor's degree preferred	Mandatory	3.0 or above recommended	Yes	Yes	CT	Yes
WASHINGTON, D.C.	Howard University College of Dentistry	4 years	Mandatory	2.8 or above preferred	Yes	No	None	Yes
FLORIDA	Lake Erie College of Osteopathic Medicine School of Dental Medicine	Minimum 3 years; bachelor's degree preferred	Mandatory	3.0 or above recommended	Yes	No	None	No
FLORIDA	Nova Southeastern University College of Dental Medicine*	Minimum 3 years	Mandatory	3.0 or above	Yes	No	None	Yes
FLORIDA	University of Florida College of Dentistry	Minimum 3 years (90 semester hours); bachelor's degree strongly recommended	Mandatory; 15 required in all scored categories	No minimum; 3.2 or above recommended	Yes	Yes	FL	No
GEORGIA	Georgia Regents University College of Dental Medicine	Minimum 90 semester hours; bachelor's degree preferred	Mandatory	Minimum 2.8	Yes	Yes	GA	No
ILLINOIS	Midwestern University College of Dental Medicine-Illinois	Bachelor's degree required	Mandatory	Minimum 2.75 overall and science (BCP)	Yes	No	None	Yes
ILLINOIS	Southern Illinois University School of Dental Medicine	Minimum 3 years; bachelor's degree preferred	Mandatory	3.0 or above recommended	Yes	Yes	IL	No

(continued)

TABLE 3-3. ADMISSIONS REQUIREMENTS BY DENTAL SCHOOL (CONTINUED)

STATE, TERRITORY OR PROVINCE	DENTAL SCHOOL	NUMBER OF YEARS OF PREDENTAL EDUCATION REQUIRED	DAT?	GPA?	INTERVIEW MANDATORY?	DISTINGUISH IN-STATE/-PROV. VS. OUT-OF-STATE/-PROV.?	PREFERENCE GIVEN TO?	ACCEPT INTER-NATIONAL?
ILLINOIS	University of Illinois at Chicago College of Dentistry	Bachelor's degree required	Mandatory	Highly competitive science and cumulative GPAs	Yes	Yes	IL only	No
INDIANA	Indiana University School of Dentistry	Minimum 3 years; bachelor's degree preferred	Mandatory	3.0 or above recommended	Yes	Yes	None	Yes
IOWA	The University of Iowa College of Dentistry & Dental Clinics	Minimum 3 years; bachelor's degree preferred	Mandatory	Minimum 2.5; 3.5 or above recommended.	Yes	Yes	IA	Yes
KENTUCKY	University of Kentucky College of Dentistry	Minimum 4 years; bachelor's degree preferred	Mandatory	No minimum	Yes	Yes	KY	Yes
KENTUCKY	University of Louisville School of Dentistry	Bachelor's degree preferred	Mandatory	3.0 or above recommended	Yes	Yes	KY	Yes
LOUISIANA	Louisiana State University Health New Orleans School of Dentistry	Complete a minimum of 90 hours; bachelor's degree preferred	Mandatory	3.6	Yes	Yes	LA	No
MAINE	University of New England College of Dental Medicine	Minimum 3 years; bachelor's degree preferred	Mandatory	No minimum requirement	Yes	No	ME, NH, VT	Yes
MARYLAND	University of Maryland School of Dentistry	Minimum 3 years; bachelor's degree preferred	Mandatory	3.0 or above recommended	Yes	Yes	MD	Yes
MASSACHUSETTS	Boston University Henry M. Goldman School of Dental Medicine	Bachelor's degree required	Mandatory	3.3 or above recommended	Yes	No	None	Yes
MASSACHUSETTS	Harvard School of Dental Medicine	Prefer 4 years	Mandatory	No minimum: All completed applications are reviewed.	Yes	No	None	Yes
MASSACHUSETTS	Tufts University School of Dental Medicine	Bachelor's degree required	Mandatory; minimum required scores: 16 (AA and TS); 17 (PAT and RC)	Preference given to those with GPA above 3.3	Yes	No	None	No
MICHIGAN	University of Detroit Mercy School of Dentistry	Minimum 2 years; bachelor's degree preferred	Mandatory	3.0 or above recommended; 3.5 or above most competitive	Yes	No	None	Yes
MICHIGAN	University of Michigan School of Dentistry	Prefer 4 years	Mandatory	3.0 or above recommended	Yes	Yes	MI	Yes
MINNESOTA	University of Minnesota School of Dentistry	Prefer 4 years	Mandatory	3.0 preferred	Yes	Yes	NR	Yes
MISSISSIPPI	University of Mississippi Medical Center School of Dentistry	4 years; bachelor's degree preferred	Mandatory	3.0 or above recommended	Yes	Yes	MS	No
MISSOURI	Missouri School of Dentistry & Oral Health	90 semester hours required; bachelor's degree preferred	Mandatory	Minumum 2.5 science and cumulative; 3.0 or above preferred	Yes	No	None	No
MISSOURI	University of Missouri - Kansas City School of Dentistry	Bachelor's degree strongly preferred	Mandatory	3.4 science/math GPA preferred	Yes	Yes	AR, HI, KS, MO, NM (highly qualified applicants from other states welcome to apply)	No
NEBRASKA	Creighton University School of Dentistry	Prefer 4 years	Mandatory	Minimum 3.2	No	No	None	Yes

NEBRASKA	University of Nebraska Medical Center College of Dentistry	Minimum 4 years; bachelor's degree preferred	Mandatory	3.5 or above recommended	Yes	Yes	NE	Yes
NEVADA	University of Nevada, Las Vegas, School of Dental Medicine	Minimum 3 years; bachelor's degree preferred	Mandatory	3.0 or above recommended	Yes	Yes	NV	Yes
NEW JERSEY	Rutgers, The State University of New Jersey, School of Dental Medicine	Minimum 3 years; bachelor's degree preferred	Mandatory	3.0 or above recommended	Yes	Yes	None	Yes
NEW YORK	Columbia University College of Dental Medicine	Bachelor's degree required	Mandatory	3.0 or above recommended	Yes	No	None	Yes
NEW YORK	New York University College of Dentistry	Minimum 3 years/90 semester credits; bachelor's degree preferred	Mandatory	3.2 and above recommended for candidates with bachelor's degrees; 3.5 and above required for applicants with total of 3 years/90 semester credits.	Yes	No	None	Yes
NEW YORK	Stony Brook University School of Dental Medicine	Minimum 3 years; bachelor's degree preferred	Mandatory	3.0 or above recommended	Yes	Yes	NY	Yes
NEW YORK	Touro College of Dental Medicine at New York Medical College	Bachelor's degree required	Mandatory	NR	Yes	No	NY	Yes
NEW YORK	University at Buffalo School of Dental Medicine	Minimum 90 credit hours of undergraduate study at an accredited U.S. or Canadian college or university prior to enrollment	Mandatory	3.0 or above recommended	Yes	Yes	NY	Yes
NORTH CAROLINA	East Carolina University School of Dental Medicine	Bachelor's degree required	Mandatory	Holistic review	Yes	Yes	NC residents only	No
NORTH CAROLINA	University of North Carolina at Chapel Hill School of Dentistry	Minimum 3 years; bachelor's degree preferred	Mandatory	3.2 or above recommended	Yes	Yes	NC	Yes
OHIO	Case Western Reserve University School of Dental Medicine	Minimum 2 years; bachelor's degree preferred	Mandatory	3.0 or above recommended	Yes	No	None	Yes
OHIO	The Ohio State University College of Dentistry	Minimum 3 years (90 semester hours); bachelor's degree preferred	Mandatory	Minimum 3.0	Yes	Yes	OH	Yes
OKLAHOMA	University of Oklahoma College of Dentistry	Minimum 3 years; bachelor's degree preferred	Mandatory	Minumum 2.5	Yes	Yes	OK	Yes
OREGON	Oregon Health & Science University School of Dentistry	Formal minimum 3 years completed at time of application; most students have 4 years; bachelor's degree strongly preferred	Mandatory; 15 required in all scored categories	3.0 or above recommended in both overall and science (BCP)	Yes	Yes	OR	Yes
PENNSYLVANIA	The Maurice H. Kornberg School of Dentistry, Temple University	Minimum 3 years; bachelor's degree preferred	Mandatory	3.0 or above recommended	Yes	Yes	DE, PA	Yes
PENNSYLVANIA	University of Pennsylvania School of Dental Medicine	Formal minimum 3 years; usual minimum 4 years	Mandatory	3.2 or above recommended	Yes	No	None	Yes
PENNSYLVANIA	University of Pittsburgh School of Dental Medicine	Minimum 3 years/90 semester credits	Mandatory	3.2 or above recommended	Yes	No	None	Yes
PUERTO RICO	University of Puerto Rico School of Dental Medicine	90 predental credits or bachelor's degree in science	Mandatory	Minimum 2.5 or above recommended	Yes	Yes	PR	Yes
SOUTH CAROLINA	Medical University of South Carolina James B. Edwards College of Dental Medicine	Bachelor's degree strongly preferred	Mandatory	Minimum 2.8	Yes	Yes	SC	Yes

(continued)

TABLE 3-3. ADMISSIONS REQUIREMENTS BY DENTAL SCHOOL (CONTINUED)

STATE, TERRITORY OR PROVINCE	DENTAL SCHOOL	NUMBER OF YEARS OF PREDENTAL EDUCATION REQUIRED	DAT?	GPA?	INTERVIEW MANDATORY?	DISTINGUISH IN-STATE/-PROV. VS. OUT-OF-STATE/-PROV.?	PREFERENCE GIVEN TO?	ACCEPT INTER-NATIONAL?
TENNESSEE	Meharry Medical College School of Dentistry	Minimum 96 credit hours; bachelor's degree preferred	Mandatory	3.0 or above recommended	Yes	No	None	Yes
TENNESSEE	University of Tennessee Health Science Center College of Dentistry	Minimum 3 years or mandatory 97 credit hours; bachelor's degree preferred (but not required)	Mandatory	3.0 or above recommended	Yes	Yes	TN	No
TEXAS	Texas A&M University Baylor College of Dentistry	Minimum 3 years; bachelor's degree preferred	Mandatory	3.0 or above recommended	Yes	Yes	AR, LA, NM, OK, TX, UT	Yes
TEXAS	University of Texas Health Science Center at San Antonio School of Dentistry	Minimum 3 years; bachelor's degree preferred	Mandatory	Above 3.0 strongly recommended	Yes	Yes	TX	Yes
TEXAS	The University of Texas School of Dentistry at Houston	Minimum 3 years; bachelor's degree preferred	Mandatory	3.0 or above recommended	Yes	Yes	TX	No
UTAH	Roseman University of Health Sciences College of Dental Medicine – South Jordan, Utah	Minimum 60 semester credit hours; bachelor's degree preferred	Mandatory	2.8 cumulative science	Yes	No	None	Yes
UTAH	University of Utah School of Dentistry	Bachelor's degree required	Mandatory	3.3 or above recommended	Yes	Yes	UT	No
VIRGINIA	Virginia Commonwealth University School of Dentistry	Formal minimum 3 years; generally acceptable minimum of 4 years	Mandatory; should be taken no later than Dec. of the year prior to desired matriculation	No specific requirements	Yes	Yes	VA	Yes
WASHINGTON	University of Washington School of Dentistry	Prefer 4 years	Mandatory	3.0 or above recommended	Yes	Yes	WICHE, WA, AK, AR, AZ, HI, MT, ND, NM, WY	No
WEST VIRGINIA	West Virginia University School of Dentistry	Minimum 3 years; applicants must have completed a minimum of 90 semester credit hours at the time of application	Mandatory	3.5 or above recommended	Yes	Yes	WV	Yes
WISCONSIN	Marquette University School of Dentistry	Minimum 3 years; bachelor's degree preferred	Mandatory	No specific requirement; 3.3 or above recommended	Yes	Yes	None	Yes
ALBERTA	University of Alberta School of Dentistry	Minimum 2 years (10 full course requirements)	Canadian DAT mandatory; minimum score 15/30 for RC, PAT, MAN	Minimum 3.0 out of 4.0	Yes	Yes	AB	Yes
BRITISH COLUMBIA	University of British Columbia Faculty of Dentistry	Minimum 3 years	Mandatory; U.S. or Canadian DAT	Minimum 70%	Yes	Yes	90% of class for in-province applicants	No
MANITOBA	University of Manitoba College of Dentistry	Minimum 2 years	Mandatory	2014: In-province 3.6 Core Course and 19 DAT average; out-of-province 3.8 Core Course and 23 DAT average to be considered for an interview	Yes	Yes	MB	No
NOVA SCOTIA	Dalhousie University Faculty of Dentistry	Minimum 2 years	Mandatory	NR	Yes	Yes	Atlantic Provinces	Yes
ONTARIO	Western University Schulich School of Medicine & Dentistry	4-year bachelor's degree required	Mandatory	Minimum 80% in 2 years; equivalent of 3.7	Yes	No	None	Yes

ONTARIO	University of Toronto Faculty of Dentistry*	Minimum 3 years	Mandatory	Minimum 3.0	Yes	Yes	ON	Yes
QUEBEC	McGill University Faculty of Dentistry	Minimum 4 years	Not required	3.5 minimum	Yes	Yes	QC	Yes
QUEBEC	Université de Montréal Faculté de Médecine Dentaire*	4 years preferred; formal minimum 1 year	Yes	NA	No	Yes	QC	Yes, for graduate students only
QUEBEC	Université Laval Faculté de Médecine Dentaire	Minimum 2 years	Mandatory	NR	Yes	Yes	NB, ON, QC	No
SASKATCHEWAN	University of Saskatchewan College of Dentistry	Minimum 2 years predentistry courses	Mandatory: 15% overall weight on Canadian DAT scores (RC [1/3], PAT [1/3], AA [1/3])	65% weight on 2 best years. Minimum acceptable overall 2-year average is 75%.	Yes	Yes	SK	Yes

SOURCES: ADEA and dental schools.
NOTES: *Information for schools with an asterisk (*) dates from the *2014 ADEA Official Guide to Dental Schools*.
NA: Not Applicable
NR: Not Reported
LIST OF COMMON CANADIAN AND U.S. DENTAL TESTING/ADMISSION ABBREVIATIONS
AA = Academic Average
BCP = Biology, Chemistry, Physics
DAT = Dental Admission Test (United States); Dental Aptitude Test (Canada)
GPA = Grade Point Average
MAN = Manual Dexterity
PA or PAT = Perceptual Ability
RC = Reading Comprehension
TS = Total Science

TABLE 3-4. CHARACTERISTICS OF THE CLASS ENTERING FALL 2014 BY DENTAL SCHOOL

STATE, TERRITORY OR PROVINCE	DENTAL SCHOOL	AGE MEAN	AGE RANGE	2 YRS.	3 YRS.	4 YRS.	BACC.	M.S. & ABOVE	MEAN DAT AA	MEAN DAT PAT	MEAN DAT SCI	DAT RANGE AA	DAT RANGE PAT	DAT RANGE SCI	MEAN CUM-LATIVE GPA SCI	MEAN CUM-LATIVE GPA TOTAL	CUMULATIVE GPA RANGE SCI	CUMULATIVE GPA RANGE TOTAL
ALABAMA	University of Alabama at Birmingham School of Dentistry	22	22-37	0	0	0	55	5	21.0	20.4	20.1	18-25	15-25	17-25	3.66	3.71	3.07-4.00	3.21-4.00
ARIZONA	Arizona School of Dentistry & Oral Health	26	21-37	0	0	3	68	5	19.0	20.0	19.0	16-23	15-30	15-23	3.27	3.37	2.59-4.09	2.78-4.11
ARIZONA	Midwestern University College of Dental Medicine-Arizona	25	21-40	0	0	6	107	27	19.8	19.9	19.7	NR	NR	NR	NR	NR	NR	NR
CALIFORNIA	Herman Ostrow School of Dentistry of the University of Southern California*	26	20-48	0	0	0	144	20	20.0	20.0	20.0	15-25	15-27	15-26	3.40	3.50	3.00-4.00	3.00-4.00
CALIFORNIA	Loma Linda University School of Dentistry*	25	21-42	0	0	0	93	0	20.0	21.0	20.0	16-25	17-26	16-27	3.20	3.30	2.40-4.30	2.50-4.30
CALIFORNIA	University of California, Los Angeles, School of Dentistry	24	21-37	0	0	1	85	1	22.3	21.6	22.6	19-27	17-27	19-30	3.71	3.75	3.17-4.00	3.22-4.00
CALIFORNIA	University of California, San Francisco, School of Dentistry	25	21-38	0	0	0	81	6	21.0	20.0	21.0	17-27	15-27	17-30	3.42	3.51	2.62-4.06	2.66-4.07
CALIFORNIA	University of the Pacific, Arthur A. Dugoni School of Dentistry	23	18-37	3	0	1	129	6	21.6	21.4	21.5	NR	NR	NR	3.45	3.50	NR	NR
CALIFORNIA	Western University of Health Sciences College of Dental Medicine	26	21-36	0	1	4	54	10	19.0	20.0	19.0	15-22	17-25	15-23	3.17	3.29	2.40-3.85	2.66-3.85
COLORADO	The University of Colorado School of Dental Medicine	25	20-45	0	0	2	65	12	19.6	19.9	19.6	15-25	15-25	15-26	3.50	3.57	2.37-4.14	2.74-4.08
CONNECTICUT	University of Connecticut School of Dental Medicine	24	21-32	0	0	0	43	3	21.0	20.0	21.0	18-24	16-25	18-26	3.54	3.61	2.94-4.00	3.02-4.00
WASHINGTON, D.C.	Howard University College of Dentistry	27	20-35	0	0	0	61	11	17.9	18.3	17.8	NR	NR	NR	3.11	NR	NR	NR
FLORIDA	Lake Erie College of Osteopathic Medicine School of Dental Medicine	25	22-41	0	0	0	90	10	19.1	19.8	19.3	17-23	15-24	17-23	NR	NR	NR	NR
FLORIDA	Nova Southeastern University College of Dental Medicine*	25	20-36	0	8	0	91	21	20.0	20.0	21.0	18-24	17-27	18-26	3.60	3.70	3.20-4.00	2.40-4.00
FLORIDA	University of Florida College of Dentistry	24	20-37	0	0	0	85	8	20.3	20.0	20.4	17-25	15-29	17-26	3.59	3.66	2.74-4.00	2.82-4.00
GEORGIA	Georgia Regents University College of Dental Medicine	23	21-35	0	0	0	76	9	19.4	20.2	19.2	16-24	15-25	15-23	3.53	3.59	2.95-4.00	2.93-4.00
ILLINOIS	Midwestern University College of Dental Medicine-Illinois	24	21-33	0	0	0	106	24	18.6	19.1	18.3	16-23	16-23	16-24	3.31	3.43	2.79-4.00	2.87-3.90
ILLINOIS	Southern Illinois University School of Dental Medicine	24	21-35	0	2	3	41	4	19.1	19.1	18.8	22-16	27-14	22-14	3.50	3.59	2.78-4.00	2.92-4.00
ILLINOIS	University of Illinois at Chicago College of Dentistry	24	21-33	0	0	0	43	7	20.0	20.0	20.0	16-23	15-25	16-25	3.61	3.68	2.85-4.14	3.01-4.14
INDIANA	Indiana University School of Dentistry	33	22-43	0	1	0	80	23	19.3	19.5	19.0	15-28	14-26	15-28	3.55	3.33	3.20-3.45	3.33-3.56
IOWA	The University of Iowa College of Dentistry & Dental Clinics	22	21-27	0	0	0	80	0	20.0	20.0	20.0	16-25	16-25	15-27	3.68	3.74	2.92-4.13	3.25-4.10
KENTUCKY	University of Kentucky College of Dentistry	21	19-38	0	1	0	58	7	19.0	19.0	18.7	16-23	14-24	16-24	3.46	3.55	2.75-4.00	2.96-4.00
KENTUCKY	University of Louisville School of Dentistry	24	22-35	0	0	2	109	8	19.3	19.4	19.1	16-24	15-25	16-26	3.40	3.50	2.60-4.00	2.80-4.00
LOUISIANA	Louisiana State University Health New Orleans School of Dentistry	23	20-43	0	0	0	60	5	19.8	20.1	19.6	18-27	15-25	17-28	3.56	3.64	2.72-4.00	2.87-4.00
MAINE	University of New England College of Dental Medicine	25	21-38	0	0	1	54	9	18.2	18.6	17.9	16-23	14-23	15-23	3.23	3.33	2.65-3.96	2.81-3.91
MARYLAND	University of Maryland School of Dentistry	24	21-33	0	0	0	112	18	20.6	20.1	20.3	18-27	13-30	17-26	3.49	3.55	2.35-4.16	2.43-4.09

TABLE 3-4. CHARACTERISTICS OF THE CLASS ENTERING FALL 2014 BY DENTAL SCHOOL (CONTINUED)

STATE, TERRITORY OR PROVINCE	DENTAL SCHOOL	AGE		PREDENTAL EDUCATION					MEAN DAT			DAT RANGE			MEAN CUMULATIVE GPA		CUMULATIVE GPA RANGE	
		MEAN	RANGE	2 YRS.	3 YRS.	4 YRS.	BACC.	M.S. & ABOVE	AA	PAT	SCI	AA	PAT	SCI	SCI	TOTAL	SCI	TOTAL
MASSACHUSETTS	Boston University Henry M. Goldman School of Dental Medicine	22	20-28	0	0	0	83	18	19.8	19.5	19.7	17-25	14-25	17-24	3.46	3.51	2.73-4.00	2.95-4.00
MASSACHUSETTS	Harvard School of Dental Medicine	23	21-30	0	0	0	33	2	23.0	21.0	23.0	21-23	17-21	19-28	3.87	3.85	3.35-4.15	3.53-4.14
MASSACHUSETTS	Tufts University School of Dental Medicine	24	21-35	0	0	0	155	40	19.8	20.2	19.7	NR	NR	NR	3.31	3.42	NR	NR
MICHIGAN	University of Detroit Mercy School of Dentistry	24	20-40	0	17	1	114	12	20.4	20.2	20.6	17-26	14-26	17-26	3.60	3.64	2.83-4.20	2.83-4.19
MICHIGAN	University of Michigan School of Denistry	24	20-34	0	3	0	95	10	20.1	20.4	20.1	17-26	16-27	16-26	3.46	3.53	2.57-4.23	2.92-4.21
MINNESOTA	University of Minnesota School of Dentistry*	24	21-34	0	2	4	87	5	20.3	20.5	20.1	NR	NR	NR	3.60	3.60	NR	NR
MISSISSIPPI	University of Mississippi Medical Center School of Dentistry	25	22-38	0	0	0	23	12	18.7	19.6	18.6	17-24	15-25	16-27	NR	NR	NR	NR
MISSOURI	Missouri School of Dentistry & Oral Health	24	21-29	0	0	0	38	4	18.4	19.2	17.8	16-21	13-24	15-22	3.34	3.46	2.74-3.89	3.05-3.86
MISSOURI	University of Missouri - Kansas City School of Dentistry	25	21-40	0	0	0	104	5	19.0	19.6	19.1	16-23	17-25	16-22	3.66	3.62	3.00-4.00	2.60-4.00
NEBRASKA	Creighton University School of Dentistry	24	21-35	0	2	83	77	6	19.1	19.9	18.8	17-24	17-24	17-26	3.44	3.61	3.17-4.00	2.85-4.00
NEBRASKA	University of Nebraska Medical Center College of Dentistry	22	21-28	0	0	1	45	1	20.1	20.8	19.7	17-27	14-30	16-28	3.65	3.74	2.90-4.00	2.90-4.00
NEVADA	University of Nevada, Las Vegas, School of Dental Medicine	26	21-57	0	0	7	72	2	19.9	20.3	20.1	17-24	14-25	18-26	3.37	3.46	2.62-4.00	2.89-4.00
NEW JERSEY	Rutgers, The State University of New Jersey, School of Dental Medicine	23	20-39	0	3	0	76	12	20.0	19.0	20.0	17-25	15-24	16-30	3.50	3.70	2.82 - 4.00	2.80 - 4.00
NEW YORK	Columbia University College of Dental Medicine	23	21-32	0	4	1	69	6	23.0	21.0	23.0	20-27	15-26	18-30	3.62	3.63	2.82-4.00	2.61-4.00
NEW YORK	New York University College of Dentistry	23	19-39	0	28	0	314	41	21.0	20.0	21.0	NR	NR	NR	3.37	3.49	NR	NR
NEW YORK	Stony Brook University School of Dental Medicine	23	21-26	0	0	0	42	0	22.0	20.0	22.0	18-26	15-25	18-26	3.68	3.72	3.18-4.00	3.41-4.00
NEW YORK	Touro College of Dental Medicine at New York Medical College	NA	NA	NA	NA	NA	NA	NA	NA	NA	NA	NA	NA	NA	NA	NA	NA	NA
NEW YORK	University at Buffalo School of Dental Medicine	25	21-36	0	7	0	59	24	20.1	20.9	20.0	16-25	15-26	16-27	3.45	3.52	2.87-4.13	2.87-4.17
NORTH CAROLINA	East Carolina University School of Dental Medicine*	24	20-42	0	0	0	52	4	18.2	18.7	17.9	15-24	14-30	14-29	3.20	3.40	2.30-4.10	2.40-4.10
NORTH CAROLINA	University of North Carolina at Chapel Hill School of Dentistry	24	21-42	0	0	2	76	4	20.4	20.0	19.7	17-27	14-29	16-30	3.49	3.59	2.41-4.18	2.51-4.17
OHIO	Case Western Reserve University School of Dental Medicine	24	20-37	0	6	1	59	8	19.9	20.4	19.9	15-24	14-25	15-23	3.52	3.60	2.28-4.00	2.90-4.00
OHIO	The Ohio State University College of Dentistry	24	21-36	0	1	0	102	7	19.7	20.5	19.2	16-27	16-26	15-26	3.49	3.61	2.49-4.00	2.72-4.00
OKLAHOMA	University of Oklahoma College of Dentistry	24	20-40	0	0	0	52	4	20.0	19.6	19.4	17-23	13-24	17-25	3.59	3.48	2.35-4.00	2.48-4.00
OREGON	Oregon Health & Science University School of Dentistry	25	21-47	0	0	0	72	4	19.7	19.8	20.1	16-25	15-27	17-26	3.57	3.61	3.04-4.00	3.00-4.00
PENNSYLVANIA	The Maurice H. Kornberg School of Dentistry, Temple University	24	21-38	0	2	0	124	13	20.0	20.0	20.0	18-25	14-26	17-27	3.41	3.50	2.65-4.00	2.91-4.00
PENNSYLVANIA	University of Pennsylvania School of Dental Medicine	23	21-34	0	4	0	114	0	21.5	21.0	21.5	18-28	16-30	18-28	3.62	3.67	2.64-4.08	2.68-4.07

(continued)

TABLE 3-4. CHARACTERISTICS OF THE CLASS ENTERING FALL 2014 BY DENTAL SCHOOL (CONTINUED)

STATE, TERRITORY OR PROVINCE	DENTAL SCHOOL	AGE MEAN	AGE RANGE	2 YRS.	3 YRS.	4 YRS.	BACC.	M.S. & ABOVE	AA	PAT	SCI	AA	PAT	SCI	SCI	TOTAL	SCI	TOTAL
				PREDENTAL EDUCATION					MEAN DAT			DAT RANGE			MEAN CUMULATIVE GPA		CUMULATIVE GPA RANGE	
PENNSYLVANIA	University of Pittsburgh School of Dental Medicine	24	21-31	0	0	0	72	6	20.7	20.0	NR	17-24	NR	17-24	3.42	3.65	2.88-4.19	2.99-4.19
PUERTO RICO	University of Puerto Rico School of Dental Medicine*	24	21-23	1	19	0	17	3	17.0	15.0	14.0	15-19	15-20	14-20	3.40	3.50	2.90-3.90	3.40-3.90
SOUTH CAROLINA	Medical University of South Carolina James B. Edwards College of Dental Medicine	24	22-32	0	0	0	71	4	20.0	21.0	NR	16-24	16-26	NR	3.61	3.66	2.77-4.00	3.02-4.00
TENNESSEE	Meharry Medical College School of Dentistry*	24	21-37	0	4	0	48	8	17.0	17.0	17.0	16-22	13-23	15-22	3.10	3.20	2.50-4.00	2.80-4.00
TENNESSEE	University of Tennessee Health Science Center College of Dentistry	25	21-42	0	1	0	83	6	19.3	20.1	18.9	17-24	16-26	16-26	NR	NR	NR	NR
TEXAS	Texas A&M University Baylor College of Dentistry	24	21-37	0	0	0	101	3	20.7	20.2	20.4	NR	NR	NR	NR	NR	NR	NR
TEXAS	University of Texas Health Science Center at San Antonio School of Dentistry	24	21-36	3	0	4	96	1	20.0	19.8	19.7	17-25	14-26	16-26	3.52	3.59	2.69-4.00	2.73-4.00
TEXAS	The University of Texas School of Dentistry at Houston	22	19-46	0	0	1	89	10	19.4	19.6	19.3	16-26	15-24	16-25	3.64	3.68	2.70-4.00	3.05-4.00
UTAH	Roseman University of Health Sciences College of Dental Medicine – South Jordan, Utah	26	21-36	0	4	0	67	11	20.0	21.0	20.0	17-25	17-27	17-26	3.23	3.52	2.61-4.00	2.67-4.00
UTAH	University of Utah School of Dentistry	25	22-35	0	0	0	23	0	21.0	21.0	20.0	18-25	17-29	17-25	3.71	3.79	3.44-3.96	3.57-3.96
VIRGINIA	Virginia Commonwealth University School of Dentistry	24	21-42	0	0	4	81	10	20.1	20.1	20.1	17-25	16-26	16-27	3.59	3.63	2.66-4.27	3.00-4.21
WASHINGTON	University of Washington School of Dentistry	25	21-39	0	1	0	60	2	20.4	20.3	20.4	17-25	14-27	18-29	3.54	3.61	3.05-4.00	3.33-4.00
WEST VIRGINIA	West Virginia University School of Dentistry	24	20-39	0	0	1	50	6	17.7	18.1	17.2	14-22	13-24	13-21	3.45	3.57	2.58-4.00	2.88-4.00
WISCONSIN	Marquette University School of Dentistry	23	20-32	0	18	0	77	5	19.8	19.8	19.4	16-26	16-25	16-26	3.58	3.65	2.72-4.00	2.96-4.00
ALBERTA	University of Alberta School of Dentistry	23	20-26	9	4	19	12	0	NA	21.6	NA	NA	17-28	NA	NA	3.90	NA	3.69-4.00
BRITISH COLUMBIA	University of British Columbia Faculty of Dentistry*	NR	NR	NA	1	0	46	1	22.0	22.0	NA	18-26	18-27	NA	NA	3.80	NA	3.40-4.30
MANITOBA	University of Manitoba College of Dentistry	NR	NR	NR	NR	NR	8	NR	19.8	21.2	19.8	18-22	21-29	18-22	3.93	4.09	NR	NR
NOVA SCOTIA	Dalhousie University Faculty of Dentistry*	24	21-32	1	2	1	34	0	NR	NR	20.0	NR	NR	NR	NR	NR	NR	NR
ONTARIO	University of Toronto, Faculty of Dentistry	NR	NR	0	20	0	37	39	22.0	21.0	NR	18-27	16-29	NR	NR	3.86	NR	NR
ONTARIO	Western University Schulich School of Medicine & Dentistry	24	23-38	0	0	0	48	6	21.5	NR	NR	18-24	NR	NR	NR	NR	NR	NR
QUEBEC	McGill University Faculty of Dentistry	23	20-35	0	0	0	24	4	NR	NR	NR	NR	NR	NR	NR	NR	NR	NR
QUEBEC	Université de Montréal Faculté de Médecine Dentaire	21	18-26	41	0	0	48	0	NR	NR	NR	NR	NR	NR	NR	NR	NR	NR
QUEBEC	Université Laval, Faculté de Médecine Dentaire	21	18-30	18	19	10	1	0	NR	18.5	NR	NR	NR	NR	NR	NR	NR	NR
SASKATCHEWAN	University of Saskatchewan College of Dentistry	23	19-32	4	5	1	11	0	19.9	19.6	NA	17-26	15-26	NA	NA	90.66	NA	82.30-96.25

SOURCES: ADEA and dental schools

NOTES: Information for schools with an asterisk (*) dates from the *2014 ADEA Official Guide to Dental Schools*. In the 2014 edition, we did not specifically request cumulative figures for mean GPAs and GPA ranges. The numbers indicated above may not match those listed by the individual schools in their profiles (in Part II) because of different reporting procedures. Neither the numbers above nor those in the school profiles are intended to provide exact statistics, but rather, a sense of the entering class profiles of each school.

TABLE 3-5. CLASS ENTERING FALL 2014 BY DENTAL SCHOOL: IN-STATE OR -PROVINCE, OUT-OF-STATE OR PROVINCE AND INTERNATIONAL ENROLLMENT

STATE, TERRITORY OR PROVINCE	DENTAL SCHOOL	TOTAL ENTERING CLASS 2014	IN-STATE OR -PROVINCE	OUT-OF-STATE OR -PROVINCE	INTERNAT'L	ORIGIN OF OUT-OF-STATE, OUT-OF-PROVINCE AND INTERNATIONAL ENROLLEES
ALABAMA	University of Alabama at Birmingham School of Dentistry	60	47	13	0	FL-3, GA-3, IL-1, MS-1, SC-1, TN-4
ARIZONA	Arizona School of Dentistry & Oral Health	76	22	53	1	CA-22, FL-1, IL-1, IN-1, ME-1, MN-2, MS-1, MT-1, ND-1, NM-2, NV-1, NY-3, OR-1, PA-1, TX-3, UT-6, VA-2, VT-1, WA-2, Iran-1
ARIZONA	Midwestern University College of Dental Medicine-Arizona	140	37	102	1	AK-2, AR-2, CA-26, CO-3, DE-1, FL-3, HI-1, IA-1, ID-1, IL-1, IN-1, KS-2, LA-1, MA-1, MD-1, MI-1, MN-2, ND-2, NE-1, NJ-3, NM-6, NV-2, NY-1, OK-1, OR-2, PA-2, TN-3, TX-6, UT-9, VA-1, WA-10, WI-2, Canada-1
CALIFORNIA	Herman Ostrow School of Dentistry of the University of Southern California*	144	88	47	9	NR
CALIFORNIA	Loma Linda University School of Dentistry	101	61	40	1	NR
CALIFORNIA	University of California, Los Angeles, School of Dentistry	87	78	8	1	AZ-1, IL-2, NV-1, NY-1, OK-1, VA-2, South Korea-1
CALIFORNIA	University of California, San Francisco, School of Dentistry	87	65	20	2	AZ-3, CT-1, GU-1, IN-1, LA-1, MA-1, MD-1, MO-1, NJ-1, NV-1, NY-2, OR-1, SC-1, TX-2, VA-1, WA-1, China-1, South Korea-1
CALIFORNIA	University of the Pacific, Arthur A. Dugoni School of Dentistry	139	110	23	6	AZ-3, CO-1, FL-2, HI-4, IA-1, IL-1, NM-1, NY-1, OR-3, UT-4, WA-2, Canada-4, China-1, South Korea-1
CALIFORNIA	Western University of Health Sciences College of Dental Medicine	69	35	33	1	AZ-1, CT-1, FL-4, GA-1, HI-1, ID-1, IL-2, NC-1, NJ-1, NM-1, NY-2, OK-1, OR-1, PA-2, TX-2, UT-2, WA-7, WI-2, South Korea-1
COLORADO	The University of Colorado School of Dental Medicine	80	55	25	0	AK-1, AZ-4, CA-3, FL-1, KS-1, MD-2, MT-2, ND-1, NE-2, NM-4, PA-1, TX-2, WA-1
CONNECTICUT	University of Connecticut School of Dental Medicine	46	21	24	1	CO-1, MA-7, ME-4, MO-1, NC-1, NH-2, NJ-1, NY-5, PA-1, RI-1, China-1
WASHINGTON, D.C.	Howard University College of Dentistry	72	0	66	6	CA-2, CO-1, DE-3, FL-6, GA-1, IL-1, MA-1, MD-19, MI-1, MS-1, NC-3, NJ-1, NY-3, OR-1, PA-1, TN-1, TX-4, VA-16, Cameroon-1, Canada-2, Rwanda-1, Vietnam-2
FLORIDA	Lake Erie College of Osteopathic Medicine School of Dental Medicine	100	34	66	0	AL-3, AZ-1, CA-1, CT-3, GA-3, IL-1, LA-4, MD-1, MI-1, MN-3, MO-1, NC-4, NE-1, NJ-1, NY-9, OH-2, OK-2, PA-8, SC-1, TX-10, UT-2, VA-2, WA-1, WI-1
FLORIDA	Nova Southeastern University College of Dental Medicine*	120	67	46	7	AL-1, CA-9, CO-2, GA-4, IL-1, MD-1, ME-1, NC-1, ND-1, NH-1, NJ-5, NY-9, OH-1, OK-1, PA-1, TX-6, UT-1, VA-4, WI-2, Canada-4, Denmark-1, Grenada-1, South Korea-1
FLORIDA	University of Florida College of Dentistry	93	87	6	0	AL-1, AR-1, GA-2, MN-1, SD-1
GEORGIA	Georgia Regents University College of Dental Medicine	85	77	8	0	IN-1, NC-3, SC-4
ILLINOIS	Midwestern University College of Dental Medicine-Illinois	130	48	81	1	AK-2, AL-3, AZ-1, CA-8, CO-1, FL-2, GA-1, HI-1, IA-2, IN-4, KS-1, MA-1, MI-15, MN-5, MO-1, NC-1, NJ-1, NY-2, OH-1, OK-1, OR-1, TX-9, UT-2, VA-2, WA-5, WI-8, China-1
ILLINOIS	Southern Illinois University School of Dental Medicine	50	48	2	0	OK-1, NY-1
ILLINOIS	University of Illinois at Chicago College of Dentistry	50	50	0	0	NA
INDIANA	Indiana University School of Dentistry	104	74	28	2	AZ-4, CA-3, FL-1, GA-1, IL-1, KS-1, KY-2, MI-4, NH-1, NJ-1, NY-1, NC-1, PA-1, UT-2, VA-2, WA-1, Canada-3, South Korea-1
IOWA	The University of Iowa College of Dentistry & Dental Clinics	80	57	23	0	CO-1, IL-8, KS-1, MI-1, MN-4, MT-1, ND-1, VA-1, WA-1, WI-4
KENTUCKY	University of Kentucky College of Dentistry	66	37	29	0	CA-1, FL-5, GA-3, IL-1, IN-2, MA-1, MD-1, MI-2, OH-6, SC-1, TN-1, TX-5
KENTUCKY	University of Louisville School of Dentistry	119	43	75		AL-4, AR-1, AZ-1, CA-4, CO-1, CT-1, FL-3, GA-6, ID-3, IO-1, IL-2, IN-11, MI-3, NC-1, NE-1, NJ-1, OH-4, SC-1, TN-9, UT-16, WI-1, India-1
LOUISIANA	Louisiana State University Health New Orleans School of Dentistry	65	58	7	0	AR-3, IL-1, IN-1, MS-1, NY-1
MAINE	University of New England College of Dental Medicine	64	15	48	1	CO-1, CT-1, IA-1, IL-3, KS-1, MA-5, MD-2, MI-1, MN-1, NC-1, NH-5, NJ-3, NY-2, OH-2, PA-2, RI-5, TX-1, UT-2, VA-4, VT-1, WI-3, Canada-1

(continued)

TABLE 3-5. CLASS ENTERING FALL 2014 BY DENTAL SCHOOL (CONTINUED)

STATE, TERRITORY OR PROVINCE	DENTAL SCHOOL	TOTAL ENTERING CLASS 2014	IN-STATE OR -PROVINCE	OUT-OF-STATE OR -PROVINCE	INTERNAT'L	ORIGIN OF OUT-OF-STATE, OUT-OF-PROVINCE AND INTERNATIONAL ENROLLEES
MARYLAND	University of Maryland School of Dentistry	130	70	56	4	AZ-1, CA-1, CO-1, DC-1, DE-2, FL-7, GA-1, HI-1, IL-1, MA-1, MI-2, MN-1, NC-4, NJ-3, NY-8, PA-6, TX-1, UT-1, VA-12, WA-1, China-3, Taiwan-1
MASSACHUSETTS	Boston University Henry M. Goldman School of Dental Medicine	101	30	64	7	CA-3, CO-1, CT-4, FL-7, GA-5, IA-1, IN-2, LA-1, MO-1, NH-1, NJ-3, NY-12, OH-2, PA-1, RI-2, TN-1, TX-4, UT-1, VA-2, VT-1, WA-1, WI-2, Canada-13
MASSACHUSETTS	Harvard School of Dental Medicine	35	0	34	1	AZ-1, CA-9, FL-4, GA-2, ID-1, IL-1, IN-1, MD-1, ME-1, MI-1, MO-1, NC-2, NJ-1, NY-1, SC-1, TX-1, UT-1, VA-3, WI-1, Canada-1
MASSACHUSETTS	Tufts University School of Dental Medicine	195	49	143	3	AR-1, AZ-1, CA-21, CO-2, CT-7, FL-22, GA-7, HI-1, IL-7, IN-8, LA-1, MA-49, MD-3, ME-1, MI-5, NC-1, NH-4, NJ-6, NY-7, NV-2, OH-1, OK-1, OR-1, PA-3, RI-2, TX-9, UT-2, VA-7, VT-2, WA-3, WI-5, South Korea-3
MICHIGAN	University of Detroit Mercy School of Dentistry	144	72	32	40	AR-1, AZ-1, CA-11, CO-1, FL-1, IL-3, NC-2, NJ-1, NY-1, OH-1, TX-3, UT-1, VA-3, WA-2, Canada-33, China-2, South Korea-3, Not Reported-2
MICHIGAN	University of Michigan School of Dentistry	108	65	35	8	AK-1, AZ-1, CA-6, FL-2, GA-2, IL-7, KS-1, MN-3, MT-1, NC-1, NJ-1, NY-1, OR-1, TX-1, VA -1, WA-2, WI-3, Canada-5, China-1, South Korea-2
MINNESOTA	University of Minnesota School of Dentistry*	98	59	35	4	AZ-1, CA-2, IL-2, MD-2, MI-1, OR-1, PA-1, VA-1, TX-3, Canada-2, Singapore-1, South Korea-1
MISSISSIPPI	University of Mississippi Medical Center School of Dentistry	35	35	0	0	NA
MISSOURI	Missouri School of Dentistry & Oral Health	42	12	30	0	AL-1, AR-1, AZ-1, CA-2, GA-2, IA-2, ID-1, IL-5, KS-5, MI-1, MN-2, NE-2, OK-2, TX-2, UT-1
MISSOURI	University of Missouri - Kansas City School of Dentistry	109	76	33	0	AL-1, CA-1, HI-3, ID-1, IL-1, KS-22, NM-3, TX-1
NEBRASKA	Creighton University School of Dentistry	84	10	74	0	AL-1, AR-1, CA-4, CO-5, FL-1, HI-6, IA-2, ID-10, IL-4, KS-9, LA-1, MN-5, ND-3, NM-6, OH-2, OK-1, OR-3, SD-3, UT-1, WA-3, WY-4
NEBRASKA	University of Nebraska Medical Center College of Dentistry	48	35	12	1	CO-1, IA-1, KS 3, SD-3, WY-4, China-1
NEVADA	University of Nevada, Las Vegas, School of Dental Medicine	81	43	37	1	CA-16, HI-2, IL-1, LA-1, MN-1, MT-1, NM-1, NY-1, TX-4, UT-8, WA-1, Canada-1
NEW JERSEY	Rutgers, The State University of New Jersey, School of Dental Medicine	91	61	30	0	CA-5, CT-1, FL-9, GA-1, MA-1, MD-1, NY-8, PA-1, TX-1, VA-1, WI-1
NEW YORK	Columbia University College of Dental Medicine	80	34	42	4	AR-1, CA-3, CO-1, CT-2, FL-4, GA-1, IL-1, MA-3, MD-2, MI-2, NC-2, NJ-13, NY-34, PA-4, PR-1, TX-2, Brazil-1, Canada-3
NEW YORK	New York University College of Dentistry	384	107	192	88	AL-1, CA-41, CT-3, FL-26, GA-8, IL-3, MA-4, MD-7, MI-1, MN-4, NC-5, ND-1, NJ-39, OH-1, OK-1, OR-2, PA-9, SC-1, TN-2, TX-10, VA-13, VT-2, WA-5, WI-1, Not Reported-2; Canada-46, China-1, Ecuador-1, India-1, Indonesia-1, Iran-2, Israel-1, Morocco-1, South Korea-14, Ukraine-1, Not Reported-19
NEW YORK	Stony Brook University School of Dental Medicine	42	39	3	0	MD-1, NJ-2
NEW YORK	Touro College of Dental Medicine at New York Medical College	NA	NA	NA	NA	NA
NEW YORK	University at Buffalo School of Dental Medicine	90	72	16	2	CA-1, DE-1, FL-1, MA-1, MI-3, NJ-3, OK-1, PA-1, TX-1, UT-1, VA-1, WA-1, India-1, South Korea-1
NORTH CAROLINA	East Carolina University School of Dental Medicine*	52	52	0	0	NA
NORTH CAROLINA	University of North Carolina at Chapel Hill School of Dentistry	82	69	13	0	FL-3, GA-4, NY-1, TN-1, TX-2, VA-2
OHIO	Case Western Reserve University School of Dental Medicine	74	21	39	14	AZ-1, CA-3, CO-1, FL-2, GA-3, IA-1, ID-1, IL-2, MA-1, MI-3, MN-1, MO-1, NJ-3, OK-1, PA-2, TX-3, UT-3, VA-1, WA-2, Not Reported-4; Canada-8, Mexico-1, South Korea-4, Vietnam-1
OHIO	The Ohio State University College of Dentistry	110	91	19	0	AZ-1, CA-3, FL-1, ID-1, IL-1, IN-1, KY-1, MD-1, MI-1, NC-1, NM-1, NY-1, PA-2, SC-1, UT-2
OKLAHOMA	University of Oklahoma College of Dentisry	56	44	11	1	AZ-2, ID-1, KS-1, MN-1, TX-2, UT-4, China-1

TABLE 3-5. CLASS ENTERING FALL 2014 BY DENTAL SCHOOL (CONTINUED)

STATE, TERRITORY OR PROVINCE	DENTAL SCHOOL	TOTAL ENTERING CLASS 2014	IN-STATE OR -PROVINCE	OUT-OF-STATE OR -PROVINCE	INTERNAT'L	ORIGIN OF OUT-OF-STATE, OUT-OF-PROVINCE AND INTERNATIONAL ENROLLEES
OREGON	Oregon Health & Science University School of Dentistry	76	52	22	1	AZ-1, CA-5, CO-1, HI-1, ID-2, MT-2, ND-1, NM-1, NV-1, UT-1, WA-4, State Not Reported-1, Mexico-1
PENNSYLVANIA	The Maurice H. Kornberg School of Dentistry, Temple University	139	61	73	5	AZ-1, CA-9, CT-1, DE-3, FL-6, GA-1, IN-2, LA-1, MD-3, MI-3, MN-1, MO-1, NC-1, NJ-21, NY-7, OH-1, TX-3, UT-1, VA-5, WA-1, WV-1, Canada-2, Kuwait-1, South Korea-2
PENNSYLVANIA	University of Pennsylvania School of Dental Medicine	118	17	84	17	CA-8, CO-1, CT-1, DC-1, DE-1, FL-7, GA-2, HI-1, ID-1, IL-5, MA-7, MD-3, MI-3, MN-1, MO-1, NC-1, NJ-16, NY-9, SC-1, TX-3, VA-8, WA-2, WI-1, Canada-10, Jamaica-1, South Korea-3, Taiwan-1, Vietnam-1
PENNSYLVANIA	University of Pittsburgh School of Dental Medicine*	80	47	29	4	AZ-1, CA-1, CO-1, FL-6, GA-2, IL-2, KY-1, MD-2, MI-2, NC-1, NY-2, OH-1, TX-4, VA-1, VT-1, WI-1, Canada-2, China-1, South Korea-1
PUERTO RICO	University of Puerto Rico School of Dental Medicine*	40	38	2	0	AL-1, UT-1
SOUTH CAROLINA	Medical University of South Carolina James B. Edwards College of Dental Medicine	75	50	25	0	CO-1, GA-2, ID-1, IL-1, KS-1, MD-1, MN-1, MS-1, NE-1, NJ-2, NY-2, OH-2, OR-1, RI-1, TN-2, UT-1, VA-3, WA-1
TENNESSEE	Meharry Medical College School of Dentistry*	60	9	49	2	AL-4, AR-1, AZ-1, CA-1, FL-6, GA-9, IL-1, IN-1, LA-1, MD-1, MI-1, MN-1, MO-2, NC-5, NY-3, PA-1, TX-7, VA-2, WI-1, Canada-2
TENNESSEE	University of Tennessee Health Science Center College of Dentistry	90	46	44	0	AL-1, AR-31, CA-1, GA-4, IL-1, IN-1, KS-1, MS-2, NY-1, TX-1
TEXAS	Texas A&M University Baylor College of Dentistry	104	94	10	0	AL-1, AR-2, CA-2, FL-1, LA-1, NM-2, OH-1
TEXAS	University of Texas Health Science Center at San Antonio School of Dentistry	104	100	4	0	AR-1, OR-1, UT-2
TEXAS	The University of Texas School of Dentistry at Houston	100	100	0	0	NA
UTAH	Roseman University of Health Sciences College of Dental Medicine – South Jordan, Utah	82	20	58	4	AK-2, AZ-2, CA-27, CO-1, FL-1, GA-1, IA-1, ID-4, KS-1, MN-1, MS-1, NE-1, NJ-1, OK-2, SC-1, TX-3, VA-1, WA-7, Canada-4
UTAH	University of Utah School of Dentistry	23	21	2	0	MO-1, MT-1
VIRGINIA	Virginia Commonwealth University School of Dentistry	95	60	29	6	CA-1, DE-1, FL-4, GA-6, IL-2, KY-1, MD-2, MA-1, NJ-2, NY-1, NC-3, PA-1, TX-1, UT-3, Canada-1, Taiwan-1, Kuwait-4
WASHINGTON	University of Washington School of Dentistry	63	49	14	0	AZ-6; HI-2; MI-1; MT-2; MO-1; NM-1, UT-1
WEST VIRGINIA	West Virginia University School of Dentistry	57	26	28	3	AZ-1, CA-1, FL-1, IN-1, MD-5, NC-2, NJ-1, NY-1, OH-2, OK-1, PA-5, TN-1, TX-1, UT-1, VA-4, Canada-1, Kuwait-2
WISCONSIN	Marquette University School of Dentistry	100	50	49	1	CA-2, FL-3, IL-28, MI-5, MN-5, NE-1, ND-1, TX-1, UT-1, WA-2, Canada-1
ALBERTA	University of Alberta School of Dentistry	32	29	3	0	NR
BRITISH COLUMBIA	University of British Columbia Faculty of Dentistry*	48	44	4	NA	AB-1, ON-3
MANITOBA	University of Manitoba College of Dentistry	29	28	1	0	NR (out-of-province), NA (international)
NOVA SCOTIA	Dalhousie University Faculty of Dentistry*	38	28	3	7	BC-11, ON-2, United States-5, Kuwait-2
ONTARIO	University of Toronto, Faculty of Dentistry	96	86	9	1	AB-4, BC-4, SK-1, ZZ-1
ONTARIO	Western University Schulich School of Medicine & Dentistry	54	47	5	2	AB-1, BC-2, QC-1, SK-1, Taiwan-1, United States-1
QUEBEC	McGill University Faculty of Dentistry	38	31	7	0	BC-1, ON-6,
QUEBEC	Université de Montréal Faculté de Médecine Dentaire	89	84	5	0	NB-4, ON-1
QUEBEC	Université Laval, Faculté de Médecine Dentaire	48	48	0	0	NA
SASKATCHEWAN	University of Saskatchewan College of Dentistry	29	21	8	0	AB-4, BC-1, ON-3

SOURCES: ADEA and Dental Schools
NOTES: Information for schools with an asterisk (*) dates from the *2014 ADEA Official Guide to Dental Schools*.
The data indicated above may not match that listed by the individual schools in their profiles (in Part II) because of different reporting procedures. Neither the data above nor that in the school profiles are intended to provide exact details, but rather, a sense of the entering class profiles of each school.
NA: Not Applicable
NR: Not Reported

TABLE 3-6. COMBINED AND OTHER DEGREE PROGRAMS BY DENTAL SCHOOL

STATE, TERRITORY OR PROVINCE	DENTAL SCHOOL	DOCTORAL DENTAL DEGREE	Ph.D.	M.S.	M.P.H.	M.D.	B.A./B.S.	Other	Additional Information
ALABAMA	University of Alabama at Birmingham School of Dentistry	D.M.D.	Yes	No	No	No	No	No	
ARIZONA	Arizona School of Dentistry & Oral Health	D.M.D.	No	No	Yes	No	No	No	
ARIZONA	Midwestern University College of Dental Medicine-Arizona	D.M.D.	No	No	No	No	No	No	
CALIFORNIA	Herman Ostrow School of Dentistry of the University of Southern California	D.D.S.	Yes	Yes	No	No	Yes	No	
CALIFORNIA	Loma Linda University School of Dentistry	D.D.S.	Yes	Yes	Yes	Yes	Yes	No	
CALIFORNIA	University of California, Los Angeles, School of Dentistry	D.D.S.	Yes	Yes	Yes	No	No	Yes	M.B.A.
CALIFORNIA	University of California, San Francisco, School of Dentistry	D.D.S.	Yes	Yes	No	No	No	Yes	M.B.A., B.S. available only on a limited basis
CALIFORNIA	University of the Pacific, Arthur A. Dugoni School of Dentistry	D.D.S.	No	No	No	No	No	No	
CALIFORNIA	Western University of Health Sciences College of Dental Medicine	D.M.D.	No	No	No	No	No	No	
COLORADO	The University of Colorado School of Dental Medicine	D.D.S.	No	No	No	No	Yes	No	
CONNECTICUT	University of Connecticut School of Dental Medicine	D.M.D.	Yes	Yes	Yes	No	Yes	No	
WASHINGTON, D.C.	Howard University College of Dentistry	D.D.S.	No	No	No	No	Yes	Yes	B.S./D.D.S. program offered to Howard undergraduates; D.D.S./M.B.A.
FLORIDA	Lake Erie College of Osteopathic Medicine School of Dental Medicine	D.M.D.	No	No	No	No	No	No	
FLORIDA	Nova Southeastern University College of Dental Medicine	D.M.D.	No	No	No	No	No	No	
FLORIDA	University of Florida College of Dentistry	D.M.D.	Yes	No	Yes	No	Yes	No	
GEORGIA	Georgia Regents University College of Dental Medicine	D.M.D.	Yes	Yes	No	No	No	No	
ILLINOIS	Midwestern University College of Dental Medicine-Illinois	D.M.D.	No	Yes	No	No	No	Yes	D.M.D./master's degree in biomedical science
ILLINOIS	Southern Illinois University School of Dental Medicine	D.M.D.	No	No	No	No	No	No	
ILLINOIS	University of Illinois at Chicago College of Dentistry	D.M.D.	Yes	Yes	No	No	No	No	
INDIANA	Indiana University School of Dentistry	D.D.S.	Yes	Yes	Yes	No	No	Yes	M.S.D. programs in most areas
IOWA	The University of Iowa College of Dentistry & Dental Clinics	D.D.S.	No	Yes	Yes	No	No	No	
KENTUCKY	University of Kentucky College of Dentistry	D.M.D.	No	No	No	No	No	No	
KENTUCKY	University of Louisville School of Dentistry	D.M.D.	Yes	Yes	No	No	No	No	
LOUISIANA	Louisiana State University Health New Orleans School of Dentistry	D.D.S.	Yes	No	No	No	No	No	
MAINE	University of New England College of Dental Medicine	D.M.D.	No	No	No	No	No	No	
MARYLAND	University of Maryland School of Dentistry	D.D.S.	Yes	Yes	Yes	Yes	No	Yes	M.S. in clinical research

TABLE 3-6. COMBINED AND OTHER DEGREE PROGRAMS BY DENTAL SCHOOL (CONTINUED)

STATE, TERRITORY OR PROVINCE	DENTAL SCHOOL	DOCTORAL DENTAL DEGREE	Ph.D.	M.S.	M.P.H.	M.D.	B.A./B.S.	Other	Additional Information
MASSACHUSETTS	Boston University Henry M. Goldman School of Dental Medicine	D.M.D.	No	No	No	No	Yes	Yes	Certificate of Advanced Graduate Study (CAGS), M.S., M.S.D., D.Sc., D.Sc.D., Ph.D. and internship; B.A./D.M.D. 7-year program offered to Boston University undergraduates; advanced dental education programs offered in Advanced Education in General Dentistry (AEGD), Dental Public Health, Digital Dentistry, Endodontics, Operative Dentistry, Oral Biology, Oral and Maxillofacial Pathology, Oral and Maxillofacial Surgery, Orthodontics, Pediatric Dentistry, Periodontics and Prosthodontics
MASSACHUSETTS	Harvard School of Dental Medicine	D.M.D.	Yes	Yes	Yes	No	No	Yes	M.B.A.
MASSACHUSETTS	Tufts University School of Dental Medicine	D.M.D.	No	Yes	Yes	No	Yes	No	
MICHIGAN	University of Detroit Mercy School of Dentistry	D.D.S.	No	No	No	No	No	Yes	B.S./D.D.S. program offered to highly qualified high school applicants enrolled in UDM 7-year combined undergraduate/dental program.
MICHIGAN	University of Michigan School of Dentistry	D.D.S.	Yes	Yes	Yes	No	No	No	
MINNESOTA	University of Minnesota School of Dentistry	D.D.S.	Yes	Yes	Yes	No	No	No	
MISSOURI	Missouri School of Dentistry & Oral Health	D.M.D.	No	No	Yes	No	No	No	
MISSOURI	University of Missouri - Kansas City School of Dentistry	D.D.S.	Yes	Yes	No	No	No	No	
MISSISSIPPI	University of Mississippi Medical Center School of Dentistry	D.M.D.	No	No	No	No	No	No	
NEBRASKA	Creighton University School of Dentistry	D.D.S.	No	No	No	No	No	No	
NEBRASKA	University of Nebraska Medical Center College of Dentistry	D.D.S.	Yes	No	No	No	No	No	
NEVADA	University of Nevada, Las Vegas, School of Dental Medicine	D.M.D.	No	No	Yes	No	No	Yes	M.B.A.; B.S./D.M.D. 7-year program offered to UNLV and UN Reno undergraduates; D.M.D./M.B.A. with Lee Business School; D.M.D./M.P.H. with School of Community Health Sciences.
NEW JERSEY	Rutgers, The State University of New Jersey, School of Dental Medicine	D.M.D.	Yes	Yes	Yes	No	Yes	No	B.S./D.M.D. program offered to highly qualified college students enrolled in 7-year combined undergraduate/dental program.
NEW YORK	Columbia University College of Dental Medicine	D.D.S.	No	Yes	Yes	No	No	Yes	D.D.S./M.B.A. with Columbia Business School; D.D.S./M.P.H. with Mailman School of Public Health; D.D.S./M.A. in science and dental education with Teachers College
NEW YORK	New York University College of Dentistry	D.D.S.	No	No	Yes	No	Yes	No	NYU's College of Arts and Science and College of Dentistry, along with Adelphi University, offer a 7-year combined B.A./D.D.S. degree program.
NEW YORK	Stony Brook University School of Dental Medicine	D.D.S.	Yes	Yes	Yes	No	No	Yes	M.B.A.
NEW YORK	Touro College of Dental Medicine at New York Medical College	D.D.S.	No	No	No	No	No	No	
NEW YORK	University at Buffalo School of Dental Medicine	D.D.S.	Yes	Yes	No	No	Yes	Yes	M.B.A.
NORTH CAROLINA	East Carolina University School of Dental Medicine	D.M.D.	No	No	No	No	No	No	
NORTH CAROLINA	University of North Carolina at Chapel Hill School of Dentistry	D.D.S.	Yes	Yes	Yes	No	No	No	
OHIO	Case Western Reserve University School of Dental Medicine	D.M.D.	No	Yes	Yes	Yes	Yes	Yes	M.C.R.T. (master's degree in clinical research training); Combined D.M.D./M.D. is pending approval.
OHIO	The Ohio State University College of Dentistry	D.D.S.	Yes	No	No	No	No	Yes	D.D.S./Ph.D.
OKLAHOMA	University of Oklahoma College of Dentistry	D.D.S.	No	Yes	No	No	No	No	Graduate periodontics and orthodontics programs confer M.S. degrees.
OREGON	Oregon Health & Science University School of Dentistry	D.M.D.	No	No	No	No	No	No	

(continued)

TABLE 3-6. COMBINED AND OTHER DEGREE PROGRAMS BY DENTAL SCHOOL (CONTINUED)

STATE, TERRITORY OR PROVINCE	DENTAL SCHOOL	DOCTORAL DENTAL DEGREE	Ph.D.	M.S.	M.P.H.	M.D.	B.A./B.S.	Other	Additional Information
PENNSYLVANIA	The Maurice H. Kornberg School of Dentistry, Temple University	D.M.D.	No	Yes	Yes	No	Yes	No	M.S. in Oral Biology
PENNSYLVANIA	University of Pennsylvania School of Dental Medicine	D.M.D.	Yes	Yes	Yes	No	Yes	Yes	M.S. in Bioethics, Education and Translational Research; M.S.E. in Bioengineering; M.B.A.; J.D.
PENNSYLVANIA	University of Pittsburgh School of Dental Medicine	D.M.D.	Yes	Yes	Yes	No	No	No	
PUERTO RICO	University of Puerto Rico School of Dental Medicine	D.M.D.	Yes	No	No	No	No	No	
SOUTH CAROLINA	Medical University of South Carolina James B. Edwards College of Dental Medicine	D.M.D.	No	No	No	No	No	Yes	D.M.D./Ph.D.
TENNESSEE	Meharry Medical College School of Dentistry	D.D.S.	No	No	No	No	No	No	
TENNESSEE	University of Tennessee Health Science Center College of Dentistry	D.D.S.	Yes	No	No	No	No	No	
TEXAS	Texas A&M University Baylor College of Dentistry	D.D.S.	Yes	No	No	No	No	No	
TEXAS	University of Texas Health Science Center at San Antonio School of Dentistry	D.D.S.	Yes	Yes	No	No	No	No	
TEXAS	The University of Texas School of Dentistry at Houston	D.D.S.	No	No	No	Yes	No	Yes	M.D. degree in conjunction with the Certificate in Oral and Maxillofacial Surgery (UT Houston Medical school); M.S.D. degree for advanced education programs in Endodontics, Orthodontics, Pediatric Dentistry, Periodontics and Prosthodontics
UTAH	Roseman University of Health Sciences College of Dental Medicine – South Jordan, Utah	D.M.D.	No	No	No	No	No	No	
UTAH	University of Utah School of Dentistry	D.D.S.	No	No	No	No	No	No	
VIRGINIA	Virginia Commonwealth University School of Dentistry	D.D.S.	Yes	Yes	Yes	No	No	No	
WASHINGTON	University of Washington School of Dentistry	D.D.S.	Yes	Yes	Yes	No	No	Yes	D.D.S./Ph.D.
WEST VIRGINIA	West Virginia University School of Dentistry	D.D.S.	No	No	Yes	No	No	Yes	A dual degree in business administration is also available.
WISCONSIN	Marquette University School of Dentistry	D.D.S.	No	No	No	No	Yes	No	
ALBERTA	University of Alberta School of Dentistry	D.D.S.	No	No	No	No	No	No	
BRITISH COLUMBIA	University of British Columbia Faculty of Dentistry	D.M.D.	No	No	No	No	No	No	
MANITOBA	University of Manitoba College of Dentistry	D.M.D.	No	No	No	No	Yes	No	
NOVA SCOTIA	Dalhousie University Faculty of Dentistry	D.D.S.	No	No	No	No	No	No	
ONTARIO	University of Toronto Faculty of Dentistry*	D.D.S.	Yes	No	No	No	No	Yes	M.Sc.
ONTARIO	Western University Schulich School of Medicine & Dentistry	D.D.S.	No	Yes	No	Yes	No	Yes	Oral and Maxillofacial Surgery degree program offering M.Sc. and M.D. degrees
QUEBEC	McGill University Faculty of Dentistry	D.M.D.	Yes	No	No	No	No	Yes	M.Sc. in Dental Sciences
QUEBEC	Université de Montréal Faculté de Médecine Dentaire*	D.M.D.	No	No	No	No	No	Yes	M.Sc. in dentistry (Pediatric Dentistry or Orthodontics) combined with an advanced dental education clinical program In Pediatric Dentistry or Orthodontics; M.Sc. in dentistry; M.Sc. in dental sciences; 1-year multidisciplinary residency program
QUEBEC	Université Laval Faculté de Médecine Dentaire	D.M.D.	No	Yes	No	No	No	No	
SASKATCHEWAN	University of Saskatchewan College of Dentistry	D.M.D.	No	No	No	No	No	No	

SOURCES: ADEA and dental schools
NOTES: Information for schools with an asterisk (*) dates from the *2014 ADEA Official Guide to Dental Schools*.

TABLE 3-7. U.S. DENTAL ADMISSIONS INFORMATION, 2013

GENDER AND RACE/ETHNICITY

	TOTAL	M	W	HISPANIC/ LATINO[1]	AMERICAN INDIAN OR ALASKA NATIVE	ASIAN	BLACK OR AFRICAN AMERICAN	NATIVE HAWAIIAN OR PACIFIC ISLANDER	WHITE	TWO OR MORE RACES	DO NOT WISH TO REPORT OR UNKNOWN
APPLICANTS	12,162	51.3%	47.4%	7.8%	0.3%	24%	5.2%	0.1%	49.5%	2.9%	4.5%
ENROLLEES	5,769	52.8%	46.1%	8.1%	0.2%	23%	4.6%	0.1%	52.6%	3.0%	4.3%

DENTAL ADMISSION TEST (DAT)

	ACADEMIC AVERAGE		PERCEPTUAL ABILITY		TOTAL SCIENCE	
	RANGE	MEAN	RANGE	MEAN	RANGE	MEAN
APPLICANTS	10–28	18.8	7–30	19.3	10–30	18.6
ENROLLEES	12–28	19.9	10–30	20.0	12–30	19.8

GRADE POINT AVERAGE (GPA)

	SCIENCE GPA		TOTAL GPA	
	RANGE	MEAN	RANGE	MEAN
APPLICANTS	0.51–4.33	3.25	1.23–4.30	3.36
ENROLLEES	2.19–4.33	3.46	2.26–4.29	3.54

Source: American Dental Education Association, U.S. Dental School Applicants and Enrollees, 2013 Entering Class

[1]Hispanic/Latino of any race

CHAPTER 4
FINANCING A DENTAL EDUCATION

ADEA partnered with Paul Garrard, M.B.A., a longtime expert in the field of higher education financing and educational debt management to present up-to-date and relevant information to those considering a dental education. Mr. Garrard has more than 32 years of experience—on university campuses, at higher education associations and in the lending industry—helping applicants, students, alumni and their institutions promote responsible borrowing and responsible repayment. He currently works with thousands of recent graduates, including new dentists, helping them determine effective repayment strategies for their student loans.

The same level of consideration you have given to applying to dental school should be given to determining how to pay for your dental education. As you learn about financing options in this chapter and consider the ways to finance your dental education, keep in mind these four things:

1. Dental education is an affordable and worthwhile investment.

2. Although you may have to borrow, there are additional options and types of financial aid—other than just student loans.

3. You can help minimize any adverse long-term implications of financing your dental education by commiting to smart budgeting and responsible borrowing.

4. You are ultimately responsible for securing financial assistance for dental school, but there is plenty of help available along the way.

This chapter is broken into a series of questions about financing your dental education. Studying the responses should help give you confidence that you can both make and effectively manage the financial commitment a dental education requires.

ADEA makes every effort to provide that the most current information is available; however, financial aid terms, conditions and programs are subject to change, especially those involving student loans and repayment. To keep abreast of any changes in available aid, keep in close contact with your dental school's financial aid office (FAO). In fact, as of this writing, the Higher Education Act (HEA), which governs federal student aid as well as federal aid to colleges, is up for reauthorization. The programs discussed below may be changing over the course of your dental education, and staying in touch with your FAO is important.

QUESTION 1

HOW MUCH DOES A DENTAL EDUCATION COST, AND HOW MUCH MONEY WILL I NEED?

Dentistry is a financially rewarding career and should provide a great return on your investment. Dentists continue to be among the top wage earners in the nation, with the American Dental Association (ADA) reporting a median net income for general practitioners in 2013 of $180,950. With some thoughtful planning, smart budgeting and responsible borrowing, the costs can be manageable.

In considering the cost of dental education, look at two different types of costs:

1. Out-of-Pocket Costs
2. Financing Costs

■ Out-of-Pocket Costs

This category includes the items you pay for directly, such as tuition and fees, books, supplies, equipment and living expenses. Your dental school's financial aid office (FAO) can provide an estimate of these costs, sometimes referred to as cost of attendance (COA) or financial aid budget. *You will find a breakdown of these numbers for each dental school in Part II of this book.* Be sure you know your yearly COA because this figure represents the maximum amount of financial aid you can receive each year from any combination of sources, including student loans.

Budgeting: Control What You Can

Your room, board and living expenses are, for the most part, the only out-of-pocket costs you can control. You can reduce the amount of money you borrow by making a realistic budget each year and sticking to it. Financial aid that does not have to be repaid, such as grants and scholarships, usually covers tuition, fees and institutional charges, with loans being used for remaining charges and living expenses. See Question 4 for more information on unsubsidized loans, including the unsubsidized Federal Stafford and Direct PLUS loans.

Note that credit card payments and other consumer obligations cannot be included in your COA. You should make every attempt to pay off consumer debts in full before starting dental school. Any financial distraction, such as trying to keep up with these payments during dental school, could adversely impact your academic work.

How Much Do You Really Need?

Determine how much you will need for each year of dental school by asking yourself three questions:

- *How much does it cost this year?* This is the COA or financial aid budget previously outlined. Use smart budgeting to reduce this number by focusing on the expenses over which you have some control. While it's important to look at your cost over the entire duration of your program, remember that you apply for financial aid each year.

- *How much do I have to contribute to this year's costs?* Once you have been admitted, your FAO will review your completed financial aid application (an important reason not to wait until you have been accepted to apply for financial aid). A combination of income, savings and other related information as reported on your Free Application for Federal Student Aid (FAFSA®)—www.fafsa.ed.gov—will be used to determine how much you have to put toward your COA. If the amount you are expected to contribute does not match what you think you have available, you can contact your FAO to discuss the discrepancy and to see if your financial aid budget and resulting financial aid can be adjusted accordingly. Be prepared to document why you need additional help.

- *How much more do I need this year to cover the cost?* The difference between your total COA and how much you can contribute will be used by your FAO to determine the type and amount of financial aid you may receive.

■ Financing Costs

The costs associated with borrowing money for dental school include the loan principal (the original amount borrowed) and financing costs. Financing costs can increase your total repayment amount, but understanding how they work may make these costs more manageable. Several variables affect financing costs and how much you must pay back: interest rates, capitalization, use of postponement options—such as deferment and forbearance—and the length of repayment, as well as the repayment plan selected. These financing costs explain how two dental students can borrow the same amount

---

Sample First-Year Cost of Attendance

Tuition	$37,000
Fees	$2,000
Instruments, books and supplies	$12,000
Living expenses	$20,400
Total	$71,400

One way to reduce how much you pay back on your student loans is to ask family members or others to pay the interest on one of your unsubsidized loans before it capitalizes (is added back to the principal), even if they can only do so on one loan.

for dental school but pay back different amounts. See the Glossary at the end of this chapter for full definitions of these and other financial aid terms.

See Question 4 for more information on student loans, their financing costs and available repayment plans.

QUESTION 2

I NEED FINANCIAL AID. ARE THERE OPTIONS OTHER THAN STUDENT LOANS?

While the majority of dental students take out student loans to help pay for school, other financing options may be available as part of a financial aid package.

Some of these options are awarded through the financial aid office (FAO). However, some types of financial aid—including outside scholarships and service-commitment scholarships—may be provided by organizations outside your school or through the armed forces, the National Health Service Corps (NHSC) or the National Institutes of Health (NIH).

■ Grants and Scholarships

Unlike student loans, grants and scholarships do not have to be repaid and may be referred to as "gift" aid; they are always preferable to loans. In general, there are three categories of grants and scholarships:

- *Institutional grants and scholarships* are awarded by the school as part of a financial aid award package. Check with your FAO about application forms and deadlines. Grants and scholarships may be awarded based on financial need, merit or a combination of the two.

- *Outside scholarships* are awarded by organizations other than the school. You must apply for these independently. They can be found through search engines or organizations, such as ADEA and www.fastweb.com. Use caution with any scholarship searches that require payment for their services. Outside scholarships should be reported to the FAO, as they may impact other aid you are receiving. Outside scholarships are often disbursed directly to your institution.

- *Service-commitment scholarships* are sometimes referred to as "up-front" service-commitment scholarships. They provide financial support while you are in school in exchange for your promise of service after graduation. Programs are offered by the armed forces, NHSC, NIH and the Indian Health Service (IHS):

  —www.goarmy.com/amedd/education/hpsp
  —www.navy.com/careers/healthcare/dentist
  —www.airforce.com/healthcare
  —www.nhsc.hrsa.gov/scholarships
  —www.ihs.gov/JobsCareerDevelop/DHPS/Scholarships

These programs may also offer loan repayment assistance programs (help repaying your student loans in exchange for a service commitment after graduation). *See Question 3 for details on these loan repayment programs.* Please note that these are not "forgiveness" programs, as these organizations are not forgiving your debt; rather, they are simply helping you pay it back in exchange for service.

■ Education Tax Breaks

A number of tax credits and deductions—including some during the repayment period—may help defray the cost of your dental education. To find detailed information on tax credits and deductions, review Internal Revenue Service Publication 970: Tax Benefits for Education, available at www.IRS.gov/publications/p970. You may want to consult a professional tax advisor or other qualified financial advisor for assistance, especially as credits and deductions are subject to change.

> Your financial aid office should always be your first point of contact for financial aid. When figuring out how to pay for your dental education, however, consider all kinds of financial aid and assistance, including:
> - Grants and scholarships with or without a service commitment.
> - Loans and loan repayment and forgiveness programs.
> - Work-study programs.
> - Research fellowships or traineeships.
> - Education tax breaks.

> The federal government offers Scholarships for Disadvantaged Students. These awards are available to students from disadvantaged backgrounds as defined by the U.S. Department of Health and Human Services. *See the Glossary for a full definition.* Contact your financial aid office for availability of funds, as well as application process and deadline information.

■ Research Fellowship or Traineeship

Your dental school may offer a scholarship or stipend that involves conducting scientific research. Contact your FAO to see if these funds are available at your school. You may also want to regularly check adea.org for occasional announcements regarding available support from these programs.

■ Work Study

Work-study programs provide an opportunity to receive income by working part time. Due to the demands of the dental school curriculum, you may find it difficult to take advantage of this kind of financial aid. Nonetheless, you may want to ask your FAO about work-study programs if you are thinking about working while in dental school.

QUESTION 3

IS ANY FINANCIAL AID AVAILABLE FOR INTERNATIONAL STUDENTS?

International students coming to the United States to attend dental school should check with their institutions' financial aid offices (FAO) regarding financial aid opportunities. While you must be a U.S. citizen or permanent resident to qualify for federal financial

---

STUDENT PROFILE

JULISSA GUERRA PERCOLLA

GUATEMALA CITY, GUATEMALA, AND BAKERSFIELD, CA
SECOND-YEAR DENTAL STUDENT
(THREE-YEAR PROGRAM)
UNIVERSITY OF THE PACIFIC,
ARTHUR A. DUGONI SCHOOL OF DENTISTRY

Why did you choose dentistry as your career path?

I chose dentistry because it offers constant opportunities, challenges and rewards. Dentists can diagnose and treat a wide range of oral diseases, educate patients and improve their appearance and confidence. We can also be creative and independent and use technology while providing an essential health care service to diverse populations. Dentistry makes me feel happy and motivated, and fulfills my need to reach out to others. Helping others gives me a feeling of gratitude, empathy and satisfaction, and has helped me break down subconscious cultural barriers, learn more about myself and have a sense of purpose. I have also realized the high level of responsibility, constructive thinking, compassion and communication skills required—physically and personally—while working with patients.

What classes, externships or experiences (including clinical) are you involved in now?

I have already put into practice all I learned during my preclinical courses—quite rewarding! Not just because I am doing what I always wanted, but because I discovered that, to my patients, I am a doctor, am competent and am able to diagnose and treat them; they trust me! During rotations, I have learned and clinically practiced almost every aspect of dentistry. I look forward to my selective classes where I can learn more about particular topics of interest.

What are your short- and long-term goals?

While in dental school, I want to learn as much as I possibly can about all aspects of dentistry. After graduation, I hope to obtain more clinical experience within an Advanced Education in General Dentistry program. In the long run, I would like to go to a couple more states or countries and become a part of a dental practice where I can continue learning about dentistry and business models. My ultimate goal is to set up my own patient-oriented group practice housing different specialties. I would also like to become an active member of a group of dentists who are providing oral health education, prevention and care to underserved populations.

As an applicant, how did you prepare for dental school? For example, did you participate in summer programs, shadowing, research or activities to improve your manual dexterity?

I was involved in different activities. All preparation was crucial to determine and demonstrate my passion for dentistry. Serving my community has always been a priority, and I could accomplish that through my predental club. Through tutoring and research, I worked with students and teachers who challenged my critical and scientific thinking. My hobbies taught me time and stress management skills. I also shadowed many dentists, which helped me explore U.S. dental practices, get an overview of a practice's business and dental operations, and how to address patients' concerns. To improve manual dexterity, I attended UCLA's predental courses in waxing, impressions and casting. I also took a dental anatomy course, where I anatomically drew and carved each tooth.

What advice would you like to share with applicants or those considering dental school?

Good grades are a great start but not enough. Dental schools look for well-rounded applicants with real-life experiences. Applicants should demonstrate their passion for dentistry through their activities. Start by becoming an active member of your predental club or any other organization. To start shaping your own clinical and business approach, shadow dentists with different practice types and take notes on the things you like and dislike. Visit dental schools you might apply to and and talk to current students. Maintain a timeline: Organization and time management are keys to success!

Did you move to a new city to attend dental school? If so, what factors helped you make the transition?

I moved to the United States from Guatemala when I was 21. As an undergraduate, I lived in Bakersfield, CA, a smaller city. Pacific Dugoni is located in the heart of San Francisco. Initially, I visited dental schools nearby and made time to explore the area during my school interviews. When it came the time to choose the best school for me, location was a priority. During my first year, I lived close to school with a roommate. Now, I feel much more comfortable and live on my own, within walking distance to the school.

Have you taken advantage of scholarships or loans? Do you plan to take advantage of loan repayment programs? What advice would you give applicants about financial aid and dental education financing?

As an international student, I wish I could take advantage of financial aid, which is very helpful for my peers. However, I am able to take advantage of student loans. I go to financial aid-related meetings arranged by my school, and I do my research: There is a lot of help out there. I am lucky to have been chosen for a private scholarship at my school, but I have also applied to others because I am always looking for opportunities to reduce the amount of money I borrow. The bottom line is to be well-informed, ask for help from the financial aid department, plan ahead of time and take advantage of all opportunities presented.

Would you like to share whether you are married, partnered or single and if you have any children?

I am single and do not have children. My goal after dental school is to get married and form my own family.

aid, other options may be available. Check out www.edupass.org/finaid for information on financial aid for international students, including scholarships, loans, helpful organizations and the process for applying for aid.

■ Loans for International Students

If you do not qualify for a federal student loan, you may be eligible for a private loan for dental school. You can expect private loan lenders to require a creditworthy cosigner who is a U.S. citizen or permanent resident. In the past, most private loans had variable rates, though it is not unusual now for lenders to offer fixed rate private loans. Private loans that carry variable interest rates often have no interest rate cap, or a maximum interest rate that is high (for example, 18%). Private loans are unsubsidized, meaning interest starts accruing (building) at the time of disbursement. If the interest is not paid as it accrues, it will eventually be added back to the principal through a process called capitalization. See the section on private loans in Question 4.

■ Scholarships for International Students

Check with your FAO to see if your school designates any scholarship funds for international students. These scholarships may be based on merit or academic interest. The cultural department or education minister's office at your embassy may also be able to offer assistance.

QUESTION 4

WHAT TYPES OF STUDENT LOANS ARE THERE AND WHAT ARE MY REPAYMENT OPTIONS?

According to preliminary results from the ADEA Survey of Dental School Seniors, 2014 Graduating Class, 89.2% of graduates surveyed left school with student loan debt. The average debt for all graduates with debt was $247,227. The average debt for graduates from public and private schools was $216,437 and $289,897, respectively. Just over three out of every 10 students in the class of 2014 graduated with $300,000 or more in student loans; on the other hand, just over two in 10 students reported leaving dental school without any educational debt or educational debt under $100,000. Please note that these figures represent the principal amount borrowed and do not include accrued interest.

Before you look at individual loan programs, consider the following:

✓ For the best financial aid possible, contact your financial aid office (FAO) early and apply as directed, making sure you meet all stated deadlines, especially for grants and scholarships.

✓ Be cautious when considering a private or consumer loan to pay for your dental education. Federal and campus-based loans almost always offer more favorable terms and conditions. These include flexible repayment plans and postponement options if you decide to pursue additional study, such as advanced education or residency programs, after dental school. In addition to having limited repayment, postponement and consolidation options, private loans are not eligible for repayment under income-driven plans, nor are they eligible for federal forgiveness programs such as Public Service Loan Forgiveness (PSLF). PLSF eligibility might be an important consideration for dental school graduates exploring careers in the nonprofit sector, such as academia.

✓ If you do not apply or qualify for any institutional financial aid, such as grants, scholarships or campus-based loans, you can borrow up to your full cost of attendance with loans such as the unsubsidized Federal Stafford Loan and the Direct PLUS Loan.

Following are the available loan programs for dental students: The unsubsidized Federal Stafford Loan and the Direct PLUS Loan make up the bulk of many dental students' loan portfolios. Campus-based loans—which are awarded by the school and usually carry better terms and conditions—may not be available at all dental schools and for all students (check with your FAO). You can find a list of all your Federal Stafford, Direct PLUS, Federal Perkins and Direct Consolidation loans on the National Student Loan Data System at www.NSLDS.ed.gov. *See the Glossary for more information on this important site.*

■ Unsubsidized Federal Stafford Loans

Federal Stafford Loans are often the foundation of a dental student's loan portfolio. All of your Stafford borrowing will be in the unsubsidized Federal Stafford Loan program. This means you will be responsible for paying the interest that accrues on all Federal Stafford Loans you borrow during dental school. That accrued interest, which can increase your total repayment costs when it is capitalized (added back to the original principal amount borrowed), presents a strong argument to borrow responsibly.

- The federal government is the *lender* for all new Stafford Loans through its William D. Ford Federal Direct Loan Program (your loans may be referred to as Direct Stafford Loans). The actual *servicing* of your loans will be provided by another organization known as a *loan servicer* (for example, FedLoan Servicing; Great Lakes Educational Loan Services, Inc.; Nelnet; SallieMae), but the federal government is the lender.

- You may currently borrow a maximum of $40,500 per year in dental school through the unsubsidized Federal Stafford Loan program, although some FAOs prorate this amount higher based on your budget duration (9 to 12 months). Through the Federal Stafford Loan program, you can borrow a cumulative maximum of $224,000— including any subsidized Stafford Loans you had as an undergraduate student.

- The *current* unsubsidized Federal Stafford Loan rate—fixed for the life of the loan—is 6.21%.

  Note:
  —This rate is for loans disbursed on or after July 1, 2014.
  —The rate for new unsubsidized Federal Stafford Loans for graduate and professional (including dental) students changes yearly on July 1, and can be as high as 9.5%.

- Stafford Loans carry a six-month grace period following graduation or a reduction to less than half-time enrollment.

- Your Stafford Loans are listed at www.NSLDS.ed.gov.

■ Federal Direct PLUS Loans

Direct PLUS Loans may be used to supplement borrowing needs beyond those that can be met by the unsubsidized Stafford Loan. Direct PLUS Loans almost always offer more favorable terms than private loans, especially with regard to repayment and postponement options. Interest accrues from the time funds are disbursed and will eventually be capitalized if not paid prior to repayment.

- Direct PLUS loans are based in part on the borrower being "credit-ready" *(see Question 5 for more information).*

- The federal government is the *lender* for all new Direct PLUS Loans through its William D. Ford Federal Direct Loan Program (your loans may be referred to as Direct PLUS Loans). Just like with your Stafford Loans, the actual *servicing* of your Direct PLUS Loans will be provided by another organization known as a *loan servicer* (for example, FedLoan Servicing; Great Lakes Educational Loan Services, Inc.; Nelnet; SallieMae), but the federal government is the lender.

- You may borrow up to the full amount of your cost of attendance with Direct PLUS Loans, minus any other financial aid, including unsubsidized Federal Stafford Loans.

- There is no annual or cumulative maximum.

Remember that interest rates on new Stafford and Direct PLUS loans change each July 1, with caps as high as 9.5% for Stafford and 10.5% for Direct PLUS—all the more reason to limit your borrowing.

- The *current* Direct PLUS Loan rate—fixed for the life of the loan—is 7.21%. Note:

  —This rate is for loans disbursed on or after July 1, 2014.
  —The rate for new Direct PLUS Loans for graduate and professional (including dental) students changes yearly on July 1, and can be as high as 10.5%.

- Direct PLUS Loans carry a six-month post-enrollment deferment (similar to the grace period on Federal Stafford Loans) following graduation or a reduction to less than half-time enrollment.

- Your Direct PLUS Loans are listed at www.NSLDS.ed.gov.

■ Federal Perkins Loans

Federal Perkins Loans are federal loans administered by your school and are sometimes referred to as "campus-based" loans. Your school acts as the lender on behalf of the federal government and the FAO awards them based on need. Typically you are automatically considered for them if you apply for financial aid with the FAO and meet established deadlines. Note that your FAO may require income information on your parents or family to determine your eligibility for Federal Perkins Loans.

- Federal Perkins Loans are interest-free during school and during grace and deferment periods.

STUDENT PROFILE

ERICA RECKER

OELWEIN, IA
SECOND-YEAR DENTAL STUDENT
THE UNIVERSITY OF IOWA COLLEGE OF DENTISTRY &
DENTAL CLINICS

Why did you choose dentistry as your career path?

I come from a family that's big into agriculture, so being the first to break into the health care industry was a big step for me. I chose dentistry because it encompasses an exquisite blend of the arts and sciences, my biggest passions. I'm a people person, and dentistry provides the perfect opportunity to interact with the public and form long-lasting relationships. As an undergraduate, I went on a dental mission trip to Panama, where I was able to observe a wide variety of dental procedures. Working with those patients opened my eyes to how something as simple as having clean teeth can have such an astonishing impact on an individual's

self-esteem and quality of life. Upon my return, there was no doubt in my mind that this was the kind of constructive impact I wanted to make each and every single day.

What classes, externships or experiences (including clinical) are you involved in now?

As a second-year student, I have transitioned into working in the operative and preventive dentistry clinics. I see patients one day a week, either assisting a partner or serving as the clinician. My current course load includes Dental Microbiology, Human Pathology, Oral Pathology, Fixed Prosthodontics, Growth & Development, Periodontic Methods, Operative Dentistry, Basic Oral & Maxillofacial Surgery and Experiential Learning.

What are your short- and long-term goals?

My short-term goals are to continue my schooling and obtain my D.D.S. My long-term goals are to specialize in pediatric dentistry and practice in a rural community, potentially followed by exploring the world of academic dentistry.

As an applicant, how did you prepare for dental school? For example, did you participate in summer programs, shadowing, research or activities to improve your manual dexterity?

I shadowed several dentists in my hometown while in high school and participated in a number of student organizations on campus in college. As a sophomore, I became involved in student research in the College of Dentistry. While involved in research, I learned basic laboratory procedures and techniques, and I also had the opportunity to present my projects at both local and national conferences. I have continued my research as a dental student, and I am extremely grateful to have the opportunity to work with world-class mentors and faculty who are making great strides in oral health research every day.

What advice would you like to share with applicants or those considering dental school?

During your undergraduate career, take as many basic science courses as possible (anatomy, physiology, etc.) because that knowledge base is extremely beneficial. When

applying to dental school, explore any and every program that intrigues you! You're going to be spending the next four years of your life there, so it's very important that you take the time to decide which program is the best fit for you. Finally, as a dental student, don't simply focus on your classes. Become involved in student organizations and participate in extracurricular activities and outreach programs. Dental school, albeit tremendously rewarding, is also extremely challenging. Having something fun to focus on outside of the classroom serves as a great stress relief.

Did you move to a new city to attend dental school? If so, what factors helped you make the transition?

In high school, I began learning about all that the University of Iowa College of Dentistry has to offer. Keeping that in mind, I decided to pursue my undergraduate education at the University of Iowa so I could get acclimated to the campus and the community. When it came time to begin dental school, I was lucky enough to be able to stay in Iowa City to continue my education.

Have you taken advantage of scholarships or loans? Do you plan to take advantage of loan repayment programs? What advice would you give applicants about financial aid and dental education financing?

Don't let the price tag deter you from attending the program that you feel fits you best. We are entering an extremely promising profession, and while paying off a large amount of debt is never easy, it is definitely possible. I have a few private scholarships, but otherwise I have taken out loans with the help of my parents. There are several methods available to finance your education. Explore every option possible, and pay special attention to interest rates and repayment timelines.

Would you like to share whether you are married, partnered or single and if you have any children?

I am single with no children.

- A 5% fixed interest rate is assigned for the life of the loan.

- Perkins Loans carry a nine-month grace period following graduation—or a drop to less than half-time enrollment—and a "six-month post-deferment grace period" for borrowers who qualify for deferment after the original nine-month grace period.

- Your Federal Perkins Loans are listed at www.NSLDS.ed.gov.

■ Health Professions Student Loans (HPSL)

The HPSL program, which is administered by your school, is part of the Title VII federal loan program provided through the U.S. Department of Health and Human Services (HHS). Usually, you are automatically considered for HPSL if you apply for financial aid with the FAO, meet established deadlines and provide additional information required (such as parental financial information). These loans are based on exceptional financial need. Check with your FAO regarding availability.

- These loans are interest-free during school and during grace and deferment periods.

- A 5% fixed interest rate is assigned for the life of the loan.

- HPSL loans carry a 12-month grace period.

■ Loans for Disadvantaged Students (LDS)

The LDS program has similar terms and conditions as HPSL. However, based on criteria established by HHS, a borrower must be from a disadvantaged background. *See the Disadvantaged Background definition in the Glossary.* Your FAO will determine your eligibility for this program.

■ Institutional Loans

Your school may offer loans with favorable terms and conditions. Check with your FAO on their availability and application requirements.

■ Private Loans

Given the availability of Direct PLUS loans with no cumulative or annual limits (other than up to COA each year), private loans should not be necessary for dental school, except in rare cases (e.g., for international students). Private loans, which are based in part on the credit of the borrower or the cosigner, or both, often have limited repayment flexibility and limited options for postponing payments, especially when compared with federal loans. Private loans are not eligible to be repaid under income-driven plans such as Income-Based Repayment (IBR) or Pay As You Earn (PAYE), nor are they eligible for federal forgiveness programs including Public Service Loan Forgiveness. Consolidation options are also limited for private loans and they may not be consolidated into a federal consolidation loan. You may need private loans to help with costs associated with residency interviews during your last year of dental school or to assist with relocation expenses during a transition period after dental school.

ADEA strongly encourages you to consult with your FAO if you're considering a private loan to help pay for dental school.

- These unsubsidized loans may have variable interest rates with no cap to the rate.

- Grace periods vary and may be anywhere from six to 36 months.

- Repayment and postponement options are usually limited.

- Private loans do not qualify for forgiveness programs.

- A creditworthy cosigner may be required.

REPAYMENT

■ Repayment Strategies and Repayment Plans

Most student loans have some type of grace or "window" period that will allow you to get settled into residency or practice before you are required to begin making regular payments. It is smart to start planning your repayment strategy well in advance of your first payment's due date. During school, you will learn about repayment plan options, which should be covered in detail at your required senior loan exit interview prior to graduation.

Below is a brief description of the current repayment options for your federal student loans. With some exceptions, there are two generally accepted industry standards to consider as you review these debt repayment plans:

1. Monthly student loan payments should not exceed 8% to 12% of your gross income.

2. To enable you to comfortably make payments on a typical 10-year repayment plan, your total student loan debt should not exceed your starting salary. When this standard is not possible, some income-driven plans, such as IBR and PAYE, are designed to help.

Remember that dentistry is a financially rewarding field. This fact, combined with the numerous repayment plans available, may help explain why dental school graduates have a strong record of repaying their student loans.

A number of factors may influence your repayment strategy, which may fall into one of the three categories:

1. *Aggressively pay back your student loans to minimize interest cost.* Someone with minimal or no other outstanding financial obligations and whose monthly cash flow allows for higher monthly payments may use this strategy. He or she pays more than the minimum required each month and may even target the additional payment amount on his or her most expensive loan (for example, Direct PLUS). There is never a penalty for early repayment of federal loans.

2. *Maximize your monthly cash flow to free up as much cash as possible for other financial commitments or obligations.* Someone with consumer debt, medical expenses, family commitments, or any combination of these, might choose this strategy. He or she uses a plan that minimizes payments, at least initially. Doing so can increase interest costs in the long term unless payments are accelerated later.

3. *Pursue a program that repays your loans in exchange for your service commitment or forgives a portion of the balance if you meet certain conditions.* Some programs allow dental graduates to receive repayment in exchange for service or loan balance forgiveness after a designated period of time and subject to certain conditions.

Remember to reassess your repayment strategy at least once a year. While there are a few restrictions for doing so, you can switch repayment plans by working directly with your loan servicer.

IMPORTANT NOTE: If you took out private student loans prior to dental school, be sure to check the terms and conditions, such as when the loans come due and what kind of repayment terms and options you have. Be sure to check on postponement options during dental school and on any postponement options that might be available during residency or advanced dental education programs you might pursue later. Checking these options is extremely important because you do not want these loans to adversely impact later career plans or your federal student loan repayment strategy.

STUDENT PROFILE

GILBERT TAPIA

DOVER, NJ
SECOND-YEAR DENTAL STUDENT
RUTGERS, THE STATE UNIVERSITY OF NEW JERSEY,
SCHOOL OF DENTAL MEDICINE

Why did you choose dentistry as your career path?

As a child, I always enjoyed going to the dentist for my routine cleaning. At the end of the appointment, the dentist would always tell me that my teeth were in excellent condition, which gave me a sense of satisfaction. As I got older, I realized that not everybody is satisfied with their teeth; my parents, family members and friends sometimes faced dental problems. I almost felt guilty that I never did. One day it occurred to me that instead of feeling guilty, I should help them by becoming their dentist! This idea made perfect sense because I enjoyed the sciences, drawing during my spare time and helping people in need. Dentistry encompasses all of these aspects because you need to engineer a solution with the aid of your tools and hands to meet the patients' needs.

What classes, externships or experiences (including clinical) are you involved in now?

This semester we're taking our Complete Dentures 2 class, which requires us to make a complete denture for our first patient ever. Our team of five students (including myself) and a doctor successfully delivered one to a happy patient. This experience was very fulfilling. When the patient came back for the post-delivery appointment, the patient told us that their family was coming over to see their new smile.

What are your short- and long-term goals?

My short-term goals are to graduate from dental school and be accepted into a residency program to further my clinical skills. My long-term goals are to own a private practice and teach dentistry.

As an applicant, how did you prepare for dental school? For example, did you participate in summer programs, shadowing, research or activities to improve your manual dexterity?

Before being accepted into dental school, I completed my master's degree at the Rutgers Graduate School of Biomedical Sciences. During my time there, I developed studying habits that prepared me for the Dental Admission Test and dental school curriculum. I also participated in an externship program, Gateway to Dentistry, at the Rutgers School of Dental Medicine during the summer of 2010, which gave me insight into the dental profession. In this program, we were given the opportunity to perform a root canal in a preclinic setting as well as other hands-on exercises.

What advice would you like to share with applicants or those considering dental school?

Dental school is a long and tough journey that yields indescribable satisfaction and fulfillment. With hard work and determination, getting into dental school is certainly achievable.

Did you move to a new city to attend dental school? If so, what factors helped you make the transition?

I moved 30 minutes away from home to an urban area. This was an easy transition for me because my master's program was in the same building as the dental school, so I was already familiar with the area. Also, you make new friendships in dental school, and these new relationships provide support and comfort during tough times.

Have you taken advantage of scholarships or loans? Do you plan to take advantage of loan repayment programs? What advice would you give applicants about financial aid and dental education financing?

I plan to continue taking out loans to help me through dental school; however, I also plan to take advantage of scholarship opportunities. I applied for a scholarship at the end of my first year in dental school and recently found out that I was chosen as a recipient. I also plan to take advantage of loan repayment programs, but it's important to research which kinds of programs are available to you. Apply to as many scholarships as possible because it never hurts to try!

Would you like to share whether you are married, partnered or single and if you have any children?

I am single and do not have any children.

Standard Repayment

- Standard repayment—based on a 10-year schedule for unconsolidated loans with the same payment each month—is generally considered the most aggressive repayment plan available.

- Monthly payments tend to be higher; however, this plan is the least expensive in the long term because the repayment term is relatively short.

- If you do not choose another repayment plan when given the option by your loan servicer, you will be assigned the standard 10-year repayment plan.

- This plan, of interest if you have a steady income high enough to manage the monthly payments, might be appropriate for someone moving into a practice right out of dental school or for someone who might have other financial resources from a spouse or partner.

- With Direct Consolidation Loans, standard repayment is up to 30 years (depending on total amount borrowed), with the same payment each month.

Graduated Repayment

- Graduated repayment is usually based on a 10-year schedule, though some plans are extended with an interest-only option for several years.

- Payments start relatively small and increase by designated amounts at designated intervals.

- Lower initial payments result in higher overall repayment costs compared to the standard 10-year plan, unless borrowers accelerate payments.

- This plan might be of interest if you have other short-term financial obligations or are moving into a practice right out of dental school.

Income-Driven Repayment

- Eligibility is determined by your federal education loan debt, your income and your family size. Similarly, payment amounts are calculated based on your income and family size. Payments usually grow each year as income increases.

- The repayment period may run from 20 to 25 years.

- Several variations exist, including IBR and PAYE, both of which cap payments at a low percentage of the borrower's discretionary income.

- Lower initial payments result in higher overall interest costs when compared to the standard repayment plan, unless borrowers accelerate payments.

- This option may interest you if you have a variable income or other financial obligations, or if you are a dental resident who has limited income initially but want to start repayment during residency as part of your repayment strategy. This option may also be of interest if you are a dental school graduate interested in the PSLF program.

Extended Repayment

- This plan offers up to 25 years of level payments on nonconsolidated eligible loans, depending on your outstanding balance.

- Due to an extended repayment term, this plan offers lower monthly payments but potentially much higher total repayment costs if the loan is held to term (in other words, if you take the entire 25 years to repay and do not accelerate payments).

- This type of repayment may be of interest to you if you:

—Have a steady income.
—Have long-term financial obligations and are moving into a practice right out of dental school.
—Are perhaps financing a mortgage and need to show your mortgage lender a lower debt-to-income ratio to help you qualify.

> ## Federal Scholarships During and After Dental School
>
> Did you know that additional federally funded scholarships are available for predoctoral and advanced dental education students with interests in research?
>
> - The National Institute of Dental and Craniofacial Research, part of the National Institutes of Health (NIH), offers numerous programs for dental students who have an interest in dental research. For more information, visit www.nidcr.nih.gov/CareersandTraining.
>
> - The Fogarty International Clinical Research Scholars & Fellows Program provides the opportunity for individuals to experience mentored research training at NIH-funded research centers in developing countries. For more information, contact the NIH/Fogarty International Center at www.fic.nih.gov.
>
> - The NIH Graduate Partnerships Program—www.training.nih.gov/programs/gpp—provides opportunities for research and funding.

As mentioned before, you can work with your loan servicer to switch repayment plans. Campus-based loans (such as Federal Perkins, HPSL and LDS) usually have 10-year standard repayment plans with level payments. Private loans tend to have 10- to 25-year repayment terms based on the amount borrowed.

■ Loan Consolidation

Loan consolidation is a debt management tool some borrowers consider as part of their repayment strategies, but it is not appropriate for all borrowers. In general, consolidation allows a borrower to pay off multiple loans with one new loan.

Many recent dental school graduates are finding that consolidation is not needed, as all of their Federal Stafford and Direct PLUS loans are with the same lender (the federal government, through the Direct Loan Program) and are all assigned to the same loan servicer.

You *may* be a candidate for consolidation if you have multiple loans with different loan servicers, and you want the convenience of having one loan provider. If you have Federal Stafford or Direct PLUS loans, or both, you likely already have only one lender and one loan servicer—the federal government—through the Direct Loan Program. If you have nondirect loans, you may be able to consolidate them into a direct loan, which would enable you to maximize your potential forgiveness in the PSLF program, assuming you meet other eligibility requirements (only direct loans qualify for PSLF).

You *may not* be a candidate for consolidation if you:

—Think at some point after school you may adopt an aggressive repayment strategy and want to preserve the ability to pay down some of your more expensive loans first (assuming you have Direct PLUS).

—Already have all your loans with one loan servicer, as referenced above.

—Meet the criteria of both of the above.

Talk with your FAO about consolidation and check out the primer on loan consolidation at adea.org under Current Students & Residents.

STUDENT PROFILE

ANDREW WELLES

WAUSAU, WI
FOURTH-YEAR DENTAL STUDENT
MARQUETTE UNIVERSITY SCHOOL OF DENTISTRY

Why did you choose dentistry as your career path?

Simply put, I decided to pursue an education in dentistry to help people. Throughout my experiences shadowing professionals in a variety of fields, I felt the strongest connection to dentistry. There is something about the way patients connect with the dentist and how these relationships are built within the community that is unlike anything else. Practicing dentistry combines desirable and rewarding experiences from multiple areas of healthcare; treatment ranges from acute care and relieving pain to decades of long-term coordinated care for a community of patients. The dental team plays an integral role in the health care community, and this relationship with people is what attracted me to dentistry.

What classes, externships or experiences (including clinical) are you involved in now?

In our fourth year of dental school at Marquette, we have already completed most of our academic classes. We have two remaining courses, senior colloquium and dental practice dynamics, which contain many important aspects of the dental education beyond general dental sciences. In my final semester at Marquette, I am excited to be participating in an externship at the Tri-County Community Dental Clinic (TCCDC) in Appleton, WI, on Mondays. The TCCDC is a community-based clinic that aims to serve a large dental need in Northeast Wisconsin. All Marquette dental students have the opportunity to rotate through this clinic for weekly scheduled rotations, and the clinic offers two externships to fourth-year dental students to continue their education in community dentistry. Tuesday through Friday, I will be gaining valuable clinical experience at the Marquette Dental Clinics and associated rotations, working toward graduation in May.

What are your short- and long-term goals?

As a dental student, my most immediate short-term goal is graduation. In May of 2015, I will earn my diploma from Marquette University as a Doctor of Dental Surgery. Following graduation, I aspire to serve the National Health Service Corps in an area of need. I want to become integrated into the community as a successful oral health care provider to those who need it most. I hope to continue a balance of my work and professional involvement by participating in my local and state dental societies. I hope to remain involved with organized dentistry as I transition from being a student to being a dental professional and have a positive impact on the profession of dentistry. An additional goal of mine as I continue my career in dentistry is to become involved with dental academia in some capacity. Whether this is as an adjunct faculty or full-time professor, dental education is an exciting and rewarding career path I hope to explore.

As an applicant, how did you prepare for dental school? For example, did you participate in summer programs, shadowing, research or activities to improve your manual dexterity?

One of the biggest benefits of attending the University of Wisconsin-Madison for my undergraduate studies was the many different opportunities available to prepare for dental school. I was able to participate in a ceramics course, which enhanced my three-dimensional creativity and under-standing of space. Dental school and dentistry have strong conceptual components relating to shapes in space, and these experiences helped to prepare me for the intellectual challenges of dentistry beyond textbooks. Another way that I prepared for dental school was by shadowing general practitioners and specialists within dentistry. Through shadowing, I was able to visualize myself helping patients as a dental professional, and these experiences helped me confirm my ambition to become a dentist.

What advice would you like to share with applicants or those considering dental school?

Keep going! You have chosen a rewarding profession unlike anything else out there. A profession in dentistry is worth the time and financial investment. Keep striving to reach your educational goals, and know that you are making a great choice.

Did you move to a new city to attend dental school? If so, what factors helped you make the transition?

I moved from Madison, WI, 90 miles east to Milwaukee. The transition was made much easier with the love and support of family and friends.

Have you taken advantage of scholarships or loans? Do you plan to take advantage of loan repayment programs? What advice would you give applicants about financial aid and dental education financing?

I am honored to have been selected as a recipient of a four-year National Health Service Corps (NHSC) scholarship. This scholarship has removed the financial burden of dental school for me and allowed me to offer my services to those who need them the most. I am very excited about my future with the NHSC and highly recommend it to all incoming dental students. The advice I have for incoming dental students is to research your options for dental education financing. There are a number of programs—like the NHSC, military programs, state-based repayment programs, etc.—that offer financial assistance to dental students. Many opportunities for assistance are out there, and I highly recommend that students investigate if any of these rewarding programs would be a good fit for them.

■ Loan Repayment Programs Tied to Service Commitment

Loan repayment programs are designed to help you manage your student loans by paying a portion of your student loan debt in exchange for a service commitment. Your debt is not forgiven with loan repayment programs; rather, you receive help paying off the debt from the organization with which you made a service commitment. If you are hesitant to make a service commitment before you start dental school to receive a scholarship, you may be interested in revisiting the service commitment as you approach graduation.

There are a number of factors to consider with any service commitment program, including loan repayment programs. Review the specifics of the programs below and contact them for additional information on requirements. In addition, pay special attention to the considerations list at the end of this section.

Armed Forces Loan Repayment Programs offer loan repayment assistance, in addition to service commitment scholarships. See www.goarmy.com, www.navy.com, or www.airforce.com for details.

Faculty Loan Repayment Program offers up to $40,000 for repayment of student loans for individuals from disadvantaged backgrounds who serve as faculty of an accredited health professions college or university for two years. For more information, visit www.hrsa.gov/loanscholarships/repayment/faculty.

Student Loan Repayment Program (Federal) is offered by individual federal agencies to recruit and retain highly trained individuals for three-year commitments. Recipients may receive $10,000 per year for eligible loans, not to exceed a total of $60,000 for any one employee. Visit www.opm.gov/oca/pay/studentloan for more information.

Indian Health Service Loan Repayment Program offers up to $20,000 for repayment of eligible student loans per year of service with a two-year minimum commitment. This program is designed to help meet the staffing needs of American Indian and Alaska Native health programs. Visit www.loanrepayment.ihs.gov or call 301-443-3396 for more information.

National Health Service Corps Loan Repayment Program offers a minimum of $50,000 for repayment of a student's loans in exchange for a minimum two-year service commitment in a Health Professional Shortage Area (HPSA), with additional amounts available for additional years of service. Visit www.nhsc.hrsa.gov/loanrepayment for more information.

National Institutes of Health Loan Repayment Program awards up to $35,000 for repayment of eligible student loans per year of research with a two-year minimum commitment. Visit www.lrp.nih.gov for more information.

Considerations with Loan Repayment Programs

If any of the above loan repayment programs are of interest to you, there are a few things to consider:

False assumptions—Some students may be turned off by loan repayment programs because they are afraid they will lose control over where they will live and work during the service commitment years. While a possibility, this scenario does not always take place. Do your homework and find out what each program will require. Ask your FAO if there are any alumni participating in these programs with whom you could talk about their experiences.

Tax implications—Find out if the money that you receive from a loan repayment program is considered taxable income. Lump-sum loan repayments can be helpful because they generally lower the amount of interest you pay over the life of your loan, but they can also result in a higher tax burden. Ask if the program will cover the cost of your taxes before you commit, or if the funds even have to be declared as income on your tax return.

Application dates—Some programs require that you sign up before you finish school.

Service contracts—Loan repayment in the majority of these programs is contingent on a specified length of service outlined by a service contract. Breach of the contract is serious and can result in heavy financial penalties (and loss of repayment funds). Be sure you do not have any future commitments that could adversely impact your completion of the required terms of service.

Eligibility requirements—Before spending time applying, make sure you are eligible for a loan repayment program. For example, eligibility may require that you come from a disadvantaged background (as certified by your educational institution).

Future goals—Do you want to eventually buy a house or help a sibling pay for his or her education? What about opening your own practice or entering academia? Perhaps you want to be a leader in community service? The better you manage your educational debts, the easier it may be to focus on these and other goals. Loan repayment programs may be a great way to help you accomplish your goals.

■ Loan Forgiveness Programs

Loan forgiveness programs forgive a portion of your student loan debt as long as you meet certain conditions. Note these are different from loan repayment programs, discussed above. With forgiveness programs, nobody pays your debt for you; rather, the balance is "waived" or forgiven at a certain point. There are at least three forgiveness programs of which you should be aware:

25-Year Forgiveness Under IBR

Borrowers who meet the following criteria should be eligible to have their remaining balance forgiven (although the amount to be forgiven is subject to tax under current law):

- They qualify for IBR

- They renew their eligibility each year and remain in the program

- They still have an outstanding balance after 25 years

20-Year Forgiveness Under PAYE

Borrowers who meet the following criteria should be eligible to have their remaining balance forgiven (although the amount to be forgiven is subject to tax under current law):

- They qualify for PAYE

- They renew their eligibility each year and remain in the program

- They still have an outstanding balance after 20 years

20-Year Forgiveness Under the "New IBR" (for first-time borrowers as of July 1, 2014)

Borrowers who meet the following criteria should be eligible to have their remaining balance forgiven (although the amount to be forgiven is subject to tax under current law):

- They qualify for the "New IBR" (similar to PAYE but with no limit to the interest amount that can be capitalized)

- They renew their eligibility each year and remain in the program

- They still have an outstanding balance after 20 years

Public Service Loan Forgiveness

This program offers borrowers meeting eligibility requirements forgiveness of a portion of their student loan portfolio. To qualify, borrowers must (1) make 120 timely, eligible, scheduled payments with a repayment plan, such as IBR or PAYE, on (2) direct loans (the only ones to qualify for PSLF forgiveness) while (3) working at least 30 hours for an eligible PSLF employer, including nonprofit organizations.

Please see www.StudentLoans.gov under Managing Repayment for details.

See Question 8 for resources that provide additional information on loan forgiveness programs, including PSLF.

QUESTION 5

WHAT DO STUDENT LOANS HAVE TO DO WITH MY CREDIT?

The short answer is "a lot." Understanding credit and how it relates to your student loans is an important part of sound educational debt management. This discussion is broken into three areas:

1. The "Double Whammy"

2. Credit-Ready and Creditworthy

3. Budgeting and Credit Education

■ The "Double Whammy"

More than one-third of your credit score comes from your repayment history. This fact can cause challenges for students, who often have "thin" credit files—that is, they are not old enough to have established a long credit history proving financial responsibility. While a thin credit file may not pose a problem (everyone starts with a thin credit file), one small mistake can have an adverse impact on your credit.

For example, if a 55-year-old man with a solid credit history is more than 30 days late with a payment, the effect on his credit score will likely be outweighed by many years of timely payments. Creditors may assume the late payment (called a delinquency) is simply an exception and not a pattern.

On the other hand, if a 23-year-old first-year dental student is more than 30 days late with a payment, his or her credit score could drop dramatically because there is not a lengthy history of timely payments. Creditors may not know if the late payment is routine behavior or an exception.

Students do not really have a chance to work on their repayment histories for their student loans until after dental school, when they start paying them back on a regular monthly basis. A thin credit history, combined with a delay in paying back your student loans, could result in a "double whammy" to your credit score. While you may not think the "double whammy" is important now, consider the negative effect it could have on a mortgage or other financing application (such as startup funds for a new practice) or even on the cost of your automobile insurance after you graduate.

■ Credit-Ready and Creditworthy

Credit-ready usually means that a borrower has no credit history or that he or she has no adverse items in his or her credit history (such as payments 30 and 60 days late), or both.

Creditworthy usually means the lender will dig deeper into a borrower's credit history. The lender will likely look for a minimum credit score and may look at a debt-to-income ratio (called DTI) that indicates whether current income is high enough to sustain loan payments.

A lender making private loans may use a combination of requirements of "credit-ready" and "creditworthy" to determine eligibility, interest rate and origination or other fees. There are no credit checks for Federal Stafford Loans and only a credit-ready check for Direct PLUS Loans.

> *Remember that you cannot include consumer debts in your cost of attendance each year, so it remains more important than ever to eliminate any outstanding credit card debt before you start dental school.*

While the financial aid office (FAO) cannot process your application for financial aid until you are accepted, you should not wait until you are accepted to start the aid application process. Complete your aid application early so that the FAO can begin reviewing your file as soon as you are accepted. Hopefully, submitting your application early will help ensure you are considered for grants and scholarships.

■ Budgeting and Credit Education

We have outlined the importance of smart budgeting and the fact that credit card and other consumer obligations cannot be included in your annual cost of attendance or student financial aid budget. There have been a number of banking and credit card changes in the lending industry that are designed to help protect you (and other consumers), but you are ultimately responsible for demonstrating your ability to use credit wisely.

If you have questions about credit, the following resources may be helpful:

- www.myfico.com/crediteducation has credit scores and detailed information about credit and how it works.

- www.annualcreditreport.com is the only government-approved site where consumers can get a free credit report on an annual basis.

- www.bankrate.com also provides information you may find helpful.

QUESTION 6

ARE THERE ANY CHANGES IN FINANCIAL AID THAT I SHOULD KNOW ABOUT?

You may see some changes in financial aid during your years in dental school, so be sure to keep in touch with your school's financial aid office (FAO), not only while you are in dental school but also after you graduate. Although loan program changes in many cases are applicable only to first-time or "new" borrowers based on a certain date, do not assume the modifications do not apply to you.

■ New rates on new loans

As previously mentioned, interest rates on *new* unsubsidized Stafford Loans and *new* Direct PLUS Loans disbursed on or after July 1 of subsequent years have new rates. Once the rate is determined, however, it is fixed throughout the life of the loan (until the loan is paid in full or perhaps forgiven). For example, you could graduate from dental school with four unsubsidized Federal Stafford—or four PLUS—loans, each of which has a different rate. Current fixed rates for new loans disbursed on or after July 1, 2014, are as follows:

- 4.66% for subsidized and unsubsidized Federal Stafford Loans for undergraduates

- 6.21% for unsubsidized Federal Stafford Loans for graduate and professional students

- 7.21% for Direct PLUS Loans (including Parent PLUS and Direct PLUS)

Remember that with caps on new loans as high as 8.25% (Federal Stafford Loans for undergraduates), 9.5% (unsubsidized Federal Stafford Loans for graduate and professional students) and 10.5% (Direct PLUS Loans), it is more important than ever to borrow responsibly and never borrow more than you need.

■ Elimination of Interest Subsidy on New Stafford Loans

Remember that new Stafford Loans for graduate and professional students (including dental) carry no interest subsidy and therefore begin to accrue interest upon disbursement. You can still borrow up to $40,500 through the Stafford Loan program each year. Although you are not required during school and the grace period to pay the interest, it will accrue. If unpaid, it will be capitalized (added to the principal amount you borrowed), increasing your total repayment amount—another reason to budget wisely and borrow responsibly. Note that this change does not impact any subsidized loans you may have borrowed—perhaps as an undergraduate or in a postbaccalaureate program—prior to July 1, 2012.

■ New Income-Driven Repayment Plan

Income-driven repayment plans ("IDRs") are designed to help borrowers with high debt and low-to-moderate incomes who cannot afford repayment under other repayment plans, such as the standard repayment plan (10 years) and the extended replayment plan. Income-driven repayment is actually the "umbrella" name of a number of different types of plans, but the most popular ones are Income-Based Repayment (IBR) and Pay As You Earn (PAYE). Monthly payments under IBR are calculated at 15% of the borrower's discretionary income, compared with 10% of discretionary income under PAYE.

There is a new income-driven repayment plan, also called IBR (the "New IBR"), which is similar to PAYE with one exception. PAYE limits the interest that can be capitalized, and the "New IBR" plan has no such cap.

The takeaway should be that there are currently a number of repayment plans tied to your income that should provide you with manageable monthly payments.

■ Proposed Changes to Income-Driven Repayment Plans and Forgiveness Programs

At the time of this writing, there are a number of proposals being considered that would alter not only the income-driven repayment plans, but also the forgiveness programs associated with them. In addition, there is a proposal to cap the amount of debt that can be forgiven under the Public Service Loan Forgiveness (PSLF) program.

While changes do tend to be applicable in the future to new or first-time borrowers, there is no guarantee that such will be the case. We therefore encourage you to work closely with your FAO to keep abreast of any changes that might impact not only your borrowing, but also your repayment strategy.

The takeaway should be that there are currently a number of repayment plans tied to your income that should provide you with manageable monthly payments.

QUESTION 7

HOW DO I GET STARTED, AND IS THERE A CHECKLIST I CAN USE TO BE SURE I DON'T FORGET ANYTHING?

We suggest several steps:

1. Contact the financial aid office (FAO) of your institution and ask the following questions:

■ Are any grants or scholarships available for me? Are they based on need, merit or both?

■ Are there any separate forms or applications I have to complete? What are the submission deadlines?

■ Does the FAO require that parental information be submitted for consideration of any campus-based grants, scholarships or loans?

■ What is the first-year cost of attendance/financial aid budget, and within that budget, what is the expected monthly living allowance?

■ What kind of student loan counseling and educational debt management help will be available to me during school and as I prepare to graduate? To avoid being surprised when I graduate, how can I estimate the impact of the loans I take out each year on my future loan payments? Is all the counseling done online or will I have the chance to talk with someone one-on-one?

Note: Look for information on the Association of American Medical Colleges/ American Dental Education Association (AAMC/ADEA) Dental Loan Organizer and Calculator under Question 8, below.

■ Are additional types of financial aid—such as fellowships, traineeships or work-study programs—available through the school?

Take advantage of the AAMC/ADEA DLOC— available at no cost to users—to help you organize your student loans.

The Association of American Medical Colleges/American Dental Education Association Dental Loan Organizer and Calculator:

✓ Provides a secure location for dental school students and residents to calculate and track student loans.

✓ Runs repayment scenarios based on career plans—including advanced dental education—following graduation.

Look for information at aamc.org/ GoDental.

■ Are there any summer internships or other paid research or work opportunities for incoming dental students during the summer before school starts?

2. Complete the Free Application for Federal Student Aid (FAFSA).

The FAFSA is available online at www.fafsa.ed.gov. Your FAO uses the results of your FAFSA application to consider you for financial aid. Check with your FAO about deadlines, but plan on completing the FAFSA as soon as possible after January 1 of your anticipated matriculation year. *Do not wait until you have been accepted to complete the FAFSA.*

3. Get your financial aid records in order, especially if you have outstanding student loans.

■ Contact your loan servicer(s) and ensure that they have your up-to-date contact information, including mail and email addresses and phone numbers. Be sure the loan servicer(s) know(s) when and where you are starting dental school and your expected graduation date. Do not have your mail sent home unless you are living at home; these are your loans, and correspondence about them should come to you.

■ Go to www.NSLDS.ed.gov and get an updated record of your outstanding Federal Stafford, Direct PLUS, Federal Perkins and Direct Consolidation loans you already have. You should be able to find your current loan servicer(s) for federal student loans at this site.

■ Set up both paper and electronic files to keep all financial aid-related documents, including:

—Copies of financial aid award letters or notices from the FAO.
—Copies of your master promissory note for federal loans.
—Disclosure notices from your lender (also called truth-in-lending disclosures, or "TILs").
—Borrower rights and responsibilities statements.

QUESTION 8

WHERE CAN I GO IF I NEED MORE HELP?

Although we always encourage you to check first with your financial aid office, below are additional resources.

■ Financial Aid

ADEA.org/GoDental (ADEA) contains a tremendous amount of information on paying for dental school, including video presentations and articles and primers on paying for school and on loan repayment.

adea.org/DLOC provides a link to the Association of American Medical Colleges/ American Dental Education Association (AAMC/ADEA) Dental Loan Organizer and Calculator (AAMC/ADEA DLOC), a secure location where dental students and residents can organize and track student loans. The AAMC/ADEA DLOC also runs repayment scenarios based on career plans, including advanced dental education.

www.NSLDS.ed.gov, from the U.S. Department of Education (ED), provides a comprehensive listing of all federal Title IV loans (Stafford, Direct PLUS, Perkins and Direct Consolidation loans), including information about loan servicers. You will need your federal PIN to access your record.

www.StudentAid.ed.gov (ED) has information about federal financial aid.

www.StudentLoans.gov (ED) offers information about federal loan programs and provides important repayment information, including the repayment estimator (calculator) for all available repayment plans. The site includes information on loan forgiveness programs (look for the "Managing Repayment" button in the top navigation bar).

www.finaid.org includes comprehensive information on all types of financial aid, a searchable database for scholarships (www.fastweb.com) and various repayment calculators.

www.ibrinfo.org contains information on the IBR Plan and the PSLF program from the nonpartisan Project on Student Debt.

■ Credit Information and Financial Planning

www.annualcreditreport.com is the only website authorized by the Federal Trade Commission to provide free credit reports. You may request a report from each of the three major credit reporting agencies once a year via this organization.

www.bankrate.com provides information on credit management, mortgages, credit cards, interest rates and more.

www.FPAnet.org, the website for the nonprofit Financial Planning Association has useful free information on basic financial planning and money management.

www.nfcc.org provides information on credit counseling from the National Foundation for Credit Counseling and its partners. The site offers calculators, budget workshops and tips to help promote financially responsible behavior.

■ Tax Information

www.irs.gov/publications/p970 has information on tax credits and deductions—including the lifetime learning credit, student loan interest deduction and the American opportunity tax credit—that are available for students with federal loans.

GLOSSARY
STUDENT FINANCIAL AID AND LOAN TERMS EVERY RESPONSIBLE BORROWER SHOULD KNOW

Accrued Interest: Interest assessed on the unpaid balance of the loan principal (the original amount borrowed) that in most cases is the borrower's responsibility to pay.

Aggregate Debt: The total amount of outstanding student loans for one borrower from all loan programs combined.

Aggregate Loan Limit: The total amount of outstanding principal borrowed in a specific student loan program.

Amortization: The process of repaying debt over an extended period of time through periodic installment payments of principal and interest. You may hear your repayment schedule referred to as your "amortization schedule" or that your student loans are "amortized" over a designated period of time.

Annual Percentage Rate (APR): An annual interest rate that reflects the total cost of a loan, including not only the stated interest rate but also loan fees and possible repayment benefits or discounts.

Borrower Benefits: Interest rate discounts or reimbursements—also referred to as "repayment incentives"—provided to a borrower by the lender as a means of reducing the cost of the loan. Check your promissory note or disclosure statement, or contact your lender for details. Other than a discount for automatic payments, borrower benefits on new loans are unlikely.

Campus-Based Aid: Financial aid programs administered directly by a dental school or institution. These include any grants and scholarships from the school, as well as from federal programs such as the Federal Perkins Loan, HPSL, LDS and work-study programs.

Capitalization: The process of adding accrued and unpaid interest to the principal of a loan. Capitalization increases the total repayment amount and the monthly payment. Capitalization usually occurs at repayment (for example, at the end of a grace period) and whenever there is a "status change" (for example, when you move from repayment into deferment or forbearance).

Cosigner Release: Process through which a lender releases a creditworthy cosigner from his or her obligation to repay a loan he or she cosigned. A borrower should contact the lender to see if such a provision exists. See Creditworthy Cosigner for more details.

COA: Cost of Attendance (also referred to as the financial aid budget).

Cost of Attendance: Total costs associated with attending dental school for a given award year. The amount usually includes tuition and fees. an allowance for books, supplies and equipment and an allowance for living expenses, including health insurance. Each institution develops its own student budget, also known as the financial aid budget.

Consolidation: A loan used to pay off multiple loans.

Creditworthy Cosigner: An individual—deemed creditworthy by a lender—who assumes responsibility for the loan if the borrower should fail to repay it. Usually applies only to private loan programs.

Credit Score: An evaluation—represented by a three-digit number—that represents the likelihood a borrower will repay a financial obligation. With regard to student loans, credit scores apply only to private loan programs.

Default: Failure of a borrower to make payments when due or to comply with loan terms as stated in the promissory note. In general, federal student loans are considered in default after being 270 days delinquent (time frame may differ for private loans). Default may result in actions by your loan holder to recover the money owed, including garnishing your wages, withholding income tax refunds and notifying national credit bureaus of the default. Defaulting on a government loan renders a borrower ineligible for future federal financial aid unless a satisfactory repayment schedule is arranged. Default adversely impacts credit and may stay on a borrower's credit record for up to seven years.

Deferment: A period of time during which a borrower may postpone payment on a loan, assuming he or she meets the requirements established by law or regulation or contained in the promissory note. Subsidized loans are interest-free to borrowers during periods of deferment, while unsubsidized loans continue to accrue interest. Use of the term "deferment" to describe periods when a borrower is allowed to postpone payments on a private loan may actually be a reference to forbearance (see Forbearance).

Delinquency: Failure of a borrower to make a payment by the due date. Delinquencies greater than 30 days may be reported to national credit reporting agencies by the lender. Once the delinquency exceeds a specified number of days (varies depending on the loan program), the borrower goes into default.

Disadvantaged Background (definition from HHS): One who comes from an environment that has inhibited the individual from obtaining the knowledge, skill and abilities required to enroll in and graduate from a health professions school or a program providing education or training in an allied health profession; or who comes from a family with an annual income below a low-income threshold according to family size published by the U.S. Census Bureau, adjusted annually for changes in the Consumer Price Index and adjusted by the Secretary of HHS for use in health professions and nursing programs.

Disbursement Date: The date on which the lender issues the loan proceeds, either by check or by electronic funds transfer, to the dental school or institution, typically directly to the student's account at the school.

Disclosure Statement: Document stating the terms and conditions of a student loan and the repayment schedule. Disclosure statements include information on the interest rate, fees and repayment terms. May also be called a "truth in lending" disclosure statement or "TIL."

ED: U.S. Department of Education

EFC: Expected family contribution

Electronic Funds Transfer (EFT): Method by which loan proceeds are disbursed to the school. Stafford and Direct PLUS loans are generally disbursed via EFT to the borrower's school and automatically applied to his or her student account.

Eligible Noncitizen: Someone who is not a U.S. citizen but is nonetheless eligible for federal student aid. Eligible noncitizens include U.S. permanent residents who hold valid green cards, U.S. nationals, those holding Form I-94 with refugee or asylum status and certain other noncitizens. A noncitizen who holds a student visa or an exchange visitor visa is not eligible for federal student aid.

Enrollment Status: An indication of whether you are a full-time, half-time or part-time student. In general, you must be enrolled at least half time to qualify for financial aid. Some financial aid programs require you to be enrolled full time.

Expected Family Contribution (EFC): The amount of money the family is expected to contribute to a student's education, as determined by the federal methodology formula that uses information provided on the FAFSA. The EFC is a student or spouse's contribution based on factors including family size, number of family members in school, taxable and non-taxable income and assets. Parental financial information is required for funds authorized by HHS and may be required by some schools for the purpose of determining eligibility for institutional funds. Some schools may use a different methodology to determine eligibility for institutional funds.

FAFSA: Free Application for Federal Student Aid

FAO: Financial aid office

Fees: Charges assessed by the lender that are usually expressed as a percentage of the principal amount borrowed and deducted from the loan proceeds at disbursement. Fees may be charged for the origination of the loan, as a guarantee against default and—in the case of some private loans—added to the repayment costs as back-end fees. Fees should be found on a loan's disclosure statement.

Financial Aid Award Letter: A listing of the financial aid you are eligible for (your financial aid award package) as determined by your school's FAO. It may be sent electronically or by postal mail, or it may be posted on your FAO's website (with secure access by a PIN or password). It may also be referred to as a financial aid notification letter.

Financial Aid Award Package: Combination of different types of financial aid, such as grants, scholarships and loans, as determined by your school's FAO.

Financial Aid Award Year: The academic period for which financial aid is requested and awarded.

Financial Aid Budget: Total costs associated with attending dental school for a given award year. The amount usually includes tuition and fees; an allowance for books, supplies and equipment; and an allowance for living expenses including health insurance. Each institution develops its own student budget, also known as the cost of attendance (COA).

Financial Aid Office (FAO): The office at the dental school or institution responsible for administering financial aid funds for their students.

Financial Need: The difference between the financial aid budget (also known as COA) and a student's available resources. Financial need is determined by the FAO and is based on the difference between COA and expected family contribution.

Fixed Interest Rate: An interest rate that does not change throughout the life of a loan (during school; during any grace, deferment or forbearance periods; and during repayment).

Forbearance: A period of time during which a borrower may postpone payment on a loan. Various types of forbearance are available on federal loans, including forbearance granted at the lender's discretion and forbearance based on a borrower's status as a dental resident. While similar to deferments as a means for postponing payments, interest accrues on all loans during forbearance. Lenders may capitalize interest more frequently during periods of forbearance, especially in the case of Direct PLUS Loans. Private loan lenders may charge a fee to postpone the payment. In addition, borrowers who use forbearance may lose borrower benefits their lenders provide on their loans.

Free Application for Federal Student Aid (FAFSA): The form approved by ED and used by students to apply for all federally sponsored student financial aid programs. The form is available at www.fafsa.ed.gov, and it can be submitted electronically or by mail. Contact your FAO for filing deadlines.

Grace Period: A period of time after graduation (or after a borrower drops below half-time status) during which a borrower is not required to begin repaying his or her student loan(s). Grace periods depend on the kind of loan, and they are attached to an individual loan. For example, a borrower who has used up a grace period on an undergraduate loan does not lose the grace periods on loans taken out in dental school. Not all loans have grace periods.

Health Professions Student Loans (HPSL): This program provides long-term, low-interest-rate loans to full-time students to pursue a degree in one of the health professions.

HHS: U.S. Department of Health and Human Services

HPSL: Health Professions Student Loans

Income-Based Repayment (IBR): One of a number of income-driven repayment plans for borrowers with high debt and low to moderate incomes. IBR sets an eligible borrower's monthly federal student loan payment at 15% of his or her discretionary income. Note there is a new version of IBR for first-time borrowers (those borrowing federal loans for the first time) on or after July 1, 2014, with repayment terms similar to PAYE.

Income-Driven Repayment: The "umbrella" name used to describe a number of different repayment plans that are tied, in part, to a borrower's income. Examples include IBR and PAYE.

Interest Rate Cap: Refers to the maximum interest a borrower may be charged over the life of the loan on a variable-rate loan (see variable interest rate). Interest rate caps apply only to variable rate loans and should be referenced in both the promissory note and disclosure statement. Not all variable rate loans have caps.

LDS: Loans for Disadvantaged Students

Loans for Disadvantaged Students: This program provides long-term, low-interest-rate loans to full-time students from disadvantaged backgrounds who need financial assistance.

Loan Terms and Conditions: The conditions of a loan, including requirements governing receipt and repayment. Specifically, loan terms usually refer to the interest rate, fees and other costs associated with receipt and repayment.

Minority: According to the U.S. government, an individual whose race/ethnicity is classified as American Indian or Alaska Native, Asian, Native Hawaiian or other Pacific Islander, Black or African American, or Hispanic/Latino.

National Health Service Corps (NHSC): NHSC connects primary health care providers to areas of the United States with limited access to care.

National Student Loan Data System (NSLDS): Federal repository accessible at www.nslds.ed.gov that provides a listing of Title IV aid (Stafford, Direct PLUS, Perkins and Direct Consolidation loans) for individual students and borrowers. You can find a list of your personal loans (with the exception of HPSL, LDS and institutional and private loans) in this database.

NHSC: National Health Service Corps

Outside Scholarship: A scholarship that comes from a source other than the dental school or institution.

Pay As You Earn (PAYE): One of a number of income-driven repayment plans for borrowers with high debt and low to moderate incomes. PAYE sets an eligible borrower's monthly federal student loan payment at 10% of his or her discretionary income.

Principal: The original amount of money borrowed or the outstanding amount immediately following capitalization of any accrued and unpaid interest.

Private Loans: Educational loans provided by private or commercial lenders and not backed by the federal government. Dental school students who already have private loans or are considering private loan programs (or both) should strongly consider speaking with their FAOs about the potential impact these loans may have on their repayment strategies after dental school.

Promissory Note: A binding legal document that must be signed by a borrower to show that he or she agrees to repay the loan according to terms specified in the document. The promissory note, which must be signed before loan funds can be disbursed by the lender, provides evidence of the borrower's willingness to repay the debt. Along with disclosure statements, the promissory note is a document a borrower should keep. A borrower is entitled to the return of the promissory note marked "paid in full" once the obligation has been met.

Repayment Schedule or Repayment Term: The time frame over which a borrower is required to repay his or her loan (also referred to as the amortization schedule). Usually stated in terms of number of monthly payments required with payment amounts and due dates, with terms of the loan listed.

Residency and Relocation Loan: A private loan used by some dental students in their fourth years to help fund expenses associated with residency interviews or relocation to their residency programs (or both) following graduation.

Satisfactory Academic Progress (SAP): The academic progress—as required and defined by the school—a student must make to continue receiving federal financial aid. If a student fails to maintain an academic standing consistent with the dental school's SAP policy, he or she is unlikely to meet the school's graduation requirements and may be ineligible to receive federal financial aid.

Student Aid Report (SAR): The report summarizing the information included in the FAFSA. The SAR, which also indicates the EFC, is provided to your school's FAO. For information on the SAR, go to www.fafsa.ed.gov.

Subsidized Loan: A loan that remains interest-free to the borrower, while he or she is enrolled at least half-time and during periods of grace and deferment. Subsidized loans are based, at least in part, on financial need.

Title IV Loans: Loan programs administered by ED. These include Stafford, Direct PLUS, Federal Perkins and Direct Consolidation loans.

Title IV School Code: The numerical code used to indicate to which school(s) you want your FAFSA results sent.

Title VII Financial Aid: Financial aid programs administered by HHS. These include the HPSL and LDS programs.

Unmet Need: The difference between your calculated need and the amount of financial aid awarded. Your school's FAO may put together unsubsidized loans to meet any unmet need.

Unsubsidized Loan: Loans that accrue interest from the date of disbursement, including during the school year and during grace and deferment periods for which the borrower may be eligible. Borrowers are responsible for the interest that accrues on unsubsidized loans. Unsubsidized loans are not based on financial need and may be used to cover the family contribution and any unmet need.

U.S. Department of Education (ED): The government department that administers Title IV federal student financial aid programs, including the federal work-study program, Perkins, Stafford, Direct PLUS and Direct Consolidation loans.

Variable Interest Rate: A loan interest rate that changes at designated intervals, sometimes monthly or quarterly.

CHAPTER 5
GETTING MORE INFORMATION

This chapter gives you lists of individuals, organizations and references that can help answer any questions left unanswered by this book.

WHO CAN ADVISE ME?

First, consider talking to people involved in dental education: They are interested in encouraging students like you to consider dentistry as a career. Next, think about approaching other professionals, such as the ones indicated here:

THESE PROFESSIONALS	CAN HELP YOU BY ...
Practicing Dentists	■ Sharing their knowledge about the education and skills needed to pursue a variety of careers in dentistry. ■ Describing day-to-day work and addressing work-life balance. ■ Offering you internship or "shadowing" opportunities.
Health Professions Advisors	■ Assisting you with a broad range of issues about dental education and dental schools. ■ Informing you about the academic preparation necessary (before you begin the application process) to be accepted into a dental school. ■ Helping provide or coordinate letters of recommendation (during the application process).
Science Professors (especially those in biological sciences)	■ Advising you on academic preparation. ■ Providing letters of recommendation. ■ Substituting for a health professions advisor if your undergraduate school does not have one.
Dental School Admissions Officers	■ Providing information about the dental schools they represent, including: —Catalogs. —Admission criteria. —Academic program highlights. —Student support services. —Other useful features.
Dental School Minority/ Diversity Affairs Officers	■ Sharing information about diversity at their schools. ■ Welcoming and assisting students from diverse backgrounds. ■ Providing information about support services.

THESE PROFESSIONALS	CAN HELP YOU BY ...	(continued)
Financial Aid Administrators	■ Advising you on ways to finance the cost of attending dental school. ■ Helping you understand the: —Financial aid application process. —Eligibility requirements for governmental, institutional and private sources of financial aid. ■ Assisting you in securing any funds for which you are eligible.	
Dental Students	■ Sharing perceptions and personal experiences about the education they are receiving. (Keep in mind that it is always a good idea to base your decisions on information collected from a variety of sources.) ■ Describing their experiences of their schools' nonacademic features, such as student support services and social atmosphere. ■ Talking about issues related to dental school in online discussion boards, such as ADEA GoDental (adea.org/GoDental).	

WHAT ORGANIZATIONS CAN HELP ME?

A number of organizations offer information about careers in dentistry, preparing for admission to dental school and seeking financial aid.

DENTAL EDUCATION		
Organization and Location	**Contact Information**	**Mission/Objectives**
American Dental Education Association (ADEA) *Washington, DC*	**Phone:** 202-289-7201 **Fax:** 202-289-7204 **Websites:** adea.org adea.org/join adea.org/GoDental	■ Provides information about dental school application and admissions processes. ■ Sponsors application services for admission to: —Dental school (ADEA AADSAS^{SM}). —Advanced dental education (ADEA PASS^{SM}). —Advanced placement for international dentists (ADEA CAAPID^{SM}). —Dental hygiene programs (DHCAS^{SM}). ■ Offers free membership to dental students.
ADEA GoDental^{SM} *Washington, DC*	**Phone:** 202-289-7201 **Email:** godental@adea.org **Website:** adea.org/GoDental	■ Sponsored by ADEA, serves as a career-building and networking Web resource for people on the pathway to careers in dentistry or dental hygiene. ■ Promotes collaboration, community and connection between prehealth and current health professionals.
American Student Dental Association *Chicago, IL*	**Phone:** 800-621-8099, ext. 2795 (central office); 312-440-2826 (membership inquiries) **Fax:** 312-440-2820 **Email:** Membership@ASDAnet.org **Website:** www.asdanet.org	■ Serves as a student-run organization with 20,000 members. ■ Protects and advances the rights, interests and welfare of dental students. ■ Provides services, information, education, representation and advocacy.

DENTAL EDUCATION			*(continued)*
Organization and Location	**Contact Information**		**Mission/Objectives**
ExploreHealthCareers.org *Washington, DC*	Phone: Email: Website:	202-289-7201 347-365-9253 feedback@explorehealthcareers. org www.ExploreHealthCareers.org	■ Serves as a free multidisciplinary website allowing users to explore more than 100 health professions careers, including dentistry and allied dentistry. ■ Provides a database with more than 500 resources about scholarships and predental enrichment programs.
International Federation of Dental Educators and Associations *San Francisco, CA*	Website:	www.ifdea.org	■ Operates a web-based knowledge-sharing resource for the dental education community. ■ Gathers international resources and expertise in dental education.

DENTAL SPECIALTY ORGANIZATIONS			
Organization and Location	**Contact Information**		**Mission/Objectives**
Academy of General Dentistry *Chicago, IL*	Phone: Fax: Website:	888-AGD-DENT or 888-243-3368 312-335-3432 www.agd.org	■ Serves the needs and represents the interests of general dentists. ■ Fosters continued proficiency of general dentists through quality dental education.
American Academy of Oral and Maxillofacial Pathology *Wheaton, IL*	Phone: Fax: Website:	888-552-2667 or 630-510-4552 630-510-4501 www.aaomp.org	■ Represents the dental specialty that identifies and manages diseases affecting the oral and maxillofacial regions and investigates the causes, processes and effects of these diseases. ■ Includes clinical practitioners, researchers, educators and microscopic diagnosticians who collaborate with other health care professionals.
American Academy of Oral and Maxillofacial Radiology *Springfield, IL*	Email: Website:	ED@aaomr.org www.aaomr.org	■ Safeguards ethical, evidence-based, and high-quality oral and maxillofacial diagnostic services to the referred public. ■ Promotes and advances the art and science of radiology in dentistry to the health care community and to the public. ■ Provides a forum for communication among its members.
American Academy of Pediatric Dentistry *Chicago, IL*	Phone: Fax: Website:	312-337-2169 312-337-6329 www.aapd.org	■ Serves as the recognized authority on children's oral health. ■ Advocates children's oral health by: —Promoting evidence-based policies and clinical guidelines. —Educating and informing policymakers, parents and guardians, and other health care professionals. —Fostering research. —Providing continuing professional education.

DENTAL SPECIALTY ORGANIZATIONS		*(continued)*
Organization and Location	*Contact Information*	*Mission/Objectives*
American Academy of Periodontology *Chicago, IL*	**Phone:** 312-787-5518 **Fax:** 312-787-3670 **Website:** www.perio.org	■ Specializes in the prevention, diagnosis and treatment of diseases affecting the gums and supporting structures of the teeth, as well as in the placement and maintenance of dental implants. ■ Advances the periodontal and general health of the public and promotes excellence in the practice of periodontics.
American Association of Endodontists *Chicago, IL*	**Phone:** 800-872-3636 (North America) or +1-312-266-7255 (International) **Website:** www.aae.org	■ Seeks to secure contributions, shepherd resources and share grant funds that support research, generate new knowledge and enhance endodontic education. ■ Works to ensure the specialty's place at the forefront of the dental health arena.
American Association of Hospital Dentists *Chicago, IL*	*See under:* **Special Care Dentistry Association**	
American Association of Oral and Maxillofacial Surgeons *Rosemont, IL*	**Phone:** 847-678-6200 or 800-822-6637 **Fax:** 847-678-6286 **Website:** www.aaoms.org	■ Represents more than 9,000 U.S. oral and maxillofacial surgeons who care for patients who experience such conditions as impacted wisdom teeth, facial and TMJ pain, and abnormal jaws, as well as for patients who have suffered from facial injuries. ■ Supports members' ability to practice their specialty through education, research and advocacy.
American Association of Orthodontists *St. Louis, MO*	**Phone:** 314-993-1700 or 800-424-2841 **Fax:** 314-997-1745 **Website:** www.mylifemysmile.org	■ Serves as the organization for specialists who diagnose, prevent, and treat dental and facial irregularities. ■ Provides information on the need and benefits of orthodontic treatment. ■ Supports research and education leading to quality patient care.
American Association of Public Health Dentistry *Springfield, IL*	**Phone:** 217-529-6941 **Fax:** 217-529-9120 **Website:** www.aaphd.org	■ Provides a focus for meeting the challenge to improve the oral health of the public. ■ Provides—through its broad membership base—numerous opportunities and a fertile environment to exchange ideas and experiences.
American College of Prosthodontists *Chicago, IL*	**Phone:** 312-573-1260 **Fax:** 312-573-1257 **Website:** www.gotoapro.org	■ Serves as a professional association of dentists with advanced specialty training in creating optimal oral health, both in function and appearance, including through the use of dental implants, dentures, veneers, crowns and teeth whitening. ■ Represents the needs and interests of prosthodontists, within organized dentistry and to the public.

DENTAL SPECIALTY ORGANIZATIONS		*(continued)*
Organization and Location	**Contact Information**	**Mission/Objectives**
Special Care Dentistry Association *Chicago, IL*	**Phone:** 312-527-6764 **Fax:** 312-673-6663 **Website:** www.scdaonline.org	▪ Brings together the following organizations: —American Association of Hospital Dentists —Academy of Dentistry for Persons with Disabilities —American Society for Geriatric Dentistry ▪ Works with oral health professionals and organizations to promote the oral health of individuals with special needs. ▪ Provides resources and opportunities for individuals interested in advancing the oral health of special needs patients.

RESEARCH		
Organization and Location	**Contact Information**	**Mission/Objectives**
American Association for Dental Research *Alexandria, VA*	**Phone:** 703-548-0066 **Fax:** 703-548-1883 **Website:** www.aadronline.org	▪ Advances research and increases knowledge for the improvement of oral health. ▪ Supports and represents the oral health research community. ▪ Facilitates the communication and application of research findings.
International Association for Dental Research *Alexandria, VA*	**Phone:** 703-548-0066 **Fax:** 703-548-1883 **Website:** www.iadr.com	▪ Advances research and increases knowledge for the improvement of oral health worldwide. ▪ Supports and represents the oral health research community. ▪ Facilitates the communication and application of research findings.
National Institute of Dental and Craniofacial Research *Bethesda, MD*	**Phone:** 301-496-4261 **Fax:** 301-480-4098 **Website:** www.nidcr.nih.gov	▪ Aims to improve dental, oral and craniofacial health through research, research training and the dissemination of health information.

PROFESSIONAL		
American Association of Women Dentists *Chicago, IL*	**Phone:** 800-920-2293 **Fax:** 312-750-1203 **Website:** www.aawd.org	▪ Celebrates the rich history of women dentists. ▪ Represents and provides support and education for women dentists across the United States, internationally and in the uniformed services. ▪ Strives toward "becoming the recognized resource for connecting and enriching the lives of women dentists."
American College of Dentists *Gaithersburg, MD*	**Phone:** 301-977-3223 **Fax:** 301-977-3330 **Email:** office@acd.org **Website:** www.acd.org	▪ Serves as the oldest national honorary organization for dentists. ▪ Promotes excellence, ethics, professionalism and leadership in dentistry. ▪ Offers conferences, programs and online resources. *Note:* Membership is by invitation only.

PROFESSIONAL		*(continued)*
Organization and Location	*Contact Information*	*Mission/Objectives*
American Dental Association *Chicago, IL*	Phone: 312-440-2500 Fax: 312-440-7494 Website: www.ada.org	▪ As the nation's largest dental association, represents more than 157,000 dentist members. ▪ Serves as the leading source of oral health-related information for dentists and their patients. ▪ Remains committed to its members and to the improvement of oral health for the public.
Association of Schools & Programs of Public Health *Washington, DC*	Phone: 202-296-1099 Fax: 202-296-1252 Website: www.aspph.org	▪ Represents the deans, faculty and students of the accredited member schools of public health and other programs seeking accreditation as schools of public health. ▪ Collects information on careers in public health.
Hispanic Dental Association *Austin, TX*	Phone: 512-904-0252 Website: www.hdassoc.org	▪ Seeks—through service, education, advocacy and leadership—to eliminate oral health disparities in the Hispanic community. ▪ Provides advocacy for Hispanic oral health professionals across the United States.
National Dental Association and Student National Dental Association *Greenbelt, MD*	Phone: 202-588-1697 Fax: 202-588-1244 Websites: www.ndaonline.org www.sndanet.org	▪ Promotes oral health equity among people of color by: —Harnessing the collective power of members. —Mentoring dental students of color and advocating their needs. —Raising the profile of the profession in our communities.
Society of American Indian Dentistry *Studio City, CA*	Phone: 310-694-4286 Email: info@thesaidonline.org Website: www.thesaidonline.org	▪ Comprises oral health professionals and students dedicated to: —Promoting and improving the oral health of the American Indian/Alaskan Native community. —Providing advocacy for the American Indian/Alaskan Native dental professionals across the United States.
Oral Health America *Chicago, IL*	Phone: 312-836-9900 Fax: 312-836-9986 Email: info@oralhealthamerica.org Website: www.oralhealthamerica.org	▪ Connects communities with resources to increase access to care. ▪ Provides education and advocacy for all Americans, especially those most vulnerable.

ARE THERE OTHER HELPFUL RESOURCES I CAN ACCESS?

College, university and public libraries generally have a range of publications about careers, undergraduate and graduate education, and financial aid. Many also offer computer use for access to electronic resources.

OTHER RESOURCES		
Dental Admission Test (DAT) Web portal	Available on ADA's website: www.ada.org/en/education-careers/dental-admission-test/dat-guide	■ Provides access to the following DAT resources, among others: —The most current DAT Program Guide (which you must read before applying to take the test) —Test preparation material and helpful information —Application procedures —Additional DAT-related information
Getting Into Dental School: ASDA's Guide for Predental Students	Available on the American Student Dental Association's website: www.asdanet.org/publications/	■ Targets predental students and those considering careers in dentistry. ■ Provides information on: —Applying to dental school. —Seeking financial aid. —Taking advantage of ASDA membership benefits. —Learning about debt management. ■ Includes dental career options and a DAT survival guide.
Getting Through Dental School: ASDA's Guide for Dental Students	Available on the American Student Dental Association's website: www.asdanet.org/publications/	■ Includes information on: —Scholarships, loans and grants. —Public health and international opportunities. —ASDA membership benefits. —Leadership opportunities.

ON TO PART II

Part I has provided you information about dentistry careers, meeting dental school acceptance criteria, financing a dental education and deciding where to apply. Part II, Learning about Dental Schools, introduces you to every dental school in the United States and Canada.

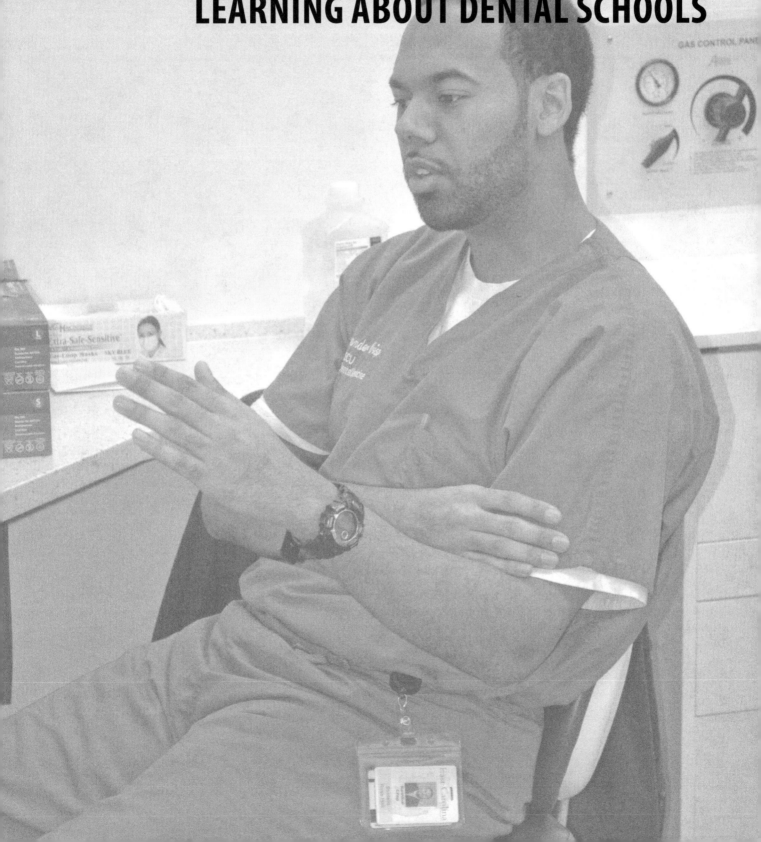

LEARNING ABOUT DENTAL SCHOOLS

Part II provides an individual introduction to each U.S. and Canadian dental school. ADEA has developed a format for Part II that is consistent from school to school to make it easier for readers to gather information. However, the narrative sections are provided by the dental schools themselves so that you can discern the distinctive qualities of each institution.

Every dental school in the United States and Canada is accredited or seeking accreditation. The Commission on Dental Accreditation accredits U.S. schools, and the Commission on Dental Accreditation of Canada accredits Canadian schools.

HOW TO USE PART II

The school entries are presented alphabetically by *state*.

Information about each school is organized into the areas that tend to be of most interest to dental school applicants:

■ **General Information** describes the type of institution, history of the dental school, location, size, facilities, doctoral dental degree offered, relationship of the dental school to other health profession schools in the university and other programs conducted by the school.

■ **Preparation** presents the school's requirements with respect to:

- Predental education (number of years, required courses, limitations on community college work and suggested additional preparation).

- Dental Admissions Test (DAT).

- Grade point average (GPA).

■ **Application and Selection** provides information on the application process and residency requirements and demographics. Demographics information is supplied by institutions, and their individual reporting procedures vary. A timetable is provided for submitting application materials and fees (if any) to be paid to the dental school and to inform applicants when they can expect to be notified. The residency section may disclose a school's participation in regional compacts, other interstate agreements or (for private schools) in-state agreements.

■ **Curriculum** introduces the dental school's educational program. Dental schools generally use this section to discuss program length, goals and objectives. Student research opportunities may also be listed.

■ **Special Programs and Services** describes assistance programs and other related student organizations that are available.

■ **Costs and Financial Aid** allows schools to briefly describe their financial aid policies or provide a website address for more information. The section also has a chart showing estimated expenses for both residents and nonresidents of the state in which the dental school is located. The costs given are for the most recent academic year the school has reported; you should adjust your estimated costs upward for the 2015–16 academic year.

■ **Contact Information** is listed on the left-hand side of the first page of the school's profile. This list usually provides the names, addresses and telephone numbers for the dental school's admissions, financial aid, minority/diversity affairs and housing offices.

As you determine where you plan to send applications, you should contact those dental schools directly for the most complete information about admission requirements. Their telephone numbers, addresses and websites are included with their entries.

UNIVERSITY OF ALABAMA AT BIRMINGHAM
SCHOOL OF DENTISTRY

Michael S. Reddy, D.M.D., D.M.Sc., Dean

GENERAL INFORMATION

The University of Alabama at Birmingham School of Dentistry (UABSOD), located on the campus of the University of Alabama at Birmingham, is an integral part of the large complex of medical facilities on this urban campus at the periphery of downtown Birmingham (metropolitan population: approximately one million). The School of Dentistry was created in 1945 by an act of the state legislature, and the first class matriculated in 1948. Students at the UABSOD pursue their professional education utilizing modern equipment in recently renovated facilities.

MISSION
To optimize oral health In Alabama and beyond

Vision: Leading oral health care

Core Values: excellence—innovation—patient centered—unity of purpose

Type of institution: Public	Doctoral dental degree offered: D.M.D.
Year opened: 1948	Targeted predoctoral enrollment: 228
Term type: Semester	Targeted entering class size: 62
Time to degree in months: 48	Campus setting: Urban
Start month: July	Campus housing available: Yes

PREPARATION

Formal minimum preparation in semester/quarter hours: Semester: 90   Quarter: 120
Baccalaureate degree preferred: Yes
Number of first-year, first-time enrollees whose highest degree is:
  Baccalaureate: 55
  Master's degree and beyond: 5
Of first-year, first-time enrollees without baccalaureates the number with:
  Equivalent of 60 undergraduate credit hours or less: 0
  Equivalent of 61–90 undergraduate credit hours: 0
  Equivalent of 91 or more undergraduate credit hours: 0

PREREQUISITE COURSE	REQUIRED	RECOMMENDED	LAB REQUIRED	CREDITS (SEMESTER/QUARTER)
BCP (biology-chemistry-physics) sciences				
Biology	✓		✓	12/18
Chemistry, general/inorganic	✓		✓	8/12
Chemistry, organic	✓		✓	8/12
Physics	✓		✓	8/12
Additional biological sciences				
Anatomy		✓		
Biochemistry		✓		
Cell biology		✓		
Histology		✓		
Immunology		✓		
Microbiology		✓		
Molecular biology/genetics		✓		
Physiology		✓		
Zoology		✓		

CONTACT INFORMATION
www.dental.uab.edu

Dr. Michael S. Reddy
Dean
SDB 406
1720 2nd Avenue South
Birmingham, AL 35294-0007
Phone: 205-934-4720
Fax: 205-975-6544

OFFICE OF ADMISSIONS
Dr. Steven Filler
Associate Dean of Student, Alumni and External Affairs
SDB 125
1720 2nd Avenue South
Birmingham, AL 35294-0007
Phone: 205-934-3387

FINANCIAL AID
Ms. Ann Little
LHL 120
1720 2nd Avenue South
Birmingham, AL 35294-0013
Phone: 205-934-8223

STUDENT AFFAIRS
Dr. Maureen Pezzementi
Director of Student Affairs
SDB 124
1720 2nd Avenue South
Birmingham, AL 35294-0007
Phone: 205-934-5470

MINORITY AFFAIRS/DIVERSITY
Dr. Michelle Robinson
SDB 631
1720 2nd Avenue South
Birmingham, AL 35294-0007
Phone: 205-934-1141

PREPARATION (CONTINUED)

PREREQUISITE COURSE	REQUIRED	RECOMMENDED	LAB REQUIRED	CREDITS (SEMESTER/QUARTER)
Other				
Mathematics	✓			6/9
English	✓			6/9
Non Science	✓			30/45

Community college coursework accepted for prerequisites: Yes
Community college coursework accepted for electives: Yes
Limits on community college credit hours: Yes
Maximum number of community college credit hours: 60
Advanced placement (AP) credit accepted for prerequisites: Yes
Advanced placement (AP) credit accepted for electives: Yes
Comments regarding AP credit: Applicants are strongly encouraged to take prerequisite courses for which they have earned AP/International Baccalaureate (IB) or other credit at the university level.
Job shadowing: Required

DAT

Mandatory: Yes
Latest DAT for consideration of application: 12/01/2015
Oldest DAT considered: 12/01/2012
When more than one DAT score is reported: Average score is considered.
Canadian DAT accepted: Yes
Application considered before DAT scores are submitted: No

DAT: 2014 ENTERING CLASS

ENROLLEE DAT SCORES	MEAN	RANGE
Academic Average	21.0	18–25
Perceptual Ability	20.4	15–25
Total Science	20.1	17–25

GPA: 2014 ENTERING CLASS

ENROLLEE GPA SCORES	UNDERGRAD. MEAN	GRADUATE MEAN	UNDERGRAD. RANGE	GRADUATE RANGE
Science GPA	3.66	NR	3.07–4.0	NR
Total GPA	3.71	NR	3.21–4.0	NR

APPLICATION AND SELECTION

TIMETABLE

Earliest filing date: 06/02/2015
Latest filing date: 11/01/2015
Earliest date for acceptance offers: 12/01/2015
Maximum time in days for applicant's response to acceptance offer:
    30 days if accepted on or after December 1
    15 days if accepted on or after February 1
Requests for deferred entrance considered: No
Fee for application: Yes, submitted only when requested.
Amount of fee for application:
    In state: $75   Out of state: $75   International: $75
Fee waiver available: No

	FIRST DEPOSIT	SECOND DEPOSIT	THIRD DEPOSIT
Required to hold place	Yes	No	No
Resident amount	$200		
Nonresident amount	$200		
Deposit due	As indicated in admission offer		
Applied to tuition	Yes		
Refundable	No		

APPLICATION PROCESS

Participates in Associated American Dental Schools Application Service (AADSAS): Yes
Accepts direct applicants: No
Secondary or supplemental application required: Yes
Secondary or supplemental application website: None
Interview is mandatory: Yes
Interview is by invitation: Yes

RESIDENCY

In-state/in-province versus out-of-state/out-of-province
Admissions process distinguishes between in-state/in-province and out-of-state/out-of-province applicants: Yes
Preference given to residents of: Alabama
Reciprocity Admissions Agreement available for legal residents of: None
Generally and over time, percentage of your first-year enrollment that is in-state: 85%
Origin of out-of-state/out-of-province enrollees: FL-3, GA-3, IL-1, MS-1, SC-1, TN-4

International
Applications are accepted from international (noncitizens/nonpermanent residents): Yes
Origin of international enrollees: NA

APPLICATION AND ENROLLMENT	NUMBER OF APPLICANTS	ESTIMATED NUMBER INTERVIEWED	ESTIMATED NUMBER ENROLLED
In-state or province applicants/enrollees	110	66	47
Out-of-state or province applicants/enrollees	646	66	13
International applicants/enrollees (noncitizens/nonpermanent residents)	8	0	0

DEMOGRAPHIC DESCRIPTIONS OF APPLICANTS: 2014 ENTERING CLASS

	APPLICANTS			ENROLLEES		
	M	W	Gender Unknown or Not Reported	M	W	Gender Unknown or Not Reported
American Indian or Alaska Native	1	1	0	0	0	0
Asian	67	79	3	5	3	0
Black or African American	12	25	0	3	2	0
Hispanic or Latino	19	23	0	0	1	0
Native Hawaiian or Other Pacific Islander	2	0	0	0	0	0
White	274	204	6	22	23	0
Two or more races	6	18	0	0	1	0
Race and ethnicity unknown	10	5	1	0	0	0
International	3	5	0	0	0	0

	MINIMUM	MAXIMUM	MEAN
2014 entering class enrollees by age	22	37	22

CURRICULUM

The objective of the program at the University of Alabama at Birmingham is to produce competent and caring oral health care providers. Our goal is to foster an academic environment that encourages the process of inquiry and the scientific method of problem solving. While much of the first two years of school is focused on basic science education, students interact with patients very early in the curriculum. The program is organized so that dental students function as assistants in their first year and hygienists in their second year; the third and fourth years are devoted to comprehensive care of patients. Specialty electives are available in the fourth year for students who progress briskly through the curriculum. The school emphasizes progressive education techniques, which include traditional lectures, small-group interactions, problem-based learning and a systems-based basic science education.

Student research opportunities: Yes

SPECIAL PROGRAMS AND SERVICES

PREDENTAL
Summer enrichment programs

DURING DENTAL SCHOOL
Academic counseling and tutoring
Community service opportunities
Internships, externships, or extramural programs
Mentoring
Personal counseling
Professional- and career-development programming
Training for those interested in academic careers

ACTIVE STUDENT ORGANIZATIONS
American Association of Dental Research Student Research Group
American Association of Pediatric Dentistry
American Association of Women Dentists
American Dental Education Association
American Student Dental Association
Hispanic Dental Association
Student Government Association
Student National Dental Association

INTERNATIONAL DENTISTS
Graduates of international dental schools considered for traditional predoctoral program: No
Advanced standing program offered for graduates of international dental schools: No

COMBINED AND ALTERNATE DEGREES

Ph.D.	M.S.	M.P.H.	M.D.	B.A./B.S.	Other
✓	—	—	—	—	—

COSTS: 2014–15 SCHOOL YEAR

	FIRST YEAR	SECOND YEAR	THIRD YEAR	FOURTH YEAR
Tuition, resident	$24,672	$24,672	$25,900	$28,350
Tuition, nonresident	$56,950	$56,950	$59,992	$66,082
Tuition, other				
Fees	$1,264	$851	$1,348	$1,397
Instruments, books, and supplies	$10,111	$8,204	$7,043	$950
Estimated living expenses	$18,901	$20,728	$24,196	$21,068
Total, resident	$54,948	$54,455	$58,487	$51,765
Total, nonresident	$87,226	$86,733	$92,579	$89,497
Total, other				

FINANCIAL AID

For more information, please visit: http://www.uab.edu/students/paying-for-UAB

A.T. STILL UNIVERSITY
ARIZONA SCHOOL OF DENTISTRY & ORAL HEALTH

Jack Dillenberg, D.D.S., M.P.H., Dean

GENERAL INFORMATION

The Arizona School of Dentistry & Oral Health (ASDOH) prepares caring, technologically adept dentists to become community and educational leaders. The school offers students an experience-rich learning environment where health professionals approach patient health as part of a team. ASDOH is part of A.T. Still University, which also includes the Kirksville College of Osteopathic Medicine, Arizona School of Health Sciences, the College of Graduate Health Studies and the School of Osteopathic Medicine in Arizona.

MISSION

- Educate caring, technologically adept, community-responsive dentists who will seek life-long learning.
- Inculcate a strong foundation comprising critical inquiry, evidence-based practice, research, and cultural competency.

Type of institution: Private
Year opened: 2003
Term type: Semester
Time to degree in months: 48
Start month: July
Doctoral dental degree offered: D.M.D.

Approximate targeted predoctoral enrollment: 300
Approximate targeted entering class size: 76
Campus setting: Suburban
Campus housing available: No

PREPARATION

Formal minimum preparation in semester/quarter hours: Semester: 90   Quarter: 135
Baccalaureate degree preferred: Yes
Number of first-year, first-time enrollees whose highest degree is:
    Baccalaureate: 68
    Master's degree and beyond: 5
Of first-year, first-time enrollees without baccalaureates, the number with:
    Equivalent of 60 undergraduate credit hours or less: 0
    Equivalent of 61–90 undergraduate credit hours: 0
    Equivalent of 91 or more undergraduate credit hours: 3

PREREQUISITE COURSE	REQUIRED	RECOMMENDED	LAB REQUIRED	CREDITS (SEMESTER/QUARTER)
BCP (biology-chemistry-physics) sciences				
Biology	✓		✓	8/12
Chemistry, general/inorganic	✓		✓	8/12
Chemistry, organic	✓		✓	8/12
Physics	✓		✓	8/12
Additional biological sciences				
Anatomy	✓			3/4
Biochemistry	✓			3/4
Cell biology				
Histology				
Immunology				
Microbiology		✓		3/4
Molecular biology/genetics				
Physiology	✓			3/4
Zoology				

(Prerequisite Courses continued)

PREPARATION (CONTINUED)

PREREQUISITE COURSE	REQUIRED	RECOMMENDED	LAB REQUIRED	CREDITS (SEMESTER/QUARTER)
Other				
English composition/technical writing	✓			3/4

Community college coursework accepted for prerequisites: Yes
Community college coursework accepted for electives: Yes
Limits on community college credit hours: No
Advanced placement (AP) credit accepted for prerequisites: Yes
Advanced placement (AP) credit accepted for electives: Yes
Job shadowing: Recommended
Number of hours of job shadowing required or recommended: 20
Other factors considered in admission: Community service experience is expected, along with a letter of recommendation from a community service supervisor.

DAT

Mandatory: Yes
Latest DAT for consideration of application: 11/15/2015
Oldest DAT considered: 01/01/2012
When more than one DAT score is reported: Highest score is considered.
Canadian DAT accepted: No
Application considered before DAT scores are submitted: No

DAT: 2014 ENTERING CLASS

ENROLLEE DAT SCORES	MEAN	RANGE
Academic Average	19.0	16–23
Perceptual Ability	20.0	15–30
Total Science	19.0	15–23

GPA: 2014 ENTERING CLASS

ENROLLEE GPA SCORES	UNDERGRAD. MEAN	GRADUATE MEAN	UNDERGRAD. RANGE	GRADUATE RANGE
Science GPA	3.26	3.49	2.52–4.09	2.79–4.00
Total GPA	3.37	3.53	2.63–4.11	3.04–4.00

APPLICATION AND SELECTION

TIMETABLE

Earliest filing date: 06/02/2015
Latest filing date: 11/15/2015
Earliest date for acceptance offers: 12/01/2015
Maximum time in days for applicant's response to acceptance offer:
    30 days if accepted on or after December 1 through January 31
    15 days if accepted on or after February 1
    48 hours after May 1
Requests for deferred entrance considered: In exceptional circumstances only
Fee for application: Yes, submitted only when requested
Amount of fee for application:
    In state: $70   Out of state: $70   International: $70
Fee waiver available: Yes

	FIRST DEPOSIT	SECOND DEPOSIT	THIRD DEPOSIT
Required to hold place	Yes	Yes	No
Resident amount	$1,000	$1,000	
Nonresident amount	$1,000	$1,000	
Deposit due	As indicated in admission offer	05/01/2016	
Applied to tuition	Yes	Yes	
Refundable	No	No	

APPLICATION PROCESS

Participates in Associated American Dental Schools Application Service (AADSAS): Yes
Accepts direct applicants: No
Secondary or supplemental application required: Yes
Secondary or supplemental application website: Invitation will be sent by email.
Interview is mandatory: Yes
Interview is by invitation: Yes

RESIDENCY

In-state/in-province versus out-of-state/out-of-province
Admissions process distinguishes between in-state/in-province and out-of-state/out-of-province applicants: No
Preference given to residents of: None
Reciprocity Admissions Agreement available for legal residents of: None
Generally and over time, percentage of your first-year enrollment that is in-state: 25%
Origin of out-of-state/out-of-province enrollees: CA-22, FL-1, IL-1, IN-1, ME-1, MN-2, MS-1, MT-1, ND-1, NM-2, NV-1, NY-3, OR-1, PA-1, TX-3, UT-6, VA-2, VT-1, WA-2

International
Applications are accepted from international (noncitizens/nonpermanent residents): Yes
Origin of international enrollees: Iran-1

APPLICATION AND ENROLLMENT	NUMBER OF APPLICANTS	ESTIMATED NUMBER INTERVIEWED	ESTIMATED NUMBER ENROLLED
In-state or province applicants/enrollees	163	77	22
Out-of-state or province applicants/enrollees	3,011	299	53
International applicants/enrollees (noncitizens/nonpermanent residents)	89	4	1

DEMOGRAPHIC DESCRIPTIONS OF APPLICANTS: 2014 ENTERING CLASS

	APPLICANTS			ENROLLEES		
	M	W	Gender Unknown or Not Reported	M	W	Gender Unknown or Not Reported
American Indian or Alaska Native	6	7	0	1	1	0
Asian	492	469	5	7	6	0
Black or African American	33	52	1	0	1	0
Hispanic or Latino	118	121	1	5	2	0
Native Hawaiian or Other Pacific Islander	9	0	0	0	0	0
White	998	600	8	26	24	0
Two or more races	76	76	4	1	0	0
Race and ethnicity unknown	53	37	8	1	0	0
International	56	32	1	0	0	1

	MINIMUM	MAXIMUM	MEAN
2014 entering class enrollees by age	21	37	26

CURRICULUM

The curriculum at the Arizona School of Dentistry & Oral Health is designed to produce graduates who are technologically adept, professionally competent, patient-centered and compassionate. The curriculum emphasizes patient-care experiences through simulation, integration of biomedical and clinical sciences, and problem-solving scenarios to achieve clinical excellence. The curriculum includes a strong component of public health, leadership and practice through weekly learning modules. Students have the opportunity to interact with faculty, practicing dentists and national leaders to discuss cases in a regularly scheduled "grand rounds" format.

Student research opportunities: Yes

SPECIAL PROGRAMS AND SERVICES

DURING DENTAL SCHOOL

Academic counseling and tutoring
Community service opportunities
Internships, externships, or extramural programs
Mentoring
Personal counseling
Transfer applicants considered if space is available

ACTIVE STUDENT ORGANIZATIONS

American Association for Dental Research National Student Research Group
American Association of Women Dentists
American Dental Education Association
American Student Dental Association
Hispanic Dental Association
Society of American Indian Dentistry, Student Chapter
Student National Dental Association

INTERNATIONAL DENTISTS

Graduates of international dental schools considered for traditional predoctoral program: Yes
Advanced standing program offered for graduates of international dental schools: No

COMBINED AND ALTERNATE DEGREES

Ph.D.	M.S.	M.P.H.	M.D.	B.A./B.S.	Other
—	—	✓	—	—	—

COSTS: 2014–15 SCHOOL YEAR

	FIRST YEAR	SECOND YEAR	THIRD YEAR	FOURTH YEAR
Tuition, resident	$62,820	$61,646	$59,343	$57,080
Tuition, nonresident	$62,820	$61,646	$59,343	$57,080
Tuition, other	$62,820	$61,646	$59,343	$57,080
Fees	$15,075	$15,295	$11,423	$12,018
Instruments, books, and supplies	$1,724	0	0	0
Estimated living expenses	$30,201	$29,876	$29,876	$33,976
Total, resident	$109,820	$106,817	$100,642	$103,074
Total, nonresident	$109,820	$106,817	$100,642	$103,074
Total, other	$109,820	$106,817	$100,642	$103,074

FINANCIAL AID

A.T. Still University Arizona School of Dentistry & Oral Health (ASDOH) participates in the U.S. Department of Education's Direct Loan Program. Student loans are available for tuition, fees and living expenses. ASDOH is also involved in a number of scholarship programs, such as the Health Professions Scholarship Program (military), the National Health Service Corps, the Indian Health Service and the Western Interstate Commission for Higher Education. Federal loans are the most common form of financial assistance, with 95% of the student body using these loans.

FINANCIAL AID AWARDS TO FIRST-YEAR STUDENTS 2014–15

Total number of first-year recipients: 65
Percentage of the first-year class: 88%
Percentage of awards that are grants? 0%
Percentage of awards that are loans? 92%

	AVERAGE AWARDS	RANGE OF AWARDS
Residents and nonresidents	$95,059	$107,820 (maximum award)

For more information, please visit: www.atsu.edu/financial_aid/index.htm

MIDWESTERN UNIVERSITY
COLLEGE OF DENTAL MEDICINE-ARIZONA

P. Bradford Smith, D.D.S., Dean

CONTACT INFORMATION

www.midwestern.edu
19555 North 59th Avenue
Glendale, AZ 85308
Phone: 623-572-3800
Fax: 623-572-3830

OFFICE OF ADMISSIONS

Mr. James Walter
Director
19555 North 59th Avenue
Glendale, AZ 85308
Phone: 623-572-3275

OFFICE OF STUDENT FINANCIAL SERVICES

Ms. Gina Wesolowki
Director
19555 North 59th Avenue
Glendale, AZ 85308
Phone: 623-572-3220

STUDENT AFFAIRS

Dr. Ross Kosinski
Dean of Students
19555 North 59th Avenue
Glendale, AZ 85308
Phone: 623-572-3329

HOUSING

Mr. José Ponce
Residence Life Coordinator
19555 North 59th Avenue
Glendale, AZ 85308
Phone: 623-572-3848

GENERAL INFORMATION

The College of Dental Medicine-Arizona is part of the Glendale, AZ, campus of Midwestern University, which was founded in 1900. The Glendale campus, situated on 146 acres, 15 miles northwest of downtown Phoenix, grew from a single building in 1996 to a full-service university with more than 34 buildings (covering 1,465,032 square feet) and more than 2,925 students. The Glendale campus comprises more than five colleges and 17 programs offering a variety of graduate degrees, including doctoral degree programs. The four-year dental curriculum leads to a D.M.D. degree. The College of Dental Medicine-Arizona graduated its first class in 2012.

MISSION

Our mission is to graduate well-qualified general dentists and to improve oral health through research, scholarly activity and service to the public.

Core Values:

- Maintaining a student-friendly environment
- Promoting ethics/professionalism
- Advocating collegiality and teamwork
- Focusing on a general dentistry curriculum
- Assuring competence for general practice
- Delivering comprehensive, patient-centered care

Type of institution: Private	Doctoral dental degree offered: D.M.D.
Year opened: 2008	Targeted predoctoral enrollment: 560
Term type: Quarter	Targeted entering class size: 140
Time to degree in months: 46	Campus setting: Suburban
Start month: August	Campus housing available: Yes

PREPARATION

Formal minimum preparation in semester/quarter hours: Semester: 90   Quarter: 120
Baccalaureate degree preferred: Yes
Number of first-year, first-time enrollees whose highest degree is:
    Baccalaureate: 107
    Master's degree and beyond: 27
Of first-year, first-time enrollees without baccalaureates, the number with:
    Equivalent of 60 undergraduate credit hours or less: 0
    Equivalent of 61–90 undergraduate credit hours: 0
    Equivalent of 91 or more undergraduate credit hours: 6

PREREQUISITE COURSE	REQUIRED	RECOMMENDED	LAB REQUIRED	CREDITS (SEMESTER/QUARTER)
BCP (biology-chemistry-physics) sciences				
Biology	✓		✓	8/12
Chemistry, general/inorganic	✓		✓	8/12
Chemistry, organic	✓		✓	4/6
Physics	✓		✓	8/12
Additional biological sciences				
Anatomy	✓		✓	3/4
Biochemistry	✓			3/4
Cell biology				
Histology		✓		
Immunology		✓		
Microbiology	✓			3/4

PREPARATION (CONTINUED)

PREREQUISITE COURSE	REQUIRED	RECOMMENDED	LAB REQUIRED	CREDITS (SEMESTER/QUARTER)
Molecular biology/genetics		✓		
Physiology	✓			3/4
Zoology		✓		
Other				
English composition/ technical writing	✓			6/9

Community college coursework accepted for prerequisites: Yes
Community college coursework accepted for electives: Yes
Limits on community college credit hours: No
Maximum number of community college credit hours: NA
Advanced placement (AP) credit accepted for prerequisites: Yes
Advanced placement (AP) credit accepted for electives: Yes
Comments regarding AP credit: We accept AP credit.
Job shadowing: Recommended
Number of hours of job shadowing required or recommended: 100

DAT

Mandatory: Yes
Latest DAT for consideration of application: 01/01/2016
Oldest DAT considered: 08/01/2013
When more than one DAT score is reported: Latest score is considered
Canadian DAT accepted: Yes
Application considered before DAT scores are submitted: No

DAT: 2014 ENTERING CLASS

ENROLLEE DAT SCORES	MEAN	RANGE
Academic Average	19.8	NR
Perceptual Ability	19.9	NR
Total Science	19.7	NR

GPA: 2014 ENTERING CLASS

ENROLLEE GPA SCORES	UNDERGRAD. MEAN	GRADUATE MEAN	UNDERGRAD. RANGE	GRADUATE RANGE
Science GPA	3.46	NR	NR	NR
Total GPA	3.52	NR	NR	NR

APPLICATION AND SELECTION

TIMETABLE

Earliest filing date: 06/02/2015
Latest filing date: 12/31/2015
Earliest date for acceptance offers: 12/01/2015
Maximum time in days for applicant's response to acceptance offer:
    30 days if accepted on or after December 1
    15 days if accepted on or after January 1
Requests for deferred entrance considered: In exceptional circumstances only
Fee for application: Yes, submitted only when requested
Amount of fee for supplemental application:
    In state: $50   Out of state: $50   International: $50
Fee waiver available: Yes

	FIRST DEPOSIT	SECOND DEPOSIT	THIRD DEPOSIT
Required to hold place	Yes	No	No
Resident amount	$1,000		
Nonresident amount	$1,000		
Deposit due	As indicated in admission offer		
Applied to tuition	Yes		
Refundable	Partially		

APPLICATION PROCESS

Participates in Associated American Dental Schools Application Service (AADSAS): Yes
Accepts direct applicants: No
Secondary or supplemental application required: Yes
Secondary or supplemental application website: Sent from admissions office if qualified
Interview is mandatory: Yes
Interview is by invitation: Yes

RESIDENCY

In-state/in-province versus out-of-state/out-of-province
Admissions process distinguishes between in-state/in-province and out-of-state/out-of-province applicants: No
Preference given to residents of: None
Reciprocity Admissions Agreement available for legal residents of: None
Generally and over time, percentage of your first-year enrollment that is in-state: 25%
Origin of out-of-state/out-of-province enrollees: AK-2, AR-2, CA-26, CO-3, DE-1, FL-3, HI-1, IA-1, ID-1, IL-1, IN-1, KS-2, LA-1, MA-1, MD-1, MI-1, MN-2, ND-2, NE-1, NJ-3, NM-6, NV-2, NY-1, OK-1, OR-2, PA-2, TN-3, TX-6, UT-9, VA-1, WA-10, WI-2

International
Applications are accepted from international (noncitizens/nonpermanent residents): Yes
Origin of international enrollees: Canada-1

APPLICATION AND ENROLLMENT	NUMBER OF APPLICANTS	ESTIMATED NUMBER INTERVIEWED	ESTIMATED NUMBER ENROLLED
In-state or province applicants/enrollees	169	72	37
Out-of-state or province applicants/enrollees	2,612	448	102
International applicants/enrollees (noncitizens/nonpermanent residents)	91	3	1

DEMOGRAPHIC DESCRIPTIONS OF APPLICANTS: 2014 ENTERING CLASS

	APPLICANTS			ENROLLEES		
	M	W	Gender Unknown or Not Reported	M	W	Gender Unknown or Not Reported
American Indian or Alaska Native	7	2	0	2	0	0
Asian	137	97	0	13	10	0
Black or African American	26	33	0	0	2	0
Hispanic or Latino	31	27	0	3	7	0
Native Hawaiian or Other Pacific Islander	1	0	0	0	0	0
White	927	490	0	63	28	0
Two or more races	469	453	0	6	4	0
Race and ethnicity unknown	42	39	0	1	0	0
International	62	29	0	1	0	0

	MINIMUM	MAXIMUM	MEAN
2014 entering class enrollees by age	21	40	25

CURRICULUM

The curriculum emphasizes integrated disciplines that both enhance learning and fully prepare students to practice general dentistry providing total patient care. The basic science curriculum is organized by body systems, rather than by biomedical discipline, and spans five academic quarters. This systems-based approach, combined with clinical case studies, improves the learning experience for entry to patient care and prepares students for Part I of the National Dental Board Examination. The preclinical curriculum is organized by tooth segments, rather than by dental disciplines. This highly integrated coursework spans six academic quarters of instruction in the simulation laboratory, emphasizing competency in a wide variety of clinical procedures. The coursework stresses patient simulation, technical quality, high efficiency and self-assessment. Students begin clinical care on a limited basis in the second year. The foundation of the clinical curriculum in the third and fourth academic years rests in the practice of general dentistry organized in practice groups led by general dentist faculty members. This eight-quarter curriculum emphasizes comprehensive patient-centered care, competency of all students in a full range of patient care services, and practice management and efficiency. The curriculum also prepares students for Part II of the National Board Dental Examination and clinical licensure examinations.

Student research opportunities: Yes

SPECIAL PROGRAMS AND SERVICES

PREDENTAL

Postbaccalaurate program in the College of Health Sciences Predental simulation courses

DURING DENTAL SCHOOL

Academic counseling and tutoring
Community service rotations in DM-2
Extramural rotations in DM-3 and DM-4 years
Mentoring
Personal counseling
Research opportunities

ACTIVE STUDENT ORGANIZATIONS

American Student Dental Association

INTERNATIONAL DENTISTS

Graduates of international dental schools considered for traditional predoctoral program: Yes
Advanced standing program offered for graduates of international dental schools: No

COMBINED AND ALTERNATE DEGREES

Ph.D.	M.S.	M.P.H.	M.D.	B.A./B.S.	Other
—	—	—	—	—	—

COSTS: 2014–15 SCHOOL YEAR

	FIRST YEAR	SECOND YEAR	THIRD YEAR	FOURTH YEAR
Tuition, resident	$65,348	$65,348	$65,348	$65,348
Tuition, nonresident	$65,348	$65,348	$65,348	$65,348
Tuition, other				
Fees	$12,082	$12,082	$12,082	$12,082
Instruments, books, and supplies	$5,358	$1,560	$150	$150
Estimated living expenses	$20,569	$19,329	$26,197	$26,465
Total, resident	$103,357	$98,319	$103,777	$104,045
Total, nonresident	$103,357	$98,319	$103,777	$104,045
Total, other				

Note: Tuition and fees do not vary based on residency status. Estimated living expenses represent an average of both on- and off-campus totals.

FINANCIAL AID

FINANCIAL AID AWARDS TO FIRST-YEAR STUDENTS 2014–15

Total number of first-year recipients: 106
Percentage of the first-year class: 75%
Percentage of awards that are grants? 0%
Percentage of awards that are loans? 74%

	AVERAGE AWARDS	RANGE OF AWARDS
Residents and Nonresidents	$101,727	$2,000–$112,412

Note: Average award is based on students only receiving federal financial aid.

For more information, please visit: https://www.midwestern.edu/programs-and-admission/student-financial-services.html

Herman Ostrow School of Dentistry of USC

HERMAN OSTROW SCHOOL OF DENTISTRY
OF THE UNIVERSITY OF SOUTHERN CALIFORNIA

Avishai Sadan, D.M.D., Dean

CONTACT INFORMATION

http://dentistry.usc.edu/
925 West 34th Street
Room 201
Los Angeles, CA 90089
Phone: 213-740-2841

FINANCIAL AID

Mr. Sergio Estavillo
Director, Financial Aid
925 West 34th Street, Room 201
Los Angeles, CA 90089
Phone: 213-740-2861
Email: uscsdfa@usc.edu

ADMISSIONS, MINORITY AND STUDENT AFFAIRS

Ms. Sandra C. Bolivar
Assistant Dean
925 West 34th Street, Room 201
Los Angeles, CA 90089
Phone: 213-740-2841
Email: uscsdadm@usc.edu

GENERAL INFORMATION

The Herman Ostrow School of Dentistry is a private institution founded in 1897. The school has become recognized for the excellence of its faculty in the clinical disciplines. Indeed, many procedures and techniques used in everyday dental practice were originated by University of Southern California faculty members. Programs of the school include those leading to a D.D.S., a B.S. in dental hygiene, certificate programs in advanced (specialty) education and continuing education for the practicing dentist, the Advanced Standing Program for International Dentists for foreign dental school graduates and the graduate program in craniofacial biology leading to the M.S. or Ph.D. degree.

MISSION

Dedicated to ongoing learning, flexibility and openness to new ideas, the Herman Ostrow School of Dentistry is committed to improving the health of all through education and training, innovation and discovery.

Type of institution: Private
Year opened: 1897
Term type: Trimester
Time to degree in months: 40
Start month: August

Doctoral dental degree offered: D.D.S.
Targeted predoctoral enrollment: 580
Targeted entering class size: 144
Campus setting: Urban
Campus housing available: Yes

PREPARATION

Formal minimum preparation in semester/quarter hours: Semester: 60   Quarter: 90
Baccalaureate degree preferred: Yes
Number of first-year, first-time enrollees whose highest degree is:
    Baccalaureate: 144
    Master's degree and beyond: 20
Of first-year, first-time enrollees without baccalaureates, and the number with:
    Equivalent of 60 undergraduate credit hours or less: 0
    Equivalent of 61–90 undergraduate credit hours: 0
    Equivalent of 91 or more undergraduate credit hours: 0

PREREQUISITE COURSE	REQUIRED	RECOMMENDED	LAB REQUIRED	CREDITS (SEMESTER/QUARTER)
BCP (biology-chemistry-physics) sciences				
Biology	✓		✓	8/10
Chemistry, general/inorganic	✓		✓	8/10
Chemistry, organic	✓		✓	8/10
Physics	✓		✓	8/10
Additional biological sciences				
Anatomy		✓		
Biochemistry		✓		
Cell biology		✓		
Histology		✓		
Immunology		✓		
Microbiology		✓		
Molecular biology/genetics		✓		
Physiology		✓		
Zoology				

(Prerequisite Courses continued)

95

PREPARATION (CONTINUED)

Community college coursework accepted for prerequisites: Yes. A very limited number may be accepted.

Community college coursework accepted for electives: Yes; maximum of 60 units

Limits on community college credit hours: Yes; 60 units

Maximum number of community college credit hours: 60

Advanced placement (AP) credit accepted for prerequisites: Yes

Advanced placement (AP) credit accepted for electives: Yes

Comments regarding AP credit: Credit must have been accepted by undergraduate college and included on transcript.

Job shadowing: Recommended

Number of hours of job shadowing required or recommended: 10-20

Other factors considered in admission: Personal background and experience, postbaccalaureate experience, letters of evaluation, research experience, advanced degrees or training and scope of academic background

DAT

Mandatory: Yes

Latest DAT for consideration of application: 02/01/2016

Oldest DAT considered: 01/01/2013

When more than one DAT score is reported: Most recent score only is considered

Canadian DAT accepted: Yes

Application considered before DAT scores are submitted: Yes

DAT: 2013 ENTERING CLASS

ENROLLEE DAT SCORES	MEAN	RANGE
Academic Average	20.0	15–25
Perceptual Ability	20.0	15–27
Total Science	20.0	15–26

GPA: 2013 ENTERING CLASS

ENROLLEE GPA SCORES	MEAN	RANGE
Science GPA	3.4	3.00–4.00
Total GPA	3.5	3.00–4.00

APPLICATION AND SELECTION

TIMETABLE

Earliest filing date: 06/02/2015

Latest filing date: 02/01/2016

Earliest date for acceptance offers: 12/01/2015

Maximum time in days for applicant's response to acceptance offer:
30 days if accepted on or after December 1
15 days if accepted on or after February 1

Requests for deferred entrance considered: No

Fee for applicat 5 ion: Yes

Amount of fee for application:
In state: $85   Out of state: $85   F-1 Visa, International: $145

Fee waiver available: Yes

	FIRST DEPOSIT	SECOND DEPOSIT	THIRD DEPOSIT
Required to hold place	Yes	Yes	Yes
Resident amount	$500	$1,000	$1,500
Nonresident amount	$500	$1,000	$1,500
Deposit due	As indicated in admission offer		
Applied to tuition	Yes	Yes	Yes
Refundable	No	No	Yes
Refundable by			08/01/2016

APPLICATION PROCESS

Participates in Associated American Dental Schools Application Service (AADSAS): Yes

Accepts direct applicants: No

Secondary or supplemental application required: No

Interview is mandatory: Yes

Interview is by invitation: Yes

RESIDENCY

In-state/in-province versus out-of-state/out-of-province

Admissions process distinguishes between in-state/in-province and out-of-state/out-of-province applicants: No

Preference given to residents of: None

Reciprocity Admissions Agreement available for legal residents of: None

Generally and over time, percentage of your first-year enrollment that is in-state: 60%

Origin of out-of-state/out-of-province enrollees: NR

International

Applications are accepted from international (noncitizens/nonpermanent residents): Yes

Origin of international enrollees: NR

APPLICATION AND ENROLLMENT	NUMBER OF APPLICANTS	ESTIMATED NUMBER INTERVIEWED	ESTIMATED NUMBER ENROLLED
In-state or province applicants/enrollees	1,128	316	89
Out-of-state or province applicants/enrollees	2,201	114	55
International applicants/enrollees (noncitizens/nonpermanent residents)	308	NR	9

DEMOGRAPHIC DESCRIPTIONS OF APPLICANTS: 2013 ENTERING CLASS

	APPLICANTS	ENROLLEES
	Total	Total
American Indian or Alaska Native	5	1
Asian	1,273	58
Black or African American	72	7
Hispanic or Latino	254	11
Native Hawaiian or Other Pacific Islander	2	2
White	1,171	62
Two or more races	109	3
Race and ethnicity unknown	89	0
International	308	9

	MINIMUM	MAXIMUM	MEAN
2013 entering class enrollees by age	20	48	26

CURRICULUM

The curricular goals are the following:

1. To use student-centered, inquiry-based methods in all aspects of basic, preclinical and clinical science instruction throughout all four years that will encourage students to develop lifelong problem-solving and group learning skills.

2. To encourage students to question materials presented and to develop a collegial interaction with the faculty—all areas of instruction occur in a professional atmosphere, and there is no activity that demeans students or creates an atmosphere in which student inquiry is repressed.

3. To vertically integrate the curriculum so that all three sciences and clinical skills are organized to emphasize the direct relevance of basic science learning outcomes to clinical problems.

4. To develop dental graduates who are:
   - Dedicated to lifelong, self-motivated learning.
   - Accomplished in the methods required to solve problems in a clinical setting.
   - Able to effectively understand and respond to changes in the profession.

Student research opportunities: Yes

SPECIAL PROGRAMS AND SERVICES

PREDENTAL
Dental Explorers Program (two-week experience for predental and high school students)
Postbaccalaureate programs
Summer enrichment programs

DURING DENTAL SCHOOL
Academic counseling and tutoring
Community service opportunities
Internships, externships, or extramural programs
Personal counseling
Professional- and career-development programming

ACTIVE STUDENT ORGANIZATIONS
American Association of Dental Research Student Research Group
American Association of Women Dentists
American Dental Education Association
American Student Dental Association
Hispanic Dental Association
Student National Dental Association
Student Professional Ethics Club
Student National Dental Association

INTERNATIONAL DENTISTS
Graduates of international dental schools considered for traditional predoctoral program: No
Advanced standing program offered for graduates of international dental schools: Yes
Advanced standing program description: Special two-year program is offered. Application is not through ADEA AADSAS but directly through ADEA Centralized Application for Advanced Placement for International Dentists (ADEA CAAPID).

COMBINED AND ALTERNATE DEGREES

Ph.D.	M.S.	M.P.H.	M.D.	B.A./B.S.	Other
✓	✓	—	—	—	—

COSTS: 2013–14 SCHOOL YEAR

	FIRST YEAR	SECOND YEAR	THIRD YEAR	FOURTH YEAR
Tuition, resident	$81,180	$81,180	$81,180	$54,120
Tuition, nonresident	$81,180	$81,180	$81,180	$54,120
Tuition, other				
Fees	$1,980	$1,980	$1,980	$1,320
Instruments, books, and supplies	$10,095	$2,834		
Estimated living expenses	$21,334	$21,334	$21,334	$14,200

FINANCIAL AID

Procedures:

- The Free Application for Federal Student Aid (FAFSA) can be completed online at www.fafsa.ed.gov on or after January 1 of the matriculation year.
- USC's School Code is 001328.
- If you wish to be considered for the Health Professional Student Loan Program (HPSL), you must complete the parental section of the FAFSA.
- After admission into the Ostrow School of Dentistry, complete the online Supplemental Form, which can be found at www.usc.edu/admission/fa/.

After your admission and following the financial aid application procedures, the Herman Ostrow School of Dentistry will determine your financial aid eligibility. Notification of financial aid eligibility will be communicated via email. Please respond to the notification of financial aid eligibility as instructed in the notification.

Please visit www.usc.edu/admission/fa/ for more detailed information.

LOMA LINDA UNIVERSITY
SCHOOL OF DENTISTRY

Ronald J. Dailey, Ph.D., Dean

GENERAL INFORMATION

Loma Linda University (LLU) represents distinction in quality Christian education. A private institution, owned and operated by the Seventh-Day Adventist Church, the university has established a reputation for leadership in mission service, clinical excellence, research and advancements in the health-related sciences. Located 60 miles from Los Angeles in one of the fastest growing areas nationwide, LLU comprises eight health science schools and has an annual enrollment of more than 4,000 students from more than 100 countries. The school offers eight advanced dental education programs and has 122 full-time faculty for an excellent student/faculty ratio of three to one.

MISSION

We seek to further the teaching and healing ministry of Jesus Christ by teaching students to provide high-quality oral health care based on sound biologic principles.

Vision: LLUSD is a preeminent health-care organization seeking to represent God in all we do. We are committed to excellent, innovative, comprehensive education and whole-person care.

Core Values: The University affirms these values as central to its view of education: COMPASSION—INTEGRITY—EXCELLENCE—FREEDOM—JUSTICE—PURITY/SELF-CONTROL—HUMILITY.

www.llu.edu/central/values.page

Type of institution: Private
Year opened: 1953
Term type: Quarter
Time to degree in months: 45
Start month: August

Doctoral dental degree offered: D.D.S.
Targeted predoctoral enrollment: 395
Targeted entering class size: 100
Campus setting: Suburban
Campus housing available: Yes

PREPARATION

Formal minimum preparation in semester/quarter hours: Semester: 96   Quarter: 144
Baccalaureate degree preferred: Yes
Number of first-year, first-time enrollees whose highest degree is:
    Baccalaureate: 93
    Master's degree and beyond: 0
Of first-year, first-time enrollees without baccalaureates, the number with:
    Equivalent of 60 undergraduate credit hours or less: 0
    Equivalent of 61–90 undergraduate credit hours: 0
    Equivalent of 91 or more undergraduate credit hours: 0

PREREQUISITE COURSE	REQUIRED	RECOMMENDED	LAB REQUIRED	CREDITS (SEMESTER/QUARTER)
BCP (biology-chemistry-physics) sciences				
Biology	✓		✓	8/12
Chemistry, general/inorganic	✓		✓	8/12
Chemistry, organic	✓		✓	8/12
Physics	✓		✓	8/12
Additional biological sciences				
Anatomy		✓		4/4
Biochemistry	✓			4/8
Cell biology		✓		4/4
Histology		✓		4/4
Immunology		✓		4/4
Microbiology		✓		4/4

PREPARATION (CONTINUED)

PREREQUISITE COURSE	REQUIRED	RECOMMENDED	LAB REQUIRED	CREDITS (SEMESTER/QUARTER)
Molecular biology/genetics		✓		4/4
Physiology		✓		4/4
Zoology				
Other				
English Composition	✓			6/12

Community college coursework accepted for prerequisites: Yes (Discouraged)
Community college coursework accepted for electives: Yes (Discouraged)
Limits on community college credit hours: Yes
Maximum number of community college credit hours: 64
Advanced placement (AP) credit accepted for prerequisites: Yes, English only
Advanced placement (AP) credit accepted for electives: Yes
Comments regarding AP credit: Must provide official Advanced Placement transcript and receive determination from LLUSD
Job shadowing: Required
Number of hours of job shadowing required or recommended: 50 hours required, more recommended

DAT

Mandatory: Yes
Latest DAT for consideration of application: 12/01/2015
Oldest DAT considered: 08/15/2014
When more than one DAT score is reported: Average score is considered
Canadian DAT accepted: Yes
Application considered before DAT scores are submitted: No

DAT: 2014 ENTERING CLASS

ENROLLEE DAT SCORES	MEAN	RANGE
Academic Average	19.9	17–25
Perceptual Ability	20.7	17–26
Total Science	19.9	17–27

GPA: 2014 ENTERING CLASS

ENROLLEE GPA SCORES	MEAN	RANGE
Science GPA	3.35	2.70–4.10
Total GPA	3.46	2.80–4.10

APPLICATION AND SELECTION

TIMETABLE

Earliest filing date: 06/02/2015
Latest filing date: 12/01/2015
Earliest date for acceptance offers: 12/01/2015
Maximum time in days for applicant's response to acceptance offer:
    30 days if accepted on or after December 1
    15 days if accepted on or after February 1
Requests for deferred entrance considered: No
Fee for application: Yes, submitted only when requested
Amount of fee for application:
    In state: $100   Out of state: $100   International: $100
Fee waiver available: Yes

	FIRST DEPOSIT	SECOND DEPOSIT	THIRD DEPOSIT
Required to hold place	Yes	Yes	No
Resident amount	$1,000	$1,000	
Nonresident amount	$1,000	$1,000	
Deposit due date	As indicated in admission offer	May 1	
Applied to tuition	Yes		
Refundable	No		

APPLICATION PROCESS

Participates in Associated American Dental Schools Application Service (AADSAS): Yes
Accepts direct applicants: No
Secondary or supplemental application required: Yes
Secondary or supplemental application website: Information is emailed to applicant
Interview is mandatory: Yes
Interview is by invitation: Yes

RESIDENCY

In-state/in-province versus out-of-state/out-of-province
Admissions process distinguishes between in-state/in-province and out-of-state/out-of-province applicants: No
Preference given to residents of: None
Reciprocity Admissions Agreement available for legal residents of: None
Generally and over time, percentage of your first-year enrollment that is in-state: 85%
Origin of out-of-state/out-of-province enrollees (2013 entering class): AR-1, CO-1, FL-5, GA-3, HI-1, IL-1, MD-1, MI-4, NC-1, ND-1, NV-1, NY-2, OH-1, OR-1, PA-2, TN-2, TX-3, WA-2

International
Applications are accepted from international (noncitizens/nonpermanent residents): Yes
Origin of international enrollees: Canada-5, South Korea-3, Taiwan-1

APPLICATION AND ENROLLMENT	NUMBER OF APPLICANTS	ESTIMATED NUMBER INTERVIEWED	ESTIMATED NUMBER ENROLLED
In-state or province applicants/ enrollees	1,125	166	46
Out-of-state or province applicants/enrollees	842	245	47
International applicants/enrollees (noncitizens/nonpermanent residents)	NR	NR	9

DEMOGRAPHIC DESCRIPTIONS OF APPLICANTS: 2014 ENTERING CLASS

	APPLICANTS			ENROLLEES		
	M	W	Gender Unknown or Not Reported	M	W	Gender Unknown or Not Reported
American Indian or Alaska Native	1	1	1	0	0	0
Asian	413	358	6	28	14	0
Black or African American	37	31	1	7	2	0
Hispanic or Latino	68	94	3	5	9	0
Native Hawaiian or Other Pacific Islander	0	0	0	0	0	0
White	533	276	8	20	15	0
Two or more races	73	83	0	3	6	0
Race and ethnicity unknown	32	27	12	3	0	1
International	109	81	3	11	1	0

	MINIMUM	MAXIMUM	MEAN
2014 entering class enrollees by age	21	42	25

CURRICULUM

LLU's program is a traditional dental curriculum with emphasis in clinical training. Graduates are skilled in providing quality dental care that is comprehensive in its scope and preventive in its goals. Year 1. Basic sciences with introduction to clinical sciences. Year 2. Applied sciences and introduction to clinical practice. Year 3. Clinical sciences with extensive patient contact. Year 4. Delivery of comprehensive dental care.

Student research opportunities: Yes

SPECIAL PROGRAMS AND SERVICES

PREDENTAL

Careers in Dentistry, Gateway Summer Program, Minority Introduction to the Health Sciences (MITHS), Minorities in Dentistry
Postbaccalaureate program
Summer enrichment programs

DURING DENTAL SCHOOL

Community service opportunities

ACTIVE STUDENT ORGANIZATIONS

American Dental Education Association
American Student Dental Association
California Dental Association
Dental Students' Association
Junior Dental Auxiliary

INTERNATIONAL DENTISTS

Graduates of international dental schools considered for traditional predoctoral program: No
Advanced standing program offered for graduates of international dental schools: Yes

COMBINED AND ALTERNATE DEGREES

Ph.D.	M.S.	M.P.H.	M.D.	B.A./B.S.	Other
✓	✓	✓	✓	✓	—

COSTS: 2014–15 SCHOOL YEAR

	FIRST YEAR	SECOND YEAR	THIRD YEAR	FOURTH YEAR
Tuition, resident	$57,207	$69,300	$69,300	$69,300
Tuition, nonresident	$57,207	$69,300	$69,300	$69,300
Tuition, other				
Fees	$4,463	$5,955	$4,660	$4,721
Instruments, books, and supplies	$13,995	$9,013	$5,242	$646
Estimated living expenses	$16,000	$19,200	$19,200	$19,200
Total, resident	$93,854	$104,979	$98,460	$96,518
Total, nonresident	$93,854	$104,979	$98,460	$96,518
Total, other				

FINANCIAL AID

Various financial aid programs and a financial advisor are available.

For more information visit our website at www.llu.edu/ssweb/finaid, call 909-558-4509 or email finaid@llu.edu.

UNIVERSITY OF CALIFORNIA, LOS ANGELES
SCHOOL OF DENTISTRY

No-Hee Park, D.M.D., Ph.D., Dean

CONTACT INFORMATION

www.dentistry.ucla.edu

DEAN'S SUITE

UCLA School of Dentistry
Los Angeles, CA 90095
Phone: 310-206-6063

ADMISSIONS

Ms. Noemi Benitez
Coordinator
Office of Student Affairs, A0-111
Los Angeles, CA 90095
Phone: 310-794-7971
Email: dds_admissions@dentistry.ucla.edu

OFFICE OF FINANCIAL AID

Ms. Connie Steppes
Office of Student Affairs, A0-111
Los Angeles, CA 90095
Phone: 310-825-6994
Email: financial_aid@dentistry.ucla.edu

STUDENT AFFAIRS

Dr. Carol A. Bibb
Associate Dean for Student Affairs
Office of Student Affairs, A0-111
Los Angeles, CA 90095
Phone: 310-825-2615

MINORITY AFFAIRS/DIVERSITY

Dr. Edmond R. Hewlett
Associate Dean for Outreach and Diversity
Office of Student Affairs and Outreach, A0-111
Los Angeles, CA 90095
Phone: 310-825-7097

HOUSING

Phone: 310-825-4271
www.housing.ucla.edu

INTERNATIONAL DENTISTS

Ms. Stephanie Cuellar
Coordinator-Professional Program
for International Dentists
Office of Student Affairs
Los Angeles, CA 90095
Phone: 310-825-6218
Email: ppid_admissions@dentistry.ucla.edu

GENERAL INFORMATION

The UCLA School of Dentistry is one of two public dental schools in California. The school has state-of-the-art facilities, a high caliber faculty, a talented and diverse student body, close collaboration with the UCLA Medical Center and convenient access to the recreational and cultural opportunities on the UCLA campus and in the LA area. The competency-based curriculum has Pass/No Pass evaluation, and students are well prepared for the National Board and licensure examinations, as well as for advanced dental education residency programs. Along with a challenging basic- and clinical-sciences curriculum, students have diverse opportunities for professional development in research, teaching, leadership and community service.

MISSION

To improve the oral and systemic health of the people of California, the nation and the world through education, research, patient care and public service.

Type of institution: Public	Doctoral dental degree offered: D.D.S.
Year opened: 1964	Targeted predoctoral enrollment: 392
Term type: Quarter	Targeted entering class size: 88
Time to degree in months: 45	Campus setting: Urban
Start month: September	Campus housing available: Yes

PREPARATION

Formal minimum preparation in semester/quarter hours: Semester: 90   Quarter: 135
Baccalaureate degree preferred: Yes
Number of first-year, first-time enrollees whose highest degree is:
    Baccalaureate: 85
    Master's degree and beyond: 1
Of first-year, first-time enrollees without baccalaureates, the number with:
    Equivalent of 60 undergraduate credit hours or less: 0
    Equivalent of 61–90 undergraduate credit hours: 0
    Equivalent of 91 or more undergraduate credit hours: 1

PREREQUISITE COURSE	REQUIRED	RECOMMENDED	LAB REQUIRED	CREDITS (SEMESTER/QUARTER)
BCP (biology-chemistry-physics) sciences				
Biology	✓		✓	8/12
Chemistry, general/inorganic	✓		✓	8/12
Chemistry, organic	✓		✓	6/8
Physics	✓		✓	8/12
Additional biological sciences				
Anatomy		✓		3/4
Biochemistry	✓			3/4
Cell biology				
Histology		✓		3/4
Immunology				
Microbiology		✓		3/4
Molecular biology/genetics				
Physiology		✓		3/4
Zoology				

(Prerequisite Courses continued)

PREPARATION (CONTINUED)

PREREQUISITE COURSE	REQUIRED	RECOMMENDED	LAB REQUIRED	CREDITS (SEMESTER/QUARTER)
Other				
English Composition	✓			6/8
Psychology	✓			3/4

Community college coursework accepted for prerequisites: Yes
Community college coursework accepted for electives: Yes
Limits on community college credit hours: Yes
Maximum number of community college credit hours: 70
Advanced placement (AP) credit accepted for prerequisites: Yes
Advanced placement (AP) credit accepted for electives: No
Comments regarding AP credit: Maximum credit of 3 semester/4 quarter hours toward prerequisites
Job shadowing: Recommended
Number of hours of job shadowing required or recommended: NR

DAT

Mandatory: Yes
Latest DAT for consideration of application: 12/31/2015
Oldest DAT considered: 01/01/2013
When more than one DAT score is reported: Most recent score only is considered
Canadian DAT accepted: No
Application considered before DAT scores are submitted: No

DAT: 2014 ENTERING CLASS

ENROLLEE DAT SCORES	MEAN	RANGE
Academic Average	22.3	19–27
Perceptual Ability	21.6	17–27
Total Science	22.6	19–30

GPA: 2014 ENTERING CLASS

ENROLLEE GPA SCORES	UNDERGRAD. MEAN	GRADUATE MEAN	UNDERGRAD. RANGE	GRADUATE RANGE
Science GPA	3.71	3.95	3.04–4.00	NA
Total GPA	3.75	3.94	3.20–4.00	NA

APPLICATION AND SELECTION

TIMETABLE

Earliest filing date: 06/02/2015
Latest filing date: 01/01/2016
Earliest date for acceptance offers: 12/01/2015
Maximum time in days for applicant's response to acceptance offer:
    30 days if accepted on or after December 1
    15 days if accepted on or after February 1
Requests for deferred entrance considered: No
Fee for application: Yes, submitted only when requested
Amount of fee for application:
    In state: $60   Out of state: $60   International: $60
Fee waiver available: Yes, contact office for details

	FIRST DEPOSIT	SECOND DEPOSIT	THIRD DEPOSIT
Required to hold place	Yes	No	No
Resident amount	$1,000		
Nonresident amount	$1,000		
Deposit due	As indicated in admission offer		
Applied to tuition	Yes		
Refundable	No		

APPLICATION PROCESS

Participates in Associated American Dental Schools Application Service (AADSAS): Yes
Accepts direct applicants: No
Secondary or supplemental application required: Yes
Secondary or supplemental application website: www.dentistry.ucla.edu
Interview is mandatory: Yes
Interview is by invitation: Yes

RESIDENCY

In-state/in-province versus out-of-state/out-of-province
Admissions process distinguishes between in-state/in-province and out-of-state/out-of-province applicants: Yes
Preference given to residents of: Alaska, Arizona, California, Hawaii, Montana, New Mexico, North Dakota, Wyoming
Reciprocity Admissions Agreement available for legal residents of: None
Generally and over time, percentage of your first-year enrollment that is in-state: 85%
Origin of out-of-state/out-of-province enrollees: AZ-1, IL-2, NV-1, NY-1, OK-1, VA-2

International
Applications are accepted from international (noncitizens/nonpermanent residents): Yes
Origin of international enrollees: South Korea-1

APPLICATION AND ENROLLMENT	NUMBER OF APPLICANTS	ESTIMATED NUMBER INTERVIEWED	ESTIMATED NUMBER ENROLLED
In-state or province applicants/enrollees	934	129	78
Out-of-state or province applicants/enrollees	669	12	8
International applicants/enrollees (noncitizens/nonpermanent residents)	108	1	1

DEMOGRAPHIC DESCRIPTIONS OF APPLICANTS: 2014 ENTERING CLASS

	APPLICANTS			ENROLLEES		
	M	W	Gender Unknown or Not Reported	M	W	Gender Unknown or Not Reported
American Indian or Alaska Native	0	1	0	0	0	0
Asian	349	326	8	28	22	1
Black or African American	24	18	1	1	0	0
Hispanic or Latino	71	79	1	2	2	0
Native Hawaiian or Other Pacific Islander	1	2	0	0	0	0
White	347	250	0	12	13	0
Two or more races	28	34	1	1	2	0
Race and ethnicity unknown	27	25	10	1	1	0
International	58	50	0	1	0	0

	MINIMUM	MAXIMUM	MEAN
2014 entering enrollees by age	21	37	24

CURRICULUM

The goals of the program are to prepare reflective practitioners who 1) possess the knowledge and skills necessary to provide patients with comprehensive dental care; 2) view their role in the profession from a humanitarian perspective; 3) are able to provide socially sensitive and responsible leadership in the community; and 4) continuously update their knowledge, techniques and practices. The length of the D.D.S. program is 45 months. The curriculum uses lectures, small group discussion, labs, CD-ROMs and web-based resources. Students supplement their educational experience through a variety of electives including teaching apprenticeships, mentored research projects, leadership training and volunteer service at UCLA-sponsored outreach clinics. Early entry into the clinic is a priority. Student dentists, organized in vertical-tier teams, provide comprehensive care to an assigned patient pool, supplemented by rotations to specialty and community clinics.

Student research opportunities: Yes

SPECIAL PROGRAMS AND SERVICES

PREDENTAL

Summer Medical and Dental Education Program
Postbaccalaureate programs

DURING DENTAL SCHOOL

Academic counseling and tutoring
Community service opportunities
Externships
Mentorship programs
Personal counseling
Professional- and career-development programming
Training for those interested in academic careers

ACTIVE STUDENT ORGANIZATIONS

American Academy of Pediatric Dentistry
American Association for Dental Research National Student Research Group
American Association of Women Dentists
American Dental Education Association
American Student Dental Association
California Dental Association
Hispanic Dental Association

INTERNATIONAL DENTISTS

Graduates of international dental schools considered for traditional predoctoral program: No
Advanced standing program offered for graduates of international dental schools: Yes
Advanced standing program description: Program awarding a dental degree.

COMBINED AND ALTERNATE DEGREES

Ph.D.	M.S.	M.P.H.	M.D.	B.A./B.S.	Other
✓	✓	✓	—	—	✓

Note: M.B.A.

COSTS: 2014–15 SCHOOL YEAR

	FIRST YEAR	SECOND YEAR	THIRD YEAR	FOURTH YEAR
Tuition, resident	$39,797	$43,737	$43,737	$43,737
Tuition, nonresident	$48,998	$52,938	$52,938	$52,938
Tuition, other				
Fees		See "Note:" below.		
Instruments, books, and supplies	$20,129	$12,148	$3,984	$4,319
Estimated living expenses	$17,886	$23,848	$23,848	$23,848
Total, resident	$77,812	$79,733	$71,569	$71,904
Total, nonresident	$87,013	$88,934	$80,770	$81,105
Total, other				

Note: Tuition fees above include tuition, student service fee, professional degree supplemental tuition and other charges, as well as UCLA campus-based fees that are assessed to all full-time students.

FINANCIAL AID

General Information: The UCLA School of Dentistry provides both need- and merit-based funds. The dental financial aid staff is available to ensure comprehensive, personal and confidential counseling services.

FINANCIAL AID AWARDS TO FIRST-YEAR STUDENTS 2014–15

Total number of first-year recipients: 75	
Percentage of the first-year class: 85%	
Percentage of awards that are grants? 15%	
Percentage of awards that are loans? 85%	

	AVERAGE AWARDS	RANGE OF AWARDS
Residents	$52,390	$3,500–$79,190
Nonresidents	$55,322	$14,300–$88,966

For more information, please visit: www.dentistry.ucla.edu

University of California
San Francisco

School of Dentistry

UNIVERSITY OF CALIFORNIA, SAN FRANCISCO
SCHOOL OF DENTISTRY

John D.B. Featherstone, M.Sc., Ph.D., Dean

GENERAL INFORMATION

The University of California, San Francisco (UCSF), School of Dentistry provides a unique balance of clinical excellence, research opportunity and community service as part of one of the leading health science centers in the nation. Established in 1881, the school has a tradition of service (beginning with care following the 1904 earthquake), strong clinical programs that prepare dentists for the future and research activities at the vanguard of contemporary science.

The four-year predoctoral curriculum (see Curriculum section of this profile) covers the broad range of science, art and technology that makes up contemporary dental practice.

MISSION

Advancing oral, craniofacial and public health through excellence in education, discovery and patient-centered care.

Vision: To be a worldwide leader in dental education and public health, clinical practice and scientific discovery.

Core Values: Excellence, integrity, respect, innovation, accountability, leadership and social responsibility.

Type of institution: Public	Doctoral dental degree offered: D.D.S.
Year opened: 1881	Targeted predoctoral enrollment: 352
Term type: Quarter	Targeted entering class size: 88
Time to degree in months: 42	Campus setting: Urban
Start month: September	Campus housing available: Yes

PREPARATION

Formal minimum preparation in semester/quarter hours: Semester: 93   Quarter: 139
Baccalaureate degree preferred: Yes
Number of first-year, first-time enrollees whose highest degree is:
    Baccalaureate: 81
    Master's degree and beyond: 6
Of first-year, first-time enrollees without baccalaureates, the number with:
    Equivalent of 60 undergraduate credit hours or less: 0
    Equivalent of 61–90 undergraduate credit hours: 0
    Equivalent of 91 or more undergraduate credit hours: 0

PREREQUISITE COURSE	REQUIRED	RECOMMENDED	LAB REQUIRED	CREDITS (SEMESTER/QUARTER)
BCP (biology-chemistry-physics) sciences				
Biology	✓		✓	8/12
Chemistry, general/inorganic	✓		✓	8/12
Chemistry, organic	✓		✓	4/8
Physics	✓		✓	8/12
Additional biological sciences				
Anatomy		✓		
Biochemistry	✓			3/4
Cell biology		✓		
Histology		✓		
Immunology		✓		
Microbiology		✓		
Molecular biology/genetics		✓		

CONTACT INFORMATION

http://dentistry.ucsf.edu

513 Parnassus Avenue, S619
San Francisco, CA 94143-0430
Phone: 415-476-2737
Fax: 415-476-4226
admissions@dentistry.ucsf.edu

ADMISSIONS

Mr. James C. Betbeze, Jr.
Assistant Dean for Enrollment Management and Outreach
513 Parnassus Avenue, S619
San Francisco, CA 94143-0430
Phone: 415-476-2737

STUDENT FINANCIAL SERVICES

500 Parnassus Avenue
Millberry Union 201, West
San Francisco, CA 94143-0246
Phone: 415-476-4181
Fax: 415-476-6652
Email: finaid@ucsf.edu
http://finaid.ucsf.edu

STUDENT ACADEMIC AFFAIRS

http://saa.ucsf.edu

DIVERSITY AND OUTREACH

http://diversity.ucsf.edu/

HOUSING

500 Parnassus Avenue
Millberry Union 102, West
San Francisco, CA 94143-0232
Phone: 415-476-2231
Fax: 415-476-6733
Email: housing@ucsf.edu
www.campuslifeservices.ucsf.edu/housing

INTERNATIONAL STUDENTS & SCHOLARS

William J. Rutter Center
1675 Owens Street, Room CC-290
San Francisco, CA 94143
Phone: 415-476-1773
Email: visa@ucsf.edu
http://isso.ucsf.edu

PREPARATION (CONTINUED)

PREREQUISITE COURSE	REQUIRED	RECOMMENDED	LAB REQUIRED	CREDITS (SEMESTER/QUARTER)
Physiology		✓		
Zoology		✓		
Other				
English composition	✓			6/8
Introductory psychology	✓			3/4
Hum. Soc. Sci. electives	✓			11/16
Additional electives	✓			42/63

Community college coursework accepted for prerequisites: Yes
Community college coursework accepted for electives: Yes
Limits on community college credit hours: Yes
Maximum number of community college credit hours: 64
Advanced placement (AP) credit accepted for prerequisites: Yes
Advanced placement (AP) credit accepted for electives: Yes
Comments regarding AP credit: Applicants must submit official Score Report (School Code 5482). Science prerequisites can only be partially fulfilled using AP credit. See our admissions website for more detailed information.
Job shadowing: Recommended

DAT

Mandatory: Yes
Latest DAT for consideration of application: Official scores must be received by 10/15/2015
Oldest DAT considered: 06/01/2013
When more than one DAT score is reported: Most recent score only is considered
Canadian DAT accepted: No
Application considered before DAT scores are submitted: No

DAT: 2014 ENTERING CLASS

ENROLLEE DAT SCORES	MEAN	RANGE
Academic Average	21.0	17–27
Perceptual Ability	20.0	15–27
Total Science	21.0	17–30

GPA: 2014 ENTERING CLASS

ENROLLEE GPA SCORES	UNDERGRAD. MEAN	GRADUATE MEAN	UNDERGRAD. RANGE	GRADUATE RANGE
Science GPA	3.42	3.17	2.62–4.06	3.23–4.08
Total GPA	3.51	3.81	2.66–4.07	3.38–4.08

APPLICATION AND SELECTION

TIMETABLE

Earliest filing date: 06/02/2015
Latest filing date: 10/15/2015
Earliest date for acceptance offers: 12/01/2015
Maximum time in days for applicant's response to acceptance offer:
    30 days if accepted on or after December 1
    15 days if accepted on or after February 1
Requests for deferred entrance considered: No
Fee for application: Yes, submitted only when requested
Amount of fee for application:
    In state: $80   Out of state: $80   International: $100
Fee waiver available: Yes; information provided with supplemental application

	FIRST DEPOSIT	SECOND DEPOSIT	THIRD DEPOSIT
Required to hold place	Yes	No	No
Resident amount	$1,000		
Nonresident amount	$1,000		
Deposit due	As indicated in admission offer		
Applied to tuition	Yes		
Refundable	No		

APPLICATION PROCESS

Participates in Associated American Dental Schools Application Service (AADSAS): Yes
Accepts direct applicants: No
Secondary or supplemental application required: Yes, accepted upon invitation only
Secondary or supplemental application website: Provided upon invitation only
Interview is mandatory: Yes
Interview is by invitation: Yes

RESIDENCY

In-state/in-province versus out-of-state/out-of-province
Admissions process distinguishes between in-state/in-province and out-of-state/out-of-province applicants: No
Preference given to residents of: None
Reciprocity Admissions Agreement available for legal residents of: None
Generally and over time, percentage of your first-year enrollment that is in-state: 80%
Origin of out-of-state/out-of-province enrollees: AZ-3, CT-1, GU-1, IN-1, LA-1, MD-1, MO-1, NJ-1, NV-1, NY-2, OR-1, SC-1, TX-2, VA-1, WA-1

International
Applications are accepted from international (noncitizens/nonpermanent residents): Yes
Origin of international enrollees: China-1, South Korea-1

APPLICATION AND ENROLLMENT	NUMBER OF APPLICANTS	ESTIMATED NUMBER INTERVIEWED	ESTIMATED NUMBER ENROLLED
In-state or province applicants/enrollees	887	162	65
Out-of-state or province applicants/enrollees	944	87	20
International applicants/enrollees (noncitizens/nonpermanent residents)	137	9	2

DEMOGRAPHIC DESCRIPTIONS OF APPLICANTS: 2014 ENTERING CLASS

	APPLICANTS			ENROLLEES		
	M	W	Gender Unknown or Not Reported	M	W	Gender Unknown or Not Reported
American Indian or Alaska Native	3	0	0	0	0	0
Asian	399	401	6	15	23	0
Black or African American	20	16	1	4	1	0
Hispanic or Latino	70	81	1	1	6	0
Native Hawaiian or Other Pacific Islander	0	4	0	0	0	0
White	392	322	1	11	19	0
Two or more races	24	32	0	2	2	0
Race and ethnicity unknown	21	30	7	1	0	0
International	76	59	2	1	1	0

	MINIMUM	MAXIMUM	MEAN
2014 entering class enrollees by age	21	38	25

CURRICULUM

The curriculum is designed to organize material into five thematic streams that emphasize and reinforce the integration of basic sciences and clinical sciences in dental education. The dental curriculum prepares students to render evidence-based, high-quality, comprehensive oral care. The curriculum emphasizes thorough understanding of diagnosis, prevention and control of disease; recognition of social needs; and knowledge of general health problems. Students are evaluated by examination and clinical competency examinations and by the quality and quantity of procedures completed. Courses are graded Passed/Not Passed/Passed With Honors.

In the first years, students experience strong scientific preparation augmented with introductory clinical activities and the fundamentals of dental therapies. During the third and fourth years, clinical experience—providing scientifically based patient-centered care—develops clinicians who graduate as competent dentists, and as men and women of science.

Details can be found at: http://dentistry.ucsf.edu/students-faculty-staff/students/curriculum.

Student research opportunities: Yes

SPECIAL PROGRAMS AND SERVICES

PREDENTAL

Postbaccalaureate programs: See school website
Special affiliation with colleges and universities: UCSF / UC Berkeley Extension – Postbaccalaureate program

DURING DENTAL SCHOOL

Academic counseling and tutoring
Community service opportunities
Internships, externships, or extramural programs
Mentoring
Personal counseling
Professional- and career-development programming
Special affiliations with colleges and universities: University of San Francisco – M.B.A. Program
Training for those interested in academic careers

ACTIVE STUDENT ORGANIZATIONS

American Association for Dental Research National Student Research Group
American Dental Education Association
American Student Dental Association
Hispanic Student Dental Association
Student National Dental Association

For a complete list of active student organizations, visit http://dentistry.ucsf.edu/node/731

INTERNATIONAL DENTISTS

Graduates of international dental schools considered for traditional predoctoral program: No
Advanced standing program offered for graduates of international dental schools: Yes
Advanced standing program description: Program awarding a dental degree

COMBINED AND ALTERNATE DEGREES

Ph.D.	M.S.	M.P.H.	M.D.	B.A./B.S.	Other
✓	✓	—	—	—	✓

Note: M.B.A., B.S. available only on a limited basis

COSTS: 2014–15 SCHOOL YEAR

	FIRST YEAR	SECOND YEAR	THIRD YEAR	FOURTH YEAR
Tuition, resident*	$44,069	$44,069	$48,632	$48,632
Tuition, nonresident	$56,314	$56,314	$60,877	$60,877
Tuition, other				
Fees	$216	$216	$216	$216
Instruments, books, and supplies	$14,229	$8,938	$7,178	$7,404
Estimated living expenses**	$20,484	$20,484	$27,312	$27,312
Total, resident	$78,998	$73,707	$83,338	$83,564
Total, nonresident	$91,243	$85,952	$95,583	$95,809
Total, other				

*Tuition and fees are subject to change by the University of California Regents and could be affected by state funding reductions. Final approved amount for 2015–16 may differ from the amounts shown above. Nonresidents have additional annual supplemental tuition of $12,245.

**Allowance assumes shared housing. Students in university-owned apartments will have a lower housing allowance if monthly rent is less than $1,040. As required by federal law, budgets used to determine financial aid eligibility can only include the student's costs; spouse and or children's expenses cannot be included in cost of living allowance.

FINANCIAL AID

Approximately 96.4% of our students receive financial aid to cover the cost of the predoctoral program. The majority of this aid is in the form of federal student loans. Admitted students should submit the Free Application for Federal Student Aid (FAFSA), College Board Profile and the UCSF Financial Aid application. Some need-based grand aid and scholarship funding is available. Admitted students do not have to apply for this separately; they will automatically be considered when they submit the above-mentioned items.

FINANCIAL AID AWARDS TO FIRST-YEAR STUDENTS 2014–15

Total number of first-year recipients: 85
Percentage of the first-year class: 26.6%
Percentage of awards that are grants? 100%
Percentage of awards that are loans? 88.2%

	AVERAGE AWARDS	RANGE OF AWARDS
Residents	$66,314	$5,000–$85,433
Nonresidents	$74,481	$8,379–$95,200

Note: Dollar figures include all awards (i.e., grants and loans).

For more information, please visit: http://finaid.ucsf.edu

UNIVERSITY OF THE PACIFIC
ARTHUR A. DUGONI SCHOOL OF DENTISTRY

Patrick J. Ferrillo, Jr., D.D.S., Dean

CONTACT INFORMATION

www.dental.pacific.edu
155 Fifth Street
San Francisco, CA 94103

OFFICE OF ADMISSIONS

Mr. Stan Constantino
Director of Admissions
155 Fifth Street
San Francisco, CA 94103
Phone: 415-929-6491

OFFICE OF FINANCIAL AID

Mr. Marco Castellanos
Director of Financial Aid
155 Fifth Street
San Francisco, CA 94103
Phone: 415-929-6452

OFFICE OF STUDENT SERVICES & HOUSING

Ms. Kathleen Candito
Associate Dean of Student Services
155 Fifth Street
San Francisco, CA 94103
Phone: 415-929-6491

MINORITY AFFAIRS/DIVERSITY

Mr. Stan Constantino
Director of Admissions
155 Fifth Street
San Francisco, CA 94103
Phone: 415-929-6491

GENERAL INFORMATION

The Arthur A. Dugoni School of Dentistry, recognized since its inception as a major resource for dental education in the western states, is the only dental school in which a four-academic-year curriculum can be completed in three calendar years.

In summer 2014, Pacific Dugoni moved to its new home at 155 Fifth Street in San Francisco's South of Market (SoMa) neighborhood. The building features modern clinical spaces, flexible learning environments, a state-of-the-art preclinical simulation laboratory, research labs and communal and study spaces to support the student experience. The sustainably designed campus is being built to LEED Gold standards.

MISSION

- To prepare oral health care providers for scientifically based practice
- To define new standards for education
- To provide patient-centered care
- To discover and disseminate knowledge

Vision: Leading the improvement of health by advancing oral health

Core Values: Humanism, Innovation, Leadership, Reflection, Stewardship, Collaboration, Philanthropy

Type of institution: Private	Doctoral dental degree offered: D.D.S.
Year opened: 1896	Targeted predoctoral enrollment: 423
Term type: Quarter	Targeted entering class size: 141
Time to degree in months: 36	Campus setting: Urban
Start month: July	Campus housing available: No

PREPARATION

Formal minimum preparation in semester/quarter hours: Semester: 90   Quarter: 135
Baccalaureate degree preferred: Yes
Number of first-year, first-time enrollees whose highest degree is:
  Baccalaureate: 129
  Master's degree and beyond: 6
Of first-year, first-time enrollees without baccalaureates, the number with:
  Equivalent of 60 undergraduate credit hours or less: 3
  Equivalent of 61–90 undergraduate credit hours: 0
  Equivalent of 91 or more undergraduate credit hours: 1

PREREQUISITE COURSE	REQUIRED	RECOMMENDED	LAB REQUIRED	CREDITS (SEMESTER/QUARTER)
BCP (biology-chemistry-physics) sciences				
Biology	✓		✓	4/6
Chemistry, general/inorganic	✓		✓	2/3
Chemistry, organic	✓			2/3
Physics	✓		✓	2/3
Additional biological sciences				
Anatomy		✓		
Biochemistry		✓		
Cell biology		✓		
Histology		✓		
Immunology		✓		
Microbiology		✓		
Molecular biology/genetics		✓		

PREPARATION (CONTINUED)

PREREQUISITE COURSE	REQUIRED	RECOMMENDED	LAB REQUIRED	CREDITS (SEMESTER/QUARTER)
Physiology		✓		
Zoology				

Community college coursework accepted for prerequisites: Yes
Community college coursework accepted for electives: Yes
Limits on community college credit hours: NA
Maximum number of community college credit hours: Courses taken at a community college will be acceptable if they are transferable as equivalent to predental courses at a four-year college.
Advanced placement (AP) credit accepted for prerequisites: Yes
Advanced placement (AP) credit accepted for electives: Yes
Comments regarding AP credit: Acceptance of advanced placement (AP) credit for prerequisites is assessed on an individual basis
Job shadowing: Required
Number of hours of job shadowing required or recommended: 40

DAT

Mandatory: Yes
Latest DAT for consideration of application: 11/01/2015
Oldest DAT considered: 11/01/2013
When more than one DAT score is reported: Most recent score only is considered
Canadian DAT accepted: Yes
Application considered before DAT scores are submitted: No

U.S. DAT: 2014 ENTERING CLASS

ENROLLEE DAT SCORES	MEAN	RANGE
Academic Average	21.6	NR
Perceptual Ability	21.4	NR
Total Science	21.5	NR

CANADIAN DAT: 2014 ENTERING CLASS

ENROLLEE DAT SCORES	MEAN	RANGE
Academic Average	21.0	NR
Manual Dexterity	NR	NR
Perceptual Ability	20.5	NR
Total Science	21.0	NR

GPA: 2014 ENTERING CLASS

ENROLLEE GPA SCORES	UNDERGRAD. MEAN	GRADUATE MEAN	UNDERGRAD. RANGE	GRADUATE RANGE
Science GPA	3.44	3.80	NR	NR
Total GPA	3.50	3.75	NR	NR

APPLICATION AND SELECTION

TIMETABLE

Earliest filing date: 06/02/2015
Latest filing date: 02/02/2016
Earliest date for acceptance offers: 12/01/2015
Maximum time in days for applicant's response to acceptance offer:
    30 days if accepted on or after December 1
    15 days if accepted on or after February 1
Requests for deferred entrance considered: Yes
Fee for application: Yes, submitted at same time as AADSAS application

Amount of fee for application:
    In state: $75   Out of state: $75   International: $75
Fee waiver available: No

	FIRST DEPOSIT	SECOND DEPOSIT	THIRD DEPOSIT
Required to hold place	Yes	Yes	No
Resident amount	$1,000	$2,000	
Nonresident amount			
Deposit due	As indicated in admission offer	As indicated in admission offer	
Applied to tuition	Yes	Yes	
Refundable	No	Yes	

APPLICATION PROCESS

Participates in AADSAS: Yes
Participates in Texas Medical and Dental Schools Application Service (for Texas applicants applying to Texas dental schools): No
Accepts direct applicants: No
Secondary or supplemental application required: No
Interview is mandatory: Yes
Interview is by invitation: Yes

RESIDENCY

In-state/in-province versus out-of-state/out-of-province
Admissions process distinguishes between in-state/in-province and out-of-state/out-of-province applicants: No
Preference given to residents of: None
Reciprocity Admissions Agreement available for legal residents of: None
Generally and over time, percentage of your first-year enrollment that is in-state: 75%
Origin of out-of-state/out-of-province enrollees: AZ-3, CO-1, FL-2, HI-4, IA-1, IL-1, NM-1, NY-1, OR-3, UT-4, WA-2

International
Applications are accepted from international (noncitizens/nonpermanent residents): Yes
Origin of international enrollees: Canada-4, China-1, South Korea-1

APPLICATION AND ENROLLMENT	NUMBER OF APPLICANTS	ESTIMATED NUMBER INTERVIEWED	ESTIMATED NUMBER ENROLLED
In-state or province applicants/enrollees	1,081	188	110
Out-of-state or province applicants/enrollees	1,370	59	23
International applicants/enrollees (noncitizens/nonpermanent residents)	336	13	6

DEMOGRAPHIC DESCRIPTIONS OF APPLICANTS: 2014 ENTERING CLASS

	APPLICANTS			ENROLLEES		
	M	W	Gender Unknown or Not Reported	M	W	Gender Unknown or Not Reported
American Indian or Alaska Native	6	1	0	0	0	0
Asian	526	507	9	32	23	1
Black or African American	19	26	1	0	0	0
Hispanic or Latino	84	94	2	3	7	0
Native Hawaiian or Other Pacific Islander	3	3	0	1	0	0
White	619	391	3	35	21	0
Two or more races	43	40	1	3	2	0
Race and ethnicity unknown	31	33	9	0	4	1
International	192	142	2	2	4	0

	MINIMUM	MAXIMUM	MEAN
2014 entering class enrollees by age	18	37	23

CURRICULUM

As suggested by the school's helix logo, biomedical, preclinical and clinical science subjects are integrated and combined with applied behavioral sciences in a program both to prepare graduates to provide excellent-quality dental care to the public and to enter a changing world that will require them to be critical thinkers and lifelong learners. The 36-month curriculum leading to the degree of Doctor of Dental Surgery begins in July and is divided into 12 quarters, each consisting of 10 weeks of instruction, one week of examinations and a vacation period of varying length (between one and four weeks). Students with research interests and ability are encouraged to undertake projects under the guidance of experienced faculty members. Student progress in the program is evaluated by academic performance committees and carefully monitored by the Academic Advisory Committees that serve to identify any problems (such as undiagnosed learning disabilities) and recommend tutorial and other support. The highest standards are maintained in preparation for National Dental Examining Boards and licensure for practice. Very few students are delayed in their progress toward graduation.

Student research opportunities: Yes

SPECIAL PROGRAMS AND SERVICES

PREDENTAL

Postbaccalaureate programs
Special affiliations with colleges and universities: University of the Pacific - Accelerated Dental Program; San Francisco State/Pacific - Postbaccalaureate Program

DURING DENTAL SCHOOL

Academic counseling and tutoring
Community service opportunities
Internships, externships, or extramural programs
Mentoring
Personal counseling
Professional- and career-development programming
Training for those interested in academic careers

ACTIVE STUDENT ORGANIZATIONS

American Association of Dental Research National Student Research Group
American Association of Women Dentists
American Dental Education Association
American Student Dental Association
Hispanic Dental Association
Pacific Dental Mission
Student Community Outreach for Public Education
Student National Dental Association
For a complete list of active student organizations, visit: http://dental.pacific.edu/Current_Students/Student_Life/Organizations_and_Clubs.html

INTERNATIONAL DENTISTS

Graduates of international dental schools considered for traditional predoctoral program: Yes
Advanced standing program offered for graduates of international dental schools: Yes

COMBINED AND ALTERNATE DEGREES

Ph.D.	M.S.	M.P.H.	M.D.	B.A./B.S.	Other
—	—	—	—	—	—

COSTS: 2014–15 SCHOOL YEAR

	FIRST YEAR	SECOND YEAR	THIRD YEAR	FOURTH YEAR
Tuition, resident	$98,105	$98,105	$98,105	NA
Tuition, nonresident	$98,105	$98,105	$98,105	NA
Tuition, other				NA
Fees	$6,451	$7,233	$8,461	NA
Instruments, books, and supplies	$15,195	$2,840	$800	NA
Estimated living expenses	$28,368	$28,368	$28,368	NA
Total, resident	$148,119	$136,546	$135,734	NA
Total, nonresident	$148,119	$136,546	$135,734	NA
Total, other				

FINANCIAL AID: 2014 ENTERING CLASS ESTIMATES

Federal loans continue to be the major source of funding for dental student. At University of the Pacific, Arthur A Dugoni School of Dentistry, 95% of entering students are borrowing some type of loan to pay for their dental education.

The financial aid office is committed to helping students find the best financing options and manage financial resources and indebtedness. While borrowing for dental school may be necessary, we encourage students to follow a budget and try to reduce expenses when possible. Budgeting and being a wise borrower will decrease student loan debt.

FINANCIAL AID AWARDS TO FIRST-YEAR STUDENTS 2014–15

Total number of first-year recipients: 107	
Percentage of the first-year class: 75%	
Percentage of awards that are grants? 11%	
Percentage of awards that are loans? 98%	

	AVERAGE AWARDS	RANGE OF AWARDS
Residents and nonresidents	$124,710	$18,000–$152,734

Additional financial aid information can be found on our school website www.dental.pacific.edu.

WESTERN UNIVERSITY OF HEALTH SCIENCES
COLLEGE OF DENTAL MEDICINE

Steven W. Friedrichsen, D.D.S., Dean

CONTACT INFORMATION

http://prospective.westernu.edu/dentistry/welcome-2/

309 East Second Street
Pomona, CA 91766
Phone: 909-706-3504
Fax: 909-706-3800

ADMISSIONS

309 East Second Street
Pomona, CA 91766
Phone: 909-469-5335
Email: admissions@westernu.edu

FINANCIAL AID

309 East Second Street
Pomona, CA 91766
Phone: 909-469-5353
Email: finaid@westernu.edu
http://prospective.westernu.edu/dentistry/financing-2/

STUDENT AFFAIRS

309 East Second Street
Pomona, CA 91766
Phone: 909-469-5340

HOUSING

309 East Second Street
Pomona, CA 91766
Phone: 909-469-5605
Email: jhutson@westernu.edu

INTERNATIONAL STUDENTS

Ms. Kathy Ford
University International Student Advisor
309 East Second Street
Pomona, CA 91766
Phone: 909-469-5542
Email: kford@westernu.edu
www.westernu.edu/international/international-welcome/

GENERAL INFORMATION

Western University of Health Sciences, founded in 1977, exists as a nonprofit, graduate university for the health professions located on 22 acres in Pomona. A city of approximately 150,000 residents, Pomona is located 35 miles east of Los Angeles near the foothills of the San Gabriel Mountains. The university emphasizes the education and preparation of interprofessional primary health care service teams. The university's philosophical perspective focuses on preparing highly skilled health care professionals who are also compassionate, humanistic caregivers.

MISSION

The College of Dental Medicine will educate and train highly competent, diverse clinical practitioners to provide complex, integrative, high-quality, evidence-based care for patients, families and communities.

Type of institution: Private
Year opened: 2009
Term type: Semester
Time to degree in months: 45
Start month: August

Doctoral dental degree offered: D.M.D.
Total predoctoral enrollment: 279
2014 entering class size: 70
Campus setting: Suburban
Campus housing available: No

PREPARATION

Formal minimum preparation in semester/quarter hours: Semester: 90   Quarter: 135
Baccalaureate degree preferred: Yes
Number of first-year, first-time enrollees whose highest degree is:
    Baccalaureate: 54
    Master's degree and beyond: 10
Of first-year, first-time enrollees without baccalaureates, the number with:
    Equivalent of 60 undergraduate credit hours or less: 0
    Equivalent of 61–90 undergraduate credit hours: 1
    Equivalent of 91 or more undergraduate credit hours: 4

PREREQUISITE COURSE	REQUIRED	RECOMMENDED	LAB REQUIRED	CREDITS (SEMESTER/QUARTER)
BCP (biology-chemistry-physics) sciences				
Biology	✓		✓	8/12
Chemistry, general/inorganic	✓		✓	8/12
Chemistry, organic	✓		✓	8/12
Physics	✓		✓	8/12
Additional biological sciences				
Anatomy		✓		4/6
Biochemistry		✓		4/6
Cell biology		✓		4/6
Histology				
Immunology				
Microbiology		✓		4/6
Molecular biology/genetics		✓		4/6
Physiology		✓		4/6
Zoology				

(Prerequisite Courses continued)

PREPARATION (CONTINUED)

PREREQUISITE COURSE	REQUIRED	RECOMMENDED	LAB REQUIRED	CREDITS (SEMESTER/QUARTER)
Other				
Calculus		✓		3/4
Psychology		✓		3/4
Conversational Spanish		✓		3/4
College English/composition	✓			6/9

Community college coursework accepted for prerequisites: Yes
Community college coursework accepted for electives: Yes
Limits on community college credit hours: No
Maximum number of community college credit hours: None
Advanced placement (AP) credit accepted for prerequisites: For English only
Advanced placement (AP) credit accepted for electives: No
Job shadowing: Required
Number of hours of job shadowing required or recommended: 30—dental-related work experience (paid or volunteer)

DAT

Mandatory: Yes. Scores valid three years from date of application
Latest DAT for consideration of application: 10/15/2015
Oldest DAT considered: 01/01/2012
When more than one DAT score is reported: Most recent score only is considered
Canadian DAT accepted: No
Application considered before DAT scores are submitted: No

DAT: 2014 ENTERING CLASS

ENROLLEE DAT SCORES	MEAN	RANGE
Academic Average	19.0	15–22
Perceptual Ability	20.0	17–25
Total Science	19.0	15–23

GPA: 2014 ENTERING CLASS

ENROLLEE GPA SCORES	UNDERGRAD. MEAN	GRADUATE MEAN	UNDERGRAD. RANGE	GRADUATE RANGE
Science GPA	3.16	3.48	2.68–3.85	2.56–3.94
Total GPA	3.26	3.53	2.66–3.85	2.56–3.92

APPLICATION AND SELECTION

TIMETABLE

Earliest filing date: 06/02/2015
Latest filing date: 12/01/2015
Earliest date for acceptance offers: 12/01/2015
Maximum time in days for applicant's response to acceptance offer:
   30 days if accepted on or after December 1
   15 days if accepted on or after February 1
   Response time lifted if offered after May 15
Requests for deferred entrance considered: In exceptional circumstances only
Fee for application: Yes, electronically paid with online supplemental application
Amount of fee for application:
   In state: $60   Out of state: $60   International: $60
Fee waiver available: Check school website for details

	FIRST DEPOSIT	SECOND DEPOSIT	THIRD DEPOSIT
Required to hold place	Yes	Yes	No
Resident amount	$1,000	$1,000	
Nonresident amount	$1,000	$1,000	
Deposit due	As indicated in admission offer	As indicated in admission offer	
Applied to tuition	Yes	Yes	
Refundable	No	No	

APPLICATION PROCESS

Participates in Associated American Dental Schools Application Service (AADSAS): Yes
Accepts direct applicants: No
Secondary or supplemental application required: Yes, to be submitted online with $60 fee via the WesternU website
Secondary or supplemental application website: http://prospective.westernu.edu/dentistry/apply
Interview is mandatory: Yes
Interview is by invitation: Yes

RESIDENCY

In-state/in-province versus out-of-state/out-of-province
Admissions process distinguishes between in-state/in-province and out-of-state/out-of-province applicants: No
Preference given to residents of: None
Reciprocity Admissions Agreement available for legal residents of: None
Generally and over time, percentage of your first-year enrollment that is in-state: 63%
Origin of out-of-state/out-of-province enrollees: AZ-1, CT-1, FL-4, GA-1, HI-1, ID-1, IL-2, NC-1, NJ-1, NM-1, NY-2, OK-1, OR-1, PA-2, TX-2, UT-2, WA-7, WI-2

International
Applications are accepted from international (noncitizens/nonpermanent residents): Yes
Origin of international enrollees: South Korea-1

APPLICATION AND ENROLLMENT	NUMBER OF APPLICANTS	ESTIMATED NUMBER INTERVIEWED	ESTIMATED NUMBER ENROLLED
In-state or province applicants/enrollees	1,003	216	35
Out-of-state or province applicants/enrollees	1,518	201	33
International applicants/enrollees (noncitizens/nonpermanent residents)	148	11	1

DEMOGRAPHIC DESCRIPTIONS OF APPLICANTS: 2014 ENTERING CLASS

	APPLICANTS			ENROLLEES		
	M	W	Gender Unknown or Not Reported	M	W	Gender Unknown or Not Reported
American Indian or Alaska Native	1	2	0	0	0	0
Asian	509	482	0	11	12	0
Black or African American	19	22	0	0	0	0
Hispanic or Latino	96	109	0	7	4	0
Native Hawaiian or Other Pacific Islander	1	2	0	0	0	0
White	646	391	0	17	9	0
Two or more races	72	81	2	1	4	0
Race and ethnicity unknown	42	40	4	0	3	0
International	83	63	2	1	0	0

	MINIMUM	MAXIMUM	MEAN
2014 entering class enrollees by age	21	36	26

CURRICULUM

The College of Dental Medicine will be a premier center for integrative educational innovation; basic and translational research; and high-quality, patient-centered, interprofessional health care, all conducted in a setting that uses advanced technology and promotes individual dignity and potential for personal and professional growth. The overarching themes of the dental curriculum are:

1. Critical thinking.
2. Professionalism.
3. Communication and interpersonal skills.
4. Health promotion.
5. Practice management and informatics.
6. Patient care.

Teaching methodologies will include small-group interaction, preclinical simulation laboratory, comprehensive patient-care clinical experience and community-based clinical care and service.

Student research opportunities: Yes

SPECIAL PROGRAMS AND SERVICES

DURING DENTAL SCHOOL

Academic counseling and tutoring
Community service opportunities
Internships, externships, or extramural programs
Mentoring
Personal counseling
Professional- and career-development programming
Training for those interested in academic careers

ACTIVE STUDENT ORGANIZATIONS

American Student Dental Association
More than 75 diverse clubs and interest groups

INTERNATIONAL DENTISTS

Graduates of international dental schools considered for traditional predoctoral program: Yes
Advanced standing program offered for graduates of international dental schools: No

COMBINED AND ALTERNATE DEGREES

Ph.D.	M.S.	M.P.H.	M.D.	B.A./B.S.	Other
—	—	—	—	—	—

COSTS: 2014–15 SCHOOL YEAR

	FIRST YEAR	SECOND YEAR	THIRD YEAR	FOURTH YEAR*
Tuition, resident	$64,870	$64,870	$64,870	$64,870
Tuition, nonresident	$64,870	$64,870	$64,870	$64,870
Tuition, other				
Fees	$8,631	$8,704	$11,966	$12,586
Instruments, books, and supplies	$7,940	$5,570	$5,570	$5,570
Estimated living expenses	$20,498	$20,498	$20,498	$20,498
Total, resident	$101,939	$99,642	$102,904	$103,524
Total, nonresident	$101,939	$99,642	$102,904	$103,524
Total, other				

FINANCIAL AID

Students need to complete the Free Application for Federal Student Aid (FAFSA) in order to apply for financial aid. The Financial Aid Office encourages all students to file the FAFSA at www.fafsa.ed.gov after January 1. Students may estimate their income in order to complete the FAFSA. The school code for Western University of Health Sciences is 024827. The Financial Aid Office will then be able to determine the student's eligibility for federal aid once the student has submitted the completed FAFSA application. An award letter will be sent electronically to the student's Western University of Health Sciences email address.

FINANCIAL AID AWARDS TO FIRST-YEAR STUDENTS 2014–15

Total number of first-year recipients: 64	
Percentage of the first-year class: 92.75%	
Percentage of awards that are grants? 7.25%	
Percentage of awards that are loans? 89.86%	

	AVERAGE AWARDS	RANGE OF AWARDS
Residents and nonresidents	$94,082	$20,000–$110,862

For more information, please visit: http://www.westernu.edu/financial/financial-welcome/

CONTACT INFORMATION

www.ucdenver.edu/sdm

MS F833, 13065 East 17th Avenue
Aurora, CO 80045
Phone: 303-724-7122
Fax: 303-724-7109
DDSadmissioninquiries@ucdenver.edu

ADMISSIONS, STUDENT LIFE AND INCLUSION

Associate Dean for Student Affairs
MS F833, 13065 East 17th Avenue
Aurora, CO 80045
Phone: 303-724-7120

STUDENT FINANCIAL AID OFFICE

CB A088, 13120 East 19th Avenue
Aurora, CO 80045
Phone: 303-724-8039
www.ucdenver.edu/finaid

OFFICE OF INCLUSION AND OUTREACH

Mr. Dominic Martinez
Senior Director
MS A049, 13120 East 19th Avenue
Aurora, CO 80045
Phone: 303-724-8003
www.ucdenver.edu/about/departments/
DiversityandInclusion

CAMPUS STUDENT SERVICES

CB A043, 13120 East 19th Avenue
Aurora, CO 80045
Phone: 303-724-7686
www.ucdenver.edu/life/services/
student-assistance

INTERNATIONAL STUDENTS

Dr. Elizabeth Towne
Director
MS 838, 13065 East 17th Avenue
Aurora, CO 80045
Phone: 303-724-7060

THE UNIVERSITY OF COLORADO
SCHOOL OF DENTAL MEDICINE

Denise K. Kassebaum, D.D.S., M.S., Dean

GENERAL INFORMATION

Since The University of Colorado School of Dental Medicine (CU SDM) enrolled its first class in 1973, the program has evolved as ongoing research has advanced the field of dentistry. CU SDM's mission and progressive vision allow the D.D.S. program to flourish and provide quality educational experiences that are personalized for each of its successful graduates. Recognized as a model institution for developing an innovative interprofessional curriculum, the school prepares graduates for team-based practice.

CU SDM offers clinical functions including general dentistry, endodontics, orthodontics, periodontics, surgery, radiology, esthetic dentistry and specialized areas of pediatric care, geriatric care and special needs care.

MISSION

CU SDM's mission is to provide programs of excellence in teaching, research, patient care, and community and professional service for Colorado and the nation.

Vision: CU SDM will be the premier public dental school, recognized for its innovative interprofessional programs of excellence in education, discovery, patient care and community engagement.

Type of institution: Public
Year opened: 1973
Term type: Semester
Time to degree in months: 46
Start month: August

Doctoral dental degree offered: D.D.S.
Targeted predoctoral enrollment: 320
Targeted entering class size: 80
Campus setting: Suburban
Campus housing available: No

PREPARATION

Formal minimum preparation in semester/quarter hours: Semester: 90   Quarter: 135
Baccalaureate degree preferred: Yes
Number of first-year, first-time enrollees whose highest degree is:
    Baccalaureate: 65
    Master's degree and beyond: 12
Of first-year, first-time enrollees without baccalaureates, the number with:
    Equivalent of 60 undergraduate credit hours or less: 0
    Equivalent of 61–90 undergraduate credit hours: 0
    Equivalent of 91 or more undergraduate credit hours: 2

PREREQUISITE COURSE	REQUIRED	RECOMMENDED	LAB REQUIRED	CREDITS (SEMESTER/QUARTER)
BCP (biology-chemistry-physics) sciences				
Biology	✓		✓	8/12
Chemistry, general/inorganic	✓		✓	8/12
Chemistry, organic	✓		✓	8/12
Physics	✓		✓	8/12
Additional biological sciences				
Anatomy		✓		4/6
Biochemistry	✓			3/5
Cell biology		✓		4/6
Histology		✓		4/6
Immunology		✓		4/6

PREPARATION (CONTINUED)

PREREQUISITE COURSE	REQUIRED	RECOMMENDED	LAB REQUIRED	CREDITS (SEMESTER/QUARTER)
Microbiology	✓			3/5
Molecular biology/genetics		✓		4/6
Physiology		✓		4/6
Other				
English composition	✓			3/5

Community college coursework accepted for prerequisites: Yes
Community college coursework accepted for electives: Yes
Limits on community college credit hours: Yes
Maximum number of community college credit hours: 60
Advanced placement (AP) credit accepted for prerequisites: Yes
Advanced placement (AP) credit accepted for electives: Yes
Comments regarding AP credit: NA
Job shadowing: Required
Number of hours of job shadowing required or recommended: 50 hour minimum

DAT

Mandatory: Yes
Latest DAT for consideration of application: 12/31/2015
Oldest DAT considered: 12/31/2011
When more than one DAT score is reported: Highest score is considered
Canadian DAT accepted: No
Application considered before DAT scores are submitted: No

DAT: 2014 ENTERING CLASS

ENROLLEE DAT SCORES	MEAN	RANGE
Academic Average	19.6	15–25
Perceptual Ability	19.9	15–25
Total Science	19.6	15–26

GPA: 2014 ENTERING CLASS

ENROLLEE GPA SCORES	UNDERGRAD. MEAN	GRADUATE MEAN	UNDERGRAD. RANGE	GRADUATE RANGE
Science GPA	3.49	3.88	2.37–4.14	3.00–4.00
Total GPA	3.56	3.64	2.53–4.08	3.16–4.00

APPLICATION AND SELECTION

TIMETABLE

Earliest filing date: 06/02/2015
Latest filing date: 12/31/2015
Earliest date for acceptance offers: 12/01/2015
Maximum time in days for applicant's response to acceptance offer:
    30 days if accepted on or after December 1
    15 days if accepted on or after February 1
Requests for deferred entrance considered: In exceptional
    circumstances only.
Fee for application: Yes, submitted only when requested
Amount of fee for application:
    In state: $50   Out of state: $50   International: $75
Fee waiver available: No

	FIRST DEPOSIT	SECOND DEPOSIT	THIRD DEPOSIT
Required to hold place	Yes	No	No
Resident amount	$1,000		
Nonsponsored amount	$1,000		
Deposit due	As indicated in admission offer		
Applied to tuition	Yes		
Refund	Yes		
Refundable by	60 days prior to matriculation		

APPLICATION PROCESS

Participates in Associated American Dental Schools Application Service
    (AADSAS): Yes
Accepts direct applicants: No
Secondary or supplemental application required: Yes, only upon request
Secondary or supplemental application website: None
Interview is mandatory: Yes
Interview is by invitation: Yes

RESIDENCY

In-state/in-province versus out-of-state/out-of-province
Admissions process distinguishes between in-state/in-province and
    out-of-state/out-of-province applicants: Yes
Preference given to residents of: Colorado and participating WICHE
    states
Reciprocity Admissions Agreement available for legal residents of: None
Generally and over time, percentage of your first-year enrollment that is
    in-state: 66%
Origin of out-of-state/out-of-province enrollees: AK-1, AZ-4, CA-3, FL-1,
    KS-1, MD-2, MT-2, ND-1, NE-2, NM-4, PA-1, TX-2, WA-1

International
Applications are accepted from international (noncitizens/
    nonpermanent residents): Yes
Origin of international enrollees: NA

APPLICATION AND ENROLLMENT	NUMBER OF APPLICANTS	ESTIMATED NUMBER INTERVIEWED	ESTIMATED NUMBER ENROLLED
In-state or province applicants/enrollees	126	90	51
Out-of-state or province applicants/enrollees	1,443	162	29
International applicants/enrollees (noncitizens/nonpermanent residents)	38	0	0

DEMOGRAPHIC DESCRIPTIONS OF APPLICANTS: 2014 ENTERING CLASS

	APPLICANTS			ENROLLEES		
	M	W	Gender Unknown or Not Reported	M	W	Gender Unknown or Not Reported
American Indian or Alaska Native	4	5	0	0	0	0
Asian	144	143	3	11	3	0
Black or African American	11	17	2	0	0	0
Hispanic or Latino	66	60	0	4	3	0
Native Hawaiian or Other Pacific Islander	2	4	0	0	0	0
White	597	401	1	29	26	0
Two or more races	28	23	0	1	0	0
Race and ethnicity unknown	23	23	2	0	2	0
International	10	27	1	0	0	0

	MINIMUM	MAXIMUM	MEAN
2014 entering class enrollees by age	20	45	25

CURRICULUM

The dental curriculum aims to graduate dentists who will be able to:

1. Prevent, diagnose and treat oral disease.
2. Apply biological, physical and social sciences to perform appropriate prevention, diagnosis and treatment.
3. Apply personal and professional skills to practice effectively and relate to patients and colleagues.
4. Recognize professional capabilities and judiciously refer patients for specialty care.
5. Continue to acquire knowledge through patterns of lifelong study.

Basic science instruction, reinforced by such courses as systemic disease, and oral and organ pathology, occurs in the first and second years.

Predoctoral dental students participate in the six-semester clinical curriculum. Early experiences include observing and assisting upperclassmen in patient treatment. Following this first year, students begin to treat patients on a limited basis, performing primarily oral diagnosis and periodontal and operative dental procedures. After accumulating a "family" of patients, students are responsible for their complete care. During the following semesters, students continue to treat patients and rotate through the Oral Surgery, Emergency and Pediatric Clinics.

While continuing to treat patients in the Comprehensive Care Clinic, dental students participate in the nationally recognized Advanced Clinical Training Service (ACTS) program, a cooperative effort with community-based providers.

Student research opportunities: Yes

SPECIAL PROGRAMS AND SERVICES

PREDENTAL

Postbaccalaureate programs: One-year structured curriculum/underrepresented (by application only)
Summer enrichment programs: The Undergraduate Pre-Health Program (UPP) has shadowing and research opportunities for underrepresented minority students.

DURING DENTAL SCHOOL

Academic counseling and tutoring
Community service opportunities
Mentoring
Opportunity to serve in Guatemala
Personal counseling
Professional and career development program
Research opportunities
Transfer applicants considered if space is available

ACTIVE STUDENT ORGANIZATIONS

American Association for Dental Research
American Association of Public Health Dentistry
American Association of Women Dentists
American Dental Education Association
American Student Dental Association
Dental fraternities, including Alpha Omega International Dental Fraternity and Delta Sigma Delta International Fraternity
Global Oral Health Student Association
Hispanic Student Dental Association
Student National Dental Association
Student chapters of the Academy of LDS Dentists, the American Academy of Pediatric Dentistry and the Christian Dental Association

INTERNATIONAL DENTISTS

Graduates of international dental schools considered for traditional predoctoral program: No
Advanced standing program offered for graduates of international dental schools: Yes
Advanced standing program description: International Student Program

COMBINED AND ALTERNATE DEGREES

Ph.D.	M.S.	M.P.H.	M.D.	B.A./B.S.	Other
—	—	—	—	✓	—

COSTS: 2014–15 SCHOOL YEAR

	FIRST YEAR	SECOND YEAR	THIRD YEAR	FOURTH YEAR
Tuition, resident	$32,125	$32,125	$32,125	$32,125
Tuition, nonresident	$57,428	$57,428	$57,428	$57,428
Tuition, other				
Fees	$605	$390	$390	$390
Instruments, books, and supplies	$9,560	$5,610	$5,610	$5,610
Estimated health fees	$3,918	$3,918	$3,918	$3,918
Estimated living expenses	$21,600	$21,600	$21,600	$16,200
Total, resident	$67,808	$63,643	$63,643	$58,243
Total, nonresident	$93,111	$88,946	$88,946	$83,546
Total, other				

FINANCIAL AID

For the 2015 Academic Award Period (Fall 2014 and Spring 2015), first-year students were awarded state and institutional grants, federal loans and institutional, governmental and private scholarships. Both grants and scholarships are included in the *Percentage of awards that are grants* below.

FINANCIAL AID AWARDS TO FIRST-YEAR STUDENTS 2014–15

Total number of first-year recipients: 75
Percentage of the first-year class: 94%
Percentage of awards that are grants? 18%
Percentage of awards that are loans? 82%

	AVERAGE AWARDS	RANGE OF AWARDS
Residents	$19,789	$734–$40,500
Nonresidents	$26,004	$602–$47,010

For more information, please visit: www.ucdenver.edu/finaid

R. Lamont MacNeil, D.D.S., M.D.S., Dean

GENERAL INFORMATION

The University of Connecticut School of Dental Medicine (UConn SDM) is a prominent leader in dental education, dental research and patient care. The predoctoral curriculum focuses on the biological and epidemiological bases of disease and provides strong preparation in diagnostic and technical skills. Sharing a basic science curriculum with the School of Medicine, UConn SDM emphasizes an integrative approach to understanding the human body's dynamics. Up to 80% of students pursue advanced dental education in the clinical specialties or general dentistry. Connecticut's only dental school and the only public dental school in New England, UConn SDM is recognized nationally and internationally for its predoctoral and advanced dental education/graduate programs.

MISSION

The School of Dental Medicine is committed to graduating dentists and specialists who are dedicated to acquiring and advancing knowledge, lifelong-learning, and serving their communities.

Core Values: The School of Dental Medicine commits to pursue excellence, embrace innovation, promote professionalism and social responsibility, provide leadership, and serve the needs of the community.

Type of institution: Public	Doctoral dental degree offered: D.M.D.
Year opened: 1968	Targeted predoctoral enrollment: 160
Term type: Semester	Targeted entering class size: 40
Time to degree in months: 45	Campus setting: Suburban
Start month: August	Campus housing available: No

PREPARATION

Formal minimum preparation in semester/quarter hours: Semester: 90   Quarter: 180
Baccalaureate degree preferred: Yes
Number of first-year, first-time enrollees whose highest degree is:
  Baccalaureate: 43
  Master's degree and beyond: 3
Of first-year, first-time enrollees without baccalaureates, the number with:
  Equivalent of 60 undergraduate credit hours or less: 0
  Equivalent of 61–90 undergraduate credit hours: 0
  Equivalent of 91 or more undergraduate credit hours: 0

PREREQUISITE COURSE	REQUIRED	RECOMMENDED	LAB REQUIRED	CREDITS (SEMESTER/QUARTER)
BCP (biology-chemistry-physics) sciences				
Biology	✓		✓	8/12
Chemistry, general/inorganic	✓		✓	8/12
Chemistry, organic	✓		✓	8/12
Physics	✓		✓	8/12
Additional biological sciences				
Anatomy				
Biochemistry	✓			4/6
Cell biology		✓		4/6
Histology				
Immunology				
Microbiology		✓		4/6
Molecular biology/genetics		✓		4/6

(Prerequisite Courses continued)

CONTACT INFORMATION

http://sdm.uchc.edu

263 Farmington Avenue
Farmington, CT 06030-3915
Phone: 860-679-2808
Fax: 860-679-1330

OFFICE OF ADMISSIONS

Ms. Tricia M. Avolt
Admissions Coordinator
263 Farmington Avenue, MC 3905
Farmington, CT 06030-3905
Phone: 860-679-2175

STUDENT FINANCIAL SERVICE CENTER

Ms. Andrea Devereux
Director
263 Farmington Avenue, MC 1827
Farmington, CT 06030-1827
Phone: 860-679-3574

OFFICE OF DENTAL STUDENT AFFAIRS

263 Farmington Avenue, MC 3905
Farmington, CT 06030-3905
Phone: 860-679-2175

MINORITY AFFAIRS/DIVERSITY

Dr. Marja Hurley
Associate Dean
263 Farmington Avenue, MC 1850
Farmington, CT 06030-1850
Phone: 860-679-3484

HOUSING

Ms. Lisa Francini
Student Affairs and Activities
263 Farmington Avenue, MC 1829
Farmington, CT 06030-1829
Phone: 860-679-2986
Fax: 860-679-6763

INTERNATIONAL STUDENTS

Ms. Tricia M. Avolt
Admissions Coordinator
263 Farmington Avenue, MC 3905
Farmington, CT 06030-3905
Phone: 860-679-2175

PREPARATION (CONTINUED)

PREREQUISITE COURSE	REQUIRED	RECOMMENDED	LAB REQUIRED	CREDITS (SEMESTER/QUARTER)
Physiology				
Zoology				

Community college coursework accepted for prerequisites: Yes
Community college coursework accepted for electives: Yes
Limits on community college credit hours: No
Advanced placement (AP) credit accepted for prerequisites: Yes
Advanced placement (AP) credit accepted for electives: Yes
Job shadowing: Required
Number of hours of job shadowing required or recommended: 75

DAT

Mandatory: Yes
Latest DAT for consideration of application: 11/01/2015
Oldest DAT considered: 06/01/2013
When more than one DAT score is reported: Most recent score only is considered
Canadian DAT accepted: Yes
Application considered before DAT scores are submitted: No

DAT: 2014 ENTERING CLASS

ENROLLEE DAT SCORES	MEAN	RANGE
Academic Average	21.0	18–24
Perceptual Ability	20.0	16–25
Total Science	21.0	18–26

GPA: 2014 ENTERING CLASS

ENROLLEE GPA SCORES	UNDERGRAD. MEAN	GRADUATE MEAN	UNDERGRAD. RANGE	GRADUATE RANGE
Science GPA	3.54	3.33	2.94–4.00	3.18–3.61
Total GPA	3.61	3.34	3.02–4.00	3.18–3.64

APPLICATION AND SELECTION

TIMETABLE

Earliest filing date: 06/02/2015
Latest filing date: 11/01/2015
Earliest date for acceptance offers: 12/01/2015
Maximum time in days for applicant's response to acceptance offer:
    30 days if accepted on or after December 1
    15 days if accepted on or after January 1
Requests for deferred entrance considered: In exceptional circumstances only
Fee for application: Yes, submitted at same time as Associated American Dental Schools Application Service (AADSAS) application
Amount of fee for application:
    In state: $75   Out of state: $75   International: $75
Fee waiver available: Yes

	FIRST DEPOSIT	SECOND DEPOSIT	THIRD DEPOSIT
Required to hold place	Yes	Yes	No
Resident amount	$1,000	$500	
Nonresident amount	$1,000	$500	
Deposit due	As indicated in admission offer	As indicated in admission offer	
Applied to tuition	Yes	Yes	
Refundable	No	No	

APPLICATION PROCESS

Participates in AADSAS: Yes
Accepts direct applicants: Yes
Secondary or supplemental application required: No
Interview is mandatory: Yes
Interview is by invitation: Yes

RESIDENCY

In-state/in-province versus out-of-state/out-of-province
Admissions process distinguishes between in-state/in-province and out-of-state/out-of-province applicants: Yes
Preference given to residents of: Connecticut
Reciprocity Admissions Agreement available for legal residents of: New England
Generally and over time, percentage of your first-year enrollment that is in-state: 50%
Origin of out-of-state/out-of-province enrollees: C0-1, MA-7, ME-4, MO-1, NC-1, NH-2, NJ-1, NY-5, PA-1, RI-1

International
Applications are accepted from international (noncitizens/ nonpermanent residents): Yes
Origin of international enrollees: China-1

APPLICATION AND ENROLLMENT	NUMBER OF APPLICANTS	ESTIMATED NUMBER INTERVIEWED	ESTIMATED NUMBER ENROLLED
In-state or province applicants/ enrollees	78	35	21
Out-of-state or province applicants/enrollees	1,086	128	24
International applicants/enrollees (noncitizens/nonpermanent residents)	82	4	1

DEMOGRAPHIC DESCRIPTIONS OF APPLICANTS: 2014 ENTERING CLASS

	APPLICANTS			ENROLLEES		
	M	W	Gender Unknown or Not Reported	M	W	Gender Unknown or Not Reported
American Indian or Alaska Native	0	1	0	0	0	0
Asian	164	179	2	1	2	0
Black or African American	12	30	1	1	2	0
Hispanic or Latino	27	54	0	1	4	0
Native Hawaiian or Other Pacific Islander	0	0	0	0	0	0
White	331	270	4	15	16	0
Two or more races	14	19	0	1	0	0
Race and ethnicity unknown	24	25	8	2	0	0
International	46	36	0	0	1	0

	MINIMUM	MAXIMUM	MEAN
2014 entering class enrollees by age	21	32	24

CURRICULUM

The curriculum is designed to provide students with a comprehensive educational experience that allows them to master the knowledge and requisite skills associated with the practice of general dentistry. The goals of the program are to help students gain an understanding of human biology and the behavioral sciences, and to develop their competency in all aspects of clinical dentistry. During the first two years, dental students follow an integrated course of study in the basic sciences along with the medical students. The third- and fourth-year clinical program extends for 22 months and emphasizes comprehensive care, prevention and the emerging epidemiologic patterns of dental diseases. Students are evaluated through written and practical examinations in the medical, dental and clinical sciences, and through observation of students' development in patient oral health care delivery. The grading system is on a pass/fail basis.

Student research opportunities: Yes

SPECIAL PROGRAMS AND SERVICES

PREDENTAL

DAT workshops
Passport to Dentistry Program
Postbaccalaureate programs
Summer enrichment programs

DURING DENTAL SCHOOL

Academic counseling and tutoring
Community service opportunities
Internships, externships, or extramural programs
Mentoring
Personal counseling
Professional- and career-development programming
Training for those interested in academic careers

ACTIVE STUDENT ORGANIZATIONS

American Dental Education Association
American Student Dental Association
Hispanic Dental Association
Student National Dental Association

INTERNATIONAL DENTISTS

Graduates of international dental schools considered for traditional predoctoral program: Yes
Advanced standing program offered for graduates of international dental schools: No
Advanced standing program description: NA

COMBINED AND ALTERNATE DEGREES

Ph.D.	M.S.	M.P.H.	M.D.	B.A./B.S.	Other
✓	✓	✓	—	✓	—

Note: The only M.S. degree offered to predoctoral students is in Clinical and Translational Research.

COSTS: 2014–15 SCHOOL YEAR

	FIRST YEAR	SECOND YEAR	THIRD YEAR	FOURTH YEAR
Tuition, resident	$25,531	$25,531	$25,531	$25,531
Tuition, nonresident	$57,494	$57,494	$57,494	$57,494
Tuition, New England resident	$43,930	$43,930	$43,930	$43,930
Fees	$6,372	$6,372	$6,372	$6,372
Instruments, books, and supplies	$9,364	$2,298	$3,512	$735
Estimated living expenses	$20,925	$20,775	$24,450	$21,600
Total, resident	$62,192	$54,976	$59,865	$54,238
Total, nonresident	$94,155	$86,939	$91,828	$86,201
Total, New England resident	$80,591	$73,375	$78,264	$72,637

FINANCIAL AID

For additional information on Financial Aid, please go to http://student-services.uchc.edu/financial/index.html.

FINANCIAL AID AWARDS TO FIRST-YEAR STUDENTS 2014–15

Total number of first-year recipients: 37
Percentage of the first-year class: 76%
Percentage of awards that are grants? 23%
Percentage of awards that are loans? 77%

	AVERAGE AWARDS	RANGE OF AWARDS
Residents	$37,960	$1,000–$64,951
Nonresidents	$74,986	$20,000–$94,712

For more information, please visit: sdm.uchc.edu

HOWARD UNIVERSITY
COLLEGE OF DENTISTRY

Leo E. Rouse, D.D.S., Dean

CONTACT INFORMATION

www.howard.edu/collegedentistry

600 W Street, NW
Washington, DC 20059
Phone: 202-806-0019
Fax: 202-806-0354

OFFICE OF ADMISSIONS

Ms. Deborah Willis
Director of Admissions
Room 126
600 W Street, NW
Washington, DC 20509
Phone: 202-806-0400

FINANCIAL AID

Mr. Joseph Smith III
Financial Aid Manager
Room 126
600 W Street, NW
Washington, DC 20059
Phone: 202-806-0368

OFFICE OF STUDENT AFFAIRS

Dr. Donna Grant-Mills
Associate Dean for Student Affairs
Room 128
600 W Street, NW
Washington, DC 20509
Phone: 202-806-0361

OFFICE OF THE DEAN

Dr. Leo E. Rouse
Dean
600 W Street, NW
Washington, DC 20059
Phone: 202-806-0019

RESIDENCE LIFE- HOWARD PLAZA

Mr. Larry Frelow
Property Manager
2401 4th Street, NW
Washington, DC 20059
Phone: 202-797-7148
www.howard.edu

GENERAL INFORMATION

Established in 1881, the Howard University College of Dentistry—the nation's fifth oldest dental school—is a leading teaching and patient care institution. The college has trained thousands of highly skilled dental professionals to serve their communities, particularly the underserved. Our graduates currently serve communities in 40 states and 53 foreign countries. Our more than 80 faculty members, who constitute one of the best-trained dental faculties in the world, are committed to producing distinguished, compassionate and culturally sensitive graduates. Furthermore, the college is dedicated to providing high-quality oral health care to patients and to improving oral health in local, national and global communities.

MISSION

To provide a dental education of exceptional quality to qualified individuals, with particular emphasis on recruiting promising African Americans and other historically underrepresented students.

Vision: To provide exemplary education, service, and research that promotes patient-centered, collaborative care and advocacy for the elimination of health disparities.

Type of institution: Private	Doctoral dental degree offered: D.D.S.
Year opened: 1881	Targeted predoctoral enrollment: 335
Term type: Semester	Targeted entering class size: 80
Time to degree in months: 42	Campus setting: Urban
Start month: August	Campus housing available: Yes

PREPARATION

Formal minimum preparation in semester/quarter hours: Semester: 8   Quarter: 12
Baccalaureate degree preferred: Yes, baccalaureate degree is required.
Number of first-year, first-time enrollees whose highest degree is:
    Baccalaureate: 61
    Master's degree and beyond: 11
Of first-year, first-time enrollees without baccalaureates, the number with:
    Equivalent of 60 undergraduate credit hours or less: 0
    Equivalent of 61–90 undergraduate credit hours: 0
    Equivalent of 91 or more undergraduate credit hours: 0

PREREQUISITE COURSE	REQUIRED	RECOMMENDED	LAB REQUIRED	CREDITS (SEMESTER/QUARTER)
BCP (biology-chemistry-physics) sciences				
Biology	✓		✓	8/12
Chemistry, general/inorganic	✓		✓	8/12
Chemistry, organic	✓		✓	8/12
Physics	✓		✓	8/12
Additional biological sciences				
Anatomy	✓			6/8
Biochemistry	✓			3/5
Cell biology		✓		4/6
Histology		✓		4/6
Immunology		✓		4/6
Microbiology		✓		4/6
Molecular biology/genetics		✓		4/6
Physiology		✓		6/8

(Prerequisite Courses continued)

PREPARATION (CONTINUED)

PREREQUISITE COURSE	REQUIRED	RECOMMENDED	LAB REQUIRED	CREDITS (SEMESTER/QUARTER)
Zoology		✓		4/6
Other				
English Composition		✓		6/8

Community college coursework accepted for prerequisites: Yes
Community college coursework accepted for electives: Yes
Limits on community college credit hours: Yes
Maximum number of community college credit hours: 60
Advanced placement (AP) credit accepted for prerequisites: No
Advanced placement (AP) credit accepted for electives: Yes
Comments regarding AP credit: None accepted.
Job shadowing: Recommended
Number of hours of job shadowing required or recommended: 100 hours—should be over a period of time.
Other factors considered in admission: Community service, number of hours spent job shadowing, leadership qualities, and interview.

DAT

Mandatory: Yes
Latest DAT for consideration of application: 03/31/2016
Oldest DAT considered: 03/31/2014
When more than one DAT score is reported: Highest score is considered
Canadian DAT accepted: Yes
Application considered before DAT scores are submitted: No

DAT: 2014 ENTERING CLASS

ENROLLEE DAT SCORES	MEAN	RANGE
Academic Average	17.9	NR
Perceptual Ability	18.3	NR
Total Science	17.8	NR

GPA: 2014 ENTERING CLASS

ENROLLEE GPA SCORES	UNDERGRAD. MEAN	GRADUATE MEAN	UNDERGRAD. RANGE	GRADUATE RANGE
Science GPA	3.11	NR	NR	NR
Total GPA	3.24	NR	NR	NR

APPLICATION AND SELECTION

TIMETABLE

Earliest filing date: 06/02/2015
Latest filing date: 02/01/2016
Earliest date for acceptance offers: 12/01/2015
Maximum time in days for applicant's response to acceptance offer:
    30 days if accepted on or after December 1
    15 days if accepted on or after February 1
Requests for deferred entrance considered: In exceptional circumstances only
Fee for application: Yes, nonrefundable, submitted only when requested
Amount of fee for application:
    In state: $75   Out of state: $75   International: $200
    (Excludes International Dentist Program Applicants)
Fee waiver available: No

	FIRST DEPOSIT	SECOND DEPOSIT	THIRD DEPOSIT
Required to hold place	Yes	No	No
Resident amount	$1,000		
Nonresident amount	$1,000		
Deposit due	As indicated in admission offer		
Applied to tuition	Yes		
Refundable	No		

Participates in Associated American Dental Schools Application Service (AADSAS): Yes
Accepts direct applicants: No
Secondary or supplemental application required: No
Secondary or supplemental application website: www.howard.edu
Interview is mandatory: Yes
Interview is by invitation: Yes

RESIDENCY

In-state/in-province versus out-of-state/out-of-province
Admissions process distinguishes between in-state/in-province and out-of-state/out-of-province applicants: No
Preference given to residents of: Alabama
Reciprocity Admissions Agreement available for legal residents of: None
Generally and over time, percentage of your first-year enrollment that is in-state: 1%
Origin of out-of-state/out-of-province enrollees: CA-2, CO-1, DE-3, FL-6, GA-1, MA-1, MD-19, IL-1, MI-1, MS-1, NC-3, NJ-1, NY-3, OR-1, PA-1, TN-1, TX-4, VA-16

International
Applications are accepted from international (noncitizens/nonpermanent residents): Yes
Origin of international enrollees: Cameroon-1, Canada-2, Rwanda-1, Vietnam-2

APPLICATION AND ENROLLMENT	NUMBER OF APPLICANTS	ESTIMATED NUMBER INTERVIEWED	ESTIMATED NUMBER ENROLLED
In-state or province applicants/enrollees	4	3	0
Out-of-state or province applicants/enrollees	1,865	137	66
International applicants/enrollees (noncitizens/nonpermanent residents)	207	11	6

DEMOGRAPHIC DESCRIPTIONS OF APPLICANTS: 2014 ENTERING CLASS

	APPLICANTS			ENROLLEES		
	M	W	Gender Unknown or Not Reported	M	W	Gender Unknown or Not Reported
American Indian or Alaska Native	1	3	0	0	0	0
Asian	326	350	11	10	9	0
Black or African American	122	215	5	7	16	0
Hispanic or Latino	79	124	1	2	4	0
Native Hawaiian or Other Pacific Islander	3	3	0	0	0	0
White	281	221	4	5	7	0
Two or more races	29	36	1	3	2	0
Race and ethnicity unknown	23	22	9	0	1	0
International	105	98	4	2	4	0

	MINIMUM	MAXIMUM	MEAN
2014 entering class enrollees by age	20	35	27

CURRICULUM

The primary objective of the curriculum is to educate individuals for the practice of general dentistry.

Specific objectives are:

1. To provide comprehensive predoctoral dental education such that the dental graduate will be competent in the prevention, diagnosis and treatment of oral diseases and disorders.
2. To inculcate in our graduates the highest standards of ethical and moral responsibility to the dental profession and to the communities they serve.

The foundation courses in the basic biomedical sciences are taught during the first two years followed by clinical courses and clinical experiences in the next two years. However, throughout the four years, the basic science and clinical science curriculum are integrated to prepare the students to be outstanding clinicians.

Student research opportunities: Students participate during the summer in our research lab or at other institutions such as The Johns Hopkins University.

They also compete and present scientific research projects nationally.

SPECIAL PROGRAMS AND SERVICES

PREDENTAL

Association of American Medical Colleges/ADEA Summer Medical and Dental Education Program (AAMC/ADEA SMDEP)
Special affiliations with colleges and universities: Howard University - Feeder School
Other summer enrichment programs

DURING DENTAL SCHOOL

Academic counseling and tutoring
Community service opportunities: Community service is part of the curriculum.
Internships, externships, or extramural programs
Mentoring
Personal counseling
Professional- and career-development programming
Training for those interested in academic careers

ACTIVE STUDENT ORGANIZATIONS

American Association for Dental Research National Student Research Group
American Association of Women Dentists
American Dental Education Association
American Student Dental Association
Hispanic Dental Association
Student National Dental Association

INTERNATIONAL DENTISTS

Graduates of international dental schools considered for traditional predoctoral program: Yes
Advanced standing program offered for graduates of international dental schools: Yes

COMBINED AND ALTERNATE DEGREES

Ph.D.	M.S.	M.P.H.	M.D.	B.A./B.S.	Other
—	—	—	—	✓	✓

Note: B.S./D.D.S. offered to Howard undergraduates.
Other Degree is D.D.S./M.B.A.

COSTS: 2014–15 SCHOOL YEAR

	FIRST YEAR	SECOND YEAR	THIRD YEAR	FOURTH YEAR
Tuition, resident	$42,631	$42,631	$42,631	$42,631
Tuition, nonresident	$42,631	$42,631	$42,631	$42,631
Tuition, other				
Fees	$1,233	$1,233	$1,233	$1,233
Instruments, books, and supplies	$11,192	$1,500	$1,500	$1,500
Estimated living expenses	$32,910	$32,910	$32,910	$32,910
Total, resident	$87,966	$78,274	$78,274	$78,274
Total, nonresident	$87,966	$78,274	$78,274	$78,274
Total, other				

FINANCIAL AID

FINANCIAL AID AWARDS TO FIRST-YEAR STUDENTS 2014–15

Total number of first-year recipients: 274	
Percentage of the first-year class: 95%	
Percentage of awards that are grants? 75%	
Percentage of awards that are loans? 96%	

	AVERAGE AWARDS	RANGE OF AWARDS
Residents	$10,000	$1,000–$20,000
Nonresidents	$10,000	$1,000–$20,000

For more information, please visit: http://healthsciences.howard.edu/education/schools-and-academics/dentistry

LAKE ERIE COLLEGE OF OSTEOPATHIC MEDICINE
SCHOOL OF DENTAL MEDICINE

Anton S. Gotlieb, D.D.S., M.S., Acting Dean

CONTACT INFORMATION

www.lecom.edu

4800 Lakewood Ranch Boulevard
Bradenton, FL 34211-4909
Phone: 941-405-1500
Fax: 941-405-1676

OFFICE OF ADMISSIONS AND STUDENT AFFAIRS

5000 Lakewood Ranch Boulevard
Bradenton, FL 34211-4909
Phone: 941-405-1500
Fax: 941-782-5721
Email: dentalfLa@lecom.edu

FINANCIAL AID

5000 Lakewood Ranch Boulevard
Bradenton, FL 34211-4909
Phone: 941-756-0690
Fax: 941-782-5721
Email: bradentonfinaid@lecom.edu

GENERAL INFORMATION

The Lake Erie College of Osteopathic Medicine School of Dental Medicine (LECOM SDM) welcomed its inaugural class in July 2012. LECOM comprises the main campus in Erie, PA; a Greensburg, PA, campus; and a Bradenton, FL, campus, where the dental school is housed in a 138,000-square-foot building. LECOM, which boasts an innovative, patient-centered curriculum, has a dual mission: to prepare students to become dentists through programs of excellence in education, research, clinical care and community service, and to enhance quality of life through improved health. The simulation and patient clinics are equipped with state-of-the-art technology. Clinical experience starts during year one and continues throughout all four years. During their fourth year, students provide patient care at an offsite facility in an underserved area.

MISSION

LECOM SDM's primary goal is to prepare dental professionals committed to providing high-quality, ethical, empathetic and patient-centered care to serve the needs of a diverse population.

Type of institution: Private	Doctoral dental degree offered: D.M.D.
Year opened: 2012	Targeted predoctoral enrollment: 400
Term type: Semester	Targeted entering class size: 100
Time to degree in months: 48	Campus setting: Suburban
Start month: July	Campus housing available: No

PREPARATION

Formal minimum preparation in semester/quarter hours: Semester: 8   Quarter: 12
Baccalaureate degree preferred: Yes
Number of first-year, first-time enrollees whose highest degree is:
  Baccalaureate: 90
  Master's degree and beyond: 10
Of first-year, first-time enrollees without baccalaureates, the number with:
  Equivalent of 60 undergraduate credit hours or less: 0
  Equivalent of 61–90 undergraduate credit hours: 0
  Equivalent of 91 or more undergraduate credit hours: 0

PREREQUISITE COURSE	REQUIRED	RECOMMENDED	LAB REQUIRED	CREDITS (SEMESTER/QUARTER)
BCP (biology-chemistry-physics) sciences				
Biology	✓		✓	8/12
Chemistry, general/inorganic	✓		✓	8/12
Chemistry, organic	✓		✓	8/12
Physics		✓*		4/6
Additional biological sciences				
Anatomy		✓*		3/6
Biochemistry	✓			3/4.5
Cell biology		✓*		
Histology		✓		
Immunology		✓		
Microbiology		✓*		4/6
Molecular biology/genetics		✓		
Physiology		✓*		4/6
Zoology				

*Strongly recommended. Students completing these courses will be more competitive.

PREPARATION (CONTINUED)

PREREQUISITE COURSE	REQUIRED	RECOMMENDED	LAB REQUIRED	CREDITS (SEMESTER/QUARTER)
Other				
English composition	✓			6/9

Community college coursework accepted for prerequisites: Yes
Community college coursework accepted for electives: Yes
Limits on community college credit hours: Yes
Maximum number of community college credit hours: NA
Advanced placement (AP) credit accepted for prerequisites: Yes
Advanced placement (AP) credit accepted for electives: Yes
Comments regarding AP credit: AP credit will be accepted for prerequisite courses only if upper-level (or more advanced) coursework is satisfactorily completed.
Job shadowing: Recommended
Number of hours of job shadowing recommended: 100
Other factors considered in admission: Community service, number of hours spent shadowing, leadership qualities, and interview

DAT

Mandatory: Yes
Latest DAT for consideration of application: 02/11/2016
Oldest DAT considered: Three years
When more than one DAT score is reported: Highest score is considered
Canadian DAT accepted: Yes
Application considered before DAT scores are submitted: No

DAT: 2014 ENTERING CLASS

ENROLLEE DAT SCORES	MEAN	RANGE
Academic Average	19.1	17–23
Perceptual Ability	19.8	15–24
Total Science	19.3	17–23

GPA: 2014 ENTERING CLASS

ENROLLEE GPA SCORES	UNDERGRAD. MEAN	GRADUATE MEAN	UNDERGRAD. RANGE	GRADUATE RANGE
Science GPA	3.29	3.62	2.39–3.98	3.00–4.00
Total GPA	3.38	3.69	2.61–3.90	3.11–4.00

APPLICATION AND SELECTION

TIMETABLE

Earliest filing date: 06/02/2015
Latest filing date: 02/01/2016
Earliest date for acceptance offers: 12/01/2015
Maximum time in days for applicant's response to acceptance offer:
    30 days if accepted on or after December 1
    15 days if accepted on or after February 1
Requests for deferred entrance considered: Exceptional circumstances only
Fee for application: Yes
Amount of fee for application:
    Resident: $50 nonrefundable
    Nonresident: $50 nonrefundable
Fee waiver available: No

	FIRST DEPOSIT	SECOND DEPOSIT	THIRD DEPOSIT
Required to hold place	Yes	No	No
Resident amount	$2,000		
Nonresident amount	$2,000		
Deposit due	As indicated in admissions offer		
Applied to tuition	Yes		
Refundable	No		

APPLICATION PROCESS

Participates in Associated American Dental Schools Application Service (AADSAS): Yes
Accepts direct applicants: No
Secondary or supplemental application required: Yes
Secondary or supplemental application website: www.lecom.edu
Interview is mandatory: Yes
Interview is by invitation: Yes

RESIDENCY

In-state/in-province versus out-of-state/out-of-province
Admissions process distinguishes between in-state/in-province and out-of-state/out-of-province applicants: No
Preference given to residents of: None
Reciprocity Admissions Agreement available for legal residents of: None
Generally and over time, percentage of your first-year enrollment that is in-state: 50%
Origin of out-of-state/out-of-province enrollees: AL-3, AZ-1, CA-1, CT-3, GA-3, IL-1, LA-4, MD-1, MI-1, MN-3, M0-1, NC-4, NE-1, NJ-1, NY-9, OH-2, OK-2, PA-8, SC-1, TX-10, UT-2, VA-2, WA-1, WI-1

International
Applications are accepted from international (noncitizens/nonpermanent residents): No
Origin of international enrollees: NA

APPLICATION AND ENROLLMENT	NUMBER OF APPLICANTS	ESTIMATED NUMBER INTERVIEWED	ESTIMATED NUMBER ENROLLED
In-state or province applicants/enrollees	491	133	34
Out-of-state or province applicants/enrollees	2,666	453	66
International applicants/enrollees (noncitizens/nonpermanent residents)	NA	NA	NA

DEMOGRAPHIC DESCRIPTIONS OF APPLICANTS: 2014 ENTERING CLASS

	APPLICANTS			ENROLLEES		
	M	W	Gender Unknown or Not Reported	M	W	Gender Unknown or Not Reported
American Indian or Alaska Native	3	2	0	1	0	0
Asian	506	549	14	9	10	0
Black or African American	54	72	3	1	1	0
Hispanic or Latino	116	192	1	3	4	0
Native Hawaiian or Other Pacific Islander	1	2	0	0	0	0
White	854	584	13	42	23	1
Two or more races	37	58	13	1	0	0
Race and ethnicity unknown	47	36	13	2	1	1
International	0	0	0	0	0	0

	MINIMUM	MAXIMUM	MEAN
2014 entering class enrollees by age	22	41	25

CURRICULUM

LECOM SDM's unique, innovative curriculum prepares students for the practice of general dentistry, specifically for underserved communities. The school's evidence-based, quality dental education trains students to provide patient-centered care and optimal therapeutic and economic outcomes, to promote disease prevention, and to enhance patient and provider education. LECOM SDM offers the D.M.D. degree through a full-time, four-year pathway. The curriculum comprises two years of basic science and preclinical instruction delivered through case-based, small-group, Problem-Based Learning (PBL) sessions, as well as through lectures, laboratories and clinical experiences. Years three and four are primarily hands-on, clinical experiences. PBL courses integrate medical and dental students. Other unique curriculum components include faculty-directed self-study of gross anatomy; early exposure to dentistry in the first year through direct comprehensive patient care in the first year (fabrication of full maxillary and mandibular removable prosthesis); a patient-based simulation clinic; and the entire fourth year devoted to primary care clinics in underserved areas of Florida and Erie, Pennsylvania. Faculty members assess the professional competencies students gain through the program. These competencies empower students with the knowledge and skills necessary to work effectively in interprofessional, interdisciplinary and multicultural environments.

Student research opportunities: Yes

SPECIAL PROGRAMS AND SERVICES

DURING DENTAL SCHOOL
Student Ambassadors
Student Tutors

ACTIVE STUDENT ORGANIZATIONS
Alpha Omega International Dental Fraternity
American Student Dental Association
Delta Alpha Phi Dental Association for Philanthropy
Hispanic Student Dental Association
Multicultural Student Dental Association
Student Government Association

INTERNATIONAL DENTISTS
Graduates of international dental schools considered for traditional predoctoral program: Yes
Advanced standing program offered for graduates of international dental schools: No

COMBINED AND ALTERNATE DEGREES

Ph.D.	M.S.	M.P.H.	M.D.	B.A./B.S.	Other
—	—	—	—	—	—

COSTS: 2014–15 SCHOOL YEAR

	FIRST YEAR	SECOND YEAR	THIRD YEAR	FOURTH YEAR
Tuition, resident	$48,480	$48,480	$48,480	NA
Tuition, nonresident	$48,480	$48,480	$48,480	NA
Tuition, other				
Fees	$4,595	$4,595	$4,595	NA
Instruments, books, and supplies	$10,998	$6,678	$5,401	NA
Estimated living expenses	$22,622	$26,479	$26,849	NA
Total, resident	$86,695	$86,232	$85,325	NA
Total, nonresident	$86,695	$86,232	$85,325	NA
Total, other				

FINANCIAL AID

Detailed financial aid information, application instructions and links to application materials may be found on the LECOM School of Dental Medicine website at http://lecom.edu/financial-aid.php under "School of Dental Medicine Tuition & Fees."

Students are required to complete the FAFSA to be considered for federal student financial aid.

If you have any questions, please call the Office of Financial Aid at 941-756-0690 or email bradentonfinaid@lecom.edu.

FINANCIAL AID AWARDS TO FIRST-YEAR STUDENTS 2014–15

Total number of first-year recipients: 82	
Percentage of the first-year class: 82%	
Percentage of awards that are grants? 5%	
Percentage of awards that are loans? 99%	

	AVERAGE AWARDS	RANGE OF AWARDS
Residents	$79,213	$475–$86,695
Nonresidents	$79,213	$475–$86,695

For more information, please visit: http://lecom.edu/school-dental-medicine.php/LECOM-School-of-Dental-Medicine/49/2205/614/2424

NOVA SOUTHEASTERN UNIVERSITY
COLLEGE OF DENTAL MEDICINE

Linda C. Niessen, D.M.D., M.P.H., M.P.P., Dean

College of Dental Medicine

CONTACT INFORMATION
http://dental.nova.edu

Dr. Hal Lippman
Executive Associate Dean of Admissions,
Student and Alumni Services and
Clinical Affairs
3200 South University Drive
Fort Lauderale, FL 33328
Phone: 954-262-1796
Email: hlippman@nova.edu

ADMISSIONS

Ms. Su-Ann Zarrett
Admissions Counselor
Enrollment Processing Services
Office of Admissions
3301 College Avenue, P.O. Box 299000
Fort Lauderdale, FL 33329-9905
Phone: 954-262-1108
Email: zarrett@nova.edu

Ms. Norma Concepcion
Admissions Services Representative I
Enrollment Processing Services
Office of Admissions
3301 College Avenue, P.O. Box 299000
Fort Lauderdale, FL 33329-9905
Phone: 954-262-1839
Email: nc548@nova.edu

STUDENT AFFAIRS

Ms. DeVaria E. Hudson
Assistant Director of Student Affairs
3200 South University Drive
Fort Lauderdale, FL 33328
Phone: 954-262-7302
Email: cdmservices@nova.edu

MINORITY AFFAIRS/DIVERSITY
3200 South University Drive
Fort Lauderdale, FL 33328
Phone: 954-262-7338
Email: rgaines@nova.edu

HOUSING, OFFICE OF RESIDENTIAL LIFE
3301 College Avenue
Fort Lauderdale, FL 33314
Phone: 954-262-7052

INTERNATIONAL STUDENTS
International Students and Scholars
3301 College Avenue
Ft. Lauderdale, FL 33314
Phone: 954-262-7240
Email: intl@nova.edu

GENERAL INFORMATION

Nova Southeastern University is the seventh largest not-for-profit university in the southeastern United States and the largest independent institution of higher learning in Florida. The College of Dental Medicine (CDM) is closely allied with the other colleges in the Health Professions Division of the University. CDM students can socialize and study with students from the colleges of Osteopathic Medicine, Pharmacy, Optometry, Medical Sciences, Health Care Sciences and Nursing. Basic biomedical sciences courses and emphasis on integrative clinical thinking, evidence-based treatment options and state-of-the-art technology prepare students to treat patients with quality care. Early introduction into clinical settings, under preceptorship of faculty group practice leaders, teaches students to manage and deliver oral health care and understand the dynamics of the dentist/patient relationship.

MISSION

Nova Southeastern complements on-campus educational opportunities and resources with accessible distance learning programs and fosters intellectual inquiry, leadership and commitment to community.

Type of institution: Private	Doctoral dental degree offered: D.M.D.
Year opened: 1997	Targeted predoctoral enrollment: 520
Term type: Semester	Targeted entering class size: 125
Time to degree in months: 46	Campus setting: Suburban
Start month: August	Campus housing available: Yes

PREPARATION

Formal minimum preparation in semester/quarter hours: Semester: 90
Baccalaureate degree preferred: Yes
Number of first-year, first-time enrollees whose highest degree is:
    Baccalaureate: 91
    Master's degree and beyond: 21
Of first-year, first-time enrollees without baccalaureates, the number with:
    Equivalent of 60 undergraduate credit hours or less: NA
    Equivalent of 61–90 undergraduate credit hours: NA
    Equivalent of 91 or more undergraduate credit hours: 8

PREREQUISITE COURSE	REQUIRED	RECOMMENDED	LAB REQUIRED	CREDITS (SEMESTER/QUARTER)
BCP (biology-chemistry-physics) sciences				
Biology	✓		✓	8/12
Chemistry, general/inorganic	✓		✓	8/12
Chemistry, organic	✓		✓	8/12
Physics	✓		✓	8/12
Additional biological sciences				
Anatomy		✓		3/5
Biochemistry	✓			3/5
Cell biology		✓		3/5
Histology		✓		3/5
Immunology				
Microbiology	✓			3/5
Molecular biology/genetics		✓		3/5
Physiology		✓		3/5

(Prerequisite Courses continued)

PREPARATION (CONTINUED)

PREREQUISITE COURSE	REQUIRED	RECOMMENDED	LAB REQUIRED	CREDITS (SEMESTER/QUARTER)
Zoology				

Note: Science classes recommended.

Community college coursework accepted for prerequisites: Yes
Community college coursework accepted for electives: Yes
Limits on community college credit hours: Yes
Maximum number of community college credit hours: 60
Advanced placement (AP) credit accepted for prerequisites: Yes
Advanced placement (AP) credit accepted for electives: Yes
Comments regarding AP credit: None
Job shadowing: Recommended
Number of hours of job shadowing required or recommended: 0
Other factors considered in admission: The College of Dental Medicine selects students based on preprofessional academic performance, DAT scores, a personal interview, an application, and letters of evaluation.

DAT

Mandatory: Yes
Latest DAT for consideration of application: 12/30/2015
Oldest DAT considered: 12/31/2013
When more than one DAT score is reported: All scores are evaluated on their merit.
Canadian DAT accepted: Yes
Application considered before DAT scores are submitted: No

DAT: 2013 ENTERING CLASS

ENROLLEE DAT SCORES	MEAN	RANGE
Academic Average	20.0	18–24
Perceptual Ability	20.0	17–27
Total Science	21.0	18–26

GPA: 2013 ENTERING CLASS

ENROLLEE GPA SCORES	MEAN	RANGE
Science GPA	3.63	3.24–4.00
Total GPA	3.67	3.20–4.00

APPLICATION AND SELECTION

TIMETABLE

Earliest filing date: 06/02/2015
Latest filing date: 12/31/2015
Earliest date for acceptance offers: 12/01/2015
Maximum time in days for applicant's response to acceptance offer:
    30 days if accepted on or after December 1
    15 days if accepted on or after February 1
Requests for deferred entrance considered: In exceptional circumstances only.
Fee for application: Yes, submitted only when requested.
Amount of fee for application:
    In state: $50   Out of state: $50   International: $50
Fee waiver available: No

	FIRST DEPOSIT	SECOND DEPOSIT	THIRD DEPOSIT
Required to hold place	Yes	Yes	No
Resident amount	$1,000	$1,000	
Nonresident amount	$1,000	$1,000	
Deposit due	As indicated in admission offer	As indicated in admission offer	
Applied to tuition	Yes	Yes	
Refundable	No	No	

APPLICATION PROCESS

Participates in Associated American Dental Schools Application Service (AADSAS): Yes
Accepts direct applicants: No
Secondary or supplemental application required: Yes
Secondary or supplemental application website: www.nova.edu
Interview is mandatory: Yes
Interview is by invitation: Yes

RESIDENCY

In-state/in-province versus out-of-state/out-of-province
Admissions process distinguishes between in-state/in-province and out-of-state/out-of-province applicants: No
Preference given to residents of: None
Reciprocity Admissions Agreement available for legal residents of: None
Generally and over time, percentage of your first-year enrollment that is in-state: 60%
Origin of out-of-state/out-of-province enrollees: AL-1, CA-9, CO-2, GA-4, IL-1, MD-1, ME-1, NC-1, ND-1, NH-1, NJ-5, NY-9, OK-1, PA-1, TX-6, UT-1, VA-4, WI-2

International
Applications are accepted from international (noncitizens/ nonpermanent residents): Yes
Origin of international enrollees: Canada-4, Denmark-1, Grenada-1, South Korea-1

APPLICATION AND ENROLLMENT	NUMBER OF APPLICANTS	ESTIMATED NUMBER INTERVIEWED	ESTIMATED NUMBER ENROLLED
In-state or province applicants/ enrollees	1,586	412	67
Out-of-state or province applicants/enrollees	1,315	334	53
International applicants/enrollees (noncitizens/nonpermanent residents)	NR	NR	7

DEMOGRAPHIC DESCRIPTIONS OF APPLICANTS: 2013 ENTERING CLASS

	APPLICANTS			ENROLLEES		
	M	W	Gender Unknown or Not Reported	M	W	Gender Unknown or Not Reported
American Indian or Alaska Native	3	2	0	1	0	0
Asian	646	334	0	29	11	0
Black or African American	27	74	0	0	2	0
Hispanic or Latino	154	157	0	15	10	0
Native Hawaiian or Other Pacific Islander	0	0	0	0	0	0
White	823	637	0	25	26	0
Two or more races	0	0	0	0	0	0
Race and ethnicity unknown	29	15	0	1	0	0
International	NR	NR	NR	0	0	0

	MINIMUM	MAXIMUM	MEAN
2014 entering class enrollees by age	20	36	25

CURRICULUM

The College of Dental Medicine's mission is to educate and train students to ensure their competency to practice the art and science of the dental profession. This competency requires graduates to be biologically knowledgeable, technically skilled, compassionate and sensitive to the needs of all patients and the community. The college fosters excellence in dental education through innovative teaching, research and community service.

Student research opportunities: Yes

SPECIAL PROGRAMS AND SERVICES

PREDENTAL
Postbaccalaureate programs
Special affiliations with colleges and universities: Shaw University - Fast track 3-4 program; St. Leo College - Fast track 3-4 program; Nova Southeastern University - Fast track 3-4 program and 4-4 program; Talladega University - 3-4 program; University of Pennsylvania (LPS) Postbaccalaureate Pre-Health Program

DURING DENTAL SCHOOL
Academic counseling and tutoring
Community service opportunities
Internships, externships, or extramural programs
Mentoring
Personal counseling
Professional- and career-development programming
Training for those interested in academic careers
Transfer applicants considered if space is available

ACTIVE STUDENT ORGANIZATIONS
American Academy of Pediatric Dentistry
American Student Dental Association
Class Councils
Hispanic Dental Student Association
Omicron Kappa Upsilon National Dental Honor Society
Psi Omega Fraternity
Student Government Association
Student National Dental Association
Women's Dental Society (student chapter of American Association of Women Dentists)

INTERNATIONAL DENTISTS
Graduates of international dental schools considered for traditional predoctoral program: Yes
Advanced standing program offered for graduates of international dental schools: Yes
Advanced standing program description: Program awarding a dental degree

COMBINED AND ALTERNATE DEGREES

Ph.D.	M.S.	M.P.H.	M.D.	B.A./B.S.	Other
—	✓	✓	—	—	✓

Other degree: D.O./D.M.D.

COSTS: 2013–14 SCHOOL YEAR

	FIRST YEAR	SECOND YEAR	THIRD YEAR	FOURTH YEAR
Tuition, resident	$55,596	$55,596	$55,596	$55,597
Tuition, nonresident	$57,270	$57,270	$57,270	$57,271
Tuition, other				
Fees	$1,728	$1,728	$1,728	$1,728
Instruments, books, and supplies	$18,549	$15,549	$11,049	$13,550
Estimated living expenses (see "Note" below)	$31,776	$31,776	$31,776	$23,830
Total, resident	$107,649	$104,649	$100,149	$94,705
Total, nonresident	$109,323	$106,323	$101,823	$96,379
Total, other				

Note: Living expenses include room and board, transportation costs and personal costs.

FINANCIAL AID

www.nova.edu/financialaid/index.html

UNIVERSITY OF FLORIDA
COLLEGE OF DENTISTRY

Isabel Garcia, D.D.S., M.P.H., Dean

CONTACT INFORMATION

admissions.dental.ufl.edu

OFFICE OF ADMISSIONS

Dr. Pamela Sandow
Assistant Dean for Admissions &
Financial Aid
P.O. Box 100445
Gainesville, FL 32610-0445
Phone: 352-273-5955
Fax: 352-846-0311
Email: DMDAdmissions@dental.ufl.edu

OFFICE OF FINANCIAL AID

P.O. Box 100445
Gainesville, FL 32610-0445
Phone: 352-273-5999
Email: FinancialAid@dental.ufl.edu

STUDENT AND MULTICULTURAL AFFAIRS

Dr. Patricia Xirau-Probert
Assistant Dean for Student and Multicultural
Affairs
P.O. Box 100445
Gainesville, FL 32610-0445
Phone: 352-273-5954

HOUSING

www.housing.ufl.edu
Phone: 352-392-2171

GENERAL INFORMATION

The University of Florida College of Dentistry is one of the top dental schools in the United States. The college is part of a large health science center with a major teaching hospital and five other health colleges: Medicine, Nursing, Pharmacy, Public Health and Health Professions, and Veterinary Medicine. The University of Florida Health Science Center is part of the comprehensive University of Florida campus, which offers rich educational and cultural opportunities, nationally ranked sports teams and everything a large university system has to offer. Students, faculty, staff and residents in the community represent a very diverse, highly educated population, who come to live, study and work from across the state, nation and from all over the world.

MISSION

The mission of the College of Dentistry is to achieve excellence in the art and science of dentistry through teaching, research, and service.

Vision: To be internationally known for innovative education, cultural diversity, discovery, transfer of scientific knowledge, our graduates' superior skills and excellence in service.

Core Values: The following values help the College of Dentistry achieve its vision and mission:

Excellence | Integrity | Fairness | Communication | Cooperation | Courtesy | Continuous Improvement

Type of institution: Public	Doctoral dental degree offered: D.M.D.
Year opened: 1971	Targeted predoctoral enrollment: 352
Term type: Semester	Targeted entering class size: 93
Time to degree in months: 45	Campus setting: Suburban
Start month: August	Campus housing available: Yes

PREPARATION

Formal minimum preparation in semester/quarter hours: Semester: 90   Quarter: 120
Baccalaureate degree preferred: Yes. A baccalaureate degree is strongly recommended.
Number of first-year, first-time enrollees whose highest degree is:
    Baccalaureate: 85
    Master's degree and beyond: 8
Of first-year, first-time enrollees without baccalaureates, the number with:
    Equivalent of 60 undergraduate credit hours or less: 0
    Equivalent of 61–90 undergraduate credit hours: 0
    Equivalent of 91 or more undergraduate credit hours: 0

PREREQUISITE COURSE	REQUIRED	RECOMMENDED	LAB REQUIRED	CREDITS (SEMESTER/QUARTER)
BCP (biology-chemistry-physics) sciences				
Biology	✓		✓	8/12
Chemistry, general/inorganic	✓		✓	8/12
Chemistry, organic	✓		✓	8/12
Physics	✓		✓	8/12
Additional biological sciences				
Anatomy		✓		4/6
Biochemistry	✓		✓	4/6
Cell biology		✓		
Histology		✓		
Immunology		✓		
Microbiology	✓		✓	4/6
Molecular biology/genetics	✓		✓	4/6

PREPARATION (CONTINUED)

PREREQUISITE COURSE	REQUIRED	RECOMMENDED	LAB REQUIRED	CREDITS (SEMESTER/QUARTER)
Physiology		✓		
Zoology		✓		
Other				
General psychology	✓			3/6
English	✓			6/6

Community college coursework accepted for prerequisites: Yes
Community college coursework accepted for electives: Yes
Limits on community college credit hours: No
Maximum number of community college credit hours: None
Advanced placement (AP) credit accepted for prerequisites: Yes
Advanced placement (AP) credit accepted for electives: Yes
Comments regarding AP credit: Applicants are strongly encouraged to take prerequisite courses at the university level for which they have earned AP/International Baccalaureate (IB) or other credit.
Job shadowing: Strongly recommended

DAT

Mandatory: Yes
Latest DAT for consideration of application: 01/01/2016
Oldest DAT considered: Varies
When more than one DAT score is reported: Most recent score is considered
Canadian DAT accepted: No
Application considered before DAT scores are submitted: No

DAT: 2014 ENTERING CLASS

ENROLLEE DAT SCORES	MEAN	RANGE
Academic Average	20.3	17–25
Perceptual Ability	20.0	15–29
Total Science	20.4	17–26

GPA: 2014 ENTERING CLASS

ENROLLEE GPA SCORES	UNDERGRAD. MEAN	GRADUATE MEAN	UNDERGRAD. RANGE	GRADUATE RANGE
Science GPA	3.57	3.81	2.56–4.00	3.56–4.00
Total GPA	3.65	3.80	2.67–4.00	3.56–4.00

APPLICATION AND SELECTION

TIMETABLE

Earliest filing date: 06/02/2015
Latest filing date: 11/01/2015
Earliest date for acceptance offers: 12/01/2015
Maximum time in days for applicant's response to acceptance offer:
    30 days if accepted on or after December 1
    15 days if accepted on or after February 1
Requests for deferred entrance considered in exceptional circumstances only
Fee for application: Yes, submitted only when requested
Amount of fee for application:
    In state: $30   Out of state: $30   International: NA
Fee waiver available: Check school website for details.

	FIRST DEPOSIT	SECOND DEPOSIT	THIRD DEPOSIT
Required to hold place	Yes	No	No
Resident amount	$200		
Nonresident amount	$200		
Deposit due	As indicated in admission offer		
Applied to tuition	Yes		
Refundable	No		

APPLICATION PROCESS

Participates in Associated American Dental Schools Application Service (AADSAS): Yes
Accepts direct applicants: No
Secondary or supplemental application required: Yes. Supplemental application by invitation.
Secondary or supplemental application website: Website address given when invited to complete a supplemental application.
Interview is mandatory: Yes
Interview is by invitation: Yes

RESIDENCY

In-state/in-province versus out-of-state/out-of-province
Admissions process distinguishes between in-state/in-province and out-of-state/out-of-province applicants: Yes
Preference given to residents of: Florida
Reciprocity Admissions Agreement available for legal residents of: None
Generally and over time, percentage of your first-year enrollment that is in-state: 90%
Origin of out-of-state/out-of-province enrollees: AL-1, AR-1, GA-2, MN-1, SD-1

International
Applications are accepted from international (noncitizens/nonpermanent residents): No
Origin of international enrollees: NA

APPLICATION AND ENROLLMENT	NUMBER OF APPLICANTS	ESTIMATED NUMBER INTERVIEWED	ESTIMATED NUMBER ENROLLED
In-state or province applicants/enrollees	536	253	87
Out-of-state or province applicants/enrollees	786	54	6
International applicants/enrollees (noncitizens/nonpermanent residents)	0	0	0

DEMOGRAPHIC DESCRIPTIONS OF APPLICANTS: 2013 ENTERING CLASS

	APPLICANTS			ENROLLEES		
	M	W	Gender Unknown or Not Reported	M	W	Gender Unknown or Not Reported
American Indian or Alaska Native	0	0	0	0	0	0
Asian	142	172	4	7	16	0
Black or African American	20	40	0	1	1	0
Hispanic or Latino	68	145	1	5	13	0
Native Hawaiian or Other Pacific Islander	0	0	0	0	0	0
White	356	278	4	20	26	0
Two or more races	14	28	1	1	1	0
Race and ethnicity unknown	20	18	5	0	2	0
International	17	10	0	0	0	0

	MINIMUM	MAXIMUM	MEAN
2013 entering class enrollees by age	20	37	24

CURRICULUM

The College of Dentistry has a dynamic curriculum relevant to the educational needs of the present and adaptable to those of the future. This curriculum applies instructional technology to enhance learning effectiveness in the classroom, preclinical simulation laboratory and clinics. Graduates will be well-prepared to practice competently, implement current dental concepts, guide the work of others and manage a dental office.

Year 1: Basic science, preclinical technique and introduction to clinics.

Year 2: Completion of basic sciences, preclinical technical courses and beginning of comprehensive patient care.

Year 3: Clinical rotations and comprehensive patient care.

Year 4: Comprehensive patient care, extramural rotations and experience in private practice concepts. Community service is incorporated into all four years of the curriculum.

D.M.D/Ph.D. program: Prospective students may apply to the D.M.D/Ph.D. program at the same time they apply to the D.M.D. program. Students already accepted to the D.M.D. program can apply for admissions to the D.M.D./Ph.D. program any time prior to their eighth consecutive semester.

D.M.D/M.P.H. program: Students can apply to this program after gaining admission to the D.M.D. program.

Student research opportunities: a summer research program for entering first-year students; a research track and research honors at graduation

SPECIAL PROGRAMS AND SERVICES

PREDENTAL

Summer enrichment programs: A Summer Learning Program for first- and second-year undergraduate students is available.

DURING DENTAL SCHOOL

Academic counseling and tutoring

Access to all University of Florida student services (for more information, visit: http://www.ufsa.ufl.edu/students/)

Community service opportunities

Internships, externships, or extramural programs

Mentoring

Opportunity to study for credit at institution abroad

Personal counseling

Professional- and career-development programming

Training for those interested in academic careers

Transfer applicants considered if space is available

ACTIVE STUDENT ORGANIZATIONS

American Academy of Pediatric Dentistry

American Association for Dental Research National Student Research Group

American Association of Public Health Dentistry

American Association of Women Dentists

American Dental Education Association Student Chapter

American Student Dental Association

Christian Dental Society

Dental fraternities, including Alpha Omega International Dental Fraternity, Psi Omega Dental Fraternity

Hispanic Student Dental Association

Student National Dental Association

For a complete list, visit: http://dental.ufl.edu/education/dmd-program/student-multicultural-affairs/student-organizations/

INTERNATIONAL DENTISTS

Graduates of international dental schools considered for traditional predoctoral program: No

Advanced standing program offered for graduates of international dental schools: No

Advanced standing program description: A four-year D.M.D. program and a two-year Advanced Education in General Dentistry certificate program. http://admissions.dental.ufl.edu/iedp/programs-application-process/

COMBINED AND ALTERNATE DEGREES

Ph.D.	M.S.	M.P.H.	M.D.	B.A./B.S.	Other
✓	—	✓	—	✓	—

COSTS: 2013–14 SCHOOL YEAR

	FIRST YEAR	SECOND YEAR	THIRD YEAR	FOURTH YEAR
Tuition, resident	$37,564	$37,564	$37,564	$37,564
Tuition, nonresident	$64,064	$64,064	$64,064	$64,064
Tuition, other				
Fees	$4,064	$4,064	$4,064	$4,064
Instruments, books, and supplies	$10,600	$9,114	$8,448	$5,596
Estimated living expenses	$19,240	$19,680	$19,753	$17,045
Total, resident	$71,468	$70,422	$69,829	$64,259
Total, nonresident	$97,950	$96,904	$96,311	$90,741
Total, other				

FINANCIAL AID

Fifty-one students each received a scholarship or grant, or both, in the D1 class. The average award for the scholarship/grant was $7,596, with the awards ranging from $2,000 to $15,000. A total of $387,418 in scholarship/grants was awarded to the D1 class for 2014–15.

In 2012, the Health Resources and Services Administration's Scholarships for Disadvantaged Students program awarded the college $645,000 for the 2012–13 academic year, with the recommended future support of $645,000 per year for the following three years—totaling more than $2.5 million over four years.

To date (from 2012 to 2015), the award has provided 126 individual scholarships of $15,000 each. These scholarships were awarded to students who have faced financial and location obstacles to gaining the skills and abilities to enroll in and graduate from health professions schools.

FINANCIAL AID AWARDS TO FIRST-YEAR STUDENTS 2014–15

Total number of first-year recipients: 78
Percentage of awards that are grants? NR
Percentage of awards that are loans? NR

	AVERAGE AWARDS	RANGE OF AWARDS
Residents	$58,117	$32,000–$79,354
Nonresidents	$82,310	$74,968–$99,850

For more information, please visit: http://admissions.dental.ufl.edu/

GEORGIA REGENTS UNIVERSITY
COLLEGE OF DENTAL MEDICINE

Carol A. Lefebvre, D.D.S., M.S., Dean

GENERAL INFORMATION

Since enrolling its first class in 1969, the Georgia Regents University College of Dental Medicine has had as its primary mission the improvement of the oral health of the citizens of Georgia. The school remains committed to this goal with programs for education, research and public service through patient care. The College of Dental Medicine is part of the Georgia Regents University, one of 31 autonomous institutions within the University System of Georgia. In addition to dentistry, the institution includes schools of allied health, graduate studies, medicine and nursing and is adjacent to a large complex of health care facilities, providing a diverse and stimulating environment for its students on the fringe of downtown Augusta.

MISSION

To educate dentists to improve overall health and reduce the burden of illness in society by discovering and applying knowledge embracing craniofacial health and disease prevention.

Vision: Our vision is to be a top-tier university that is a destination of choice for education, health care, discovery, creativity and innovation.

Core Values: Collegiality, Compassion, Excellence, Inclusivity, Integrity

Type of institution: Public	Doctoral dental degree offered: D.M.D.
Year opened: 1969	Targeted predoctoral enrollment: 322
Term type: Semester	Targeted entering class size: 86
Time to degree in months: 46	Campus setting: Urban
Start month: August	Campus housing available: Yes

PREPARATION

Formal minimum preparation in semester/quarter hours: Semester: 90   Quarter: 120
Baccalaureate degree preferred: Yes
Number of first-year, first-time enrollees whose highest degree is:
   Baccalaureate: 76
   Master's degree and beyond: 9
Of first-year, first-time enrollees without baccalaureates, the number with:
   Equivalent of 60 undergraduate credit hours or less: 0
   Equivalent of 61–90 undergraduate credit hours: 0
   Equivalent of 91 or more undergraduate credit hours: 0

PREREQUISITE COURSE	REQUIRED	RECOMMENDED	LAB REQUIRED	CREDITS (SEMESTER/QUARTER)
BCP (biology-chemistry-physics) sciences				
Biology	✓		✓	8/12
Chemistry, general/inorganic	✓		✓	8/12
Chemistry, organic	✓		✓	8/12
Physics	✓		✓	4/6
Additional biological sciences				
Anatomy		✓		4/6
Biochemistry	✓			3/5
Cell biology		✓		3/5
Histology		✓		3/5
Immunology		✓		3/5
Microbiology		✓		3/5
Molecular biology/genetics		✓		3/5

PREPARATION (CONTINUED)

PREREQUISITE COURSE	REQUIRED	RECOMMENDED	LAB REQUIRED	CREDITS (SEMESTER/QUARTER)
Physiology				
Zoology				
Other				
English	✓			6/10
Drafting/Pottery		✓		3/5
Psychology		✓		3/5

Community college coursework accepted for prerequisites: Yes
Community college coursework accepted for electives: Yes
Limits on community college credit hours: Yes
Maximum number of community college credit hours: 90
Advanced placement (AP) credit accepted for prerequisites: Yes
Advanced placement (AP) credit accepted for electives: Yes
Job shadowing: Required
Number of hours of job shadowing required or recommended: At least 200 hours is recommended.
Other factors considered in admission: Leadership roles, community service, home county, and experience related to dentistry.

DAT

Mandatory: Yes
Latest DAT for consideration of application: 09/30/2015
Oldest DAT considered: 06/01/2013
When more than one DAT score is reported: Highest score is considered
Canadian DAT accepted: No
Application considered before DAT scores are submitted: Yes

DAT: 2014 ENTERING CLASS

ENROLLEE DAT SCORES	MEAN	RANGE
Academic Average	19.4	16–24
Perceptual Ability	20.2	15–25
Total Science	19.2	15–23

GPA: 2014 ENTERING CLASS

ENROLLEE GPA SCORES	UNDERGRAD. MEAN	GRADUATE MEAN	UNDERGRAD. RANGE	GRADUATE RANGE
Science GPA	3.53	3.26	2.95–4.00	3.23–4.00
Total GPA	3.59	3.71	2.93–4.00	3.31–4.00

APPLICATION AND SELECTION

TIMETABLE

Earliest filing date: 06/02/2015
Latest filing date: 09/30/2015
Earliest date for acceptance offers: 12/01/2015
Maximum time in days for applicant's response to acceptance offer: 30 days
Requests for deferred entrance considered: In exceptional circumstances only.
Fee for application: Yes
Amount of fee for application:
In state: $30   Out of state: $30   International: NA
Fee waiver available: No

	FIRST DEPOSIT	SECOND DEPOSIT	THIRD DEPOSIT
Required to hold place	Yes	No	No
Resident amount	$500		
Nonresident amount	$1,000		
Deposit due	As indicated in admission offer		
Applied to tuition	Yes		
Refundable	No		
Refundable by	NA		

APPLICATION PROCESS

Participates in Associated American Dental Schools Application Service (AADSAS): Yes
Accepts direct applicants: No
Secondary or supplemental application required: Yes
Interview is mandatory: Yes
Interview is by invitation: Yes

RESIDENCY

In-state/in-province versus out-of-state/out-of-province
Admissions process distinguishes between in-state/in-province and out-of-state/out-of-province applicants: Yes
Preference given to residents of: Georgia
Reciprocity Admissions Agreement available for legal residents of: None
Generally and over time, percentage of your first-year enrollment that is in-state: 90%
Origin of out-of-state/out-of-province enrollees: IN-1, NC-3, SC-4

International
Applications are accepted from international (noncitizens/nonpermanent residents): No
Origin of international enrollees: 0

APPLICATION AND ENROLLMENT	NUMBER OF APPLICANTS	ESTIMATED NUMBER INTERVIEWED	ESTIMATED NUMBER ENROLLED
In-state or province applicants/enrollees	337	167	77
Out-of-state or province applicants/enrollees	544	53	8
International applicants/enrollees (noncitizens/nonpermanent residents)	0	0	0

DEMOGRAPHIC DESCRIPTIONS OF APPLICANTS: 2014 ENTERING CLASS

	APPLICANTS			ENROLLEES		
	M	W	Gender Unknown or Not Reported	M	W	Gender Unknown or Not Reported
American Indian or Alaska Native	1	0	0	0	0	0
Asian	103	118	2	7	3	0
Black or African American	21	42	0	3	5	0
Hispanic or Latino	3	5	0	2	3	0
Native Hawaiian or Other Pacific Islander	0	0	0	0	0	0
White	274	241	0	33	22	0
Two or more races	14	18	0	2	4	0
Race and ethnicity unknown	20	19	0	0	1	0
International	0	0	0	0	0	0

Notes: There were 881 total applicants, and 85 students enrolled in the entering class of 2014.

	MINIMUM	MAXIMUM	MEAN
2014 entering class enrollees by age	21	35	23

CURRICULUM

The College of Dental Medicine awards the D.M.D. degree. The program of study consists of 11 semesters spread over approximately 45 months. Students are enrolled for eight regular semesters (fall and spring) of 15 weeks and for summer semesters of eight, 12, and 12 weeks after the first, second and third years, respectively. Clinical and basic science courses are taught throughout the eight regular semesters, and elementary clinical treatment of patients, including restorative dentistry, begins in the second year. The placement of clinical experiences in the first year shifts some basic science courses to the third year.

Student research opportunities: Yes

SPECIAL PROGRAMS AND SERVICES

PREDENTAL
Summer Educational Enrichment Program

DURING DENTAL SCHOOL
Academic counseling and tutoring
Community service opportunities
Internships, externships, or extramural programs
Mentoring

Personal counseling
Professional- and career-development programming
Training for those interested in academic careers

ACTIVE STUDENT ORGANIZATIONS

American Association of Dental Research Student Research Group
American Association of Public Health Dentistry
American Student Dental Association
America's Tooth Fairy
Give a Smile Foundation
Hispanic Student Dental Association
Operation Smile
Student National Dental Association
Student Professionalism and Ethics Association In Dentistry

INTERNATIONAL DENTISTS

Graduates of international dental schools considered for traditional predoctoral program: No
Advanced standing program offered for graduates of international dental schools: No

COMBINED AND ALTERNATE DEGREES

Ph.D.	M.S.	M.P.H.	M.D.	B.A./B.S.	Other
✓	✓	—	—	✓	—

COSTS: 2014–15 SCHOOL YEAR

	FIRST YEAR	SECOND YEAR	THIRD YEAR	FOURTH YEAR
Tuition, resident	$27,354	$27,354	$27,354	$18,236
Tuition, nonresident	$68,610	$68,610	$68,610	$45,740
Tuition, other				
Fees	$4,956	$4,956	$4,956	$2,150
Instruments, books, and supplies	$7,508	$7,218	$5,492	$3,820
Estimated living expenses	$19,692	$19,692	$19,692	$13,128
Total, resident	$59,510	$59,220	$57,494	$37,334
Total, nonresident	$100,766	$100,476	$98,750	$64,838
Total, other				

FINANCIAL AID

In addition to mandatory disability and student health insurance, fees include the following: student activity, student health, technology, special institutional, student center facility, wellness center, athletic, parking and transportation. For additional financial aid information, we encourage you to contact the Enrollment Service Center at 706-737-1524 or email osfa@gru.edu.

FINANCIAL AID AWARDS TO FIRST-YEAR STUDENTS 2014–15

Total number of first-year recipients: 70
Percentage of the first-year class: 82%
Percentage of awards that are grants? 0%
Percentage of awards that are loans? 85%

	AVERAGE AWARDS	RANGE OF AWARDS
Residents	$47,167	$30,000–$71,167
Nonresidents	$80,246	$30,000–$87,167

For more information, please visit: http://www.gru.edu/finaid/

MIDWESTERN UNIVERSITY
COLLEGE OF DENTAL MEDICINE-ILLINOIS

M.A.J. Lex MacNeil, D.D.S., Dean

CONTACT INFORMATION

www.midwestern.edu
555 31st Street
Downers Grove, IL 60515-1235
Phone: 630-515-7350
Fax: 630-515-7290

OFFICE OF ADMISSIONS

Office of Admissions
555 31st Street
Downers Grove, IL 60515-1235
Phone: 800-458-6253 or 630-515-7200
Fax: 630-971-6086
Email: admissil@midwestern.edu

FINANCIAL AID

Phone: 630-515-6101

STUDENT AFFAIRS

Phone: 630-515-6470

MINORITY AFFAIRS/DIVERSITY

Phone: 630-515-6470

HOUSING

Phone: 630-971-6400

GENERAL INFORMATION

At Midwestern University-Illinois, health care education is what we do. We are an established leader with an exciting vision for the future. Midwestern University-Illinois offers programs that give you solid footing in the sciences, extensive hands-on experience in outstanding clinical rotations and a compassionate perspective toward your patients. You will learn side-by-side with students in other health professions, modeling the team approach to 21st century health care practice. And you will learn from faculty mentors who are dedicated to preparing their future colleagues for the realities of patient care. Our graduates are found in leading hospitals, private practices, laboratories, pharmacies and health care facilities across the United States. The new College of Dental Medicine-Illinois uses state-of-the-art technology to provide high-quality, integrated dental education.

MISSION

We are dedicated to the education of dentists who will demonstrate excellence in comprehensive oral health care and the discovery and dissemination of knowledge.

Type of institution: Private
Year opened: 2011
Term type: Quarter
Time to degree in months: 46
Start month: August
Doctoral dental degree offered: D.M.D.

Targeted predoctoral enrollment: 520 when fully enrolled
Targeted entering class size: 130
Campus setting: Suburban
Campus housing available: Yes

PREPARATION

Formal minimum preparation in semester/quarter hours: Semester: 120   Quarter: 180
Baccalaureate degree preferred: Yes. Bachelor's degree required.
Number of first-year, first-time enrollees whose highest degree is:
    Baccalaureate: 106
    Master's degree and beyond: 24
Of first-year, first-time enrollees without baccalaureates, the number with:
    Equivalent of 60 undergraduate credit hours or less: 0
    Equivalent of 61–90 undergraduate credit hours: 0
    Equivalent of 91 or more undergraduate credit hours: 0

PREREQUISITE COURSE	REQUIRED	RECOMMENDED	LAB REQUIRED	CREDITS (SEMESTER/QUARTER)
BCP (biology-chemistry-physics) sciences				
Biology	✓		✓	8/12
Chemistry, general/inorganic	✓		✓	8/12
Chemistry, organic	✓		✓	4/6
Physics	✓		✓	8/12
Additional biological sciences				
Anatomy	✓			3/4
Biochemistry	✓			3/4
Cell biology				
Histology		✓		
Immunology		✓		
Microbiology	✓			3/4
Molecular biology/genetics		✓		
Physiology	✓			3/4
Zoology		✓		

(Prerequisite Courses continued)

PREPARATION (CONTINUED)

PREREQUISITE COURSE	REQUIRED	RECOMMENDED	LAB REQUIRED	CREDITS (SEMESTER/QUARTER)
Other				
English composition/ technical writing	✓			6/9

Community college coursework accepted for prerequisites: Yes
Community college coursework accepted for electives: Yes
Limits on community college credit hours: No
Maximum number of community college credit hours: Not specified
Advanced placement (AP) credit accepted for prerequisites: Yes
Advanced placement (AP) credit accepted for electives: Yes
Comments regarding AP credit: Reviewed by Admissions Office
Job shadowing: Recommended
Number of hours of job shadowing required or recommended: Not specified
Other factors considered in admission: Demonstration of a sincere understanding of, and interest in, the humanitarian ethos of health care and, particularly, dental medicine

DAT

Mandatory: Yes
Oldest DAT considered: 01/01/2013
When more than one DAT score is reported: Most recent score is considered
Canadian DAT accepted: Yes
Application considered before DAT scores are submitted: No

DAT: 2014 ENTERING CLASS

ENROLLEE DAT SCORES	MEAN	RANGE
Academic Average	18.6	16–23
Perceptual Ability	19.1	16–23
Total Science	18.3	16–24

GPA: 2014 ENTERING CLASS

ENROLLEE GPA SCORES	UNDERGRAD. MEAN	GRADUATE MEAN	UNDERGRAD. RANGE	GRADUATE RANGE
Science GPA	3.31	NR	2.79–4.00	NR
Total GPA	3.43	NR	2.87–3.90	NR

APPLICATION AND SELECTION

TIMETABLE

Earliest filing date: 06/02/2015
Latest filing date: 01/01/2016
Earliest date for acceptance offers: 12/01/2015
Maximum time in days for applicant's response to acceptance offer:
    30 days if accepted on or after December 1
    15 days if accepted on or after February 1
Requests for deferred entrance considered: In exceptional circumstances
Fee for application: Yes, submit only when requested
Amount of fee for application:
    In state: $50   Out of state: $50   International: $50
Fee waiver available: No

	FIRST DEPOSIT	SECOND DEPOSIT	THIRD DEPOSIT
Required to hold place	Yes	No	No
Resident amount	$1,000		
Nonresident amount	$1,000		
Deposit due	As indicated in admission offer		
Applied to tuition	Partially		
Refundable	No		
Refundable by	NR		

APPLICATION PROCESS

Participates in Associated American Dental Schools Application Service (AADSAS): Yes
Accepts direct applicants: No
Secondary or supplemental application required: Yes
Secondary or supplemental application website: Sent from Office of Admissions if qualified
Interview is mandatory: Yes
Interview is by invitation: Yes

RESIDENCY

In-state/in-province versus out-of-state/out-of-province
Admissions process distinguishes between in-state/in-province and out-of-state/out-of-province applicants: No
Preference given to residents of: None
Reciprocity Admissions Agreement available for legal residents of: None
Generally and over time, percentage of your first-year enrollment that is in-state: 40%
Origin of out-of-state/out-of-province enrollees: AL-3, AK-2, AZ-1, CA-8, CO-1, FL-2, GA-1, HI-1, IA-2, IN-4, KS-1, MA-1, MI-15, MN-5, MO-1, NC-1, NJ-1, NY-2, OH-1, OK-1, OR-1, TX-9, UT-2, VA-2, WA-5, WI-8

International
Applications are accepted from international (noncitizens/ nonpermanent residents): Yes
Origin of international enrollees: China-1

APPLICATION AND ENROLLMENT	NUMBER OF APPLICANTS	ESTIMATED NUMBER INTERVIEWED	ESTIMATED NUMBER ENROLLED
In-state or province applicants/enrollees	350	109	48
Out-of-state or province applicants/enrollees	2,481	256	81
International applicants/enrollees (noncitizens/nonpermanent residents)	107	4	1

DEMOGRAPHIC DESCRIPTIONS OF APPLICANTS: 2014 ENTERING CLASS

	APPLICANTS			ENROLLEES		
	M	W	Gender Unknown or Not Reported	M	W	Gender Unknown or Not Reported
American Indian or Alaska Native	0	4	0	0	1	0
Asian	413	426	11	20	20	0
Black or African American	17	29	2	0	0	0
Hispanic or Latino	66	77	1	5	0	0
Native Hawaiian or Other Pacific Islander	3	0	0	1	0	0
White	728	206	6	44	36	0
Two or more races	47	43	0	0	2	0
Race and ethnicity unknown	221	206	12	0	0	0
International	62	43	2	0	1	0

	MINIMUM	MAXIMUM	MEAN
2014 entering class enrollees by age	21	33	24

CURRICULUM

The Midwestern University College of Dental Medicine-Illinois provides an integrated, clinically based, interactive learning environment that incorporates the clinical, behavioral and basic sciences. In the fourth year of the program students will spend approximately 10% of their time in community health situations.

Student research opportunities: Yes

SPECIAL PROGRAMS AND SERVICES

DURING DENTAL SCHOOL
Academic counseling and tutoring
Community service opportunities
Internships, externships, and extramural programs
Mentoring
Personal counseling
Professional- and career-development programming
Training for those interested in academic careers

ACTIVE STUDENT ORGANIZATIONS
American Academy of Pediatric Dentistry
American Association for Dental Research National Student Research Group
American Association of Women Dentists
American Dental Education Association
American Student Dental Association
Hispanic Student Dental Association
Student National Dental Association
Student Professionalism and Ethics Association in Dentistry

INTERNATIONAL DENTISTS
Graduates of international dental schools considered for traditional predoctoral program: Yes
Advanced standing program offered for graduates of international dental schools: No

COMBINED AND ALTERNATE DEGREES

Ph.D.	M.S.	M.P.H.	M.D.	B.A./B.S.	Other
—	✓	—	—	—	✓

Other degree: D.M.D./Master's in Biomedical Science

COSTS: 2014–15 SCHOOL YEAR

	FIRST YEAR	SECOND YEAR	THIRD YEAR	FOURTH YEAR
Tuition, resident	$67,624	NR	NR	NR
Tuition, nonresident	$67,624	NR	NR	NR
Tuition, other				
Fees	$14,847	NR	NR	NR
Instruments, books, and supplies	$3,349	NR	NR	NR
Estimated living expenses	$21,863	NR	NR	NR
Total, resident	$107,683	NR	NR	NR
Total, nonresident	$107,683	NR	NR	NR
Total, other				

FINANCIAL AID

The Office of Student Financial Services is committed to providing the highest level of customer service to support our students in achieving their academic goals. We intend to ensure that each student graduates from Midwestern University with the lowest possible educational debt and guarantee that the distribution of financial aid funds will be fair and equitable. We are committed to providing a comprehensive financial literacy program supporting our students and alumni that will serve as a model to other institutions. Our goal is to create an environment that embraces teamwork and collaborative partnerships within the educational community.

FINANCIAL AID AWARDS TO FIRST-YEAR STUDENTS 2014–15

Total number of first-year recipients: 112
Percentage of the first-year class: 85.5%
Percentage of awards that are grants? 3.1%
Percentage of awards that are loans? 84%

	AVERAGE AWARDS	RANGE OF AWARDS
Residents and nonresidents	$93,946	$40,500–$113,087

For more information, please visit: https://www.midwestern.edu/programs-and-admission/student-financial-services.html

SOUTHERN ILLINOIS UNIVERSITY
SCHOOL OF DENTAL MEDICINE

Bruce E. Rotter, D.M.D., M.S., Dean

GENERAL INFORMATION

Southern Illinois University (SIU), a state-supported institution, established the School of Dental Medicine (SDM) in 1969. The dental school is located on the campus of the former Shurtleff College in Alton, 15 miles from the Edwardsville campus. Situated within the metropolitan St. Louis area, SIU-SDM offers the social and cultural attractions of an urban environment while it identifies with predominantly rural southern Illinois. This unique circumstance enables SDM students to apply their knowledge and skills in the treatment of the broadest spectrum of oral health care needs.

MISSION

Our mission is to improve the oral health of the region through education and patient care, in conjunction with scholarship/research and service.

Type of institution: Public
Year opened: 1972
Term type: Semester
Time to degree in months: 44
Start month: August

Doctoral dental degree offered: D.M.D.
Targeted predoctoral enrollment: 198
Targeted entering class size: 50
Campus setting: Suburban
Campus housing available: No

PREPARATION

Formal minimum preparation in semester/quarter hours: Semester: 90   Quarter: 120
Baccalaureate degree preferred: Yes
Number of first-year, first-time enrollees whose highest degree is:
  Baccalaureate: 41
  Master's degree and beyond: 4
Of first-year, first-time enrollees without baccalaureates, the number with:
  Equivalent of 60 undergraduate credit hours or less: 0
  Equivalent of 61–90 undergraduate credit hours: 2
  Equivalent of 91 or more undergraduate credit hours: 3

PREREQUISITE COURSE	REQUIRED	RECOMMENDED	LAB REQUIRED	CREDITS (SEMESTER/QUARTER)
BCP (biology-chemistry-physics) sciences				
Biology	✓		✓	8/12
Chemistry, general/inorganic	✓		✓	8/12
Chemistry, organic	✓		✓	8/12
Physics	✓		✓	6/9
Additional biological sciences				
Anatomy		✓		3/5
Biochemistry	✓			3/5
Cell biology		✓		3/5
Histology		✓		3/5
Immunology		✓		3/5
Microbiology		✓		3/5
Molecular biology/genetics		✓		3/5
Physiology		✓		3/5
Zoology		✓		3/5
Other				
English	✓			6/9
Statistics		✓		3/5

PREPARATION (CONTINUED)

Community college coursework accepted for prerequisites: Yes
Community college coursework accepted for electives: Yes
Limits on community college credit hours: Yes
Maximum number of community college credit hours: 60
Advanced placement (AP) credit accepted for prerequisites: No
Advanced placement (AP) credit accepted for electives: Yes
Comments regarding AP credit: None
Job shadowing: Recommended
Number of hours of job shadowing required or recommended: 30

DAT

Mandatory: Yes
Latest DAT for consideration of application: 04/01/2016
Oldest DAT considered: 08/01/2013
When more than one DAT score is reported: Most recent score only is considered
Canadian DAT accepted: Yes
Application considered before DAT scores are submitted: No

DAT: 2014 ENTERING CLASS

ENROLLEE DAT SCORES	MEAN	RANGE
Academic Average	19.1	22–16
Perceptual Ability	19.1	27–14
Total Science	18.8	22–14

GPA: 2014 ENTERING CLASS

ENROLLEE GPA SCORES	UNDERGRAD. MEAN	GRADUATE MEAN	UNDERGRAD. RANGE	GRADUATE RANGE
Science GPA	3.45	3.72	2.58–4.00	3.20–4.00
Total GPA	3.57	3.62	2.97–4.00	3.24–3.83

APPLICATION AND SELECTION

TIMETABLE

Earliest filing date: 06/02/2015
Latest filing date: 01/15/2016
Earliest date for acceptance offers: 12/01/2015
Maximum time in days for applicant's response to acceptance offer:
    30 days if accepted on or after December 1
    15 days if accepted on or after February 1
Requests for deferred entrance considered: No
Fee for application: Yes, submitted at same time as AADSAS application
Amount of fee for application:
    In state: $20   Out of state: $20   International: NA
Fee waiver available: No

	FIRST DEPOSIT	SECOND DEPOSIT	THIRD DEPOSIT
Required to hold place	Yes	No	No
Resident amount	$300		
Nonresident amount	$300		
Deposit due	As indicated in admission offer		
Applied to tuition	Yes		
Refundable	No		

APPLICATION PROCESS

Participates in Associated American Dental Schools Application Service (AADSAS): Yes
Accepts direct applicants: No
Secondary or supplemental application required: Yes
Secondary or supplemental application website: www.siue.edu/dentalmedicine/prospective/app_process.shtml
Interview is mandatory: Yes
Interview is by invitation: Yes

RESIDENCY

In-state/in-province versus out-of-state/out-of-province
Admissions process distinguishes between in-state/in-province and out-of-state/out-of-province applicants: Yes
Preference given to residents of: Illinois
Reciprocity Admissions Agreement available for legal residents of: None
Generally and over time, percentage of your first-year enrollment that is in-state: 98%
Origin of out-of-state/out-of-province enrollees: OK-1, NY-1

International
Applications are accepted from international (noncitizens/nonpermanent residents): No
Origin of international enrollees: NA

APPLICATION AND ENROLLMENT	NUMBER OF APPLICANTS	ESTIMATED NUMBER INTERVIEWED	ESTIMATED NUMBER ENROLLED
In-state or province applicants/enrollees	358	112	48
Out-of-state or province applicants/enrollees	456	4	2
International applicants/enrollees (noncitizens/nonpermanent residents)	41	0	0

DEMOGRAPHIC DESCRIPTIONS OF APPLICANTS: 2014 ENTERING CLASS

	APPLICANTS			ENROLLEES		
	M	W	Gender Unknown or Not Reported	M	W	Gender Unknown or Not Reported
American Indian or Alaska Native	1	3	0	0	0	0
Asian	106	118	3	4	3	0
Black or African American	11	30	3	1	0	0
Hispanic or Latino	21	28	0	1	2	0
Native Hawaiian or Other Pacific Islander	1	0	0	0	0	0
White	222	194	3	19	17	0
Two or more races	9	10	0	1	1	0
Race and ethnicity unknown	11	9	3	1	0	0
International	26	14	1	0	0	0

	MINIMUM	MAXIMUM	MEAN
2014 entering class enrollees by age	21	35	24

CURRICULUM

The School of Dental Medicine's curriculum develops the critical thinking and intellectual curiosity necessary for its students to maintain a state of continuous self-improvement. The program is divided into four academic years consisting of biomedical sciences, clinical sciences and behavioral sciences, as well as study and consultation time.

Student research opportunities: Yes

SPECIAL PROGRAMS AND SERVICES

DURING DENTAL SCHOOL
Academic counseling and tutoring
Community service opportunities
Personal counseling
Research opportunities

ACTIVE STUDENT ORGANIZATIONS
American Dental Education Association
American Student Dental Association
Illinois State Dental Society

INTERNATIONAL DENTISTS
Graduates of international dental schools considered for traditional predoctoral program: No
Advanced standing program offered for graduates of international dental schools: No
Advanced standing program description: NA

COMBINED AND ALTERNATE DEGREES

Ph.D.	M.S.	M.P.H.	M.D.	B.A./B.S.	Other
—	—	—	—	—	—

COSTS: 2014–15 SCHOOL YEAR

	FIRST YEAR	SECOND YEAR	THIRD YEAR	FOURTH YEAR
Tuition, resident	$28,552	$34,897	$34,897	$28,552
Tuition, nonresident	$85,656	$104,691	$104,691	$85,656
Tuition, other				
Fees	$5,394	$6,785	$6,785	$5,394
Instruments, books, and supplies	$10,532	$8,485	$2,329	$3,432
Estimated living expense	$15,500	$15,500	$15,500	$15,500
Total, resident	$59,978	$65,667	$59,511	$52,878
Total, nonresident	$117,082	$135,461	$129,305	$109,982
Total, other				

FINANCIAL AID

The SIU School of Dental Medicine offers eligible students financial aid in the form of loans and scholarships. The kind of aid received can be categorized into two different types: gift aid and self-help aid. Self-help aid most often comes in the form of loans, and it must be repaid. Gift aid normally comes in the form of scholarships and usually does not have to be repaid.

FINANCIAL AID AWARDS TO FIRST-YEAR STUDENTS 2014–15

Total number of first-year recipients: 39
Percentage of the first-year class: 78%
Percentage of awards that are grants? 3%
Percentage of awards that are loans? 97%

	AVERAGE AWARDS	RANGE OF AWARDS
Residents	$35,765	$26,265–$40,245
Nonresidents	$64,192	$64,192–$64,192

For more information, please visit: http://www.siue.edu/dentalmedicine/misc/fin_aid.shtml

THE UNIVERSITY OF ILLINOIS AT CHICAGO DENTISTRY

UNIVERSITY OF ILLINOIS AT CHICAGO
COLLEGE OF DENTISTRY

Clark M. Stanford, D.D.S., Ph.D., Dean

CONTACT INFORMATION
http://dentistry.uic.edu
801 South Paulina Street, MC 621
Chicago, IL 60612
Phone: 312-996-1020
Fax: 312-413-9050

OFFICE OF STUDENT & DIVERSITY
Dr. Darryl D. Pendleton
Associate Dean for Student and Diversity Affairs
801 South Paulina Street, MC 621
Chicago, IL 60612
Phone: 312-355-1670

Ms. Millie Mendez
Director of Student Affairs
801 S. Paulina Street, MC 621
Chicago, IL 60612
Phone: 312-413-1209

OFFICE OF ADMISSIONS
Ms. Braulia Espinosa
Director of Admissions
801 South Paulina Street, MC 621
Chicago, IL 60612
Phone: 312-355-0320
Email: bespin1@uic.edu

Ms. Carolyn Feller
Director of Admissions
801 South Paulina Street, MC 621
Chicago, IL 60612
Phone: 312-996-2873
Email: cfeller@uic.edu

OFFICE OF STUDENT FINANCIAL AID
1800 Student Services Building
1200 West Harrison, MC 334
Chicago, IL 60612
Phone: 312-996-3126
www.uic.edu/depts/financialaid

CAMPUS HOUSING
Campus Housing
818 South Wolcott Street, MC 579
Chicago, IL 60612
Phone: 312-355-6300
www.housing.uic.edu

GENERAL INFORMATION

The University of Illinois at Chicago College of Dentistry (UIC COD) is focused on preparing highly qualified dental professionals. By addressing the oral health needs of vulnerable and underserved populations, UIC COD trains dentists both to be empathetic, highly ethical and humanistic practitioners and to play their part in eliminating health disparities. Student training is integrated into a patient-centered and evidence-based curriculum.

Renovated research and clinical facilities highlight the college's reputation as a world renowned research and clinical center. UIC COD engages all fourth-year students in service-learning experiences in community-based clinics in Chicago, rural areas of Illinois, clinics in Colorado and international locations including China, Africa and Guatemala.

Upon graduation, students may pursue a variety of specialty programs.

MISSION
To promote optimum oral and general health to the people of Illinois and worldwide by striving for perfection in education, patient care, research and service.

Vision: Continue as a worldwide leader in:

- Patient-centered, evidence-based clinical care founded on preventive and public health sciences.
- Integrated advanced technology-based education programs.
- Interdisciplinary, innovative research.

Core Values:

- Education
- Patient Care
- Research
- Service

Type of institution: Public
Year opened: 1891
Term type: Semester
Time to degree in months: 44
Start month: August

Doctoral dental degree offered: D.M.D.
Targeted predoctoral enrollment: 200
Targeted entering class size: 70
Campus setting: Urban
Campus housing available: Yes

PREPARATION

Formal minimum preparation in semester/quarter hours: Applicants must have a minimum of a bachelor's degree conferred no later than June of the matriculation year from a U.S. institution. Additional upper-level science coursework is strongly preferred.

Number of first-year, first-time enrollees whose highest degree is:
Baccalaureate: 43
Master's degree and beyond: 7
Of first-year, first-time enrollees without baccalaureates, the number with:
Equivalent of 60 undergraduate credit hours or less: 0
Equivalent of 61–90 undergraduate credit hours: 0
Equivalent of 91 or more undergraduate credit hours: 0

PREREQUISITE COURSE	REQUIRED	RECOMMENDED	LAB REQUIRED	CREDITS (SEMESTER/QUARTER)
BCP (biology-chemistry-physics) sciences				
Biology	✓		✓	6/9
Chemistry, general/inorganic	✓		✓	14/21
Chemistry, organic	✓		✓	4/6
Physics	✓		✓	6/9

(Prerequisite Courses continued)

PREPARATION (CONTINUED)

Additional biological sciences

Anatomy*	✓
Biochemistry*	✓
Cell biology	✓
Histology	✓
Immunology	✓
Microbiology*	✓
Molecular biology/genetics	✓
Physiology	✓
Zoology	

Other

English	✓	6/9

*STRONGLY RECOMMENDED

Note: Advanced Placement credits not accepted for College of Dentistry prerequisites.

Disclaimer: Please continue to check the UIC College of Dentistry website for any updates or changes to school requirements.

Community college coursework accepted for prerequisites: Yes
Community college coursework accepted for electives: Yes
Limits on community college credit hours: No
Maximum number of community college credit hours: None
Advanced placement (AP) credit accepted for prerequisites: Advanced Placement (AP) courses are not accepted as course requirements.
Job shadowing: Strongly recommended
Number of hours of job shadowing required or recommended: 100

DAT

Mandatory: Yes
Latest DAT for consideration of application: 12/01/2015
Oldest DAT considered: 01/01/2014
When more than one DAT score is reported: Highest score is considered
Canadian DAT accepted: No
Application considered before DAT scores are submitted: No

DAT: 2014 ENTERING CLASS

ENROLLEE DAT SCORES	MEAN	RANGE
Academic Average	20.0	16–23
Perceptual Ability	20.0	15–25
Total Science	20.0	16–25

GPA: 2014 ENTERING CLASS

ENROLLEE GPA SCORES	UNDERGRAD. MEAN	GRADUATE MEAN	UNDERGRAD. RANGE	GRADUATE RANGE
Science GPA	3.61	3.63	2.85–4.14	3.29–4.00
Total GPA	3.68	3.71	3.01–4.14	3.29–4.00

APPLICATION AND SELECTION

TIMETABLE

Earliest filing date: 06/02/2015
Latest filing date: 12/01/2015
Earliest date for acceptance offers: 12/01/2015

Maximum time in days for applicant's response to acceptance offer:
30 days if accepted on or after December 1
15 days if accepted on or after February 1
Requests for deferred entrance considered: In exceptional circumstances only
Fee for application: Yes
Amount of fee for application:
In state: $85   Out of state: $85   International: NA
Fee waiver available: No

	FIRST DEPOSIT	SECOND DEPOSIT	THIRD DEPOSIT
Required to hold place	Yes	No	No
Resident amount	$500		
Nonresident amount (Ph.D./D.M.D. only)	$1,500		
Deposit due	As indicated in admission offer		
Applied to tuition	Yes		
Refundable	No		

APPLICATION PROCESS

Participates in Associated American Dental Schools Application Service (AADSAS): Yes. Letters of recommendation are accepted electronically via AADSAS only.
Accepts direct applicants: No
Secondary or supplemental application required: Yes
Interview is mandatory: Yes
Interview is by invitation: Yes

RESIDENCY

In-state/in-province versus out-of-state/out-of-province

Admissions process distinguishes between in-state/in-province and out-of-state/out-of-province applicants: Yes

Preference given to residents of: Illinois

Reciprocity Admissions Agreement available for legal residents of: None

Generally and over time, percentage of your first-year enrollment that is in-state: 100%

Origin of out-of-state/out-of-province enrollees: NA

International

Applications are accepted from international (noncitizens/nonpermanent residents): No

Origin of international enrollees: NA

APPLICATION AND ENROLLMENT	NUMBER OF APPLICANTS	ESTIMATED NUMBER INTERVIEWED	ESTIMATED NUMBER ENROLLED
In-state or province applicants/enrollees	458	138	50
Out-of-state or province applicants/enrollees	0	1	0
International applicants/enrollees (noncitizens/nonpermanent residents)	0	0	0

DEMOGRAPHIC DESCRIPTIONS OF APPLICANTS: 2014 ENTERING CLASS

	APPLICANTS			ENROLLEES		
	M	W	Gender Unknown or Not Reported	M	W	Gender Unknown or Not Reported
American Indian or Alaska Native	1	0	0	0	0	0
Asian	60	73	0	9	6	0
Black or African American	10	15	0	0	2	0
Hispanic or Latino	22	12	0	2	5	0
Native Hawaiian or Other Pacific Islander	0	0	0	0	0	0
White	132	133	0	15	11	0
Two or more races	4	5	0	0	0	0
Race and ethnicity unknown	0	0	0	0	0	0
International	0	0	0	0	0	0

	MINIMUM	MAXIMUM	MEAN
2014 entering class enrollees by age	21	33	24

CURRICULUM

In 2011, UIC COD faculty changed the Doctor of Dental Surgery to the Doctor of Dental Medicine (D.M.D.) degree to emphasize oral health's integral role in general health. The faculty then implemented a new curriculum replacing lectures with faculty-facilitated small learning groups focused on patient health care scenarios. This new curriculum is one of only two patient-case-based dental education programs in the United States.

The UIC COD curriculum, supported by innovative information technologies, provides an interdisciplinary, collaborative learning environment in which students achieve the competencies for oral health care in the context of patient management for the 21st century. The curriculum features small-group and independent learning, combined with experiential laboratory activities in biomedical, clinical and behavioral sciences, and extensive time in community clinical experiences. Biomedical, clinical and behavioral education all span the entire four years of the curriculum, from the first week of the D1 year until graduation. The college prides itself on its student and faculty culture of collegiality, intellectual rigor, high standards of competence and ethical behavior, commitment to improve access to care, and service to diverse communities.

Student research opportunities: Yes, throughout students' dental education. Undergraduate and incoming D1 summer research programs are available.

SPECIAL PROGRAMS AND SERVICES

PREDENTAL

DAT workshops

Illinois Predental Consortium

Postbaccalaureate programs

Summer enrichment programs

DURING DENTAL SCHOOL

Academic counseling and tutoring

Community service opportunities

Internships, externships, or extramural programs

Mentoring

Personal counseling

Professional- and career-development programming

Training for those interested in academic careers

ACTIVE STUDENT ORGANIZATIONS

Alpha Omega International Dental Fraternity

American Academy of Pediatric Dentistry

American Association of Women Dentists

American Student Dental Association

Association of Muslim Dental Students

Christian Medical & Dental Associations

Chinese American, Hispanic, Korean and Middle Eastern student dental associations

Illinois Academy of General Dentistry

Student National Dental Association

Student Research Group

INTERNATIONAL DENTISTS

Graduates of international dental schools considered for traditional predoctoral program: No

Advanced standing program offered for graduates of international dental schools: Yes

Advanced standing program description: Program awarding a dental degree

COMBINED AND ALTERNATE DEGREES					
Ph.D.	M.S.	M.P.H.	M.D.	B.A./B.S.	Other
✓	✓	—	—	—	—

COSTS: 2014–15 SCHOOL YEAR

	FIRST YEAR	SECOND YEAR	THIRD YEAR	FOURTH YEAR
Tuition, resident	$30,846	$46,269	$46,269	$46,269
Tuition, nonresident	$55,514	$83,271	$83,271	$83,271
Tuition, other*				
Fees	$4,004	$5,235	$5,235	$5,235
Instruments, books, and supplies	$11,060	$16,590	$16,590	$16,590
Estimated living expenses	$25,000	$25,000	$25,000	$25,000
Total, resident	$70,910	$93,094	$93,094	$93,094
Total, nonresident	$95,578	$130,096	$130,096	$130,096
Total, other				

FINANCIAL AID

Although moderate, the cost of a UIC education is still beyond the financial resources of many students and their families. The UIC Office of Student Financial Aid provides a wide range of financial services designed to help students and their families meet the cost of attending the university. Financial aid is available for those students who need assistance with their education-related expenses (e.g., tuition, fees, books, supplies, child care, rental and miscellaneous expenses). To be considered for various types of aid, students must complete the Free Application for Federal Student Aid (also called "FAFSA") application.

FINANCIAL AID AWARDS TO FIRST-YEAR STUDENTS 2014–15

Total number of first-year recipients: 87
Percentage of the first-year class: 96%
Percentage of awards that are grants? 0%
Percentage of awards that are loans? 100%

	AVERAGE AWARDS	RANGE OF AWARDS
Residents	$79,833	$60,167–$91,466
Nonresidents	$86,449	$70,000–$95,488

For more information, please visit: http://www.uic.edu/depts/financialaid/

INDIANA UNIVERSITY
SCHOOL OF DENTISTRY

John N. Williams, D.M.D., M.B.A., Dean

GENERAL INFORMATION

Indiana University School of Dentistry (IUSD) houses the state's only professional D.D.S. program. IUSD, integral to IU's Medical Center, includes a medical school, a nursing school and a complex of hospitals with more than 600 beds. Clinical facilities are excellent. Patients are drawn from a population area of over one million. The school maintains dental clinics in Riley Hospital for Children at Indiana University Health, the Regenstrief Institute and IU Health University Hospital on the Medical Center campus. Graduate students are candidates for either M.S. or M.S.D. degrees in most dental school departments. A limited number of Ph.D. programs are offered. A dual D.D.S./M.P.H. option is also available. An International Dentist Program for dentists trained outside of the United States was adopted in 2013.

MISSION

IUSD promotes optimal oral and general health through the IUSD Indiana Model of Dental Education program and through the school's research, patient-care and service programs.

Vision: The IU School of Dentistry will be one of the best dental schools for the 21st century.

Core Values: Excellence, Integrity, Scholarship, Patient-Centered Care, Collaboration, Diversity, Stewardship

Type of institution: Public	Doctoral dental degree offered: D.D.S.
Year opened: 1879	Targeted predoctoral enrollment: 400
Term type: Semester	Targeted entering class size: 104
Time to degree in months: 48	Campus setting: Urban
Start month: July (D1) / August (D2, D3, D4)	Campus housing available: Yes

PREPARATION

Formal minimum preparation in semester/quarter hours: Semester: 90   Quarter: 135
Baccalaureate degree preferred: Yes; preferred but not required
Number of first-year, first-time enrollees whose highest degree is:
  Baccalaureate: 80
  Master's degree and beyond: 23
Of first-year, first-time enrollees without baccalaureates, the number with:
  Equivalent of 60 undergraduate credit hours or less: 0
  Equivalent of 61–90 undergraduate credit hours: 1
  Equivalent of 91 or more undergraduate credit hours: 0

PREREQUISITE COURSE	STRONGLY RECOMMENDED	RECOMMENDED	LAB REQUIRED	CREDITS (SEMESTER/QUARTER)
BCP (biology-chemistry-physics) sciences				
Biology[1]	✓		✓	Please refer to footnotes below.
Chemistry, general/inorganic[2]	✓		✓	
Chemistry, organic[2]	✓		✓	
Physics	✓		✓	8/12
Additional biological sciences				
Anatomy[1] (or Zoology[1])	✓		✓	
Biochemistry[2]	✓			
Cell biology[1]	✓			Please refer to footnotes below.
Histology[1]	✓		✓	
Immunology[1] (or Microbiology[1])	✓			
Microbiology[1] (or Immunology[1])	✓			
Molecular biology/genetics				

CONTACT INFORMATION

https://www.dentistry.iu.edu/
1121 West Michigan Street
Indianapolis, IN 46202

OFFICE OF ADMISSIONS AND STUDENT AFFAIRS

Dr. Melanie Peterson
Assistant Dean for Admissions and Student Affairs
Director, International Dentist Program
1121 West Michigan Street, Room 105
Indianapolis, IN 46202
Phone: 317-274-8173
Fax: 317-278-9066
Email: ds-stdnt@iupui.edu
https://www.dentistry.iu.edu/index.php/prospective-students/

OFFICE OF STUDENT FINANCIAL AID

Ms. Jennifer Vines
Assistant Director, Dentistry
IUPUI Office of Student Financial Services
1121 West Michigan Street, Room 109
Indianapolis, IN 46202
Phone: 317-278-1549
Fax: 317-278-9066
https://www.dentistry.iu.edu/prospective-students/financial-aid/

OFFICE OF DIVERSITY, EQUITY AND INCLUSION

Dr. Pamella P. Shaw
Associate Dean for Diversity, Equity, and Inclusion
1121 West Michigan Street, Room 130
Indianapolis, IN 46202
Phone: 317-274-6573
Fax: 317-278-0173
Email: dsdivsty@iupui.edu

HOUSING

Mr. Aaron Hart
Director, Housing and Residence Life
IUPUI Division of Student Affairs
Riverwalk Apartments, Orvis 150
Indianapolis, IN 46202
Phone: 317-274-7200
Fax: 317-274-3934
Email: aarohart@iupui.edu
www.life.iupui.edu/housing

INTERNATIONAL STUDENTS

Office of International Affairs
Indiana University – Purdue University Indianapolis
902 W New York Street, Room 2126
Indianapolis, IN 46202
Phone: 317-274-7000

PREPARATION (CONTINUED)

PREREQUISITE COURSE	STRONGLY RECOMMENDED	RECOMMENDED	LAB REQUIRED	CREDITS (SEMESTER/QUARTER)
Physiology[1]	✓			Please refer to footnotes below.
Zoology[1] (or Anatomy[1])	✓		✓	
Other				

Social sciences, which may include:
    Psychology
    Sociology
    Anthropology
    Comunication studies
	✓			3/4.5

Humanities, which may include:
    English composition
    Literature
    Philosophy
    History
    Foreign Language
	✓			3/4.5

[1]Students must complete the equivalent of 20/30 semester/quarter hours in the biological sciences. Only courses intended for science majors, as determined by applicant's undergraduate institution, count toward prerequisite. Students may choose biology or zoology, anatomy and/or histology, microbiology or immunology.

[2]Students must complete the equivalent of 15/22.5 semester/quarter hours in chemistry. Only courses intended for science majors, as defined by applicant's undergraduate institution, count. Students may choose general chemistry or inorganic chemistry.

For additional details on prerequisites, please visit: https://www.dentistry.iu.edu/index.php?cID=578

Community college coursework accepted for prerequisites: Yes; prefer science prerequisites from four-year colleges

Community college coursework accepted for electives: Yes

Limits on community college credit hours: Yes; science classes should be from a four-year college.

Maximum number of community college credit hours: 60

Advanced placement (AP) credit accepted for prerequisites: No

Advanced placement (AP) credit accepted for electives: Yes

Job shadowing: Required

Number of hours of job shadowing required or recommended: 40—must shadow general practice dentists in private practice settings

Other factors considered in admission: Community service, campus involvement, volunteerism, communication skills, and manual dexterity skills

DAT

Mandatory: Yes

Latest DAT for consideration of application: 02/01/16

Oldest DAT considered: 01/01/2009

When more than one DAT score is reported: Most recent score only is considered

Canadian DAT accepted: Yes

Application considered before DAT scores are submitted: No

DAT: 2014 ENTERING CLASS

ENROLLEE DAT SCORES	MEAN	RANGE
Academic Average	19.3	15–28
Perceptual Ability	19.5	14–26
Total Science	19.0	15–28

GPA: 2014 ENTERING CLASS

ENROLLEE GPA SCORES	MEAN	RANGE
Science GPA	3.50	2.80–4.20
Total GPA	3.50	2.60–4.20

APPLICATION AND SELECTION

TIMETABLE

Earliest filing date: 06/02/2015

Latest filing date: 11/01/2015

Earliest date for acceptance offers: 12/01/2015

Maximum time in days for applicant's response to acceptance offer:
    30 days if accepted on or after December 1
    15 days if accepted on or after February 1

Requests for deferred entrance considered: In exceptional circumstances only

Fee for application: Yes
Amount of fee for application:
In state: $60   Out of state: $60   International: $62.50
Fee waiver available: No

	FIRST DEPOSIT	SECOND DEPOSIT	THIRD DEPOSIT
Required to hold place	Yes	No	No
Resident amount	$1,000		
Nonresident amount	$1,000		
Deposit due	As indicated in admission offer		
Applied to tuition	Yes		
Refundable	No		

APPLICATION PROCESS

Participates in Associated American Dental Schools Application Service (AADSAS): Yes
Accepts direct applicants: No
Secondary or supplemental application required: Yes
Interview is mandatory: Yes
Interview is by invitation: Yes

RESIDENCY

In-state/in-province versus out-of-state/out-of-province
Admissions process distinguishes between in-state/in-province and out-of-state/out-of-province applicants: Yes
Preference given to residents of: None
Reciprocity Admissions Agreement available for legal residents of: None
Generally and over time, percentage of your first-year enrollment that is in-state: 67%
Origin of out-of-state/out-of-province enrollees: AZ-4, CA-3, FL-1, GA-1, IL-1, KS-1, KY-2, MI-4, NH-1, NJ-1, NY-1, NC-1, PA-1, UT-2, VA-2, WA-1

International
Applications are accepted from international (noncitizens/nonpermanent residents): Yes
Origin of international enrollees: Canada-3, South Korea-1

APPLICATION AND ENROLLMENT	NUMBER OF APPLICANTS	ESTIMATED NUMBER INTERVIEWED	ESTIMATED NUMBER ENROLLED
In-state or province applicants/enrollees	203	146	74
Out-of-state or province applicants/enrollees	1,209	229	30
International applicants/enrollees (noncitizens/nonpermanent residents)	NR	NR	2

DEMOGRAPHIC DESCRIPTIONS OF APPLICANTS: 2013 ENTERING CLASS

	APPLICANTS			ENROLLEES		
	M	W	Gender Unknown or Not Reported	M	W	Gender Unknown or Not Reported
American Indian or Alaska Native	2	2	0	0	0	0
Asian	208	193	2	2	2	0
Black or African American	15	26	0	1	4	0
Hispanic or Latino	37	44	1	2	2	0
Native Hawaiian or Other Pacific Islander	0	0	0	0	0	0
White	481	334	8	52	38	0
Two or more races	15	27	0	0	0	0
Race and ethnicity unknown	0	0	0	0	0	0
International	112	68	0	4	1	0

	MINIMUM	MAXIMUM	MEAN
2014 entering class enrollees by age	22	43	33

CURRICULUM

Launched in 1997, the Indiana Model of Dental Education offers a dynamic blend of contemporary and traditional learning environments designed and continually refined so as to maximally promote the principles of student centeredness, critical thinking, problem solving, evidence-based decision-making, competency-based clinical care and lifelong learning.

Student research opportunities: Yes

SPECIAL PROGRAMS AND SERVICES

DURING DENTAL SCHOOL

Academic counseling and tutoring
Community service opportunities
Internships, externships, or extramural programs
Mentoring
Personal counseling
Professional and career development programming
Training for those interested in academic careers

ACTIVE STUDENT ORGANIZATIONS

American Academy of Pediatric Dentistry
American Association for Dental Research National Student Research Group
American Association of Public Health Dentistry
American Student Dental Association
Christian Medical & Dental Associations
Delta Sigma Delta International Fraternity
Hispanic Dental Association
Society of American Indian Dentistry
Student National Dental Association
Student Professionalism & Ethics Association in Dentistry
For more information, visit https://www.dentistry.iu.edu/index.php?cID=1113

INTERNATIONAL DENTISTS

Graduates of international dental schools considered for traditional predoctoral program: Yes

Advanced standing program offered for graduates of international dental schools: Yes

COMBINED AND ALTERNATE DEGREES

Ph.D.	M.S.	M.P.H.	M.D.	B.A./B.S.	Other
✓	✓	✓	—	—	✓

Other degree: M.S.D. programs in most areas

COSTS: 2014–15 SCHOOL YEAR

	FIRST YEAR	SECOND YEAR	THIRD YEAR	FOURTH YEAR
Tuition, resident	$31,549	$31,549	$31,549	$31,549
Tuition, nonresident	$66,036	$66,036	$66,036	$66,036
Tuition, other				
Fees	$3,789	$3,789	$3,789	$3,789
Instruments, books, and supplies	$12,768	$13,691	$4,720	$3,416
Estimated living expenses	$18,134	$18,134	$18,134	$18,134
Total, resident	$63,097	$65,270	$55,889	$54,585
Total, nonresident	$98,424	$99,757	$90,376	$89,072
Total, other				

FINANCIAL AID

www.dentistry.iu.edu/index.php/prospective-students/financial-aid/

THE UNIVERSITY OF IOWA
COLLEGE OF DENTISTRY & DENTAL CLINICS

David C. Johnsen, D.D.S., M.S., Dean

CONTACT INFORMATION

www.dentistry.uiowa.edu
University of Iowa College of Dentistry &
Dental Clinics
801 Newton Road
Iowa City, IA 52242
Phone: 319-335-9650
Fax: 319-335-7155

OFFICE OF ADMISSIONS

Ms. Elaine Brown
Director, Dental Admissions
311 Dental Science Building N
Iowa City, IA 52242-1010
Phone: 319-335-7157

OFFICE FOR STUDENT FINANCIAL AID

208 Calvin Hall
Iowa City, IA 52242
Phone: 319-335-1450

STUDENT AFFAIRS

Ms. Catherine M. Solow
Associate Dean for Student Affairs
311 Dental Science Building N
Iowa City, IA 52242-1010
Phone: 319-335-7164

MINORITY AFFAIRS/FINANCIAL AID/ADMISSIONS

311 Dental Science Building N
Iowa City, IA 52242-1010
Phone: 319-335-7164

HOUSING

Housing Service Building
Iowa City, IA 52242
Phone: 319-335-9199
www.uiowa.edu

INTERNATIONAL STUDENTS

www.dentistry.uiowa.edu

GENERAL INFORMATION

The University of Iowa (UI) is a state-supported institution with an enrollment of more than 30,000, located on a 1,700-acre campus spanning the Iowa River Valley and merging with the business center of Iowa City, a community of 60,000. The College of Dentistry, founded in 1882, has an enrollment of about 320 dental students and a faculty of 90. The Dental Science Building includes patient care clinics, academic classrooms, a simulation clinic and preclinical research laboratories. In addition to the D.D.S. program, the College of Dentistry is the only dental school that offers advanced dental education programs in all dental specialties recognized by the American Dental Association. The college also offers additional outstanding programs and residencies with study toward master's and Ph.D. degrees.

MISSION

To embrace both the academic values of a university and the ethical responsibilities implicit in the education of future members of a health care profession.

Vision: To educate dentists through scholarly research, deliver high-quality oral health care to Iowa and the region, and serve as a resource to Iowa and dentistry.

Type of institution: Public	Doctoral dental degree offered: D.D.S.
Year opened: 1882	Targeted predoctoral enrollment: 320
Term type: Semester	Targeted entering class size: 80
Time to degree in months: 48	Campus setting: Urban
Start month: August	Campus housing available: Yes

PREPARATION

Formal minimum preparation in semester/quarter hours: Semester: 90
Baccalaureate degree preferred: Yes
Number of first-year, first-time enrollees whose highest degree is:
   Baccalaureate: 80
   Master's degree and beyond: 0
Of first-year, first-time enrollees without baccalaureates, the number with:
   Equivalent of 60 undergraduate credit hours or less: 0
   Equivalent of 61–90 undergraduate credit hours: 0
   Equivalent of 91 or more undergraduate credit hours: 0

PREREQUISITE COURSE	REQUIRED	RECOMMENDED	LAB REQUIRED	CREDITS (SEMESTER/QUARTER)
BCP (biology-chemistry-physics) sciences				
Biology	✓		✓	8
Chemistry, general/inorganic	✓		✓	8
Chemistry, organic	✓		✓	8
Physics	✓		✓	8
Additional biological sciences				
Anatomy		✓		
Biochemistry	✓			3
Cell biology		✓		
Histology		✓		
Immunology		✓		
Microbiology		✓		
Molecular biology/genetics		✓		
Physiology		✓		

(Prerequisite Courses continued)

PREPARATION (CONTINUED)

PREREQUISITE COURSE	REQUIRED	RECOMMENDED	LAB REQUIRED	CREDITS (SEMESTER/QUARTER)
Zoology		✓		
Other				
English	✓			
Mathematics	✓			

Community college coursework accepted for prerequisites: Yes
Community college coursework accepted for electives: Yes
Limits on community college credit hours: Yes
Maximum number of community college credit hours: 60
Advanced placement (AP) credit accepted for prerequisites: Yes
Advanced placement (AP) credit accepted for electives: Yes
Comments regarding AP credit: AP credit in math and physics is acceptable; prefer biology and chemistry be taken at a four-year institution
Job shadowing: Recommended (hours not specified)
Other factors considered in admission: Personal essay, letters of recommendation, diversity, community service, leadership qualities, college attended and course load

DAT

Mandatory: Yes
Latest DAT for consideration of application: 08/01/2015
Oldest DAT considered: 08/01/2010
When more than one DAT score is reported: Most recent score only is considered
Canadian DAT accepted: Yes
Application considered before DAT scores are submitted: No

DAT: 2014 ENTERING CLASS

ENROLLEE DAT SCORES	MEAN	RANGE
Academic Average	20	16–25
Perceptual Ability	20	16–25
Total Science	20	15–27

GPA: 2014 ENTERING CLASS

ENROLLEE GPA SCORES	UNDERGRAD. MEAN	GRADUATE MEAN	UNDERGRAD. RANGE	GRADUATE RANGE
Science GPA	3.68	NR	2.92–4.13	NR
Total GPA	3.74	NR	3.25–4.10	NR

APPLICATION AND SELECTION

TIMETABLE

Earliest filing date: 06/02/2015
Latest filing date: 10/01/2015
Earliest date for acceptance offers: 12/01/2015
Maximum time in days for applicant's response to acceptance offer:
  30 days if accepted on or after December 1
  15 days if accepted on or after February 1
Requests for deferred entrance considered: Yes
Fee for application: Yes, submitted only when requested.
Amount of fee for application:
  In state: $60   Out of state: $60   International: $100
Fee waiver available: Yes

	FIRST DEPOSIT	SECOND DEPOSIT	THIRD DEPOSIT
Required to hold place	Yes	No	No
Resident amount	$500		
Nonresident amount	$500		
Deposit due	As indicated in admission offer		
Applied to tuition	Yes		
Refundable	No		

APPLICATION PROCESS

Participates in Associated American Dental Schools Application Service (AADSAS): Yes
Accepts direct applicants: No
Secondary or supplemental application required: Yes
Secondary or supplemental application website: www.dentistry.uiowa.edu
Interview is mandatory: Yes
Interview is by invitation: Yes

RESIDENCY

In-state/in-province versus out-of-state/out-of-province
Admissions process distinguishes between in-state/in-province and out-of-state/out-of-province applicants: Yes
Preference given to residents of: Iowa
Reciprocity Admissions Agreement available for legal residents of: None
Generally and over time, percentage of your first-year enrollment that is in-state: 71%
Origin of out-of-state/out-of-province enrollees: CO-1, IL-8, KS-1 MI-1, MN-4, MT-1, ND-1, VA-1, WA-1, WI-4

International
Applications are accepted from international (noncitizens/nonpermanent residents): Yes
Origin of international enrollees: NA

APPLICATION AND ENROLLMENT	NUMBER OF APPLICANTS	ESTIMATED NUMBER INTERVIEWED	ESTIMATED NUMBER ENROLLED
In-state or province applicants/enrollees	106	73	57
Out-of-state or province applicants/enrollees	779	143	23
International applicants/enrollees	45	8	0

DEMOGRAPHIC DESCRIPTIONS OF APPLICANTS: 2014 ENTERING CLASS

	APPLICANTS			ENROLLEES		
	M	W	Gender Unknown or Not Reported	M	W	Gender Unknown or Not Reported
American Indian or Alaska Native	4	0	0	0	1	0
Asian	64	68	0	4	6	0
Black or African American	13	23	0	2	0	0
Hispanic or Latino	29	28	0	0	1	0
Native Hawaiian or Other Pacific Islander	0	1	0	0	0	0
White	344	260	0	39	27	0
Two or more races	9	15	0	0	0	0
Race and ethnicity unknown	12	10	0	0	0	0
International	40	27	0	0	0	0

	MINIMUM	MAXIMUM	MEAN
2014 entering class enrollees by age	21	27	22

CURRICULUM

The University of Iowa College of Dentistry is committed to providing a high-quality dental education to aspiring dentists to help them meet the health needs of a large and diverse population.

Year 1: Basic sciences, laboratory and technique courses, and an introduction to clinical experiences.

Year 2: Continuation of basic sciences and technical courses, plus definitive clinical patient treatment.

Year 3: Rotation through a series of clerkships in each of the seven clinical disciplines.

Year 4: Delivery of comprehensive dental care under conditions approximating those in private practice; seniors' participation in extramural programs in locations primarily throughout the Midwest.

Student research opportunities: Yes

SPECIAL PROGRAMS AND SERVICES

PREDENTAL
Summer enrichment programs

DURING DENTAL SCHOOL
Academic counseling and tutoring
Community service opportunities
Internships, externships, or extramural programs
Mentoring
Opportunity to study for credit at institution abroad
Personal counseling
Professional- and career-development programming
Training for those interested in academic careers

ACTIVE STUDENT ORGANIZATIONS
American Academy of Pediatric Dentistry
American Association for Dental Research National Student Research Group
American Association of Public Health Dentistry
American Association of Women Dentists
American Dental Education Association

American Student Dental Association
Christian Dental Association
Dentistry Gay-Straight Alliance
Hispanic Student Dental Association
Student National Dental Association
For more information, visit: http://www.dentistry.uiowa.edu/education-dds and select "Student Organizations" in the left-hand navigation.

INTERNATIONAL DENTISTS
Graduates of international dental schools considered for traditional predoctoral program: Yes
Advanced standing program offered for graduates of international dental schools: No

COMBINED AND ALTERNATE DEGREES

Ph.D.	M.S.	M.P.H.	M.D.	B.A./B.S.	Other
—	✓	✓	—	—	✓

Other degree: The opportunity exists for students to complete a defined set of requirements for the M.S. in Public Health program while in dental school and have advanced standing in the M.S. program at the completion of the D.D.S.

COSTS: 2014–15 SCHOOL YEAR

	FIRST YEAR	SECOND YEAR	THIRD YEAR	FOURTH YEAR
Tuition, resident	$41,007	$41,007	$37,953	$37,953
Tuition, nonresident	$64,173	$64,173	$61,119	$61,119
Tuition, other				
Fees	$2,656	$2,110	$1,700	$4,603
Instruments, books, and supplies	$14,063	$9,368	$4,823	$1,478
Estimated living expenses	$16,852	$16,852	$17,618	$17,618
Total, resident	$74,578	$69,337	$62,094	$61,652
Total, nonresident	$97,744	$92,503	$85,260	$84,818
Total, other				

FINANCIAL AID

Students are not encouraged to have jobs during the first two years due to the intensity of their course of study. Financial aid eligibility is based on need established by the completed Free Application for Federal Student Aid. Eligible dental students may receive the following: Health Professions Student Loans, Federal Perkins Loans, Federal Stafford Loans and PLUS Loans, on which interest accrues at a comparatively low rate. These loans are repayable over an extended period of time after completion of studies. Additionally, some loans are available from the American Dental Association, and sources within the University of Iowa College of Dentistry. Information on dental student scholarships and loans may be obtained from the University of Iowa Office of Student Financial Aid, 208 Calvin Hall.

FINANCIAL AID AWARDS TO FIRST-YEAR STUDENTS 2014–15

Total number of first-year recipients: 75
Percentage of the first-year class: 93%
Percentage of awards that are grants? 21%
Percentage of awards that are loans? 78%

	AVERAGE AWARDS	RANGE OF AWARDS
Residents	$18,660	$240–$51,006
Nonresidents	$19,844	$1,340–$73,972

For more information, please visit: http://www.dentistry.uiowa.edu/education-financial-aid

CONTACT INFORMATION

www.mc.uky.edu/dentistry
M-134 Chandler Medical Center
Lexington, KY 40536
Phone: 859-323-1884

OFFICE OF ADMISSIONS AND STUDENT AFFAIRS

Ms. Christine Harper
Assistant Dean, Admissions and Student Affairs

Ms. Missy Shelton
Admissions Coordinator

Ms. Leslie LeRoy
Student Affairs Coordinator
Admissions and Student Affairs
M-134 Chandler Medical Center
Lexington, KY 40536
Phone: 859-323-6071
leslie.leroy@uky.edu

FINANCIAL AID

Mr. Don Brown
Financial Aid Coordinator
D-155 Chandler Medical Center
Lexington, KY 40536
Phone: 859-323-5280

ACADEMIC AFFAIRS

M-134 Chandler Medical Center
Lexington, KY 40536
Phone: 859-323-5656

UNIVERSITY OF KENTUCKY
COLLEGE OF DENTISTRY

Sharon P. Turner, D.D.S., J.D., Dean

GENERAL INFORMATION

The University of Kentucky College of Dentistry (UKCD), a public institution with a statewide mission, is located on UK's main campus, a suburban setting in Lexington (population 297,000) situated in the heart of Kentucky's scenic bluegrass region. Along with the D.M.D. program, UKCD offers advanced dental education programs in oral and maxillofacial surgery, orthodontics, pediatric dentistry, periodontics, general practice dentistry and orofacial pain. In addition to strong research and continuing education programs, the college conducts many public service activities throughout Kentucky, especially with pediatric patients. Today it has an enrollment of 243 student dentists and 59 advanced dental education students. There are 67 full-time faculty in the college for an excellent student/faculty ratio of 1:3.6.

MISSION

To promote oral health literacy, to improve oral and general health, and to reduce health disparities within Kentucky and beyond through teaching, research, and service.

Type of institution: Public	Doctoral dental degree offered: D.M.D.
Year opened: 1962	Targeted predoctoral enrollment: 260
Term type: Semester	Targeted entering class size: 65
Time to degree in months: 43	Campus setting: Urban
Start month: August	Campus housing available: Yes

PREPARATION

Formal minimum preparation in semester/quarter hours: Semester: 120
Baccalaureate degree preferred: Yes
Number of first-year, first-time enrollees whose highest degree is:
    Baccalaureate: 58
    Master's degree and beyond: 7
Of first-year, first-time enrollees without baccalaureates, the number with:
    Equivalent of 60 undergraduate credit hours or less: 0
    Equivalent of 61–90 undergraduate credit hours: 0
    Equivalent of 91 or more undergraduate credit hours: 1

PREREQUISITE COURSE	REQUIRED	RECOMMENDED	LAB REQUIRED	CREDITS (SEMESTER/QUARTER)
BCP (biology-chemistry-physics) sciences				
Biology	✓		✓	2 semesters
Chemistry, general/inorganic	✓		✓	2 semesters
Chemistry, organic	✓		✓	2 semesters
Physics	✓		✓	1 semester
Additional biological sciences				
Anatomy		✓		
Biochemistry	✓			1 semester
Cell biology		✓		
Histology		✓		
Immunology		✓		
Microbiology	✓			1 semester
Molecular biology/genetics		✓		
Physiology		✓		
Zoology				

PREPARATION (CONTINUED)

PREREQUISITE COURSE	REQUIRED	RECOMMENDED	LAB REQUIRED	CREDITS (SEMESTER/QUARTER)
Other				
English	✓			2 semesters

Community college coursework accepted for prerequisites: Yes
Community college coursework accepted for electives: No
Limits on community college credit hours: Yes
Maximum number of community college credit hours: 60
Advanced placement (AP) credit accepted for prerequisites: Yes
Advanced placement (AP) credit accepted for electives: No
Job shadowing: Required
Number of hours of job shadowing required or recommended: 20 hours minimum
Other factors considered in admission: Noncognitive factors

DAT

Mandatory: Yes
Latest DAT for consideration of application: 12/01/2015
Oldest DAT considered: 01/01/2012
When more than one DAT score is reported: Highest score is considered
Canadian DAT accepted: Yes
Application considered before DAT scores are submitted: No

DAT: 2014 ENTERING CLASS

ENROLLEE DAT SCORES	MEAN	RANGE
Academic Average	19.0	16–23
Perceptual Ability	19.0	14–24
Total Science	18.7	16–24

GPA: 2014 ENTERING CLASS

ENROLLEE GPA SCORES	UNDERGRAD. MEAN	GRADUATE MEAN	UNDERGRAD. RANGE	GRADUATE RANGE
Science GPA	3.40	3.51	2.11–4.00	2.91–4.00
Total GPA	3.51	3.50	2.50–4.00	3.00–3.76

APPLICATION AND SELECTION

TIMETABLE

Earliest filing date: 06/02/2015
Latest filing date: 12/01/2015
Earliest date for acceptance offers: 12/01/2015
Maximum time in days for applicant's response to acceptance offer:
    30 days if accepted on or after December 1
    15 days if accepted on or after February 1
Requests for deferred entrance considered: In exceptional
    circumstances only
Fee for application: Yes, submitted only when requested
Amount of fee for application:
    In state: $75   Out of state: $75   International: $75
Fee waiver available: No

	FIRST DEPOSIT	SECOND DEPOSIT	THIRD DEPOSIT
Required to hold place	Yes	No	No
Resident amount	$250		
Nonresident amount	$1,000		
Deposit due	As indicated in admission offer		
Applied to tuition	Yes		
Refundable	No		

APPLICATION PROCESS

Participates in Associated American Dental Schools Application Service (AADSAS): Yes
Accepts direct applicants: No
Secondary or supplemental application required: Yes, only when contacted
Secondary or supplemental application website: No
Interview is mandatory: Yes
Interview is by invitation: Yes

RESIDENCY

In-state/in-province versus out-of-state/out-of-province
Admissions process distinguishes between in-state/in-province and out-of-state/out-of-province applicants: Yes
Preference given to residents of: Kentucky
Reciprocity Admissions Agreement available for legal residents of: None
Generally and over time, percentage of your first-year enrollment that is in-state: 65%
Origin of out-of-state/out-of-province enrollees: CA-1, FL-5, GA-3, IL-1, IN-2, MA-1, MD-1, MI-2, OH-6, SC-1, TN-1, TX-5

International
Applications are accepted from international (noncitizens/ nonpermanent residents): Yes
Origin of international enrollees: NA

APPLICATION AND ENROLLMENT	NUMBER OF APPLICANTS	ESTIMATED NUMBER INTERVIEWED	ESTIMATED NUMBER ENROLLED
In-state or province applicants/ enrollees	152	93	37
Out-of-state or province applicants/enrollees	1,578	119	29
International applicants/enrollees (noncitizens/nonpermanent residents)	71	11	0

DEMOGRAPHIC DESCRIPTIONS OF APPLICANTS: 2014 ENTERING CLASS

	APPLICANTS			ENROLLEES		
	M	W	Gender Unknown or Not Reported	M	W	Gender Unknown or Not Reported
American Indian or Alaska Native	2	3	0	1	0	0
Asian	193	188	4	6	3	0
Black or African American	15	42	2	0	3	0
Hispanic or Latino	43	70	0	0	3	0
Native Hawaiian or Other Pacific Islander	2	0	0	0	0	0
White	618	464	4	21	24	0
Two or more races	17	25	2	1	4	0
Race and ethnicity unknown	21	15	3	0	0	0
International	38	32	1	0	0	0

	MINIMUM	MAXIMUM	MEAN
2014 entering class enrollees by age	19	38	21

CURRICULUM

The College of Dentistry's program integrates basic science, preclinical lab, technique, clinical and related courses throughout the curriculum. Basic science courses begin at enrollment. Clinical course time and patient contact start early in the first year and expand as the basic science and preclinical curriculum decreases. The dental curriculum has four primary areas of study: basic sciences, behavioral sciences, preclinical dentistry and clinical dentistry. The basic sciences, such as anatomy, biochemistry and pharmacology, as well as the didactic portion of the preclinical courses, are taught mainly by lecture, seminar, some self-instruction or any combination of these teaching methods. The technical skills of the preclinical subjects, such as restorations, denture construction and periodontal therapy, are taught in laboratory and clinical settings.

Student research opportunities: Yes

SPECIAL PROGRAMS AND SERVICES

PREDENTAL
Open House
Sim Lab Experience

DURING DENTAL SCHOOL
Academic counseling and tutoring
Community service opportunities
Internships, externships and extramural programs
Mentoring
Professional- and career-development programming
Summer enrichment program

ACTIVE STUDENT ORGANIZATIONS
American Association for Dental Research National Student Research Group
American Association of Women Dentists
American Association of Public Health Dentistry
American Dental Education Association
American Student Dental Association
Hispanic Dental Association
Student National Dental Association
Student Professionalism and Ethics Association in Dentistry

INTERNATIONAL DENTISTS
Graduates of international dental schools considered for traditional predoctoral program: Yes
Advanced standing program offered for graduates of international dental schools: No

COMBINED AND ALTERNATE DEGREES

Ph.D.	M.S.	M.P.H.	M.D.	B.A./B.S.	Other
—	—	—	—	—	—

COSTS: 2014–15 SCHOOL YEAR

	FIRST YEAR	SECOND YEAR	THIRD YEAR	FOURTH YEAR
Tuition, resident	$28,800	$28,800	$28,800	$28,800
Tuition, nonresident	$60,240	$60,240	$60,240	$60,240
Tuition, other				
Fees	$1,388	$1,388	$1,388	$1,388
Instruments, books, and supplies	$11,212	$9,682	$4,556	$6,322
Estimated living expenses	$22,300	$22,300	$22,300	$22,300
Total, resident	$63,700	$62,170	$57,044	$58,810
Total, nonresident	$95,140	$93,610	$88,484	$90,250
Total, other				

FINANCIAL AID

FINANCIAL AID AWARDS TO FIRST-YEAR STUDENTS 2014–15

Total number of first-year recipients: 65
Percentage of the first-year class: 96%
Percentage of awards that are grants? 0%
Percentage of awards that are loans? 89%

	AVERAGE AWARDS	RANGE OF AWARDS
Residents	$47,516	$1,200–$65,444
Nonresidents	$74,109	$1,000–$95,640

For more information, please visit: http://www.mc.uky.edu/Dentistry/financial-aid

UNIVERSITY OF LOUISVILLE
SCHOOL OF DENTISTRY

John J. Sauk, D.D.S., M.S., Dean

CONTACT INFORMATION

www.dental.louisville.edu/dental

501 S. Preston Street
Louisville, KY 40202
Phone: 502-852-5081

ADMISSIONS

Ms. Robin R. Benningfield
Admissions Counselor
Room 234, School of Dentistry
501 S. Preston Street
Louisville, KY 40202
Phone: 502-852-5081
Email: dmdadms@louisville.edu

FINANCIAL AID

Ms. Barbara Dagnan
Financial Aid Coordinator
Room 230, HSC Instructional Building
Louisville, KY 40202
Phone: 502-852-5076
Email: dmdadms@louisville.edu

STUDENT AFFAIRS

Ms. Dianne Foster
Assistant Dean for Student Affairs
Room 234, School of Dentistry
501 S. Preston Street
Louisville, KY 40202
Phone: 502-852-5081
Email: dmdadms@louisville.edu

MINORITY AFFAIRS

Dr. Sherry Babbage
Diversity & Inclusion Coordinator
Room 234, School of Dentistry
501 S. Preston Street
Louisville, KY 40202
Phone: 502-852-5081
Email: dmdadms@louisville.edu

HOUSING

Ms. Shannon Staten
Director of Residence Administration
Phone: 502-852-6636
Email: shannon.staten@louisville.edu
http://louisville.edu/housing

INTERNATIONAL CENTER

Ms. Sharolyn Pepper
International Student Coordinator
Phone: 502-852-6602
Email: pepper@louisville.edu
www.louisville.edu/internationalcenter

GENERAL INFORMATION

Offering outstanding clinical education through state-of-the art simulation education, technology and leadership in biomedical research, the University of Louisville School of Dentistry (ULSD) considers students partners in learning and seeks to provide them with the knowledge and skills they need to meet the challenges of today's diverse dental profession. Many ULSD graduates choose to practice general dentistry, while others continue their education in a specialty, engage in dental research or prepare for a career in education. A state-supported institution, ULSD is located within the University Health Sciences Center (HSC) in downtown Louisville (metropolitan population of more than one million). A total renovation of ULSD's clinics and classrooms, including the addition of state-of-the-art technology, was completed in fall 2011.

MISSION

Through excellence in teaching and research, we educate competent dental professionals, provide quality dental care and serve the community to fulfill urban and statewide missions.

Vision:

- Educate competent oral health practitioners.
- Provide lifelong learning opportunities.
- Promote mutual trust and respect in an environment of inclusiveness.
- Advance knowledge through research.
- Serve communities.

Type of institution: Public	Doctoral dental degree offered: D.M.D.
Year opened: 1887	Targeted predoctoral enrollment: 478
Term type: Semester	Targeted entering class size: 120
Time to degree in months: 46	Campus setting: Urban
Start month: July	Campus housing available: Yes

PREPARATION

Formal minimum preparation in semester/quarter hours: Semester: 90   Quarter: 120
Baccalaureate degree preferred: Yes
Number of first-year, first-time enrollees whose highest degree is:
   Baccalaureate: 109
   Master's degree and beyond: 8
Of first-year, first-time enrollees without baccalaureates, the number with:
   Equivalent of 60 undergraduate credit hours or less: 0
   Equivalent of 61–90 undergraduate credit hours: 0
   Equivalent of 91 or more undergraduate credit hours: 2

PREREQUISITE COURSE	REQUIRED	RECOMMENDED	LAB REQUIRED	CREDITS (SEMESTER/QUARTER)
BCP (biology-chemistry-physics) sciences				
Biology	✓		✓	16/24
Chemistry, general/inorganic	✓		✓	8/12
Chemistry, organic	✓		✓	8/12
Physics	✓	✓		3/5
Additional biological sciences				
Anatomy		✓		4/6
Biochemistry		✓		4/6
Cell biology		✓		4/6
Histology		✓		4/6
Immunology		✓		4/6

(Prerequisite Courses continued)

PREPARATION (CONTINUED)

PREREQUISITE COURSE	REQUIRED	RECOMMENDED	LAB REQUIRED	CREDITS (SEMESTER/QUARTER)
Microbiology		✓		4/6
Molecular biology/genetics		✓		4/6
Physiology		✓		4/6
Zoology		✓		4/6

Community college coursework accepted for prerequisites: Yes
Community college coursework accepted for electives: Yes
Limits on community college credit hours: Yes
Maximum number of community college credit hours: 60
Advanced placement (AP) credit accepted for prerequisites: Yes
Advanced placement (AP) credit accepted for electives: Yes
Comments regarding AP credit: Accepted by ULSD if accepted by institution granting under-graduate degree
Job shadowing: Highly recommended shadowing in general dentistry
Number of hours of job shadowing required or recommended: Minimum of 40 hours highly recommended
Other factors considered in admission: Social awareness, volunteerism, critical thinking, ethical reasoning and community service

DAT

Mandatory: Yes
Latest DAT for consideration of application: 02/01/2016
Oldest DAT considered: 06/01/2013
When more than one DAT score is reported: Most recent score is considered.
Canadian DAT accepted: Yes
Application considered before DAT scores are submitted: No

DAT: 2014 ENTERING CLASS

ENROLLEE DAT SCORES	MEAN	RANGE
Academic Average	19.3	16–24
Perceptual Ability	19.4	15–25
Total Science	19.1	16–26

GPA: 2014 ENTERING CLASS

ENROLLEE GPA SCORES	MEAN	RANGE
Science GPA	3.45	2.19–4.03
Total GPA	3.55	2.23–4.02

APPLICATION AND SELECTION

TIMETABLE

Earliest filing date: 06/02/2015
Latest filing date: 01/01/2016
Earliest date for acceptance offers: 12/01/2015
Maximum time in days for applicant's response to acceptance offer:
    30 days if accepted on or after December 1
    15 days if accepted on or after February 1
Requests for deferred entrance considered: In exceptional circumstances only.
Fee for application: Yes, submitted only after email request is sent from ULSD.

Amount of fee for application:
    In state: $65   Out of state: $65   International: $65
Fee waiver available: No

	FIRST DEPOSIT	SECOND DEPOSIT	THIRD DEPOSIT
Required to hold place	Yes	No	No
Resident amount	$200		
Nonresident amount	$1,000		
Deposit due	As indicated in admission offer		
Applied to tuition	Yes		
Refundable	No		

APPLICATION PROCESS

Participates in Associated American Dental Schools Application Service (AADSAS): Yes
Accepts direct applicants: No
Secondary or supplemental application required: No
Interview is mandatory: Yes
Interview is by invitation: Yes

RESIDENCY

In-state/in-province versus out-of-state/out-of-province
Admissions process distinguishes between in-state/in-province and out-of-state/out-of-province applicants: Yes
Preference given to residents of: Kentucky
Reciprocity Admissions Agreement available for legal residents of: Arkansas
Generally and over time, percentage of your first-year enrollment that is in-state: 37%
Origin of out-of-state/out-of-province enrollees: AL-4, AR-1, AZ-1, CA-4, CO-1, CT-1, FL-3, GA-6, IA-1, ID-3, IL-2, IN-11, MI-3, NC-1, NE-1, NJ-1, OH-4, SC-1, TN-9, UT-16, WI-1

International
Applications are accepted from international (noncitizens/nonpermanent residents): Yes
Origin of international enrollees: India-1

APPLICATION AND ENROLLMENT	NUMBER OF APPLICANTS	ESTIMATED NUMBER INTERVIEWED	ESTIMATED NUMBER ENROLLED
In-state or province applicants/enrollees	154	102	42
Out-of-state or province applicants/enrollees	2,824	332	76
International applicants/enrollees (noncitizens/nonpermanent residents)	138	7	1

DEMOGRAPHIC DESCRIPTIONS OF APPLICANTS: 2014 ENTERING CLASS

	APPLICANTS			ENROLLEES		
	M	W	Gender Unknown or Not Reported	M	W	Gender Unknown or Not Reported
American Indian or Alaska Native	2	7	0	0	0	0
Asian	323	323	8	10	3	0
Black or African American	46	69	1	2	1	0
Hispanic or Latino	86	98	0	4	5	0
Native Hawaiian or Other Pacific Islander	1	3	0	0	0	0
White	1,123	712	10	57	31	1
Two or more races	46	42	2	2	1	0
Race and ethnicity unknown	35	34	7	1	0	0
International	74	60	4	0	1	0

	MINIMUM	MAXIMUM	MEAN
2014 entering class enrollees by age	22	35	24

CURRICULUM

The evidence-based curriculum is designed to develop competent practitioners, some of who may seek advanced or specialty training. The first two years focus on basic science and preclinical instruction. The following two years emphasize patient care augmented by further education in all clinical disciplines, as well as strengthening professional values. The treatment of patients occurs in the group-based comprehensive general practice clinic, specialty clinics and extramural rotations, providing the student with experience in treating a diverse population of patients in a variety of settings. Extramural experiences may also include delivering oral health care through agencies such as the U.S. Public Health Service and the Indian Health Service. Elective courses permit the student to pursue more in-depth knowledge in different aspects of the profession.

SPECIAL PROGRAMS AND SERVICES

PREDENTAL

Summer Medical and Dental Education Program
DAT workshops
Other summer enrichment programs

DURING DENTAL SCHOOL

Academic counseling and tutoring
Community service opportunities
International health service and exchange program opportunities
Internships, externships and extramural programs
Mentoring
Personal counseling
Professional- and career-development programming
Transfer applicants considered if space is available

ACTIVE STUDENT ORGANIZATIONS

Alpha Omega International Dental Fraternity
American Association of Women Dentists
American Dental Education Association
American Student Dental Association
Christian Medical and Dental Society
Hispanic Student Dental Association
Psi Omega
Student National Dental Association
Student Professionalism and Ethics Association in Dentistry
Student Remote Area Medical Association

INTERNATIONAL DENTISTS

Graduates of international dental schools considered for traditional predoctoral program: Yes
Advanced standing program offered for graduates of international dental schools: Yes, Advanced Standing Placement option
Advanced Standing Placement description: The University of Louisville School of Dentistry (ULSD) offers Advanced Standing Placement in the traditional D.M.D. program for selected individuals who have received their dental degree from an institution outside the United States or Canada. Advanced standing admission is dependent upon the school's available resources.

COMBINED AND ALTERNATE DEGREES

Ph.D.	M.S.	M.P.H.	M.D.	B.A./B.S.	Other
✓	✓	—	—	—	—

COSTS: 2014–15 SCHOOL YEAR

	FIRST YEAR	SECOND YEAR	THIRD YEAR	FOURTH YEAR
Tuition, resident	$29,972	$29,972	$29,972	$29,972
Tuition, nonresident	$62,474	$62,474	$62,474	$62,474
Tuition, other				
Fees	$7,660	$7,660	$7,660	$7,660
Instruments, books, and supplies	$1,500	$1,266	$1,000	$3,234
Estimated living expenses	$23,016	$23,016	$23,016	$19,180
Total, resident	$62,148	$61,914	$61,648	$60,046
Total, nonresident	$94,650	$94,416	$94,150	$92,548
Total, other				

FINANCIAL AID

Approximately 90% of all dental students receive some form of financial aid. Both scholarships and loans are offered, although the majority of financial aid comes in the form of student loans. Most financial aid is federally based and is available only to U.S. citizens or qualified nonresidents. All applicants for federal student aid must annually submit a Free Application for Federal Aid (FASFA). A student's financial aid award cannot exceed the cost of attendance. Cost of attendance is a standard figure computed for each category of student and includes:

- Tuition and fees.
- Dental instrument rental.
- Books and supplies.
- Personal and living expenses.

Federal regulations require that coast of attendance be based on the student only and not include the student's family.

FINANCIAL AID AWARDS TO FIRST-YEAR STUDENTS 2014–15

Total number of first-year recipients: 107
Percentage of the first-year class: 90%
Percentage of awards that are grants? 33%
Percentage of awards that are loans? 67%

	AVERAGE AWARDS	RANGE OF AWARDS
Residents	$46,662	$1,000–$62,148
Nonresidents	$82,980	$3,100–$94,650

For more information, please visit: http://louisville.edu/dentistry/financialaid

LOUISIANA STATE UNIVERSITY HEALTH NEW ORLEANS
SCHOOL OF DENTISTRY

Henry A. Gremillion, D.D.S., Dean

School of Dentistry

GENERAL INFORMATION

The Louisiana State University School of Dentistry (LSUSD) admitted its first class in September 1968. The $16 million dental school building was dedicated in 1972. The dental school complex provides excellent basic sciences, preclinical and clinical facilities. The School of Dentistry is a public, state-supported institution and is an integral part of the Louisiana State University (LSU) Health Sciences Center in New Orleans. The school serves as a center for education, research and service related to oral health for the state of Louisiana and, as such, offers a variety of educational opportunities, including advanced education and programs in dental hygiene and dental laboratory technology.

MISSION

To serve the needs of Louisiana's citizens by educating future general dentists, specialists and allied dental professionals to provide excellent and current health care.

Vision:

- Lead research into new disease prevention and management approaches.
- Develop innovative treatment modalities.
- Expedite knowledge transfer for clinical use and to enhance health care delivery.

Type of institution: Public
Year opened: 1968
Term type: Academic Year
Time to degree in months: 48
Start month: July

Doctoral dental degree offered: D.D.S.
Targeted predoctoral enrollment: 260
Targeted entering class size: 65
Campus setting: Urban
Campus housing available: Yes

PREPARATION

Formal minimum preparation in semester/quarter hours: Semester: 90
Baccalaureate degree preferred: Yes
Number of first-year, first-time enrollees whose highest degree is:
    Baccalaureate: 60
    Master's degree and beyond: 5
Of first-year, first-time enrollees without baccalaureates, the number with:
    Equivalent of 60 undergraduate credit hours or less: 0
    Equivalent of 61–90 undergraduate credit hours: 0
    Equivalent of 91 or more undergraduate credit hours: 0

PREREQUISITE COURSE	REQUIRED	RECOMMENDED	LAB REQUIRED	CREDITS (SEMESTER/QUARTER)
BCP (biology-chemistry-physics) sciences				
Biology	✓		✓	12/18
Chemistry, general/inorganic	✓		✓	8/12
Chemistry, organic	✓		✓	8/12
Physics	✓		✓	8/12
Additional biological sciences				
Anatomy		✓		3/6
Biochemistry	✓			3/6
Cell biology		✓		3/6
Histology		✓		3/6
Immunology		✓		3/6
Microbiology	✓			3/6
Molecular biology/genetics		✓		3/6
Physiology		✓		3/6

(Prerequisite Courses continued)

PREPARATION (CONTINUED)

PREREQUISITE COURSE	REQUIRED	RECOMMENDED	LAB REQUIRED	CREDITS (SEMESTER/QUARTER)
Other				
English	✓			9 hours

Community college coursework accepted for prerequisites: Yes
Community college coursework accepted for electives: Yes
Limits on community college credit hours: No
Advanced placement (AP) credit accepted for prerequisites: Yes
Advanced placement (AP) credit accepted for electives: Yes
Job shadowing: Required
Number of hours of job shadowing required or recommended: Minimum of 50 hours. Seventeen hours each at three different general dentists' offices.

DAT

Mandatory: Yes
Latest DAT for consideration of application: 10/01/2015
Oldest DAT considered: 10/01/2011
When more than one DAT score is reported: Latest score is considered
Canadian DAT accepted: No
Application considered before DAT scores are submitted: No

DAT: 2014 ENTERING CLASS

ENROLLEE DAT SCORES	MEAN	RANGE
Academic Average	19.8	18–27
Perceptual Ability	20.1	15–25
Total Science	19.6	17–28

GPA: 2014 ENTERING CLASS

ENROLLEE GPA SCORES	UNDERGRAD. MEAN	GRADUATE MEAN	UNDERGRAD. RANGE	GRADUATE RANGE
Science GPA	3.56	3.44	2.72–4.00	3.06–3.83
Total GPA	3.64	3.51	2.87–4.00	3.06–3.84

APPLICATION AND SELECTION

TIMETABLE

Earliest filing date: 06/02/2015
Latest filing date: 09/01/2015
Earliest date for acceptance offers: 12/01/2015
Maximum time in days for applicant's response to acceptance offer:
    30 days if accepted on or after December 1
    15 days if accepted on or after February 1
Requests for deferred entrance considered: No
Fee for application: Yes
Amount of fee for application:
    In state: $175   Out of state: $175   International: NA
Fee waiver available: No

	FIRST DEPOSIT	SECOND DEPOSIT	THIRD DEPOSIT
Required to hold place	Yes	No	No
Resident amount	$200		
Nonresident amount	$200		
Deposit due	As indicated in admission offer		
Applied to tuition	Yes		
Refundable	No		

APPLICATION PROCESS

Participates in Associated American Dental Schools Application Service (AADSAS): Yes
Accepts direct applicants: No
Secondary or supplemental application required: Yes, by invitation only
Secondary or supplemental application website: Sent by Admissions Office
Interview is mandatory: Yes
Interview is by invitation: Yes

RESIDENCY

In-state/in-province versus out-of-state/out-of-province
Admissions process distinguishes between in-state/in-province and out-of-state/out-of-province applicants: Yes
Preference given to residents of: Louisiana
Reciprocity Admissions Agreement available for legal residents of: Arkansas
Generally and over time, percentage of your first-year enrollment that is in-state: 86%
Origin of out-of-state/out-of-province enrollees: AR-3, IL-1, IN-1, MS-1, NY-1

International
Applications are accepted from international (noncitizens/nonpermanent residents): No
Origin of international enrollees: NA

APPLICATION AND ENROLLMENT	NUMBER OF APPLICANTS	ESTIMATED NUMBER INTERVIEWED	ESTIMATED NUMBER ENROLLED
In-state or province applicants/enrollees	180	93	58
Out-of-state or province applicants/enrollees	474	40	7
International applicants/enrollees (noncitizens/nonpermanent residents)	5	0	0

DEMOGRAPHIC DESCRIPTIONS OF APPLICANTS: 2014 ENTERING CLASS

	APPLICANTS			ENROLLEES		
	M	W	Gender Unknown or Not Reported	M	W	Gender Unknown or Not Reported
American Indian or Alaska Native	2	2	0	1	0	0
Asian	72	71	0	4	3	0
Black or African American	8	31	0	0	3	0
Hispanic or Latino	16	26	1	2	4	0
Native Hawaiian or Other Pacific Islander	0	0	0	0	0	0
White	221	175	1	24	21	0
Two or more races	10	6	0	0	1	0
Race and ethnicity unknown	6	5	1	1	1	0
International	3	2	0	0	0	0

	MINIMUM	MAXIMUM	MEAN
2014 entering class enrollees by age	20	43	23

CURRICULUM

LSUSD follows a vertical curriculum providing a blend of basic, clinical, and behavioral sciences and practice management. This approach allows early introduction to clinical experience and integration of basic science material into the clinical curriculum.

Year 1: Basic sciences, preclinical technical courses and behavioral science with clinical experience in oral diagnostics.

Year 2: Continuation of basic sciences and preclinical technical courses with clinical patient treatment in operative dentistry, oral diagnosis and periodontics.

Year 3: Clinical didactic courses and clinical patient treatment in a comprehensive care format, which includes operative dentistry, fixed and removable prosthodontics, pediatric dentistry, periodontics, oral and maxillofacial surgery, orthodontics, oral diagnosis and endodontics.

Year 4: Total comprehensive patient care in general dentistry; elective courses available in many departments.

Student research opportunities: Yes, optional

SPECIAL PROGRAMS AND SERVICES

PREDENTAL
Mini Admissions Workshops
Predental 101-College Workshop
Summer enrichment programs

DURING DENTAL SCHOOL
Academic counseling/Mentoring and tutoring
Community service opportunities
Internships, externships, or extramural programs
Personal counseling
Transfer applicants considered if space is available and their reason is compelling

ACTIVE STUDENT ORGANIZATIONS
American Association for Dental Research National Student Research Group
American Dental Education Association
American Student Dental Association
Delta Sigma Delta International Fraternity
Student National Dental Association

INTERNATIONAL DENTISTS
Graduates of international dental schools considered for traditional predoctoral program: No
Advanced standing program offered for graduates of international dental schools: No

COMBINED AND ALTERNATE DEGREES

Ph.D.	M.S.	M.P.H.	M.D.	B.A./B.S.	Other
✓	—	—	—	—	—

COSTS: 2014–15 SCHOOL YEAR

	FIRST YEAR	SECOND YEAR	THIRD YEAR	FOURTH YEAR
Tuition, resident	$22,466	$22,466	$22,466	$22,466
Tuition, nonresident	$56,135	$56,135	$56,135	$56,135
Tuition, other				
Fees	$5,398	$5,744	$6,629	$7,613
Instruments, books, and supplies	$10,453	$7,150	$4,275	$3,275
Estimated living expenses	$21,791	$21,791	$21,791	$21,791
Total, resident	$60,109	$57,151	$55,161	$55,145
Total, nonresident	$93,777	$90,820	$88,830	$88,814
Total, other				

FINANCIAL AID

The Student Financial Aid Office administers grants, loans, scholarships and part-time employment. Students interested in receiving financial aid should contact this office well in advance of their expected enrollment. Each student's need will be evaluated on information supplied and in accordance with the Financial Aid Policy of the Health Sciences Center.

Although the primary responsibility for financing an education rests with the student and the student's immediate family, it is recognized that many students require additional assistance in order to meet their educational costs.

Awards from aid programs funded by the federal or State governments are administered according to laws and regulations governing those programs. Priority is given to students with the greatest documented need whose completed applications are received by the appropriate deadline.

FINANCIAL AID AWARDS TO FIRST-YEAR STUDENTS 2014–15

Total number of first-year recipients: 57
Percentage of the first-year class: 87.69%
Percentage of awards that are grants? 6.12%
Percentage of awards that are loans? 93.88%

	AVERAGE AWARDS	RANGE OF AWARDS
Residents	$47,273	$500–$60,916
Nonresidents	$80,358	$61,978–$94,585

For more information, please visit: http://www.lsuhsc.edu/FinancialAid/

UNIVERSITY OF NEW ENGLAND
COLLEGE OF DENTAL MEDICINE

James B. Hanley, D.M.D., Dean

CONTACT INFORMATION

www.une.edu/dentalmedicine

716 Stevens Avenue
Portland, ME 04103
Phone: 207-221-4700
Fax: 207-523-1915

GRADUATE & PROFESSIONAL ADMISSIONS

Mr. Isaac Stickney
Graduate Admissions Counselor
716 Stevens Avenue
Portland, ME 04103
Phone: 207-221-4480
Fax: 207-523-1925
Email: gradadmissions@une.edu
www.une.edu/dentalmedicine/admissions

FINANCIAL AID

Ms. Kendra St. Gelais
Assistant Director of Financial Aid
716 Stevens Avenue
Portland, ME 04103
Phone: 207-602-2342
Fax: 207-221-4890
Email: finaid@une.edu
www.une.edu/financialaid

GRADUATE & PROFESSIONAL STUDENT AFFAIRS

Mr. Ray Handy
Assistant Dean of Students
716 Stevens Avenue
Portland, ME 04103
Phone: 207-221-4213
Fax: 207-523-1903
Email: rhandy@une.edu
www.une.edu/studentlife/portland

MINORITY AFFAIRS/DIVERSITY

Ms. Donna Gaspar
Director of Multicultural Affairs
11 Hills Beach Road
Biddeford, ME 04005
Phone: 207-602-2461
Fax: 207-602-5980
Email: dgaspar@une.edu
www.une.edu/studentlife/multicultural

HOUSING

Mr. Travis Erikson
Director, Student and Community Life
716 Stevens Avenue
Portland, ME 04103
Phone: 207-221-4213
Fax: 207-523-1903
Email: terickson@une.edu
www.une.edu/studentlife/portland

GENERAL INFORMATION

The University of New England College of Dental Medicine (UNE-CDM) matriculated its inaugural class in August 2013.

A top-ranked independent, coeducational, nonprofit university and leading provider of health care professionals in Maine, UNE has recognized strengths in osteopathic medicine; in health, biological, marine and environmental sciences; and in select areas of the liberal arts.

Three original colleges—St. Francis College, The New England College of Osteopathic Medicine, and Westbrook College (with a history dating to 1831)—formed UNE, which has six academic units on two campuses:

- The College of Osteopathic Medicine and the College of Arts and Sciences (Biddeford)
- The Westbrook College of Health Professions, the Center for Public and Community Health, the College of Pharmacy and the College of Dental Medicine (Portland)

MISSION

To improve the health of Northern New England and shape the future of dentistry through excellence in education, discovery and service.

Type of institution: Private
Year opened: 2013
Term type: Trimester
Time to degree in months: 46
Start month: August

Doctoral dental degree offered: D.M.D.
Targeted predoctoral enrollment: 128
Targeted entering class size: 64
Campus setting: Suburban
Campus housing available: No

PREPARATION

Formal minimum preparation in semester/quarter hours: Semester: 90 Quarter: 135
Baccalaureate degree preferred: Yes
Number of first-year, first-time enrollees whose highest degree is:
  Baccalaureate: 54
  Master's degree and beyond: 9
Of first-year, first-time enrollees without baccalaureates, the number with:
  Equivalent of 60 undergraduate credit hours or less: 0
  Equivalent of 61–90 undergraduate credit hours: 0
  Equivalent of 91 or more undergraduate credit hours: 1

PREREQUISITE COURSE	REQUIRED	RECOMMENDED	LAB REQUIRED	CREDITS (SEMESTER/QUARTER)
BCP (biology-chemistry-physics) sciences				
Biology	✓		✓	4/6
Chemistry, general/inorganic	✓		✓	4/6
Chemistry, organic	✓		✓	4/6
Physics		✓		
Additional biological sciences				
Anatomy		✓		
Biochemistry	✓			3/4
Cell biology		✓		
Histology		✓		
Immunology				
Microbiology	✓		✓	4/6
Molecular biology/genetics		✓		
Physiology		✓		

PREPARATION (CONTINUED)

PREREQUISITE COURSE	REQUIRED	RECOMMENDED	LAB REQUIRED	CREDITS (SEMESTER/QUARTER)
Zoology				
Other				
Additional biology, chemistry, and/or physics courses	✓			16/24
English composition/technical writing	✓			3/4
Business		✓		
Computers		✓		
Three-Dimensional art		✓		
Communications		✓		
Ethics		✓		

Community college coursework accepted for prerequisites: Yes
Community college coursework accepted for electives: Yes
Limits on community college credit hours: No
Maximum number of community college credit hours: NA
Advanced placement (AP) credit accepted for prerequisites: No
Advanced placement (AP) credit accepted for electives: No
Comments regarding AP credit: None
Job shadowing: Required
Number of hours of job shadowing required or recommended: 30
Other factors considered in admission: Demonstrated Community Service—Applicants must demonstrate community service through volunteerism or service-oriented employment.

DAT

Mandatory: Yes
Latest DAT for consideration of application: 10/15/2014
Oldest DAT considered: NA
When more than one DAT score is reported: We look at trends.
Canadian DAT accepted: Yes
Application considered before DAT scores are submitted: No

U.S. DAT: 2014 ENTERING CLASS

ENROLLEE DAT SCORES	MEAN	RANGE
Academic Average	18.2	16–23
Perceptual Ability	18.6	14–23
Total Science	17.9	15–23

CANADIAN DAT: 2014 ENTERING CLASS

ENROLLEE DAT SCORES	MEAN	RANGE
Academic Average	16	16–16
Manual Dexterity	NA	16–16
Perceptual Ability	16	16–16
Total Science	16	16–16

GPA: 2014 ENTERING CLASS

ENROLLEE GPA SCORES	UNDERGRAD. MEAN	GRADUATE MEAN	UNDERGRAD. RANGE	GRADUATE RANGE
Science GPA	3.21	3.43	2.65–3.91	2.82–4.00
Total GPA	3.33	3.47	2.81–3.91	2.90–4.00

APPLICATION AND SELECTION

TIMETABLE

Earliest filing date: 06/02/2015
Latest filing date: 11/01/2015
Earliest date for acceptance offers: 12/01/2015
Maximum time in days for applicant's response to acceptance offer: 30
Requests for deferred entrance considered: No
Fee for application: Yes
Amount of fee for application:
In state: $55   Out of state: $55   International: $55
Fee waiver available: No

	FIRST DEPOSIT	SECOND DEPOSIT	THIRD DEPOSIT
Required to hold place	Yes	Yes	No
Resident amount	$500	$1,500	
Nonresident amount	$500	$1,500	
Deposit due	30 days	03/01/15	
Applied to tuition	Yes	Yes	
Refundable	No	No	

APPLICATION PROCESS

Participates in Associated American Dental Schools Application Service (AADSAS): Yes
Accepts direct applicants: No
Secondary or supplemental application required: Yes
Secondary or supplemental application website: TBD
Interview is mandatory: Yes
Interview is by invitation: Yes

RESIDENCY

In-state/in-province versus out-of-state/out-of-province
Admissions process distinguishes between in-state/in-province and out-of-state/out-of-province applicants: No
Preference given to residents of: Maine, New Hampshire, Vermont
Reciprocity Admissions Agreement available for legal residents of: NA
Generally and over time, percentage of your first-year enrollment that is in-state: Not reported by institution
Origin of out-of-state/out-of-province enrollees: CO-1, CT-1, IA-1, IL-3, KS-1, MA-5, MD-2, MI-1, MN-1, NC-1, NH-5, NJ-3, NY-2, OH-2, PA-2, RI-5, TX-1, UT-2, VA-4, VT-2, WI-3

International
Applications are accepted from international (noncitizens/nonpermanent residents): Yes
Origin of international enrollees: Canada-1

APPLICATION AND ENROLLMENT	NUMBER OF APPLICANTS	ESTIMATED NUMBER INTERVIEWED	ESTIMATED NUMBER ENROLLED
In-state or province applicants/enrollees	35	34	15
Out-of-state or province applicants/enrollees	1,129	244	48
International applicants/enrollees	64	13	1

DEMOGRAPHIC DESCRIPTIONS OF APPLICANTS: 2014 ENTERING CLASS

	APPLICANTS			ENROLLEES		
	M	W	Gender Unknown or Not Reported	M	W	Gender Unknown or Not Reported
American Indian or Alaska Native	0	0	0	0	0	0
Asian	193	191	6	1	5	0
Black or African American	8	15	0	0	0	0
Hispanic or Latino	31	39	0	0	1	0
Native Hawaiian or Other Pacific Islander	0	2	0	0	0	0
White	362	239	4	28	21	0
Two or more races	17	18	0	2	1	0
Race and ethnicity unknown	15	21	3	1	3	0
International	31	33	0	1	0	0

	MINIMUM	MAXIMUM	MEAN
2014 entering class enrollees by age	21	38	25

CURRICULUM

Along with early and extensive clinical experiences, the program uses lectures, small group sessions, online courses and self-directed learning to deliver curriculum grounded in the biomedical and behavioral sciences.

The program, which emphasizes the linkages between basic, behavioral and clinical sciences and the clinical practice of dentistry (including principles of community and public health) provides extensive clinical education in UNE's main dental clinic and in community-based clinics and practices.

Beginning clinical experiences in the state-of-the-art simulation clinic by treating simulated patients with electronic records and digital images, students learn to evaluate health histories and develop and implement comprehensive treatment plans. Students also work in teams to learn and practice hands-on diagnosis and assessment skills on each other. Faculty-led group practices include student associates from each of the program's four years.

During the program, students:

- Begin to provide care to clinical patients in the latter part of the second year.
- Further develop their clinical knowledge and skills through the third year in the campus teaching clinic.
- Spend the majority of time in the fourth year providing oral health care in community-based clinics and practices throughout northern New England.

Student research opportunities: Yes

SPECIAL PROGRAMS AND SERVICES

DURING DENTAL SCHOOL

Academic counseling and tutoring
Community service opportunities (extensive)
Internships, externships, or extramural programs
Mentoring
Personal counseling
Professional- and career-development programming
Training for those interested in academic careers
Research opportunities

ACTIVE STUDENT ORGANIZATIONS

Graduate and Professional Student Association
American Student Dental Association

INTERNATIONAL DENTISTS

Graduates of international dental schools considered for traditional predoctoral program: Yes
Advanced standing program offered for graduates of international dental schools: No

COMBINED AND ALTERNATE DEGREES

Ph.D.	M.S.	M.P.H.	M.D.	B.A./B.S.	Other
—	—	—	—	—	—

ESTIMATED COSTS: 2014–15 SCHOOL YEAR

	FIRST YEAR	SECOND YEAR	THIRD YEAR	FOURTH YEAR
Tuition, resident	$58,540	$58,540	NA	NA
Tuition, nonresident	$58,540	$58,540	NA	NA
Tuition, other				
Fees	$15,255	$15,255	NA	NA
Program fee (instruments, books, and supplies, etc.)	$1,250	$1,250	NA	NA
Estimated living expenses	$16,290	$21,720	NA	NA
Total, resident	$91,335	$96,765	NA	NA
Total, nonresident	$91,335	$96,765	NA	NA
Total, other				

FINANCIAL AID

FINANCIAL AID AWARDS TO FIRST-YEAR STUDENTS 2014–15

Total number of first-year recipients: 55
Percentage of the first-year class: 86%
Percentage of awards that are grants? 0%
Percentage of awards that are loans? 100%

	AVERAGE AWARDS	RANGE OF AWARDS
Residents	$92,109	$74,253–$95,513
Nonresidents	$86,644	$40,500–$95,513

For more information, please visit: www.une.edu/sfs/graduate/costs/dental-medicine

CONTACT INFORMATION

www.dental.umaryland.edu
650 West Baltimore Street, 6-South
Baltimore, MD 21201

ADMISSIONS
Dr. Judith A. Porter
**Assistant Dean of Admissions
and Recruitment**
650 West Baltimore Street, 6-South
Room 6410
Baltimore, MD 21201
Phone: 410-706-7472

ACADEMIC AFFAIRS
Dr. Patricia E. Meehan
Associate Dean for Academic Affairs
650 West Baltimore Street, 6-South
Room 6408
Baltimore, MD 21201
Phone: 410-706-7461

STUDENT AFFAIRS
Dr. Karen Faraone
Assistant Dean for Student Affairs
650 West Baltimore Street, 6-South
Room 6414
Baltimore, MD 21201
Phone: 410-706-7461

RECRUITMENT AND STUDENT ADVOCACY
Dr. Andrea Morgan
**Dental Recruitment Coordinator
Director of Student Advocacy and
Cultural Affairs**
650 West Baltimore Street, 6-South
Room 6410
Baltimore, MD 21201
Phone: 410-706-7472

STUDENT FINANCIAL ASSISTANCE AND EDUCATION
601 West Lombard Street
Suite 221
Baltimore, MD 21201
Phone: 410-706-7347
Email: Aidtalk@umaryland.edu

HOUSING
518 West Fayette Street
Baltimore, MD 21201
Phone: 410-706-5523
Email: umbhousing@umaryland.edu
www.housing.umaryland.edu

UNIVERSITY OF MARYLAND
SCHOOL OF DENTISTRY
Mark Reynolds, D.D.S., Ph.D., M.A., Dean

GENERAL INFORMATION

Founded In 1840, the University of Maryland School of Dentistry (UMSOD) is a public institution that began as the Baltimore College of Dental Surgery, the first school in history to offer a course in dental education. UMSOD has maintained its position as a leader in dental education and offers a very strong curriculum, supported by well-trained, highly committed faculty. Biological and clinical science faculty are recognized as leaders in education, research and service. UMSOD enjoys the advantages of sharing an urban campus with the schools of Medicine, Law, Pharmacy, Nursing, and Social Work, and with the Veterans Administration and University Medical Centers. The new dental school facility, completed in and operational since the fall of 2006, is located in Baltimore's famous revitalized downtown center.

MISSION

To graduate exceptional health care professionals, advance the scientific basis of treatments for diseases of the oral and craniofacial complex, and deliver consistently outstanding health care.

Vision: To improve the quality of life—on a state, national and International level—through education, research and service focusing on dental, oral and craniofacial health.

Type of institution: Public	Doctoral dental degree offered: D.D.S.
Year opened: 1840	Targeted predoctoral enrollment: 520
Term type: Semester	Targeted entering class size: 130
Time to degree in months: 46	Campus setting: Urban
Start month: August	Campus housing available: Yes

PREPARATION

Formal minimum preparation in semester/quarter hours: Semester: 90   Quarter: 135
Baccalaureate degree preferred: Yes, baccalaureate degree strongly preferred
Number of first-year, first-time enrollees whose highest degree is:
  Baccalaureate: 112
  Master's degree and beyond: 18
Of first-year, first-time enrollees without baccalaureates, the number with:
  Equivalent of 60 undergraduate credit hours or less: 0
  Equivalent of 61–90 undergraduate credit hours: 0
  Equivalent of 91 or more undergraduate credit hours: 0

PREREQUISITE COURSE	REQUIRED	RECOMMENDED	LAB REQUIRED	CREDITS (SEMESTER/QUARTER)
BCP (biology-chemistry-physics) sciences				
Biology	✓		✓	8/12
Chemistry, general/inorganic	✓		✓	8/12
Chemistry, organic	✓		✓	8/12
Physics	✓		✓	8/12
Additional biological sciences				
Anatomy		✓		
Biochemistry	✓			3/5
Cell biology		✓		
Histology		✓		
Immunology		✓		
Microbiology		✓		
Molecular biology/genetics		✓		
Physiology		✓		

PREPARATION (CONTINUED)

PREREQUISITE COURSE	REQUIRED	RECOMMENDED	LAB REQUIRED	CREDITS (SEMESTER/QUARTER)
Zoology		✓		
Other				
English composition	✓			6/9

Community college coursework accepted for prerequisites: Yes
Community college coursework accepted for electives: Yes
Limits on community college credit hours: Yes
Maximum number of community college credit hours: 60
Advanced placement (AP) credit accepted for prerequisites: Yes
Advanced placement (AP) credit accepted for electives: Yes
Comments regarding AP credit: AP credits for prerequisites will be reviewed by the Admissions Committee.
Job shadowing: Highly recommended
Number of hours of job shadowing required or recommended: Minimum recommended is 100 hours
Other factors considered in admission: Academic performance, performance on the DAT, knowledge of the profession, personal statement, letters of recommendation, extracurricular activities including leadership and community service, the personal interview, and personal factors

DAT

Mandatory: Yes
Latest DAT for consideration of application: 12/01/2015
Oldest DAT considered: 01/01/2013
When more than one DAT score is reported: Most recent score only is considered
Canadian DAT accepted: Yes
Application considered before DAT scores are submitted: No

DAT: 2014 ENTERING CLASS

ENROLLEE DAT SCORES	MEAN	RANGE
Academic Average	20.6	18–27
Perceptual Ability	20.1	13–30
Total Science	20.3	17–26

GPA: 2014 ENTERING CLASS

ENROLLEE GPA SCORES	UNDERGRAD. MEAN	GRADUATE MEAN	UNDERGRAD. RANGE	GRADUATE RANGE
Science GPA	3.46	3.65	2.13–4.16	2.87–4.33
Total GPA	3.53	3.68	2.29–4.09	2.93–4.17

APPLICATION AND SELECTION

TIMETABLE

Earliest filing date: 06/02/2015
Latest filing date: 012/31/2015
Earliest date for acceptance offers: 12/01/2015
Maximum time in days for applicant's response to acceptance offer:
    30 days if accepted on or after December 1
    15 days if accepted on or after February 1
Requests for deferred entrance considered: In exceptional circumstances only.
Fee for application: Yes, submitted at same time as Associated American Dental Schools Application Service (AADSAS) application.
Amount of fee for application:
    In state: $85   Out of state: $85   International: $85
Fee waiver available: No

	FIRST DEPOSIT	SECOND DEPOSIT	THIRD DEPOSIT
Required to hold place	Yes	Yes	No
Resident amount	$1,000	$1,000	
Nonresident amount	$1,000	$1,000	
Deposit due	As indicated in offer letter	04/01/2016	
Applied to tuition	Yes	Yes	
Refundable	No	No	

APPLICATION PROCESS

Participates in AADSAS: Yes
Accepts direct applicants: No
Secondary or supplemental application required: Yes, by invitation
Secondary or supplemental application website: NA
Interview is mandatory: Yes
Interview is by invitation: Yes

RESIDENCY

In-state/in-province versus out-of-state/out-of-province
Admissions process distinguishes between in-state/in-province and out-of-state/out-of-province applicants: Yes
Preference given to residents of: Maryland
Reciprocity Admissions Agreement available for legal residents of: None
Generally and over time, percentage of your first-year enrollment that is in-state: UMSOD does not report this percentage.
Origin of out-of-state/out-of-province enrollees: AZ-1, CA-1, CO-1, DC-1, DE-2, FL-7, GA-1, HI-1, IL-1, MA-1, MI-2, MN-1, NC-4, NJ-3, NY-8, PA-6, TX-1, UT-1, VA-12, WA-1

International
Applications are accepted from international (noncitizens/nonpermanent residents): Yes
Origin of international enrollees: China-3, Taiwan-1

APPLICATION AND ENROLLMENT	NUMBER OF APPLICANTS	ESTIMATED NUMBER INTERVIEWED	ESTIMATED NUMBER ENROLLED
In-state or province applicants/enrollees	253	152	70
Out-of-state or province applicants/enrollees	2,240	333	56
International applicants/enrollees (noncitizens/nonpermanent residents)	127	13	4

DEMOGRAPHIC DESCRIPTIONS OF APPLICANTS: 2014 ENTERING CLASS

	APPLICANTS			ENROLLEES		
	M	W	Gender Unknown or Not Reported	M	W	Gender Unknown or Not Reported
American Indian or Alaska Native	1	0	0	0	0	0
Asian	385	434	7	9	16	0
Black or African American	39	94	2	5	16	0
Hispanic or Latino	66	89	0	3	4	0
Native Hawaiian or Other Pacific Islander	0	2	0	0	0	0
White	690	506	6	41	25	0
Two or more races	30	32	0	2	3	0
Race and ethnicity unknown	47	52	11	1	1	0
International	57	69	1	2	2	0

	MINIMUM	MAXIMUM	MEAN
2014 entering class enrollees by age	21	33	24

CURRICULUM

The D.D.S. program combines a strong base of biological sciences and an outstanding clinical education, with a focus on application of latest research findings. Working in a highly collegial manner, nationally recognized faculty provide excellent educational services for students. Students have the opportunity to use innovative educational methodologies, including online learning activities. The outstanding clinical education program, featuring patient-centered and student-centered general practices, simulates the structure of a dental practice. Various cooperative efforts with local, state and federal agencies also provide dental services for special-needs populations. Additionally, the UMSOD-Perryville is a satellite school staffed by faculty and students providing contemporary dental care to an underserved population in Cecil County and surrounding areas. This 26-chair facility is equipped with state-of-the-art equipment. Students engage in service learning experiences at this facility under the supervision of faculty. Dental graduates are well prepared to enter advanced dental education programs and to practice their professions in a wide range of private practice, public service and academic settings.

Student research opportunities: Yes

SPECIAL PROGRAMS AND SERVICES

PREDENTAL
Summer enrichment programs

DURING DENTAL SCHOOL
Academic counseling and tutoring
Community service opportunities
Internships, externships, or extramural programs
Mentoring
Advanced standing considered if space is available
Senior Selectives

ACTIVE STUDENT ORGANIZATIONS

American Association for Dental Research National Student Research Group
American Association of Pediatric Dentistry
American Association of Women Dentists
American Dental Education Association
American Student Dental Association
Hispanic Dental Association
Student National Dental Association

INTERNATIONAL DENTISTS

Graduates of international dental schools considered for traditional predoctoral program: No
Advanced standing program offered for graduates of international dental schools: Yes, in special circumstances
Advanced standing program description: UMSOD does not have a specific program designed for candidates seeking admission to the Doctor of Dental Surgery (D.D.S.) program with advanced standing. However, it may be possible for exceptionally talented graduates of non-U.S./non-Canadian dental schools or dental students currently enrolled in U.S./Canadian dental schools to gain admission to the University of Maryland's D.D.S. program with advanced standing.

COMBINED AND ALTERNATE DEGREES

Ph.D.	M.S.	M.P.H.	M.D.	B.A./B.S.	Other
✓	✓	✓	—	—	✓

Other degree: Master of Science in Clinical Research

COSTS: 2014–15 SCHOOL YEAR

	FIRST YEAR	SECOND YEAR	THIRD YEAR	FOURTH YEAR
Tuition, resident	$29,801	$29,801	$29,801	$29,801
Tuition, nonresident	$59,566	$59,566	$59,566	$59,566
Tuition, other				
Fees	$1,885	$1,885	$1,885	$1,885
Instruments, books, and supplies	$8,042	$5,658	$3,132	$2,532
Other costs	$21,500	$19,350	$25,800	$25,800
Estimated living expenses	$9,080	$9,080	$9,277	$9,537
Total, resident	$70,308	$65,774	$69,895	$69,555
Total, nonresident	$100,073	$95,539	$99,660	$99,320
Total, other				

FINANCIAL AID

Applicants are strongly encouraged to complete the Free Application for Federal Student Aid no later than March 1 each year. Students can complete the form using estimated income and asset information to meet the deadline and can make corrections once taxes have been filed.

FINANCIAL AID AWARDS TO FIRST-YEAR STUDENTS 2014–15

Total number of first-year recipients: 112
Percentage of the first-year class: 86%
Percentage of awards that are grants? 72%
Percentage of awards that are loans? 75%

	AVERAGE AWARDS	RANGE OF AWARDS
Residents	$40,500	Up to cost of attendance
Nonresidents	$65,000	Up to cost of attendance

For more information, please visit: http://www.umaryland.edu/fin/

BOSTON UNIVERSITY
HENRY M. GOLDMAN SCHOOL OF DENTAL MEDICINE

Jeffrey W. Hutter, D.M.D., M.Ed., Dean

CONTACT INFORMATION

www.bu.edu/dental

Boston University Henry M. Goldman
School of Dental Medicine
100 East Newton Street, G-305
Boston, MA 02118
Phone: 617-638-4787
Fax: 617-638-4798

ADMISSIONS

Ms. Catherine Sarkis
Assistant Dean for Admissions
Boston University Henry M. Goldman
School of Dental Medicine
100 East Newton Street, G-305
Boston, MA 02118
Phone: 617-638-4787
www.bu.edu/dental/admissions

STUDENT FINANCIAL SERVICES

Mr. Joseph Corbett and Mr. Emir Morais
Co-Directors ad interim
Boston University Medical Campus
72 East Concord Street, A-303
Boston, MA 02118
Phone: 617-638-5130
www.bumc.bu.edu/osfs

STUDENT AFFAIRS

Dr. Joseph Calabrese
Assistant Dean of Students
Boston University Henry M. Goldman
School of Dental Medicine
100 East Newton Street, G-305
Boston, MA 02118
Phone: 617-638-4790
http://www.bu.edu/dental/about/offices/
student-affairs/

MINORITY AFFAIRS/DIVERSITY

Dr. Larry G. Dunham
Director of Diversity and Multicultural Affairs
Boston University Henry M. Goldman
School of Dental Medicine
100 East Newton Street, G-305
Boston, MA 02118
Phone: 617-638-4738
www.bu.edu/dental/admissions

HOUSING RESOURCES

Ms. Barbara Attianese
Housing Resources Manager
Boston University Medical Campus
72 East Concord Street, A-303
Boston, MA 02118
Phone: 617-638-5125
www.bumc.bu.edu/ohr

INTERNATIONAL STUDENTS AND SCHOLARS OFFICE

Ms. Jeanne Kelley
Director
Boston University ISSO
888 Commonwealth Avenue
Boston, MA 02215
Phone: 617-353-3565
www.bu.edu/isso

GENERAL INFORMATION

Boston University Henry M. Goldman School of Dental Medicine (BU GSDM) is a forward-thinking educational institution that produces a highly competent dentist in a challenging and exciting environment. A comfortable class size combined with a dedicated, talented faculty provides an exceptionally stimulating educational experience. The curriculum successfully integrates the biomedical sciences with the clinical care of patients both within the school and in selected extramural sites. The Extramural Program, composed of an Applied Professional Experience (APEX) Program in the first year and an externship during the fourth year, provides students with practical clinical experience in preparation for their professional careers upon graduation.

MISSION

We will be the premier academic dental institution promoting excellence in dental education, research, oral health care and community service to improve the global population's overall health.

Vision: We will provide outstanding service to a diverse group of students, patients, faculty, staff, alumni and health care professionals within our facilities, our community and the world.

Type of institution: Private	Doctoral dental degree offered: D.M.D.
Year opened: 1963	Targeted predoctoral enrollment: 460
Term type: Semester	Targeted entering class size: 115
Time to degree in months: 48	Campus setting: Urban
Start month: July	Campus housing available: No

PREPARATION

Formal minimum preparation in semester/quarter hours: Semester: 120   Quarter: 200
Baccalaureate degree preferred: Yes, required
Number of first-year, first-time enrollees whose highest degree is:
    Baccalaureate: 83
    Master's degree and beyond: 18
Of first-year, first-time enrollees without baccalaureates, the number with:
    Equivalent of 60 undergraduate credit hours or less: 0
    Equivalent of 61–90 undergraduate credit hours: 0
    Equivalent of 91 or more undergraduate credit hours: 0

PREREQUISITE COURSE	REQUIRED	RECOMMENDED	LAB REQUIRED	CREDITS (SEMESTER/QUARTER)
BCP (biology-chemistry-physics) sciences				
Biology	✓		✓	12/18
Chemistry, general/inorganic	✓		✓	8/12
Chemistry, organic	✓		✓	8/12
Physics	✓		✓	8/12

(Prerequisite Courses continued)

PREPARATION (CONTINUED)

PREREQUISITE COURSE	REQUIRED	RECOMMENDED	LAB REQUIRED	CREDITS (SEMESTER/QUARTER)
Additional biological sciences				
Anatomy		✓		4/6
Biochemistry		✓		4/6
Cell biology		✓		4/6
Histology		✓		4/6
Immunology		✓		4/6
Microbiology		✓		4/6
Molecular biology/genetics		✓		4/6
Physiology		✓		4/6
Zoology		✓		4/6
Other				
Math with calculus	✓			8/12
English or composition	✓			8/12
Social sciences selections/ Humanities		✓		20/26
Economics, business		✓		4/6

Community college coursework accepted for prerequisites: No. Prerequisites only from four-year accredited U.S./Canada colleges.
Community college coursework accepted for electives: Yes
Limits on community college credit hours: Yes
Maximum number of community college credit hours: 30
Advanced placement (AP) credit accepted for prerequisites: No
Advanced placement (AP) credit accepted for electives: Yes
Comments regarding AP credit: Applicants with AP in prerequisites should take upper-level courses in the same field of study. Credits earned at an accredited four-year U.S./Canadian college or university should match or exceed the prerequisite requirement in the subject.
Job shadowing: Strongly recommended
Other factors considered in admission: Undergraduate record, quality and difficulty of courses taken, demonstrated leadership ability, motivation for the study of dentistry, references, DAT, extracurricular endeavors, community engagement and communication skills.

DAT

Mandatory: Yes
Latest DAT for consideration of application: 12/01/2015
Oldest DAT considered: 06/01/2013
When more than one DAT score is reported: Highest score is considered.
Canadian DAT accepted: Yes, carving section not required
Application considered before DAT scores are submitted: No

U.S. DAT: 2014 ENTERING CLASS

ENROLLEE DAT SCORES	MEAN	RANGE
Academic Average	19.8	17–25
Perceptual Ability	19.5	14–25
Total Science	19.7	17–24

CANADIAN DAT: 2014 ENTERING CLASS

ENROLLEE DAT SCORES	MEAN	RANGE
Academic Average	19.6	18–22
Manual Dexterity	NA	NA
Perceptual Ability	20.1	18–23
Total Science	20.3	18–23

GPA: 2014 ENTERING CLASS

ENROLLEE GPA SCORES	UNDERGRAD. MEAN	GRADUATE MEAN	UNDERGRAD. RANGE	GRADUATE RANGE
Science GPA	3.46	3.65	2.73–4.00	3.10–4.00
Total GPA	3.51	3.65	2.95–4.00	3.16–4.00

APPLICATION AND SELECTION

TIMETABLE

Earliest filing date: 06/02/2015
Latest filing date: 12/01/2015
Earliest date for acceptance offers: 12/01/2015
Maximum time in days for applicant's response to acceptance offer:
   30 days if accepted on or after December 1
   15 days if accepted on or after February 1
Requests for deferred entrance considered: Yes
Fee for application: Yes, submitted only when requested
Amount of fee for application:
   In state: $75   Out of state: $75   International: $105
Fee waiver available: Yes

	FIRST DEPOSIT	SECOND DEPOSIT	THIRD DEPOSIT
Required to hold place	Yes	No	No
Amount for all enrolling applicants	$3,000		
Deposit due	As indicated in admission offer		
Applied to tuition	Yes		
Refundable	No		

APPLICATION PROCESS

Participates in Associated American Dental Schools Application Service (AADSAS): Yes
Accepts direct applicants: No
Secondary or supplemental application required: Yes
Interview is mandatory: Yes
Interview is by invitation: Yes

RESIDENCY

In-state/in-province versus out-of-state/out-of-province
Admissions process distinguishes between in-state/in-province and out-of-state/out-of-province applicants: No
Preference given to residents of: None
Reciprocity Admissions Agreement available for legal residents of: None
Generally and over time, percentage of your first-year enrollment that is in-state: 25%
Origin of out-of-state/out-of-province enrollees: CA-3, CO-1, CT-4, FL-7, GA-5, IA-1, IN-2, LA-1, MO-1, NH-1, NJ-3, NY-12, OH-2, PA-1, RI-2, TN-1, TX-4, UT-1, VA-2, VT-1, WA-1, WI-2

International
Applications are accepted from international (noncitizens/nonpermanent residents): Yes
Origin of international enrollees: Canada-13 (AB -5, BC-2, MB-1, ON-5)

APPLICATION AND ENROLLMENT	NUMBER OF APPLICANTS	ESTIMATED NUMBER INTERVIEWED	ESTIMATED NUMBER ENROLLED
In-state or province applicants/enrollees	155	57	29
Out-of-state or province applicants/enrollees	3,453	160	59
International applicants/enrollees (noncitizens/nonpermanent residents)	507	28	13

DEMOGRAPHIC DESCRIPTIONS OF APPLICANTS: 2014 ENTERING CLASS

	APPLICANTS			ENROLLEES		
	M	W	Gender Unknown or Not Reported	M	W	Gender Unknown or Not Reported
American Indian or Alaska Native	1	2	0	0	0	0
Asian	631	713	14	17	11	0
Black or African American	26	56	3	1	1	0
Hispanic or Latino	113	163	2	2	6	0
Native Hawaiian or Other Pacific Islander	1	3	0	0	0	0
White	926	725	6	29	16	0
Two or more races	46	59	2	3	8	0
Race and ethnicity unknown	53	50	13	0	1	0
International	264	233	10	6	7	0

	MINIMUM	MAXIMUM	MEAN
2014 entering class enrollees by age	20	28	22

CURRICULUM

Integrated learning experiences provide the student with the ability to ultimately deliver the highest level of oral health care. Year 1 starts with biomedical science courses and an introduction to general dentistry. It continues with simulated dental experiences and culminates with APEX, an internship experience in a dental practice. Year 2 continues with biomedical and behavioral sciences, simulated dental experiences and clinical sciences. Emphasis is on integrating biomedical and behavioral sciences with clinical sciences. Years 3 and 4 focus on comprehensive patient care. Faculty mentors oversee clinical activities of students in a group practice model. A 10-week externship experience in Year 4 serves as a capstone activity that fosters students' development into independent clinical practitioners.

Student research opportunities: Yes

SPECIAL PROGRAMS AND SERVICES

PREDENTAL

Postbaccalaureate programs
Special affiliations with colleges and universities: Boston University School of Medicine Division of Graduate Medical Sciences - Master of Arts in Medical Sciences Concentration in Oral Health Sciences; Boston University College of Liberal Arts - 7 Year B.A./D.M.D.; Boston University Metropolitan College Postbaccalaureate Certificate in Premedical Studies

DURING DENTAL SCHOOL

Academic counseling and tutoring
Community service opportunities
Internships, externships, or extramural programs
Mentoring
Personal counseling
Professional- and career-development programming
Training for those interested in academic careers

ACTIVE STUDENT ORGANIZATIONS

Alpha Omega International Dental Fraternity

American Association for Dental Research National Student Research Group

American Association of Public Health Dentistry

American Association of Women Dentists

American Dental Education Association

American Student Dental Association, BU GSDM Chapter

BUMC Pride: Boston University Medical Campus LGBTQ+ and Allies

Multicultural dental associations, including Asian Dental Student Organization, Hispanic Student Dental Association, Muslim Student Association

Student National Dental Association

Uniformed Services Student Dental Association

INTERNATIONAL DENTISTS

Graduates of international dental schools considered for traditional predoctoral program: No

Advanced standing program offered for graduates of international dental schools: Yes

Advanced standing program description: 24-month program for internationally trained dentists awarding the D.M.D. degree

COMBINED AND ALTERNATE DEGREES

Ph.D.	M.S.	M.P.H.	M.D.	B.A./B.S.	Other
—	—	—	—	✓	✓

Other degrees: CAGS, M.S., M.S.D., D.Sc., D.Sc.D., Ph.D. and Internship; B.A./D.M.D. 7-year program offered to Boston University undergraduates; advanced dental education programs offered in Advanced Education in General Dentistry (AEGD), Dental Public Health, Digital Dentistry, Endodontics, Operative Dentistry, Oral Biology, Oral and Maxillofacial Pathology, Oral and Maxillofacial Surgery, Orthodontics, Pediatric Dentistry, Periodontics and Prosthodontics

COSTS: 2014–15 SCHOOL YEAR

	FIRST YEAR	SECOND YEAR	THIRD YEAR	FOURTH YEAR
Tuition, resident	$67,000	$67,000	$67,000	$67,000
Tuition, nonresident	$67,000	$67,000	$67,000	$67,000
Tuition, other				
Fees	$1,698	$1,718	$2,248	$1,778
Instruments, books, and supplies	$9,620	$8,334	$1,794	$0
Estimated living expenses	$20,776	$20,776	$17,328	$20,776
Total, resident	$99,094	$97,828	$88,370	$89,554
Total, nonresident	$99,094	$97,828	$88,370	$89,554
Total, other				

Note: Health Insurance and travel expenses not included in costs indicated above.

Student Financial Services (SFS) provides information about available resources that can help make dental education affordable while also assisting students to become proactive about financing their education. The role of SFS includes:

- Counseling for pre-admissions.

- Delivering orientation, debt-management and financial-awareness programs.

- Administering institutional and federal aid programs.

- Certifying credit-based private loan applications.

- Providing student financial need documentation to outside scholarship agencies.

- Conducting entrance and exit counseling sessions.

- Revising and re-evaluating student financial aid packages.

- Making provisions for eligible students to receive advances for living expenses.

- Ensuring that all aspects of the financial aid process are completed thoroughly and accurately as determined by institutional and federal policies.

- Maintaining available a comprehensive website, http://www. bumc.bu.edu/osfs/.

Contact us at 617-638-5130 or osfs-sdm@bu.edu.

FINANCIAL AID AWARDS TO FIRST-YEAR STUDENTS 2014–15

Total number of first-year recipients: 87	
Percentage of the first-year class: 76%	
Percentage of awards that are grants? 21%	
Percentage of awards that are loans? 79%	

	AVERAGE AWARDS	RANGE OF AWARDS
Residents	$5,100	$600–$10,000
Nonresidents	$5,100	$600–$10,000

For more information, please visit: http://www.bumc.bu.edu/osfs

HARVARD SCHOOL OF DENTAL MEDICINE

R. Bruce Donoff, D.M.D., M.D., Dean

CONTACT INFORMATION

www.hsdm.harvard.edu

188 Longwood Avenue
Boston, MA 02115

OFFICE OF ADMISSIONS

188 Longwood Avenue
Boston, MA 02115
Phone: 617-432-1443
Email: hsdm_dmd_admissions@hsdm.harvard.edu

FINANCIAL AID

Mr. Gardner Key
Director of Financial Aid
188 Longwood Avenue
Boston, MA 02115
Phone: 617-432-1527

OFFICE OF DENTAL EDUCATION

Ms. Anne Berg
Director of Admissions
188 Longwood Avenue
Boston, MA 02115
Phone: 617-432-1447

OFFICE OF DIVERSITY INCLUSION

Dr. Peggy Timothé
Director
188 Longwood Avenue
Boston, MA 02115
Phone: 617-432-1401

HOUSING

Vanderbilt Hall
107 Louis Pasteur Avenue
Boston, MA 02115
Email: vanderbilt_hall@hms.harvard.edu

INTERNATIONAL STUDENTS

Office of Admissions
188 Longwood Avenue
Boston, MA 02115
Phone: 617-432-0569
Email: hsdm_dmd_admissions@hsdm.harvard.edu

GENERAL INFORMATION

The Harvard School of Dental Medicine (HSDM) was established in 1867 as the first university-based dental school in the United States. This relationship with a great university and its associated world-renowned medical center and teaching hospitals shapes the education of dental students. The Harvard School of Dental Medicine has achieved success in its mission of producing leaders in the field of dental medicine in clinical care, teaching and research by being educationally innovative and by providing a professional school education that presents multiple opportunities for enrichment. The education of a Harvard dental student prepares women and men for a career of lifelong learning whether that be in clinical practice, teaching, research, oral health care delivery or a combination of these.

MISSION

The Harvard School of Dental Medicine's mission is to develop and foster a community of global leaders advancing oral and systemic health.

Vision: The vision of the Harvard School of Dental Medicine is to set the standard of excellence in and to define the future of dental education, practice and research.

Type of institution: Private	Doctoral dental degree offered: D.M.D.
Year opened: 1867	Targeted predoctoral enrollment: 145
Term type: Semester	Targeted entering class size: 35
Time to degree in months: 41	Campus setting: Urban
Start month: August	Campus housing available: Yes

PREPARATION

Formal minimum preparation in semester/quarter hours: Semester: 90 credit hours
Baccalaureate degree preferred: Yes
Number of first-year, first-time enrollees whose highest degree is:
  Baccalaureate: 33
  Master's degree and beyond: 2
Of first-year, first-time enrollees without baccalaureates, the number with:
  Equivalent of 60 undergraduate credit hours or less: 0
  Equivalent of 61–90 undergraduate credit hours: 0
  Equivalent of 91 or more undergraduate credit hours: 0

PREREQUISITE COURSE	REQUIRED	RECOMMENDED	LAB REQUIRED	CREDITS (SEMESTER/QUARTER)
BCP (biology-chemistry-physics) sciences				
Biology	✓		✓	8/12
Chemistry, general/inorganic	✓		✓	8/12
Chemistry, organic	✓		✓	8/12
Physics	✓		✓	8/12
Additional biological sciences				
Anatomy				
Biochemistry	✓			3/5
Cell biology		✓		
Histology				
Immunology				
Microbiology		✓		
Molecular biology/genetics				
Physiology		✓		
Zoology				

(Prerequisite Courses continued)

PREPARATION (CONTINUED)

PREREQUISITE COURSE	REQUIRED	RECOMMENDED	LAB REQUIRED	CREDITS (SEMESTER/QUARTER)
Other				
Calculus	✓			3/5
English (preferably writing)	✓			3/5
Statistics/biostatistic		✓		

Community college coursework accepted for prerequisites: Yes, but prefer courses be taken at four-year institution
Community college coursework accepted for electives: Yes
Limits on community college credit hours: Yes, but prefer science courses at four-year institutions
Maximum number of community college credit hours: 60
Advanced placement (AP) credit accepted for prerequisites: Yes
Advanced placement (AP) credit accepted for electives: Yes
Comments regarding AP credit: Accepted for calculus and one English course
Prefer all science prerequisite courses be taken at a four-year institution
Job shadowing: Recommended

DAT

Mandatory: Yes
Latest DAT for consideration of application: 11/01/2015
Oldest DAT considered: 01/01/2013
When more than one DAT score is reported: Highest score is considered
Canadian DAT accepted: Yes
Application considered before DAT scores are submitted: No

DAT: 2014 ENTERING CLASS

ENROLLEE DAT SCORES	MEAN	RANGE
Academic Average	23.0	21–23
Perceptual Ability	21.0	17–21
Total Science	23.0	19–28

GPA: 2014 ENTERING CLASS

ENROLLEE GPA SCORES	UNDERGRAD. MEAN	GRADUATE MEAN	UNDERGRAD. RANGE	GRADUATE RANGE
Science GPA	3.87	3.75	3.35–4.15	3.69–3.81
Total GPA	3.85	3.75	3.53–4.14	3.69–3.81

APPLICATION AND SELECTION

TIMETABLE

Earliest filing date: 06/02/2015
Latest filing date: 12/01/2015
Earliest date for acceptance offers: 12/01/2015
Maximum time in days for applicant's response to acceptance offer:
    30 days if accepted between December 1 and January 31
    15 days if accepted on or after February 1
    Response period may be lifted after April 15
Requests for deferred entrance considered: No
Fee for application: Yes, submit to school when Associated American Dental Schools Application Service (AADSAS) application is submitted.
Amount of fee for application:
    In state: $75   Out of state: $75   International: $75
Fee waiver available: Yes, if AADSAS fee has been waived: Provide a copy of AADSAS fee waiver.

	FIRST DEPOSIT	SECOND DEPOSIT	THIRD DEPOSIT
Required to hold place	No	No	No

APPLICATION PROCESS

Participates in AADSAS: Yes
Accepts direct applicants: No
Secondary or supplemental application required: Yes, only when selected for interview
Interview is mandatory: Yes
Interview is by invitation: Yes

RESIDENCY

In-state/in-province versus out-of-state/out-of-province
Admissions process distinguishes between in-state/in-province and out-of-state/out-of-province applicants: No
Preference given to residents of: None
Reciprocity Admissions Agreement available for legal residents of: None
Generally and over time, number of your first-year enrollment that is in-state: 4 to 5
Origin of out-of-state/out-of-province enrollees: AZ-1, CA-9, FL-4, GA-2, ID-1, IL-1, IN-1, MD-1, ME-1, MI-1, MO-1, NC-2, NJ-1, NY-1, SC-1, TX-1, UT-1, VA-3, WI-1

International
Applications are accepted from international (noncitizens/nonpermanent residents): Yes
Origin of international enrollees: Canada-1

APPLICATION AND ENROLLMENT	NUMBER OF APPLICANTS	ESTIMATED NUMBER INTERVIEWED	ESTIMATED NUMBER ENROLLED
In-state or province applicants/enrollees	68	2	0
Out-of-state or province applicants/enrollees	804	108	34
International applicants/enrollees (noncitizens/nonpermanent residents)	140	8	1

DEMOGRAPHIC DESCRIPTIONS OF APPLICANTS: 2014 ENTERING CLASS

	APPLICANTS			ENROLLEES		
	M	W	Gender Unknown or Not Reported	M	W	Gender Unknown or Not Reported
American Indian or Alaska Native	1	0	0	0	0	0
Asian	134	152	2	3	4	0
Black or African American	10	17	0	0	1	0
Hispanic or Latino	30	34	1	4	3	0
Native Hawaiian or Other Pacific Islander	0	0	0	0	0	0
White	233	188	0	7	8	0
Two or more races	12	14	0	2	1	0
Race and ethnicity unknown	19	19	6	0	1	0
International	74	64	2	0	1	0

	MINIMUM	MAXIMUM	MEAN
2014 entering class enrollees by age	21	30	23

CURRICULUM

The philosophy of education at HSDM is that dentistry is a specialty of medicine. In keeping with this belief, medical and dental students study together in the New Pathway curriculum at Harvard Medical School during the first two years. Dental clinical instruction occurs in treatment teams that utilize a comprehensive approach to patient care. Both didactic and clinical courses are taught by problem-based method of study and discussion in small tutorial groups. In this approach, cases based on actual clinical records or investigative problems are utilized to set the learning objectives. Students learn critical thinking and problem-solving techniques that will equip them for lifelong learning in the field of dental medicine. Students also take courses in research and complete a research project, thesis and formal presentation over the course of the four-year training period.

Student research opportunities: Yes

SPECIAL PROGRAMS AND SERVICES

DURING DENTAL SCHOOL

Academic counseling and tutoring
Significant community service opportunities
Internships, externships, or extramural programs
Mentoring
Opportunity to study for credit at institution abroad (available only during elective periods)
Personal counseling

ACTIVE STUDENT ORGANIZATIONS

American Association for Dental Research National Student Research Group
American Academy of Pediatric Dentistry
American Association of Women Dentists
American Dental Education Association
Alpha Omega International Dental Fraternity, Delta Chapter
American Student Dental Association
Hispanic Dental Association
Student National Dental Association

INTERNATIONAL DENTISTS

Graduates of international dental schools considered for traditional predoctoral program: Yes; if prerequisite courses are taken at a U.S. college/university
Advanced standing program offered for graduates of international dental schools: No

COMBINED AND ALTERNATE DEGREES

Ph.D.	M.S.	M.P.H.	M.D.	B.A./B.S.	Other
✓	✓	✓	—	—	✓

Other degree: M.B.A.

COSTS: 2014–15 SCHOOL YEAR

	FIRST YEAR	SECOND YEAR	THIRD YEAR	FOURTH YEAR
Tuition, resident	$54,200	$54,200	$54,200	$54,200
Tuition, nonresident	$54,200	$54,200	$54,200	$54,200
Tuition, other				
Fees	$1,970	$15,402	$14,556	$17,050
Instruments, books, and supplies	$1,950	$5,062	$3,025	$260
Estimated living expenses	$20,412	$25,208	$29,784	$22,912
Total, resident	$78,532	$99,872	$101,565	$94,422
Total, nonresident	$78,532	$99,872	$101,565	$94,422
Total, other				

Note: Year 1=10 months; year 2=11 months; year 3=13 months; year 4=10 months.

FINANCIAL AID

All financial aid offered by the Harvard School of Dental Medicine is based solely on financial need. Merit awards are not available.

FINANCIAL AID AWARDS TO FIRST-YEAR STUDENTS 2014–15

Total number of first-year recipients: 24	
Percentage of the first-year class: 69%	
Percentage of awards that are grants? 37%	
Percentage of awards that are loans? 67%	

	AVERAGE AWARDS	RANGE OF AWARDS
Residents	$53,400	$42,722–$72,822
Nonresidents	$53,400	$42,722–$72,822

For more information, please visit: http://hsdm.harvard.edu/about/admin/financial_aid

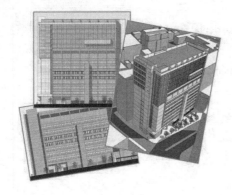

TUFTS UNIVERSITY
SCHOOL OF DENTAL MEDICINE

Huw F. Thomas, B.D.S., M.S., Ph.D., Dean

GENERAL INFORMATION

Tufts University School of Dental Medicine (TUSDM), a private institution, is located in downtown Boston adjacent to the Tufts Medical Center. In addition to being home to TUSDM, the Boston Health Sciences Campus is home to the School of Medicine, the Sackler School of Graduate Biomedical Sciences, the Gerald J. and Dorothy R. Friedman School of Nutrition Science and Policy, the Jaharis Family Center for Graduate Biomedical and Nutrition Research, the Jean Mayer Human Nutrition Research Center on Aging and five hospitals. TUSDM offers the D.M.D. program and an Advanced Standing Program for International Students, as well as accredited advanced education programs in eight dental specialties (each leading to a certificate or M.S. degree) and nonaccredited advanced education programs in six dental specialties.

MISSION

To educate diverse predoctoral and advanced dental education students to practice dentistry with knowledge of different patient populations, all dental specialties and varied practice settings.

Vision: Education committed to clinical excellence

Core Values:

- Professional excellence and integrity
- Commitment to advance dentistry
- Respect
- A culture of open communication

Type of institution: Private
Year opened: 1868
Term type: Semester
Time to degree in months: 42
Start month: September

Doctoral dental degree offered: D.M.D.
Targeted predoctoral enrollment: 733
Targeted entering class size: 195
Campus setting: Urban
Campus housing available: No

PREPARATION

Formal minimum preparation in semester/quarter hours: Semester: 31   Quarter: 46
Baccalaureate degree preferred: Yes, bachelor's degree required prior to matriculation
Number of first-year, first-time enrollees whose highest degree is:
  Baccalaureate: 155
  Master's degree and beyond: 40
Of first-year, first-time enrollees without baccalaureates, the number with:
  Equivalent of 60 undergraduate credit hours or less: 0
  Equivalent of 61–90 undergraduate credit hours: 0
  Equivalent of 91 or more undergraduate credit hours: 0

PREREQUISITE COURSE	REQUIRED	RECOMMENDED	LAB REQUIRED	CREDITS (SEMESTER/QUARTER)
BCP (biology-chemistry-physics) sciences				
Biology	✓		✓	8
Chemistry, general/inorganic	✓		✓	8
Chemistry, organic	✓		✓	4
Physics	✓		✓	8
Additional biological sciences *(Please see notes below table.)*				
Anatomy		✓		
Biochemistry	✓			3/5
Cell biology		✓		
Histology		✓		
Immunology		✓		
Microbiology		✓		

PREPARATION (CONTINUED)

PREREQUISITE COURSE	REQUIRED	RECOMMENDED	LAB REQUIRED	CREDITS (SEMESTER/QUARTER)
Molecular biology/genetics		✓		
Physiology		✓		
Zoology		✓		
Other				
Statistics		✓		
Writing intensive courses	✓			4

Note: In addition to the above required courses, we also require one semester (3 credits) of an upper-division biology course. Any of the recommended biology courses would meet this requirement.

Community college coursework accepted for prerequisites: No
Community college coursework accepted for electives: No
Limits on community college credit hours: See above
Advanced placement (AP) credit accepted for prerequisites: No
Advanced placement (AP) credit accepted for electives: Yes
Comments regarding AP credit: The Admissions Committee will not recognize prerequisites completed by earning AP credits. Applicants who have received college credit and/or placed out of prerequisite courses because of AP credits must either retake those courses at a four-year institution or take an equal number of credits in upper-level coursework in the same discipline at a four-year institution.
Job shadowing: Required
Number of hours of job shadowing required or recommended: 75; 40 hours with General Dentist required

DAT

Mandatory: Yes
Latest DAT for consideration of application: 02/01/2016
Oldest DAT considered: 06/01/2013
When more than one DAT score is reported: Most recent score is considered
Canadian DAT accepted: Yes
Application considered before DAT scores are submitted: No

DAT: 2014 ENTERING CLASS

ENROLLEE DAT SCORES	MEAN	RANGE
Academic Average	19.8	NR
Perceptual Ability	20.2	NR
Total Science	19.7	NR

GPA: 2014 ENTERING CLASS

ENROLLEE GPA SCORES	UNDERGRAD. MEAN	GRADUATE MEAN	UNDERGRAD. RANGE	GRADUATE RANGE
Science GPA	3.29	3.47	NR	NR
Total GPA	3.40	3.59	NR	NR

APPLICATION AND SELECTION

TIMETABLE

Earliest filing date: 06/02/2015
Latest filing date: 02/01/2016
Earliest date for acceptance offers: 12/01/2015
Maximum time in days for applicant's response to acceptance offer:
    30 days if accepted on or after December 1
    15 days if accepted on or after February 1
Requests for deferred entrance considered: In exceptional circumstances only

Fee for application: Yes, submitted only when requested via credit card
Amount of fee for application:
    In state: $75   Out of state: $75   International: NA
Fee waiver available: No

	FIRST DEPOSIT	SECOND DEPOSIT	THIRD DEPOSIT
Required to hold place	Yes	Yes	No
Resident amount	$1,500	$500	
Nonresident amount	$1,500	$500	
Deposit due	When admission offer made	04/15/2016	
Applied to tuition	Yes	Yes	
Refundable	No	No	

APPLICATION PROCESS

Participates in Associated American Dental Schools Application Service (AADSAS): Yes
Accepts direct applicants: No
Secondary or supplemental application required: Yes, sent to interviewed candidates only
Secondary or supplemental application website: No
Interview is mandatory: Yes
Interview is by invitation: Yes

RESIDENCY

In-state/in-province versus out-of-state/out-of-province
Admissions process distinguishes between in-state/in-province and out-of-state/out-of-province applicants: No
Preference given to residents of: NA
Reciprocity Admissions Agreement available for legal residents of: NA
Generally and over time, percentage of your first-year enrollment that is in-state: NA (private school)
Origin of out-of-state/out-of-province enrollees: AR-1, AZ-1, CA-21, CO-2, CT-7, FL-22, GA-7, HI-1, IL-7, IN-8, LA-1, MD-3, ME-1, MI-5, NC-1, NH-4, NJ-6, NY-7, NV-2, OH-1, OK-1, OR-1, PA-3, RI-2, TX-9, UT-2, VA-7, VT-2, WA-3, WI-5

International
Applications are accepted from international (noncitizens/
   nonpermanent residents): No
Origin of international enrollees: South Korea-3

APPLICATION AND ENROLLMENT	NUMBER OF APPLICANTS	ESTIMATED NUMBER INTERVIEWED	ESTIMATED NUMBER ENROLLED
In-state or province applicants/enrollees	161	72	49
Out-of-state or province applicants/enrollees	3,493	427	143
International applicants/enrollees (noncitizens/nonpermanent residents)	25	3	3

DEMOGRAPHIC DESCRIPTIONS OF APPLICANTS: 2014 ENTERING CLASS

	APPLICANTS			ENROLLEES		
	M	W	Gender Unknown or Not Reported	M	W	Gender Unknown or Not Reported
American Indian or Alaska Native	1	3	0	0	0	0
Asian	655	691	12	24	42	0
Black or African American	41	68	1	0	9	0
Hispanic or Latino	115	162	2	4	15	0
Native Hawaiian or Other Pacific Islander	0	3	0	0	0	0
White	983	662	9	49	36	0
Two or more races	53	64	0	3	5	0
Race and ethnicity unknown	58	57	14	2	3	0
International	15	10	0	2	1	0

	MINIMUM	MAXIMUM	MEAN
2014 entering class enrollees by age	21	35	24

CURRICULUM

TUSDM's curriculum has been designed and modified over the years to reflect the changing needs of the dental profession and the public. The school's primary goal is to develop dental practitioners who are able to utilize their knowledge of the basic principles of human biology and human behavior in conjunction with their technical skills in diagnosing, treating and preventing oral disease. The D.M.D. program, which extends over a four-year period, consists of a series of didactic, laboratory and clinical experiences, resulting in the logical development of concepts and skills. Upon completion of the curriculum, the graduate will be both intellectually and technically prepared to practice the profession of dentistry as it exists today, to adapt to future changes and to initiate and contribute to those changes, all of which will enhance the delivery of dental care. Please visit http://dental.tufts.edu for more information regarding our curriculum.

Student research opportunities: Yes

SPECIAL PROGRAMS AND SERVICES

PREDENTAL
Postbaccalaureate programs
Special affiliations with colleges and universities: Tufts University School of Arts and Sciences 8-Year Early Assurance Program and Post-baccalaureate Joint Degree program; Marist College—Early Assurance Program; Tougaloo College—Early Assurance Program; Fisk University—Early Assurance Program

DURING DENTAL SCHOOL
Academic counseling and tutoring
Community service opportunities
Internships, externships, or extramural programs
Mentoring
Personal counseling
Professional- and career-development programming
Training for those interested in academic careers
Transfer applicants considered if space is available

ACTIVE STUDENT ORGANIZATIONS
American Association for Dental Research National Student Research Group
American Association of Women Dentists
American Dental Education Association
American Student Dental Association
Hispanic Dental Association
Student National Dental Association
Uniformed Services Dental Student Association
Please see our website (http://dental.tufts.edu/student-gateway/student-organizations/) for a complete list of student organizations offered at TUSDM.

INTERNATIONAL DENTISTS
Graduates of international dental schools considered for traditional predoctoral program: No
Advanced standing program offered for graduates of international dental schools: Yes
Advanced standing program description: Program awarding a dental degree

COMBINED AND ALTERNATE DEGREES

Ph.D.	M.S.	M.P.H.	M.D.	B.A./B.S.	Other
—	✓	✓	—	✓	✓

Other degrees: Combined D.M.D./M.P.H. and D.M.D./M.S. degrees are available.

COSTS: 2014–15 SCHOOL YEAR

	FIRST YEAR	SECOND YEAR	THIRD YEAR	FOURTH YEAR
Tuition, resident	$66,010	$66,010	$66,010	$66,010
Tuition, nonresident	$66,010	$66,010	$66,010	$66,010
Tuition, other				
Fees	$4,355	$4,651	$4,945	$4,945
Instruments, books, and supplies	$12,675	$11,710	$7,700	$3,800
Estimated living expenses	$21,000	$21,000	$23,100	$18,900
Total, resident	$104,040	$103,371	$101,755	$93,655
Total, nonresident	$104,040	$103,371	$101,755	$93,655
Total, other				

FINANCIAL AID

Students enrolled in the D.M.D. program, Advanced Standing Program for International Students and accredited postgraduate programs can access a wide variety of both federal and institutional financial aid. Both merit- and need-based grants are available to students who qualify. The majority of funding available consists of student loans, which include both federal and institutional loans. International students can apply for private education loans if they have a qualified cosigner. Financial aid application information for the 2016–17 academic year will be released in February 2016. The deadline for submitting a financial aid application for the 2016–17 academic year is May 2016. Award notices are released in mid-June. Application materials and further information are available on TUSDM's Financial Aid Office website: http://dental.tufts.edu/financial_aid.

FINANCIAL AID AWARDS TO FIRST-YEAR STUDENTS 2014–15

Total number of first-year recipients: 152

Percentage of the first-year class: 78%

Percentage of awards that are grants? 14%

Percentage of awards that are loans? 86%

	AVERAGE AWARDS	RANGE OF AWARDS
All first year students	$90,615	$4,200–$104,498

For more information, please visit: http://dental.tufts.edu/admissions/financial-aid/

UNIVERSITY OF DETROIT MERCY
SCHOOL OF DENTISTRY

Mert N. Aksu, D.D.S., J.D., M.H.S.A., Dean

CONTACT INFORMATION

www.dental.udmercy.edu
Office of the Dean
2700 Martin Luther King Jr. Boulevard
Detroit, MI 48208-2576

OFFICE OF DENTAL ADMISSIONS

Dr. Gary E. Jeffers
Director of Dental Admissions
Office of Dental Admissions
University of Detroit Mercy School of Dentistry
2700 Martin Luther King Jr. Boulevard
Detroit, MI 48208-2576
Phone: 313-494-6650
Email: jefferge@udmercy.edu
http://dental.udmercy.edu/admission

OFFICE OF FINANCIAL AID

Ms. Caren Bendes
Coordinator, Financial Aid
Office of Financial Aid
University of Detroit Mercy School of Dentistry
2700 Martin Luther King Jr. Boulevard
Detroit, MI 48208-2576
Phone: 313-993-3341
Email: bendescm@udmercy.edu
http://dental.udmercy.edu/admission/financial/
index.htm

OFFICE OF STUDENT AFFAIRS

Ms. Juliette Daniels
Director of Student Affairs
Office of Student Affairs
University of Detroit Mercy School of Dentistry
2700 Martin Luther King Jr. Boulevard
Detroit, MI 48208-2576
Phone: 313-494-6850
Email: danieljc@udmercy.edu

OFFICE OF MULTICULTURAL AFFAIRS

Dr. Deirdre D. Young
Director of Multicultural Affairs
University of Detroit Mercy School of Dentistry
2700 Martin Luther King Jr. Boulevard
Detroit, MI 48208-2576
Phone: 313-494-6653
Email: youngdd@udmercy.edu

HOUSING OFFICE OF DENTAL ADMISSIONS

Ms. Carol J. Blackburn
Administrative Assistant, Dental Admissions
Office of Dental Admissions
University of Detroit Mercy School of Dentistry
2700 Martin Luther King Jr. Boulevard
Detroit, MI 48208-2576
Phone: 313-494-6650
Email: blackbcj@udmercy.edu

GENERAL INFORMATION

The University of Detroit Mercy School of Dentistry (UDM SOD), an independent Catholic institution, is an urban-based school located in metropolitan Detroit. UDM SOD provides opportunities to deliver oral health care to an extensive patient population, as well as continue its history of community outreach activities. The school also provides classrooms, preclinical laboratories, clinics, cafeteria and library—an improved environment for learning, research and patient care. A clinical simulation laboratory containing patient simulator mannequins and clinical work stations enhances learning. A 42-chair hospital-based satellite clinic, with additional patient-care opportunities, is located nearby at the University Health Center of Detroit Receiving Hospital. UDM SOD educates dentists who are patient-care oriented and skilled in the art of self-evaluation and lifelong learning.

MISSION

Through excellence in teaching, scholarship and service, UDM SOD, in the Jesuit and Mercy traditions, develops scientifically based, socially and ethically sensitive oral health professionals.

Vision: UDM SOD will meet the oral health care and educational needs of southeast Michigan by serving as a benchmark for effective community and professional collaborations.

Core Values: The following values guide our daily activities and future planning:

Excellence	Service	Respect	Lifelong Learning	Integrity

Type of institution: Private and state-related
Year opened: 1932
Term type: Semester
Time to degree in months: 44
Start month: August

Doctoral dental degree offered: D.D.S.
Targeted predoctoral enrollment: 576
Targeted entering class size: 144
Campus setting: Urban
Campus housing available: No

PREPARATION

Formal minimum preparation in semester/quarter hours: Semester: 60   Quarter: 90
Baccalaureate degree preferred: Yes,
Number of first-year, first-time enrollees whose highest degree is:
   Baccalaureate: 114
   Master's degree and beyond: 12
Of first-year, first-time enrollees without baccalaureates, the number with:
   Equivalent of 60 undergraduate credit hours or less: 0
   Equivalent of 61–90 undergraduate credit hours: 17
   Equivalent of 91 or more undergraduate credit hours: 1

PREREQUISITE COURSE	REQUIRED	RECOMMENDED	LAB REQUIRED	CREDITS (SEMESTER/QUARTER)
BCP (biology-chemistry-physics) sciences				
Biology	✓		✓	8/12
Chemistry, general/inorganic	✓		✓	8/12
Chemistry, organic	✓		✓	8/12
Physics	✓		✓	8/12
Additional biological sciences				
Anatomy		✓		4/6
Biochemistry	✓			3/5
Cell biology		✓		4/6
Histology		✓		4/6
Immunology		✓		4/6
Microbiology	✓			3/5

PREPARATION (CONTINUED)

Molecular biology/genetics	✓	4/6
Physiology	✓	8/12
Zoology	✓	4/6
Other		
English/Writing Skills	✓	6/9
Computer Skills/Technology	✓	3/5
Statistics	✓	3/5
Psychology	✓	
Sociology	✓	
Business courses	✓	
Communications courses	✓	

Community college coursework accepted for prerequisites: Yes; four-year college/university preferred
Community college coursework accepted for electives: Yes; four-year college/university preferred
Limits on community college credit hours: Yes; 60 semester hours/90 quarter hours.
Maximum number of community college credit hours: 60
Advanced placement (AP) credit accepted for prerequisites: Yes
Advanced placement (AP) credit accepted for electives: Yes
Comments regarding AP credit: If the prospective candidate has received AP credits in a prerequisite discipline(s) from his or her "home" college/university, he or she is strongly encouraged to pursue additional upper-division coursework within the discipline for which credit was received—equal to the number of recognized AP credits.
Job shadowing: Required
Number of hours of job shadowing required or recommended: Minimally, 60 hours within a general practice setting. A letter of recommendation also attests to activities and time in office.
Other factors considered in admission: Difficulty of a curriculum and achievement, letters of recommendation, personal statement, experience/exposure to the profession, research experience, motivation, community service, time management, and intrinsic values

DAT

Mandatory: Yes; recommended minimum of 20 on each section (20+ competitive)
Latest DAT for consideration of application: 12/31/2015
Oldest DAT considered: 12/31/2013
When more than one DAT score is reported: Most recent score only is considered
Canadian DAT accepted: Yes
Application considered before DAT scores are submitted: No

U.S. DAT: 2014 ENTERING CLASS

ENROLLEE DAT SCORES	MEAN	RANGE
Academic Average	20.4	17–26
Perceptual Ability	20.2	14–26
Total Science	20.6	17–26

CANADIAN DAT: 2014 ENTERING CLASS

ENROLLEE DAT SCORES	MEAN	RANGE
Academic Average	20.2	18–22
Manual Dexterity	NA	NA
Perceptual Ability	19.8	17–22
Total Science	20.1	18–22

GPA: 2014 ENTERING CLASS

ENROLLEE GPA SCORES	UNDERGRAD. MEAN	GRADUATE MEAN	UNDERGRAD. RANGE	GRADUATE RANGE
Science GPA	3.60	NA	2.83–4.20	NA
Total GPA	3.64	NA	2.83–4.19	NA

APPLICATION AND SELECTION

TIMETABLE
Earliest filing date: 06/02/2015
Latest filing date: 12/31/2015
Earliest date for acceptance offers: 12/01/2015
Maximum time in days for applicant's response to acceptance offer:
    30 days if accepted on or after December 1
    14 days if accepted on or after February 1
    7 days if accepted on or after March 1
    3 days if accepted after July 1
Requests for deferred entrance considered: Yes, in exceptional circumstances only
Fee for application: Yes, submitted at same time as Associated American Dental Schools Application Service (AADSAS) application.
Amount of fee for application:
    In state: $75   Out of state: $75   International: $75
Fee waiver available: Yes, in exceptional circumstances only

	FIRST DEPOSIT	SECOND DEPOSIT	THIRD DEPOSIT
Required to hold place	Yes	No	No
Resident amount	$1,500		
Nonresident amount	$1,500		
Deposit due	As indicated in admission offer		
Applied to tuition	Yes		
Refundable	No		

APPLICATION PROCESS

Participates in AADSAS: Yes
Accepts direct applicants: No
Secondary or supplemental application required: No; only requirement
is submission of $75 application fee and photo.
Interview is mandatory: Yes
Interview is by invitation: Yes

RESIDENCY

In-state/in-province versus out-of-state/out-of-province
Admissions process distinguishes between in-state/in-province and
out-of-state/out-of-province applicants: No
Preference given to residents of: None
Reciprocity Admissions Agreement available for legal residents of: NR
Generally and over time, percentage of your first-year enrollment that is
in-state: 50%
Origin of out-of-state/out-of-province enrollees: AR-1, AZ-1, CA-11,
CO-1, FL-1, IL-3, NC-2, NJ-1, NY-1, OH-1, TX-3, UT-1, VA-3, WA-2

International
Applications are accepted from international (noncitizens/
nonpermanent residents): Yes
Origin of international enrollees: Canada-33, China-2, South Korea-3,
Not Reported-2

APPLICATION AND ENROLLMENT	NUMBER OF APPLICANTS	ESTIMATED NUMBER INTERVIEWED	ESTIMATED NUMBER ENROLLED
In-state or province applicants/enrollees	357	163	72
Out-of-state or province applicants/enrollees	965	437	32
International applicants/enrollees (noncitizens/nonpermanent residents)	325	NR	40

DEMOGRAPHIC DESCRIPTIONS OF APPLICANTS: 2014 ENTERING CLASS

	APPLICANTS			ENROLLEES		
	M	W	Gender Unknown or Not Reported	M	W	Gender Unknown or Not Reported
American Indian or Alaska Native	0	2	0	0	0	0
Asian	244	217	6	12	16	0
Black or African American	22	43	1	0	5	0
Hispanic or Latino	29	47	0	1	4	0
Native Hawaiian or Other Pacific Islander	0	1	0	0	0	0
White	376	242	4	35	25	0
Two or more races	14	15	1	3	1	0
Race and ethnicity unknown	23	14	5	2	0	0
International	186	136	3	25	15	0

	MINIMUM	MAXIMUM	MEAN
2014 entering class enrollees by age	20	40	24

CURRICULUM

The majority of biomedical, behavioral and preclinical sciences are concentrated in the first two years. The freshman curriculum is divided between biomedical and dental sciences, while the sophomore year is devoted primarily to dental sciences taught in a simulation environment. Limited patient care experiences occur in the first and second years. More than 75% of the curricular time during the third and fourth years is devoted to clinical practice. Patient care experiences are based on an evidence-based, comprehensive care model using the expertise of generalists and specialists. Individual students are assigned a patient family and are responsible for addressing all the patient's dental needs. Outreach clinical rotations occurring during the fourth year expose the students to alternative practice settings in a community-based environment. Ethics, patient management and current issues are addressed throughout the curriculum.

Student research opportunities: Yes

SPECIAL PROGRAMS AND SERVICES

PREDENTAL
American Student Dental Association (ASDA) Predental Workshop
Association of American Medical Colleges/ADEA Summer Medical and
Dental Education Program (AAMC/ADEA SMDEP)
DAT workshops
Postbaccalaureate programs
Special affiliations with colleges and universities: Academic program
enabling students to earn a combined baccalaureate/D.D.S. degree
in seven calendar years.

DURING DENTAL SCHOOL
Academic counseling and tutoring
Community service opportunities
Mentoring
Personal counseling
Professional- and career-development programming
Training for those interested in academic careers
Transfer applicants considered if space is available—Considered rarely
and only in exceptional circumstances; curricula must be compatible

ACTIVE STUDENT ORGANIZATIONS

Alpha Omega International Dental Fraternity

American Association for Dental Research National Student
  Research Group

American Dental Education Association

American Student Dental Association

Canadian Student Association

Christian Dental Association

Delta Sigma Delta International Fraternity

Hispanic Student Dental Association

Student National Dental Association

INTERNATIONAL DENTISTS

Graduates of international dental schools considered for traditional
  predoctoral program: Yes

Advanced standing program offered for graduates of international
  dental schools: No

Accelerated program offered to international dental school graduates:
  Yes (Preferred candidates are those who have specialty certification
  from an American Dental Association-accredited program or have
  completed, at a minimum, a two-year program in advanced clinical
  dentistry at a U.S. dental school.)

COMBINED AND ALTERNATE DEGREES

Ph.D.	M.S.	M.P.H.	M.D.	B.A./B.S.	Other
—	—	—	—	—	✓

Other degree: B.S./D.D.S. for highly qualified high school applicants enrolled
in UDM 7-year combined undergraduate/dental program

COSTS: 2014–15 SCHOOL YEAR

	FIRST YEAR	SECOND YEAR	THIRD YEAR	FOURTH YEAR
Tuition, resident	$64,940	$64,940	$64,940	$64,940
Tuition, nonresident	$64,940	$64,940	$64,940	$64,940
Tuition, other				
Fees	$5,493	$2,947	$2,763	$3,007
Instruments, books, and supplies	$9,338	$11,015	$6,512	$6,033
Estimated living expenses[1]	$12,042	$12,042	$12,042	$12,042
Health Insurance[2]	$1,338	$1,338	$1,338	$1,338
Total, resident	$93,151	$92,282	$87,595	$87,360
Total, nonresident	$93,151	$92,282	$87,595	$87,360
Total, other				

Notes:

[1] If a student does not live with his or her parents, the estimated annual
living expenses are $20,043, and in such cases, the total costs per year
would need to be adjusted accordingly.

[2] Health insurance can be waived.

FINANCIAL AID

FINANCIAL AID AWARDS TO FIRST-YEAR STUDENTS 2014–15

Total number of first-year recipients: 88

Percentage of the first-year class: 62%

Percentage of awards that are grants? 3%

Percentage of awards that are loans? 97%

	AVERAGE AWARDS	RANGE OF AWARDS
Residents	$88,733	$12,443–$99,999
Nonresidents	$84,899	$44,944–$99,814

For more information, please visit: dental.udmercy.edu/admission/
financial/index.htm

UNIVERSITY OF MICHIGAN
SCHOOL OF DENTISTRY

Laurie K. McCauley, D.D.S., M.S., Ph.D., Dean

GENERAL INFORMATION

The University of Michigan School of Dentistry (U-M SOD), organized in 1875, was the first dental school established as an integral part of a state university and the second to become a part of any university. The University of Michigan is located in Ann Arbor, a city of 114,000 about 40 miles west of Detroit. Approximately 500 students are enrolled annually in various programs offered by U-M SOD:

1. The D.D.S. degree program
2. Advanced education programs, each leading to an M.S. degree
3. A B.S. program in dental hygiene
4. A Ph.D. in Oral Health Sciences
5. A dual D.D.S./Ph.D. program

U-M SOD also offers comprehensive program offerings in continuing dental education.

MISSION

Advancing health through education, service, research and discovery.

Core Value: Compassion, Leadership, Excellence, Responsibility, Trust, Creativity, Inclusion

Type of institution: Public	Doctoral dental degree offered: D.D.S.
Year opened: 1875	Targeted predoctoral enrollment: 434
Term type: Semester	Targeted entering class size: 108
Time to degree in months: 46	Campus setting: Suburban
Start month: June	Campus housing available: Yes

PREPARATION

Formal minimum preparation in semester/quarter hours: Semester: 90   Quarter: 135
Baccalaureate degree preferred: Yes
Number of first-year, first-time enrollees whose highest degree is:
    Baccalaureate: 95
    Master's degree and beyond: 10
Of first-year, first-time enrollees without baccalaureates, the number with:
    Equivalent of 60 undergraduate credit hours or less: 0
    Equivalent of 61–90 undergraduate credit hours: 0
    Equivalent of 91 or more undergraduate credit hours: 3

PREREQUISITE COURSE	REQUIRED	RECOMMENDED	LAB REQUIRED	CREDITS (SEMESTER/QUARTER)
BCP (biology-chemistry-physics) sciences				
Biology	✓		✓	8/12
Chemistry, general/inorganic	✓		✓	8/12
Chemistry, organic	✓		✓	8/12
Physics	✓		✓	8/12
Additional biological sciences				
Anatomy		✓		
Biochemistry	✓			3/5
Cell biology				
Histology		✓		
Immunology				
Microbiology	✓			3/5
Molecular biology/genetics				
Physiology		✓		

PREPARATION (CONTINUED)

PREREQUISITE COURSE	REQUIRED	RECOMMENDED	LAB REQUIRED	CREDITS (SEMESTER/QUARTER)
Zoology				
Other				
Psychology	✓			3/5
Sociology	✓			3/5
English composition	✓			6/9

Community college coursework accepted for prerequisites: Yes
Community college coursework accepted for electives: Yes
Limits on community college credit hours: Yes
Maximum number of community college credit hours: 60
Advanced placement (AP) credit accepted for prerequisites: Yes
Advanced placement (AP) credit accepted for electives: Yes
Comments regarding AP credit: Applicants must receive credit for AP classes on their under-
graduate transcripts.
Job shadowing: Required
Number of hours of job shadowing required: 100 hours
Other factors considered in admission: All prerequisite courses must have a grade of C or
better. Candidates must present strong letters of recommendation; strong examples of
extracurricular, volunteer, work and research experiences; an original essay and evidence
of leadership capacity.

DAT

Mandatory: Yes
Latest DAT for consideration of application: 08/31/2015
Oldest DAT considered: 01/01/2012
When more than one DAT score is reported: Primary attention to most
recent scores
Canadian DAT accepted: Yes
Application considered before DAT scores are submitted: No

U.S. DAT: 2014 ENTERING CLASS

ENROLLEE DAT SCORES	MEAN	RANGE
Academic Average	20.1	17–26
Perceptual Ability	20.4	16–27
Total Science	20.1	16–26

CANADIAN DAT: 2014 ENTERING CLASS

ENROLLEE DAT SCORES	MEAN	RANGE
Academic Average	20.0	19–21
Manual Dexterity	14.7	12–16
Perceptual Ability	20.0	18–24
Total Science	20.3	19–21

GPA: 2014 ENTERING CLASS

ENROLLEE GPA SCORES	UNDERGRAD. MEAN	GRADUATE MEAN	UNDERGRAD. RANGE	GRADUATE RANGE
Science GPA	3.46	3.68	2.57–4.23	3.59–4.00
Total GPA	3.53	3.71	2.92–4.21	3.03–4.00

APPLICATION AND SELECTION

TIMETABLE

Earliest filing date: 06/02/2015
Latest filing date: 10/15/2015
Earliest date for acceptance offers: 12/01/2015
Maximum time in days for applicant's response to acceptance offer:
30 days if accepted on or after December 1
15 days if accepted on or after February 1
Requests for deferred entrance considered: No
Fee for application: Yes, submitted at same time as Associated American
Dental Schools Application Service (AADSAS) application
Amount of fee for application:
In state: $75   Out of state: $75   International: $75
Fee waiver available: Yes

	FIRST DEPOSIT	SECOND DEPOSIT	THIRD DEPOSIT
Required to hold place	Yes	No	No
Resident amount	$1,500		
Nonresident amount	$1,500		
Deposit due	As indicated in admission offer		
Applied to tuition	Yes		
Refundable	No		

APPLICATION PROCESS

Participates in AADSAS: Yes
Accepts direct applicants: No
Secondary or supplemental application required: No
Secondary or supplemental application website: NA
Interview is mandatory: Yes
Interview is by invitation: Yes

RESIDENCY

In-state/in-province versus out-of-state/out-of-province
Admissions process distinguishes between in-state/in-province and
out-of-state/out-of-province applicants: Yes
Preference given to residents of: Michigan
Reciprocity Admissions Agreement available for legal residents of: None

Generally and over time, percentage of your first-year enrollment that is in-state: 60%

Origin of out-of-state/out-of-province enrollees: AK-1, AZ-1, CA-6, FL-2, GA-2, IL-7, KS-1, MN-3, MT-1, NC-1, NJ-1, NY-1, OR-1, TX-1, VA-1, WA-2, WI-3

International

Applications are accepted from international (noncitizens/nonpermanent residents): Yes

Origin of international enrollees: Canada-5, China-1, South Korea-2

APPLICATION AND ENROLLMENT	NUMBER OF APPLICANTS	ESTIMATED NUMBER INTERVIEWED	ESTIMATED NUMBER ENROLLED
In-state or province applicants/enrollees	299	108	65
Out-of-state or province applicants/enrollees	1,497	197	35
International applicants/enrollees (noncitizens/nonpermanent residents)	165	16	8

DEMOGRAPHIC DESCRIPTIONS OF APPLICANTS: 2014 ENTERING CLASS

	APPLICANTS			ENROLLEES		
	M	W	Gender Unknown or Not Reported	M	W	Gender Unknown or Not Reported
American Indian or Alaska Native	2	1	0	0	0	0
Asian	278	283	2	5	9	0
Black or African American	20	35	0	1	1	0
Hispanic or Latino	39	60	0	1	5	0
Native Hawaiian or Other Pacific Islander	0	1	0	0	0	0
White	567	415	2	43	34	0
Two or more races	21	21	0	0	1	0
Race and ethnicity unknown	25	19	5	0	0	0
International	90	74	1	4	4	0

	MINIMUM	MAXIMUM	MEAN
2014 entering class enrollees by age	20	34	24

CURRICULUM

The general objectives of dental education are to accomplish the following:

1. Provide opportunities within a stimulating academic environment for students to develop an appreciation for and understanding of philosophical, social and intellectual problems.
2. Strongly orient the student to study the physical and biological sciences on which the practice of contemporary dentistry is based.
3. Offer opportunities and experiences enabling the student to develop the essential clinical skills and critical thinking needed to provide the highest quality oral health service to patients.
4. Foster the student's appreciation for the value, design and methodology of dental research.
5. Ensure the graduating student is able to make decisions affecting the practice of dentistry based on ethical principles and as prescribed by law.

6. Encourage students to consider career possibilities in dental research, dental education, dental leadership and alternative health care delivery pathways, including dental public health.
7. Develop the potential of the dental graduate to adapt and to thrive in a diverse and dynamic practice environment.

Student research opportunities: Yes

SPECIAL PROGRAMS AND SERVICES

PREDENTAL

Summer enrichment program for 3rd and 4th year undergraduates

DURING DENTAL SCHOOL

Academic counseling and tutoring
Community service opportunities
Internships, externships, or extramural programs
Mentoring
Personal counseling
Training for those interested in academic careers

ACTIVE STUDENT ORGANIZATIONS

http://www.dent.umich.edu/student-life/extracurricular/student-organizations

INTERNATIONAL DENTISTS

Graduates of international dental schools considered for traditional predoctoral program: Yes

Advanced standing program offered for graduates of international dental schools: Yes

Advanced standing program description: D.D.S. awarded after successful completion of a 2 1/2 year program that includes preclinical, didactic, and clinical courses, as well as clinical rotations.

COMBINED AND ALTERNATE DEGREES

Ph.D.	M.S.	M.P.H.	M.D.	B.A./B.S.	Other
✓	✓	✓	—	—	—

COSTS: 2014–15 SCHOOL YEAR

	FIRST YEAR	SECOND YEAR	THIRD YEAR	FOURTH YEAR
Tuition, resident	$29,561	$35,356	$35,356	$35,356
Tuition, nonresident	$46,247	$55,321	$55,321	$55,321
Tuition, other				
Fees	$409	$490	$490	$490
Instruments, books, and supplies	$7,675	$7,147	$5,311	$7,753
Estimated living expenses	$25,220	$30,330	$30,330	$30,330
Total, resident	$62,865	$73,323	$71,487	$73,929
Total, nonresident	$79,551	$93,288	$91,452	$93,894
Total, other				

FINANCIAL AID

The University of Michigan School of Dentistry is committed to helping dental students with the process of funding their dental education. Please visit the Office of Financial Aid: Dentistry website at the URL listed below. This site provides the most up-to-date information on cost of attendance, financial aid guides and available loan programs for students of the School of Dentistry.

For more information, please visit: www.finaid.umich.edu/Home/HowtoApplyforAid/DentalDDSStudents

UNIVERSITY OF MINNESOTA
SCHOOL OF DENTISTRY

Leon A. Assael, D.M.D., C.M.M., Dean

CONTACT INFORMATION

www.dentistry.umn.edu

15-163 Malcolm Moos Health Sciences Tower
515 Delaware Street SE
Minneapolis, MN 55455

OFFICE OF ADMISSIONS AND DIVERSITY

Dr. Naty Lopez
Assistant Dean, Admissions and Diversity
15-163 Malcolm Moos Health Sciences Tower
515 Delaware Street SE
Minneapolis, MN 55455
Phone: 612-625-7477

OFFICE OF FINANCIAL AID

Ms. Elizabeth Holm
Financial Aid Advisor
210 Fraser Hall
Minneapolis, MN 55455
Phone: 612-624-4138
Email: holmx029@umn.edu

STUDENT AFFAIRS

Ms. Sara Johnson
Director, Student Affairs
15-106 Malcolm Moos Health Sciences Tower
515 Delaware Street SE
Minneapolis, MN 55455
Phone: 612-625-0927

MINORITY AFFAIRS/DIVERSITY

Dr. Naty Lopez
Assistant Dean, Admissions and Diversity
15-163 Malcolm Moos Health Sciences Tower
515 Delaware Street SE
Minneapolis, MN 55455
Phone: 612-625-7477

HOUSING AND RESIDENTIAL LIFE

Comstock Hall East
210 Delaware Street SE
Minneapolis, MN 55455
Phone: 612-624-2994
Email: housing@umn.edu
www.housing.umn.edu

INTERNATIONAL STUDENT AND SCHOLAR SERVICES

190 Hubert H. Humphrey Center
301 19th Avenue South
Minneapolis, MN 55455
Phone: 612-626-7100
www.isss.umn.edu

GENERAL INFORMATION

The University of Minnesota School of Dentistry (U of M SOD), established in 1888, is part of a great university health center located on the Minneapolis campus in the center of the Minneapolis-St. Paul area, which has a population of more than 3.1 million. Dental students enjoy a variety of academic, cultural and recreational opportunities. U of M SOD's teaching and research facilities are in a health sciences building that holds shared basic science laboratories and lecture rooms. U of M SOD conducts a wide range of programs, including dentistry, dental hygiene, dental therapy, dental specialties, oral biology and other advanced dental education and clinical training programs, as well as a comprehensive research program.

MISSION

U of M SOD improves oral and craniofacial health by educating clinicians and scientists who translate knowledge and experience into clinical practice.

Vision: U of M SOD is committed to graduating professionals who provide the highest quality care and service to the people of Minnesota and the world.

Core Values:

- Discovering knowledge through research
- Inspiring innovation in the health sciences
- Providing oral health care to a diverse patient population in a variety of settings

Type of institution: Public
Year opened: 1888
Term type: Semester
Time to degree in months: 45
Start month: August
Doctoral dental degree offered: D.D.S.

Targeted predoctoral enrollment (including our PASS program for international dentists): 413
Targeted entering class size: 98
Campus setting: Urban
Campus housing available: Yes

PREPARATION

Formal minimum preparation in semester/quarter hours: Semester: 87   Quarter: 130
Baccalaureate degree preferred: Yes
Number of first-year, first-time enrollees whose highest degree is:
    Baccalaureate: 87
    Master's degree and beyond: 5
Of first-year, first-time enrollees without baccalaureates, the number with:
    Equivalent of 60 undergraduate credit hours or less: 0
    Equivalent of 61–90 undergraduate credit hours: 2
    Equivalent of 91 or more undergraduate credit hours: 4

PREREQUISITE COURSE	REQUIRED	RECOMMENDED	LAB REQUIRED	CREDITS (SEMESTER/QUARTER)
BCP (biology-chemistry-physics) sciences				
Biology	✓		✓	8/12
Chemistry, general/inorganic	✓		✓	8/12
Chemistry, organic	✓		✓	8/12
Physics	✓		✓	8/12
Additional biological sciences				
Anatomy		✓		3/5
Biochemistry	✓			3/5
Cell biology		✓		3/5
Histology		✓		3/5
Immunology		✓		3/5

(Prerequisite Courses continued)

PREPARATION (CONTINUED)

PREREQUISITE COURSE	REQUIRED	RECOMMENDED	LAB REQUIRED	CREDITS (SEMESTER/QUARTER)
Microbiology		✓		3/5
Molecular biology/genetics		✓		3/5
Physiology		✓		3/5
Zoology		✓		3/5

Community college coursework accepted for prerequisites: Yes
Community college coursework accepted for electives: Yes
Limits on community college credit hours: Yes
Maximum number of community college credit hours: 64
Advanced placement (AP) credit accepted for prerequisites: Yes
Advanced placement (AP) credit accepted for electives: No
Job shadowing: Required
Number of hours of job shadowing required or recommended: Minimum 30
Other factors considered in admission: DAT scores, GPA, and noncognitive factors

DAT

Mandatory: Yes
Latest DAT for consideration of application: 12/01/2015
Oldest DAT considered: 06/01/2012
When more than one DAT score is reported: Most recent score only is considered
Canadian DAT accepted: Yes
Application considered before DAT scores are submitted: No

DAT: 2014 ENTERING CLASS

ENROLLEE DAT SCORES	MEAN	RANGE
Academic Average	20.1	16–27
Perceptual Ability	20.9	15–27
Total Science	19.9	16–30

GPA: 2014 ENTERING CLASS

ENROLLEE GPA SCORES	MEAN	RANGE
Science GPA	3.51	2.65–4.20
Total GPA	3.57	2.84–4.18

APPLICATION AND SELECTION

TIMETABLE

Earliest filing date: 06/02/2015
Latest filing date: 12/01/2015
Earliest date for acceptance offers: 12/01/2015
Maximum time in days for applicant's response to acceptance offer: Varies
Requests for deferred entrance considered: For special circumstances
Fee for application: Yes, submitted at same time as AADSAS application
Amount of fee for application:
   In state: $85   Out of state: $85   International: $85
Fee waiver available: No

	FIRST DEPOSIT	SECOND DEPOSIT	THIRD DEPOSIT
Required to hold place	Yes	Yes	No
Resident amount	$1,000	$500	
Nonresident amount	$1,000	$500	
International amount	$1,000	$500	
Deposit due	Varies	Varies	
Applied to tuition	Yes	Yes	
Refundable	No		

APPLICATION PROCESS

Participates in Associated American Dental Schools Application Service (AADSAS): Yes
Accepts direct applicants: No
Secondary or supplemental application required: Yes
Secondary or supplemental application website: www.dentistry.umn.edu
Interview is mandatory: Yes
Interview is by invitation: Yes

RESIDENCY

In-state/in-province versus out-of-state/out-of-province
Admissions process distinguishes between in-state/in-province and out-of-state/out-of-province applicants: Yes
Preference given to residents of: NA
Reciprocity Admissions Agreement available for legal residents of: NA
Generally and over time, percentage of your first-year enrollment that is in-state: 60%
Origin of out-of-state/out-of-province enrollees: AZ-1, CA-3, IA-2, IL-1, MI-2, MT-2, ND-6, PR-1, SD-2, TX-3, VA-1, WA-1, WI-4

International
Applications are accepted from international (noncitizens/ nonpermanent residents): Yes
Origin of international enrollees: Canada-6, Vietnam-1

APPLICATION AND ENROLLMENT	NUMBER OF APPLICANTS	ESTIMATED NUMBER INTERVIEWED	ESTIMATED NUMBER ENROLLED
In-state or province applicants/ enrollees	224	102	65
Out-of-state or province applicants/enrollees	928	153	35
International applicants/enrollees (noncitizens/nonpermanent residents)	172	37	6

DEMOGRAPHIC DESCRIPTIONS OF APPLICANTS: 2014 ENTERING CLASS

	APPLICANTS			ENROLLEES		
	M	W	Gender Unknown or Not Reported	M	W	Gender Unknown or Not Reported
American Indian or Alaska Native	3	12	0	1	1	0
Asian	194	158	5	12	4	0
Black or African American	9	20	1	1	2	0
Hispanic or Latino	19	20	0	2	2	0
Native Hawaiian or Other Pacific Islander	0	2	0	0	0	0
White	410	313	6	45	32	0
Two or more races	26	33	0	3	2	0
Race and ethnicity unknown	26	18	6	3	0	0
International	99	70	4	5	2	0

	MINIMUM	MAXIMUM	MEAN
2014 entering class enrollees by age	20	41	24

CURRICULUM

U of M SOD has a strong reputation for educating fine clinicians and diagnosticians through a curriculum that involves progressive introduction to clinical training, integration of basic and applied clinical skills, and group and problem-based learning situations. During the students' final year, U of M SOD offers experiences in outreach clinical practice sites and a comprehensive-care clinic setting within the school. The school also encourages students to take elective courses in dental and other disciplines to enhance their clinical, didactic and research knowledge base. The goal of the dental curriculum is to educate dental professionals whose scholarly capabilities, scientific acumen, cultural competency and interpersonal skills are commensurate with their clinical mastery. This goal will provide graduates with the flexibility to adapt to continuing changes in health care and to developments in the practice of dentistry.

Student research opportunities: The summer research fellowship program during the first and second years provides a great opportunity for qualified students to conduct research with faculty mentors and contribute to the progress of dental and craniofacial research.

SPECIAL PROGRAMS AND SERVICES

PREDENTAL
American Student Dental Association Drill and Fill Experience

DURING DENTAL SCHOOL
Academic counseling and tutoring
Community service opportunities
Internships, externships, or extramural programs
Mentoring
Opportunity to study for credit at institution abroad
Personal counseling
Professional- and career-development programming
Research fellowships
Training for those interested in academic careers
Transfer applicants considered if space is available

ACTIVE STUDENT ORGANIZATIONS
American Association of Public Health Dentistry
American Dental Education Association
American Student Dental Association
Hispanic Student Dental Association
Student Council

INTERNATIONAL DENTISTS
Graduates of international dental schools considered for traditional predoctoral program: Yes
Advanced standing program offered for graduates of international dental schools: Yes
Advanced standing program description: The program awards a dental degree.

COMBINED AND ALTERNATE DEGREES

Ph.D.	M.S.	M.P.H.	M.D.	B.A./B.S.	Other
✓	✓	✓	—	✓	—

COSTS: 2013–14 SCHOOL YEAR

	FIRST YEAR	SECOND YEAR	THIRD YEAR	FOURTH YEAR
Tuition, resident	$31,304	$39,304	$39,800	$38,923
Tuition, nonresident	$56,624	$72,124	$71,124	$70,766
Tuition, other	$56,942	$72,601	$72,601	$72,601
Fees	$5,340	$5,912	$5,215	$4,498
Instruments, books, and supplies	$6,058	$6,848	$6,408	$5,640
Estimated living expenses	$10,188	$13,584	$13,584	$13,584
Total, resident	$55,640	$69,811	$68,674	$66,371
Total, nonresident	$80,960	$101,735	$100,598	$98,214
Total, other	$81,278	$102,212	$101,075	$98,601

FINANCIAL AID

Students in need of financial aid to help meet their educational costs must complete the Free Application for Federal Student Aid, available after January 1. The application for financial aid starts in January. There is no application priority date, but please submit the application by the end of April. Apply online at www.fafsa.ed.gov. The University of Minnesota Twin Cities Federal Code Number is 003969. Financial aid packets are mailed in February. The School of Dentistry offers a limited number of scholarships. For more information on financial aid and scholarships, visit our website at www.dentistry.umn.edu or email Liz Holm at holmx029@umn.edu.

CONTACT INFORMATION

http://dentistry.umc.edu
School of Dentistry
2500 North State Street
Jackson, MS 39216
Phone: 601-984-6000
Fax: 601-984-6014

ADMISSIONS

Dr. John B. Smith
Assistant Dean
School of Dentistry
2500 North State Street
Jackson, MS 39216
Phone: 601-984-6060

OFFICE OF STUDENT FINANCIAL AID

Ms. Carrie Cooper
Director-Student Financial Aid
Office of Financial Aid
2500 North State Street
Jackson, MS 39216
Phone: 601-815-4174
Email: cecooper@umc.edu

UNIVERSITY OF MISSISSIPPI
SCHOOL OF DENTISTRY

Gary W. Reeves, D.M.D., Dean

GENERAL INFORMATION

The University of Mississippi School of Dentistry's diverse student body, faculty and staff exemplify qualities of leadership and dedication not only to preparing competent, ethical dentists for the state of Mississippi, but also to furthering the health of its citizens. The School of Dentistry fosters an environment of lifelong learning, collaborative teaching, service and research through partnerships within the Medical Center and with community organizations and dental health practitioners throughout the State of Mississippi.

Vision: The University of Mississippi School of Dentistry will be a nationally recognized center of excellence in education, patient care, research and services for the citizens of Mississippi.

Core Values: Integrity and Excellence, Leadership and Professionalism, Continuous Improvement, Diversity, Caring

Type of institution: Public
Year opened: 1975
Term type: Semester
Time to degree in months: 48
Start month: August

Doctoral dental degree offered: D.M.D.
Targeted predoctoral enrollment: 140
Targeted entering class size: 35
Campus setting: Urban
Campus housing available: No

PREPARATION

Formal minimum preparation in semester/quarter hours: Semester: 90   Quarter: 120
Baccalaureate degree preferred: Yes
Number of first-year, first-time enrollees whose highest degree is:
    Baccalaureate: 23
    Master's degree and beyond: 12
Of first-year, first-time enrollees without baccalaureates, the number with:
    Equivalent of 60 undergraduate credit hours or less: 0
    Equivalent of 61–90 undergraduate credit hours: 0
    Equivalent of 91 or more undergraduate credit hours: 0

PREREQUISITE COURSE	REQUIRED	RECOMMENDED	LAB REQUIRED	CREDITS (SEMESTER/QUARTER)
BCP (biology-chemistry-physics) sciences				
Biology (or Zoology)	✓		✓	2/3
Chemistry, general/inorganic	✓		✓	2/3
Chemistry, organic	✓		✓	2/3
Physics	✓		✓	2/3
Additional biological sciences				
Anatomy*	✓			2/3
Biochemistry*	✓			2/3
Cell biology		✓		
Histology		✓		
Immunology		✓		
Microbiology*	✓			2/3
Molecular biology/genetics		✓		
Physiology		✓		
Zoology (or Biology)	✓		✓	2/3

*Note: One course in comparative anatomy, biochemistry, or microbiology is required.

PREPARATION (CONTINUED)

PREREQUISITE COURSE	REQUIRED	RECOMMENDED	LAB REQUIRED	CREDITS (SEMESTER/QUARTER)
Other				
English	✓			2/3
Mathematics (college algebra and trigonometry or higher level)	✓			2/3
Statistics or biostatistics (general, business, or scientific statistics), in addition to one-year mathematics requirement)	✓			1/1

Community college coursework accepted for prerequisites: Yes
Community college coursework accepted for electives: Yes
Limits on community college credit hours: Yes
Maximum number of community college credit hours: 65
Advanced placement (AP) credit accepted for prerequisites: No
Advanced placement (AP) credit accepted for electives: Yes
Job shadowing: Required
Number of hours of job shadowing required or recommended: 100

DAT

Mandatory: Yes
Latest DAT for consideration of application: 10/31/2015
Oldest DAT considered: 10/31/2012
When more than one DAT score is reported: Highest score is considered
Canadian DAT accepted: No
Application considered before DAT scores are submitted: No

DAT: 2014 ENTERING CLASS

ENROLLEE DAT SCORES	MEAN	RANGE
Academic Average	18.7	17–24
Perceptual Ability	19.6	15–25
Total Science	18.6	16–27

GPA: 2014 ENTERING CLASS

ENROLLEE GPA SCORES	UNDERGRAD. MEAN	GRADUATE MEAN	UNDERGRAD. RANGE	GRADUATE RANGE
Science GPA	3.53	3.65	2.26–4.00	3.00–4.00
Total GPA	3.62	3.65	2.56–4.00	3.00–4.00

APPLICATION AND SELECTION

TIMETABLE

Earliest filing date: 06/02/2015
Latest filing date: 09/25/2015
Earliest date for acceptance offers: 12/01/2015
Maximum time in days for applicant's response to acceptance offer: 30 days from receipt of offer letter
Requests for deferred entrance considered: In exceptional circumstances only
Fee for application: Yes
Amount of fee for application:
    In state: $245   Out of state: NA   International: NA
Fee waiver available: No

	FIRST DEPOSIT	SECOND DEPOSIT	THIRD DEPOSIT
Required to hold place	No	No	No

APPLICATION PROCESS

Participates in Associated American Dental Schools Application Service (AADSAS): Yes
Accepts direct applicants: No
Secondary or supplemental application required: Yes
Interview is mandatory: Yes
Interview is by invitation: Yes

RESIDENCY

In-state/in-province versus out-of-state/out-of-province
Admissions process distinguishes between in-state/in-province and out-of-state/out-of-province applicants: Yes
Preference given to residents of: Mississippi
Reciprocity Admissions Agreement available for legal residents of: None
Generally and over time, percentage of your first-year enrollment that is in-state: 100%
Origin of out-of-state/out-of-province enrollees: NA

International
Applications are accepted from international (noncitizens/nonpermanent residents): No
Origin of international enrollees: NA

APPLICATION AND ENROLLMENT	NUMBER OF APPLICANTS	ESTIMATED NUMBER INTERVIEWED	ESTIMATED NUMBER ENROLLED
In-state or province applicants/enrollees	119	89	35
Out-of-state or province applicants/enrollees	0	0	0
International applicants/enrollees (noncitizens/nonpermanent residents)	NA	NA	NA

DEMOGRAPHIC DESCRIPTIONS OF APPLICANTS: 2014 ENTERING CLASS

	APPLICANTS			ENROLLEES		
	M	W	Gender Unknown or Not Reported	M	W	Gender Unknown or Not Reported
American Indian or Alaska Native	0	0	0	0	0	0
Asian	7	11	0	2	1	0
Black or African American	4	7	0	2	2	0
Hispanic or Latino	1	4	0	0	2	0
Native Hawaiian or Other Pacific Islander	0	0	0	0	0	0
White	47	30	0	15	9	0
Two or more races	3	1	0	0	1	0
Race and ethnicity unknown	3	1	0	0	1	0
International	0	0	0	0	0	0

	MINIMUM	MAXIMUM	MEAN
2014 entering class enrollees by age	22	38	25

CURRICULUM

The major emphasis of the dental curriculum is to train practitioners of general dentistry to provide total health care. This training is accomplished by employing a systems approach to a problem-oriented curriculum. Clinical experience begins in the second year, and a team approach to patient care is used on a limited basis through all four years. A team comprises one student from each class. Basic science and clinical science courses are integrated. Off-campus clinical experiences begin in the first year with a one-week community project somewhere in the state. These continue throughout the four years. All clinical faculty are evaluated yearly by the third and fourth year students, and all courses are evaluated on a four-year cycle. Student learning laboratories, including a patient-simulation suite, are utilized by all classes.

Student research opportunities: Yes

SPECIAL PROGRAMS AND SERVICES

PREDENTAL
DAT workshops
Impressions Program (Student National Dental Association)
Postbaccalaureate programs
Summer enrichment programs

DURING DENTAL SCHOOL
Academic counseling and tutoring
Community service opportunities
Internships, externships, or extramural programs
Mentoring
Personal counseling
Professional- and career development programming
Training for those interested in academic careers

ACTIVE STUDENT ORGANIZATIONS
American Academy of Pediatric Dentistry
American Association for Dental Research National Student Research Group
American Association of Women Dentists
American Dental Education Association
American Student Dental Association
Hispanic Student Dental Association
Student National Dental Association

INTERNATIONAL DENTISTS
Graduates of international dental schools considered for traditional predoctoral program: No
Advanced standing program offered for graduates of international dental schools: No

COMBINED AND ALTERNATE DEGREES

Ph.D.	M.S.	M.P.H.	M.D.	B.A./B.S.	Other
—	—	—	—	—	—

COSTS: 2014–15 SCHOOL YEAR

	FIRST YEAR	SECOND YEAR	THIRD YEAR	FOURTH YEAR
Tuition, resident	$24,310	$24,310	$24,310	$24,310
Tuition, nonresident	$24,310	$24,310	$24,310	$24,310
Tuition, other				
Fees	$0	$350	$2,340	$650
Instruments, books, and supplies	$7,000	$3,200	$1,950	$1,240
Estimated living expenses	$23,612	$23,612	$30,663	$30,663
Total, resident	$54,922	$51,472	$59,263	$56,863
Total, nonresident	$54,922	$51,472	$59,263	$56,863
Total, other				

FINANCIAL AID

FINANCIAL AID AWARDS TO FIRST-YEAR STUDENTS 2014–15

Total number of first-year recipients: 32
Percentage of the first-year class: 86.4%
Percentage of awards that are grants? 22%
Percentage of awards that are loans? 78%

	AVERAGE AWARDS	RANGE OF AWARDS
Residents	$41,068	Up to $53,250
Nonresidents	NA	NA

For more information, please visit: http://www.umc.edu/sod/

A.T. STILL UNIVERSITY
MISSOURI SCHOOL OF DENTISTRY & ORAL HEALTH

Christopher G. Halliday, D.D.S., M.P.H., Dean

GENERAL INFORMATION

The Missouri School of Dentistry & Oral Health (MOSDOH) prepares caring, technologically adept dentists to become community and educational leaders. The school offers students an experience-rich learning environment where health professionals approach patient health as part of a team. MOSDOH is part of A.T. Still University, which also includes the Kirksville College of Osteopathic Medicine, Arizona School of Health Sciences, College of Graduate Health Studies, Arizona School of Dentistry & Oral Health, and School of Osteopathic Medicine in Arizona.

MISSION

To graduate caring, technologically adept dentists who will become community and educational leaders, serving those in need and leading the lifelong education of community-responsive oral health providers.

Core Values:

- Optimal patient care delivery
- Transfer of newly acquired knowledge, skills and technology to the profession and to the community

Type of institution: Private
Year opened: 2013
Term type: Semester
Time to degree in months: 48
Start month: July

Doctoral dental degree offered: D.M.D.
Targeted predoctoral enrollment: 168
Targeted entering class size: 42
Campus setting: Rural
Campus housing available: Yes

PREPARATION

Formal minimum preparation in semester/quarter hours: Semester: 90   Quarter: 135
Baccalaureate degree preferred: Yes
Number of first-year, first-time enrollees whose highest degree is:
    Baccalaureate: 38
    Master's degree and beyond: 4
Of first-year, first-time enrollees without baccalaureates, the number with:
    Equivalent of 60 undergraduate credit hours or less: 0
    Equivalent of 61–90 undergraduate credit hours: 0
    Equivalent of 91 or more undergraduate credit hours: 0

PREREQUISITE COURSE	REQUIRED	RECOMMENDED	LAB REQUIRED	CREDITS (SEMESTER/QUARTER)
BCP (biology-chemistry-physics) sciences				
Biology	✓		✓	8/12
Chemistry, general/inorganic	✓		✓	8/12
Chemistry, organic	✓		✓	8/12
Physics	✓		✓	8/12
Additional biological sciences				
Anatomy		✓		
Biochemistry	✓			3/4
Cell biology				
Histology				
Immunology				
Microbiology		✓		
Molecular biology/genetics				
Physiology	✓			3/4

(Prerequisite Courses continued)

PREPARATION (CONTINUED)

PREREQUISITE COURSE	REQUIRED	RECOMMENDED	LAB REQUIRED	CREDITS (SEMESTER/QUARTER)
Zoology				
Other				
English composition/technical writing	✓			3/4

Community college coursework accepted for prerequisites: Yes
Community college coursework accepted for electives: Yes
Limits on community college credit hours: No
Advanced placement (AP) credit accepted for prerequisites: Yes
Advanced placement (AP) credit accepted for electives: Yes
Job shadowing: Recommended
Number of hours of job shadowing required or recommended: 75
Other factors considered in admission: Community service experience is expected.

DAT

Mandatory: Yes
Latest DAT for consideration of application: 12/01/2015
Oldest DAT considered: 01/01/2012
When more than one DAT score is reported: Highest academic average score is considered.
Canadian DAT accepted: No
Application considered before DAT scores are submitted: No

DAT: 2014 ENTERING CLASS

ENROLLEE DAT SCORES	MEAN	RANGE
Academic Average	18.4	16–21
Perceptual Ability	19.2	13–24
Total Science	17.8	15–22

GPA: 2014 ENTERING CLASS

ENROLLEE GPA SCORES	UNDERGRAD. MEAN	GRADUATE MEAN	UNDERGRAD. RANGE	GRADUATE RANGE
Science GPA	3.33	3.67	2.74–3.89	3.12–4.00
Total GPA	3.45	3.63	3.05–3.86	3.19–3.88

APPLICATION AND SELECTION

TIMETABLE

Earliest filing date: 06/02/2015
Latest filing date: 12/01/2015
Earliest date for acceptance offers: 12/01/2015
Maximum time in days for applicant's response to acceptance offer:
    30 days if accepted on or after December 1 through January 31
    15 days if accepted on or after February 1
    48 hours after May 1
Requests for deferred entrance considered: In exceptional circumstances only
Fee for application: Yes, submitted only when requested
Amount of fee for application:
    In state: $70   Out of state: $70   International: NA
Fee waiver available: Yes

	FIRST DEPOSIT	SECOND DEPOSIT	THIRD DEPOSIT
Required to hold place	Yes	Yes	No
Resident amount	$1,000	$1,000	
Nonresident amount	$1,000	$1,000	
Deposit due	As indicated in admission offer	05/01/2016	
Applied to tuition	Yes	Yes	
Refundable	No	No	

APPLICATION PROCESS

Participates in Associated American Dental Schools Application Service (AADSAS): Yes
Accepts direct applicants: No
Secondary or supplemental application required: Yes
Secondary or supplemental application website: Invitation will be sent by email.
Interview is mandatory: Yes
Interview is by invitation: Yes

RESIDENCY

In-state/in-province versus out-of-state/out-of-province
Admissions process distinguishes between in-state/in-province and out-of-state/out-of-province applicants: No
Preference given to residents of: None
Reciprocity Admissions Agreement available for legal residents of: NR
Generally and over time, percentage of your first-year enrollment that is in-state: 25%
Origin of out-of-state/out-of-province enrollees: AL-1, AR-1, AZ-1, CA-2, GA-2, IA-2, ID-1, IL-5, KS-5, MI-1, MN-2, NE-2, OK-2, TX-2, UT-1

International
Applications are accepted from international (noncitizens/nonpermanent residents): No
Origin of international enrollees: NA

APPLICATION AND ENROLLMENT	NUMBER OF APPLICANTS	ESTIMATED NUMBER INTERVIEWED	ESTIMATED NUMBER ENROLLED
In-state or province applicants/enrollees	107	28	12
Out-of-state or province applicants/enrollees	922	86	30
International applicants/enrollees (noncitizens/nonpermanent residents)	0	0	0

DEMOGRAPHIC DESCRIPTIONS OF APPLICANTS: 2014 ENTERING CLASS

	APPLICANTS			ENROLLEES		
	M	W	Gender Unknown or Not Reported	M	W	Gender Unknown or Not Reported
American Indian or Alaska Native	1	5	0	0	1	0
Asian	145	128	3	5	0	0
Black or African American	14	19	0	0	0	0
Hispanic or Latino	30	27	0	1	1	0
Native Hawaiian or Other Pacific Islander	1	0	0	0	0	0
White	351	204	2	9	22	0
Two or more races	26	32	0	1	0	0
Race and ethnicity unknown	26	11	4	1	1	0
International	0	0	0	0	0	0

	MINIMUM	MAXIMUM	MEAN
2014 entering class enrollees by age	21	29	24

CURRICULUM

The curriculum at MOSDOH is designed to produce graduates who are technologically adept, professionally competent, patient-centered and compassionate. The curriculum emphasizes patient care experiences through simulation, integration of biomedical and clinical sciences, and problem-solving scenarios to achieve clinical excellence. The curriculum includes a strong component of public health, leadership and practice through weekly learning modules.

Student research opportunities: Yes

SPECIAL PROGRAMS AND SERVICES

DURING DENTAL SCHOOL
Academic counseling and tutoring
Community service opportunities
Internships, externships, or extramural programs
Mentoring
Personal counseling

INTERNATIONAL DENTISTS

Graduates of international dental schools considered for traditional predoctoral program: No
Advanced standing program offered for graduates of international dental schools: No

COMBINED AND ALTERNATE DEGREES

Ph.D.	M.S.	M.P.H.	M.D.	B.A./B.S.	Other
—	—	✓	—	—	—

COSTS: 2014–15 SCHOOL YEAR

	FIRST YEAR	SECOND YEAR	THIRD YEAR	FOURTH YEAR
Tuition, resident	$61,344	$61,344	NR	NR
Tuition, nonresident	$61,344	$61,344		
Tuition, other				
Fees	$16,348	$14,517		
Instruments, books, and supplies	$1,724			
Estimated living expenses	$23,033	$22,583		
Total, resident	$102,449	$98,444		
Total, nonresident	$102,449	$98,444		
Total, other				

FINANCIAL AID

A.T. Still University (ATSU) Missouri School of Dentistry & Oral Health (MOS-DOH) participates in the Federal Direct Loan Program. Student loans are available for tuition, fees and living expenses. MOSDOH is also involved in a number of scholarship programs, such as the Health Professions Scholarship Program (military). Federal loans are the most common form of financial assistance, with 95% of the student body using these loans.

FINANCIAL AID AWARDS TO FIRST-YEAR STUDENTS 2014–15

Total number of first-year recipients: 38
Percentage of the first-year class: 90%
Percentage of awards that are grants? 0%
Percentage of awards that are loans? 95%

	AVERAGE AWARDS	RANGE OF AWARDS
Residents and nonresidents	$89,377	Up to $100,439

For more information, please visit: www.atsu.edu/financial_aid/index.htm

UNIVERSITY OF MISSOURI - KANSAS CITY
SCHOOL OF DENTISTRY

Marsha A. Pyle, D.D.S., M.Ed., Dean

GENERAL INFORMATION

The University of Missouri - Kansas City School of Dentistry (UMKC SOD), which has maintained a tradition of excellence for more than a century, offers a varied and complete range of education experiences for dental, dental hygiene, graduate and continuing education students. The first-rate faculty comprises scholars, scientists and specialists dedicated to providing a quality and comprehensive education adapted to students' needs and goals.

UMKC, which has a paperless clinic with 279 dental operatories, delivers clinical care to more than 60,000 patients annually. With neighbors including the UMKC schools of Medicine and Nursing, Children's Mercy Hospital, Truman Medical Center and several other private and public medical facilities, students can learn, work and interact with scholars, researchers and professionals in many related health care areas.

MISSION

To provide educational programs that develop engaged learners who are also competent, compassionate and caring clinicians who are involved in their communities.

Vision: To gain national and international recognition for excellence in research and improved services to the community.

Type of institution: Public	Doctoral dental degree offered: D.D.S.
Year opened: 1881	Targeted predoctoral enrollment: 436
Term type: Semester	Targeted entering class size: 109
Time to degree in months: 40	Campus setting: Urban
Start month: August	Campus housing available: Yes, on the Volker Campus.

PREPARATION

Formal minimum preparation in semester/quarter hours: Semester: 120   Quarter: 180
Baccalaureate degree preferred: Yes
Number of first-year, first-time enrollees whose highest degree is:
    Baccalaureate: 104
    Master's degree and beyond: 5
Of first-year, first-time enrollees without baccalaureates, the number with:
    Equivalent of 60 undergraduate credit hours or less: 0
    Equivalent of 61–90 undergraduate credit hours: 0
    Equivalent of 91 or more undergraduate credit hours: 0

PREREQUISITE COURSE	REQUIRED	RECOMMENDED	LAB REQUIRED	CREDITS (SEMESTER/QUARTER)
BCP (biology-chemistry-physics) sciences				
Biology	✓		✓	8/12
Chemistry, general/inorganic	✓		✓	8/12
Chemistry, organic	✓		✓	8/12
Physics	✓		✓	8/12
Additional biological sciences				
Anatomy	✓		✓	4/6
Biochemistry	✓			4/6
Cell biology	✓			4/6
Histology		✓		
Immunology				
Microbiology		✓		3

PREPARATION (CONTINUED)

PREREQUISITE COURSE	REQUIRED	RECOMMENDED	LAB REQUIRED	CREDITS (SEMESTER/QUARTER)
Molecular biology/genetics		✓		
Physiology	✓		✓	4/6
Zoology				

Community college coursework accepted for prerequisites: Yes, contact Director of Admissions for guidance.
Community college coursework accepted for electives: Yes
Limits on community college credit hours: Yes
Maximum number of community college credit hours: 60
Advanced placement (AP) credit accepted for prerequisites: No
Advanced placement (AP) credit accepted for electives: May be applied to undergraduate degree
Comments regarding AP credit: (1) May be applied to the undergraduate degree prior to entry into the D.D.S. program; (2) Do not meet prerequisite requirements unless have additional advanced courses in subject
Job shadowing: Required
Number of hours of job shadowing required or recommended: Minimum of five office settings, 100-120 hours
Other factors considered in admission: Investigation of dentistry, commitment to community, personal character, critical thinking/problem solving skills, interpersonal communication skills, and time management skills

DAT

Mandatory: Yes
Latest DAT for consideration of application: 10/01/2014
Oldest DAT for consideration of application: 10/01/2010
When more than one DAT score is reported: Most recent score only is considered
Canadian DAT accepted: Yes
Application considered before DAT scores are submitted: Applications are reviewed after the DAT scores arrive.

DAT: 2014 ENTERING CLASS

ENROLLEE DAT SCORES	MEAN	RANGE
Academic Average	18.9	16–23
Perceptual Ability	19.6	17–25
Total Science	19.1	16–22

GPA: 2014 ENTERING CLASS

ENROLLEE GPA SCORES	UNDERGRAD. MEAN	GRADUATE MEAN	UNDERGRAD. RANGE	GRADUATE RANGE
Science GPA	3.60	NR	3.10–4.00	NR
Total GPA	3.60	NR	3.00–4.00	NR

APPLICATION AND SELECTION

TIMETABLE

Earliest filing date: 06/02/2015
Latest filing date: 10/01/2015 (09/01/2015 preference deadline)
Earliest date for acceptance offers: 12/01/2015
Maximum time in days for applicant's response to acceptance offer:
  30 days if accepted on or after December 1
  15 days if accepted on or after February 1
Requests for deferred entrance considered: In exceptional circumstances only
Fee for application: Yes, submitted only when requested

Amount of fee for application:
  In state: $35   Out of state: $35   International: NA
Fee waiver available: No

	FIRST DEPOSIT	SECOND DEPOSIT	THIRD DEPOSIT
Required to hold place	Yes	No	No
Resident amount	$200		
Nonresident amount	$200		
Deposit due	As indicated in admission offer		
Applied to tuition	Yes		
Refundable	No		

APPLICATION PROCESS

Participates in Associated American Dental Schools Application Service (AADSAS): Yes
Accepts direct applicants: Yes
Secondary or supplemental application required: Yes, with interview invitation
Secondary or supplemental application website: The UMKC School of Dentistry Survey is only available from our office.
Interview is mandatory: Yes
Interview is by invitation: Yes

RESIDENCY

In-state/in-province versus out-of-state/out-of-province
Admissions process distinguishes between in-state/in-province and out-of-state/out-of-province applicants: Yes
Preference given to residents of: Arkansas, Hawaii, Kansas, Missouri, and New Mexico. Highly qualified applicants outside these states are welcome to apply.
Reciprocity Admissions Agreement available for legal residents of: Arkansas, Kansas, New Mexico
Generally and over time, percentage of your first-year enrollment that is in-state: 70%
Origin of out-of-state/out-of-province enrollees: AL-1, CA-1, HI-3, ID-1, IL-1, KS-22, NM-3, TX-1

International
Applications are accepted from international (noncitizens/nonpermanent residents): No
Origin of international enrollees: NA

APPLICATION AND ENROLLMENT	NUMBER OF APPLICANTS	ESTIMATED NUMBER INTERVIEWED	ESTIMATED NUMBER ENROLLED
In-state or province applicants/enrollees	150	76	76
Out-of-state or province applicants/enrollees	660	61	33
International applicants/enrollees (noncitizens/nonpermanent residents)	12	NR	NA

DEMOGRAPHIC DESCRIPTIONS OF APPLICANTS: 2014 ENTERING CLASS

	APPLICANTS			ENROLLEES		
	M	W	Gender Unknown or Not Reported	M	W	Gender Unknown or Not Reported
American Indian or Alaska Native	1	4	0	0	1	0
Asian	98	96	1	2	5	0
Black or African American	10	11	0	0	1	0
Hispanic or Latino	21	20	0	5	3	0
Native Hawaiian or Other Pacific Islander	1	0	0	0	0	0
White	286	211	4	54	33	0
Two or more races	17	10	0	2	2	0
Race and ethnicity unknown	9	7	4	0	0	1
International	4	7	1	0	0	0

	MINIMUM	MAXIMUM	MEAN
2014 entering year enrollees by age	21	40	25

CURRICULUM

The curriculum (eight semesters and two summer terms) offers an education leading to an effective and enriching career of public service, professional growth and contribution. The program provides a sound background in the biomedical, behavioral and clinical sciences with an emphasis on comprehensive oral health care delivered through a generalist-based team system of clinical education. Practice management courses are also built into the curriculum. The early exposure to clinical dentistry and the multidisciplinary, integrated preclinical curriculum is a hallmark of the program. Degrees Offered: Dental Degree—D.D.S. Additional Degrees: B.S. in Dental Hygiene; M.S. in Dental Hygiene Education; M.S. in Oral Biology; interdisciplinary Ph.D. program; graduate professional certificates in advanced dental education in general dentistry, oral and maxillofacial surgery, orthodontics and dentofacial orthopedics, pediatric dentistry, periodontics, and endodontics; and a variety of continuing education courses.

Student research opportunities: Yes: Summer Scholars Research Program following the first year of the D.D.S. program

SPECIAL PROGRAMS AND SERVICES

PREDENTAL

Online DAT Preparatory course available at www.cewebinar.com
Admissions Enhancement Program
Dental Explorer's Post

DURING DENTAL SCHOOL

Academic counseling and tutoring
Community service opportunities
Internships, externships, or extramural programs
Mentoring
Online National Board Dental Examination Part II preparatory course
Personal counseling
Professional- and career-development programming
Senior Departmental Advanced Studies Program
Training for those interested in academic careers
Transfer applicants considered if space is available

ACTIVE STUDENT ORGANIZATIONS

Academy of LDS Dentists
American Association for Dental Research National Student Research Group
American Academy of Pediatric Dentistry
American Association of Women Dentists
American Dental Education Association
American Society of Dentistry for Children
Fraternities, including Interfraternity Council, Delta Sigma Delta International Dental Fraternity, Psi Omega Fraternity and Xi Psi Dental Fraternity.
Hispanic Dental Association
Student dental associations, including American Student Dental Association and Student National Dental Association
Students Take Action

INTERNATIONAL DENTISTS

Graduates of international dental schools considered for traditional predoctoral program: Yes, they are considered only if space is available in the second year. They must be permanent residents or U.S. citizens. Additionally, their legal state of residence must be Missouri or Kansas.

Advanced standing program offered for graduates of international dental schools: No

COMBINED AND ALTERNATE DEGREES

Ph.D.	M.S.	M.P.H.	M.D.	B.A./B.S.	Other
✓	✓	—	—	—	—

COSTS: 2014–15 SCHOOL YEAR

	FIRST YEAR	SECOND YEAR	THIRD YEAR	FOURTH YEAR
Tuition, resident	$28,349	$28,349	$35,346	$35,346
Tuition, nonresident	$55,210	$55,210	$69,334	$69,334
Tuition, other*	$42,524	$42,524	$53,019	$53,019
Fees				
Instruments, books, and supplies	$11,525	$9,125	$8,500	$9,165
Estimated living expenses	$17,230	$17,230	$17,230	$17,230
Total, resident	$57,104	$54,704	$61,076	$61,741-
Total, nonresident	$83,965	$81,565	$95,064	$95,729
Total, other*	$71,279	$68,879	$78,749	$79,414

*Midwest Student Exchange Program (150% of in-state tuition)

FINANCIAL AID

The University of Missouri-Kansas City Cashiers Office makes public current tuition rates, other costs and payment information. For more information visit www.umkc.edu.

For more information, please visit: www.umkc.edu/dentistry

CREIGHTON
UNIVERSITY
SCHOOL OF
DENTISTRY

CREIGHTON UNIVERSITY
SCHOOL OF DENTISTRY

Mark A. Latta, D.M.D., M.S., Dean

GENERAL INFORMATION

Creighton University, a private Jesuit school with a total enrollment of approximately 7,000 students, is one of the most diverse educational institutions of its size in the nation. Creighton University School of Dentistry (Creighton SOD) was established in 1905. Although Creighton SOD directs its major effort toward its D.D.S. degree program, the school also offers continuing education courses and cooperates with several local junior colleges in the training of allied dental professionals. In addition, Creighton SOD conducts research, provides dental health and dental health education services to the local community, and participates in an outreach program to the Dominican Republic. Creighton SOD is a regional resource. Creighton students come from all parts of the United States, its territories and other countries.

MISSION

To care for the oral health needs of society, particularly those with inadequate dental health due to isolation or the unavailability of dental health facilities.

Vision: To educate dental practitioners who are biologically oriented, clinically competent, socially sensitive, and ethically and morally responsible.

Core Values: Adhering to principles set forth by the Society of Jesus during its half millennium of existence, Creighton SOD promotes values that are Judeo-Christian in philosophy.

Type of institution: Private
Year opened: 1905
Term type: Semester
Time to degree in months: 44
Start month: August

Doctoral dental degree offered: D.D.S.
Targeted predoctoral enrollment: 340
Targeted entering class size: 85
Campus setting: Urban
Campus housing available: Yes

PREPARATION

Formal minimum preparation in semester/quarter hours: Semester: 64   Quarter: 96
Baccalaureate degree preferred: Yes
Number of first-year, first-time enrollees whose highest degree is:
   Baccalaureate: 77
   Master's degree and beyond: 6
Of first-year, first-time enrollees without baccalaureates, the number with:
   Equivalent of 60 undergraduate credit hours or less: 0
   Equivalent of 61–90 undergraduate credit hours: 0
   Equivalent of 91 or more undergraduate credit hours: 85

PREREQUISITE COURSE	REQUIRED	RECOMMENDED	LAB REQUIRED	CREDITS (SEMESTER/QUARTER)
BCP (biology-chemistry-physics) sciences				
Biology	✓		✓	6/10
Chemistry, general/inorganic	✓		✓	8/12
Chemistry, organic	✓		✓	6/10
Physics	✓		✓	6/10
Additional biological sciences				
Anatomy		✓		3/5
Biochemistry		✓		3/5
Cell biology		✓		3/5
Histology		✓		3/5
Immunology		✓		3/5
Microbiology		✓		3/5

(Prerequisite Courses continued)

CONTACT INFORMATION
www.creighton.edu/dentalschool
2500 California Plaza
Omaha, NE 68178
Phone: 402-280-5092
Fax: 402-280-5094

ADMISSIONS
2500 California Plaza
Omaha, NE 68178
Phone: 402-280-2695 or 402-280-2881

FINANCIAL AID
2500 California Plaza
Omaha, NE 68178
Phone: 402-280-2731
www.creighton.edu/financial aid

MINORITY AFFAIRS/DIVERSITY
2500 California Plaza
Omaha, NE 68178
Phone: 402-280-2459
www.creighton.edu/about/diversity

HOUSING
2500 California Plaza
Omaha, NE 68178
Phone: 402-280-3016
www.creighton.edu

INTERNATIONAL STUDENTS
2500 California Plaza
Omaha, NE 68178
Phone: 402-280-2221
www.admissions.creighton.edu/international-students

PREPARATION (CONTINUED)

PREREQUISITE COURSE	REQUIRED	RECOMMENDED	LAB REQUIRED	CREDITS (SEMESTER/QUARTER)
Molecular biology/genetics		✓		3/5
Physiology		✓		3/5
Zoology				
Other				
English	✓			6/10

Community college coursework accepted for prerequisites: No
Community college coursework accepted for electives: Yes
Limits on community college credit hours: Yes
Maximum number of community college credit hours: 64
Advanced placement (AP) credit accepted for prerequisites: No
Advanced placement (AP) credit accepted for electives: No
Job shadowing: Recommended
Number of hours of job shadowing required or recommended: 40

DAT

Mandatory: Yes
Latest DAT for consideration of application: 02/28/2015
Oldest DAT considered: 12/31/2010
When more than one DAT score is reported: Most recent score only is considered
Canadian DAT accepted: Yes
Application considered before DAT scores are submitted: No

DAT: 2014 ENTERING CLASS

ENROLLEE DAT SCORES	MEAN	RANGE
Academic Average	19.1	17–24
Perceptual Ability	19.9	17–24
Total Science	18.8	17–26

GPA: 2014 ENTERING CLASS

ENROLLEE GPA SCORES	UNDERGRAD. MEAN	GRADUATE MEAN	UNDERGRAD. RANGE	GRADUATE RANGE
Science GPA	3.44	NR	3.17–4.00	NR
Total GPA	3.61	NR	2.85–4.00	NR

APPLICATION AND SELECTION

TIMETABLE

Earliest filing date: 06/02/2015
Latest filing date: 02/01/2016
Earliest date for acceptance offers: 12/01/2015
Maximum time in days for applicant's response to acceptance offer:
    30 days if accepted on or after December 1
    15 days if accepted on or after February 1
Requests for deferred entrance considered: In exceptional circumstances only.
Fee for application: Yes, submitted at same time as Associated American Dental Schools Application Service (AADSAS) application
Amount of fee for application:
    In state: $60   Out of state: $60   International: $60
Fee waiver available: No

	FIRST DEPOSIT	SECOND DEPOSIT	THIRD DEPOSIT
Required to hold place	Yes	Yes	No
Resident amount	$500	$300	
Nonresident amount	$500	$300	
Deposit due	As indicated in admission offer	As indicated in admission offer	
Applied to tuition	Yes	Yes	
Refundable	No	No	

APPLICATION PROCESS

Participates in AADSAS: Yes
Accepts direct applicants: No
Secondary or supplemental application required: Yes
Secondary or supplemental application website:
    www.creighton.edu/dentalschool/admissions/prospectivestudents/index.php
Interview is mandatory: No
Interview is by invitation: Yes

RESIDENCY

In-state/in-province versus out-of-state/out-of-province
Admissions process distinguishes between in-state/in-province and out-of-state/out-of-province applicants: No
Preference given to residents of: None
Reciprocity Admissions Agreement available for legal residents of: NR
Generally and over time, percentage of your first-year enrollment that is in-state: 12%
Origin of out-of-state/out-of-province enrollees: AL-1, AR-1, CA-4, CO-5, FL-1, HI-6, IA-2, ID-10, IL-4, KS-9, LA-1, MN-5, NM-6, ND-3, OH-2, OK-1, OR-3, SD-3, UT-1, WA-3, WY-4

International
Applications are accepted from international (noncitizens/nonpermanent residents): Yes
Origin of international enrollees: NA

APPLICATION AND ENROLLMENT	NUMBER OF APPLICANTS	ESTIMATED NUMBER INTERVIEWED	ESTIMATED NUMBER ENROLLED
In-state or province applicants/enrollees	66	13	10
Out-of-state or province applicants/enrollees	1,996	233	74
International applicants/enrollees (noncitizens/nonpermanent residents)	144	0	0

DEMOGRAPHIC DESCRIPTIONS OF APPLICANTS: 2014 ENTERING CLASS

	APPLICANTS			ENROLLEES		
	M	W	Gender Unknown or Not Reported	M	W	Gender Unknown or Not Reported
American Indian or Alaska Native	6	5	0	3	0	0
Asian	252	265	4	3	4	0
Black or African American	25	25	1	0	2	0
Hispanic or Latino	64	59	0	0	3	0
Native Hawaiian or Other Pacific Islander	5	1	0	3	0	0
White	782	450	4	32	29	0
Two or more races	32	26	0	4	0	0
Race and ethnicity unknown	27	23	6	0	0	1
International	90	52	2	0	0	0

	MINIMUM	MAXIMUM	MEAN
2014 entering class enrollees by age	21	35	24

CURRICULUM

The four-year program is designed to provide maximum opportunity for clinical application of basic concepts. Essentially, the curriculum is a progression of experiences from basic and preclinical sciences to mastery of clinical skills. Basic sciences are cooperatively taught by both dental and medical school faculty under the aegis of the Department of Oral Biology. Clinical sciences are taught by full-time clinical faculty with the assistance of part-time faculty. The full-time faculty, representing both basic and clinical science disciplines by training and experience, ensure integration of basic and clinical sciences. The part-time faculty bring extensive and varied experience, based on their own private practices, to add another dimension to the program and to reinforce the concepts being taught.

Student research opportunities: Yes

SPECIAL PROGRAMS AND SERVICES

PREDENTAL

Postbaccalaureate programs: Please see website.
Summer enrichment programs: Please see website.

DURING DENTAL SCHOOL

Academic counseling and tutoring
Community service opportunities
Internships, externships, or extramural programs
Mentoring
Opportunity to study for credit at institution abroad
Personal counseling
Professional- and career-development programming
Training for those interested in academic careers
Transfer applicants considered if space is available

ACTIVE STUDENT ORGANIZATIONS

American Association for Dental Research National Student Research Group
American Student Dental Association

INTERNATIONAL DENTISTS

Graduates of international dental schools considered for traditional predoctoral program: No
Advanced standing program offered for graduates of international dental schools: Yes, space-available program only
Advanced standing program description: Program awarding a dental degree

COMBINED AND ALTERNATE DEGREES

Ph.D.	M.S.	M.P.H.	M.D.	B.A./B.S.	Other
—	—	—	—	—	—

COSTS: 2014–15 SCHOOL YEAR

	FIRST YEAR	SECOND YEAR	THIRD YEAR	FOURTH YEAR
Tuition, resident	$54,474	$54,474	$54,474	$54,474
Tuition, nonresident	$54,474	$54,474	$54,474	$54,474
Tuition, other				
Fees	$1,564	$1,564	$1,564	$1,564
Instruments, books, and supplies	$7,686	$8,046	$7,386	$9,941
Estimated living expenses	$17,600	$17,600	$17,600	$14,400
Total, resident	$81,324	$81,684	$81,024	$80,379
Total, nonresident	$81,324	$81,684	$81,024	$80,379
Total, other				

FINANCIAL AID

FINANCIAL AID AWARDS TO FIRST-YEAR STUDENTS 2014–15

Total number of first-year recipients: 74
Percentage of the first-year class: 88%
Percentage of awards that are grants? 3%
Percentage of awards that are loans? 97%

	AVERAGE AWARDS	RANGE OF AWARDS
Residents and nonresidents	$64,808	$1,000–$84,100

For more information, please visit: www.creighton.edu/finaid/

CONTACT INFORMATION
www.unmc.edu/dentistry
4000 East Campus Loop South
Lincoln, NE 68583-0740
Phone: 402-472-1301
Fax: 402-472-5290

ADMISSIONS
Ms. Joyce Hurst
Enrollment Manager
4000 East Campus Loop South
Lincoln, NE 68583-0740
Phone: 402-472-1363
Email: joyce.hurst@unmc.edu

OFFICE OF FINANCIAL AID
Ms. Judith D. Walker
Executive Director, Student Services
Financial Aid
984265 Nebraska Medical Center
Omaha, NE 68198-4265
Phone: 402-559-4199
Email: jdwalker@unmc.edu

STUDENT AFFAIRS
Dr. Merlyn W. Vogt
Assistant Dean for Student Affairs
4000 East Campus Loop South
Lincoln, NE 68583-0740
Phone: 402-472-1479
Email: mvogt@unmc.edu

UNIVERSITY OF NEBRASKA MEDICAL CENTER
COLLEGE OF DENTISTRY

Janet M. Guthmiller, D.D.S., Ph.D., Dean

GENERAL INFORMATION

The University of Nebraska Medical Center College of Dentistry (UNMC COD) has its origins in the Lincoln Dental College, founded in 1899 and operated as a private school until 1917, when it became affiliated with the University of Nebraska. The college became part of the university's Medical Center on July 1, 1979. Located in Lincoln (population 258,000), UNMC COD has a total student enrollment of 270, including 48 two-year dental hygiene students and 50 advanced dental education and graduate students. Advanced dental programs are offered in endodontics, general practice residency, orthodontics, pediatric dentistry and periodontics. A graduate program in dentistry leads to a clinically oriented M.S. degree. A graduate program in the oral biology department leads to a more traditional M.S. or Ph.D. degree.

MISSION

UNMC College of Dentistry seeks to admit academically qualified, diverse applicants from Nebraska and the region with consideration given to Nebraska applicants from rural backgrounds.

Vision: UNMC's vision is to be a world-renowned health sciences center that delivers state-of-the-art health care through academic and private practice.

Type of institution: Public	Doctoral dental degree offered: D.D.S.
Year opened: 1899	Targeted predoctoral enrollment: 180
Term type: Semester	Targeted entering class size: 47
Time to degree in months: 45	Campus setting: Suburban
Start month: August	Campus housing available: Yes

PREPARATION

Formal minimum preparation in semester/quarter hours: Semester: 90   Quarter: 120
Baccalaureate degree preferred: Yes
Number of first-year, first-time enrollees whose highest degree is:
    Baccalaureate: 45
    Master's degree and beyond: 1
Of first-year, first-time enrollees without baccalaureates, the number with:
    Equivalent of 60 undergraduate credit hours or less: 0
    Equivalent of 61–90 undergraduate credit hours: 0
    Equivalent of 91 or more undergraduate credit hours: 1

PREREQUISITE COURSE	REQUIRED	RECOMMENDED	LAB REQUIRED	CREDITS (SEMESTER/QUARTER)
BCP (biology-chemistry-physics) sciences				
Biology	✓		✓	8/12
Chemistry, general/inorganic	✓		✓	8/12
Chemistry, organic	✓		✓	8/12
Physics	✓		✓	8/12
Additional biological sciences				
Anatomy		✓		4/6
Biochemistry		✓		4/6
Cell biology		✓		4/6
Histology		✓		4/6
Immunology		✓		4/6
Microbiology		✓		4/6
Molecular biology/genetics				
Physiology		✓		4/6

PREPARATION (CONTINUED)

PREREQUISITE COURSE	REQUIRED	RECOMMENDED	LAB REQUIRED	CREDITS (SEMESTER/QUARTER)
Zoology				
Other				
English Composition	✓			6/9

Community college coursework accepted for prerequisites: Yes
Community college coursework accepted for electives: Yes
Limits on community college credit hours: No
Maximum number of community college credit hours: NR
Advanced placement (AP) credit accepted for prerequisites: Yes
Advanced placement (AP) credit accepted for electives: Yes
Comments regarding AP credit: Contact school for information.
Job shadowing: Required
Number of hours of job shadowing required or recommended: 35

DAT

Mandatory: Yes
Latest DAT for consideration of application: 11/15/2015
Oldest DAT considered: 08/01/2011
When more than one DAT score is reported: Most recent score only is considered.
Canadian DAT accepted: Yes
Application considered before DAT scores are submitted: Yes

DAT: 2014 ENTERING CLASS

ENROLLEE DAT SCORES	MEAN	RANGE
Academic Average	20.1	17–27
Perceptual Ability	20.8	14–30
Total Science	19.7	16–28

GPA: 2014 ENTERING CLASS

ENROLLEE GPA SCORES	UNDERGRAD. MEAN	GRADUATE MEAN	UNDERGRAD. RANGE	GRADUATE RANGE
Science GPA	3.65	NR	2.90–4.00	NR
Total GPA	3.74	NR	2.90–4.00	NR

APPLICATION AND SELECTION

TIMETABLE

Earliest filing date: 06/02/2015
Latest filing date: 02/01/2016
Earliest date for acceptance offers: 12/01/2015
Maximum time in days for applicant's response to acceptance offer:
    30 days if accepted on or after December 1
    15 days if accepted on or after February 1
Requests for deferred entrance considered: Yes
Fee for application: Yes
Amount of fee for application:
    In state: $50   Out of state: $50   International: $50
Fee waiver available: Yes

	FIRST DEPOSIT	SECOND DEPOSIT	THIRD DEPOSIT
Required to hold place	Yes	No	No
Resident amount	$200		
Nonresident amount	$200		
Deposit due	As indicated in admission offer		
Applied to tuition	Yes		
Refundable	No		

APPLICATION PROCESS

Participates in Associated American Dental Schools Application Service (AADSAS): Yes
Accepts direct applicants: No
Secondary or supplemental application required: No
Interview is mandatory: Yes
Interview is by invitation: Yes

RESIDENCY

In-state/in-province versus out-of-state/out-of-province
Admissions process distinguishes between in-state/in-province and out-of-state/out-of-province applicants: Yes
Preference given to residents of: Nebraska
Reciprocity Admissions Agreement available for legal residents of: Wyoming
Generally and over time, percentage of your first-year enrollment that is in-state: 70%
Origin of out-of-state/out-of-province enrollees: CO-1, IA-1, KS-3, SD-3, WY-4

International
Applications are accepted from international (noncitizens/nonpermanent residents): Yes
Origin of international enrollees: China-1

APPLICATION AND ENROLLMENT	NUMBER OF APPLICANTS	ESTIMATED NUMBER INTERVIEWED	ESTIMATED NUMBER ENROLLED
In-state or province applicants/enrollees	86	65	35
Out-of-state or province applicants/enrollees	558	50	12
International applicants/enrollees (noncitizens/nonpermanent residents)	46	1	1

DEMOGRAPHIC DESCRIPTIONS OF APPLICANTS: 2014 ENTERING CLASS

	APPLICANTS			ENROLLEES		
	M	W	Gender Unknown or Not Reported	M	W	Gender Unknown or Not Reported
American Indian or Alaska Native	0	2	0	0	0	0
Asian	55	67	0	0	1	0
Black or African American	10	9	1	0	0	0
Hispanic or Latino	25	20	0	1	0	0
Native Hawaiian or Other Pacific Islander	1	1	0	0	0	0
White	233	177	4	30	13	0
Two or more races	12	12	0	0	2	0
Race and ethnicity unknown	6	8	1	0	0	0
International	27	18	1	0	1	0

	MINIMUM	MAXIMUM	MEAN
2014 entering class enrollees by age	21	28	22

CURRICULUM

The dental program is 44.5 months in duration with 36.5 months in actual attendance. There are eight semesters of 16 weeks each. In addition, attendance is required at three summer sessions (eight weeks each), one between each academic year until graduation. Objectives of the UNMC COD are to:

1. Select applicants who have the personal and moral qualifications, technical potential and scholastic ability for a professional career in dentistry.

2. Provide, within a flexible curriculum, a solid foundation of fundamental scientific knowledge and the basic technical skills necessary for using this education.

3. Motivate students to recognize and fulfill their social and moral responsibilities to their patients, their civic responsibility to the community and their ethical obligation to the profession of dentistry.

4. Inspire students to see the need for continuing education and for personal and professional evaluation throughout their dental careers.

Student research opportunities: Yes

SPECIAL PROGRAMS AND SERVICES

PREDENTAL

Summer Medical and Dental Education Program (SMDEP)
Other summer enrichment programs: American Student Dental Association Simulation Clinic

DURING DENTAL SCHOOL

Academic counseling and tutoring
Community service opportunities
Internships, externships, or extramural programs
Mentoring
Personal counseling
Professional- and career-development programming
Training for those interested in academic careers

ACTIVE STUDENT ORGANIZATIONS

American Association for Dental Research National Student Research Group
American Association of Women Dentists
American Dental Education Association
American Student Dental Association

INTERNATIONAL DENTISTS

Graduates of international dental schools considered for traditional predoctoral program: Yes
Advanced standing program offered for graduates of international dental schools: Yes
Advanced standing program description: Program awarding a dental degree.

COMBINED AND ALTERNATE DEGREES

Ph.D.	M.S.	M.P.H.	M.D.	B.A./B.S.	Other
✓	—	—	—	—	—

COSTS: 2014–15 SCHOOL YEAR

	FIRST YEAR	SECOND YEAR	THIRD YEAR	FOURTH YEAR
Tuition, resident	$28,692	$28,692	$28,692	$22,954
Tuition, nonresident	$70,403	$70,403	$70,403	$56,322
Tuition, other				
Fees	$1,965	$1,973	$1,969	$1,680
Instruments, books, and supplies	$10,000	$9,890	$9,890	$9,890
Estimated living expenses	$20,400	$20,400	$20,400	$15,300
Total, resident	$61,057	$60,955	$60,951	$49,824
Total, nonresident	$102,768	$102,666	$102,662	$83,192
Total, other				

FINANCIAL AID

For more information, please visit: http://unmc.edu/financialaid/

UNIVERSITY OF NEVADA, LAS VEGAS
SCHOOL OF DENTAL MEDICINE

Karen P. West, D.M.D., M.P.H., Dean

CONTACT INFORMATION

http://dentalschool.unlv.edu
1001 Shadow Lane MS7410
Las Vegas, NV 89106
Phone: 702-774-2500

ADMISSIONS AND STUDENT AFFAIRS

Dr. Christine C. Ancajas
Assistant Dean for Admissions and
Student Affairs
1001 Shadow Lane MS7411
Las Vegas, NV 89106
Phone: 702-774-2520
Fax: 702-774-2521
Email: christine.ancajas@unlv.edu

OFFICE OF FINANCIAL AID AND MINORITY AFFAIRS/DIVERSITY

Dr. Christopher A. Kypuros
Director of Financial Aid, Scholarships and
Academic Endeavors
Director of Diversity
UNLV Title IX Deputy Coordinators
1001 Shadow Lane MS7411
Las Vegas, NV 89106-4124
Phone: 702-774-2526
Fax: 702-774-2506
Email: christopher.kypuros@unlv.edu

GENERAL INFORMATION

The University of Nevada, Las Vegas, School of Dental Medicine (UNLV SDM), located on the new Shadow Lane Campus, occupies 154,000 square feet in three buildings, including an 84-seat, state-of-the-art simulation laboratory, smart classrooms and 231 ultramodern operatories. More than 43,000 patients receive treatment annually in a fully electronic environment. Advanced dental education programs include General Practice, Orthodontics and Dentofacial Orthopedics, and Pediatric Dentistry, with other programs in the planning stages. With one of the most diverse faculties in dental education, UNLV SDM is dedicated to serving the Las Vegas community and has touched the lives of more than 175,000 citizens. UNLV has seen dramatic growth in its student population (now more than 28,000) and its academic offerings (comprising more than 220 undergraduate and graduate degrees).

MISSION

To be a driving force toward improving the health of Nevada's citizens through unique oral health care services; integrated biomedical, professional, and clinical curricula; and biomedical discovery.

Vision: UNLV is committed to excellence in education, research and patient care.

Core Values:

- Excellence in patient-centered clinical care/education and statewide community outreach programs.
- Innovative curriculum ensuring competent oral health care providers.
- Environment conducive to scholarly activities and collaborative research.

Type of institution: Public	Doctoral dental degree offered: D.M.D.
Year opened: 2002	Targeted predoctoral enrollment: 318
Term type: Trimester	Targeted entering class size: 82
Time to degree in months: 45	Campus setting: Urban
Start month: September	Campus housing available: No

PREPARATION

Formal minimum preparation in semester/quarter hours: Semester: 90   Quarter: 120
Baccalaureate degree preferred: Yes; not required but highly recommended
Number of first-year, first-time enrollees whose highest degree is:
    Baccalaureate: 72
    Master's degree and beyond: 2
Of first-year, first-time enrollees without baccalaureates, the number with:
    Equivalent of 60 undergraduate credit hours or less: 0
    Equivalent of 61–90 undergraduate credit hours: 0
    Equivalent of 91 or more undergraduate credit hours: 7

PREREQUISITE COURSE	REQUIRED	RECOMMENDED	LAB REQUIRED	CREDITS (SEMESTER/QUARTER)
BCP (biology-chemistry-physics) sciences				
Biology	✓		✓	8/12
Chemistry, general/inorganic	✓		✓	8/12
Chemistry, organic	✓		✓	8/12
Physics	✓		✓	8/12
Additional biological sciences				
Anatomy, Human*	✓			4/6
Biochemistry	✓			3/5
Cell biology		✓		3/5
Histology		✓		3/5
Immunology		✓		3/5

(Prerequisite Courses continued)

PREPARATION (CONTINUED)

PREREQUISITE COURSE	REQUIRED	RECOMMENDED	LAB REQUIRED	CREDITS (SEMESTER/QUARTER)
Microbiology		✓		4/6
Molecular biology/genetics		✓		4/6
Physiology		✓		4/6
Zoology		✓		4/6

*Anatomy and Physiology I and II (8/12 semester/quarter credits) may be substituted for Human Anatomy.

Community college coursework accepted for prerequisites: Yes
Community college coursework accepted for electives: Yes
Limits on community college credit hours: Yes; maximum of 60 semester credits
Maximum number of community college credit hours: 60
Minimum number of credits from a 4-year institution: 30
Minimum number of semester units or equivalent at accredited U.S. or Canadian college/university: 90
Advanced placement (AP) credit accepted for prerequisites: No
Advanced placement (AP) credit accepted for electives: Yes
Job shadowing: Required
Number of job shadowing hours required or recommended: Consistency over a long period of time
Other factors considered in admission: Dental experience, extracurricular activities, community service, and letters of recommendation (4 total: 2 science, 1 dental professional, 1 personal)

DAT

Mandatory: Yes, scores are good for 3 years.
Latest DAT for consideration of application: 02/01/2016
Oldest DAT considered: 01/01/2013
When more than one DAT score is reported: Highest score is considered
Canadian DAT accepted: No
Application considered before DAT scores are submitted: No

DAT: 2014 ENTERING CLASS

ENROLLEE DAT SCORES	MEAN	RANGE
Academic Average	19.9	17–24
Perceptual Ability	20.3	14–25
Total Science	20.1	16–26

GPA: 2014 ENTERING CLASS

ENROLLEE GPA SCORES	UNDERGRAD. MEAN	GRADUATE MEAN	UNDERGRAD. RANGE	GRADUATE RANGE
Science GPA	3.38	3.37	2.49–4.00	2.82–3.42
Total GPA	3.47	3.44	2.74–4.00	3.07–3.68

APPLICATION AND SELECTION

TIMETABLE

Earliest filing date: 06/02/2015
Latest filing date: 01/01/2016
Earliest date for acceptance offers: 12/01/2015
Maximum time in days for applicant's response to acceptance offer:
30 days if accepted on or after December 1
15 days if accepted on or after February 1
Requests for deferred entrance considered: In exceptional circumstances only

Fee for application: Yes, submitted at same time as AADSAS application
Amount of fee for application:
In state: $50   Out of state: $50   International: $50
Fee waiver available: No

	FIRST DEPOSIT	SECOND DEPOSIT	THIRD DEPOSIT
Required to hold place	Yes	Yes	No
Resident amount	$750	$1,000	
Nonresident amount	$750	$1,000	
Deposit due	As indicated in admission offer	04/01/2016	
Applied to tuition	Yes	Yes	
Refundable	No	No	

APPLICATION PROCESS

Participates in Associated American Dental Schools Application Service (AADSAS): Yes
Accepts direct applicants: No
Secondary or supplemental application required: Yes
Secondary or supplemental application website: http://dentalschool.unlv.edu
Interview is mandatory: Yes
Interview is by invitation: Yes

RESIDENCY

In-state/in-province versus out-of-state/out-of-province
Admissions process distinguishes between in-state/in-province and out-of-state/out-of-province applicants: Yes
Preference given to residents of: Nevada
Reciprocity Admissions Agreement available for legal residents of: None
Generally and over time, percentage of your first-year enrollment that is in-state: 50%
Origin of out-of-state/out-of-province enrollees: CA-16, HI-2, IL-1, LA-1, MN-1, MT-1, NM-1, NY-1, UT-8, TX-4, WA-1

International
Applications are accepted from international (noncitizens/nonpermanent residents): Yes
Origin of international enrollees: Canada-1

APPLICATION AND ENROLLMENT	NUMBER OF APPLICANTS	ESTIMATED NUMBER INTERVIEWED	ESTIMATED NUMBER ENROLLED
In-state or province applicants/enrollees	70	56	43
Out-of-state or province applicants/enrollees	1,802	290	37
International applicants/enrollees (noncitizens/nonpermanent residents)	105	10	1

DEMOGRAPHIC DESCRIPTIONS OF APPLICANTS: 2014 ENTERING CLASS

	APPLICANTS			ENROLLEES		
	M	W	Gender Unknown or Not Reported	M	W	Gender Unknown or Not Reported
American Indian or Alaska Native	3	1	0	1	0	0
Asian	374	290	10	17	16	0
Black or African American	16	19	1	2	0	0
Hispanic or Latino	72	77	0	1	1	0
Native Hawaiian or Other Pacific Islander	2	2	0	0	0	0
White	603	274	6	24	10	0
Two or more races	30	39	1	4	4	0
Race and ethnicity unknown	23	23	6	1	0	0
International	62	43	0	0	1	0

	MINIMUM	MAXIMUM	MEAN
2014 entering class enrollees by age	21	57	26

CURRICULUM

The UNLV SDM is a driving force toward improving the health of the citizens of Nevada through unique programs of oral health care services to the community. A highly integrated and timed approach toward discovery in the biomedical, professional and clinical sciences encourages a continuous learning professional. Patient-centered clinical care, patient education and community outreach reinforces the horizontally and vertically integrated curriculum. Scholarship provides an environment to produce collaborative research and scholarly activities. With faculty cultivated toward excellence, professionalism and the medical model of total patient care, the school's mission is a constant goal: Toward perfect health through oral health.

Student research opportunities: Yes

SPECIAL PROGRAMS AND SERVICES

PREDENTAL

Special affiliations with colleges and universities
Summer enrichment programs: We provide a two-day UNLV Dental Simulation Course that involves a hands-on experience for predental students.

DURING DENTAL SCHOOL

Academic counseling and tutoring
Community service opportunities
Internships, externships, or extramural programs
Mentoring
Personal counseling
Professional- and career-development programming

ACTIVE STUDENT ORGANIZATIONS

American Association of Women Dentists
American Dental Education Association
American Student Dental Association
Hispanic Dental Association
Student National Dental Association

INTERNATIONAL DENTISTS

Graduates of international dental schools considered for traditional predoctoral program: Yes
Advanced standing program offered for graduates of international dental schools: No

COMBINED AND ALTERNATE DEGREES

Ph.D.	M.S.	M.P.H.	M.D.	B.A./B.S.	Other
—	—	✓	—	—	✓

Other degree: M.B.A.

COSTS: 2014–15 SCHOOL YEAR

	FIRST YEAR	SECOND YEAR	THIRD YEAR	FOURTH YEAR
Tuition, resident	$35,760	$35,760	$35,760	$23,840
Tuition, nonresident	$71,070	$71,070	$71,070	$47,380
Tuition, other				
Fees	$19,020	$19,020	$19,020	$13,431
Instruments, books, and supplies	See *"Note"* below.			
Estimated living expenses	$36,576	$35,276	$35,276	$23,483
Total, resident	$91,356	$90,056	$90,056	$60,754
Total, nonresident	$126,666	$125,366	$125,366	$84,294
Total, other				

Note: Tuition costs include mandatory yearly health insurance, a computer, books and supplies.

FINANCIAL AID

FINANCIAL AID AWARDS TO FIRST-YEAR STUDENTS 2014–15

Total number of first-year recipients: 72
Percentage of the first-year class: 79%
Percentage of awards that are grants? 7.6%
Percentage of awards that are loans? 89%

	AVERAGE AWARDS	RANGE OF AWARDS
Residents	$80,054	$24,999–$92,856
Nonresidents	$110,758	$27,389–$129,291

For more information, please visit: http://www.unlv.edu/dental/financialaid

CONTACT INFORMATION

sdm.rutgers.edu
110 Bergen Street
Newark, NJ 07103-2400
Phone: 973-972-5362
Fax: 973-972-0309

OFFICE OF ADMISSIONS

Dr. Rosa Chaviano-Moran
Assistant Dean of Admissions and
Student Recruitment
110 Bergen Street
Room B-829
Newark, NJ 07103-2400
Phone: 973-972-5362

OFFICE OF STUDENT FINANCIAL AID

Ms. Cheryl White
Campus Director
30 Bergen Street
ADMC #1208
Newark, NJ 07103-2400
Phone: 973-972-4376

STUDENT AFFAIRS

Dr. Kim Fenesy
Senior Associate Dean for Academic Affairs
110 Bergen Street
Room B-825
Newark, NJ 07103-2400
Phone: 973-972-1699

OFFICE OF MULTICULTURAL AFFAIRS

Dr. Herminio Perez
Director of Student and Multicultural Affairs
110 Bergen Street
Room B-828
Newark, NJ 07103-2400
Phone: 973-972-7816

HOUSING

180 West Market Street
Newark, NJ 07103-2400
Phone: 973-972-8796

RUTGERS, THE STATE UNIVERSITY OF NEW JERSEY
SCHOOL OF DENTAL MEDICINE

Cecile A. Feldman, D.M.D., M.B.A., Dean

GENERAL INFORMATION

Rutgers School of Dental Medicine (RSDM), formerly known as the New Jersey Dental School, was established as part of the Seton Hall College of Medicine and Dentistry, admitting its first students in 1956. The school has since grown into New Jersey's major resource for dental education, research and community service. RSDM offers graduate dental educational specialty training in six areas: endodontics, oral surgery, orthodontics, pediatric dentistry, periodontics and prosthodontics. Hospital residencies are offered in general practice and in oral and maxillofacial surgery. A fellowship in oral medicine is also available.

MISSION

RSDM's mission comprises:

- The scientific exploration of factors contributing to oral health.
- The dissemination/application of knowledge toward the community's health and well-being.

Core Values: RSDM accomplishes its mission in a collegial environment through four interrelated activities: education, patient care, research and community service.

Type of institution: Public	Doctoral dental degree offered: D.M.D.
Year opened: 1956	Targeted predoctoral enrollment: 410
Term type: Trimester	Targeted entering class size: 90
Time to degree in months: 48	Campus setting: Urban
Start month: August	Campus housing available: Yes

PREPARATION

Formal minimum preparation in semester/quarter hours: Semester: 90
Baccalaureate degree preferred: Yes
Number of first-year, first-time enrollees whose highest degree is:
    Baccalaureate: 76
    Master's degree and beyond: 12
Of first-year, first-time enrollees without baccalaureates, the number with:
    Equivalent of 60 undergraduate credit hours or less: 0
    Equivalent of 61–90 undergraduate credit hours: 3
    Equivalent of 91 or more undergraduate credit hours: 0

PREREQUISITE COURSE	REQUIRED	RECOMMENDED	LAB REQUIRED	CREDITS (SEMESTER/QUARTER)
BCP (biology-chemistry-physics) sciences				
Biology	✓		✓	8/12
Chemistry, general/inorganic	✓		✓	8/12
Chemistry, organic	✓		✓	8/12
Physics	✓		✓	8/12
Additional biological sciences				
Anatomy		✓		
Biochemistry		✓		
Cell biology		✓		
Histology		✓		
Immunology		✓		
Microbiology		✓		
Molecular biology/genetics		✓		
Physiology		✓		

PREPARATION (CONTINUED)

PREREQUISITE COURSE	REQUIRED	RECOMMENDED	LAB REQUIRED	CREDITS (SEMESTER/QUARTER)
Zoology		✓		
Other				
Sculpture/art		✓		
English	✓			6/12
Intensive writing courses		✓		

Community college coursework accepted for prerequisites: Yes (but, prerequisite coursework from four-year colleges preferred)
Community college coursework accepted for electives: Yes
Limits on community college credit hours: Yes
Maximum number of community college credit hours: 60
Advanced placement (AP) credit accepted for prerequisites: No
Advanced placement (AP) credit accepted for electives: Yes; AP credit must appear on undergraduate transcript
Comments regarding AP credit: Check school website for details.
Job shadowing: Required
Number of hours of job shadowing required or recommended: A minimum of 50 hours is recommended.

DAT

Mandatory: Yes
Latest DAT for consideration of application: 11/01/2015
Oldest DAT considered: 01/01/2012
When more than one DAT score is reported: Most recent score only is considered
Canadian DAT accepted: Yes
Application considered before DAT scores are submitted: No

U.S. DAT: 2014 ENTERING CLASS

ENROLLEE DAT SCORES	MEAN	RANGE
Academic Average	20.0	17–25
Perceptual Ability	19.0	15–24
Total Science	20.0	16–30

CANADIAN DAT: 2014 ENTERING CLASS

ENROLLEE DAT SCORES	MEAN	RANGE
Academic Average	22.0	NR
Manual Dexterity	22.0	NR
Perceptual Ability	19.0	NR
Total Science	20.0	NR

GPA: 2014 ENTERING CLASS

ENROLLEE GPA SCORES	CUMULATIVE MEAN	CUMULATIVE RANGE
Science GPA	3.50	2.82–4.00
Total GPA	3.70	2.80–4.00

APPLICATION AND SELECTION

TIMETABLE

Earliest filing date: 06/02/2015
Latest filing date: 11/01/2015
Earliest date for acceptance offers: 12/01/2015

Maximum time in days for applicant's response to acceptance offer:
30 days if accepted on or after December 1
21 days if accepted on or after January 1
15 days if accepted on or after February 1
Requests for deferred entrance considered: Only at the discretion of the Admissions Committee
Fee for application: Yes, submitted at the request of Admissions Office
Amount of fee for application:
In state: $85   Out of state: $85
Fee waiver available: No

	FIRST DEPOSIT	SECOND DEPOSIT	THIRD DEPOSIT
Required to hold place	Yes	Yes	No
Resident amount	$1,500	$1,000	
Nonresident amount	$1,500	$1,000	
Deposit due	As indicated in admission offer	As indicated in admission offer	
Applied to tuition	Yes	Yes	
Refundable	No	No	

APPLICATION PROCESS

Participates in Associated American Dental Schools Application Service (AADSAS): Yes
Accepts direct applicants: No
Secondary or supplemental application required: No
Interview is mandatory: Yes
Interview is by invitation: Yes

RESIDENCY

In-state/in-province versus out-of-state/out-of-province
Admissions process distinguishes between in-state/in-province and out-of-state/out-of-province applicants: Yes
Preference given to residents of: NA
Reciprocity Admissions Agreement available for legal residents of: NA
Generally and over time, percentage of your first-year enrollment that is in-state: 70%
Origin of out-of-state/out-of-province enrollees: CA-5, CT-1, FL-9, GA-1, MA-1, MD-1, NY-8, PA-1, TX-1, VA-1, WI-1

International
Applications are accepted from international (noncitizens/nonpermanent residents): Yes
Origin of international enrollees: NA

APPLICATION AND ENROLLMENT	NUMBER OF APPLICANTS	ESTIMATED NUMBER INTERVIEWED	ESTIMATED NUMBER ENROLLED
In-state or province applicants/enrollees	326	155	61
Out-of-state or province applicants/enrollees	1,415	157	30
International applicants/enrollees (noncitizens/nonpermanent residents)	101	NR	0

DEMOGRAPHIC DESCRIPTIONS OF APPLICANTS: 2014 ENTERING CLASS

	APPLICANTS			ENROLLEES		
	M	W	Gender Unknown or Not Reported	M	W	Gender Unknown or Not Reported
American Indian or Alaska Native	0	1	0	0	0	0
Asian	282	358	7	9	17	0
Black or African American	23	48	1	2	7	0
Hispanic or Latino	57	94	0	9	10	0
Native Hawaiian or Other Pacific Islander	0	1	0	0	0	0
White	395	334	5	17	15	0
Two or more races	17	27	1	0	0	0
Race and ethnicity unknown	33	47	10	4	0	0
International	57	44	0	0	0	0

	MINIMUM	MAXIMUM	MEAN
2014 entering class enrollees by age	20	39	23

CURRICULUM

RSDM is a publicly supported institution. Its mission is to promote professional standards of excellence among its students, faculty and staff, while meeting the health needs of New Jersey citizens through the coordination of education, research and service. The goal of the dental curriculum is to prepare competent general practitioners, who are able to manage the oral health care of the public. The curriculum also provides a foundation for graduates who seek advanced training in the dental specialties, biomedical research and/or dental education. To accomplish our mission, graduates must understand the interrelationship of the biological, physical, clinical, and behavioral sciences to effectively practice three overlapping areas of professional responsibility: 1) comprehensive patient care; 2) participation in community dental-health programs; and 3) continuation of professional development.

Student research opportunities: Yes

SPECIAL PROGRAMS AND SERVICES

PREDENTAL

College Level Pipeline Programs: Gateway to Dentistry and Summer Medical and Dental Education Program
Other enrichment programs: High School Level: Decision for Dentistry. Elementary School Level: Dental Express and Dental Exploration
BS/DMD Articulation Programs with: Caldwell College; Fairleigh Dickinson University; New Jersey City University; Montclair State University; New Jersey Institute of Technology; North Carolina Central University; Ramapo College; Rowan University; Rutgers University; St. Peters College; The Richard Stockton College of New Jersey

DURING DENTAL SCHOOL

Academic counseling and tutoring
Service opportunities (local, national and international)
Internships, externships, or extramural programs
Mentoring
Personal counseling
Professional- and career-development programming
Research/translational research
Training for those interested in academic careers

ACTIVE STUDENT ORGANIZATIONS

American Association of Women Dentists
American Dental Education Association
American Student Dental Association
Hispanic Dental Association
Indian Student Dental Association
Student National Dental Association

INTERNATIONAL DENTISTS

Graduates of international dental schools considered for traditional predoctoral program: No
Advanced standing program offered for graduates of international dental schools: Yes
Advanced standing program description: Program awarding a dental degree (D.M.D.) following a 27-month didactic and clinical program.

COMBINED AND ALTERNATE DEGREES

Ph.D.	M.S.	M.P.H.	M.D.	B.A./B.S.	Other
✓	✓	✓	—	✓	—

COSTS: 2013–14 SCHOOL YEAR

	FIRST YEAR	SECOND YEAR	THIRD YEAR	FOURTH YEAR
Tuition, resident	$35,823	$35,823	$35,823	$35,823
Tuition, nonresident	$57,479	$57,479	$57,479	$57,479
Tuition, other				
Fees	$2,526	$2,826	$3,126	$3,486
Instruments, books, and supplies	$9,812	$6,726	$6,256	$2,900
Estimated living expenses	$13,860	$12,474	$16,632	$15,246
Total, resident	$62,021	$57,848	$61,836	$57,455
Total, nonresident	$83,676	$79,504	$83,492	$79,111
Total, other				

FINANCIAL AID

For more information, please visit: http://sdm.rutgers.edu/students/prospective/financing.html

COLUMBIA UNIVERSITY
COLLEGE OF DENTAL MEDICINE

Christian S. Stohler, D.M.D., Dr.Med.Dent., Dean

CONTACT INFORMATION

www.dental.columbia.edu
630 West 168th Street
New York, NY 10032
Phone: 212-305-3478
Fax: 212-305-1034

ADMISSIONS AND STUDENT AFFAIRS

Dr. Laureen Zubiaurre Bitzer
Associate Dean
Phone: 212-305-3478
Email: laz1@columbia.edu

Ms. Sandra Garcia
Assistant Dean
Phone: 212-342-1697
Email: sb64@columbia.edu

FINANCIAL AID

Ms. Ellen Spilker
Executive Director
Phone: 212-305-4100
Email: cpmc-sfp@columbia.edu

OFFICE OF DIVERSITY AFFAIRS

Dr. Dennis Mitchell
Senior Associate Dean
Phone: 212-342-3716
http://www.dental.columbia.edu/page/
office-diversity-affairs

HOUSING

50 Haven Avenue
Bard Hall, 1st floor
New York, NY 10032
Phone: 212-304-7000
http://www.cumc.columbia.edu/facilities-
management/housing/housing

INTERNATIONAL STUDENTS

Ms. Bonnie Garner
Assistant Manager
650 West 168th Street
New York, NY 10032
Phone: 212-305-5455
Email: bLg12@columbia.edu

GENERAL INFORMATION

The Columbia University College of Dental Medicine (Columbia CDM), an integral part of the Columbia University Medical Center, traces its origin to the year 1852, when the New York State legislature chartered the college. When dentistry was recognized as an integral part of the health sciences, the college in 1916 became the School of Dental and Oral Surgery of Columbia University. Many departments of the university contribute to and collaborate in the education of dental and advanced dental education students, who are thus assured a broad foundation for sound professional development. Columbia CDM remains one of the few dental colleges whose students during the first year and half share the biomedical courses with the medical students—in this instance, of the College of Physicians and Surgeons.

MISSION

Education: Emphasizing the biomedical basis of comprehensive dental care.
Research: Inspiring, promoting and supporting participation in research.
Community care: Providing comprehensive dental care for northern Manhattan's underserved.

Type of institution: Private
Year opened: 1852
Term type: Semester
Time to degree in months: 45
Start month: August

Doctoral dental degree offered: D.D.S.
Targeted predoctoral enrollment: 320
Targeted entering class size: 80
Campus setting: Urban
Campus housing available: Yes

PREPARATION

Formal minimum preparation in semester/quarter hours: Semester: 90 Quarter: 120
Baccalaureate degree preferred: Yes
Number of first-year, first-time enrollees whose highest degree is:
　Baccalaureate: 69
　Master's degree and beyond: 6
Of first-year, first-time enrollees without baccalaureates, the number with:
　Equivalent of 60 undergraduate credit hours or less: 0
　Equivalent of 61–90 undergraduate credit hours: 0
　Equivalent of 91 or more undergraduate credit hours: 5 (from a linkage pilot program)

PREREQUISITE COURSE	REQUIRED	RECOMMENDED	LAB REQUIRED	CREDITS (SEMESTER/QUARTER)
BCP (biology-chemistry-physics) sciences				
Biology	✓		✓	8/12
Chemistry, general/inorganic	✓		✓	8/12
Chemistry, organic	✓		✓	8/12
Physics	✓		✓	8/12
Additional biological sciences				
Anatomy		✓		4/6
Biochemistry	✓			4/6
Cell biology		✓		4/6
Histology				
Immunology				
Microbiology				
Molecular biology/genetics				
Physiology		✓		
Zoology				

(Prerequisite Courses continued)

PREPARATION (CONTINUED)

PREREQUISITE COURSE	REQUIRED	RECOMMENDED	LAB REQUIRED	CREDITS (SEMESTER/QUARTER)
Other				
English	✓			6/9
Mathematics	✓			6/9

Community college coursework accepted for prerequisites: Yes
Community college coursework accepted for electives: Yes
Limits on community college credit hours: No
Maximum number of community college credit hours: NA
Advanced placement (AP) credit accepted for prerequisites: Yes
Advanced placement (AP) credit accepted for electives: Yes
Comments regarding AP credit: None
Job shadowing: Recommended
Number of hours of job shadowing required or recommended: Not specified
Other factors considered in admission: Noncognitive factors including community service/ volunteerism and other extracurricular activities

DAT

Mandatory: Yes
Latest DAT for consideration of application: 12/01/2015
Oldest DAT considered: 01/01/2013
When more than one DAT score is reported: Highest score is considered.
Canadian DAT accepted: Yes
Application considered before DAT scores are submitted: No

DAT: 2014 ENTERING CLASS

ENROLLEE DAT SCORES	MEAN	RANGE
Academic Average	23.0	20–27
Perceptual Ability	21.0	15–26
Total Science	23.0	18–30

GPA: 2014 ENTERING CLASS

ENROLLEE GPA SCORES	UNDERGRAD. MEAN	GRADUATE MEAN	UNDERGRAD. RANGE	GRADUATE RANGE
Science GPA	3.62	3.78	2.82–4.00	3.28–4.00
Total GPA	3.63	3.78	2.61–4.00	3.28–4.00

APPLICATION AND SELECTION

TIMETABLE

Earliest filing date: 06/02/2015
Latest filing date: 12/30/2015
Earliest date for acceptance offers: 12/01/2015
Maximum time in days for applicant's response to acceptance offer:
   30 days if accepted on or after December 1
   15 days if accepted on or after February 1
Requests for deferred entrance considered: No
Fee for application: Yes, submitted at same time as Associated American Dental Schools Application Service (AADSAS) application
Amount of fee for application:
   In state: $75   Out of state: $75   International: $75
Fee waiver available: Yes, upon documentation by college of high financial need

	FIRST DEPOSIT	SECOND DEPOSIT	THIRD DEPOSIT
Required to hold place	Yes	Yes	No
Resident amount	$2,000	$1,000	
Nonresident amount	$2,000	$1,000	
Deposit due	As indicated in admission offer	As indicated in admission offer	
Applied to tuition	Yes	Yes	
Refundable	No	No	

APPLICATION PROCESS

Participates in Associate American Dental Schools Application Service (AADSAS): Yes
Accepts direct applicants: No
Secondary or supplemental application required: Yes, a fee of $75 at the time application is submitted
Secondary or supplemental application website: None
Interview is mandatory: Yes
Interview is by invitation: Yes, by invitation only

RESIDENCY

In-state/in-province versus out-of-state/out-of-province
Admissions process distinguishes between in-state/in-province and out-of-state/out-of-province applicants: No
Preference given to residents of: NA
Reciprocity Admissions Agreement available for legal residents of: None
Generally and over time, percentage of your first-year enrollment that is in-state: 25%
Origin of out-of-state/out-of-province enrollees: AR-1, CA-3, CO-1, CT-2, FL-4, GA-1, IL-1, MA-3, MD-2, MI-2, NC-2, NJ-13, NY-34, PA-4, PR-1, TX-2

International
Applications are accepted from international (noncitizens/ nonpermanent residents): Yes
Origin of international enrollees: Brazil-1, Canada-3

APPLICATION AND ENROLLMENT	NUMBER OF APPLICANTS	ESTIMATED NUMBER INTERVIEWED	ESTIMATED NUMBER ENROLLED
In-state or province applicants/ enrollees	369	67	34
Out-of-state or province applicants/enrollees	1,452	190	42
International applicants/enrollees (noncitizens/nonpermanent residents)	235	8	4

DEMOGRAPHIC DESCRIPTIONS OF APPLICANTS: 2014 ENTERING CLASS

	APPLICANTS			ENROLLEES		
	M	W	Gender Unknown or Not Reported	M	W	Gender Unknown or Not Reported
American Indian or Alaska Native	1	1	0	0	0	0
Asian	329	368	6	11	12	0
Black or African American	36	51	1	3	2	0
Hispanic or Latino	65	89	0	4	1	0
Native Hawaiian or Other Pacific Islander	1	2	0	0	0	0
White	380	348	4	21	16	0
Two or more races	22	29	1	1	2	0
Race and ethnicity unknown	41	37	9	2	1	0
International	113	117	5	2	2	0

Notes: Hispanic applicants/students reporting more than one race appear under the category of two or more ethnicities.

	MINIMUM	MAXIMUM	MEAN
2014 entering class enrollees by age	21	32	23

CURRICULUM

Interdisciplinary integration characterizes the curriculum's three phases: biomedical, preclinical and clinical.

One and half years of study are shared with medical students in four biomedical foundation courses: Molecular Mechanisms in Health and Disease, Clinical Human Anatomy and The Body in Health and Disease. Dental faculty provide dental correlations using small group sessions and case- and team-based-learning approaches.

Clinical clerkships occur in the second and third semesters enabling students to apply biomedical coursework (medical history, physical diagnosis) and behavioral science coursework (patient interviewing, wellness counseling, nutritional assessment, addictive behavior counseling).

Semester 4 targets basic dental science courses and an intensive, case-based preclinical dental simulation course. Interdisciplinary faculty work with the students to develop comprehensive dental care skills.

During the curriculum's clinical phase, students—guided by faculty mentors—provide comprehensive general dental care to a panel of patients.

In year 3, students have four rotations to affiliated hospitals: two 2-week rotations in physical diagnosis (fall semester) and two 2-week rotations in general dentistry (spring semester). Primary medicine grand rounds provide opportunities to integrate biomedical information into the dental care of the students' patients. An honors program is available for a select group of students during the final semester.

Extensive student research opportunities are available.

SPECIAL PROGRAMS AND SERVICES

PREDENTAL
Summer Medical and Dental Education Program

DURING DENTAL SCHOOL
Academic counseling and tutoring: shared with medical school
Community service opportunities

Internships, externships, or extramural programs: extensive, supported Global Health Externship Program
Mentoring
Personal and career counseling
Professional- and career-development programming
Training for those interested in academic and research careers

ACTIVE STUDENT ORGANIZATIONS
American Academy of Pediatric Dentistry
American Association for Dental Research National Student Research Group
American Association of Women Dentists
American Student Dental Association
Hispanic Dental Association
Student National Dental Association
For more information on student organizations, visit http://dental.columbia.edu/page/cdm-club-and-student-organizations

INTERNATIONAL DENTISTS
Graduates of international dental schools considered for traditional predoctoral program: No

COMBINED AND ALTERNATE DEGREES

Ph.D.	M.S.	M.P.H.	M.D.	B.A./B.S.	Other
—	✓	✓	—	—	✓

Other degrees: M.A. in Education, M.B.A.

COSTS: 2014–15 SCHOOL YEAR

	FIRST YEAR	SECOND YEAR	THIRD YEAR	FOURTH YEAR
Tuition, resident	$60,312	$58,324	$58,324	$58,324
Tuition, nonresident	$60,312	$58,324	$58,324	$58,324
Tuition, other				
Fees	$15,526	$15,421	$15,421	$15,421
Instruments, books, and supplies	$1,550	$1,555	$645	$3,150
Estimated living expenses	$20,058	$21,485	$25,785	$22,560
Total, resident	$97,446	$96,785	$100,175	$99,455
Total, nonresident	$97,446	$96,785	$100,175	$99,455
Total, other				

Note: Fees include:
- Student health service ($1,776).
- Student health insurance premium ($3,581), which can be waived.
- Disability insurance ($68).
- Student activity fee ($260); D.D.S. technology fee ($9,966), which includes dental kit.
- CUMC network fee ($370).
- First-year students' one-time transcript fee ($105).

FINANCIAL AID

FINANCIAL AID AWARDS TO FIRST-YEAR STUDENTS 2014–15

Total number of first-year recipients: 62	
Percentage of the first-year class: 78%	
Percentage of awards that are grants? 9%	
Percentage of awards that are loans? 91%	

	AVERAGE AWARDS	RANGE OF AWARDS
Residents	$71,702	$2,593–$102,386
Nonresidents	$71,702	$2,593–$102,386

For more information, please visit: www.cumc.columbia.edu/student/finaid

NEW YORK UNIVERSITY
COLLEGE OF DENTISTRY

Charles N. Bertolami, D.D.S., D.Med.Sc., Herman Robert Fox Dean

GENERAL INFORMATION

New York University College of Dentistry (NYUCD) offers students the advantage of a metropolitan setting. Founded in 1865, NYUCD is the largest and third oldest dental school in the nation. NYUCD offers professional training leading to the D.D.S. degree, as well as advanced dental education and specialty training. NYUCD is administered by the David B. Kriser Dental Center, New York University (NYU), which comprises three buildings in New York City. Additional programs include a bachelor's degree and associate degree in dental hygiene, continuing dental education programs, the Program for Advanced Study in Dentistry for International Graduates, a master's degree in Oral Biology in collaboration with NYU's Graduate School of Arts and Sciences, a master's degree in Clinical Research and a master's degree in Biomaterials.

MISSION

To partner with students in achieving academic excellence; providing the best oral health care; and engaging in research to improve the health of diverse populations.

Type of institution: Private
Year opened: 1865
Term type: Semester
Time to degree in months: 48
Start month: August

Doctoral dental degree offered: D.D.S.
Targeted predoctoral enrollment: 1,441
Targeted entering class size: 365
Campus setting: Urban
Campus housing available: No, the majority of students live in off-campus apartments.

PREPARATION

Formal minimum preparation in semester/quarter hours: Semester: 90   Quarter: 120
Baccalaureate degree preferred: Yes
Number of first-year, first-time enrollees whose highest degree is:
    Baccalaureate: 314
    Master's degree and beyond: 41
Of first-year, first-time enrollees without baccalaureates, the number with:
    Equivalent of 60 undergraduate credit hours or less: 0
    Equivalent of 61–90 undergraduate credit hours: 0
    Equivalent of 91 or more undergraduate credit hours: 28

PREREQUISITE COURSE	REQUIRED	RECOMMENDED	LAB REQUIRED	CREDITS (SEMESTER/QUARTER)
BCP (biology-chemistry-physics) sciences				
Biology	✓		✓	8/12
Chemistry, general/inorganic	✓		✓	6/9
Chemistry, organic	✓		✓	6/9
Physics	✓		✓	6/9
Additional biological sciences				
Anatomy		✓		4/6
Biochemistry		✓		4/6
Cell biology		✓		4/6
Histology		✓		4/6
Immunology		✓		4/6
Microbiology		✓		4/6
Molecular biology/genetics		✓		4/6
Physiology				
Zoology				

CONTACT INFORMATION

www.nyu.edu/dental

433 East 1st Avenue
New York, NY 10010
Phone: 212-998-9818
Fax: 212-995-4240
Email: dental.admissions@nyu.edu

OFFICE OF ADMISSIONS

Dr. Eugenia E. Mejia
Assistant Dean of Admissions and Enrollment Management
Phone: 212-998-9818
Email: dental.admissions@nyu.edu

OFFICE OF FINANCIAL AID

Email: dental.financial.aid@nyu.edu

OFFICE OF STUDENT AFFAIRS

Ms. Staci Lynn Ripkey
Assistant Dean, Student Affairs & Academic Support Services
Email: staci.ripkey@nyu.edu

Diversity Initiatives
Dr. Eugenia E. Mejia
Assistant Dean of Admissions and Enrollment Management
Phone: 212-998-9818
Email: dental.admissions@nyu.edu

PREPARATION (CONTINUED)

PREREQUISITE COURSE	REQUIRED	RECOMMENDED	LAB REQUIRED	CREDITS (SEMESTER/QUARTER)
Other				
English	✓			6/9

Community college coursework accepted for prerequisites: Yes; prefer courses be taken at four-year college
Community college coursework accepted for electives: Yes
Limits on community college credit hours: Yes, 60 credit hours
Maximum number of community college credit hours: 60
Advanced placement (AP) credit accepted for prerequisites: No
Advanced placement (AP) credit accepted for electives: Yes
Comments regarding AP credit: Students with AP credits in the sciences are expected to take a higher-level science course in that discipline.
Job shadowing: Required
Number of hours of job shadowing required or recommended: 100
Other factors considered in admissions: Yes

DAT

Mandatory: Yes
Latest DAT for consideration of application: 02/01/2016
Oldest DAT considered: 01/01/2013
When more than one DAT score is reported: Highest score is considered
Canadian DAT accepted: Yes
Application considered before DAT scores are submitted: No

U.S. DAT: 2014 ENTERING CLASS

ENROLLEE DAT SCORES	MEAN	RANGE
Academic Average	21.0	NR
Perceptual Ability	20.0	NR
Total Science	21.0	NR

CANADIAN DAT: 2014 ENTERING CLASS

ENROLLEE DAT SCORES	MEAN	RANGE
Academic Average	21.0	NR
Manual Dexterity	18.0	NR
Perceptual Ability	20.0	NR
Total Science	21.0	NR

GPA: 2014 ENTERING CLASS

ENROLLEE GPA SCORES	UNDERGRAD. MEAN	GRADUATE MEAN	UNDERGRAD. RANGE	GRADUATE RANGE
Science GPA	3.34	3.40	NR	NR
Total GPA	3.46	3.62	NR	NR

APPLICATION AND SELECTION

TIMETABLE

Earliest filing date: 06/02/2015
Latest filing date: 02/01/2016
Earliest date for acceptance offers: 12/01/2015
Maximum time in days for applicant's response to acceptance offer:
30 days if accepted on or after December 1
15 days if accepted on or after February 1

Requests for deferred entrance considered: In exceptional circumstances only
Fee for application: Yes, submitted at same time as Associated American Dental Schools Application Service (AADSAS) application
Amount of fee for application:
In state: $80   Out of state: $80   International: $80
Fee waiver available: Yes

	FIRST DEPOSIT	SECOND DEPOSIT	THIRD DEPOSIT
Required to hold place	Yes	Yes	No
Resident amount	$1,500	$3,500	
Nonresident amount	$1,500	$3,500	
Deposit due	As indicated in admission offer	As indicated in admission offer	
Applied to tuition	Yes	Yes	
Refundable	No	No	

APPLICATION PROCESS

Participates in Associated American Dental Schools Application Service (AADSAS): Yes
Accepts direct applicants: No
Secondary or supplemental application required: Yes, at time of interview
Secondary or supplemental application website: None
Interview is mandatory: Yes
Interview is by invitation: Yes

RESIDENCY

In-state/in-province versus out-of-state/out-of-province
Admissions process distinguishes between in-state/in-province and out-of-state/out-of-province applicants: No
Preference given to residents of: NR
Reciprocity Admissions Agreement available for legal residents of: NR
Generally and over time, percentage of your first-year enrollment that is in-state: 30%
Origin of out-of-state/out-of-province enrollees: AL-1, CA-41, CT-3, FL-26, GA-8, IL-3, MA-4, MD-7, MI-1, MN-4, NC-5, ND-1, NJ-39, OH-1, OK-1, OR-2, PA-9, SC-1, TN-2, TX-10, VA-13, VT-2, WA-5, WI-1, State Not Reported-2

International
Applications are accepted from international (noncitizens/nonpermanent residents): Yes
Origin of international enrollees: Canada-46, China-1, Ecuador-1, India-1, Indonesia-1, Iran-2, Israel-1, Morocco-1, South Korea-14, Ukraine-1, ZZ-19

APPLICATION AND ENROLLMENT	NUMBER OF APPLICANTS	ESTIMATED NUMBER INTERVIEWED	ESTIMATED NUMBER ENROLLED
In-state or province applicants/enrollees	563	NR	107
Out-of-state or province applicants/enrollees	3,436	NR	192
International applicants/enrollees (noncitizens/nonpermanent residents)	585	NR	88

DEMOGRAPHIC DESCRIPTIONS OF APPLICANTS: 2014 ENTERING CLASS

	APPLICANTS			ENROLLEES		
	M	W	Gender Unknown or Not Reported	M	W	Gender Unknown or Not Reported
American Indian or Alaska Native	1	3	0	0	0	0
Asian	760	800	21	62	53	0
Black or African American	46	87	4	2	3	0
Hispanic or Latino	141	194	2	4	12	0
Native Hawaiian or Other Pacific Islander	0	3	0	0	1	0
White	941	736	5	76	59	0
Two or more races	58	62	1	2	6	0
Race and ethnicity unknown	65	58	16	9	7	0
International	302	272	11	39	49	0

	MINIMUM	MAXIMUM	MEAN
2014 entering class enrollees by age	19	39	23

CURRICULUM

NYUCD's educational philosophy is based on the conviction that real life is not the rote repetition of information; rather, it is the application of knowledge to solve problems associated with disease. Thus, NYUCD has initiated a hands-on approach early in the learning process in combination with a rigorous program that requires critical thinking and problem-solving. NYUCD's four-year curriculum is fully integrated and does not teach along traditional departmental structure. The biomedical sciences are taught in three segments over the first three years. The clinical sciences emphasize general dentistry and are also fully integrated. Education is broad in scope, yet focused and applied to real-world problems and issues. Patient contact begins in the first year, and students earn patient care privileges through achievement.

Student research opportunities: Dental students may be introduced to research at an early stage in their careers. Their first opportunity to participate in research occurs the summer before they begin their studies. Participants in the eight-week summer program work with faculty mentors on their research studies full time and attend seminars three times a week. The Honors in Research Program provides dental students with the opportunity to participate in a research project from their D1 to D4 years.

SPECIAL PROGRAMS AND SERVICES

PREDENTAL

Special affiliations with colleges and universities: NYU College of Arts and Science - B.A./D.D.S. 7-year combined degree program; Adelphi University - B.A./D.D.S. 7-year combined degree program
Summer enrichment programs: Research program available for high school and undergraduate students

DURING DENTAL SCHOOL

Academic counseling and tutoring
Community service opportunities: national and international outreach programs
Mentoring
Personal counseling
Professional- and career-development programming
Training for those interested in academic careers
Transfer applicants considered if space is available

ACTIVE STUDENT ORGANIZATIONS

American Association for Dental Research National Student Research Group
American Dental Education Association
American Student Dental Association
Asian dental clubs
Community Service Club
Hispanic Dental Association
Student National Dental Association
Women of Color in Dentistry

INTERNATIONAL DENTISTS

Graduates of international dental schools considered for traditional predoctoral program: Yes
Advanced standing program offered for graduates of international dental schools: No
Advanced standing program description: None

COMBINED AND ALTERNATE DEGREES

Ph.D.	M.S.	M.P.H.	M.D.	B.A./B.S.	Other
—	—	✓	—	✓	—

Note: A seven-year combined B.A./D.D.S. degree program is available through collaboration with the NYU College of Arts and Science and Adelphi University.

COSTS: 2014–15 SCHOOL YEAR

	FIRST YEAR	SECOND YEAR	THIRD YEAR	FOURTH YEAR
Tuition, resident	$67,403	$67,403	$67,403	$67,403
Tuition, nonresident	$67,403	$67,403	$67,403	$67,403
Tuition, other				
Fees	$6,688	$5,936	$6,084	$6,024
Instruments, books, and supplies	$7,305	$5,330	$7,305	$5,330
Estimated living expenses	$28,772	$31,333	$31,333	$26,111
Total, resident	$110,168	$110,002	$112,125	$104,868
Total, nonresident	$110,168	$110,002	$112,125	$104,868
Total, other				

FINANCIAL AID

NYUCD requires applicants to submit the Free Application for Federal Student Aid (FAFSA). New York State residents may also submit the New York State Tuition Assistance Program (TAP) application. NYUCD recommends filing the FAFSA before March in the year admission is sought. The online FAFSA form opens on January 1. The applicants should complete all required sections, including parents' financial data, even if s/he is financially independent. The completed form should be submitted to the central processor (not NYUCD), who will forward the data to NYUCD electronically. Each year, the school awards a limited number of scholarships to admitted applicants. Eligibility for a Dean's Award is based on the overall GPA, DAT scores and the overall competitiveness of the application.

For more information, please visit: http://dental.nyu.edu/student-life/financial-services.html

CONTACT INFORMATION

http://dentistry.stonybrookmedicine.edu
Phone: 631-632-8900
Fax: 631-632-7130

OFFICE OF EDUCATION

Rockland Hall, Room 115
Stony Brook, NY 11794
Phone: 631-632-3745
http://dentistry.stonybrookmedicine.edu/
dental/student/admissions

OFFICE OF FINANCIAL AID

Rockland Hall, Room 148
Stony Brook, NY 11794-8709
Phone: 631-632-3027
http://dentistry.stonybrookmedicine.edu/
dentalfinancial

MINORITY AFFAIRS/DIVERSITY

Dr. Fred Ferguson
Rockland Hall, Room 126
Stony Brook, NY 11794
Phone: 631-632-8902

THE DIVISON OF CAMPUS RESIDENCE

Stony Brook University
Stony Brook, NY 11794
Phone: 631-632-6966
Email: reside@stonybrook.edu
www.studentaffairs.stonybrook.edu/res/
housing_facilities/apartments.shtml

STONY BROOK UNIVERSITY
SCHOOL OF DENTAL MEDICINE

Mary R. Truhlar, D.D.S., M.S., Dean

GENERAL INFORMATION

The School of Dental Medicine (SDM) is a major component of the Health Sciences Center of Stony Brook University, a leading New York public university located on Long Island. The school is internationally recognized for excellence in education, clinical rigor and innovative personalized curricula via its small size relative to peer institutions. Predoctoral dental students routinely participate in providing early and comprehensive clinical care, interprofessional training, global and community outreach programs, and research experiences. Opportunities to pursue concurrent master's degrees and combined D.D.S./Ph.D. degrees provide additional educational enrichment. The SDM's comprehensive educational programs and supportive learning environment graduate professionals who are competent to enter clinical general practice, committed to lifelong learning, and who become leaders in patient care, academia, research and service/engagement.

MISSION

To advance the oral and general health of the local and global communities through continuous pursuit of excellence in education, patient care, discovery and leadership.

Type of institution: Public	Doctoral dental degree offered: D.D.S.
Year opened: 1973	Targeted predoctoral enrollment: 168
Term type: Semester	Targeted entering class size: 42
Time to degree in months: 44	Campus setting: Suburban
Start month: August	Campus housing available: Yes

PREPARATION

Formal minimum preparation in semester/quarter hours: Semester: 60   Quarter: 90
Baccalaureate degree preferred: Yes
Number of first-year, first-time enrollees whose highest degree is:
   Baccalaureate: 42
   Master's degree and beyond: 0
Of first-year, first-time enrollees without baccalaureates, the number with:
   Equivalent of 60 undergraduate credit hours or less: 0
   Equivalent of 61–90 undergraduate credit hours: 0
   Equivalent of 91 or more undergraduate credit hours: 0

PREREQUISITE COURSE	REQUIRED	RECOMMENDED	LAB REQUIRED	CREDITS (SEMESTER/QUARTER)
BCP (biology-chemistry-physics) sciences				
Biology	✓		✓	8/12
Chemistry, general/inorganic	✓		✓	8/12
Chemistry, organic	✓		✓	8/12
Physics	✓		✓	8/12
Additional biological sciences				
Anatomy		✓		4/6
Biochemistry	✓			3
Cell biology		✓		4/6
Histology		✓		4/6
Immunology		✓		4/6
Microbiology		✓		4/6
Molecular biology/genetics		✓		4/6
Physiology		✓		4/6
Zoology		✓		4/6

PREPARATION (CONTINUED)

PREREQUISITE COURSE	REQUIRED	RECOMMENDED	LAB REQUIRED	CREDITS (SEMESTER/QUARTER)
Other				
Calculus 1	✓			4/6
Calculus 2 or Statistics	✓			4/6
Intensive Writing Course	✓			6/9

Community college coursework accepted for prerequisites: Yes, but prerequisites from four-year college preferred
Community college coursework accepted for electives: Yes
Limits on community college credit hours: Yes
Maximum number of community college credit hours: 60
Advanced placement (AP) credit accepted for prerequisites: Must score 4 or above for credit
Advanced placement (AP) credit accepted for electives: Must score 4 or above for credit
Comments regarding AP credit: For prerequisite courses, additional course(s) should be taken within that discipline to demonstrate scholastic ability at the college level.
Job shadowing: Required
Number of hours of job shadowing required or recommended: 60 hours or more preferred.
Other factors considered in admission: Academic experience and performance, DAT, letters of evaluation, exposure to and comprehension of the dental profession, communication skills, life experiences, prior research, service and/or leadership, and interview performance

DAT

Mandatory: Yes
Oldest DAT considered: Current score obtained after 06/01/2012
When more than one DAT score is reported: All scores are reviewed.
Canadian DAT accepted: No
Application considered before DAT scores are submitted: No

DAT: 2014 ENTERING CLASS

ENROLLEE DAT SCORES	MEAN	RANGE
Academic Average	22.0	18–26
Perceptual Ability	20.0	15–25
Total Science	22.0	18–26

GPA: 2014 ENTERING CLASS

ENROLLEE GPA SCORES	UNDERGRAD. MEAN	GRADUATE MEAN	UNDERGRAD. RANGE	GRADUATE RANGE
Science GPA	3.68	NA	3.18–4.00	NA
Total GPA	3.72	NA	3.41–4.00	NA

APPLICATION AND SELECTION

TIMETABLE

Earliest filing date: 06/02/2015
Latest filing date: 12/01/2015
Earliest date for acceptance offers: 12/01/2015
Maximum time in days for applicant's response to acceptance offer:
    30 days if accepted between 12/01 and 01/31
    15 days if accepted between 02/01 and 05/15
    Applicants accepted after 05/15 may be asked for an immediate response to an admissions offer
Requests for deferred entrance considered: Yes

Fee for application: Yes, submitted at same time as Associated American Dental Schools Application Service (AADSAS) application.
Amount of fee for application:
    In state: $100   Out of state: $100   International: $100
Fee waiver available: No

	FIRST DEPOSIT	SECOND DEPOSIT	THIRD DEPOSIT
Required to hold place	Yes	No	No
Resident amount	$350		
Nonresident amount	$350		
Deposit due	As indicated in admission offer		
Applied to tuition	Yes		
Refundable	Yes		
Refundable by	As indicated in admission offer		

APPLICATION PROCESS

Participates in AADSAS: Yes
Accepts direct applicants: No
Secondary or supplemental application required: No
Interview is mandatory: Yes
Interview is by invitation: Yes

RESIDENCY

In-state/in-province versus out-of-state/out-of-province
Admissions process distinguishes between in-state/in-province and out-of-state/out-of-province applicants: Yes
Preference given to residents of: New York State
Reciprocity Admissions Agreement available for legal residents of: None
Generally and over time, percentage of your first-year enrollment that is in-state: 90%
Origin of out-of-state/out-of-province enrollees: MD-1, NJ-2

International
Applications are accepted from international (noncitizens/nonpermanent residents): Yes
Origin of international enrollees: NA

APPLICATION AND ENROLLMENT	NUMBER OF APPLICANTS	ESTIMATED NUMBER INTERVIEWED	ESTIMATED NUMBER ENROLLED
In-state or province applicants/enrollees	453	NR	39
Out-of-state or province applicants/enrollees	571	NR	3
International applicants/enrollees (noncitizens/nonpermanent residents)	82	NR	0

DEMOGRAPHIC DESCRIPTIONS OF APPLICANTS: 2014 ENTERING CLASS

	APPLICANTS			ENROLLEES		
	M	W	Gender Unknown or Not Reported	M	W	Gender Unknown or Not Reported
American Indian or Alaska Native	1	1	0	0	0	0
Asian	137	193	2	6	8	0
Black or African American	13	19	0	1	1	0
Hispanic or Latino	38	41	0	1	0	0
Native Hawaiian or Other Pacific Islander	0	0	0	0	0	0
White	250	253	1	8	14	0
Two or more races	12	16	0	0	0	0
Race and ethnicity unknown	16	25	6	3	0	0
International	38	43	1	0	0	0

	MINIMUM	MAXIMUM	MEAN
2014 entering class enrollees by age	21	26	23

CURRICULUM

Stony Brook University School of Dental Medicine predoctoral curriculum provides a comprehensive learning model, which includes an integrated biomedical education, early entry to clinical patient care, research opportunities and community service learning. Education in the basic, behavioral and clinical sciences emphasizes development of critical thinking skills leading to excellence in the practice of dentistry. Predoctoral dental students are integrated with medical school colleagues in the basic science curriculum of year 1. In addition, preclinical training begins in year 1, leading to early patient care delivery at the end of that year followed by extensive, patient-centered experiences in years 2, 3 and 4. Students engage in local, regional and global community outreach programs (e.g., through the U.S. Indian Health Service, and in Chile, Madagascar and Jamaica). Research experience is encouraged and provided as early as the summer prior to matriculation.

Student research opportunities: Yes, newly accepted students may begin research opportunities during the summer prior to matriculation.

SPECIAL PROGRAMS AND SERVICES

PREDENTAL

Summer enrichment programs: Research opportunities

DURING DENTAL SCHOOL

Academic counseling and tutoring
Community service opportunities (local, national, and international)

Internships, externships, or extramural programs
Interprofessional training and adjunctive degree program
Mentoring
Personal counseling
Professional- and career-development programming
Research/translational research

ACTIVE STUDENT ORGANIZATIONS

American Academy of Pediatric Dentistry, Student Chapter
American Academy of Public Health Dentistry
American Dental Education Association, Stony Brook Chapter
American Student Dental Association
Business in Dentistry
Community Outreach Interfaith Network
Cosmetic and Aesthetic Dentistry Club
Dental Student Research Society
Hispanic Student Dental Association
Minority Student Dental Association

INTERNATIONAL DENTISTS

Graduates of international dental schools considered for traditional predoctoral program: Yes
Advanced standing program offered for graduates of international dental schools: No
Advanced standing program description: NA

COMBINED AND ALTERNATE DEGREES

Ph.D.	M.S.	M.P.H.	M.D.	B.A./B.S.	Other
✓	✓	✓	—	—	✓

Other degree: M.B.A.

COSTS: 2014–15 SCHOOL YEAR

	FIRST YEAR	SECOND YEAR	THIRD YEAR	FOURTH YEAR
Tuition, resident	$30,240	$30,240	$30,240	$30,240
Tuition, nonresident	$62,950	$62,950	$62,950	$62,950
Tuition, other				
Fees	$12,854	$12,636	$12,786	$12,636
Instruments, books, and supplies	$12,382	$15,554	$4,877	$3,515
Estimated living expenses	$20,130	$20,130	$20,130	$20,130
Total, resident	$75,606	$78,560	$68,033	$66,521
Total, nonresident	$108,316	$111,270	$100,743	99,231
Total, other				

FINANCIAL AID

To be considered for financial aid from the federal Title IV programs, students must meet basic eligibility requirements. Please review the U.S. Department of Education's Funding Education Beyond High School: The Guide to Federal Student Aid for specific eligibility details at http://studentaid.ed.gov/students/publications/student_guide/index.html. The federal financial aid application process begins with the completion of the Free Application for Federal Student Aid (FAFSA). In order for us to receive a copy of their FAFSA results, student must include Stony Brook University federal code 002838 when completing their FAFSA. Students are strongly encouraged to file their FAFSA before April 1, 2015. To be awarded any financial aid, students must first be admitted into a degree-granting program at Stony Brook University.

For more information, please visit: http://dentistry.stonybrookmedicine.edu/dentalfinancial

TOURO COLLEGE OF DENTAL MEDICINE AT
NEW YORK MEDICAL COLLEGE

Jay P. Goldsmith, D.M.D., Founding Dean

CONTACT INFORMATION

www.nymc.edu/
19 Skyline Drive
Hawthorne, NY 12332
Phone: 914-594-3936
Fax: 914-594-4415

OFFICE OF ADMISSIONS
40 Sunshine Cottage Road
Valhalla, N.Y. 10595
Phone: 914-594-4507

FINANCIAL AID
Mr. Anthony M. Sozzo
Director of Student Financial Planning
40 Sunshine Cottage Road
Valhalla, NY 10595
Phone: 914-594-4491
Fax: 914-594-4613

STUDENT AFFAIRS
Ms. Tanya L. Hodges
Director, Student Affairs
40 Sunshine Cottage Road
Valhalla, NY 10595
Phone: 914-594-4498
Fax: 914-594-4613

MINORITY AFFAIRS/DIVERSITY
Ms. Joan Y. June
Associate Dean for Student Diversity
40 Sunshine Cottage Road
Valhalla, NY 10595
Phone: 914-594-3016
Fax: 914-594-4613

HOUSING
Ms. Katherine Dillon Smith
Director of Student and Residential Life
40 Sunshine Cottage Road
Valhalla, NY 10595
Phone: 914-594-4832
Fax: 914-594-4613

GENERAL INFORMATION

The Touro College of Dental Medicine at New York Medical College (TCDM NYMC), scheduled to accept its first class in summer 2016, will be the first U.S. dental school opened under Jewish auspices. Situated just north of New York City on NYMC's campus in Westchester County, TCDM will offer its students a robust education delivered in a new state-of-the art clinical facility. The basic sciences will be taught by distinguished NYMC faculty, and students will develop their clinical skills in a technologically advanced comprehensive practice clinic where they will have the latest available digital dentistry tools. Students will participate in community education and outreach within the diverse Westchester community.

MISSION

To graduate outstanding dental professionals who will use a complex knowledge base and sophisticated perceptual skills.

Vision: To deliver excellent health care service to diverse communities.

Core Values: Integrity | Compassion | Empathy

Type of institution: Public	Doctoral dental degree offered: D.D.S.
Year opened: 2016	Targeted predoctoral enrollment: 440
Term type: Trimester	Targeted entering class size: 110
Time to degree in months: 46	Campus setting: Suburban
Start month: July	Campus housing available: Yes

PREPARATION

Formal minimum preparation in semester/quarter hours: Semester: 90   Quarter: 135
Baccalaureate degree preferred: Yes
Number of first-year, first-time enrollees whose highest degree is:
  Baccalaureate: NA
  Master's degree and beyond: NA
Of first-year, first-time enrollees without baccalaureates, the number with:
  Equivalent of 60 undergraduate credit hours or less: NA
  Equivalent of 61–90 undergraduate credit hours: NA
  Equivalent of 91 or more undergraduate credit hours: NA

PREREQUISITE COURSE	REQUIRED	RECOMMENDED	LAB REQUIRED	CREDITS (SEMESTER/QUARTER)
BCP (biology-chemistry-physics) sciences				
Biology	✓		✓	4/6
Chemistry, general/inorganic	✓		✓	4/6
Chemistry, organic	✓		✓	4/6
Physics		✓		
Additional biological sciences				
Anatomy		✓		
Biochemistry	✓			3/4
Cell biology		✓		
Histology		✓		
Immunology				
Microbiology				
Molecular biology/genetics		✓		

(Prerequisite Courses continued)

PREPARATION (CONTINUED)

PREREQUISITE COURSE	REQUIRED	RECOMMENDED	LAB REQUIRED	CREDITS (SEMESTER/QUARTER)
Physiology		✓		
Zoology				
Other				
Additional biology, chemistry, and/or physics courses	✓			16/24
English composition/technical writing	✓			3/4

Community college coursework accepted for prerequisites: Yes
Community college coursework accepted for electives: Yes
Limits on community college credit hours: No
Maximum number of community college credit hours: NA
Advanced placement (AP) credit accepted for prerequisites: No
Advanced placement (AP) credit accepted for electives: No
Comments regarding AP credit: None
Job shadowing: Recommended
Number of hours of job shadowing required or recommended: 30

DAT

Mandatory: Yes
Latest DAT for consideration of application: 12/01/2015
Oldest DAT considered: 01/01/2013
When more than one DAT score is reported: Highest score is considered
Canadian DAT accepted: Yes
Application considered before DAT scores are submitted: No

APPLICATION AND SELECTION

TIMETABLE

Earliest filing date: 06/02/2015
Latest filing date: 12/30/2015
Earliest date for acceptance offers: 12/01/2015
Maximum time in days for applicant's response to acceptance offer: 30 days
Requests for deferred entrance considered: No
Fee for application: Yes
Amount of fee for application:
In state: $100   Out of state: $100   International: $100
Fee waiver available: Yes

	FIRST DEPOSIT	SECOND DEPOSIT	THIRD DEPOSIT
Required to hold place	Yes	Yes	No
Resident amount	$2,000	TBD	
Nonresident amount	$2,000	TBD	
International amount			
Deposit due	As indicated on acceptance	As indicated on acceptance	
Applied to tuition	Yes	Yes	
Refundable	No	No	

APPLICATION PROCESS

Participates in Associated American Dental Schools Application Service (AADSAS): Yes
Accepts direct applicants: No
Secondary or supplemental application required: Yes
Secondary or supplemental application website: To be determined
Interview is mandatory: Yes
Interview is by invitation: Yes

RESIDENCY

In-state/in-province versus out-of-state/out-of-province
Admissions process distinguishes between in-state/in-province and out-of-state/out-of-province applicants: No
Preference given to residents of: Westchester, Lower Hudson Valley, New York State
Reciprocity Admissions Agreement available for legal residents of: None
Generally and over time, percentage of your first-year enrollment that is in-state: NA
Origin of out-of-state/out-of-province enrollees: NA

International
Applications are accepted from international (noncitizens/nonpermanent residents): Yes
Origin of international enrollees: NA

CURRICULUM

Across its curriculum, TCDM emphasizes the important link connecting basic, behavioral and clinical dental sciences. Although implemented at a new school, the rigorous basic science and behavioral science curricula will taught by distinguished faculty who teach the corresponding coursework at NYMC. These faculty members are seasoned teaching professionals known for their commitment to helping each student maximize his or her potential.

The teamwork concepts learned in the preclinical simulation lab will be integrated into clinical training. The clinic is designed to be a working replica of an everyday dental practice, with the students making decisions and performing the type of procedures they will be doing in their future clinical practices. In the past 15 years, dentistry has seen tremendous change in the available technologies and techniques. The clinical curriculum at TCDM will employ these advancements to help our students focus on the knowledge, skills and values necessary to provide culturally competent, comprehensive, patient-centered care.

The TCDM program will also provide students with extensive opportunities to experience multiple clinical practice scenarios using our extensive and diverse network of affiliated hospitals and community clinics.

Student research opportunities: Yes

SPECIAL PROGRAMS AND SERVICES

PREDENTAL

Summer enrichment programs

DURING DENTAL SCHOOL

Academic counseling and tutoring
Community service opportunities
Internships, externships, or extramural programs
Mentoring
Personal counseling
Professional- and career-development programming
Training for those interested in academic careers
Transfer applicants considered if space is available

ACTIVE STUDENT ORGANIZATIONS

Alpha Omega International Dental Fraternity

INTERNATIONAL DENTISTS

Graduates of international dental schools considered for traditional predoctoral program: Yes
Advanced standing program offered for graduates of international dental schools: No

COMBINED AND ALTERNATE DEGREES

Ph.D.	M.S.	M.P.H.	M.D.	B.A./B.S.	Other
—	—	—	—	—	—

COSTS: 2014–15 SCHOOL YEAR

	FIRST YEAR	SECOND YEAR	THIRD YEAR	FOURTH YEAR
Tuition, resident				
Tuition, nonresident				
Tuition, other				
Fees				
Instruments, books, and supplies		To be determined		
Estimated living expenses				
Total, resident				
Total, nonresident				
Total, other				

University at Buffalo
The State University of New York

UNIVERSITY AT BUFFALO
SCHOOL OF DENTAL MEDICINE

Michael Glick, D.M.D., Dean

GENERAL INFORMATION

The University at Buffalo School of Dental Medicine (UB SDM) has its origins in the private University of Buffalo, which later became a member of the State University of New York system. Today, UB SDM is part of UB's South Campus Health Sciences Center. The school improves the oral and general health of the people of New York through teaching, research and service by educating general practitioners and specialists to provide the highest quality of patient-centered care. This education is based on a dynamic curriculum employing the latest information technologies and emphasizing the interactions among basic biomedical and behavioral sciences, clinical sciences and clinical practice. Additionally, the school prepares individuals for leadership roles in the basic and oral health sciences and in dental education.

MISSION

UB School of Dental Medicine Mission: Leading innovation in oral health education, research and service to improve quality of life

Vision: UB School of Dental Medicine Vision: Defining excellence in global health

Type of institution: Public
Year opened: 1892
Term type: Semester
Time to degree in months: 43
Start month: August

Doctoral dental degree offered: D.D.S.
Targeted predoctoral enrollment: 408
Targeted entering class size: 90
Campus setting: Urban
Campus housing available: Yes

PREPARATION

Formal minimum preparation in semester/quarter hours: Semester: 90   Quarter: 120
Baccalaureate degree preferred: Yes
Number of first-year, first-time enrollees whose highest degree is:
    Baccalaureate: 59
    Master's degree and beyond: 24
Of first-year, first-time enrollees without baccalaureates, the number with:
    Equivalent of 60 undergraduate credit hours or less: 0
    Equivalent of 61–90 undergraduate credit hours: 7
    Equivalent of 91 or more undergraduate credit hours: 0

PREREQUISITE COURSE	REQUIRED	RECOMMENDED	LAB REQUIRED	CREDITS (SEMESTER/QUARTER)
BCP (biology-chemistry-physics) sciences				
Biology	✓		✓	8/12
Chemistry, general/inorganic	✓		✓	8/12
Chemistry, organic	✓		✓	8/12
Physics	✓		✓	8/12
Additional biological sciences				
Anatomy		✓		
Biochemistry		✓		
Cell biology		✓		
Histology		✓		
Immunology		✓		
Microbiology		✓		
Molecular biology/genetics		✓		
Physiology		✓		
Zoology				

PREPARATION (CONTINUED)

PREREQUISITE COURSE	REQUIRED	RECOMMENDED	LAB REQUIRED	CREDITS (SEMESTER/QUARTER)
Other				
English	✓			8/12

Comment: English prerequisite must include composition.

Community college coursework accepted for prerequisites: Yes, strongly preferred from four-year college
Community college coursework accepted for electives: Yes, preferred from four-year college
Limits on community college credit hours: No, courses preferred from four-year college
Maximum number of community college credit hours: None; courses preferred from four-year college
Advanced placement (AP) credit accepted for prerequisites: Yes
Advanced placement (AP) credit accepted for electives: Yes
Comments regarding AP credit: AP credit will be accepted by UB SDM if your undergraduate institution accepted your AP credit, with the exception of biology. The biology prerequisite must be taken at an undergraduate institution.
Job shadowing: Required
Number of hours of job shadowing required or recommended: 100
Other factors considered in admission: Prior to application, candidates are strongly encouraged to acquire a minimum of 100 hours experience in the field of clinical dentistry in a variety of settings (general practice, specialty, hospital).

DAT

Mandatory: Yes
Latest DAT for consideration of application: 11/01/2015 (official scores must be received by Associated American Dental Schools Application Service [AADSAS] prior to 12/01/2015)
Oldest DAT considered: 01/01/2013 for fall 2016 admission
When more than one DAT score is reported: Most recent score only is considered
Canadian DAT accepted: Yes
Application considered before DAT scores are submitted: No

DAT: 2014 ENTERING CLASS

ENROLLEE DAT SCORES	MEAN	RANGE
Academic Average	20.1	16–25
Perceptual Ability	20.9	15–26
Total Science	20.0	16–27

GPA: 2014 ENTERING CLASS

ENROLLEE GPA SCORES	UNDERGRAD. MEAN	GRADUATE MEAN	UNDERGRAD. RANGE	GRADUATE RANGE
Science GPA	3.50	3.75	2.60–4.13	3.00–4.00
Total GPA	3.52	3.75	2.77–4.17	3.00–4.00

APPLICATION AND SELECTION

TIMETABLE

Earliest filing date: 06/02/2015
Latest filing date: 12/01/2015
Earliest date for acceptance offers: 12/01/2015
Maximum time in days for applicant's response to acceptance offer:
   30 days if accepted on or after December 1
   15 days if accepted on or after February 1
Requests for deferred entrance considered: In exceptional circumstances only

Fee for application: Yes, submitted at same time as AADSAS application
Amount of fee for application:
   In state: $75   Out of state: $75   International: $75
Fee waiver available: Yes

	FIRST DEPOSIT	SECOND DEPOSIT	THIRD DEPOSIT
Required to hold place	Yes	No	No
Resident amount	$350		
Nonresident amount	$350		
Deposit due	As indicated in admission offer		
Applied to tuition	Yes		
Refundable	Yes		
Refundable by	03/01/2016		

APPLICATION PROCESS

Participates in AADSAS: Yes
Accepts direct applicants: No
Secondary or supplemental application required: No
Interview is mandatory: Yes
Interview is by invitation: Yes

RESIDENCY

In-state/in-province versus out-of-state/out-of-province
Admissions process distinguishes between in-state/in-province and out-of-state/out-of-province applicants: Yes
Preference given to residents of: New York State
Reciprocity Admissions Agreement available for legal residents of: None
Generally and over time, percentage of your first-year enrollment that is in-state: 76%
Origin of out-of-state/out-of-province enrollees: CA-1, DE-1, FL-1, MA-1, MI-3, NJ-3, OK-1, PA-1, TX-1, UT-1, VA-1, WA-1

International
Applications are accepted from international (noncitizens/nonpermanent residents): Yes
Origin of international enrollees: India-1, South Korea-1

APPLICATION AND ENROLLMENT	NUMBER OF APPLICANTS	ESTIMATED NUMBER INTERVIEWED	ESTIMATED NUMBER ENROLLED
In-state or province applicants/enrollees	488	150	72
Out-of-state or province applicants/enrollees	1,029	99	16
International applicants/enrollees (noncitizens/nonpermanent residents)	275	20	2

DEMOGRAPHIC DESCRIPTIONS OF APPLICANTS: 2014 ENTERING CLASS

	APPLICANTS			ENROLLEES		
	M	W	Gender Unknown or Not Reported	M	W	Gender Unknown or Not Reported
American Indian or Alaska Native	0	3	0	0	0	0
Asian	251	270	6	8	14	0
Black or African American	15	21	0	0	1	0
Hispanic or Latino	44	47	0	3	2	0
Native Hawaiian or Other Pacific Islander	1	0	0	0	0	0
White	416	307	1	25	25	0
Two or more races	16	22	1	4	1	0
Race and ethnicity unknown	20	32	12	1	4	0
International	143	128	4	1	1	0

	MINIMUM	MAXIMUM	MEAN
2014 entering class enrollees by age	21	36	25

CURRICULUM

The D.D.S. program provides students with the basic science training, clinical expertise and analytical skills necessary to attain the highest level of proficiency as practitioners. Our graduates practice across the country, in many different settings, in all areas of dental medicine as general practitioners and specialists in private practice, as dental researchers, health care administrators, faculty in dental schools and managers in the private sector.

Student research opportunities: Yes

SPECIAL PROGRAMS AND SERVICES

DURING DENTAL SCHOOL

Academic counseling and tutoring
Community service opportunities: Buffalo Outreach and Community Assistance (BOCA)
Internships, externships, or extramural programs
Mentoring
Personal counseling
Professional- and career-development programming
Training for those interested in academic careers

ACTIVE STUDENT ORGANIZATIONS

Alpha Omega International Dental Fraternity
American Association for Dental Research
American Association of Women Dentists
American Student Dental Association
Buffalo Outreach and Community Assistance
Delta Sigma Delta International Dental Fraternity
Dental Student Research Group
Finance Club
Hispanic Dental Association
Pediatric Education and Dental Outreach Club

INTERNATIONAL DENTISTS

Graduates of international dental schools considered for traditional predoctoral program: Yes, if they meet the eligibility criteria, including the minimum of 90 credit hours of undergraduate study prior to enrollment in the D.D.S. program, with a minimum of 60 credit hours—two full years—completed at an accredited U.S. or Canadian college or university prior to application.
Advanced standing program offered for graduates of international dental schools: Yes
Advanced standing program description: Available at http://dental.buffalo.edu/Education/DDSProgram/InternationalDentistProgram%28DDS%29.aspx

COMBINED AND ALTERNATE DEGREES

Ph.D.	M.S.	M.P.H.	M.D.	B.A./B.S.	Other
✓	✓	—	—	✓	✓

Other degree: M.B.A.

COSTS: 2014–15 SCHOOL YEAR

	FIRST YEAR	SECOND YEAR	THIRD YEAR	FOURTH YEAR
Tuition, resident	$30,240	$30,240	$30,240	$30,240
Tuition, nonresident	$62,950	$62,950	$62,950	$62,950
Tuition, other				
Fees	$2,434	$2,434	$2,434	$2,434
Instruments, books, and supplies	$14,418	$11,380	$8,232	$7,335
Estimated living expenses	$19,568	$19,568	$19,568	$19,568
Total, resident	$66,660	$63,622	$60,474	$59,577
Total, nonresident	$99,370	$96,332	$93,184	$92,287
Total, other				

FINANCIAL AID

FINANCIAL AID AWARDS TO FIRST-YEAR STUDENTS 2014–15

Total number of first-year recipients: 88
Percentage of the first-year class: 98%
Percentage of awards that are grants? 5%
Percentage of awards that are loans? 95%

	AVERAGE AWARDS	RANGE OF AWARDS
Residents	$17,992	$1,500–$28,448
Nonresidents	$24,804	$2,000–$59,255

For more information, please visit: http://financialaid.buffalo.edu/graduate/dentalschool.php

EAST CAROLINA UNIVERSITY
SCHOOL OF DENTAL MEDICINE

D. Gregory Chadwick, D.D.S., M.S., Dean

GENERAL INFORMATION

East Carolina University School of Dental Medicine (ECU SDM) is part of a major health sciences center that includes the Brody School of Medicine and the colleges of Nursing and Allied Health Sciences. East Carolina University—with a total enrollment of more than 25,000 students—is a member institution of the University of North Carolina System. Students spend the first three years of the predoctoral program in the school's new 188,000-square-foot, state-of-the-art building. Training in the fourth year is provided in university-owned, community-based service learning centers located across North Carolina. Advanced dental education resident programs are also available. ECU SDM prepares outstanding, community-minded primary care clinicians ready to serve all segments of society, with an emphasis on rural areas and underserved communities.

MISSION

- To educate academically qualified individuals from underrepresented groups, disadvantaged backgrounds and underserved areas.
- To prepare ethical leaders with outstanding clinical skills, sound judgment and a passion to serve.

Type of institution: Public
Year opened: 2011
Term type: Trimester
Time to degree in months: 44
Start month: August

Doctoral dental degree offered: D.M.D.
Targeted predoctoral enrollment: 200
Targeted entering class size: 52
Campus setting: Health Sciences Center
Campus housing available: No

PREPARATION

Formal minimum preparation in semester/quarter hours: Bachelor's degree is required.
Baccalaureate degree preferred: Bachelor's degree is required.
Number of first-year, first-time enrollees whose highest degree is:
  Baccalaureate: 52
  Master's degree and beyond: 4
Of first-year, first-time enrollees without baccalaureates, the number with:
  Equivalent of 60 undergraduate credit hours or less: 0
  Equivalent of 61–90 undergraduate credit hours: 0
  Equivalent of 91 or more undergraduate credit hours: 0

PREREQUISITE COURSE	REQUIRED	RECOMMENDED	LAB REQUIRED	CREDITS (SEMESTER/QUARTER)
BCP (biology-chemistry-physics) sciences				
Biology	✓		✓	1 year
Chemistry, general/inorganic	✓		✓	1 year
Chemistry, organic	✓		✓	1 year
Physics	✓		✓	1 year
Additional biological sciences				
Anatomy		✓		
Biochemistry		✓		
Cell biology		✓		
Histology		✓		
Immunology		✓		
Microbiology		✓		
Molecular biology/genetics		✓		
Physiology		✓		

(Prerequisite Courses continued)

CONTACT INFORMATION
www.ecu.edu/dentistry
1851 MacGregor Downs Road, MS 701
Greenville, NC 27834-4300

OFFICE OF STUDENT AFFAIRS
Dr. Margaret B. Wilson
Associate Dean for Student Affairs

Mr. B. Lamont Lowery
Director of Admissions
Phone: 252-737-7043

PREPARATION (CONTINUED)

PREREQUISITE COURSE	REQUIRED	RECOMMENDED	LAB REQUIRED	CREDITS (SEMESTER/QUARTER)
Zoology		✓		
Other				
English	✓			1 year
College mathematics	✓			1 year

Community college coursework accepted for prerequisites: In some instances
Community college coursework accepted for electives: Yes
Limits on community college credit hours: Yes
Maximum number of community college credit hours: 60
Advanced placement (AP) credit accepted for prerequisites: In some instances
Advanced placement (AP) credit accepted for electives: Yes
Comments regarding AP credit: We strongly recommend applicants who receive AP credit to then avail themselves of the opportunity to take additional higher-level courses.
Job shadowing: Strongly recommended
Number of hours of job shadowing required or recommended: No specific requirement
Other factors considered in admission: Demonstrated commitment to and leadership in community service, particularly related to promoting health

DAT

Mandatory: Yes
Latest DAT for consideration of application: December 2015
Oldest DAT considered: 07/01/2013
When more than one DAT score is reported: All scores will be reviewed, with emphasis on the most recent set of scores.
Canadian DAT accepted: No
Application considered before DAT scores are submitted: Yes, but decision regarding applicant cannot occur until DAT scores are received and favorably reviewed.

DAT: 2013 ENTERING CLASS

ENROLLEE DAT SCORES	MEAN	RANGE
Academic Average	18.2	15–24
Perceptual Ability	18.7	14–30
Total Science	17.9	14–29

GPA: 2013 ENTERING CLASS

ENROLLEE GPA SCORES	MEAN	RANGE
Science GPA	3.20	2.30–4.10
Total GPA	3.40	2.40–4.10

APPLICATION AND SELECTION

TIMETABLE

Earliest filing date: 06/02/2015
Latest filing date: 12/01/2015
Earliest date for acceptance offers: 12/01/2015
Maximum time in days for applicant's response to acceptance offer:
    30 days if accepted on or after December 1
    15 days if accepted on or after February 1
Requests for deferred entrance considered: In exceptional circumstances only

Fee for application: Yes, nonrefundable
Amount of fee for application:
    In state: $80   Out of state: NA   International: NA
Fee waiver available: No

	FIRST DEPOSIT	SECOND DEPOSIT	THIRD DEPOSIT
Required to hold place	Yes	No	No
Resident amount	$300		
Nonresident amount	NA		
Deposit due	As indicated in admissions offer		
Applied to tuition	Yes		
Refundable	No		

APPLICATION PROCESS

Participates in Associated American Dental Schools Application Service (AADSAS): Yes
Accepts direct applicants: No
Secondary or supplemental application required: Yes
Secondary or supplemental application website: Provided to applicants at time AADSAS is received
Interview is mandatory: Yes
Interview is by invitation: Yes

RESIDENCY

In-state/in-province versus out-of-state/out-of-province
Admissions process distinguishes between in-state/in-province and out-of-state/out-of-province applicants: Yes
Preference given to residents of: Only residents of North Carolina are eligible for admission
Reciprocity Admissions Agreement available for legal residents of: None
Generally and over time, percentage of your first-year enrollment that is in-state: 100%
Origin of out-of-state/out-of-province enrollees: NA

International
Applications are accepted from international (noncitizens/nonpermanent residents): No
Origin of international enrollees: NA

APPLICATION AND ENROLLMENT	NUMBER OF APPLICANTS	ESTIMATED NUMBER INTERVIEWED	ESTIMATED NUMBER ENROLLED
In-state or province applicants/enrollees	361	249	32
Out-of-state or province applicants/enrollees	31	1	0
International applicants/enrollees (noncitizens/nonpermanent residents)	6	NR	0

DEMOGRAPHIC DESCRIPTIONS OF APPLICANTS: 2013 ENTERING CLASS

	APPLICANTS			ENROLLEES		
	M	W	Gender Unknown or Not Reported	M	W	Gender Unknown or Not Reported
American Indian or Alaska Native	2	0	0	0	0	0
Asian	34	35	3	0	5	0
Black or African American	17	29	1	3	6	0
Hispanic or Latino	10	9	0	2	1	0
Native Hawaiian or Other Pacific Islander	0	0	0	0	0	0
White	135	92	1	21	14	0
Two or more races	4	3	0	0	0	0
Race and ethnicity unknown	6	3	2	0	0	0
International	2	4	0	0	0	0

	MINIMUM	MAXIMUM	MEAN
2014 entering class enrollees by age	20	42	24

CURRICULUM

The goal of the curriculum is to interlace problem solving into all aspects of didactic and clinical experiences. Every basic science and preclinical course has a seminar component that will involve group collaboration on increasingly difficult cases and topical problems intended to make problem assessment, solution research and self-reflection equal components of knowledge acquisition. This philosophy continues throughout the four years of clinical training. Unique to ECU SDM are the clinical experiences in the Community Service Learning Centers, located in rural and underserved communities across North Carolina. Utilizing the best practices in health science informatics, the curriculum is designed to provide the highest level of educational experiences in a collaborative and challenging environment. The students are required to play an active role in their success as young professionals.

SPECIAL PROGRAMS AND SERVICES

DURING DENTAL SCHOOL

Academic counseling and tutoring
Community service opportunities
Internships, externships, or extramural programs
Mentoring
Personal counseling
Professional- and career-development programming
Training for those interested in academic careers

ACTIVE STUDENT ORGANIZATIONS

Academy of General Dentistry
American Academy of Pediatric Dentistry
American Association for Dental Research National Student
    Research Group
American Association of Women Dentists
American Dental Education Association
American Student Dental Association
Christian Medical & Dental Associations
Hispanic Dental Association
Student National Dental Association
Student Professionalism and Ethics Association in Dentistry

INTERNATIONAL DENTISTS

Graduates of international dental schools considered for traditional predoctoral program: Only if they are North Carolina residents and have completed all other requirements
Advanced standing program offered for graduates of international dental schools: We do not offer an advanced program for internationally trained dentists.

COMBINED AND ALTERNATE DEGREES

Ph.D.	M.S.	M.P.H.	M.D.	B.A./B.S.	Other
—	—	—	—	—-	—

COSTS: 2013–14 SCHOOL YEAR

	FIRST YEAR	SECOND YEAR	THIRD YEAR	FOURTH YEAR
Tuition, resident	$23,716	$23,716	$23,716	NA
Tuition, nonresident	$23,716	$23,716	$23,716	NA
Tuition, other				
Fees	$6,673	$6,673	$6,673	NA
Instruments, books, and supplies	$8,374	$3,940	$2,500	NA
Estimated living expenses	$20,841	$20,841	$20,841	
Total, resident	$59,604	$55,170	$53,730	NA
Total, nonresident	$59,604	$55,170	$53,730	NA
Total, other				

FINANCIAL AID

Our finalized, approved tuition and fee schedule is posted on our website. On admissions interview day, a financial aid counselor meets with applicants, providing them a summary of the projected education cost. The counselor describes available financial aid options, directing applicants to the Federal Student Aid website. Applicants must complete a Free Application for Federal Student Aid soon after January 1, but no later than February 14, of the matriculation year.

Based on student-provided information, the U.S. Department of Education prepares need analyses, sending them electronically to our Office of Student Financial Aid, which determines each student's financial need level and awards funds accordingly. The Office of Student Financial Aid conveys the information to each student via award letter, which includes award acceptance instructions.

UNIVERSITY OF NORTH CAROLINA AT CHAPEL HILL
SCHOOL OF DENTISTRY

Jane A. Weintraub, D.D.S., M.P.H., Dean

CONTACT INFORMATION

www.dentistry.unc.edu
University of North Carolina at Chapel Hill
School of Dentistry
Manning Drive and Columbia Street
Chapel Hill, NC 27599-7450
Phone: 919-537-3737
Fax: 919-966-4049

ADMISSIONS

1611 Koury Oral Health Sciences Building
Campus Box 7450
Chapel Hill, NC 27599-7450
Phone: 919-537-3348
Fax: 919-966-5795

FINANCIAL AID

University of North Carolina at Chapel Hill
111 Pettigrew Hall
Chapel Hill, NC 27599-2300
Phone: 919-962-3620
www.studentaid.unc.edu

ACADEMIC AFFAIRS

1611 Koury Oral Health Sciences Bldg
Campus Box 7450
Chapel Hill, NC 27599-7450
Phone: 919-537-3347
Fax: 919-966-5795

GENERAL INFORMATION

The University of North Carolina at Chapel Hill (UNC) has the distinction of being the nation's first state university. Close to the Research Triangle Park near the center of the state, Chapel Hill is a college community of 57,000. UNC School of Dentistry (UNC SOD) occupies four buildings—its original building; a five-story, 110,000-square-foot building providing teaching and clinical facilities; a six-story patient care facility, and a new 216,000-square-foot facility, opened in March 2012, for teaching and research. The dental school offers graduate education in 13 areas including nine dental specialties, Advanced Education in General Dentistry and General Practice Residency programs, oral biology and clinical research.

MISSION

To promote the health of the people of North Carolina, the nation and the world through excellence in teaching, patient care, research and service.

Type of institution: Public	Doctoral dental degree offered: D.D.S.
Year opened: 1950	Targeted predoctoral enrollment: 325
Term type: Semester	Targeted entering class size: 82
Time to degree in months: 46	Campus setting: Suburban
Start month: August	Campus housing available: Yes

PREPARATION

Formal minimum preparation in semester/quarter hours: Semester: 96   Quarter: 144
Baccalaureate degree preferred: Yes
Number of first-year, first-time enrollees whose highest degree is:
 Baccalaureate: 76
 Master's degree and beyond: 4
Of first-year first-time enrollees without baccalaureates, the number with:
 Equivalent of 60 undergraduate credit hours or less: 0
 Equivalent of 61–90 undergraduate credit hours: 0
 Equivalent of 91 or more undergraduate credit hours: 2

PREREQUISITE COURSE	REQUIRED	RECOMMENDED	LAB REQUIRED	CREDITS (SEMESTER/QUARTER)
BCP (biology-chemistry-physics) sciences				
Biology	✓		✓	4/6
Chemistry, general/inorganic	✓		✓	8/12
Chemistry, organic	✓			6/10
Physics	✓			6/10
Additional biological sciences				
Anatomy	✓		✓	4/6
Biochemistry	✓			3/5
Cell biology				
Histology				
Immunology				
Microbiology				
Molecular biology/genetics				
Physiology				
Zoology				

PREPARATION (CONTINUED)

PREREQUISITE COURSE	REQUIRED	RECOMMENDED	LAB REQUIRED	CREDITS (SEMESTER/QUARTER)
Other				
English	✓			6/10

Community college coursework accepted for prerequisites: Yes, but prerequisite courses preferred from four-year college/university

Community college coursework accepted for electives: Yes

Limits on community college credit hours: Yes

Maximum number of community college credit hours: 64

Advanced placement (AP) credit accepted for prerequisites: Yes

Advanced placement (AP) credit accepted for electives: Yes

Job shadowing: Required

Number of hours of job shadowing required or recommended: Not specified

Other factors considered in admission: Academic abilities, psychomotor skills, service commitment, self-directed learner and knowledge of the dental profession

DAT

Mandatory: Yes

Latest DAT for consideration of application: 11/01/2015

Oldest DAT considered: 11/01/2012

When more than one DAT score is reported: Highest score is considered

Canadian DAT accepted: Yes

Application considered before DAT scores are submitted: No

DAT: 2014 ENTERING CLASS

ENROLLEE DAT SCORES	MEAN	RANGE
Academic Average	20.4	17–27
Perceptual Ability	20.0	14–29
Total Science	19.7	16–30

GPA: 2014 ENTERING CLASS

ENROLLEE GPA SCORES	UNDERGRAD. MEAN	GRADUATE MEAN	UNDERGRAD. RANGE	GRADUATE RANGE
Science GPA	3.52	3.60	2.04–4.00	3.33–4.00
Total GPA	3.58	3.78	2.15–4.00	2.93–4.00

APPLICATION AND SELECTION

TIMETABLE

Earliest filing date: 06/02/2015

Latest filing date: 11/15/2015

Earliest date for acceptance offers: 12/01/2015

Maximum time in days for applicant's response to acceptance offer:
30 days if accepted on or after December 1 (after first selection meeting)
21 days if accepted on or after February 1 (after second selection meeting)

Requests for deferred entrance considered: No

Fee for application: Yes, submitted at same time as Associated American Dental Schools Application Service (AADSAS) application.

Amount of fee for application:
In-state: $84   Out-of-state: $84   International: $84

Fee waiver available: No

	FIRST DEPOSIT	SECOND DEPOSIT	THIRD DEPOSIT
Required to hold place	Yes	No	No
Resident amount	$500		
Non-resident amount	$500		
Deposit due	As indicated in admission offer		
Applied to tuition	Yes		
Refundable	No		

APPLICATION PROCESS

Participates in AADSAS: Yes

Accepts direct applicants: No

Secondary or supplemental application required: Yes

Secondary or supplemental application website: https://www.dentistry.unc.edu/secure/academic/dds/supplementalapplication/index.cfm

Interview is by invitation: Yes

Interview is mandatory: Yes

RESIDENCY

In-state/in-province versus out-of-state/out-of-province

Admissions process distinguishes between in-state/in-province and out-of-state/out-of-province applicants: Yes

Preference given to residents of: North Carolina

Reciprocity Admissions Agreement available for legal residents of: None

Generally and over time, percentage of your first-year enrollment that is in-state: 82%

Origin of out-of-state/out-of-province enrollees: FL-3, GA-4, NY-1, TN-1, TX-2, VA-2

International

Applications are accepted from international (noncitizens/nonpermanent residents): Yes

Origin of international enrollees: NA

APPLICATION AND ENROLLMENT	NUMBER OF APPLICANTS	ESTIMATED NUMBER INTERVIEWED	ESTIMATED NUMBER ENROLLED
In-state or province applicants/enrollees	345	174	69
Out-of-state or province applicants/enrollees	1,283	82	13
International applicants/enrollees (noncitizens/nonpermanent residents)	72	0	0

DEMOGRAPHIC DESCRIPTIONS OF APPLICANTS: 2014 ENTERING CLASS

	APPLICANTS			ENROLLEES		
	M	W	Gender Unknown or Not Reported	M	W	Gender Unknown or Not Reported
American Indian or Alaska Native	3	6	0	0	0	0
Asian	172	202	3	12	8	0
Black or African American	36	69	1	3	7	0
Hispanic or Latino	39	60	0	1	1	0
Native Hawaiian or Other Pacific Islander	0	0	0	0	0	0
White	542	456	9	24	26	0
Two or more races	1	3	0	0	0	0
Race and ethnicity unknown	14	9	3	0	0	0
International	46	26	0	0	0	0

	MINIMUM	MAXIMUM	MEAN
2014 entering class enrollees by age	21	42	24

CURRICULUM

The program consists of eight semesters of 16 weeks each, plus three required 10-week summer semesters. Most students meet the degree requirements in four years; circumstances may necessitate an extended period of study. The first year includes basic science core courses, introductory dental sciences and introduction to patient management. Students begin patient care in the summer of the first year. During the second year, students continue taking biological science courses, and the next series of dental science and health care delivery systems courses. They also assume full patient care privileges, begin delivering comprehensive care services, and are responsible for providing both therapeutic and preventive treatment for their patients. In the third year, students spend a significant amount of time providing comprehensive care for their patients. A series of intermediate dental science courses are offered. During the summer of their third year, students complete two required externships (community and hospital settings) at in-state and out-of-state extramural sites. In a mentored, general dentistry group practice, fourth-year students assume responsibility for patients requiring more advanced dental care. Advanced dental science courses, updates and practice-related material are offered during the fourth year.

Student research opportunities: Yes

SPECIAL PROGRAMS AND SERVICES

PREDENTAL

Summer enrichment programs: the Medical Education Program (MED) and the Science Enrichment Preparation Program (SEP)

DURING DENTAL SCHOOL

Academic counseling and tutoring
Community service opportunities
Internships, externships and extramural programs
Mentoring
Personal counseling
Training for those interested in academic careers
Transfer applicants considered if space is available

ACTIVE STUDENT ORGANIZATIONS

American Association for Dental Research National Student Research Group
American Association of Women Dentists
American Dental Education Association
American Student Dental Association
Hispanic Dental Association
Student National Dental Association

INTERNATIONAL DENTISTS

Graduates of international dental schools considered for traditional predoctoral program: Yes
Advanced standing program offered for graduates of international dental schools: No

COMBINED AND ALTERNATE DEGREES

Ph.D.	M.S.	M.P.H.	M.D.	B.A./B.S.	Other
✓	✓	✓	—	—	—

COSTS: 2014–15 SCHOOL YEAR

	FIRST YEAR	SECOND YEAR	THIRD YEAR	FOURTH YEAR
Tuition, resident	$30,858	$32,258	$31,758	$27,485
Tuition, nonresident	$63,152	$69,152	$67,152	$50,152
Tuition, other				
Fees (Lease Fee)	$6,715	$6,953	$3,455	$2,925
Instruments, books, and supplies	$5,940	$3,765	$3,500	$5,525
Estimated living expenses	NR	NR	NR	NR
Total, resident	$43,513	$42,976	$38,713	$35,935
Total, nonresident	$75,807	$79,870	$74,107	$58,602
Total, other				

FINANCIAL AID

FINANCIAL AID AWARDS TO FIRST-YEAR STUDENTS 2014–15

Total number of first-year recipients: 78
Percentage of the first-year class: 93%
Percentage of awards that are grants? 11%
Percentage of awards that are loans? 89%

	AVERAGE AWARDS	RANGE OF AWARDS
Residents	$65,954	$3,975–$66,800
Nonresidents	$89,494	$3,975–$89,494

For more information, please visit: http://studentaid.unc.edu

CASE WESTERN RESERVE UNIVERSITY
SCHOOL OF DENTAL MEDICINE

Kenneth B. Chance, Sr., D.D.S., Dean

GENERAL INFORMATION

Case Western Reserve University School of Dental Medicine (CWRU SDM) was originally the Dental Department of Western Reserve University. Since 1969, CWRU SDM's facilities have been located in the university's Health Science Center adjacent to the schools of medicine and nursing, as well as to the University Hospitals of Cleveland. Students study the basic sciences and technique, and they undertake preclinical laboratory work in individually assigned areas of the multidisciplinary laboratories. The 50,000-square-foot dental clinic comprises two major and five specialty clinics. The major clinics are made up of cubicles fully equipped as operatories. Drawing from a population of more than one million, the clinics afford students substantial clinical experience by providing a broad spectrum of care. CWRU SDM has conferred degrees on more than 5,500 graduates.

MISSION

To provide outstanding programs in oral health education, patient care, focused research and scholarship, and service that are of value to our constituents.

Type of institution: Private
Year opened: 1892
Term type: Semester
Time to degree in months: 48
Start month: August

Doctoral dental degree offered: D.M.D.
Targeted predoctoral enrollment: 282
Targeted entering class size: 75
Campus setting: Urban
Campus housing available: No

PREPARATION

Formal minimum preparation in semester/quarter hours: Semester: 60   Quarter: 90
Baccalaureate degree preferred: Yes, strongly recommended
Number of first-year, first-time enrollees whose highest degree is:
   Baccalaureate: 59
   Master's degree and beyond: 8
Of first-year, first-time enrollees without baccalaureates, the number with:
   Equivalent of 60 undergraduate credit hours or less: 0
   Equivalent of 61–90 undergraduate credit hours: 6
   Equivalent of 91 or more undergraduate credit hours: 1

PREREQUISITE COURSE	REQUIRED	RECOMMENDED	LAB REQUIRED	CREDITS (SEMESTER/QUARTER)
BCP (biology-chemistry-physics) sciences				
Biology	✓		✓	6/10
Chemistry, general/inorganic	✓		✓	6/10
Chemistry, organic	✓		✓	6/10
Physics	✓		✓	6/10
Additional biological sciences				
Anatomy		✓		3/5
Biochemistry		✓		3/5
Cell biology		✓		3/5
Histology		✓		3/5
Immunology		✓		3/5
Microbiology		✓		3/5
Molecular biology/genetics		✓		3/5
Physiology		✓		3/5

PREPARATION (CONTINUED)

Community college coursework accepted for prerequisites: Yes, majority of prerequisites taken at a four-year college

Community college coursework accepted for electives: Yes

Limits on community college credit hours: Yes

Maximum number of community college credit hours: 60

Advanced placement (AP) credit accepted for prerequisites: Yes

Advanced placement (AP) credit accepted for electives: Yes

Comments regarding AP credit: Provided they appear on official transcript—additional upper level coursework in the subject is strongly recommended.

Job shadowing: Recommended

Number of hours of job shadowing required or recommended: 20—Shadowing of multiple dentists recommended

Other factors considered in admission: Academic performance, DAT scores, personal essay, and faculty letters of recommendation

DAT

Mandatory: Yes

Latest DAT for consideration of application: 01/31/2016

Oldest DAT considered: 01/01/2013

When more than one DAT score is reported: Highest score is considered

Canadian DAT accepted: Yes

Application considered before DAT scores are submitted: No

U.S. DAT: 2014 ENTERING CLASS

ENROLLEE DAT SCORES	MEAN	RANGE
Academic Average	19.9	15–24
Perceptual Ability	20.4	14–25
Total Science	19.9	15–23

CANADIAN DAT: 2014 ENTERING CLASS

ENROLLEE DAT SCORES	MEAN	RANGE
Academic Average	21.3	21–22
Manual Dexterity	19.0	13–25
Perceptual Ability	20.5	20–21
Total Science	20.8	20–21

GPA: 2014 ENTERING CLASS

ENROLLEE GPA SCORES	UNDERGRAD. MEAN	GRADUATE MEAN	UNDERGRAD. RANGE	GRADUATE RANGE
Science GPA	3.51	3.62	2.28–4.00	3.38–4.00
Total GPA	3.61	3.58	2.89–4.00	3.27–4.00

APPLICATION AND SELECTION

TIMETABLE

Earliest filing date: 06/02/2015

Latest filing date: 01/01/2016

Earliest date for acceptance offers: 12/01/2015

Maximum time in days for applicant's response to acceptance offer:
30 days if accepted on or after December 1
15 days if accepted on or after February 1

Requests for deferred entrance considered: In exceptional circumstances only

Fee for application: Yes, submitted at same time as Associated American Dental Schools Application Service (AADSAS) application.

Amount of fee for application:
In state: $60   Out of state: $60   International: $60

Fee waiver available: Yes, the applicant must provide a copy of an ADEA Fee Assistance Program approval letter or a DAT partial fee approval letter.

	FIRST DEPOSIT	SECOND DEPOSIT	THIRD DEPOSIT
Required to hold place	Yes	No	No
Resident amount	$1,000		
Nonresident amount	$1,000		
Deposit due	30 or 15 days from date of acceptance		
Applied to tuition	Yes		
Refundable	No		

APPLICATION PROCESS

Participates in AADSAS: Yes

Accepts direct applicants: Yes, for formal 3+4 programs and CWRU PPSP program only

Secondary or supplemental application required: No, only AADSAS application required

Interview is mandatory: Yes

Interview is by invitation: Yes

RESIDENCY

In-state/in-province versus out-of-state/out-of-province

Admissions process distinguishes between in-state/in-province and out-of-state/out-of-province applicants: No

Preference given to residents of: Alabama

Reciprocity Admissions Agreement available for legal residents of: None

Generally and over time, percentage of your first-year enrollment that is in-state: 15%

Origin of out-of-state/out-of-province enrollees: AZ-1, CA-3, CO-1, FL-2, GA-3, ID-1, IL-2, IA-1, MA-1, MI-3, MN-1, MO-1, NJ-3, OK-1, PA-2, TX-3, UT-3, VA-1, WA-2, Not Reported-4

International

Applications are accepted from international (noncitizens/nonpermanent residents): Yes

Origin of international enrollees: Canada-8, Mexico-1, South Korea-4, Vietnam-1

APPLICATION AND ENROLLMENT	NUMBER OF APPLICANTS	ESTIMATED NUMBER INTERVIEWED	ESTIMATED NUMBER ENROLLED
In-state or province applicants/enrollees	174	41	21
Out-of-state or province applicants/enrollees	2,156	225	39
International applicants/enrollees (noncitizens/nonpermanent residents)	389	50	14

DEMOGRAPHIC DESCRIPTIONS OF APPLICANTS: 2014 ENTERING CLASS

	APPLICANTS			ENROLLEES		
	M	W	Gender Unknown or Not Reported	M	W	Gender Unknown or Not Reported
American Indian or Alaska Native	2	2	0	0	0	0
Asian	392	390	10	8	9	0
Black or African American	26	41	0	0	0	0
Hispanic or Latino	64	76	0	1	1	0
Native Hawaiian or Other Pacific Islander	2	1	0	0	0	0
White	710	464	5	22	17	0
Two or more races	35	31	0	0	0	0
Race and ethnicity unknown	33	35	11	0	2	0
International	220	164	5	8	6	0

	MINIMUM	MAXIMUM	MEAN
2014 entering class enrollees by age	20	37	24

CURRICULUM

CWRU SDM has created the new model for dental education. The new curriculum is grounded in principles that exemplify educational formats embracing experiential learning. Key features of our curriculum are small group learning environments where students retain responsibility for learning; time allocated for independent study, integration of concepts and reflection; and cornerstone experiences that integrate multiple content areas in powerful learning scenarios within the school and the larger community.

Student research opportunities: Yes

SPECIAL PROGRAMS AND SERVICES

PREDENTAL

Summer Medical and Dental Education Program
Special affiliations with colleges and universities:
    Denison University: 3+4 Program
    University of Toledo: 3+4 Program
    Walsh University: 3+4 Program
    Westminster College: 3+4 Program
    Wooster College: 3+4 Program

DURING DENTAL SCHOOL

Academic counseling and tutoring
Community service opportunities: Healthy Smiles dental sealant program in first year
Internships, externships, or extramural programs
Mentoring
Personal counseling
Professional- and career-development programming
Training for those interested in academic careers

ACTIVE STUDENT ORGANIZATIONS

American Dental Education Association
American Student Dental Association

INTERNATIONAL DENTISTS

Graduates of international dental schools considered for traditional predoctoral program: Yes
Advanced standing program offered for graduates of international dental schools: Yes
Advanced standing program description: Program awarding a dental degree

COMBINED AND ALTERNATE DEGREES

Ph.D.	M.S.	M.P.H.	M.D.	B.A./B.S.	Other
—	✓	✓	*	✓	✓

Other degrees: M.C.R.T. (master's degree in clinical research training)
*D.M.D./M.D. (pending approval)

COSTS: 2014–15 SCHOOL YEAR

	FIRST YEAR	SECOND YEAR	THIRD YEAR	FOURTH YEAR
Tuition, resident	$58,095	$60,789	$62,585	$62,585
Tuition, nonresident	$58,095	$60,789	$62,585	$62,585
Tuition, other				
Fees	$2,907	$2,923	$2,923	$2,923
Instruments, books, and supplies	$15,896	$9,592	$3,778	$5,050
Estimated living expenses	$18,044	$18,044	$22,064	$22,064
Total, resident	$94,942	$91,348	$91,350	$92,622
Total, nonresident	$94,942	$91,348	$91,350	$92,622
Total, other				

FINANCIAL AID

Case Western Reserve University School of Dental Medicine participates in the federal student loan programs: Stafford, Perkins, Health Professions and federal Graduate Plus loans. We therefore require that the Free Application for Federal Student Aid (FAFSA), which can be found on www.fafsa.ed.gov, as well as our own online application form, be completed before May 15 of the year you matriculate. Please note that these programs are available for U.S. citizens and eligible noncitizens.

For the 2013 academic year, 7% of our students were recipients of the Health Professions Scholarship Program offered by the U.S. Air Force, Army or Navy.

The median 2014 graduate indebtedness, including undergraduate indebtedness, was $307,843.

FINANCIAL AID AWARDS TO FIRST-YEAR STUDENTS 2014–15

Total number of first-year recipients: 48

Percentage of the first-year class: 66%

Percentage of awards that are grants? 0%

Percentage of awards that are loans? 100%

	AVERAGE AWARDS	RANGE OF AWARDS
Residents and nonresidents	$81,055	$12,454–$98,925

For more information, please visit: http://dental.case.edu/admissions/dmd/finaid/

THE OHIO STATE UNIVERSITY
COLLEGE OF DENTISTRY

Patrick M. Lloyd, D.D.S., M.S., Dean

CONTACT INFORMATION

www.dentistry.osu.edu
305 West 12th Avenue
Columbus, OH 43210
Phone: 614-292-3361

RECRUITMENT AND ADMISSIONS

Ms. Annette McMurry
Director of Admissions
305 West 12th Avenue
Columbus, OH 43210
Phone: 614-292-3361
Email: mcmurry.7@osu.edu
www.dentistry.osu.edu/admission

REGISTRAR AND FINANCIAL AID

Ms. Jami Conway
Financial Aid Advisor
305 West 12th Avenue
Columbus, OH 43210
Phone: 614-292-8155
Email: conway.244@osu.edu

Mr. Michael Murray
Registrar
305 West 12th Avenue
Columbus, OH 43210
Phone: 614-292-4404
Email: murray.287@osu.edu
www.dentistry.osu.edu/oaa

OFFICE OF ACADEMIC AFFAIRS AND STUDENT SERVICES

Ms. Susannah Turner
Director of Student Affairs
0116 Postle Hall
305 West 12th Avenue
Columbus, OH 43210
Phone: 614-688-1103
Email: turner.647@osu.edu
www.dentistry.osu.edu/studentaffairs

MINORITY AFFAIRS/DIVERSITY

www.osu.edu/diversity

GRADUATE & PROFESSIONAL HOUSING

http://housing.osu.edu

GENERAL INFORMATION

The Ohio State University College of Dentistry (OSU COD) has a long-standing history of academic excellence and research innovation. The nation's fourth largest dental school, OSU COD offers a dynamic working and learning environment. Part of a thriving metropolitan community, OSU COD, located in a medical center complex, is part of a top national research university. Drawing on a unique combination of strengths, the college offers a full range of dental specialty programs on campus, as well as extensive clinical training that includes service work at a variety of statewide outreach sites. A high-profile research program draws extensive support from the National Institutes of Health and the National Science Foundation. Please visit us at www.dentistry.osu.edu/admission.

MISSION

OSU COD's mission is to produce dental professionals who are prepared for entry into practice, advanced dental education or specialized practice.

Vision:

- To prepare graduates to meet state- and nationwide oral health care needs.
- To conduct research expanding the scientific base of dental practice.
- To provide service to the profession.

Type of institution: Public	Doctoral dental degree offered: D.D.S.
Year opened: 1890	Targeted predoctoral enrollment: 440
Term type: Semester	Targeted entering class size: 110
Time to degree in months: 45	Campus setting: Urban
Start month: August	Campus housing available: Yes

PREPARATION

Formal minimum preparation in semester/quarter hours: Semester: 60   Quarter: 90
Baccalaureate degree preferred: Yes
Number of first-year, first-time enrollees whose highest degree is:
    Baccalaureate: 102
    Master's degree and beyond: 7
Of first-year, first-time enrollees without baccalaureates, the number with:
    Equivalent of 60 undergraduate credit hours or less: 0
    Equivalent of 61–90 undergraduate credit hours: 1
    Equivalent of 91 or more undergraduate credit hours: 0

PREREQUISITE COURSE	REQUIRED	RECOMMENDED	LAB REQUIRED	CREDITS (SEMESTER/QUARTER)
BCP (biology-chemistry-physics) sciences				
Biology	✓		✓	6/10
Chemistry, general/inorganic	✓		✓	9/15
Chemistry, organic	✓		✓	6/10
Physics	✓		✓	3/5
Additional biological sciences				
Anatomy	✓		✓	3/5
Biochemistry	✓			3/5
Cell biology		✓		
Histology		✓		
Immunology		✓		
Microbiology	✓			3/5
Molecular biology/genetics		✓		

(Prerequisite Courses continued)

PREPARATION (CONTINUED)

PREREQUISITE COURSE	REQUIRED	RECOMMENDED	LAB REQUIRED	CREDITS (SEMESTER/QUARTER)
Physiology	✓			3/5
Zoology				
Other				
Freshman English	✓			3/3
English composition	✓			3/3

Community college coursework accepted for prerequisites: Not recommended
Community college coursework accepted for electives: Yes
Limits on community college credit hours: No
Maximum number of community college credit hours: None
Advanced placement (AP) credit accepted for prerequisites: Yes
Advanced placement (AP) credit accepted for electives: Yes
Job shadowing: Required
Number of hours of job shadowing required or recommended: 20
Other factors considered in admission: Nonacademic experiences are considered and include teaching, volunteer hours, research, leadership, military service, athletic participation, employment, teaching and other noncognitive factors.

DAT

Mandatory: Yes
Latest DAT for consideration of application: NA
Oldest DAT considered: Scores good for 2 years prior to submitting application
When more than one DAT score is reported: Most recent score only is considered
Canadian DAT accepted: Yes
Application considered before DAT scores are submitted: No

DAT: 2014 ENTERING CLASS

ENROLLEE DAT SCORES	MEAN	RANGE
Academic Average	19.7	16–27
Perceptual Ability	20.5	16–26
Total Science	19.2	15–26

GPA: 2014 ENTERING CLASS

ENROLLEE GPA SCORES	UNDERGRAD. MEAN	GRADUATE MEAN	UNDERGRAD. RANGE	GRADUATE RANGE
Science GPA	3.49	3.58	2.49–4.00	2.98–4.00
Total GPA	3.61	3.56	2.72–4.00	3.05–4.00

APPLICATION AND SELECTION

TIMETABLE

Earliest filing date: 06/02/2015
Latest filing date: 09/01/2015
Earliest date for acceptance offers: 12/01/2015
Maximum time in days for applicant's response to acceptance offer:
    30 days if accepted between December 1 and January 1
    15 days if accepted on or after January 1
Requests for deferred entrance considered: In exceptional circumstances only

Fee for application: Yes, submitted only when requested
Amount of fee for application:
    In state: $60   Out of state: $60   International: $70
Fee waiver available: No
Transfer: $80

	FIRST DEPOSIT	SECOND DEPOSIT	THIRD DEPOSIT
Required to hold place	Yes	Yes	No
Resident amount	$200	$500	
Nonresident amount	$200	$500	
Deposit due	At time of acceptance	At time of acceptance	
Applied to tuition	No	Yes	
Refundable	No	No	

APPLICATION PROCESS

Participates in Associated American Dental Schools Application Service (AADSAS): Yes
Accepts direct applicants: No
Secondary or supplemental application required: Yes
Secondary or supplemental application website: Link sent to applicants via email
Interview is mandatory: Yes
Interview is by invitation: Yes

RESIDENCY

In-state/in-province versus out-of-state/out-of-province
Admissions process distinguishes between in-state/in-province and out-of-state/out-of-province applicants: Yes
Preference given to residents of: Ohio
Reciprocity Admissions Agreement available for legal residents of: None
Generally and over time, percentage of your first-year enrollment that is in-state: 75–85%
Origin of out-of-state/out-of-province enrollees: AZ-1, CA-3, FL-1, ID-1, IL-1, IN-1, KY-1, MD-1, MI-1, NC-1, NM-1, NY-1, PA-2, SC-1, UT-2

International
Applications are accepted from international (noncitizens/nonpermanent residents): Yes
Origin of international enrollees: NA

APPLICATION AND ENROLLMENT	NUMBER OF APPLICANTS	ESTIMATED NUMBER INTERVIEWED	ESTIMATED NUMBER ENROLLED
In-state or province applicants/ enrollees	218	117	91
Out-of-state or province applicants/enrollees	766	101	19
International applicants/enrollees (noncitizens/nonpermanent residents)	19	0	0

DEMOGRAPHIC DESCRIPTIONS OF APPLICANTS: 2014 ENTERING CLASS

	APPLICANTS			ENROLLEES		
	M	W	Gender Unknown or Not Reported	M	W	Gender Unknown or Not Reported
American Indian or Alaska Native	2	1	0	0	0	0
Asian	109	122	0	7	6	0
Black or African American	7	16	0	3	3	0
Hispanic or Latino	7	6	0	1	1	0
Native Hawaiian or Other Pacific Islander	0	0	0	0	0	0
White	361	260	0	48	29	0
Two or more races	31	31	0	5	5	0
Race and ethnicity unknown	16	15	0	1	1	0
International	10	9	0	0	0	0

	MINIMUM	MAXIMUM	MEAN
2014 entering class enrollees by age	21	36	24

CURRICULUM

The D.D.S. curriculum includes 11 semesters of instruction over four years, including three summer sessions. During the first and second years, an emphasis is placed on the basic sciences and preclinical dentistry courses, including didactic and laboratory instruction. Students also participate in early clinic experiences beginning their first academic term. During the third and fourth years, the focus shifts to patient treatment experiences. Students provide treatment in one of the college's eight comprehensive care clinic groups, with approximately 25 students assigned to each group. Additionally, students receive a wide range of experiences with oversight provided by general practitioners and dental specialists. Students have many opportunities to treat patients with special needs, and they also rotate through several specialty clinics and areas in which they have an opportunity to use cutting-edge technology. During the fourth year, students spend 10 weeks treating patients in external clinics that are primarily located in Ohio's underserved communities. All instruction emphasizes patient-centered, evidence-based care. Throughout the curriculum, instruction includes a blend of in-person (large and small group) presentations and online delivery. The curriculum also includes coursework in other areas essential to provision of oral health care, such as communication skills and practice management.

Student research opportunities: Yes

SPECIAL PROGRAMS AND SERVICES

PREDENTAL
DAT workshops
Postbaccalaureate programs

DURING DENTAL SCHOOL
Academic counseling and tutoring
Community service opportunities
Internships, externships, or extramural programs
Mentoring
Personal counseling
Professional- and career-development programming
Training for those interested in academic careers
Transfer applicants considered if space is available

ACTIVE STUDENT ORGANIZATIONS
Alpha Omega International Dental Fraternity
American Association for Dental Research National Student Research Group
American Association of Women Dentists
American Student Dental Association
Christian Dental Association, a branch of the Christian Medical and Dental Associations
Delta Sigma Delta (international dental fraternity)
Dental Entrepreneurs Society
Hispanic Student Dental Association
Psi Omega Fraternity
Student National Dental Association

INTERNATIONAL DENTISTS
Graduates of international dental schools considered for traditional predoctoral program: Yes
Advanced standing program offered for graduates of international dental schools: No

COMBINED AND ALTERNATE DEGREES

Ph.D.	M.S.	M.P.H.	M.D.	B.A./B.S.	Other
✓	—	—	—	—	✓

Other degree: D.D.S./Ph.D.

COSTS: 2014–15 SCHOOL YEAR

	FIRST YEAR	SECOND YEAR	THIRD YEAR	FOURTH YEAR
Tuition, resident	$32,688	$43,572	$43,572	$43,572
Tuition, nonresident	$70,370	$93,682	$93,682	$93,682
Tuition, other				
Fees	$2,952	$3,927	$3,927	$3,927
Instruments, books, and supplies	$2,816	$2,131	$1,417	$1,117
Estimated living expenses	$16,215	$21,614	$21,614	$21,614
Total, resident	$54,671	$71,244	$70,530	$70,230
Total, nonresident	$92,353	$121,354	$120,640	$120,340
Total, other				

FINANCIAL AID

Scholarship awards are based on merit, need and community relations. Some awards are made at the time of admissions and do not require an application, while others require the student to complete a general university scholarship application. Scholarship awards are both annual and renewable, depending on the award.

Loan assistance is available to eligible students who complete the Free Application for Federal Student Aid (OSU deadline: February 15). Students commonly use federal loan programs and university-administered loans.

Nonresident students may be eligible for residency. Ohio high school graduates who attended non-Ohio colleges and/or moved out of state after graduation, are considered Ohioans for tuition purposes.

The average 2013 graduate indebtedness was $199,338.

FINANCIAL AID AWARDS TO FIRST-YEAR STUDENTS 2014–15

Total number of first-year recipients: 109
Percentage of the first-year class: 100%
Percentage of awards that are grants? 6%
Percentage of awards that are loans? 91%

	AVERAGE AWARDS	RANGE OF AWARDS
Residents	$46,339*	$5,000–$70,863
Nonresidents	$82,259*	$25,000–$92,998

*Includes scholarships and loans.

For more information, please visit: www.dentistry.osu.edu/admission

UNIVERSITY OF OKLAHOMA
COLLEGE OF DENTISTRY

Raymond A. Cohlmia, D.D.S., Dean

GENERAL INFORMATION

The University of Oklahoma College of Dentistry program promotes high standards in clinical and professional preparation. Through a well-designed and rigorous curriculum, students develop their knowledge and skills under the guidance of a capable and dedicated teaching faculty. Early on and throughout the course of their education, students engage in significant patient-care opportunities, designed to build a strong clinical foundation and patient centered perspective. Modern and well-appointed facilities provide an optimal learning environment featuring the best equipment and latest technology. The College of Dentistry is part of the Health Sciences Center in Oklahoma City, a 15-block campus near city center that includes several major teaching hospitals, research facilities and colleges of Allied Health, Medicine, Nursing, Pharmacy and Public Health.

MISSION

To improve Oklahomans' health and shape dentistry's future by developing highly qualified dental practitioners/scientists through excellence in education/research, patient care, facilities and community service.

Vision: To be recognized as an innovative leader in transforming dental education and as a vibrant, stimulating place to work and learn.

Type of institution: Public
Year opened: 1972
Term type: Semester
Time to degree in months: 48
Start month: June

Doctoral dental degree offered: D.D.S.
Targeted predoctoral enrollment: 232
Targeted entering class size: 56
Campus setting: Urban
Campus housing available: Yes

PREPARATION

Formal minimum preparation in semester/quarter hours: Semester: 90   Quarter: 135
Baccalaureate degree preferred: Yes
Number of first-year, first-time enrollees whose highest degree is:
    Baccalaureate: 52
    Master's degree and beyond: 4
Of first-year, first-time enrollees without baccalaureates, the number with:
    Equivalent of 60 undergraduate credit hours or less: 0
    Equivalent of 61–90 undergraduate credit hours: 0
    Equivalent of 91 or more undergraduate credit hours: 0

PREREQUISITE COURSE	REQUIRED	RECOMMENDED	LAB REQUIRED	CREDITS (SEMESTER/QUARTER)
BCP (biology-chemistry-physics) sciences				
Biology	✓		✓	16/24
Chemistry, general/inorganic	✓		✓	8/12
Chemistry, organic	✓		✓	8/12
Physics	✓		✓	8/12
Additional biological sciences				
Anatomy		✓		
Biochemistry	✓			3/5
Cell biology		✓		
Histology				
Immunology				
Microbiology		✓		
Molecular biology/genetics		✓		

(Prerequisite Courses continued)

PREPARATION (CONTINUED)

PREREQUISITE COURSE	REQUIRED	RECOMMENDED	LAB REQUIRED	CREDITS (SEMESTER/QUARTER)
Physiology		✓		
Zoology		✓		
Other				
English (Composition)	✓			6/9
Psychology (Introduction)	✓			3/4

Community college coursework accepted for prerequisites: Yes
Community college coursework accepted for electives: Yes
Limits on community college credit hours: No
Maximum number of community college credit hours: No maximum number.
Advanced placement (AP) credit accepted for prerequisites: Yes
Advanced placement (AP) credit accepted for electives: Yes
Comments regarding AP credit: We will accept AP credit for prerequisites in English and psychology. Prerequisites in science may also be met by AP, but students are advised to take additional upper-division coursework.
Job shadowing: Required
Number of hours of job shadowing required or recommended: 100
Other factors considered in admission: Strength of schedule, term course load, Grade Point Average (GPA) for last 60 credits and history of course withdrawals

DAT

Mandatory: Yes
Latest DAT for consideration of application: 11/01/2015
Oldest DAT considered: 06/2010
When more than one DAT score is reported: Highest score is considered
Canadian DAT accepted: Yes
Application considered before DAT scores are submitted: No

DAT: 2014 ENTERING CLASS

ENROLLEE DAT SCORES	MEAN	RANGE
Academic Average	20.0	17–23
Perceptual Ability	19.6	13–24
Total Science	19.4	17–25

GPA: 2014 ENTERING CLASS

ENROLLEE GPA SCORES	UNDERGRAD. MEAN	GRADUATE MEAN	UNDERGRAD. RANGE	GRADUATE RANGE
Science GPA	3.59	NR	2.35–4.00	NR
Total GPA	3.48	NR	2.48–4.00	NR

APPLICATION AND SELECTION

TIMETABLE

Earliest filing date: 06/02/2015
Latest filing date: 10/01/2015
Earliest date for acceptance offers: 12/01/2015
Maximum time in days for applicant's response to acceptance offer:
  30 days if accepted on or after December 1
  15 days if accepted on or after February 1
Requests for deferred entrance considered: Exceptional circumstances only

Fee for application: Yes, Associated American Dental Schools Application Service (AADSAS) application fee and Supplemental application fee.
Amount of fee for application:
  In state: $98   Out of state: $98   International: $98
Fee waiver available: No

	FIRST DEPOSIT	SECOND DEPOSIT	THIRD DEPOSIT
Required to hold place	Yes	No	No
Resident amount	$800		
Nonresident amount	$800		
Deposit due	As indicated in admission offer		
Applied to tuition	Yes		
Refundable	No		

APPLICATION PROCESS

Participates in AADSAS: Yes
Accepts direct applicants: No
Secondary or supplemental application required: Yes, $98 application fee
Secondary or supplemental application website: https://apps.ouhsc.edu/admissions
Interview is mandatory: Yes
Interview is by invitation: Yes

RESIDENCY

In-state/in-province versus out-of-state/out-of-province
Admissions process distinguishes between in-state/in-province and out-of-state/out-of-province applicants: Yes
Preference given to residents of: Oklahoma
Reciprocity Admissions Agreement available for legal residents of: None
Generally and over time, percentage of your first-year enrollment that is in-state: 79%
Origin of out-of-state/out-of-province enrollees: AZ-2, ID-1, KS-1, MN-1, TX-2, UT-4

International
Applications are accepted from international (noncitizens/nonpermanent residents): Yes
Origin of international enrollees: China-1

APPLICATION AND ENROLLMENT	NUMBER OF APPLICANTS	ESTIMATED NUMBER INTERVIEWED	ESTIMATED NUMBER ENROLLED
In-state or province applicants/enrollees	123	86	44
Out-of-state or province applicants/enrollees	537	74	11
International applicants/enrollees (noncitizens/nonpermanent residents)	34	1	1

DEMOGRAPHIC DESCRIPTIONS OF APPLICANTS: 2014 ENTERING CLASS

	APPLICANTS			ENROLLEES		
	M	W	Gender Unknown or Not Reported	M	W	Gender Unknown or Not Reported
American Indian or Alaska Native	6	5	0	2	1	0
Asian	75	70	3	2	3	0
Black or African American	5	13	0	0	1	0
Hispanic or Latino	22	14	0	2	1	0
Native Hawaiian or Other Pacific Islander	0	0	0	0	0	0
White	238	152	2	22	15	0
Two or more races	20	16	0	4	1	0
Race and ethnicity unknown	13	6	0	1	0	0
International	15	18	1	0	1	0

	MINIMUM	MAXIMUM	MEAN
2014 entering class enrollees by age	20	40	24

CURRICULUM

The curriculum integrates theory, applied technique and clinical experience. The early curriculum develops a solid foundation in both the biomedical sciences and dental sciences. As students progress in the program, instruction shifts to hands-on, preclinical exercises teaching students to perform procedures in a laboratory or simulated patient environments. By year 3, students learn more sophisticated aspects of dental care and spend substantially more time treating patients, under faculty supervision. In year 4, the curriculum emphasizes comprehensive patient management and treatment. Starting in year 1, and continuing throughout the four years, the curriculum presents opportunities for students to interact with patients and provide appropriate care commensurate with their advancing level of experience and expertise. These opportunities are a hallmark of the College of Dentistry's curriculum and undergird our reputation for providing an excellent clinical education with a strong patient contact component. Competency assessments and overall clinical requirements ensure that students attain appropriate skill levels and experience a sufficient number of practice opportunities to develop clinical proficiency. The curriculum addresses knowledge and development in other areas—including direct service-outreach, research and scholarship, and practice management—key to preparing graduates for roles as responsible health care professionals.

Student research opportunities: Yes

SPECIAL PROGRAMS AND SERVICES

PREDENTAL
Summer enrichment programs

DURING DENTAL SCHOOL
Academic counseling and tutoring
Community service opportunities
Dentist-student mentoring
Internships, externships, or extramural programs
Peer mentoring
Personal counseling
Professional- and career-development programming
Training for those interested in academic careers

ACTIVE STUDENT ORGANIZATIONS
Academy of General Dentistry™
Albert Staples Society
American Association for Dental Research National Student Research Group
American Association of Women Dentists
American Student Dental Association
Christian Medical & Dental Associations
Good Shepherd Mission
Rural Interest Group
Student Government Association/Student Council
Student Professionalism and Ethics Association in Dentistry

INTERNATIONAL DENTISTS
Graduates of international dental schools considered for traditional predoctoral program: Yes
Advanced standing program offered for graduates of international dental schools: Yes

COMBINED AND ALTERNATE DEGREES

Ph.D.	M.S.	M.P.H.	M.D.	B.A./B.S.	Other
—	—	—	—	—	—

COSTS: 2014–15 SCHOOL YEAR

	FIRST YEAR	SECOND YEAR	THIRD YEAR	FOURTH YEAR
Tuition, resident	$20,927	$20,927	$20,927	$20,927
Tuition, nonresident	$49,672	$49,672	$49,672	$49,672
Tuition, other				
Fees	$7,860	$7,860	$7,860	$7,860
Instruments, books, and supplies	$14,573	$13,293	$3,613	$4,200
Estimated living expenses	$27,900	$27,900	$27,900	$27,900
Total, resident	$71,260	$69,980	$60,300	$60,887
Total, nonresident	$100,005	$98,725	$89,045	$89,632
Total, other				

FINANCIAL AID

Students apply for aid by using the Free Application for Federal Student Aid. Details on aid types are available on the University of Oklahoma Health Sciences Center Financial Services website: http://www.ouhsc.edu/financialservices/SFA/.

FINANCIAL AID AWARDS TO FIRST-YEAR STUDENTS 2014–15

Total number of first-year recipients: 52

Percentage of the first-year class: 92%

Percentage of awards that are grants? 16%

Percentage of awards that are loans? 84%

	AVERAGE AWARDS	RANGE OF AWARDS
Residents	$43,000	$500–$64,945
Nonresidents	$59,898	$700–$78,565

For more information, please visit: http://www.ouhsc.edu/financialservices/SFA/

OREGON HEALTH & SCIENCE UNIVERSITY
SCHOOL OF DENTISTRY

Phillip T. Marucha, D.M.D., Ph.D., Dean

CONTACT INFORMATION

www.ohsu.edu/sod

2730 SW Moody Avenue
Mail code: SD-DEAN
Portland, OR 97201-5042
Phone: 503-494-8801
Fax: 503-494-8351

OFFICE OF ADMISSIONS AND STUDENT AFFAIRS

2730 SW Moody Avenue
Mail code: SD-SA
Portland, OR 97201-5042
Phone: 503-494-5274
Fax: 503-494-6244

FINANCIAL AID OFFICE

3181 SW Sam Jackson Park Road, L109
Portland, OR 97239-3098
Phone: 503-494-7800
www.ohsu.edu/finaid

GENERAL INFORMATION

Located in Portland, a city of 603,106 residents in a greater metropolitan area of approximately 2.3 million, the Oregon Health & Science University School of Dentistry (OHSU SOD) is located in a brand new state-of-the-art facility on the bank of the Willamette River on OHSU's South Waterfront Campus. Paths for joggers, bicyclists and pedestrians connect the university with the heart of the city just two miles away. The objectives of the dental program are to impart the scientific knowledge and clinical skills needed in the practice of dentistry, to instill standards of professional conduct as a way of life, and to promote a dedication to continuous, lifelong professional study and self-improvement.

MISSION

To provide educational programs, basic and clinical research, and high-quality care and community programs through an environment promoting mutual respect and the free exchange of ideas.

Vision: The School of Dentistry is a leader and innovator in oral health education, care and discovery.

Core Values:

- Optimize and integrate missions.
- Provide an exceptional educational experience.
- Provide an outstanding patient experience.
- Promote a community of scholarship.
- Develop and diversify sustainable funding.

Type of institution: Public
Year opened: 1898
Term type: Quarter
Time to degree in months: 47
Start month: August

Doctoral dental degree offered: D.M.D.
Targeted predoctoral enrollment: 300
Targeted entering class size: 75
Campus setting: Urban
Campus housing available: No

PREPARATION

Formal minimum preparation in semester/quarter hours: Semester: 90   Quarter: 135 (completed at the time of application). Coursework must be completed at an accredited U.S. or Canadian college or university. Other than Canadian, no international coursework is accepted.
Baccalaureate degree preferred: Yes
Number of first-year, first-time enrollees whose highest degree is:
    Baccalaureate: 72
    Master's degree and beyond: 4
Of first-year, first-time enrollees without baccalaureates, the number with:
    Equivalent of 60 undergraduate credit hours or less: 0
    Equivalent of 61–90 undergraduate credit hours: 0
    Equivalent of 91 or more undergraduate credit hours: 0

PREREQUISITE COURSE	REQUIRED	RECOMMENDED	LAB REQUIRED	CREDITS (SEMESTER/QUARTER)
BCP (biology-chemistry-physics) sciences				
Biology	✓		✓	8/12
Chemistry, general/inorganic	✓		✓	8/12
Chemistry, organic	✓		✓	8/12
Physics	✓		✓	8/12
Additional biological sciences				
Anatomy	✓		✓	4/6
Biochemistry	✓			4/6
Cell biology		✓		4/6
Histology		✓		4/6

(Prerequisite Courses continued)

PREPARATION (CONTINUED)

PREREQUISITE COURSE	REQUIRED	RECOMMENDED	LAB REQUIRED	CREDITS (SEMESTER/QUARTER)
Immunology		✓		4/6
Microbiology		✓		3/5
Molecular biology/genetics		✓		4/6
Physiology	✓		✓	4/6
Zoology		✓		4/6
Other				
English composition	✓			8/12

Community college coursework accepted for prerequisites: Yes
Community college coursework accepted for electives: Yes
Limits on community college credit hours: Yes
Maximum number of community college credit hours: 32 preferred
Advanced placement (AP) credit accepted for prerequisites: Yes
Advanced placement (AP) credit accepted for electives: Yes
Comments regarding AP credit: AP/International Baccalaureate (IB) credit is accepted. To receive credit for a prerequisite requirement, the course name and number receiving AP/IB credit must appear on an official transcript. No other documentation of AP/IB credit will replace an official transcript.
Job shadowing: Required
Number of hours of job shadowing required or recommended: A required minimum of 50 documented hours completed prior to submission of one's application is required in a clinical setting of which 25 hours must occur in one or more general practices.
Other factors considered in admission: Community service, work experience, research experience, extracurricular activities, leadership and demonstrated passion for dentistry

DAT

Mandatory: Yes. No less than 15 in all scored areas will be considered.
Latest DAT for consideration of application: 11/01/2015
Oldest DAT considered: 01/01/2012
When more than one DAT score is reported: Most recent score only is considered
Canadian DAT accepted: No
Application considered before DAT scores are submitted: No

DAT: 2014 ENTERING CLASS

ENROLLEE DAT SCORES	MEAN	RANGE
Academic Average	19.7	16–25
Perceptual Ability	19.8	15–27
Total Science	20.1	17–26

GPA: 2014 ENTERING CLASS

ENROLLEE GPA SCORES	UNDERGRAD. MEAN	GRADUATE MEAN	UNDERGRAD. RANGE	GRADUATE RANGE
Science GPA	3.56	3.77	3.04–4.00	3.52–4.00
Total GPA	3.61	3.80	3.00–4.00	3.52–4.00

APPLICATION AND SELECTION

TIMETABLE

Earliest filing date: 06/02/2015
Latest filing date: 11/01/2015
Earliest date for acceptance offers: 12/01/2015

Maximum time in days for applicant's response to acceptance offer:
30 days if accepted on or after December 1
15 days if accepted on or after February 1
5 days if accepted on or after May 15
Requests for deferred entrance considered: No
Fee for application: Yes, submitted at same time as Associated American Dental Schools Application Service (AADSAS) application
Amount of fee for application:
In state: $75   Out of state: $75   International: $75
Fee waiver available: Check school website for details.

	FIRST DEPOSIT	SECOND DEPOSIT	THIRD DEPOSIT
Required to hold place	Yes	No	No
Resident amount	$1,000		
Nonresident amount	$1,000		
Deposit due	As indicated in admission offer		
Applied to tuition	Yes		
Refundable	No		

APPLICATION PROCESS

Participates in AADSAS: Yes
Accepts direct applicants: No
Secondary or supplemental application required: Yes, only for those applicants invited to interview
Interview is mandatory: Yes
Interview is by invitation: Yes

RESIDENCY

In-state/in-province versus out-of-state/out-of-province

Admissions process distinguishes between in-state/in-province and out-of-state/out-of-province applicants: Yes

Preference given to residents of: Oregon

Reciprocity Admissions Agreement available for legal residents of: Alaska, Arizona, Hawaii, Montana, New Mexico, North Dakota, Wyoming

Generally and over time, percentage of your first-year enrollment that is in-state: 64%

Origin of out-of-state/out-of-province enrollees: AZ-3, CA-5, CO-1, HI-1, ID-2, MT-2, ND-1, NM-1, NV-1, UT-1, WA-4, Not Reported-1

International

Applications are accepted from international (noncitizens/nonpermanent residents): Yes

Origin of international enrollees: Mexico-1

APPLICATION AND ENROLLMENT	NUMBER OF APPLICANTS	ESTIMATED NUMBER INTERVIEWED	ESTIMATED NUMBER ENROLLED
In-state or province applicants/enrollees	110	58	52
Out-of-state or province applicants/enrollees	1,148	56	24
International applicants/enrollees (noncitizens/nonpermanent residents)	70	1	0

DEMOGRAPHIC DESCRIPTIONS OF APPLICANTS: 2014 ENTERING CLASS

	APPLICANTS			ENROLLEES		
	M	W	Gender Unknown or Not Reported	M	W	Gender Unknown or Not Reported
American Indian or Alaska Native	2	0	0	0	0	0
Asian	192	170	1	11	4	0
Black or African American	7	2	0	0	0	0
Hispanic or Latino	44	32	1	4	0	0
Native Hawaiian or Other Pacific Islander	3	2	0	1	0	0
White	470	249	3	31	21	0
Two or more races	28	20	0	1	1	0
Race and ethnicity unknown	16	11	5	1	0	1
International	45	26	0	0	0	0

	MINIMUM	MAXIMUM	MEAN
2014 entering class enrollees by age	21	47	25

CURRICULUM

Year 1 provides an integrated approach to teaching the basic sciences. Students learn the fundamentals of oral radiology, dental materials, restorative dentistry, periodontology and prevention of dental disease.

Year 2, which emphasizes dental technique skills development, includes didactic and laboratory courses in facial growth, prosthodontics, oral surgery, periodontology, endodontology and dental materials application.

Years 3 and 4 emphasize clinical practice supported by lecture and seminar sessions covering oral disease diagnosis, treatment planning and clinical treatment procedures. Dental students may also participate in supervised off-campus educational experiences and are encouraged to strengthen personal qualities to meet patient needs and professional standards. The school fosters high ethical and moral values, a liking for people and unselfish service, human relations and communications skills, and a broad understanding of community and national health goals.

Through OHSU's Interprofessional Initiative (IPI), students work collaboratively across university schools and programs to build an interprofessional education (IPE) model that makes team-based, patient-centered care the new standard. OHSU IPI prepares OHSU students to work together to build a safer and more effective patient-centered and community-oriented health care system within Oregon and across the nation, ultimately impacting the health and well-being of populations worldwide.

Student research opportunities: Yes

SPECIAL PROGRAMS AND SERVICES

PREDENTAL

During the academic year, OU SOD offers two enrichment programs for students interested in a dental career. Dental Explorers is a seven-month program for high school or college students. Students may also register for a one-quarter course—referred to as Aspects of Dentistry (CHEM 199)—through Portland State University. OHSU SOD administers both programs, which feature lecture and laboratory components and emphasize "hands-on" experience.

DURING DENTAL SCHOOL

Academic counseling and tutoring
Community service opportunities
Internships, externships or extramural programs
Mentoring
Personal counseling
Research opportunities
Rural rotations
Student Health & Wellness

ACTIVE STUDENT ORGANIZATIONS

Academy of LDS Dentists
American Student Dental Association
Christian Medical & Dental Associations
Dental fraternities, including Delta Sigma Delta International Dental Fraternity and Omicron Kappa Upsilon National Dental Honor Society
Dental Student Research Group
Hispanic Dental Association
Queers and Allies in Health Care
Student government, including for OHSU and SOD
Student interest groups, including Global Health Center Student Interest Group and Women in Dentistry Interest Group
Professionalism & Ethics Association in Dentistry

INTERNATIONAL DENTISTS

Graduates of international dental schools considered for traditional predoctoral program: No
Advanced standing program offered for graduates of international dental schools: No

COMBINED AND ALTERNATE DEGREES

Ph.D.	M.S.	M.P.H.	M.D.	B.A./B.S.	Other
—	—	—	—	—	—

COSTS: 2013–14 SCHOOL YEAR

	FIRST YEAR	SECOND YEAR	THIRD YEAR	FOURTH YEAR
Tuition, resident	$43,016	$40,203	$41,880	$41,428
Tuition, nonresident	$69,432	$64,891	$67,666	$67,292
Tuition, other				
Fees	$2,116	$2,116	$2,116	$2,116
Instruments, books, and supplies	$14,183	$10,642	$7,933	$7,155
Estimated living expenses	$19,085	$19,085	$19,085	$19,085
Total, resident	$76,284	$69,930	$68,898	$67,736
Total, nonresident	$102,700	$94,618	$94,684	$93,560
Total, other				

FINANCIAL AID

FINANCIAL AID AWARDS TO FIRST-YEAR STUDENTS 2014–15

Total number of first-year recipients: 67
Percentage of the first-year class: 88%
Percentage of awards that are grants? NA
Percentage of awards that are loans? NA

	AVERAGE AWARDS	RANGE OF AWARDS
Residents	$68,680	$3,000–$79,678
Nonresidents	$87,796	$25,400–$107,187

For more information, please visit: www.ohsu.edu/sod/admissions

THE MAURICE H. KORNBERG SCHOOL OF DENTISTRY, **TEMPLE UNIVERSITY**

Amid I. Ismail, B.D.S., M.P.H., M.B.A., Dr.P.H., Dean

CONTACT INFORMATION

www.temple.edu/dentistry
3223 North Broad Street
Philadelphia, PA 19140

ADMISSIONS

Mr. Brian F. Hahn
Senior Director, Admissions, Diversity and Student Services
3223 North Broad Street
Philadelphia, PA 19140
Phone: 215-707-2801

STUDENT FINANCIAL SERVICES

Mr. Thomas Maiorano
Assistant Director
3340 North Broad Street
Philadelphia, PA 19140
Phone: 215-707-2667
Email: thomas.maiorano@temple.edu

RECRUITMENT

Mr. Brian Hahn
Senior Director, Office of Admissions, Diversity and Student Services
3223 North Broad Street
Philadelphia, PA 19140
Phone: 215-707-7663
Email: brian.hahn@temple.edu

HOUSING & FINANCIAL AID SUPPORT SERVICES

Ms. C. Terry Griffin
Student Services Coordinator
3223 North Broad Street
Philadelphia, PA 19140
Phone: 215-707-2952
Email: terry.griffin@temple.edu

GENERAL INFORMATION

The Maurice H. Kornberg School of Dentistry at Temple University is the second oldest dental school in continuous existence. As a major urban institution in the heart of a federally designated health professional shortage area, the dental school has a diverse patient population from a variety of socio-economic and cultural backgrounds. The large size and the diversity of this patient pool contribute immeasurably to a student's dental education. The student body is among the most diverse in the country. Most states and several countries are represented by Temple students. The relaxed and friendly team-oriented atmosphere generates strong relationships among students, staff and faculty.

MISSION

To educate diverse general and specialty dentists whose advanced skills enable them to provide comprehensive, patient-centered, evidence-based care and engage in research, scholarship and community service.

Vision: To promote oral health by serving as a center for excellence in clinical dental education, patient care, research and community-based service.

Type of institution: Private and state-related	Doctoral dental degree offered: D.M.D.
Year opened: 1863	Targeted predoctoral enrollment: 557
Term type: Semester	Targeted entering class size: 140
Time to degree in months: 48	Campus setting: Urban
Start month: August	Campus housing available: No

PREPARATION

Formal minimum preparation in semester/quarter hours: Semester: 90   Quarter: 120
Baccalaureate degree preferred: Yes
Number of first-year, first-time enrollees whose highest degree is:
    Baccalaureate: 124
    Master's degree and beyond: 13
Of first-year, first-time enrollees without baccalaureates, the number with:
    Equivalent of 60 undergraduate credit hours or less: 0
    Equivalent of 61–90 undergraduate credit hours: 2
    Equivalent of 91 or more undergraduate credit hours: 0

PREREQUISITE COURSE	REQUIRED	RECOMMENDED	LAB REQUIRED	CREDITS (SEMESTER/QUARTER)
BCP (biology-chemistry-physics) sciences				
Biology	✓		✓	8/12
Chemistry, general/inorganic	✓		✓	8/12
Chemistry, organic	✓		✓	8/12
Physics	✓		✓	8/12
Additional biological sciences				
Anatomy		✓		4/6
Biochemistry		✓		4/6
Cell biology		✓		4/6
Histology		✓		4/6
Immunology		✓		4/6
Microbiology		✓		4/6
Molecular biology/genetics		✓		4/6
Physiology		✓		4/6

(Prerequisite Courses continued)

PREPARATION (CONTINUED)

PREREQUISITE COURSE	REQUIRED	RECOMMENDED	LAB REQUIRED	CREDITS (SEMESTER/QUARTER)
Zoology		✓		4/6

Community college coursework accepted for prerequisites: No
Community college coursework accepted for electives: Yes
Limits on community college credit hours: Yes
Maximum number of community college credit hours: 6
Advanced placement (AP) credit accepted for prerequisites: No
Advanced placement (AP) credit accepted for electives: Yes
Job shadowing: Recommended
Number of hours of job shadowing required or recommended: The applicant should demonstrate substantial exposure to the dental profession.
Other factors considered in admission: Number of schools attended and credit hours per semester

DAT

Mandatory: Yes
Latest DAT for consideration of application: 01/15/2015
Oldest DAT considered: 06/01/2013
When more than one DAT score is reported: Highest academic average scores are considered
Canadian DAT accepted: Yes
Application considered before DAT scores are submitted: No

U.S. DAT: 2014 ENTERING CLASS

ENROLLEE DAT SCORES	MEAN	RANGE
Academic Average	20.0	18–25
Perceptual Ability	20.0	14–26
Total Science	20.0	17–27

CANADIAN DAT: 2014 ENTERING CLASS

ENROLLEE DAT SCORES	MEAN	RANGE
Academic Average	22.0	NR
Manual Dexterity	22.0	NR
Perceptual Ability	19.0	NR
Total Science	20.0	NR

GPA: 2014 ENTERING CLASS

ENROLLEE GPA SCORES	UNDERGRAD. MEAN	GRADUATE MEAN	UNDERGRAD. RANGE	GRADUATE RANGE
Science GPA	3.41	3.60	2.65–4.00	3.00–4.00
Total GPA	3.50	3.65	2.91–4.00	3.10–4.00

APPLICATION AND SELECTION

TIMETABLE

Earliest filing date: 06/02/2015
Latest filing date: 01/15/2016
Earliest date for acceptance offers: 12/01/2015
Maximum time in days for applicant's response to acceptance offer:
    30 days if accepted on or after December 1
    15 days if accepted on or after February 1
Requests for deferred entrance considered: No
Fee for application: Yes, submitted only when requested

Amount of fee for application:
    In state: $50   Out of state: $50   International: $50
Fee waiver available: No

	FIRST DEPOSIT	SECOND DEPOSIT	THIRD DEPOSIT
Required to hold place	Yes	Yes	No
Resident amount	$1,000	$500	
Nonresident amount	$1,000	$500	
Deposit due	As indicated in admission offer	As indicated in admission offer	
Applied to tuition	Yes	Yes	
Refundable	No	No	

APPLICATION PROCESS

Participates in Associated American Dental Schools Application Service (AADSAS): Yes
Accepts direct applicants: No
Secondary or supplemental application required: Yes
Secondary or supplemental application website: No
Interview is mandatory: Yes
Interview is by invitation: Yes

RESIDENCY

In-state/in-province versus out-of-state/out-of-province
Admissions process distinguishes between in-state/in-province and out-of-state/out-of-province applicants: Yes
Preference given to residents of: Delaware, Pennsylvania
Reciprocity Admissions Agreement available for legal residents of: None
Generally and over time, percentage of your first-year enrollment that is in-state: 50%
Origin of out-of-state/out-of-province enrollees: AZ-1, CA-9, CT-1, DE-3, FL-6, GA-1, IN-2, LA-1, MD-3, MI-3, MN-1, MO-1, NC-1, NJ-21, NY-7, OH-1, TX-3, UT-1, VA-5, WA-1, WV-1

International
Applications are accepted from international (noncitizens/nonpermanent residents): Yes
Origin of international enrollees: Canada-2, Kuwait-1, South Korea-2

APPLICATION AND ENROLLMENT	NUMBER OF APPLICANTS	ESTIMATED NUMBER INTERVIEWED	ESTIMATED NUMBER ENROLLED
In-state or province applicants/enrollees	273	132	61
Out-of-state or province applicants/enrollees	2,781	268	73
International applicants/enrollees (noncitizens/nonpermanent residents)	320	10	5

DEMOGRAPHIC DESCRIPTIONS OF APPLICANTS: 2014 ENTERING CLASS

	APPLICANTS			ENROLLEES		
	M	W	Gender Unknown or Not Reported	M	W	Gender Unknown or Not Reported
American Indian or Alaska Native	0	3	0	0	0	0
Asian	526	561	16	23	16	0
Black or African American	44	76	1	3	1	0
Hispanic or Latino	88	124	1	4	4	0
Native Hawaiian or Other Pacific Islander	2	4	0	0	0	0
White	833	566	6	44	30	1
Two or more races	49	47	1	0	3	0
Race and ethnicity unknown	44	50	12	2	2	1
International	176	138	6	2	3	0

	MINIMUM	MAXIMUM	MEAN
2014 entering class enrollees by age	21	38	24

CURRICULUM

The primary emphasis of the predoctoral program is to prepare graduates for the general practice of dentistry. The curriculum provides students with significant experience in all phases of dental practice and instills the basic science and patient management skills they will rely on as dental practitioners. The curriculum also lays a solid foundation for careers in the specialties of dentistry, dental education and research.

Student research opportunities: Yes

SPECIAL PROGRAMS AND SERVICES

PREDENTAL

Special affiliations with colleges and universities: Alvernia College, Cabrini College, Caldwell University, Coppin State University, Edinboro University of Pennsylvania, Elizabethtown College, Indiana University of Pennsylvania, Juniata College, King's College, Mansfield University, Moravian College, Pennsylvania State University at Erie, Philadelphia University, Rosemont College, Rowan University, Saint Francis College, Shippensburg University, Susquehanna University, Temple University, University of Pittsburgh at Titusville, University of the Sciences in Philadelphia, West Chester University, Widener University, Wilkes University, William Paterson University

DURING DENTAL SCHOOL

Academic counseling and tutoring
Internships, externships, or extramural programs
Transfer applicants considered if space is available

ACTIVE STUDENT ORGANIZATIONS

American Association of Women Dentists
American Student Dental Association
Asian American Student Dental Association
Hispanic Dental Association
Student National Dental Association

INTERNATIONAL DENTISTS

Graduates of international dental schools considered for traditional predoctoral program: Yes
Advanced standing program offered for graduates of international dental schools: No

COMBINED AND ALTERNATE DEGREES

Ph.D.	M.S.	M.P.H.	M.D.	B.A./B.S.	Other
—	✓	✓	—	✓	—

Note: M.S. in Oral Biology

COSTS: 2014–15 SCHOOL YEAR

	FIRST YEAR	SECOND YEAR	THIRD YEAR	FOURTH YEAR
Tuition, resident	$48,808	$48,808	$48,808	$48,808
Tuition, nonresident	$57,012	$57,012	$57,012	$57,012
Tuition, other				
Fees	$690	$690	$690	$690
Instruments, books, and supplies	$8,414	$8,171	$5,800	$5,300
Estimated living expenses	$23,638	$28,158	$28,158	$21,288
Total, resident	$81,550	$85,827	$83,456	$76,086
Total, nonresident	$89,754	$94,031	$91,660	$84,290
Total, other				

FINANCIAL AID

Students who wish to be considered for any type of federal financial aid must complete the Free Application for Federal Student Aid (FAFSA) by March 1 of the award year for priority consideration. There are a limited number of scholarships and loans for students from disadvantaged backgrounds and students with extremely high need. In order to be considered for such scholarships and loans, students must provide complete parental information on the FAFSA form and provide complete copies of their and their parents' IRS tax return(s) for the 2015 filing year (including W-2s). More information on the types of financial aid available can be found at www. temple.edu/sfs. The average 2014 graduate indebtedness was $236,095.

FINANCIAL AID AWARDS TO FIRST-YEAR STUDENTS 2014–15

Total number of first-year recipients: 114
Percentage of the first-year class: 82%
Percentage of awards that are grants? 0%
Percentage of awards that are loans? 60%

	AVERAGE AWARDS	RANGE OF AWARDS
Residents	$59,872	$1,531–$82,840
Nonresidents	$68,427	$25,000–$91,420

For more information, please visit: www.temple.edu/sfs

UNIVERSITY OF PENNSYLVANIA
SCHOOL OF DENTAL MEDICINE

Denis F. Kinane, B.D.S., Ph.D., Morton Amsterdam Dean

GENERAL INFORMATION

The University of Pennsylvania School of Dental Medicine (Penn Dental Medicine) adapts its programs to remain at dental medicine's forefront, preparing graduates to follow suit. Among the nation's oldest university-affiliated dental institutions, Penn Dental Medicine attracts students throughout the country and around the world.

Association with other Penn graduate and professional schools facilitates interdisciplinary study/research. Viewing scholarship as a central component of excellence in instruction and patient care, Penn Dental Medicine places a high priority on research, offering students many multidisciplinary, basic- and clinical-science based research opportunities. A leading Philadelphia community dental care provider, Penn Dental Medicine offers students a large, diverse patient population and a depth of clinical experiences.

Programs for internationally trained dentists, several advanced dental education specialties and combined degrees are available.

MISSION
The mission of Penn Dental Medicine is to educate predoctoral and graduate dental students in the highest quality clinical and research environment.

Type of institution: Private	Doctoral dental degree offered: D.M.D.
Year opened: 1878	Targeted predoctoral enrollment: 541
Term type: Semester	Targeted entering class size: 120
Time to degree in months: 45	Campus setting: Urban
Start month: August	Campus housing available: Yes

PREPARATION

Formal minimum preparation in semester/quarter hours: Semester: NR   Quarter: NR
Baccalaureate degree preferred: Yes
Number of first-year, first-time enrollees whose highest degree is:
    Baccalaureate: 114
    Master's degree and beyond: 0
Of first-year, first-time enrollees without baccalaureates, the number with:
    Equivalent of 60 undergraduate credit hours or less: 0
    Equivalent of 61–90 undergraduate credit hours: 4
    Equivalent of 91 or more undergraduate credit hours: 0

PREREQUISITE COURSE	REQUIRED	RECOMMENDED	LAB REQUIRED	COURSES (SEMESTER/QUARTER)
BCP (biology-chemistry-physics) sciences				
Biology	✓		✓	2/3
Chemistry, general/inorganic	✓		✓	2/3
Chemistry, organic	✓		✓	2/3
Physics	✓		✓	2/3
Additional biological sciences				
Anatomy		✓		
Biochemistry	✓			1/1
Cell biology		✓		
Histology		✓		
Immunology		✓		
Microbiology		✓		
Molecular biology/genetics		✓		

CONTACT INFORMATION
www.dental.upenn.edu
University of Pennsylvania
School of Dental Medicine
The Robert Schattner Center
240 South 40th Street
Philadelphia, PA 19104-6030

OFFICE OF ADMISSIONS
Dr. Olivia Sheridan
Assistant Dean for Admissions
The Robert Schattner Center
240 South 40th Street
Room 122
Philadelphia, PA 19104-6030
Phone: 215-898-8943

OFFICE OF ADMISSIONS
Ms. Corky Cacas
Director of Admissions
The Robert Schattner Center
240 South 40th Street
Room 122
Philadelphia, PA 19104-6030
Phone: 215-898-8943

FINANCIAL AID & OFFICE OF STUDENT AFFAIRS
Ms. Susan Schwartz
Assistant Dean for Student Affairs
The Robert Schattner Center
240 South 40th Street
Philadelphia, PA 19104-6030
Phone: 215-898-4550

MINORITY AFFAIRS/DIVERSITY
Dr. Beverley Crawford
Director of Diversity
The Robert Schattner Center
240 South 40th Street
Philadelphia, PA 19104-6030
Phone: 215-898-2840
Email: beverlyc@dental.upenn.edu

PREPARATION (CONTINUED)

PREREQUISITE COURSE	REQUIRED	RECOMMENDED	LAB REQUIRED	COURSES (SEMESTER/QUARTER)
Physiology		✓		
Zoology		✓		
Other				
Mathematics	✓			1/2
English or intensive writing course	✓			2/3

Community college coursework accepted for prerequisites: Yes
Community college coursework accepted for electives: Yes
Limits on community college credit hours: Yes
Maximum number of community college credit hours: 60
Advanced placement (AP) credit accepted for prerequisites: Yes
Advanced placement (AP) credit accepted for electives: Yes
Comments regarding AP credit: AP credit is allowed as long as it appears on the official college transcript from the applicant's undergraduate institution.
Job shadowing: Required
Other factors considered in admission: Yes

DAT

DAT Mandatory: Yes
Latest DAT for consideration of application: 12/01/2015
Oldest DAT considered: 01/01/2013
When more than one DAT score is reported: Highest score is considered.
Canadian DAT accepted: Yes
Application considered before DAT scores are submitted: Yes

DAT: 2014 ENTERING CLASS

ENROLLEE DAT SCORES	MEAN	RANGE
Academic Average	21.5	18–28
Perceptual Ability	21.0	16–30
Total Science	21.5	18–28

GPA: 2014 ENTERING CLASS

ENROLLEE GPA SCORES	UNDERGRAD. MEAN	GRADUATE MEAN	UNDERGRAD. RANGE	GRADUATE RANGE
Science GPA	3.62	NA	2.64–4.08	NA
Total GPA	3.67	NA	2.68–4.07	NA

APPLICATION AND SELECTION

TIMETABLE

Earliest filing date: 06/02/2015
Latest filing date: 12/01/2015
Earliest date for acceptance offers: 12/01/2015
Maximum time in days for applicant's response to acceptance offer:
    40 days if accepted on or after December 1
    15 days if accepted on or after February 1
Requests for deferred entrance considered: No
Fee for application: Yes, submitted at same time as Associated American Dental Schools Application Service (AADSAS) application
Amount of fee for application:
    In state: $60   Out of state: $60   International: $60
Fee waiver available: No

	FIRST DEPOSIT	SECOND DEPOSIT	THIRD DEPOSIT
Required to hold place	Yes	Yes	No
Resident amount	$500	$500	
Nonresident amount	$500	$500	
Deposit due	As indicated in admission offer	As indicated in admission offer	
Applied to tuition	Yes	Yes	
Refundable	No	No	

APPLICATION PROCESS

Participates in AADSAS: Yes
Accepts direct applicants: No
Secondary or supplemental application required: Yes.
    All applicants must complete supplemental application, available on website: www.dental.upenn.edu
Interview is mandatory: Yes
Interview is by invitation: Yes

RESIDENCY

In-state/in-province versus out-of-state/out-of-province
Admissions process distinguishes between in-state/in-province and out-of-state/out-of-province applicants: No
Preference given to residents of: None
Reciprocity Admissions Agreement available for legal residents of: NR
Generally and over time, percentage of your first-year enrollment that is in-state: 14%
Origin of out-of-state/out-of-province enrollees: CA-8, CO-1, CT-1, DC-1, DE-1, FL-7, GA-2, HI-1, ID-1, IL-5, MA-7, MD-3, MI-3, MN-1, MO-1, NC-1, NJ-16, NY-9, SC-1, TX-3, VA-8, WA-2, WI-1

International
Applications are accepted from international (noncitizens/nonpermanent residents): Yes
Origin of international enrollees: Canada-10, Jamaica-1, South Korea-3, Taiwan-1, Vietnam-1

APPLICATION AND ENROLLMENT	NUMBER OF APPLICANTS	ESTIMATED NUMBER INTERVIEWED	ESTIMATED NUMBER ENROLLED
In-state or province applicants/enrollees	149	34	17
Out-of-state or province applicants/enrollees	1,980	291	84
International applicants/enrollees (noncitizens/nonpermanent residents)	105	23	17

DEMOGRAPHIC DESCRIPTIONS OF APPLICANTS: 2014 ENTERING CLASS

	APPLICANTS			ENROLLEES		
	M	W	Gender Unknown or Not Reported	M	W	Gender Unknown or Not Reported
American Indian or Alaska Native	1	3	0	0	1	0
Asian	428	435	0	11	28	0
Black or African American	18	37	0	1	2	0
Hispanic or Latino	48	80	0	3	2	0
Native Hawaiian or Other Pacific Islander	1	3	0	0	0	0
White	532	437	17	24	24	0
Two or more races	18	36	0	0	5	0
Race and ethnicity unknown	20	14	0	0	0	0
International	54	51	0	13	4	0

	MINIMUM	MAXIMUM	MEAN
2014 entering class enrollees by age	21	34	23

CURRICULUM

Four-week summer sessions between years 1 and 2, and between years 3 and 4, are mandatory. Year 1 continues through June. The basic science courses are taught during years 1 and 2 through lectures, seminars and laboratory experiences. Clinical training begins with dental health education in community settings and dental assisting in year 1 and continuing through year 2.

Years 3 and 4 emphasize the general practice of dentistry, and fourth-year students gain additional clinical skills in a hospital setting through a four-week externship. The basic and clinical sciences are integrated throughout the four years. Program highlights include an offering of more than 40 elective courses during years 2, 3 and 4; a community service component; interdisciplinary dual degree programs; an optional international externship during year 4; and an honors program in clinical, community dentistry and research for eligible students.

Student research opportunities: Yes—Penn Dental Medicine views scholarship as a central component of excellence in instruction and patient care and places a high priority on research. With its own basic science faculty (unusual among dental schools nationwide), the school's research enterprise is multidisciplinary, spanning both the basic and clinical sciences and offering many student research opportunities.

SPECIAL PROGRAMS AND SERVICES

PREDENTAL

Special affiliations with colleges and universities: University of Pennsylvania; Hampton University; Lehigh University; Muhlenberg College; Villanova University

Summer enrichment programs: Introduction to dentistry and dental simulation lab

DURING DENTAL SCHOOL

Academic counseling and tutoring

Community service opportunities: Mandatory graduation requirement

Internships, externships, or extramural programs: Hospital-based externships in U.S. or abroad

Mentoring

Personal counseling

Professional- and career-development programming

Training for those interested in academic careers

ACTIVE STUDENT ORGANIZATIONS

AMALGAM (A Mosaic of Allies, Lesbians, Gays, and More)

American Student Dental Association

Christian Dental Society

Community Health and Service Organization

Dental fraternities, including Alpha Omega International Dental Fraternity, Delta Sigma Delta International Fraternity, Psi Omega Fraternity

Dental specialty societies (predoctoral)

Hispanic Student Dental Association

Indian Student Dental Association

Korean Student Dental Association

Student National Dental Association

INTERNATIONAL DENTISTS

Graduates of international dental schools considered for traditional predoctoral program: Yes

Advanced standing program offered for graduates of international dental schools: Yes

Advanced standing program description: Program awarding a dental degree

COMBINED AND ALTERNATE DEGREES

Ph.D.	M.S.	M.P.H.	M.D.	B.A./B.S.	Other
✓	✓	✓	—	✓	✓

Other degrees: M.S. in Bioethics, Education and Translational Research; M.S.E. in Bioengineering; M.B.A. (Business Administration); J.D. (Law)

COSTS: 2014–15 SCHOOL YEAR

	FIRST YEAR	SECOND YEAR	THIRD YEAR	FOURTH YEAR
Tuition, resident	$68,278	$68,278	$68,278	$68,278
Tuition, nonresident	$68,278	$68,278	$68,278	$68,278
Tuition, other				
Fees	$3,870	$3,870	$3,870	$3,870
Instruments, books, and supplies	$18,314	$14,819	$16,736	$15,306
Estimated living expenses	$17,302	$19,094	$19,094	$17,302
Total, resident	$107,764	$106,061	$107,978	$104,756
Total, nonresident	$107,764	$106,061	$107,978	$104,756
Total, other				

FINANCIAL AID

Penn Dental Medicine makes every effort to assist students in pursuing their education. The university helps students locate financial aid resources according to their need and eligibility. Available resources include need-based and non-need-based loans. To be considered for need-based financial aid, applicants must be U.S. citizens or permanent residents. Aid is awarded based on level of need after reviewing a student's entire financial situation, including parental information, which must be submitted. A student may borrow the expected family contribution from other funding sources. International students will be considered for non-university-based funding (private educational loans). Each year the school awards a limited number of Dean's Scholarships to the applicant pool's incoming students. Please refer to www.dental.upenn.edu for information regarding available financial assistance, application procedures and requirements.

For more information, please visit: www.dental.upenn.edu

CONTACT INFORMATION

www.dental.pitt.edu

Dr. Christine Wankiiri-Hale
Associate Dean
3501 Terrace Street
Dean's Suite, 4th Floor Salk Hall
Pittsburgh, PA 15261
Phone: 412-648-8422

ADMISSIONS

Dr. Elizabeth Bilodeau
Director of Admissions

Ms. Katherine Adomitis
Admissions Officer
3501 Terrace Street
Suite 2114 Salk
Pittsburgh, PA 15261
Phone: 412-648-8422

FINANCIAL AID

Ms. Tracey Wassel
3501 Terrace Street
Suite 2114 Salk
Pittsburgh, PA 15261
Phone: 412-648-9806

STUDENT AFFAIRS

Ms. Aileen Brasacchio
3501 Terrace Street
Suite 2114 Salk
Pittsburgh, PA 15261
Phone: 412-648-8406

MINORITY PROGRAMS

Dr. Christine Wankiiri-Hale
Ms. Aileen Brasacchio
3501 Terrace Street
Suite 2114 Salk
Pittsburgh, PA 15261
Phone: 412-648-8406

ADVANCED STANDING PROGRAM FOR FOREIGN TRAINED DENTISTS

Dr. Anitha Potluri
Ms. Katherine Adomitis
3501 Terrace Street
Pittsburgh, PA 15261
Phone: 412-648-8422
Email: dentaladmissions@dental.pitt.edu

UNIVERSITY OF PITTSBURGH
SCHOOL OF DENTAL MEDICINE

Thomas W. Braun, D.M.D., M.S., Ph.D., Dean

GENERAL INFORMATION

The University of Pittsburgh is a state-related institution located in the city's Oakland District. The School of Dental Medicine, founded in 1896, is one of the schools in the University Health Complex, which consists of the schools of Medicine, Nursing, Pharmacy, Health Related Professions and Public Health, as well as affiliated university hospitals. With an emphasis on competency-based performance, our first professional students are educated to provide optimal dental care for the public. Furthermore, our dental residency programs and dental hygiene program provide predoctoral students the opportunity to work cooperatively with other members of the dental profession. Dental residency programs are offered in advanced dental education in general dentistry, endodontics, pediatric dentistry, periodontics, prosthodontics, orthodontics, anesthesiology, dental informatics, maxillofacial surgery, oral and maxillofacial pathology, and general practice residency.

MISSION

Please visit www.dental.pitt.edu to read the complete mission statement for the University of Pittsburgh School of Dental Medicine (Pitt SDM).

Type of institution: State-related	Doctoral dental degree offered: D.M.D.
Year opened: 1896	Targeted predoctoral enrollment: 320
Term type: Semester	Targeted entering class size: 80
Time to degree in months: 45	Campus setting: Urban
Start month: August	Campus housing available: Limited

PREPARATION

Formal minimum preparation in semester/quarter hours: Three years/90 Semester Credits
Baccalaureate degree preferred: Yes
Number of first-year, first-time enrollees whose highest degree is:
  Baccalaureate: 72
  Master's degree and beyond: 6
Of first-year, first-time enrollees without baccalaureates, the number with:
  Equivalent of 60 undergraduate credit hours or less: 0
  Equivalent of 61–90 undergraduate credit hours: 0
  Equivalent of 91 or more undergraduate credit hours: 0

PREREQUISITE COURSE	REQUIRED	RECOMMENDED	LAB REQUIRED	CREDITS (SEMESTER/QUARTER)
BCP (biology-chemistry-physics) sciences				
Biology	✓		✓	8/12
Chemistry, general/inorganic	✓		✓	8/12
Chemistry, organic	✓		✓	8/12
Physics		✓		6/10
Additional biological sciences				
Anatomy		✓		3/4
Biochemistry	✓			3/4
Cell biology		✓		3/4
Histology		✓		3/4
Immunology				
Microbiology		✓		3/4
Molecular biology/genetics				
Physiology		✓		3/4
Zoology				

PREPARATION (CONTINUED)

PREREQUISITE COURSE	REQUIRED	RECOMMENDED	LAB REQUIRED	CREDITS (SEMESTER/QUARTER)
Other				
English	✓			6/10

Community college coursework accepted for prerequisites: Yes, up to 30% of prerequisites
Community college coursework accepted for electives: Yes, up to 30% of coursework
Limits on community college credit hours: Yes
Maximum number of community college credit hours: 30%
Advanced placement (AP) credit accepted for prerequisites: Yes
Advanced placement (AP) credit accepted for electives: Yes
Job shadowing: Required
Number of hours of job shadowing required or recommended: 50—Ongoing shadowing is required at various practices.

DAT

Mandatory: Yes
Latest DAT for consideration of application: 09/30/2015
Oldest DAT considered: 01/01/2012
When more than one DAT score is reported: Highest score is considered
Canadian DAT accepted: Yes
Application considered before DAT scores are submitted: No, scores must be submitted with application.

DAT: 2014 ENTERING CLASS

ENROLLEE DAT SCORES	MEAN	RANGE
Academic Average	20.7	17–24
Perceptual Ability	20.3	NR
Total Science	NR	17–24

GPA: 2014 ENTERING CLASS

ENROLLEE GPA SCORES	MEAN	RANGE
Science GPA	3.42	2.80–4.10
Total GPA	3.65	2.90–4.10

APPLICATION AND SELECTION

TIMETABLE

Earliest filing date: 06/02 of application cycle
Latest filing date: 11/01 of application cycle
Earliest date for acceptance offers: 12/01 of application cycle
Maximum time in days for applicant's response to acceptance offer:
    30 days if accepted on or after December 1
    15 days if accepted on or after January 1
Requests for deferred entrance considered: No
Fee for application: Yes, submitted at same time as Associated American Dental Schools Application Service (AADSAS) application
Amount of fee for application:
    In state: $50   Out of state: $50   International: $75 (U.S.)
Fee waiver available: No

	FIRST DEPOSIT	SECOND DEPOSIT	THIRD DEPOSIT
Required to hold place	Yes	Yes	No
Resident amount	$1,000	$1,000	
Nonresident amount	$1,000	$1,000	
Deposit due	As indicated in admission offer	04/01 of application cycle	
Applied to tuition	Yes	Yes	
Refundable	No	No	

APPLICATION PROCESS

Participates in AADSAS: Yes
Accepts direct applicants: No
Secondary or supplemental application required: No; application fee and a recent 2x2 head shot photo only
Interview is mandatory: Yes
Interview is by invitation: Yes

RESIDENCY

In-state/in-province versus out-of-state/out-of-province
Admissions process distinguishes between in-state/in-province and out-of-state/out-of-province applicants: No
Preference given to residents of: None
Reciprocity Admissions Agreement available for legal residents of: NR
Generally and over time, percentage of your first-year enrollment that is in-state: NR
Origin of out-of-state/out-of-province enrollees: AZ-1 CA-1, CO-1, FL-6, GA-2, IL-2, KY-1, MD-2, MI-2, NC-1 NY-2, OH-1, TX-4, VA-1, VT-1, WI-1

International
Applications are accepted from international (noncitizens/nonpermanent residents): Yes
Origin of international enrollees: Canada-2, China-1, South Korea-1

APPLICATION AND ENROLLMENT	NUMBER OF APPLICANTS	ESTIMATED NUMBER INTERVIEWED	ESTIMATED NUMBER ENROLLED
In-state or province applicants/enrollees	199	82	NR
Out-of-state or province applicants/enrollees	1,692	317	NR
International applicants/enrollees (noncitizens/nonpermanent residents)	NR	NR	NR

DEMOGRAPHIC DESCRIPTIONS OF APPLICANTS: 2014 ENTERING CLASS

	MINIMUM	MAXIMUM	MEAN
2014 entering class enrollees by age	20	38	23

CURRICULUM

Pitt SDM combines rigorous classroom instruction with innovative hands-on experience in a clinical setting. Students in the first and second years train in state-of-the-art simulation clinics, balanced with a mix of traditional classroom lectures and small group situations. Third- and fourth-year students simulate private practice in module clinics under close supervision of clinical faculty. Students are encouraged to individualize their programs through elective courses in their third and fourth years. Elective study may range from a minimum of two courses to any number the student feels he or she can schedule comfortably. Additionally, clinical practice and social perspectives are expanded through elective study; the program provides opportunities for enrichment through electives at off-campus sites.

Student research opportunities: Yes

SPECIAL PROGRAMS AND SERVICES

PREDENTAL
Postbaccalaureate programs

DURING DENTAL SCHOOL
Academic counseling and tutoring
Community service opportunities
Internships, externships, or extramural programs
Mentoring
Personal counseling
Professional- and career-development programming
Training for those interested in academic careers
Transfer applicants considered if space is available

ACTIVE STUDENT ORGANIZATIONS
American Academy of Pediatric Dentistry, student chapter
American Association for Dental Research National Student
    Research Group
American Association of Women Dentists
American Student Dental Association
Asian Pacific American Student Dental Association
Dentist Anesthesiologist Club for Students
Hispanic Dental Association
Muslim Students' Association
Student National Dental Association
For additional information, visit: http://www.dental.pitt.edu/students/
    student_organizations.php

INTERNATIONAL DENTISTS
Graduates of international dental schools considered for traditional
    predoctoral program: Yes
Advanced standing program offered for graduates of international
    dental schools: Yes
Advanced standing program description: Program awarding a dental
    degree, Other: two-year program

COMBINED AND ALTERNATE DEGREES

Ph.D.	M.S.	M.P.H.	M.D.	B.A./B.S.	Other
✓	✓	✓	—	—	—

COSTS: 2014–15 SCHOOL YEAR

	FIRST YEAR	SECOND YEAR	THIRD YEAR	FOURTH YEAR
Tuition, resident	$43,136	$43,136	$43,136	$43,136
Tuition, nonresident	$49,952	$49,952	$49,952	$49,952
Tuition, other				
Fees	$1,110	$1,110	$1,110	$1,110
Instruments, books, and supplies	$13,200	$10,040	$5,504	$4,521
Estimated living expenses	$21,000	$21,000	$21,000	$21,000
Total, resident	$78,446	$75,286	$70,750	$69,767
Total, nonresident	$85,262	$82,102	$77,566	$76,583
Total, other				

FINANCIAL AID

http://dental.pitt.edu/financing-your-dental-education

CONTACT INFORMATION

http://dental.rcm.upr.edu
P.O. Box 365067
San Juan, PR 00936-5067
Phone: 787-758-2525, ext. 1113
Fax: 787-751-0990

OFFICE OF ADMISSIONS

P.O. Box 365067
San Juan, PR 00936-5067
Phone: 787-758-2525

OFFICE OF FINANCIAL AID

Mr. Rafael Solis
Director
P.O. Box 365067
San Juan, PR 00936-5067
Phone: 787-758-2525
Email: rafael.solis@upr.edu
www.rcm.upr.edu

STUDENT AFFAIRS

Dr. Elaine Pagan
Acting Assistant Dean for Student Affairs
P.O. Box 365067
San Juan, PR 00936-5067
Phone: 787-758-2525
Email: elaine.pagan@upr.edu

MINORITY AFFAIRS/DIVERSITY

Dr. Elaine Pagan
Acting Assistant Dean for Student Affairs
P.O. Box 365067
San Juan, PR 00936-5067
Phone: 787-758-2525
Email: elaine.pagan@upr.edu

HOUSING OFFICE

P.O. Box 365067
San Juan, PR 00936-5067
Phone: 787-758-2525
Email: nitza.rivera@upr.edu

INTERNATIONAL STUDENTS

Dr. Elaine Pagan
International Program Director
P.O. Box 365067
San Juan, PR 00936-5067
Phone: 787-758-2525
Email: elaine.pagan@upr.edu

UNIVERSITY OF PUERTO RICO
SCHOOL OF DENTAL MEDICINE

Ana López-Fuentes, D.M.D., M.P.H., Dean

GENERAL INFORMATION

On June 21, 1956, the legislature of Puerto Rico, on the recommendation of the University's Superior Education Council, approved legislation establishing the School of Dental Medicine. The first class started in August 1957. The School of Dental Medicine (SDM) is one of the faculties forming the University of Puerto Rico (UPR) and is located in the Medical Sciences Campus in Río Piedras, Puerto Rico. UPR SDM is fully accredited by the Council of Dental Education of the American Dental Association. It offers the following academic programs: 1) a four-year program leading to the D.M.D. degree; 2) advanced education programs in dental specialties of oral and maxillofacial surgery, general practice, prosthodontics, pediatric dentistry, endodontics (in conjunction with Lutheran Medical Center) and orthodontics; and 3) continuing education.

MISSION

Training dentists to become an integral part of the multidisciplinary health professional team who will satisfy the needs of the people of Puerto Rico.

Type of institution: Public	Doctoral dental degree offered: D.M.D.
Year opened: 1957	Targeted predoctoral enrollment: 194
Term type: Semester	Targeted entering class size: 40
Time to degree in months: 41	Campus setting: Urban
Start month: August	Campus housing available: No

PREPARATION

Formal minimum preparation in semester/quarter hours: Semester: 90   Quarter: 135
Baccalaureate degree preferred: Yes
Number of first-year, first-time enrollees whose highest degree is:
    Baccalaureate: 0
    Master's degree and beyond: 3
Of first-year, first-time enrollees without baccalaureates, the number with:
    Equivalent of 60 undergraduate credit hours or less: 1
    Equivalent of 61–90 undergraduate credit hours: 19
    Equivalent of 91 or more undergraduate credit hours: 17

PREREQUISITE COURSE	REQUIRED	RECOMMENDED	LAB REQUIRED	CREDITS (SEMESTER/QUARTER)
BCP (biology-chemistry-physics) sciences				
Biology	✓		✓	8/12
Chemistry, general/inorganic	✓		✓	8/12
Chemistry, organic	✓		✓	8/12
Physics	✓		✓	8/12
Additional biological sciences				
Anatomy		✓		
Biochemistry		✓		3/5
Cell biology		✓		
Histology		✓		
Immunology		✓		
Microbiology		✓		3/4
Molecular biology/genetics		✓		
Physiology		✓		3/5
Zoology				

(Prerequisite Courses continued)

PREPARATION (CONTINUED)

PREREQUISITE COURSE	REQUIRED	RECOMMENDED	LAB REQUIRED	CREDITS (SEMESTER/QUARTER)
Other				
English	✓			12/18
Spanish	✓			12/18
Social Sciences	✓			6/9

Community college coursework accepted for prerequisites: Yes
Community college coursework accepted for electives: Yes
Limits on community college credit hours: No
Maximum number of community college credit hours: 90
Advanced placement (AP) credit accepted for prerequisites: Yes
Advanced placement (AP) credit accepted for electives: Yes
Comments regarding AP credit: AP credits must appear on college transcript as accepted by college.
Job shadowing: Recommended
Number of hours of job shadowing required or recommended: No minimum
Other factors considered in admission: Extra science credits, research work done, and community service

DAT

Mandatory: Yes
Latest DAT for consideration of application: 11/30/2015
Oldest DAT considered: 11/30/2012
When more than one DAT score is reported: Highest score is considered.
Canadian DAT accepted: No
Application considered before DAT scores are submitted: No

DAT: 2013 ENTERING CLASS

ENROLLEE DAT SCORES	MEAN	RANGE
Academic Average	17.0	15–19
Perceptual Ability	15.0	15–20
Total Science	14.0	14–20

GPA: 2013 ENTERING CLASS

ENROLLEE GPA SCORES	MEAN	RANGE
Science GPA	3.40	2.90–3.90
Total GPA	3.50	3.40–3.90

APPLICATION AND SELECTION

TIMETABLE

Earliest filing date: 06/02/2015
Latest filing date: 12/01/2015
Earliest date for acceptance offers: 03/30/2016
Maximum time in days for applicant's response to acceptance offer:
    15 days if accepted on or after December 1
    15 days if accepted on or after February 1
Requests for deferred entrance considered: In exceptional circumstances only
Fee for application: Yes, submitted at same time as Associated American Dental Schools Application Service (AADSAS) application.
Amount of fee for application:
    In state: $20   Out of state: $20   International: $25
Fee waiver available: No

	FIRST DEPOSIT	SECOND DEPOSIT	THIRD DEPOSIT
Required to hold place	Yes	No	No
Resident amount	$100		
Nonresident amount	$100		
Deposit due	As indicated in admission offer		
Applied to tuition	Yes		
Refundable	No		

APPLICATION PROCESS

Participates in AADSAS: Yes
Accepts direct applicants: No
Secondary or supplemental application required: Yes
Secondary or supplemental application website: www.rcm.upr.edu
Yes, applicant must contact the school
Interview is mandatory: Yes
Interview is by invitation: Yes

RESIDENCY

In-state/in-province versus out-of-state/out-of-province
Admissions process distinguishes between in-state/in-province and out-of-state/out-of-province applicants: Yes
Preference given to residents of: Puerto Rico
Reciprocity Admissions Agreement available for legal residents of: NR
Generally and over time, percentage of your first-year enrollment that is in-state: 65%
Origin of out-of-state/out-of-province enrollees: AL-1, UT-1

International
Applications are accepted from international (noncitizens/nonpermanent residents): Yes
Origin of international enrollees: NA

APPLICATION AND ENROLLMENT	NUMBER OF APPLICANTS	ESTIMATED NUMBER INTERVIEWED	ESTIMATED NUMBER ENROLLED
In-state or province applicants/enrollees	77	58	38
Out-of-state or province applicants/enrollees	319	9	2
International applicants/enrollees (noncitizens/nonpermanent residents)	0	NA	0

DEMOGRAPHIC DESCRIPTIONS OF APPLICANTS: 2013 ENTERING CLASS

	APPLICANTS			ENROLLEES		
	M	W	Gender Unknown or Not Reported	M	W	Gender Unknown or Not Reported
American Indian or Alaska Native	2	1	0	0	0	0
Asian	38	37	0	0	0	0
Black or African American	10	11	0	0	0	0
Hispanic or Latino	49	98	0	10	29	0
Native Hawaiian or Other Pacific Islander	0	0	0	0	0	0
White	76	56	0	1	0	0
Two or more races	0	2	0	0	0	0
Race and ethnicity unknown	5	2	0	0	0	0
International	0	0	0	0	0	0

	MINIMUM	MAXIMUM	MEAN
2014 entering class enrollees by age	21	23	24

CURRICULUM

Year 1. Basic science with introduction to clinic situations.

Year 2. Continuation of basic science and technical courses.

Year 3. Clinic rotations through each of the different disciplines in dentistry.

Year 4. Delivery of comprehensive dental care under conditions that approximate private practice, with extramural community programs in locations nationwide. Dental Degree Offered: D.M.D.

Student research opportunities: Yes

SPECIAL PROGRAMS AND SERVICES

PREDENTAL

Special affiliations with colleges and universities: University of Rochester (combined double D.M.D./Ph.D. degree); Lutheran Medical Center (advanced dental education programs in Endodontics and Advanced Education in General Dentistry)
Summer enrichment programs

DURING DENTAL SCHOOL

Academic counseling and tutoring
Community service opportunities
Internships, externships, or extramural programs
Mentoring
Opportunity to study for credit at institution abroad
Personal counseling
Training for those interested in academic careers
Transfer applicants considered if space is available

ACTIVE STUDENT ORGANIZATIONS

American Association of Women Dentists
American Dental Education Association
American Student Dental Association
Hispanic Dental Association
Student Council

INTERNATIONAL DENTISTS

Graduates of international dental schools considered for traditional predoctoral program: No
Advanced standing program offered for graduates of international dental schools: Yes
Advanced standing program description: Two-year program awarding a dental degree

COMBINED AND ALTERNATE DEGREES

Ph.D.	M.S.	M.P.H.	M.D.	B.A./B.S.	Other
✓	—	—	—	—	—

COSTS: 2013–14 SCHOOL YEAR

	FIRST YEAR	SECOND YEAR	THIRD YEAR	FOURTH YEAR
Tuition, resident	$9,495	$9,101	$8,751	$8,415
Tuition, nonresident	See "Note" below.			
Tuition, other (international)	$18,377	$18,377	$18,377	$18,377
Fees	$414	$381	$612	$249
Instruments, books, and supplies	$11,534	$10,929	$3,193	$1,966
Estimated living expenses	$13,483	$14,396	$14,481	$13,398
Total, resident	$34,926	$34,807	$27,037	$24,028
Total, nonresident	See "Note" below.			
Total, other (international)	$43,808	$44,083	$36,663	$33,990

Note: Tuition for nonresidents determined according to geographical residence of applicant.

FINANCIAL AID

For more information, please visit: eps.rcm.upr.edu/asistenciaeconomica.asp or contact: lvelez@rcm.upr.edu

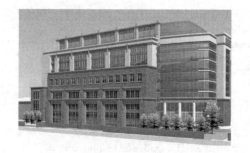

MEDICAL UNIVERSITY OF SOUTH CAROLINA
JAMES B. EDWARDS COLLEGE OF DENTAL MEDICINE

John J. Sanders, D.D.S., Dean

CONTACT INFORMATION

www.musc.edu/dentistry

OFFICE OF ENROLLMENT MANAGEMENT

Mr. Bill Liner
Dental Medicine Admissions Specialist
45 Courtenay Drive
MSC 203
Charleston, SC 29425-2030
Phone: 843-792-4892
academicdepartments.musc.edu/esl/em/

FINANCIAL AID

Ms. Ashley Stuckey
Dental Medicine Financial Aid Counselor
45 Courtenay Drive, SS-354
MSC 176
Charleston, SC 29425
Phone: 843-792-0205
academicdepartments.musc.edu/esl/em/fin_aid/

ACADEMIC & STUDENT AFFAIRS

Dr. Tariq Javed
Associate Dean for Academic and Student Affairs
173 Ashley Avenue, BSB-443
MSC 507
Charleston, SC 29425
Phone: 843-792-2345

MINORITY AFFAIRS/DIVERSITY

Dr. Gwendolyn B. Brown
Director of Diversity
173 Ashley Avenue, BSB-123
MSC 507
Charleston, SC 29425
Phone: 843-792-4425
academicdepartments.musc.edu/dentistry/about/diversity/

MUSC OFF-CAMPUS HOUSING

Ms. Nadia Mariutto
Housing Coordinator
45 Courtenay Drive, SW-213
MSC 171
Charleston, SC 29425
Phone: 843-792-0394
academicdepartments.musc.edu/housing/index.html

INTERNATIONAL SUPPORT SERVICES

Ms. Denise Smith
Administrative Coordinator
45 Courtenay Drive
MSC 203
Charleston, SC 29425
Phone: 843-792-7083
academicdepartments.musc.edu/immigrationservices/

GENERAL INFORMATION

Medical University of South Carolina James B. Edwards College of Dental Medicine (MUSC CDM) is located in the university complex's Basic Science Building. The Dental Medicine Scientist Training Program enables selected students to earn D.M.D. and Ph.D. degrees simultaneously. Faculty—from a wide variety of backgrounds and experiences—have generated a scholarly and self-critical educational environment. Students are exposed to a broad range of research activities, with multiple opportunities to participate. Predoctoral education focuses on state-of-the-art clinical instruction, including radiology and information technology, to ensure graduates' competency in clinical dentistry. MUSC CDM also offers residency/graduate programs in Advanced Education in General Dentistry, Endodontics, Oral and Maxillofacial Surgery, Orthodontics, Pediatric Dentistry and Periodontics.

MISSION

To develop principled, skilled, compassionate oral health care practitioners and leaders, and to expand the body of knowledge about oral and related diseases.

Vision: To serve the citizens South Carolina and beyond by providing exemplary oral health care.

Type of institution: Public	Doctoral dental degree offered: D.M.D.
Year opened: 1967	Targeted predoctoral enrollment: 286
Term type: Semester	Targeted entering class size: 74
Time to degree in months: 48	Campus setting: Urban
Start month: June	Campus housing available: No

PREPARATION

Formal minimum preparation in semester/quarter hours: Semester: 120 Quarter: 180
Baccalaureate degree preferred: Yes
Number of first-year, first-time enrollees whose highest degree is:
  Baccalaureate: 71
  Master's degree and beyond: 4
Of first-year, first-time enrollees without baccalaureates, the number with:
  Equivalent of 60 undergraduate credit hours or less: 0
  Equivalent of 61–90 undergraduate credit hours: 0
  Equivalent of 91 or more undergraduate credit hours: 0

PREREQUISITE COURSE	REQUIRED	RECOMMENDED	LAB REQUIRED	CREDITS (SEMESTER/QUARTER)
BCP (biology-chemistry-physics) sciences				
Biology	✓		✓	8/12
Chemistry, general/inorganic	✓		✓	8/12
Chemistry, organic	✓		✓	8/12
Physics	✓		✓	8/12
Additional biological sciences				
Anatomy		✓		8/12
Biochemistry		✓		4/6
Cell biology		✓		4/6
Histology		✓		4/6
Immunology		✓		4/6
Microbiology		✓		4/6
Molecular biology/genetics		✓		4/6
Physiology		✓		4/6

PREPARATION (CONTINUED)

PREREQUISITE COURSE	REQUIRED	RECOMMENDED	LAB REQUIRED	CREDITS (SEMESTER/QUARTER)
Zoology		✓		8/12

Community college coursework accepted for prerequisites: Yes
Community college coursework accepted for electives: Yes
Limits on community college credit hours: Yes
Maximum number of community college credit hours: 60
Advanced placement (AP) credit accepted for prerequisites: Yes
Advanced placement (AP) credit accepted for electives: Yes
Job shadowing: Recommended
Number of hours of job shadowing required or recommended: 50

DAT

Mandatory: Yes
Latest DAT for consideration of application: 12/01/2015
Oldest DAT considered: 12/01/2010
When more than one DAT score is reported: Highest score is considered.
Canadian DAT accepted: No
Application considered before DAT scores are submitted: No

DAT: 2014 ENTERING CLASS

ENROLLEE DAT SCORES	MEAN	RANGE
Academic Average	20.0	16–24
Perceptual Ability	21.0	16–26
Total Science	NR	NR

GPA: 2014 ENTERING CLASS

ENROLLEE GPA SCORES	UNDERGRAD. MEAN	GRADUATE MEAN	UNDERGRAD. RANGE	GRADUATE RANGE
Science GPA	3.61	NR	2.77–4.00	NR
Total GPA	3.66	NR	3.02–4.00	NR

APPLICATION AND SELECTION

TIMETABLE

Earliest filing date: 06/02/2015
Latest filing date: 01/15/2016
Earliest date for acceptance offers: 12/01/2015
Maximum time in days for applicant's response to acceptance offer:
    30 days if accepted on or after December 1
    15 days if accepted on or after February 1
Requests for deferred entrance considered: No
Fee for application: Yes, submitted only when requested.
Amount of fee for application:
    In state: $95   Out of state: $95   International: $95
Fee waiver available: No

	FIRST DEPOSIT	SECOND DEPOSIT	THIRD DEPOSIT
Required to hold place	Yes	No	No
Resident amount	$485		
Nonresident amount	$485		
Deposit due	As indicated in offer letter		
Applied to tuition	No		
Refundable	No		

APPLICATION PROCESS

Participates in Associated American Dental Schools Application Service (AADSAS): Yes
Accepts direct applicants: No
Secondary or supplemental application required: Yes
Secondary or supplemental application website: http://academic departments.musc.edu/em/admissions/apply.htm
Interview is mandatory: Yes
Interview is by invitation: Yes

RESIDENCY

In-state/in-province versus out-of-state/out-of-province
Admissions process distinguishes between in-state/in-province and out-of-state/out-of-province applicants: Yes
Preference given to residents of: South Carolina
Reciprocity Admissions Agreement available for legal residents of: None
Generally and over time, percentage of your first-year enrollment that is in-state: 75%
Origin of out-of-state/out-of-province enrollees: CO-1, GA-2, ID-1, IL-1, KS-1, MD-1, MN-1, MS-1, NE-1, NJ-2, NY-2, OH-2, OR-1, RI-1, TN-2, UT-1, VA-3, WA-1

International
Applications are accepted from international (noncitizens/nonpermanent residents): Yes
Origin of international enrollees: NA

APPLICATION AND ENROLLMENT	NUMBER OF APPLICANTS	ESTIMATED NUMBER INTERVIEWED	ESTIMATED NUMBER ENROLLED
In-state or province applicants/enrollees	141	93	50
Out-of-state or province applicants/enrollees	852	109	25
International applicants/enrollees (noncitizens/nonpermanent residents)	21	3	0

DEMOGRAPHIC DESCRIPTIONS OF APPLICANTS: 2014 ENTERING CLASS

	APPLICANTS			ENROLLEES		
	M	W	Gender Unknown or Not Reported	M	W	Gender Unknown or Not Reported
American Indian or Alaska Native	1	3	0	0	1	0
Asian	75	104	0	0	8	0
Black or African American	13	27	1	1	2	0
Hispanic or Latino	31	38	0	3	0	0
Native Hawaiian or Other Pacific Islander	0	1	0	0	0	0
White	354	293	0	26	31	0
Two or more races	11	18	1	1	0	0
Race and ethnicity unknown	14	7	1	0	2	0
International	10	11	0	0	0	0

	MINIMUM	MAXIMUM	MEAN
2014 entering class enrollees by age	22	32	24

CURRICULUM

Year 1: Basic sciences and preclinical dental courses.

Year 2: Additional basic science courses and preclinical courses.

Year 3: Clinical instruction and patient treatment in all disciplines.

Year 4: Clinical instruction, patient treatment and extramural rotations; senior seminars for treatment planning, implantology and practice administration.

Student research opportunities: Yes

SPECIAL PROGRAMS AND SERVICES

DURING DENTAL SCHOOL

Academic counseling and tutoring
Internships, externships, or extramural programs
Community service opportunities
Mentoring
Personal counseling
Professional- and career-development programming
Training for those interested in academic careers

ACTIVE STUDENT ORGANIZATIONS

American Association for Dental Research National Student Research Group
American Association of Women Dentists
American Dental Education Association
American Student Dental Association
Student National Dental Association

INTERNATIONAL DENTISTS

Graduates of international dental schools considered for traditional predoctoral program: Yes
Advanced standing program offered for graduates of international dental schools: No

COMBINED AND ALTERNATE DEGREES

Ph.D.	M.S.	M.P.H.	M.D.	B.A./B.S.	Other
—	—	—	—	—	✓

Other degree: D.M.D./Ph.D.

COSTS: 2014–15 SCHOOL YEAR

	FIRST YEAR	SECOND YEAR	THIRD YEAR	FOURTH YEAR
Tuition, resident	$44,699	$32,592	$44,699	$44,699
Tuition, nonresident	$78,497	$56,892	$78,497	$78,497
Tuition, other				
Fees	$19,970	$19,620	$19,660	$19,660
Instruments, books, and supplies	$4,802	$2,155	$2,895	$5,695
Estimated living expenses	$23,352	$19,460	$23,352	$23,352
Total, resident	$92,823	$73,827	$90,606	$93,406
Total, nonresident	$126,621	$98,127	$124,404	$127,204
Total, other				

FINANCIAL AID

Internal scholarships are not available to first-year dental students.

FINANCIAL AID AWARDS TO FIRST-YEAR STUDENTS 2014–15

Total number of first-year recipients: 65
Percentage of the first-year class: 86.6%
Percentage of awards that are grants? 4.4%
Percentage of awards that are loans? 95.6%

	AVERAGE AWARDS	RANGE OF AWARDS
Residents	$88,443	$26,357–$014,774
Nonresidents	$115,774	$24,067–$133,086

For more information, please visit: academicdepartments.musc.edu/dentistry/

MEHARRY MEDICAL COLLEGE
SCHOOL OF DENTISTRY

Cherae Farmer-Dixon, D.D.S., M.S.P.H., Dean

CONTACT INFORMATION
www.mmc.edu/education/sod

1005 Dr. D.B. Todd Jr. Boulevard
Nashville, TN 37208
Phone: 615-327-6207
Fax: 615-327-6213

OFFICE OF ADMISSIONS AND RECRUITMENT

1005 Dr. D.B. Todd Jr. Boulevard
Nashville, TN 37208
Phone: 615-327-6998
Email: admissions@mmc.edu
www.mmc.edu/prospectivestudents

OFFICE OF FINANCIAL AID
Ms. Barbara Tharpe
Director of Financial Aid
1005 Dr. D.B. Todd Jr. Boulevard
Nashville, TN 37208
Phone: 615-327-6826
Email: financial aid@mmc.edu
www.mmc.edu/prospectivestudents

STUDENT AFFAIRS
Dr. Sandra Harris
Associate Dean of Academic and
Student Affairs
1005 Dr. D.B. Todd Jr. Boulevard
Nashville, TN 37208
Phone: 615-327-6076

GENERAL INFORMATION

The School of Dentistry at Meharry Medical College (Meharry SOD) is a private, nonprofit institution committed to training dentists who are devoted to improving the quality of oral health care within the nation's underserved communities. The college was founded in 1876 to educate physicians; however, ten years later, the School of Dentistry was established with other health profession disciplines—including public health, health policy and biomedical sciences—soon following. A world leader in health disparity research, Meharry offers four national research centers and Meharry SOD offers high-tech clinical and training facilities, the aim of which is to train dentists to meet the diverse academic and human challenges of today's ever-changing dental profession.

MISSION

To improve the health and health care of minority and underserved communities by offering excellent education and training programs in the health sciences.

Vision: To place special emphasis on providing opportunities to people of color and individuals from disadvantaged backgrounds regardless of race or ethnicity.

Core Values: Commitment to delivering high-quality health services and conducting research that fosters the elimination of health disparities.

Type of institution: Private
Year opened: 1886
Term type: Semester
Time to degree in months: 48
Start month: June

Doctoral dental degree offered: D.D.S.
Targeted predoctoral enrollment: 218
Targeted entering class size: 60
Campus setting: Urban
Campus housing available: Yes

PREPARATION

Formal minimum preparation in semester/quarter hours: Semester: 96   Quarter: 144
Baccalaureate degree required: Preferred prior to matriculation
Number of first-year, first-time enrollees whose highest degree is:
    Baccalaureate: 48
    Master's degree and beyond: 8
Of first-year, first-time enrollees without baccalaureates, the number with:
    Equivalent of 60 undergraduate credit hours or less: 0
    Equivalent of 61–90 undergraduate credit hours: 0
    Equivalent of 91 or more undergraduate credit hours: 4

PREREQUISITE COURSE	REQUIRED	RECOMMENDED	LAB REQUIRED	CREDITS (SEMESTER/QUARTER)
BCP (biology-chemistry-physics) sciences				
Biology	✓		✓	8/12
Chemistry, general/inorganic	✓		✓	8/12
Chemistry, organic	✓		✓	8/12
Physics	✓		✓	4/6
Additional biological sciences				
Anatomy		✓		3/5
Biochemistry	✓			3/5
Cell biology		✓		3/5
Histology		✓		3/5
Immunology		✓		3/5
Microbiology		✓		3/5
Molecular biology/genetics		✓		3/5

(Prerequisite Courses continued)

PREPARATION (CONTINUED)

PREREQUISITE COURSE	REQUIRED	RECOMMENDED	LAB REQUIRED	CREDITS (SEMESTER/QUARTER)
Physiology		✓		3/5
Zoology		✓		3/5
Other				
English composition	✓			6/9
English literature		✓		
Calculus/statistics	✓			3/5

Community college coursework accepted for prerequisites: Yes
Community college coursework accepted for electives: Yes
Limits on community college credit hours: No
Maximum number of community college credit hours: NA
Advanced placement (AP) credit accepted for prerequisites: No
Advanced placement (AP) credit accepted for electives: Yes
Comments regarding AP credit: AP credits are not accepted.
Job shadowing: Recommended
Number of hours of job shadowing required or recommended: 50
Other factors considered in admission: Yes

DAT

Mandatory: Yes
Latest DAT for consideration of application: 12/15/2015
Oldest DAT considered: 01/15/2013
When more than one DAT score is reported: Most recent score only is considered
Canadian DAT accepted: Yes
Application considered before DAT scores are submitted: No

DAT: 2013 ENTERING CLASS

ENROLLEE DAT SCORES	MEAN	RANGE
Academic Average	17.0	16–22
Perceptual Ability	17.0	13–23
Total Science	17.0	15–22

GPA: 2013 ENTERING CLASS

ENROLLEE GPA SCORES	MEAN	RANGE
Science GPA	3.10	2.50–4.00
Total GPA	3.20	2.80–4.00

APPLICATION AND SELECTION

TIMETABLE

Earliest filing date: 06/02/2015
Latest filing date: 12/15/2015
Earliest date for acceptance offers: 12/01/2015
Maximum time in days for applicant's response to acceptance offer:
    30 days if accepted on or after December 1
    15 days if accepted on or after February 1
Fee for application: Yes, supplemental application completed online
Amount of fee for application:
    In state: $65   Out of state: $65   International: $65
Fee waiver available: No

	FIRST DEPOSIT	SECOND DEPOSIT	THIRD DEPOSIT
Required to hold place	Yes		
Resident amount	$800		
Nonresident amount	$800		
Deposit due	As indicated in admission offer		
Applied to tuition	Yes		
Refundable	No		

APPLICATION PROCESS

Participates in Associated American Dental Schools Application Service (AADSAS): Yes
Accepts direct applicants: No
Secondary or supplemental application required: Yes
Secondary or supplemental application website: www.mmc.edu/prospectivestudents/admissions/sod
Interview is mandatory: Yes
Interview is by invitation: Yes

RESIDENCY

In-state/in-province versus out-of-state/out-of-province
Admissions process distinguishes between in-state/in-province and out-of-state/out-of-province applicants: No
Preference given to residents of: None
Reciprocity Admissions Agreement available for legal residents of: NR
Generally and over time, percentage of your first-year enrollment that is in-state: 15%
Origin of out-of-state/out-of-province enrollees: AL-4, AR-1, AZ-1, CA-1, FL-6, GA-9, IL-1, IN-1, LA-1, MD-1, MI-1, MN-1, MO-2, NC-5, NY-3, PA-1, TX-7, VA-2, WI-1

International
Applications are accepted from international (noncitizens/nonpermanent residents): Yes
Origin of international enrollees: Canada-2

APPLICATION AND ENROLLMENT	NUMBER OF APPLICANTS	ESTIMATED NUMBER INTERVIEWED	ESTIMATED NUMBER ENROLLED
In-state or province applicants/enrollees	92	24	9
Out-of-state or province applicants/enrollees	1,629	201	51
International applicants/enrollees (noncitizens/nonpermanent residents)	97	NR	2

DEMOGRAPHIC DESCRIPTIONS OF APPLICANTS: 2013 ENTERING CLASS

	APPLICANTS	ENROLLEES
	Total	Total
American Indian or Alaska Native	7	0
Asian	496	4
Black or African American	344	38
Hispanic or Latino	169	9
Native Hawaiian or Other Pacific Islander	0	0
White	522	7
Two or more races	56	0
Race and ethnicity unknown	30	0
International	97	2

	MINIMUM	MAXIMUM	MEAN
2013 entering class enrollees by age	21	37	24

CURRICULUM

Meharry SOD's curriculum combines both educational tradition and innovation that allow students the ability to develop the appropriate foundation of knowledge and skills that will enable them to become the best in their respective dental specialties. The educational program of the School of Dentistry is composed of a multifaceted curriculum, which includes both independent and collaborative learning, and an iterative instructional pattern that ensures a sound knowledge base in general dentistry. Instructional efforts strike a balance between cognitive/intellective preparation, practical application and the inculcation of professional ethical standards.

Year 1. Most academic effort is devoted to basic sciences.

Year 2. Preclinical courses are emphasized to prepare students for the clinical diagnosis and treatment of patients.

Years 3 and 4. The final two years are devoted to clinical instruction.

Student research opportunities: Yes

SPECIAL PROGRAMS AND SERVICES

PREDENTAL

Postbaccalaureate programs: By invitation only

DURING DENTAL SCHOOL

Academic counseling and tutoring
Community service opportunities
Internships, externships, or extramural programs
Mentoring
Personal counseling
Professional- and career-development programming
Training for those interested in academic careers

ACTIVE STUDENT ORGANIZATIONS

American Academy of Pediatric Dentistry
American Association for Dental Research National Student Research Group
American Association of Women Dentists, Student Chapter
American Dental Education Association Council of Students, Residents and Fellows
American Student Dental Association
Hispanic Student Dental Association
Student National Dental Association

INTERNATIONAL DENTISTS

Graduates of international dental schools considered for traditional predoctoral program: No
Advanced standing program offered for graduates of international dental schools: No

COMBINED AND ALTERNATE DEGREES

Ph.D.	M.S.	M.P.H.	M.D.	B.A./B.S.	Other
—	—	—	—	—	—

COSTS: 2013–14 SCHOOL YEAR

	FIRST YEAR	SECOND YEAR	THIRD YEAR	FOURTH YEAR
Tuition, resident	$42,235	$42,235	$42,235	$42,235
Tuition, nonresident	$42,235	$42,235	$42,235	$42,235
Tuition, other				
Fees	$11,824	$20,124	$10,124	$6,664
Instruments, books, and supplies	$1,500	$2,000	$2,000	$1,600
Estimated living expenses	$27,367	$24,986	$24,986	$23,754
Total, resident	$82,926	$89,345	$79,345	$74,253
Total, nonresident	$82,926	$89,345	$79,345	$74,253
Total, other				

FINANCIAL AID

For the 2013–14 year, there were 218 full-time dental students enrolled in the School of Dentistry at Meharry Medical College Cost of attendance totals ranged from $74,253 to $89,345 for the academic year. Ninety percent (90%) of the student body relied on financial assistance to help finance their health professions education. Federal direct unsubsidized loan amounts could not exceed $40,500. Federal Graduate PLUS (Grad PLUS) loans ranged up to $48,845. The average scholarship awards ranged from $500 to $43,000 depending on the scholarship fund.

Timothy L. Hottel, D.D.S., M.S., M.B.A., Dean

CONTACT INFORMATION

www.uthsc.edu/dentistry
University of Tennessee Health Science Center
875 Union Avenue
Memphis, TN 38163
Phone: 800-788-0040
Fax: 901-448-1625

OFFICE OF ADMISSIONS

Dr. J. Stansill Covington, III
Associate Dean
875 Union Avenue
Memphis, TN 38163
Phone: 901-448-6268

OFFICE OF FINANCIAL AID

Mr. Samuel Matheny
Director
910 Madison Avenue
Suite 520
Memphis, TN 38163
Phone: 901-448-5568

STUDENT AFFAIRS

Dr. J. Stansill Covington, III
Associate Dean
875 Union Avenue
Memphis, TN 38163
Phone: 901-448-6268

MINORITY AFFAIRS

Dr. Michael Alston, Director
920 Madison Avenue
Suite 420
Memphis, TN 38163
Phone: 901-448-2112

HOUSING OFFICE

(No on-campus housing is available.)

INTERNATIONAL STUDENTS

Dr. J. Stansill Covington, III
Associate Dean
875 Union Avenue
Memphis, TN 38163
Phone: 901-448-6268

GENERAL INFORMATION

The University of Tennessee Health Science Center College of Dentistry (UTHSC COD), the oldest state-assisted institution in the South, is located in Memphis (area population about one million). The college accepts 90 students per year into the program. UTHSC is the state's health sciences campus and contains educational, research and service programs in all health-related fields in an environment of integrated activities. Advanced dental education programs in General Practice Residencies (GPR), Orthodontics and Dentofacial Orthopedics, Oral and Maxillofacial Surgery, Pediatric Dentistry, Periodontics, Endodontics and Prosthodontics are offered on the Memphis campus. Programs in Oral and Maxillofacial Surgery and GPR are also offered at the hospital-based unit of the college at Knoxville. The college participates in the Southern Regional Education Board, providing for enrollment of Arkansas residents.

MISSION

To improve human oral health through education, research, clinical care and public service

Type of institution: Public	Doctoral dental degree offered: D.D.S.
Year opened: 1878	Targeted predoctoral enrollment: 366
Term type: Semester	Targeted entering class size: 94
Time to degree in months: 46	Campus setting: Urban
Start month: August	Campus housing available: No

PREPARATION

Formal minimum preparation in semester/quarter hours: Semester: 98   Quarter: 150
Baccalaureate degree preferred: Yes, but is not required.
Number of first-year, first-time enrollees whose highest degree is:
  Baccalaureate: 83
  Master's degree and beyond: 6
Of first-year, first-time enrollees without baccalaureates, the number with:
  Equivalent of 60 undergraduate credit hours or less: 0
  Equivalent of 61–90 undergraduate credit hours: 0
  Equivalent of 91 or more undergraduate credit hours: 1

PREREQUISITE COURSE	REQUIRED	RECOMMENDED	LAB REQUIRED	CREDITS (SEMESTER/QUARTER)
BCP (biology-chemistry-physics) sciences				
Biology	✓		✓	2/8 (8 semester hours)
Chemistry, general/inorganic	✓		✓	2/8 (8 semester hours)
Chemistry, organic	✓		✓	2/8 (8 semester hours)
Physics	✓		✓	2/8 (8 semester hours)
Additional biological sciences				
Anatomy		✓		1/2 (4 semester hours)
Biochemistry	✓			1/2 (3 semester hours)
Cell biology		✓		
Histology	✓			1/2 (4 semester hours)
Immunology		✓		
Microbiology	✓			1/2 (4 semester hours)
Molecular biology/genetics		✓		
Physiology		✓		
Zoology		✓		

PREPARATION (CONTINUED)

PREREQUISITE COURSE	REQUIRED	RECOMMENDED	LAB REQUIRED	CREDITS (SEMESTER/QUARTER)
Other				
English Composition	✓			2/8 (8 semester hours)

Note: Applicants must take one of the following: histology, microbiology, comparative anatomy.

Community college coursework accepted for prerequisites: Yes, but not encouraged
Community college coursework accepted for electives: Yes
Limits on community college credit hours: No
Advanced placement (AP) credit accepted for prerequisites: Yes
Advanced placement (AP) credit accepted for electives: Yes
Comments regarding AP credit: NR
Job shadowing: Required
Number of hours of job shadowing required or recommended: At least 50 under a General Dentist

DAT

Mandatory: Yes
Latest DAT for consideration of application: 09/30/2015
Oldest DAT considered: 01/01/2012
When more than one DAT score is reported: Most recent score only is considered
Canadian DAT accepted: No
Application considered before DAT scores are submitted: No

DAT: 2014 ENTERING CLASS

ENROLLEE DAT SCORES	MEAN	RANGE
Academic Average	19.3	17–24
Perceptual Ability	20.1	16–26
Total Science	18.9	16–26

GPA: 2014 ENTERING CLASS

ENROLLEE GPA SCORES	UNDERGRAD. MEAN	GRADUATE MEAN	UNDERGRAD. RANGE	GRADUATE RANGE
Science GPA	3.51	NR	2.76–4.00	NR
Total GPA	3.58	NR	2.66–4.00	NR

APPLICATION AND SELECTION

TIMETABLE

Earliest filing date: 06/02/2015
Latest filing date: 9/30/2015
Earliest date for acceptance offers: First business day of December 2015
Maximum time in days for applicant's response to acceptance offer:
 30 days if accepted on or after December 1
 15 days if accepted on or after January 1
 15 days if accepted on or after February 1
Requests for deferred entrance considered: Yes
Fee for application: Yes, submitted only when requested by the admissions committee when applicant is accepted
Amount of fee for application:
 In state: $75 Out of state: $75 International: $75
Fee waiver available: No

	FIRST DEPOSIT	SECOND DEPOSIT	THIRD DEPOSIT
Required to hold place	Yes	No	No
Resident amount	$1,000		
Nonresident amount	$1,000		
Deposit due	As indicated in admission offer		
Applied to tuition	Yes		
Refundable	No		

APPLICATION PROCESS

Participates in Associated American Dental Schools Application Service (AADSAS): Yes
Accepts direct applicants: No
Secondary or supplemental application required: No
Interview is mandatory: Yes
Interview is by invitation: Yes

RESIDENCY

In-state/in-province versus out-of-state/out-of-province
Admissions process distinguishes between in-state/in-province and out-of-state/out-of-province applicants: Yes
Preference given to residents of: Tennessee
Reciprocity Admissions Agreement available for legal residents of: Arkansas
Generally and over time, percentage of your first-year enrollment that is in-state: 52%
Origin of out-of-state/out-of-province enrollees: AL-1, AR-31, CA-1, GA-4, IL-1, IN-1, KS-1, MS-2, NY-1, TX-1

International
Applications are accepted from international (noncitizens/nonpermanent residents): No
Origin of international enrollees: NA

APPLICATION AND ENROLLMENT	NUMBER OF APPLICANTS	ESTIMATED NUMBER INTERVIEWED	ESTIMATED NUMBER ENROLLED
In-state or province applicants/enrollees	163	94	46
Out-of-state or province applicants/enrollees	1,025	150	44
International applicants/enrollees (noncitizens/nonpermanent residents)	14	0	0

DEMOGRAPHIC DESCRIPTIONS OF APPLICANTS: 2014 ENTERING CLASS

	APPLICANTS			ENROLLEES		
	M	W	Gender Unknown or Not Reported	M	W	Gender Unknown or Not Reported
American Indian or Alaska Native	1	1	0	0	0	0
Asian	130	123	5	4	8	0
Black or African American	9	32	2	2	2	0
Hispanic or Latino	32	42	0	1	0	0
Native Hawaiian or Other Pacific Islander	0	1	0	0	0	0
White	447	303	4	41	29	0
Two or more races	12	19	0	1	1	0
Race and ethnicity unknown	19	5	1	1	0	0
International	5	8	1	0	0	0

	MINIMUM	MAXIMUM	MEAN
2014 entering class enrollees by age	21	42	25

CURRICULUM

The educational philosophy of the UTHSC COD is to provide opportunities for students to learn how to think in a problem-solving manner. The principal objective of the curriculum is to graduate a general practitioner who is professional, ethical, people-oriented, knowledgeable and skillful in delivering comprehensive patient care. The basic sciences are presented in carefully planned lecture/laboratory procedures by each department. However, selected segments of material have been combined into interdepartmental team teaching programs. Students are oriented to clinical activities in the first year, and delivery of patient care begins in the second year. Comprehensive, total patient care is delivered in individual student cubicles. Basic science and clinical science faculty members use a team approach to teaching in some general areas, such as growth and development, oral diagnosis and pain control.

Student research opportunities: Yes

SPECIAL PROGRAMS AND SERVICES

PREDENTAL
DAT workshops

DURING DENTAL SCHOOL
Academic counseling and tutoring
Community service opportunities
Internships, externships, or extramural programs
Mentoring
Personal counseling
Professional- and career-development programming

ACTIVE STUDENT ORGANIZATIONS
American Academy of Pediatric Dentistry
American Association for Dental Research National Student Research Group
American Association of Women Dentists
American Dental Education Association
American Student Dental Association
Psi Omega (dental fraternity)
Student National Dental Association
Xi Psi Phi (international dental fraternity)

INTERNATIONAL DENTISTS
Graduates of international dental schools considered for traditional predoctoral program: Yes
Advanced standing program offered for graduates of international dental schools: Yes, but only if space is available
Advanced standing program description: A 3-year program awarding a dental degree to dentists trained in other countries.

COMBINED AND ALTERNATE DEGREES

Ph.D.	M.S.	M.P.H.	M.D.	B.A./B.S.	Other
✓	—	—	—	—	—

COSTS: 2014–15 SCHOOL YEAR

	FIRST YEAR	SECOND YEAR	THIRD YEAR	FOURTH YEAR
Tuition, resident	$27,900	$27,900	$27,900	$27,900
Tuition, nonresident	$66,070	$66,070	$66,070	$66,070
Tuition, other				
Fees	$3,578	$3,325	$3,325	3,325
Instruments, books, and supplies	$15,881	$12,151	$7,011	$3,061
Estimated living expenses	$21,318	$23,256	$23,256	$21,318
Total, resident	$68,677	$66,632	$61,492	$55,604
Total, nonresident	$106,847	$104,802	$99,662	$93,774
Total, other				

FINANCIAL AID

Most of the College of Dentistry's students receive financial aid from a variety of sources. The Office of Financial Aid assists students in completing the application process. This office also submits approved applicants to participating lending institutions. Available programs are subsidized Federal Stafford Loans, Federal Perkins Loans, unsubsidized Federal Stafford Loans, Loans for Disadvantaged Students (Health Resources and Services Administration [HRSA]) and Health Professions Loans (HRSA). Scholarships offered include Exceptional Financial Need Scholarship (National Health Service Corps), Financial Assistance for Disadvantaged Health Professions Students and Scholarship for Disadvantaged Students (HRSA).

For application forms and information, contact:
The University of Tennessee Health Science Center
Office of Student Financial Aid
910 Madison Avenue, Suite 520
Memphis, Tennessee 38163

or phone: 901-448-5568
or email: osfa@uthsc.edu.

For more information, please visit: http://www.uthsc.edu/finaid

TEXAS A&M UNIVERSITY
BAYLOR COLLEGE OF DENTISTRY

Lawrence E. Wolinsky, Ph.D., D.M.D., Dean

CONTACT INFORMATION
www.bcd.tamhsc.edu
3302 Gaston Avenue
Dallas, TX 75246
Phone: 214-828-8100

OFFICE OF RECRUITMENT AND ADMISSIONS
Dr. Barbara Miller
Executive Director
Phone: 214-828-8231
Email: admissions-bcd@bcd.tamhsc.edu

OFFICE OF FINANCIAL AID
Ms. Kay Egbert
Director
Phone: 214-828-8236
Email: kegbert@bcd.tamhsc.edu

STUDENT AFFAIRS
Dr. Jack Long
Associate Dean
Phone: 214-828-8240
Email: jlong@bcd.tamhsc.edu

CENTER OF EXCELLENCE IN DIVERSITY
Dr. Ernestine Lacy
**Office of Student Development and
Multicultural Affairs**
Phone: 214-828-8374
Email: eslacy@bcd.tamhsc.edu

HOUSING
Ms. Moira Allen
Director
Phone: 214-828-8210
Email: mallen@bcd.tamhsc.edu

GENERAL INFORMATION

In 1905, Texas A&M University Baylor College of Dentistry (TAMBCD)—as State Dental College—opened its doors to 40 students. With a commitment to excellence, the college evolved in 1918 to an affiliation—as Baylor University College of Dentistry—with Baylor University. The affiliation lasted until 1971. The college continued for an additional 25 years as an independent private institution. In 1996, Baylor College of Dentistry entered a new era as a public institution and member of the Texas A&M University System. On January 1, 1999, the college became one of five founding components of the Texas A&M Health Science Center.

TAMBCD is located in the Dallas metropolitan area, about one mile from the downtown business district within the Baylor University Medical Center complex.

MISSION
To improve the oral health of Texans and shape the future of dentistry by developing exemplary clinicians, educators and scientists.

Vision: To care for the needs of a diverse community, serve as a leader in health professions education and seek innovations in science, education and health care delivery.

Type of institution: Public
Year opened: 1905
Term type: Semester
Time to degree in months: 48
Start month: August

Doctoral dental degree offered: D.D.S.
Targeted predoctoral enrollment: 402
Targeted entering class size: 100
Campus setting: Urban
Campus housing available: No

PREPARATION

Formal minimum preparation in semester/quarter hours: Semester: 90   Quarter: 120
Baccalaureate degree preferred: Yes
Number of first-year, first-time enrollees whose highest degree is:
    Baccalaureate: 101
    Master's degree and beyond: 3
Of first-year, first-time enrollees without baccalaureates, the number with:
    Equivalent of 60 undergraduate credit hours or less: 0
    Equivalent of 61–90 undergraduate credit hours: 0
    Equivalent of 91 or more undergraduate credit hours: 0

PREREQUISITE COURSE	REQUIRED	RECOMMENDED	LAB REQUIRED	CREDITS (SEMESTER/QUARTER)
BCP (biology-chemistry-physics) sciences				
Biochemistry	✓			3/5
Biology	✓		✓	14/21
Chemistry, general/inorganic	✓		✓	8/12
Chemistry, organic	✓		✓	8/12
Physics	✓		✓	8/12
Additional biological sciences				
Anatomy		✓		4/6
Biochemistry 2		✓		3/5
Cell biology		✓		3/5
Histology		✓		3/5
Immunology		✓		3/5
Microbiology		✓		3/5
Molecular biology/genetics		✓		3/5

(Prerequisite Courses continued)

PREPARATION (CONTINUED)

PREREQUISITE COURSE	REQUIRED	RECOMMENDED	LAB REQUIRED	CREDITS (SEMESTER/QUARTER)
Physiology		✓		3/5
Zoology		✓		3/5
Other required courses				
English	✓			6/10
Statistics	✓			3/5

Community college coursework accepted for prerequisites: Yes
Community college coursework accepted for electives: Yes
Limits on community college credit hours: Yes
Maximum number of community college credit hours: 60
Advanced placement (AP) credit accepted for prerequisites: Yes
Advanced placement (AP) credit accepted for electives: Yes
Job shadowing: Required
Number of hours of job shadowing required or recommended: 75 minimum with a general dentist
Other factors considered in admission: Noncognitive factors are considered. Volunteer work and community service are also required.

DAT

Mandatory: Yes
Latest DAT for consideration of application: 12/01/2015
Oldest DAT considered: 01/01/2010
When more than one DAT score is reported: Most recent score is considered
Canadian DAT accepted: Yes
Application considered before DAT scores are submitted: No

DAT: 2014 ENTERING CLASS

ENROLLEE DAT SCORES	MEAN	RANGE
Academic Average	20.7	NR
Perceptual Ability	20.2	NR
Total Science	20.4	NR

GPA: 2014 ENTERING CLASS

ENROLLEE GPA SCORES	UNDERGRAD. MEAN	GRADUATE MEAN	UNDERGRAD. RANGE	GRADUATE RANGE
Science GPA	3.48	NR	NR	NR
Total GPA	3.57	NR	NR	NR

APPLICATION AND SELECTION

TIMETABLE

Earliest filing date: 05/01/2015 (Texas Medical & Dental Schools Application Service [TMDSAS])
06/02/2015 (Associated American Dental Schools Application Service [AADSAS])
Latest filing date: 09/30/2015
Earliest date for acceptance offers: 12/01/2015
Maximum time in days for applicant's response to acceptance offer:
    30 days if accepted on or after December 1
    15 days if accepted on or after February 1
Requests for deferred entrance considered: Yes

Fee for application: Yes
Amount of fee for application:
    In state: $0   Out of state: $50   International: $50
Fee waiver available: Check school website for details.

	FIRST DEPOSIT	SECOND DEPOSIT	THIRD DEPOSIT
Required to hold place	Yes	No	No
Resident amount	$200		
Nonresident amount	$200		
Deposit due	As indicated in admission offer		
Applied to tuition	Yes		
Refundable	No		

APPLICATION PROCESS

Participates in AADSAS: Yes
Participates in TMDSAS: Yes, Texas residents MUST apply through TMDSAS.
Accepts direct applicants: Yes, for non-Texas residents only
Secondary or supplemental application required: Yes
Secondary or supplemental application website: www.bcd.tamhsc.edu
Interview is mandatory: Yes
Interview is by invitation: Yes

RESIDENCY

In-state/in-province versus out-of-state/out-of-province
Admissions process distinguishes between in-state/in-province and out-of-state/out-of-province applicants: Yes
Preference given to residents of: Texas, New Mexico, Arkansas, Louisiana, Oklahoma, Utah
Reciprocity Admissions Agreement available for legal residents of: Arkansas, New Mexico
Generally and over time, percentage of your first-year enrollment that is in-state: 90%
Origin of out-of-state/out-of-province enrollees: AL-1, AR-2, CA-2, FL-1, LA-1, NM-2, OH-1

International
Applications are accepted from international (noncitizens/nonpermanent residents): Yes
Origin of international enrollees: NA

APPLICATION AND ENROLLMENT	NUMBER OF APPLICANTS	ESTIMATED NUMBER INTERVIEWED	ESTIMATED NUMBER ENROLLED
In-state or province applicants/enrollees	898	210	94
Out-of-state or province applicants/enrollees	708	30	10
International applicants/enrollees (noncitizens/nonpermanent residents)	5	0	0

DEMOGRAPHIC DESCRIPTIONS OF APPLICANTS: 2014 ENTERING CLASS

	APPLICANTS			ENROLLEES		
	M	W	Gender Unknown or Not Reported	M	W	Gender Unknown or Not Reported
American Indian or Alaska Native	12	8	0	2	0	0
Asian	242	253	0	9	9	0
Black or African American	33	54	0	8	4	0
Hispanic or Latino	70	106	0	7	13	0
Native Hawaiian or Other Pacific Islander	0	0	0	0	0	0
White	426	325	0	26	23	0
Two or more races	10	14	0	0	0	0
Race and ethnicity unknown	28	25	0	2	1	0
International	3	2	0	0	0	0

	MINIMUM	MAXIMUM	MEAN
2014 entering class enrollees by age	21	37	24

CURRICULUM

Our comprehensive clinical curriculum prepares our graduates for general practice and specialty programs, as well as academic, administrative and public service dentistry.

Year D1: Emphasis on basic science courses; introduction to clinics with rotations for observation; preclinical technique courses. The summer break after the first year allows time for an optional research and/or clinical experience.

Year D2: Emphasis on preclinical technique instruction in a simulated clinic environment optimizes the transition to the clinics; introduction to practice management and clinic computer systems; beginnings of preliminary patient treatment.

Year D3: Continuation of clinical dentistry studies and direct patient treatment within a discipline-supervised comprehensive care clinic.

Year D4: General dentistry program encompassing comprehensive patient care with advanced procedures and approximating private practice; extramural rotations and selective courses allowing for experience in specialty areas.

Courses in evidence-based dentistry, professional ethics, and cultural competency enhance the clinically focused curriculum.

Student research opportunities: Yes

SPECIAL PROGRAMS AND SERVICES

PREDENTAL

DAT workshops
Postbaccalaureate programs
Special affiliations with colleges and universities
Summer enrichment programs

DURING DENTAL SCHOOL

Academic counseling and tutoring
Community service opportunities
Internships, externships, or extramural programs
Personal counseling
Professional- and career-development programming
Training for those interested in academic careers
Transfer applicants considered if space is available

ACTIVE STUDENT ORGANIZATIONS

American Academy of Pediatric Dentistry
American Association for Dental Research National Student Research Group
American Dental Education Association
American Student Dental Association
Asian-American Dental Society
Dental fraternities and honor societies
Hispanic Student Dental Association
Muslim Student Dental Association
Student National Dental Association
Texas Association of Women Dentists

INTERNATIONAL DENTISTS

Graduates of international dental schools considered for traditional predoctoral program: No, U.S. college coursework requirements must be met.
Advanced standing program offered for graduates of international dental schools: Not at the present time

COMBINED AND ALTERNATE DEGREES					
Ph.D.	M.S.	M.P.H.	M.D.	B.A./B.S.	Other
✓	—	—	—	—	—

COSTS: 2014–15 SCHOOL YEAR

	FIRST YEAR	SECOND YEAR	THIRD YEAR	FOURTH YEAR
Tuition, resident	$14,315	$14,315	$14,315	$14,315
Tuition, nonresident	$25,115	$25,115	$25,115	$25,115
Tuition, other				
Fees	$4,407	$4,497	$3,738	$3,331
Instruments, books, and supplies	$8,632	$7,740	$6,900	$5,706
Estimated living expenses	$21,154	$25,211	$25,211	$28,386
Total, resident	$48,508	$51,763	$50,164	$51,738
Total, nonresident	$59,308	$62,563	$60,964	$62,538
Total, other				

FINANCIAL AID

FINANCIAL AID AWARDS TO FIRST-YEAR STUDENTS 2014–15

Total number of first-year recipients: 89
Percentage of the first-year class: 83%
Percentage of awards that are grants? 7%
Percentage of awards that are loans? 93%

	AVERAGE AWARDS	RANGE OF AWARDS
Residents	$42,394	$1,500–$48,508
Nonresidents	$38,177	$28,000–$54,222

For more information, please visit: https://www.bcd.tamhsc.edu

UNIVERSITY OF TEXAS HEALTH SCIENCE CENTER AT SAN ANTONIO
SCHOOL OF DENTISTRY

William W. Dodge, D.D.S., Dean

CONTACT INFORMATION

www.dental.uthscsa.edu
7703 Floyd Curl Drive
San Antonio, TX 78229
Phone: 210-567-3160
Fax: 210-567-6721

REGISTRAR'S OFFICE

7703 Floyd Curl Drive
San Antonio, TX 78229-3900
registrars@uthscsa.edu
210-567-2621

FINANCIAL AID OFFICE

Dental School Financial Aid Counselor
7703 Floyd Curl Drive
San Antonio, TX 78229
Phone: 210-567-2635
http://students.uthscsa.edu/financialaid/

DENTAL DEAN'S OFFICE

Dr. Adriana Segura
Associate Dean for Student Affairs
7703 Floyd Curl Drive
San Antonio, TX 78229
Phone: 210-567-3180

INTERNATIONAL EDUCATION

Dr. Rita Parma
Director, International Dentist Education Program
7703 Floyd Curl Drive
San Antonio, TX 78229
Phone: 210-567-1411
http://dental.uthscsa.edu/admissions/IDEP.php

GENERAL INFORMATION

Located in the heart of the South Texas Medical Center, the University of Texas Health Science Center at San Antonio School of Dentistry (UTHSCSA SOD) is one of five Health Science Center schools. A leader in research, UTHSCSA SOD also has strong clinical and didactic programs. Numerous research opportunities are available to students, and the interdisciplinary aspect of many research programs is one of the institution's strengths. Clinical training occurs in the school's clinics and at various extramural sites in San Antonio and southern Texas. UTHSCSA SOD also offers advanced education in all of the dental specialties and advanced training in general dentistry.

Situated in northwest San Antonio, UTHSCA SOD benefits from a large selection of excellent nearby housing.

MISSION

To acquire, disseminate and use knowledge—through education and research; patient care; community, faculty and staff; and infrastructure—to enhance oral health.

Type of institution: Public	Doctoral dental degree offered: D.D.S.
Year opened: 1970	Targeted predoctoral enrollment: 410
Term type: Semester	Targeted entering class size: 100
Time to degree in months: 48	Campus setting: Suburban
Start month: July	Campus housing available: No

PREPARATION

Formal minimum preparation in semester/quarter hours: Semester: 90   Quarter: 120
Baccalaureate degree preferred: Yes
Number of first-year, first-time enrollees whose highest degree is:
    Baccalaureate: 96
    Master's degree and beyond: 1
Of first-year, first-time enrollees without baccalaureates, the number with:
    Equivalent of 60 undergraduate credit hours or less: 0
    Equivalent of 61–90 undergraduate credit hours: 3
    Equivalent of 91 or more undergraduate credit hours: 4

PREREQUISITE COURSE	REQUIRED	RECOMMENDED	LAB REQUIRED	CREDITS (SEMESTER/QUARTER)
BCP (biology-chemistry-physics) sciences				
Biology	✓		✓	14/21
Chemistry, general/inorganic	✓		✓	8/12
Chemistry, organic	✓		✓	8/12
Physics	✓		✓	8/12
Additional biological sciences				
Anatomy		✓		
Biochemistry	✓			3/5
Cell biology		✓		
Histology		✓		
Immunology		✓		
Microbiology		✓		
Molecular biology/genetics		✓		

(Prerequisite Courses continued)

PREPARATION (CONTINUED)

PREREQUISITE COURSE	REQUIRED	RECOMMENDED	LAB REQUIRED	CREDITS (SEMESTER/QUARTER)
Physiology		✓		
Zoology		✓		
Other				
English	✓			6/10
Statistics	✓			3/5

Community college coursework accepted for prerequisites: Yes
Community college coursework accepted for electives: Yes
Limits on community college credit hours: No
Maximum number of community college credit hours: NA
Advanced placement (AP) credit accepted for prerequisites: No
Advanced placement (AP) credit accepted for electives: No
Comments regarding AP credit: AP credit is accepted only if the undergraduate student is awarded credit for a specific course, including department, catalog number, and title. Lump sum credit is not accepted.
Other factors considered in admission: Academic history, community service, research activities, leadership, interpersonal skills, communication skills, and knowledge of the profession

DAT

Mandatory: Yes
Latest DAT for consideration of application: 12/01/2015
Oldest DAT considered: 12/01/2010
When more than one DAT score is reported: Most recent score is considered
Canadian DAT accepted: Yes
Application considered before DAT scores are submitted: No

DAT: 2014 ENTERING CLASS

ENROLLEE DAT SCORES	MEAN	RANGE
Academic Average	20.0	17–25
Perceptual Ability	19.8	14–26
Total Science	19.7	16–26

GPA: 2014 ENTERING CLASS

ENROLLEE GPA SCORES	UNDERGRAD. MEAN	GRADUATE MEAN	UNDERGRAD. RANGE	GRADUATE RANGE
Science GPA	3.52	NR	2.69–4.0	NR
Total GPA	3.59	NR	2.73–4.0	NR

APPLICATION AND SELECTION

TIMETABLE

Earliest filing date: 05/01/2015 (Texas Medical & Dental Schools Application Service [TMDSAS])
06/02/2015 (Associated American Dental Schools Application Service [AADSAS])
Latest filing date: 10/01/2015
Earliest date for acceptance offers: 12/01/2015
Maximum time in days for applicant's response to acceptance offer:
30 days if accepted on or after December 1
15 days if accepted on or after January 1
Requests for deferred entrance considered: In exceptional circumstances only.

Fee for application: Yes, submitted only when requested.
Amount of fee for application: $140 through Texas Medical and Dental Application Service; $245 through ADEA AADSAS
Fee waiver available: No

	FIRST DEPOSIT	SECOND DEPOSIT	THIRD DEPOSIT
Required to hold place	Yes	No	No
Resident amount	$60		
Non-Resident amount	$60		
Deposit due	As indicated in admission offer		
Applied to tuition	No		
Refundable	No		

APPLICATION PROCESS

Participates in AADSAS: Yes
Participates in TMDSAS (for Texas applicants applying to Texas Dental Schools): Yes
Accepts direct applicants: No
Secondary or supplemental application required: No
Interview is mandatory: Yes
Interview is by invitation: Yes

RESIDENCY

In-state/in-province versus out-of-state/out-of-province
Admissions process distinguishes between in-state/in-province and out-of-state/out-of-province applicants: Yes
Preference given to residents of: Texas
Reciprocity Admissions Agreement available for legal residents of: None
Generally and over time, percentage of your first-year enrollment that is in-state: 92%
Origin of out-of-state/out-of-province enrollees: AR-1, OR-1, UT-2

International
Applications are accepted from international (noncitizens/nonpermanent residents): Yes
Origin of international enrollees: NA

APPLICATION AND ENROLLMENT	NUMBER OF APPLICANTS	ESTIMATED NUMBER INTERVIEWED	ESTIMATED NUMBER ENROLLED
In-state or province applicants/enrollees	883	296	103
Out-of-state or province applicants/enrollees	502	29	4
International applicants/enrollees (noncitizens/nonpermanent residents)	44	0	0

DEMOGRAPHIC DESCRIPTIONS OF APPLICANTS: 2014 ENTERING CLASS

	APPLICANTS			ENROLLEES		
	M	W	Gender Unknown or Not Reported	M	W	Gender Unknown or Not Reported
American Indian or Alaska Native	1	1	0	0	0	0
Asian	219	205	1	5	15	0
Black or African American	23	35	0	1	3	0
Hispanic or Latino	73	105	1	14	11	0
Native Hawaiian or Other Pacific Islander	1	1	0	0	0	0
White	373	273	1	28	21	0
Two or more races	14	20	0	0	0	0
Race and ethnicity unknown	23	13	2	5	1	0
International	24	20	0	0	0	0

	MINIMUM	MAXIMUM	MEAN
2014 entering class enrollees by age	21	36	24

CURRICULUM

The educational program embraces the philosophy of comprehensive care. Dental preclinical courses begin the freshman year so that a significant component of patient care may be incorporated into the sophomore year. Clinical patient care and research activities for students are emphasized in our program. An electronic curriculum support system uses a specifically configured laptop computer to access current information through integrated multimedia searches. The ability to access information in real time is an important feature of the curriculum and directly supports the school's mission of developing forward-thinking dentists capable of independent learning throughout their practicing careers.

Student research opportunities: Yes

SPECIAL PROGRAMS AND SERVICES

PREDENTAL

Special affiliations with colleges and universities in Texas: Dual Degree/Early Acceptance (3+4) Program

DURING DENTAL SCHOOL

Academic counseling and tutoring
Community service opportunities
Hispanic Center of Excellence
Internships, externships, or extramural programs
Mentoring
Personal counseling
Professional- and career-development programming
Research opportunities
Training for those interested in academic careers
Transfer applicants considered if space is available

ACTIVE STUDENT ORGANIZATIONS

American Academy of Pediatric Dentistry
American Association for Dental Research National Student Research Group
American Association of Women Dentists
American Dental Education Association
American Student Dental Association
Hispanic Student Dental Association
Student Government Association
Uniformed Services Student Dental Association

INTERNATIONAL DENTISTS

Graduates of international dental schools considered for traditional predoctoral program: Yes
Advanced standing program offered for graduates of international dental schools: Yes
Advanced standing program description: Program awarding a dental degree to International Dentists

COMBINED AND ALTERNATE DEGREES

Ph.D.	M.S.	M.P.H.	M.D.	B.A./B.S.	Other
✓	✓	✓	—	—	—

COSTS: 2014–15 SCHOOL YEAR

	FIRST YEAR	SECOND YEAR	THIRD YEAR	FOURTH YEAR
Tuition, resident	$18,150	$18,150	$17,425	$17,425
Tuition, nonresident	$28,950	$28,950	$28,225	$28,225
Tuition, other				
Fees	$4,023	$3,450	$2,895	$2,550
Instruments, books, and supplies	$10,221	$5,510	$3,650	$3,250
Estimated living expenses	$27,536	$27,536	$27,536	$27,536
Total, resident	$59,930	$54,646	$51,506	$50,761
Total, nonresident	$70,730	$65,446	$62,306	$61,561
Total, other				

FINANCIAL AID

FINANCIAL AID AWARDS TO FIRST-YEAR STUDENTS 2014–15

Total number of first-year recipients: 92
Percentage of the first-year class: 85.19%
Percentage of awards that are grants? 1.89%
Percentage of awards that are loans? 85.34%

	AVERAGE AWARDS	RANGE OF AWARDS
Residents	$46,242	$4,000–$59,377
Nonresidents	$53,1232	$2,000–$70,177

For more information, please visit: http://students.uthscsa.edu/financial-aid/2013/04/dental-school-financial-aid/

THE UNIVERSITY OF TEXAS
SCHOOL OF DENTISTRY AT HOUSTON

John A. Valenza, D.D.S., Dean

CONTACT INFORMATION

http://dentistry.uth.edu

7500 Cambridge
Suite 6350
Houston, TX 77054
Phone: 713-486-4021
Fax: 713-486-4425

ADMISSIONS

7500 Cambridge
Suite 4120
Houston, TX 77054
Phone: 713-486-4151

OFFICE OF STUDENT FINANCIAL AID

7000 Fannin Street
Suite 2220
Houston, TX 77030
Phone: 713-500-3860
www.uthouston.edu/sfs

OFFICE OF STUDENT AND ALUMNI AFFAIRS

7500 Cambridge
Suite 4120
Houston, TX 77054
Phone: 713-486-4151
www.db.uth.tmc.edu/administration/student-alumni-affairs

UNIVERSITY HOUSING

1885 El Paseo
Houston, TX 77054
Phone: 713-500-8444
http://www.uth.edu/auxiliary-enterprises/

INTERNATIONAL STUDENTS

Office of International Affairs
P. O. Box 20036
Houston, TX 77225-0036
Phone: 713-500-3176
http://www.uthouston.edu/international-affairs/

GENERAL INFORMATION

The University of Texas School of Dentistry at Houston (UTSD), located in the world-renowned Texas Medical Center, is a public professional school with a unique heritage. The first dental school in Texas, UTSD has a long, proud tradition of educating quality oral health care professionals. One of the cornerstones of excellence that contributes to the strengths of The University of Texas Health Science Center at Houston, UTSD offers an excellent clinical education in an established research and service climate. UTSD's primary focus is to educate highly competent oral health care professionals for Texas. In pursuit of excellence, the school teaches the basic and clinical sciences, along with professional and ethical standards, in an environment of collegiality. UTSD moved into its new state-of-the-art building in 2012.

MISSION

UTSD's central mission is to advance human health by providing high-quality education, patient care and research in oral health for Texas, the nation and the world.

Vision: Attract and retain high-quality, diverse faculty, staff and students; develop comprehensive, contemporary dental education programs; disseminate new knowledge through research; provide compassionate, ethical oral health care.

Core Values: Professionalism and culture are based on our commitment to the core values of excellence, integrity, respect, responsibility, innovation, collaboration and leadership.

Type of institution: Public
Year opened: 1905
Term type: Semester
Time to degree in months: 46
Start month: August

Doctoral dental degree offered: D.D.S.
Targeted predoctoral enrollment: 400
Targeted entering class size: 100
Campus setting: Urban
Campus housing available: Yes

PREPARATION

Formal minimum preparation in semester/quarter hours: Semester: 90   Quarter: 134
Baccalaureate degree preferred: Yes
Number of first-year, first-time enrollees whose highest degree is:
  Baccalaureate: 89
  Master's degree and beyond: 10
Of first-year, first-time enrollees without baccalaureates, the number with:
  Equivalent of 60 undergraduate credit hours or less: 0
  Equivalent of 61–90 undergraduate credit hours: 0
  Equivalent of 91 or more undergraduate credit hours: 1

PREREQUISITE COURSE	REQUIRED	RECOMMENDED	LAB REQUIRED	CREDITS (SEMESTER/QUARTER)
BCP (biology-chemistry-physics) sciences				
Biology	✓		✓	14/21
Chemistry, general/inorganic	✓		✓	8/12
Chemistry, organic	✓		✓	8/12
Physics	✓		✓	8/12
Additional biological sciences				
Anatomy		✓		
Biochemistry	✓			3/5
Cell biology		✓		
Histology		✓		

PREPARATION (CONTINUED)

PREREQUISITE COURSE	REQUIRED	RECOMMENDED	LAB REQUIRED	CREDITS (SEMESTER/QUARTER)
Immunology		✓		
Microbiology	✓			3/5
Molecular biology/genetics		✓		
Physiology		✓		
Zoology		✓		
Other				
English	✓			3/5
Statistics	✓			6/10

Community college coursework accepted for prerequisites: Yes
Community college coursework accepted for electives: Yes
Limits on community college credit hours: Yes
Maximum number of community college credit hours: No more than 60 credit hours recommended
Advanced placement (AP) credit accepted for prerequisites: Yes
Advanced placement (AP) credit accepted for electives: Yes
Job shadowing: Required
Other factors considered in admission: Academic history, leadership, service, communication and interpersonal skills, knowledge of profession, goals, potential for serving underrepresented or underserved populations, and integrity

DAT

Mandatory: Yes
Latest DAT for consideration of application: 12/01/2015
Oldest DAT considered: 2011
When more than one DAT score is reported: Most recent score only is considered
Canadian DAT accepted: No
Application considered before DAT scores are submitted: No

DAT: 2014 ENTERING CLASS

ENROLLEE DAT SCORES	MEAN	RANGE
Academic Average	19.4	16–26
Perceptual Ability	19.6	15–24
Total Science	19.3	16–25

GPA: 2014 ENTERING CLASS

ENROLLEE GPA SCORES	UNDERGRAD. MEAN	GRADUATE MEAN	UNDERGRAD. RANGE	GRADUATE RANGE
Science GPA	3.64	3.67	2.70–4.00	2.19–4.00
Total GPA	3.68	3.72	3.05–4.00	2.20–4.00

APPLICATION AND SELECTION

TIMETABLE

Earliest filing date: 05/01/2015 (Texas Medical & Dental Schools Application Service [TMDSAS])
06/02/2015 (Associated American Dental Schools Application Service [AADSAS])
Latest filing date: 10/01/2015
Earliest date for acceptance offers: 12/01/2015
Maximum time in days for applicant's response to acceptance offer:
30 days if accepted on or after December 1
15 days if accepted on or after February 1

Requests for deferred entrance considered: In exceptional circumstances only
Fee for application: Yes, submitted at time of application
Amount of fee for application: $140 via TMDSAS
Fee waiver available: No

	FIRST DEPOSIT	SECOND DEPOSIT	THIRD DEPOSIT
Required to hold place	No	No	No
Resident amount	NA		
Nonresident amount	NA		
Deposit due	NA		
Applied to tuition	NA		
Refundable	NA		

APPLICATION PROCESS

Participates in AADSAS: Yes
Participates in TMDSAS (for Texas applicants applying to Texas dental schools): Yes
Accepts direct applicants: No
Secondary or supplemental application required: No
Interview is mandatory: Yes
Interview is by invitation: Yes

RESIDENCY

In-state/in-province versus out-of-state/out-of-province
Admissions process distinguishes between in-state/in-province and out-of-state/out-of-province applicants: Yes
Preference given to residents of: Texas
Reciprocity Admissions Agreement available for legal residents of: None
Generally and over time, percentage of your first-year enrollment that is in-state: 99%
Origin of out-of-state/out-of-province enrollees: NA

International
Applications are accepted from international (noncitizens/nonpermanent residents): No
Origin of international enrollees: NA

APPLICATION AND ENROLLMENT	NUMBER OF APPLICANTS	ESTIMATED NUMBER INTERVIEWED	ESTIMATED NUMBER ENROLLED
In-state or province applicants/enrollees	902	280	100
Out-of-state or province applicants/enrollees	462	1	0
International applicants/enrollees (noncitizens/nonpermanent residents)	49	0	0

DEMOGRAPHIC DESCRIPTIONS OF APPLICANTS: 2014 ENTERING CLASS

	APPLICANTS			ENROLLEES		
	M	W	Gender Unknown or Not Reported	M	W	Gender Unknown or Not Reported
American Indian or Alaska Native	10	4	0	0	0	0
Asian	89	95	3	9	4	0
Black or African American	29	48	0	0	3	0
Hispanic or Latino	67	100	1	8	16	0
Native Hawaiian or Other Pacific Islander	0	0	0	0	0	0
White	291	215	1	26	29	0
Two or more races	13	10	0	0	2	0
Race and ethnicity unknown	196	190	2	3	0	0
International	30	19	0	0	0	0

	MINIMUM	MAXIMUM	MEAN
2014 entering class enrollees by age	19	46	22

CURRICULUM

The curriculum utilizes a basic lecture system that is supplemented with seminars, discussion groups, laboratories/simulation and online resources. There is intentional integration of basic science material into preclinical and clinical disciplines to ensure development of sound critical thinking and clinical skills. First exposure to clinic occurs in the first year, and responsibility for comprehensive patient care begins the fall semester of second year.

Year 1: Basic and preclinical sciences with introduction to clinical situations.

Year 2: Continuation of basic sciences and clinical courses plus definitive clinical patient treatment.

Year 3: Didactic clinical sciences and clinical care within vertically integrated practices.

Year 4: Didactic clinical sciences and delivery of comprehensive dental care in a competency-based, vertically integrated group practice and community-based environment.

Student research opportunities: Yes

SPECIAL PROGRAMS AND SERVICES

PREDENTAL

Summer Medical and Dental Education Program
Special affiliations with colleges and universities: Pipeline programs with The University of Texas at Brownsville; The University of Texas-Pan American; The University of Texas at El Paso; The University of Houston-Downtown; Prairie View A&M University; Texas A&M University-Corpus Christi; Texas A&M International University; Texas A&M University-Kingsville

DURING DENTAL SCHOOL

Academic counseling and tutoring
Community service opportunities
Internships, externships, or extramural programs
Mentoring
Personal counseling
Professional- and career-development programming
Training for those interested in academic careers
Transfer applicants considered if space is available

ACTIVE STUDENT ORGANIZATIONS

American Association for Dental Research National Student Research Group
American Association of Women Dentists
American Dental Education Association
American Student Dental Association
Asian American Student Dental Association
Christian Dental Fellowship
Dental fraternities, including Delta Sigma Delta, Alpha Omega International Dental Fraternity and Psi Omega Fraternity
Hispanic Student Dental Association
Student National Dental Association
For a list of additional student organizations, visit http://db.uth.tmc.edu/sites/utdb/files/pdfs/SchoolofDentistry2012-2014Catalog.pdf

INTERNATIONAL DENTISTS

Graduates of international dental schools considered for traditional predoctoral program: No
Advanced standing program offered for graduates of international dental schools: Yes
Advanced standing program description: Program awarding a D.D.S. degree: Advanced standing may be awarded to international graduates allowing them to enter the D.D.S. program as a DS2. Offers are extended only if space is available in the DS2 class.

COMBINED AND ALTERNATE DEGREES

Ph.D.	M.S.	M.P.H.	M.D.	B.A./B.S.	Other
—	—	—	✓	—	✓

Other degrees: M.D. degree granted through The University of Texas Health Science Center at Houston Medical School via the six-year Oral and Maxillofacial Surgery Program.

M.S.D. granted through UTSD via advanced education programs in endodontics, orthodontics, pediatric dentistry, periodontics and prosthodontics.

COSTS: 2014–15 SCHOOL YEAR

	FIRST YEAR	SECOND YEAR	THIRD YEAR	FOURTH YEAR
Tuition, resident	$19,382	$19,382	$19,382	$19,382
Tuition, nonresident	$30,974	$30,974	$30,974	$30,974
Tuition, other				
Fees	$6,115	$5,615	$6,490	$6,565
Instruments, books, and supplies	$8,931	$6,461	$641	$685
Estimated living expenses	$24,624	$24,624	$24,624	$20,520
Total, resident	$59,052	$56,082	$51,137	$47,152
Total, nonresident	$70,644	$67,674	$62,729	$58,744
Total, other				

FINANCIAL AID

FINANCIAL AID AWARDS TO FIRST-YEAR STUDENTS 2014–15

Total number of first-year recipients: 76
Percentage of the first-year class: 75%
Percentage of awards that are grants? 5%
Percentage of awards that are loans? 95%

	AVERAGE AWARDS	RANGE OF AWARDS
Residents	$45,623	$15,000–$58,964
Nonresidents	0	NA

For more information, please visit: http://www.uth.edu/sfs/

ROSEMAN UNIVERSITY OF HEALTH SCIENCES
COLLEGE OF DENTAL MEDICINE – SOUTH JORDAN, UTAH

Frank W. Licari, D.D.S., M.P.H., M.B.A., Dean

CONTACT INFORMATION

www.roseman.edu

10920 South River Front Parkway
South Jordan, UT 84095
Phone: 801-878-1405
Fax: 801-878-1320

OFFICE OF ADMISSIONS AND STUDENT SERVICES

Dr. William Harman
Associate Dean for Admissions and
Student Services

Ms. Rebecca Haviland
Admissions Coordinator
10894 South River Front Parkway
South Jordan, UT 84095
Phone: 801-878-1405
Fax: 801-878-1320
Email: wharman@roseman.edu
        rhaviland@roseman.edu

FINANCIAL AID

Ms. Francisca Aquino
Assistant Director of Financial Aid
10920 South River Front Parkway
South Jordan, UT 84095
Phone: 801-878-1031
Fax: 801-254-7191
Email: faquino@roseman.edu

ACADEMIC AFFAIRS/MINORITY AFFAIRS/DIVERSITY

Dr. William Carroll
Associate Dean for Academic Affairs
10894 South River Front Parkway
South Jordan, UT 84095
Phone: 801-878-1410
Fax: 801-878-1305
Email: wcarroll@roseman.edu

GENERAL INFORMATION

The Roseman University of Health Sciences prepares students and residents to become competent, caring, ethical health care professionals and lifelong learners dedicated to providing exceptional service. The College of Dental Medicine's D.M.D. program is located on the South Jordan, Utah campus. To explore Roseman's unique educational model, visit http://www.roseman.edu/learn-about-us/the-roseman-difference/educational-philosophy.

Roseman's College of Dental Medicine (CODM) encourages students, faculty and staff to develop one another as lifelong colleagues during the educational program and throughout their professional careers. Each student, faculty and staff also agrees to abide by the honor code: I will not lie, cheat, steal, disrespect others nor tolerate among us anyone who does. To learn specific information about the D.M.D. program, go to http://www.roseman.edu/explore-our-colleges/college-of-dental-medicine/doctor-of-dental-medicine-dmd/.

MISSION

To transform health care education by providing individuals the freedom to learn and grow in a collaborative, noncompetitive and supportive environment that fosters success.

Vision: To be universally recognized as an innovative, transforming force in health care education and as a vibrant, stimulating place to work and learn.

Core Values: Subscribing to the foundational, cultural and behavioral norms—professionalism, integrity, diversity, accountability, collegiality, social responsibility and ethical behavior—of all best-in-class institutions of higher learning.

Type of institution: Private, nonprofit	Doctoral dental degree offered: D.M.D.
Year D.M.D. program opened: 2011	Targeted predoctoral enrollment: 306
Term type: Academic Year	Targeted entering class size: 82
Time to degree in months: 45	Campus setting: Suburban
Start month: August	Campus housing available: No

PREPARATION

Formal minimum preparation in semester/quarter hours: Semester: 60   Quarter: 90
Baccalaureate degree preferred: Yes
Number of first-year, first-time enrollees whose highest degree is:
    Baccalaureate: 67
    Master's degree and beyond: 11
Of first-year, first-time enrollees without baccalaureates, the number with:
    Equivalent of 60 undergraduate credit hours or less: 0
    Equivalent of 61–90 undergraduate credit hours: 0
    Equivalent of 91 or more undergraduate credit hours: 4

PREREQUISITE COURSE	REQUIRED	RECOMMENDED	LAB REQUIRED	CREDITS (SEMESTER/QUARTER)
BCP (biology-chemistry-physics) sciences				
Biology	✓		✓	4 semester courses
Chemistry, general/inorganic	✓		✓	2 semester courses
Chemistry, organic	✓		✓	2 semester courses
Physics	✓		✓	2 semester courses
Additional biological sciences				
Anatomy		✓		
Biochemistry	✓			1 semester course
Cell biology		✓		
Histology				

PREPARATION (CONTINUED)

PREREQUISITE COURSE	REQUIRED	RECOMMENDED	LAB REQUIRED	CREDITS (SEMESTER/QUARTER)
Immunology				
Microbiology				
Molecular biology/genetics		✓		
Physiology		✓		
Zoology				
Other				
Statistics		✓		
English, speech, communication	✓			2 semester courses

Note: Refer to www.roseman.edu for complete information on prerequisites.

Community college coursework accepted for prerequisites: Yes
Community college coursework accepted for electives: Yes
Limits on community college credit hours: No
Advanced placement (AP) credit accepted for prerequisites: Yes
Advanced placement (AP) credit accepted for electives: Yes
Comments regarding AP credit: Credit must be shown on undergraduate transcript.
Job shadowing: Recommended
Number of hours of job shadowing recommended: Sufficient to make informed career decision
Other factors considered in admission: Refer to www.roseman.edu for specific information on admissions requirements.

DAT

Mandatory: Yes
Latest DAT for consideration of application: Preference for scores submitted by December 1 of the year prior to matriculation
Oldest DAT considered: 3 years prior to date of Associated American Dental Schools Application Service (AADSAS) application
When more than one DAT score is reported: Roseman will consider the most recent score submitted.
Canadian DAT accepted: Yes
Application considered before DAT scores are submitted: No

U.S. DAT: 2014 ENTERING CLASS

ENROLLEE DAT SCORES	MEAN	RANGE
Academic Average	20.0	17–25
Perceptual Ability	21.0	17–27
Total Science	20.0	17–26

CANADIAN DAT: 2014 ENTERING CLASS

ENROLLEE DAT SCORES	MEAN	RANGE
Academic Average	19.0	18–19
Manual Dexterity	16.0	15–16
Perceptual Ability	20.0	18–21
Total Science	19.0	18–20

GPA: 2014 ENTERING CLASS

ENROLLEE GPA SCORES	UNDERGRAD. MEAN	GRADUATE MEAN	UNDERGRAD. RANGE	GRADUATE RANGE
Science GPA	3.23	3.52	2.61–4.00	2.49–4.00
Total GPA	3.32	3.64	2.67–4.00	2.97–4.00

APPLICATION AND SELECTION

TIMETABLE

Earliest filing date: 06/02/2015
Latest filing date: 12/01/2015
Earliest date for acceptance offers: 12/01/2015
Maximum time in days for applicant's response to acceptance offer: Roseman University follows the ADEA AADSAS Traffic Rules.
Requests for deferred entrance considered: Yes
Fee for application: Yes, see www.roseman.edu for information.
Fee waiver available: Considered on an individual basis with appropriate documentation from ADEA AADSAS Fee Assistance Program (FAP)

	FIRST DEPOSIT	SECOND DEPOSIT	THIRD DEPOSIT
Required to hold place	Yes	No	No
Resident amount	$1,000		
Nonresident amount	$1,000		
Deposit due	As indicated in admission letter		
Applied to tuition	100%		
Refundable	No		

APPLICATION PROCESS

Participates in AADSAS: Yes
Accepts direct applicants: No
Secondary or supplemental application required: No
Interview is mandatory: Yes
Interview is by invitation: Yes

RESIDENCY

In-state/in-province versus out-of-state/out-of-province
Admissions process distinguishes between in-state/in-province and out-of-state/out-of-province applicants: No
Preference given to residents of: None
Reciprocity Admissions Agreement available for legal residents of: NR

Generally and over time, percentage of your first-year enrollment that is in-state: Unknown

Origin of out-of-state/out-of-province enrollees: AK-2, AZ-2, CA-27, CO-1, FL-1, GA-1, IA-1, ID-4, KS-1, MN-1, MS-1, NE-1, NJ-1, OK-2, SC-1, TX-3, VA-1, WA-7

International

Applications are accepted from international (noncitizens/ nonpermanent residents): Yes

Origin of international enrollees: Canada-4

APPLICATION AND ENROLLMENT	NUMBER OF APPLICANTS	ESTIMATED NUMBER INTERVIEWED	ESTIMATED NUMBER ENROLLED
In-state or province applicants/ enrollees	151	63	20
Out-of-state or province applicants/enrollees	1,517	370	58
International applicants/enrollees (noncitizens/nonpermanent residents)	148	36	4

DEMOGRAPHIC DESCRIPTIONS OF APPLICANTS: 2014 ENTERING CLASS

	APPLICANTS			ENROLLEES		
	M	W	Gender Unknown or Not Reported	M	W	Gender Unknown or Not Reported
American Indian or Alaska Native	3	2	0	0	0	0
Asian	334	284	10	8	17	0
Black or African American	10	15	0	0	0	0
Hispanic or Latino	57	48	1	2	0	0
Native Hawaiian or Other Pacific Islander	4	1	0	0	0	0
White	581	219	3	27	19	1
Two or more races	27	17	1	0	0	0
Race and ethnicity unknown	26	16	9	1	2	1
International	88	58	2	2	2	0

	MINIMUM	MAXIMUM	MEAN
2014 entering class enrollees by age	21	36	26

CURRICULUM

Roseman University of Health Sciences is committed to the following educational strategies: mastery learning, unique classroom complex, block curriculum, outcomes-based education, active and collaborative learning, contemporary technology and clinics.

With an emphasis on student-centered, active learning, Roseman teaches using the "Block Curriculum System" rather than the traditional semester/ quarter system. The system allows students to concentrate on one or two didactic subjects at a time, enabling them to attain mastery of the content. To promote students' high achievement, the system also necessitates that faculty provide varied instructional activities that both support active learning techniques and strategies, and accommodate different learning styles.

Roseman CODM's classroom complexes have been designed to emphasize active and collaborative learning, as well as support the use of advanced technology in instructional activities. The design produces an inclusive classroom atmosphere—one that allows the instructor to engage students

directly and one in which students can see and interact with their class-mates, encouraging student involvement and participation.

Detailed information about the classroom complex design, mastery learning and the block curriculum is available at www.roseman.edu under Educational Philosophy.

Student research opportunities: Yes

SPECIAL PROGRAMS AND SERVICES

ACTIVE STUDENT ORGANIZATIONS

American Association of Women Dentists
American Dental Education Association
American Student Dental Association
Dental Student Association (Student Council)
Student Professional and Ethics Association in Dentistry

INTERNATIONAL DENTISTS

Graduates of international dental schools considered for traditional predoctoral program: Yes
Advanced standing program offered for graduates of international dental schools: No

COMBINED AND ALTERNATE DEGREES

Ph.D.	M.S.	M.P.H.	M.D.	B.A./B.S.	Other
—	—	—	—	—	—

COSTS: 2014–15 SCHOOL YEAR

	FIRST YEAR	SECOND YEAR	THIRD YEAR	FOURTH YEAR
Tuition, resident	$65,870	$65,870	$65,870	$65,870
Tuition, nonresident	$65,870	$65,870	$65,870	$65,870
Tuition, other				
Fees	$4,570	$2,170	$2,170	$2,370
Instruments, books, and supplies	$12,354	$8,983	$9,400	$8,400
Estimated living expenses	NR	NR	NR	NR
Total, resident	$82,794	$77,023	$77,440	$76,640
Total, nonresident	$82,794	$77,023	$77,440	$76,640
Total, other				

FINANCIAL AID

Roseman University participates in Title IV federal loan programs, various outside scholarship and grant programs and numerous private loan programs. We have dedicated financial aid staff to assist dental students and process financial aid awards. The Financial Aid Office is open Monday–Friday from 8 a.m. to 5 p.m. Appointments are available with a counselor to answer questions or assist with applications. General questions/inquiries can be directed to financialaid@roseman.edu.

FINANCIAL AID AWARDS TO FIRST-YEAR STUDENTS 2014–15

Total number of first-year recipients: 76	
Percentage of the first-year class: 93%	
Percentage of awards that are grants? 1%	
Percentage of awards that are loans? 99%	

	AVERAGE AWARDS	RANGE OF AWARDS
Residents and nonresidents	$92,624	$42,722–$125,788

For more information, please visit: http://www.roseman.edu/financial-aid

UNIVERSITY OF UTAH
SCHOOL OF DENTISTRY

Glen R. Hanson, Ph.D., D.D.S., Interim Dean

CONTACT INFORMATION
www.dentistry.utah.edu
530 S. Wakara Way
Salt Lake City, UT 84108
Phone: 801-581-8951
Fax: 801-585-6485

ADMISSIONS
Dr. Gary W. Lowder
Assistant Dean
530 S. Wakara Way
Salt Lake City, UT 84108
Phone: 801-581-8951
Fax: 801-585-6485
Email: dental.admissions@hsc.utah.edu

FINANCIAL AID
Ms. Julie Oyler
Director
530 S. Wakara Way
Salt Lake City, UT 84108
Phone: 801-581-8951
Fax: 801-585-6485
Email: julie.oyler@hsc.utah.edu

STUDENT LIFE
Dr. Lea E. Erickson
Associate Dean
530 S. Wakara Way
Salt Lake City, UT 84108
Phone: 801-581-8951
Fax: 801-585-6485
Email: lea.erickson@hsc.utah.edu

MINORITY AFFAIRS/DIVERSITY
Associate Vice President
Health Sciences
CNC 5th Floor
Salt Lake City, UT 84132
Phone: 801-585-0574
Fax: 801-585-3109

HOUSING
Housing and Residential Education
www.housing.utah.edu
Phone: 801-587-2002

GENERAL INFORMATION

The University of Utah School of Dentistry (U of U SOD), which will grant its first D.D.S. degree in 2017, is part of U of U Health Sciences, the Intermountain West's only academic medical center. Our new building was completed in early 2015. The Health Sciences, which comprise U of U Health Care, the schools of Medicine and Dentistry, and the colleges of Pharmacy, Nursing and Health, provides unlimited cross-professional education and collaboration opportunities. U of U ranks first in the country in spinoff companies resulting from university research and innovations, while U of U Health Care has ranked among the country's top 10 academic medical centers. U of U Health Sciences serve people in Utah, Idaho, Montana, Wyoming and portions of Nevada and Colorado.

MISSION
- To train compassionate and ethical dentists to partner with health care providers to serve our community and beyond.
- To further our understanding of the therapeutic management of oral structures/functions.

Type of institution: State	Doctoral dental degree offered: D.D.S.
Year opened: 2013	Targeted predoctoral enrollment: 80
Term type: Semester	Targeted entering class size: 30
Time to degree in months: 46	Campus setting: Urban
Start month: August	Campus housing available: Yes

PREPARATION

Formal minimum preparation in semester hours: Semester: 90
Baccalaureate degree preferred: Yes
Number of first-year, first-time enrollees whose highest degree is:
  Baccalaureate: 23
  Master's degree and beyond: 0
Of first-year, first-time enrollees without baccalaureates, the number with:
  Equivalent of 60 undergraduate credit hours or less: 0
  Equivalent of 61–90 undergraduate credit hours: 0
  Equivalent of 91 or more undergraduate credit hours: 0

PREREQUISITE COURSE	REQUIRED	RECOMMENDED	LAB REQUIRED	CREDITS (SEMESTER/QUARTER)
BCP (biology-chemistry-physics) sciences				
Biology	✓			6
Chemistry, general/inorganic	✓		✓	8
Chemistry, organic	✓		✓	6
Physics	✓			6
Additional biological sciences				
Anatomy		✓		
Biochemistry	✓			3
Cell biology		✓		
Histology		✓		
Immunology				
Microbiology	✓			3
Molecular biology/genetics		✓		
Physiology	✓			3
Zoology				

(Prerequisite Courses continued)

PREPARATION (CONTINUED)

PREREQUISITE COURSE	REQUIRED	RECOMMENDED	LAB REQUIRED	CREDITS (SEMESTER/QUARTER)
Other				
Additional biology, chemistry, and/or physics courses		✓		
English composition/technical writing	✓			6
Business		✓		
Computers		✓		
Three-dimensional art		✓		
Communications		✓		
Ethics		✓		

Community college coursework accepted for prerequisites: Yes, if the credits can be transferred to an accredited four-year institution

Community college coursework accepted for electives: Yes, if the credits can be transferred to an accredited four-year institution

Limits on community college credit hours: Yes

Maximum number of community college credit hours: 60

Advanced placement (AP) credit accepted for prerequisites: No

Advanced placement (AP) credit accepted for electives: Yes, if the credits can be applied toward a bachelor's degree

Comments regarding AP credit: It is recommended to take course work beyond introductory classes waived by AP

Job shadowing: Required

DAT

Mandatory: Yes

Latest DAT for consideration of application: 11/01/2015

Oldest DAT considered: 11/01/2012

When more than one DAT score is reported: Highest score within the past three years is considered.

Canadian DAT accepted: No

Application considered before DAT scores are submitted: No

DAT: 2014 ENTERING CLASS

ENROLLEE DAT SCORES	MEAN	RANGE
Academic Average	21.0	18–25
Perceptual Ability	21.0	17–29
Total Science	20.0	17–25

GPA: 2014 ENTERING CLASS

ENROLLEE GPA SCORES	UNDERGRAD. MEAN	GRADUATE MEAN	UNDERGRAD. RANGE	GRADUATE RANGE
Science GPA	3.71	NA	3.44–3.96	NA
Total GPA	3.79	NA	3.57–3.96	NA

APPLICATION AND SELECTION

TIMETABLE

Earliest filing date: 06/03/2015

Latest filing date: 01/01/2016

Earliest date for acceptance offers: 12/01/2015

Maximum time in days for applicant's response to acceptance offer: 30

Requests for deferred entrance considered: No

Fee for application: Yes, upon invitation

Amount of fee for application:

    In state: $75   Out of state: $75   International: NA

Fee waiver available: No

	FIRST DEPOSIT	SECOND DEPOSIT	THIRD DEPOSIT
Required to hold place	Yes	Yes	No
Resident amount	$500	$500	
Nonresident amount	$500	$500	
Deposit due	30 days	July 2015	
Applied to tuition	Yes	Yes	
Refundable	No	No	

APPLICATION PROCESS

Participates in Associated American Dental Schools Application Service (AADSAS): Yes

Accepts direct applicants: No

Secondary or supplemental application required: Yes

Secondary or supplemental application website: By invitation

Interview is mandatory: Yes

Interview is by invitation: Yes

RESIDENCY

In-state/in-province versus out-of-state/out-of-province

Admissions process distinguishes between in-state/in-province and out-of-state/out-of-province applicants: Yes

Preference given to residents of: Utah

Reciprocity Admissions Agreement available for legal residents of: NA

Generally and over time, percentage of your first-year enrollment that is in-state: 95%

Origin of out-of-state/out-of-province enrollees: MO-1, MT-1

International

Applications are accepted from international (noncitizens/nonpermanent residents): No

Origin of international enrollees: NA

APPLICATION AND ENROLLMENT	NUMBER OF APPLICANTS	ESTIMATED NUMBER INTERVIEWED	ESTIMATED NUMBER ENROLLED
In-state or province applicants/enrollees	144	45	21
Out-of-state or province applicants/enrollees	521	6	2
International applicants/enrollees (noncitizens/nonpermanent residents)	25	0	0

DEMOGRAPHIC DESCRIPTIONS OF APPLICANTS: 2014 ENTERING CLASS

	APPLICANTS			ENROLLEES		
	M	W	Gender Unknown or Not Reported	M	W	Gender Unknown or Not Reported
American Indian or Alaska Native	3	1	0	0	0	0
Asian	91	77	1	0	0	0
Black or African American	1	4	0	0	0	0
Hispanic or Latino	28	11	1	3	1	0
Native Hawaiian or Other Pacific Islander	2	1	0	0	0	0
White	315	91	1	13	5	0
Two or more races	11	6	1	0	0	0
Race and ethnicity unknown	9	6	4	1	0	0
International	16	8	1	0	0	0

	MINIMUM	MAXIMUM	MEAN
2014 entering class enrollees by age	22	35	25

CURRICULUM

U of U SOD will combine dental education innovations with time-tested methods. Professionalism and ethical conduct will be the core elements in providing quality, comprehensive dental care to our patients. The program will provide students with an excellent clinical education in our dental clinics and U of U's community clinics. The curriculum—based progressively presenting oral health topics and subjects of increasing depth and complexity—will support academic excellence in the oral health sciences through professional interaction with University Health Sciences disciplines such as medicine and pharmacy, among others. Students will actively participate in their education process. Most student education will take place in our new Oral Health Sciences Education Building, which will include lecture and seminar rooms, technique and simulation labs, and comprehensive and specialty care clinics. In addition to clinical experiences in the new building, students will participate in community and mobile clinics reaching out to Utah's underserved populations.

The school will promote research to enhance knowledge, advance oral health care and transition findings to the practice of dentistry.

SPECIAL PROGRAMS AND SERVICES

PREDENTAL
Pre-Dental Advising Office: ppa@uc.utah.edu

DURING DENTAL SCHOOL
Academic counseling and tutoring
Community service opportunities
Internships, externships, or extramural programs
Mentoring
Personal counseling
Professional- and career-development programming
Research opportunities
Training for those interested in academic careers

ACTIVE STUDENT ORGANIZATIONS
American Student Dental Association

INTERNATIONAL DENTISTS
Graduates of international dental schools considered for traditional Predoctoral program: No
Advanced standing program offered for graduates of international dental schools: No

COMBINED AND ALTERNATE DEGREES

Ph.D.	M.S.	M.P.H.	M.D.	B.A./B.S.	Other
—	—	—	—	—	—

ESTIMATED COSTS: 2014–15 SCHOOL YEAR

	FIRST YEAR	SECOND YEAR	THIRD YEAR	FOURTH YEAR
Tuition, resident	$32,883	$32,883	$32,883	$32,883
Tuition, nonresident	$63,107	$63,107	$63,107	$63,107
Tuition, other				
Fees	$952	$952	$952	$952
Instruments, books, and supplies	$11,812	$11,812	$11,812	$11,812
Estimated living expenses	$21,984	$21,984	$21,984	$21,984
Total, resident	$67,631	$67,631	$67,631	$67,631
Total, nonresident	$97,855	$97,855	$97,855	$97,855
Total, other				

FINANCIAL AID

The University of Utah has a campus-wide financial aid and scholarship office with a designated School of Dentistry counselor. The office is located in the Student Services Building, Room 105. Staff members are available to assist dental students between 8:00 a.m. and 5:00 p.m. on Monday, Wednesday, Thursday and Friday, as well as on Tuesday from noon to 5:00 p.m. Students may contact the office at 801-581-6211. All applicants are encouraged to complete the FAFSA (Free Application for Federal Student Aid) application prior to March 1.

FINANCIAL AID AWARDS TO FIRST-YEAR STUDENTS 2014–15

Total number of first-year recipients: 16
Percentage of the first-year class: 70%
Percentage of awards that are grants? 0%
Percentage of awards that are loans? 100%

	AVERAGE AWARDS	RANGE OF AWARDS
Residents	$42,874	$3,000–$52,473
Nonresidents	$81,039	$81,039

For more information, please visit: www.dentistry.utah.edu or www.financialaid.sa.utah.edu

VIRGINIA COMMONWEALTH UNIVERSITY
SCHOOL OF DENTISTRY
David C. Sarrett, D.M.D., M.S., Dean

CONTACT INFORMATION

www.dentistry.vcu.edu
520 North 12th Street
P.O. Box 980566
Richmond, VA 23298-0566
Phone: 804-828-9196

OFFICE OF ADMISSIONS
Dr. Riki Gottlieb
Director for Admissions
520 North 12th Street
P.O. Box 980566
Richmond, VA 23298
Phone: 804-828-9196
Email: rgottlieb@vcu.edu

OFFICE OF FINANCIAL AID
Ms. Karen D. Gilliam
Director for Financial Aid
P.O. Box 980566
Richmond, VA 23298-0566
Phone: 804-828-6374

STUDENT SERVICES
Dr. Michael Healy
Senior Associate Dean for Student Services
520 North 12th Street
P.O. Box 980566
Richmond, VA 23298-0566
Phone: 804-828-9953

OFFICE OF ACADEMIC AFFAIRS
Dr. Ellen Byrne
Associate Dean for Academic Affairs
520 North 12th Street
P.O. Box 980566
Richmond, VA 23298-0566
Phone: 804-828-3784
Email: bebyrne@vcu.edu

STUDENT RECRUITMENT
Dr. Susie Goolsby
Director for Recruitment
520 North 12th Street
Richmond, VA 23298-0566
Phone: 804-828-9196
Email: srgoolsby@vcu.edu

HOUSING
P.O. Box 980243
Richmond, VA 23298-0243
Phone: 804-828-1800

INTERNATIONAL STUDENTS
Dr. Riki Gottlieb
Director for Admissions
520 North 12th Street
P.O. Box 980566
Richmond, VA 23298
Phone: 804-828-9196
Email: rgottlieb@vcu.edu

GENERAL INFORMATION

Virginia Commonwealth University School of Dentistry (VCU SOD), a state-supported, urban, research dental school founded in 1893, is located in a historic district of Richmond, which has a population of 200,000, with approximately 1,000,000 residing in the metropolitan area. VCU has two major campuses that are less than three miles from each other: the Monroe Park Campus with an enrollment of more than 26,000 students and the VCU Medical Campus with 3,500 students. VCU's Medical campus, the site of a nationally ranked comprehensive academic health center, comprises the VCU Medical Center and the schools of Allied Health Professions, Dentistry, Medicine, Nursing and Pharmacy.

MISSION
- Education of highly qualified dental professionals
- Research that advances oral health, disease and effective treatment
- Service to the community
- Improved oral and general health

Vision: The school's overall higher purpose includes enhancing the quality of life through improved oral health and maintaining a commitment to Virginia residents' oral health needs.

Core Values: Excellence in teaching | Promotion of learning | Advancement of scholarship | Ethical, compassionate, evidence-based care | Lifelong learning | Professional/social responsibility | Respect

Type of institution: Public	Doctoral dental degree offered: D.D.S.
Year opened: 1893	Targeted predoctoral enrollment: 400
Term type: Semester	Targeted entering class size: 95
Time to degree in months: 44	Campus setting: Urban
Start month: August	Campus housing available: Yes

PREPARATION

Formal minimum preparation in semester/quarter hours: Semester: 90   Quarter: 120
Baccalaureate degree preferred: Yes
Number of first-year, first-time enrollees whose highest degree is:
    Baccalaureate: 81
    Master's degree and beyond: 10
Of first-year, first-time enrollees without baccalaureates, the number with:
    Equivalent of 60 undergraduate credit hours or less: 0
    Equivalent of 61–90 undergraduate credit hours: 0
    Equivalent of 91 or more undergraduate credit hours: 4

PREREQUISITE COURSE	REQUIRED	RECOMMENDED	LAB REQUIRED	CREDITS (SEMESTER/QUARTER)
BCP (biology-chemistry-physics) sciences				
Biology	✓		✓	8/12
Chemistry, general/inorganic	✓		✓	8/12
Chemistry, organic	✓		✓	8/12
Physics	✓		✓	8/12
Additional biological sciences				
Anatomy		✓		3/5
Biochemistry	✓			3/5
Cell biology		✓		3/5
Histology		✓		3/5
Immunology		✓		3/5
Microbiology		✓		3/5

PREPARATION (CONTINUED)

PREREQUISITE COURSE	REQUIRED	RECOMMENDED	LAB REQUIRED	CREDITS (SEMESTER/QUARTER)
Molecular biology/genetics		✓		3/5
Physiology		✓		3/5
Zoology		✓		3/5
Other				
Math/Statistics	✓			3/5
English	✓			3/5

Community college coursework accepted for prerequisites: Yes
Community college coursework accepted for electives: Yes
Limits on community college credit hours: Yes
Maximum number of community college credit hours: 60
Advanced placement (AP) credit accepted for prerequisites: Yes
Advanced placement (AP) credit accepted for electives: Yes
Comments regarding AP credit: Must be accepted by undergraduate institution
Job shadowing: Highly recommended
Number of hours of job shadowing required or recommended: 150 (of which at least 75 hours with a general dentist)
Other factors considered in admission: Whole file review

DAT

Mandatory: Yes
Latest DAT for consideration of application: 12/15/2015
Oldest DAT considered: 12/15/2012
When more than one DAT score is reported: Highest DAT exam is considered
Canadian DAT accepted: Yes
Application considered before DAT scores are submitted: No

DAT: 2014 ENTERING CLASS

ENROLLEE DAT SCORES	MEAN	RANGE
Academic Average	20.1	17–25
Perceptual Ability	20.1	16–26
Total Science	20.1	16–27

GPA: 2014 ENTERING CLASS

ENROLLEE GPA SCORES	UNDERGRAD. MEAN	GRADUATE MEAN	UNDERGRAD. RANGE	GRADUATE RANGE
Science GPA	3.57	3.78	2.39–4.27	3.33–4.23
Total GPA	3.62	3.78	2.76–4.21	3.33–4.21

APPLICATION AND SELECTION

TIMETABLE

Earliest filing date: 06/02/2015
Latest filing date: 11/01/2015
Earliest date for acceptance offers: 12/01/2015
Maximum time in days for applicant's response to acceptance offer:
30 days if accepted on or after December 1
15 days if accepted on or after February 1
Requests for deferred entrance considered: In exceptional circumstances only

Fee for application: Yes, submitted at same time as Associated American Dental Schools Application Service (AADSAS) application
Amount of fee for application:
In state: $80　　　Out of state: $80　　　International: $80
Fee waiver available: No

	FIRST DEPOSIT	SECOND DEPOSIT	THIRD DEPOSIT
Required to hold place	Yes	No	No
Resident amount	$800		
Nonresident amount	$800		
Deposit due	Indicated in acceptance offer		
Applied to tuition	Yes		
Refundable	No		

APPLICATION PROCESS

Participates in AADSAS: Yes
Accepts direct applicants: No
Secondary or supplemental application required: Yes, for candidates invited for interview
Secondary or supplemental application website: Please visit www. dentistry.vcu.edu
Interview is mandatory: Yes
Interview is by invitation: Yes

RESIDENCY

In-state/in-province versus out-of-state/out-of-province
Admissions process distinguishes between in-state/in-province and out-of-state/out-of-province applicants: Yes
Preference given to residents of: Virginia
Reciprocity Admissions Agreement available for legal residents of: None
Generally and over time, percentage of your first-year enrollment that is in-state: 65%
Origin of out-of-state/out-of-province enrollees: CA-1, DE-1, FL-4, GA-6, IL-2, KY-1, MD-2, MA-1, NC-3, NJ-2, NY-1, PA-1, TX-1, UT-3

International
Applications are accepted from international (noncitizens/ nonpermanent residents): Yes
Origin of international enrollees: Canada-1, Kuwait-4, Taiwan-1

APPLICATION AND ENROLLMENT	NUMBER OF APPLICANTS	ESTIMATED NUMBER INTERVIEWED	ESTIMATED NUMBER ENROLLED
In-state or province applicants/enrollees	325	124	60
Out-of-state or province applicants/enrollees	1,690	160	29
International applicants/enrollees (noncitizens/nonpermanent residents)	128	14	6

DEMOGRAPHIC DESCRIPTIONS OF APPLICANTS: 2014 ENTERING CLASS

	APPLICANTS			ENROLLEES		
	M	W	Gender Unknown or Not Reported	M	W	Gender Unknown or Not Reported
American Indian or Alaska Native	1	1	0	0	0	0
Asian	278	332	8	10	14	1
Black or African American	30	70	0	0	0	0
Hispanic or Latino	58	62	0	0	2	0
Native Hawaiian or Other Pacific Islander	1	2	0	0	0	0
White	634	421	5	33	22	1
Two or more races	24	32	0	3	0	0
Race and ethnicity unknown	27	23	9	2	1	0
International	69	55	4	4	2	0

	MINIMUM	MAXIMUM	MEAN
2014 entering class enrollees by age	21	42	24

CURRICULUM

The curriculum incorporates the basic sciences, preclinical sciences and clinical skills experiences to develop competent practitioners who are life-long learners. Students begin their preclinical-skills development as early as the first semester of their first-year curriculum, utilizing virtual-reality type simulation. A continuing skills development program progresses throughout the first and second years. Patient treatment progresses from hygiene re-care appointments in the first year into a comprehensive treatment planning appointment by the end of the second year. During the third year, students reinforce clinical skill development in each of the dental specialties and general practice clinics. Clinical rotations are included to provide students a broad experience in patient management and treatment. During the fourth year, the multidisciplinary practice group model of our clinical component provides a diverse patient population for a variety of dental treatments. Our patient-centered clinical emphasis, including rural community-based clinics and elective courses in the school's specialty clinics, promote a strong clinical experience and provides a cul-turally competent environment to our students. Our integrated preclinical and clinical curriculum educates dental professionals in critical thinking, professionalism and practice management. The hallmark of our program is clinical dentistry, while our strength is our student body.

Student research opportunities: Yes

SPECIAL PROGRAMS AND SERVICES

PREDENTAL

Dental Career Exploration Program
Postbaccalaureate programs
Summer enrichment programs: VCU Summer Academic Enrichment Program (SAEP)
VCU Scholars Academic Year High School Program

DURING DENTAL SCHOOL

Academic counseling and tutoring
Community service opportunities: Required rotations
Internships, externships, or extramural programs
Mentoring
Personal counseling
Professional- and career-development programming
Training for those interested in academic careers
Transfer applicants considered if space is available: Sophomore year

ACTIVE STUDENT ORGANIZATIONS

Academy of General Dentistry™
American Association for Dental Research National Student Research Group
American Dental Education Association
American Student Dental Association
Social Awareness and Multicultural Education
Student National Dental Association
Uniformed Services Student Dental Association

INTERNATIONAL DENTISTS

Graduates of international dental schools considered for traditional predoctoral program: Yes
Advanced standing program offered for graduates of international dental schools: Yes
Advanced standing program description: International Dentist Program (IDP) provides a limited number of internationally trained dentists an opportunity to continue their U.S. degree requirements in a 28-month D.D.S. program. Upon successful completion of this pro-gram, the IDP student will be awarded a dental degree (D.D.S.).

COMBINED AND ALTERNATE DEGREES

Ph.D.	M.S.	M.P.H.	M.D.	B.A./B.S.	Other
✓	✓	✓	—	—	—

COSTS: 2014–15 SCHOOL YEAR

	FIRST YEAR	SECOND YEAR	THIRD YEAR	FOURTH YEAR
Tuition, resident	$26,800	$26,800	$26,800	$26,800
Tuition, nonresident	$51,195	$51,195	$51,195	$51,195
Tuition, VCU International Dentist Program*			$68,361	$64,858
Fees	$13,750	$11,492	$11,292	$11,292
Instruments, books, and supplies	$9,060	$7,600	$6,793	$9,460
Estimated living expenses	$17,246	$17,246	$17,246	$15,679
Total, resident	$66,856	$63,138	$62,131	$63,231
Total, nonresident	$91,251	$87,533	$86,526	$87,626
Total, VCU International Dentist Program*			$103,692	$101,289

*Third- and fourth-year costs indicated are for international students with dental degrees from their home countries. These students are enrolled in the VCU International Dentist Program.

FINANCIAL AID

The Financial Aid Office at Virginia Commonwealth University (VCU) seeks to assist students and their families so that any qualified student who desires to pursue an education at VCU may do so without the hindrance of financial barriers. We support enrollment and retention by identifying resources and educating students so that they may make sound financial decisions.

FINANCIAL AID AWARDS TO FIRST-YEAR STUDENTS 2014–15

Total number of first-year recipients: 88

Percentage of the first-year class: 89%

Percentage of awards that are grants? 30%

Percentage of awards that are loans? 89%

	AVERAGE AWARDS	RANGE OF AWARDS
Residents	$61,472	$44,944–$78,000
Nonresidents	$73,972	$44,944–$103,000

For more information, please visit: http://www.enrollment.vcu.edu/finaid/

UNIVERSITY OF WASHINGTON
SCHOOL OF DENTISTRY

Joel H. Berg, D.D.S., M.S., Dean

GENERAL INFORMATION

The University of Washington School of Dentistry (UW SOD), an oral health care center of excellence serving Washington and the Pacific Northwest, offers an excellent education leading to a professional health care career. UW SOD is located on the university's main campus, which occupies approximately 700 acres along Portage Bay and Lake Washington. UW SOD is one of six professional schools that are components of the state-supported Warren G. Magnuson Health Sciences Center, an internationally recognized teaching, research and patient-care facility.

MISSION

Our primary mission—through educational, research and service programs—is to prepare students to be competent oral health care professionals.

Vision: Educate a progressive workforce, develop collaborations and bring advances in science to address the oral health needs of our state, the nation and the world.

Core Values: We fully embrace the social responsibility and public trust of our role as an international leader in education, research and clinical services.

Type of institution: Public	Doctoral dental degree offered: D.D.S.
Year opened: 1945	Targeted predoctoral enrollment: 252
Term type: Quarter	Targeted entering class size: 63
Time to degree in months: 40	Campus setting: Urban
Start month: July	Campus housing available: Yes

PREPARATION

Formal minimum preparation in semester/quarter hours: Semester: 120   Quarter: 180
Baccalaureate degree preferred: Yes
Number of first-year, first-time enrollees whose highest degree is:
   Baccalaureate: 60
   Master's degree and beyond: 2
Of first-year, first-time enrollees without baccalaureates, the number with:
   Equivalent of 60 undergraduate credit hours or less: 0
   Equivalent of 61–90 undergraduate credit hours: 0
   Equivalent of 91 or more undergraduate credit hours: 1

PREREQUISITE COURSE	REQUIRED	RECOMMENDED	LAB REQUIRED	CREDITS (SEMESTER/QUARTER)
BCP (biology-chemistry-physics) sciences				
Biology	✓			12/18
Chemistry, general/inorganic	✓			8/12
Chemistry, organic	✓			8/12
Physics	✓			12/18
Additional biological sciences				
Anatomy		✓		
Biochemistry	✓			8/12
Cell biology				
Histology		✓		
Immunology				
Microbiology	✓			8/12
Molecular biology/genetics				
Physiology				

CONTACT INFORMATION

www.dental.washington.edu
D322 Health Sciences Building
Box 356365
Seattle, WA 98195
Phone: 206-543-5982
Fax: 206-616-2612

STUDENT SERVICES AND ADMISSIONS

Ms. Kathleen Craig
Admissions Officer, Student Services and Admissions
D322 Health Sciences Building
Box 356365
Seattle, WA 98195-6365
Phone: 206-685-9484

Ms. Carol Brown
Director, Student Services
D322 Health Sciences Building
Box 356365
Seattle, WA 98195-6365
Phone: 206-685-2372

Dr. Susan Coldwell
Associate Dean for Student Services and Admissions
D322 Health Sciences Building
Box 356365
Seattle, WA 98195-6365
Phone: 206-685-9484

EDUCATIONAL PARTNERSHIPS AND DIVERSITY

Dr. Beatrice Gandara
Director, Educational Partnerships and Diversity
D322 Health Sciences Building
Box 356365
Seattle, WA 98195-6365
Phone: 206-616-6010

INTERNATIONAL DDS PROGRAM

Ms. Memory Brock, Program Manager
D322 Health Sciences Building
Box 356365
Seattle, WA 98195-6365
Phone: 206-685-7309

HOUSING

http://hfs.washington.edu

PREPARATION (CONTINUED)

PREREQUISITE COURSE	REQUIRED	RECOMMENDED	LAB REQUIRED	CREDITS (SEMESTER/QUARTER)
Zoology		✓		

Community college coursework accepted for prerequisites: Yes
Community college coursework accepted for electives: Yes
Limits on community college credit hours: No
Maximum number of community college credit hours: 90
Advanced placement (AP) credit accepted for prerequisites: Yes
Advanced placement (AP) credit accepted for electives: Yes
Dental shadowing or volunteer experience: Required
Number of hours of dental shadowing or volunteer experience required: Minimum 100 hours

DAT

Mandatory: Yes
DAT: Must complete by October 31 one year prior
Latest DAT for consideration of application: 10/31/2015
Oldest DAT considered: 06/01/2011
When more than one DAT score is reported: Most recent score is considered.
Canadian DAT accepted: Yes
Application considered before DAT scores are submitted: No

DAT: 2014 ENTERING CLASS

ENROLLEE DAT SCORES	MEAN	RANGE
Academic Average	20.4	17–25
Perceptual Ability	20.3	14–27
Total Science	20.4	18–29

GPA: 2014 ENTERING CLASS

ENROLLEE GPA SCORES	UNDERGRAD. MEAN	GRADUATE MEAN	UNDERGRAD. RANGE	GRADUATE RANGE
Science GPA	3.54	3.85	3.05–4.0	3.80–3.90
Total GPA	3.61	3.85	3.33–4.0	3.80–3.90

APPLICATION AND SELECTION

TIMETABLE

Earliest filing date: 06/02/2015
Latest filing date: 11/01/2015
Earliest date for acceptance offers: 12/01/2015
Maximum time in days for applicant's response to acceptance offer:
    30 days if accepted on or after December 1
    15 days if accepted on or after January 1
Requests for deferred entrance considered: No
Fee for application: Yes, submitted only when requested.
Amount of fee for application:
    In state: $100   Out of state: $100   International: NA
Fee waiver available: Yes

	FIRST DEPOSIT	SECOND DEPOSIT	THIRD DEPOSIT
Required to hold place	Yes	No	No
Resident amount	$500		
Nonresident amount	$500		
Deposit due	As indicated in admission offer		
Applied to tuition	Yes		
Refundable	No		

APPLICATION PROCESS

Participates in Associated American Dental Schools Application Service (AADSAS): Yes
Accepts direct applicants: No
Secondary or supplemental application required: Yes. Applicants are screened to receive a supplemental application.
Secondary or supplemental application website: NA
Interview is mandatory: Yes
Interview is by invitation: Yes

RESIDENCY

In-state/in-province versus out-of-state/out-of-province
Admissions process distinguishes between in-state/in-province and out-of-state/out-of-province applicants: Yes
Preference given to residents of: Washington, followed by Western Interstate Commission for Higher Education (WICHE) state residents
Reciprocity Admissions Agreement available for legal residents of: None
Generally and over time, percentage of your first-year enrollment that is in-state: 90%
Origin of out-of-state/out-of-province enrollees: AZ-6, HI-2, MI-1, MO-1, MT-2, NM-1, UT-1

International
Applications are accepted from international (noncitizens/nonpermanent residents): No
Origin of international enrollees: NA

APPLICATION AND ENROLLMENT	NUMBER OF APPLICANTS	ESTIMATED NUMBER INTERVIEWED	ESTIMATED NUMBER ENROLLED
In-state or province applicants/enrollees	254	113	49
Out-of-state or province applicants/enrollees	792	48	14
International applicants/enrollees (noncitizens/nonpermanent residents)	0	0	0

DEMOGRAPHIC DESCRIPTIONS OF APPLICANTS: 2014 ENTERING CLASS

	APPLICANTS			ENROLLEES		
	M	W	Gender Unknown or Not Reported	M	W	Gender Unknown or Not Reported
American Indian or Alaska Native	6	3	0	0	0	0
Asian	170	188	1	7	10	0
Black or African American	11	11	0	0	0	0
Hispanic or Latino	36	33	0	3	2	0
Native Hawaiian or Other Pacific Islander	2	1	0	0	0	0
White	303	209	3	23	16	0
Two or more races	21	22	0	1	1	0
Race and ethnicity unknown	15	6	5	0	0	0
International	0	0	0	0	0	0

	MINIMUM	MAXIMUM	MEAN
2014 entering class enrollees by age	21	39	25

CURRICULUM

The School of Dentistry's four-year D.D.S. curriculum provides students with opportunities to learn the fundamental principles significant to the entire body of oral health. Students (approximately 63 per class) learn the basic health sciences, attain proficiency in clinical skills, develop an understanding of professional and ethical principles, and develop reasoning and critical decision-making skills that will enable implementation of the dental knowledge base. Elective courses are offered by all departments, including opportunities in independent study, research, seminars on various topics and special clinical topics.

Year 1. Divided among lecture, laboratory and preclinical activities in the basic sciences, dental anatomy, occlusion and dental materials. There are also early clinical experiences in preventive dentistry and periodontics.

Year 2. Development of additional preclinical skills and learning how basic science principles are applied to the clinical setting.

Student research opportunities: Yes

SPECIAL PROGRAMS AND SERVICES

PREDENTAL

Summer Medical and Dental Education Program (SMDEP)
Other summer enrichment programs

DURING DENTAL SCHOOL

Academic counseling and tutoring
Community service opportunities
Mentoring

ACTIVE STUDENT ORGANIZATIONS

American Association for Dental Research National Student Research Group
American Student Dental Association
Hispanic Dental Association

INTERNATIONAL DENTISTS

Graduates of international dental schools considered for traditional predoctoral program: No
Advanced standing program offered for graduates of international dental schools: Yes (International Doctor of Dental Surgery [IDDS] program)

COMBINED AND ALTERNATE DEGREES

Ph.D.	M.S.	M.P.H.	M.D.	B.A./B.S.	Other
✓	✓	✓	—	—	✓

Other degree: D.D.S./Ph.D.

COSTS: 2014–15 SCHOOL YEAR

	FIRST YEAR	SECOND YEAR	THIRD YEAR	FOURTH YEAR
Tuition, resident	$38,565	$38,565	$49,364	$46,448
Tuition, nonresident	$59,466	$59,466	$77,990	$77,990
Tuition, other				
Fees	$1,089	$1,089	$1,412	$1,412
Instruments, books, and supplies	$10,500	$10,614	$5,436	$3,280
Estimated living expenses	$17,637	$17,637	$23,516	$23,516
Total, resident	$67,791	$67,905	$79,728	$74,656
Total, nonresident	$88,692	$88,806	$108,354	$106,198
Total, other				

FINANCIAL AID

Financial aid for students attending the University of Washington (UW) School of Dentistry is provided through loans, scholarships and grants. See the UW's Office of Student Financial Aid website at www.washington.edu/students/osfa for more information. All students who anticipate a need for financial aid must complete the Free Application for Federal Student Aid by February 28 each year.

FINANCIAL AID AWARDS TO FIRST-YEAR STUDENTS 2014–15

Total number of first-year recipients: 50
Percentage of the first-year class: 81%
Percentage of awards that are grants? 13%
Percentage of awards that are loans? 87%

	AVERAGE AWARDS	RANGE OF AWARDS
Residents	$58,995	$9,000–$79,887
Nonresidents	$78,156	$36,058–$92,952

For more information, please visit: www.washington.edu/students/osfa

WEST VIRGINIA UNIVERSITY
SCHOOL OF DENTISTRY

A. Thomas Borgia, D.D.S., Interim Dean

CONTACT INFORMATION

http://dentistry.hsc.wvu.edu
P.O. Box 9400
Morgantown, WV 26506-9400
Phone: 304-293-2521
Fax: 304-293-5829

OFFICE OF ADMISSIONS

Dr. Shelia S. Price
Associate Dean for Admissions,
Recruitment and Access
P.O. Box 9407
Morgantown, WV 26506-9407
Phone: 304-293-6646
Fax: 304-293-8561
Email: dentaladmit@hsc.wvu.edu

FINANCIAL AID

Ms. Candi Frazier
Associate Director
P.O. Box 9810
Morgantown, WV 26506-9810
Phone: 304-293-3706
http://financialaid.wvu.edu/home/hsc-office

STUDENT AND ALUMNI AFFAIRS

Dr. Robert L. Wanker
Assistant Dean
P.O. 9404
Morgantown, WV 26506-9404
Phone: 304-293-5589

HOUSING AND RESIDENTIAL EDUCATION

Ms. Trish Cendana
Director
P.O. Box 6430
Morgantown, WV 26506-6430
Phone: 304-293-4491
http://housing.wvu.edu

OFFICE OF INTERNATIONAL STUDENTS AND SCHOLARS

Mr. Michael Wilhelm
Director
P.O. Box 6411
Morgantown, WV 26506-6411
Phone: 304-293-3519
http://oiss.wvu.edu

GENERAL INFORMATION

The West Virginia University (WVU) School of Dentistry is located in Morgantown, a vibrant community of 30,000 that has garnered national recognitions, such as "number one small city." The School offers the D.D.S. program, B.S. and M.S. programs in Dental Hygiene, training in several dental specialties and a curricular option for dental students to pursue combined degrees in either Public Health or Business Administration. Enrollment is approximately 300 in the various degree programs. As part of the WVU Health Sciences Center, the School provides learning experiences with the schools of Medicine, Nursing, Pharmacy and Public Health. State-of-the-art technology includes electronic health records, digital radiography and implant planning, and dental simulation technology. Students engage in local, state, regional and global community outreach.

MISSION

Promote a diverse and dynamic learning environment that addresses the present and future oral health needs of the citizens of West Virginia and beyond.

Vision: To be a recognized leader in eliminating oral health disparities in rural West Virginia and beyond through a dynamic, evidence-based and interprofessional approach to wellness.

Core Values: Accountability | Communication | Collaboration | Excellence | Integrity | Service-mindedness

Type of institution: Public	Doctoral dental degree offered: D.D.S.
Year opened: 1957	Targeted predoctoral enrollment: 225
Term type: Semester	Targeted entering class size: 48
Time to degree in months: 45	Campus setting: Rural
Start month: August	Campus housing available: Yes

PREPARATION

Formal minimum preparation in semester/quarter hours: Semester: 90
Baccalaureate degree preferred: Yes
Number of first-year, first-time enrollees whose highest degree is:
  Baccalaureate: 50
  Master's degree and beyond: 6
Of first-year, first-time enrollees without baccalaureates, the number with:
  Equivalent of 60 undergraduate credit hours or less: 0
  Equivalent of 61–90 undergraduate credit hours: 0
  Equivalent of 91 or more undergraduate credit hours: 1

PREREQUISITE COURSE	REQUIRED	RECOMMENDED	LAB REQUIRED	CREDITS (SEMESTER/QUARTER)
BCP (biology-chemistry-physics) sciences				
Biology	✓		✓	8/12
Chemistry, general/inorganic	✓		✓	8/12
Chemistry, organic	✓		✓	8/12
Physics	✓		✓	8/12
Additional biological sciences				
Anatomy*	✓			3/5
Biochemistry	✓			3/5
Cell biology		✓		4/6
Histology		✓		4/6
Immunology		✓		4/6
Microbiology		✓		4/6

(Prerequisite Courses continued)

PREPARATION (CONTINUED)

PREREQUISITE COURSE	REQUIRED	RECOMMENDED	LAB REQUIRED	CREDITS (SEMESTER/QUARTER)
Molecular biology/genetics		✓		4/6
Physiology		✓		4/6
Zoology		✓		4/6
Other				
English composition	✓			6/10
Psychology		✓		3/5

*Comparative or human anatomy

Community college coursework accepted for prerequisites: Yes
Community college coursework accepted for electives: Yes
Limits on community college credit hours: Yes
Maximum number of community college credit hours: 64
Advanced placement (AP) credit accepted for prerequisites: No
Advanced placement (AP) credit accepted for electives: Yes
Comments regarding AP credit: AP credits accepted for English prerequisite.
Job shadowing: Required
Number of hours of job shadowing required or recommended: 50 minimum; variety of experiences recommended
Other factors considered in admission: The committee focuses on seven parameters: academic achievement; DAT scores; dental shadowing; career, life, and volunteer experiences; communication abilities; letters of recommendation; and personal interview.

DAT

Mandatory: Yes
Latest DAT for consideration of application: 11/01/2015
Oldest DAT considered: 11/01/2010
When more than one DAT score is reported: Highest overall score is considered.
Canadian DAT accepted: Yes
Application considered before DAT scores are submitted: Yes

DAT: 2014 ENTERING CLASS

ENROLLEE DAT SCORES	MEAN	RANGE
Academic Average	17.7	14–22
Perceptual Ability	18.1	13–24
Total Science	17.2	13–21

GPA: 2014 ENTERING CLASS

ENROLLEE GPA SCORES	UNDERGRAD. MEAN	GRADUATE MEAN	UNDERGRAD. RANGE	GRADUATE RANGE
Science GPA	3.45	3.71	2.58–4.00	3.00–4.00
Total GPA	3.57	3.70	2.88–4.00	3.45–4.00

APPLICATION AND SELECTION

TIMETABLE

Earliest filing date: 06/02/2015
Latest filing date: 11/01/2015
Earliest date for acceptance offers: 12/01/2015
Maximum time in days for applicant's response to acceptance offer:
    30 days if accepted on or after December 1
    15 days if accepted on or after February 1
Requests for deferred entrance considered: No
Fee for application: Yes, submitted only when requested.

Amount of fee for application:
    In state: $50   Out of state: $50   International: $50
Fee waiver available: No

	FIRST DEPOSIT	SECOND DEPOSIT	THIRD DEPOSIT
Required to hold place	Yes	No	No
Resident amount	$400		
Nonresident amount	$800		
Deposit due	As indicated in admission offer		
Applied to tuition	Yes		
Refundable	Yes		
Refundable by	May 1		

APPLICATION PROCESS

Participates in Associated American Dental Schools Application Service (AADSAS): Yes
Accepts direct applicants: No
Secondary or supplemental application required: Yes, submitted only when requested from applicants
Secondary or supplemental application website: NA
Interview is mandatory: Yes
Interview is by invitation: Yes

RESIDENCY

In-state/in-province versus out-of-state/out-of-province
Admissions process distinguishes between in-state/in-province and out-of-state/out-of-province applicants: Yes
Preference given to residents of: West Virginia
Reciprocity Admissions Agreement available for legal residents of: None
Generally and over time, percentage of your first-year enrollment that is in-state: 70%
Origin of out-of-state/out-of-province enrollees: AZ-1, CA-1, FL-1, IN-1, MD-5, NC-2, NJ-1, NY-1, OH-2, OK-1, PA-5, TN-1, TX-1, UT-1, VA-4

International
Applications are accepted from international (noncitizens/nonpermanent residents): Yes
Origin of international enrollees: Canada-1, Kuwait-2

APPLICATION AND ENROLLMENT	NUMBER OF APPLICANTS	ESTIMATED NUMBER INTERVIEWED	ESTIMATED NUMBER ENROLLED
In-state or province applicants/enrollees	49	48	26
Out-of-state or province applicants/enrollees	988	95	28
International applicants/enrollees (noncitizens/nonpermanent residents)	108	11	3

DEMOGRAPHIC DESCRIPTIONS OF APPLICANTS: 2014 ENTERING CLASS

	APPLICANTS			ENROLLEES		
	M	W	Gender Unknown or Not Reported	M	W	Gender Unknown or Not Reported
American Indian or Alaska Native	1	1	0	0	0	0
Asian	128	142	1	4	6	0
Black or African American	14	22	0	1	0	0
Hispanic or Latino	18	32	0	1	1	0
Native Hawaiian or Other Pacific Islander	1	1	0	0	0	0
White	365	246	2	18	21	0
Two or more races	13	15	0	0	1	0
Race and ethnicity unknown	16	12	3	0	1	0
International	63	45	4	3	0	0

	MINIMUM	MAXIMUM	MEAN
2014 entering class enrollees by age	20	39	24

CURRICULUM

WVU SOD recognizes its obligation to produce professionals capable of meeting the oral health needs of the public and providing leadership for the dental profession. The school offers a four-year program leading to the D.D.S. and provides students with a dynamic learning environment in which to develop the technical competence, intellectual capacity and professional responsibility necessary to meet the oral health needs of a globally diverse society in a state of constant transformation. The predoctoral curriculum comprises eight semesters and three summer sessions. Students are enrolled in courses designed primarily to prepare them for the general practice of dentistry. Student progress is monitored regularly by the Academic and Professional Standards Committee and a team leader program, which exists to ensure students have varied and appropriate learning experiences to achieve competency and to provide comprehensive health care to a family of patients.

Training is provided in a humanistic learning environment with state-of-the art technology, including electronic health records, digital radiography, digital implant planning and dental simulation technology. Our students actively engage in outreach to local, state, regional and global communities. Dynamic educational, service and research experiences help students become clinically competent and culturally aware oral health professionals.

Student research opportunities: Yes

SPECIAL PROGRAMS AND SERVICES

PREDENTAL

Special affiliations with colleges and universities: Shepherd University – Dental Early Admission Program; Slippery Rock University of Pennsylvania – Dental Early Admission Program; West Liberty University – Dental Early Admission Program
Summer enrichment programs

DURING DENTAL SCHOOL

Academic counseling and tutoring
Community service opportunities
Mentoring
Personal counseling
Professional- and career-development programming
Training for those interested in academic careers
Transfer applicants considered if space is available

ACTIVE STUDENT ORGANIZATIONS

American Association for Dental Research National Student Research Group
American Dental Education Association
American Student Dental Association
Delta Sigma Delta International Fraternity

INTERNATIONAL DENTISTS

Graduates of international dental schools considered for traditional predoctoral program: Yes
Advanced standing program offered for graduates of international dental schools: No
Advanced standing program description: NA

COMBINED AND ALTERNATE DEGREES

Ph.D.	M.S.	M.P.H.	M.D.	B.A./B.S.	Other
—	—	✓	—	—	✓

Other degree: A dual master's degree in business administration degree is also available.

COSTS: 2014–15 SCHOOL YEAR

	FIRST YEAR	SECOND YEAR	THIRD YEAR	FOURTH YEAR
Tuition, resident	$26,217	$26,217	$26,217	$17,478
Tuition, nonresident	$65,475	$65,475	$65,475	$43,650
Tuition, other				
Fees	$1,863	$1,863	$1,863	$1,242
Instruments, books, and supplies	$15,354	$8,005	$5,830	$6,800
Estimated living expenses	$14,582	$14,582	$14,582	$11,412
Total, resident	$58,016	$50,667	$48,492	$36,932
Total, nonresident	$97,274	$89,925	$87,750	$63,104
Total, other				

FINANCIAL AID

To apply for financial aid at West Virginia University (WVU) School of Dentistry, complete the Free Application for Federal Student Aid (FAFSA) online with the federal processor at www.fafsa.gov. WVU's school code is 003827. Although not required, including parent information on the FAFSA is recommended to be considered for all available aid programs. Students should apply by March 1 for maximum consideration. When WVU Financial Aid Office receives the results from the federal processor, eligibility is determined and award notifications are sent to students. Visit the WVU Financial Aid Office website for more information on the application process, eligibility requirements, types of aid, etc. http://financial.wvu.edu/

FINANCIAL AID AWARDS TO FIRST-YEAR STUDENTS 2014–15

Total number of first-year recipients: 53
Percentage of the first-year class: 90%
Percentage of awards that are grants? 6%
Percentage of awards that are loans? 94%

	AVERAGE AWARDS	RANGE OF AWARDS
Residents	$60,149	$25,428–$60,149
Nonresidents	$99,407	$47,167–$118,761

For more information, please visit: http://financialaid.wvu.edu/

MARQUETTE UNIVERSITY
SCHOOL OF DENTISTRY

William K. Lobb, D.D.S., M.S., M.P.H., Dean

GENERAL INFORMATION

The Marquette University School of Dentistry (Marquette SOD) is an independent, coeducational institution of professional training founded in 1907 when the Milwaukee Medical College affiliated with Marquette College to become Marquette University. By August 2014, Marquette SOD had graduated almost 9,300 dentists. The school is located near the business and cultural center of Milwaukee, Wisconsin, a city with a population of approximately 600,000. The campus includes 54 buildings and 90 acres, forming an attractive, self-contained campus in the heart of a major urban center.

MISSION

Marquette SOD is committed to excellence in education, scholarship and the provision of high-quality oral health care.

Core Values: Following Marquette University values, the school recruits and educates a diverse student body, fosters personal and professional excellence, and promotes leadership in service to others.

Type of institution: Private and state-related	Doctoral dental degree offered: D.D.S.
Year opened: 1894	Targeted predoctoral enrollment: 360
Term type: Semester	Targeted entering class size: 100
Time to degree in months: 45	Campus setting: Urban
Start month: August	Campus housing available: No

PREPARATION

Formal minimum preparation in semester/quarter hours: Semester: 90   Quarter: 120
Baccalaureate degree preferred: Yes
Number of first-year, first-time enrollees whose highest degree:
    Baccalaureate: 77
    Master's degree and beyond: 5
Of first-year, first-time enrollees without baccalaureates, the number with:
    Equivalent of 60 undergraduate credit hours or less: 0
    Equivalent of 61–90 undergraduate credit hours: 0
    Equivalent of 91 or more undergraduate credit hours: 18

PREREQUISITE COURSE	REQUIRED	RECOMMENDED	LAB REQUIRED	CREDITS (SEMESTER/QUARTER)
BCP (biology-chemistry-physics) sciences				
Biology	✓		✓	8/12
Chemistry, general/inorganic	✓		✓	8/12
Chemistry, organic	✓		✓	8/12
Physics	✓		✓	8/12
Additional biological sciences				
Anatomy		✓		
Biochemistry	✓			3/5
Cell biology		✓		
Histology		✓		
Immunology		✓		
Microbiology		✓		
Molecular biology/genetics		✓		
Physiology		✓		
Zoology		✓		

(Prerequisite Courses continued)

CONTACT INFORMATION

www.marquette.edu/dentistry
P.O. Box 1881
Milwaukee, WI 53201
Phone: 414-288-7485
Fax: 414-288-3586

OFFICE OF ADMISSIONS

Mr. Brian T. Trecek
Director of Admissions
P.O. Box 1881
Milwaukee, WI 53201
Phone: 800-445-5385

OFFICE OF FINANCIAL AID

Ms. Linda Gleason
Director of Student Services
P.O. Box 1881
Milwaukee, WI 53201
Phone: 414-288-5408

STUDENT SERVICES

Ms. Linda Gleason
Director of Student Services
P.O. Box 1881
Milwaukee, WI 53201
Phone: 414-288-5408

OFFICE OF DIVERSITY

Ms. Yvonne Roland
Director of Diversity
P.O. Box 1881
Milwaukee, WI 53201
Phone: 414-288-1533

UNIVERSITY APARTMENTS AND OFF-CAMPUS STUDENT SERVICES

1500 West Wells Street
Milwaukee, WI 53233
Phone: 414-288-7281
www.marquette.edu

OFFICE OF INTERNATIONAL EDUCATION

P.O. Box 1881
Milwaukee, WI 53201
Phone: 414-288-7289

PREPARATION (CONTINUED)

PREREQUISITE COURSE	REQUIRED	RECOMMENDED	LAB REQUIRED	CREDITS (SEMESTER/QUARTER)
Other				
English	✓			6/9

Community college coursework accepted for prerequisites: Yes, but prerequisites from four-year college preferred

Community college coursework accepted for electives: Yes

Limits on community college credit hours: Yes

Maximum number of community college credit hours: 60

Advanced placement (AP) credit accepted for prerequisites: English only

Advanced placement (AP) credit accepted for electives: Yes

Comments regarding AP credit: The amount of AP credit accepted is subject to change at the discretion of the Admissions Committee.

Job shadowing: Recommended

Other factors considered in admission: Trend of performance, rigor of university coursework and quality of undergraduate institution attended

DAT

Mandatory: Yes

Latest DAT for consideration of application: 01/01/2016

Oldest DAT considered: 01/01/2013

When more than one DAT score is reported: Most recent score only is considered

Canadian DAT accepted: Yes

Application considered before DAT scores are submitted: No

DAT: 2014 ENTERING CLASS

ENROLLEE DAT SCORES	MEAN	RANGE
Academic Average	19.8	16–26
Perceptual Ability	19.8	16–25
Total Science	19.4	16–26

GPA: 2014 ENTERING CLASS

ENROLLEE GPA SCORES	UNDERGRAD. MEAN	GRADUATE MEAN	UNDERGRAD. RANGE	GRADUATE RANGE
Science GPA	3.58	3.49	2.72–4.00	3.23–3.78
Total GPA	3.65	3.58	2.91–4.00	3.24–3.93

APPLICATION AND SELECTION

TIMETABLE

Earliest filing date: 06/02/2015

Latest filing date: 01/01/2016

Earliest date for acceptance offers: 12/01/2015

Maximum time in days for applicant's response to acceptance offer:
30 days if accepted on or after December 1
15 days if accepted on or after February 1

Requests for deferred entrance considered: In exceptional circumstances only

Fee for application: Yes

Amount of fee for application:
In state: $45   Out of state: $45   International: $45

Fee waiver available: Yes, on case-by-case basis

	FIRST DEPOSIT	SECOND DEPOSIT	THIRD DEPOSIT
Required to hold place	Yes	No	No
Resident amount	$1,000		
Nonresident amount	$1,000		
Deposit due	As indicated in admission offer		
Applied to tuition	Yes		
Refundable	No		

APPLICATION PROCESS

Participates in AADSAS: Yes

Accepts direct applicants: No

Secondary or supplemental application required: No

Interview is mandatory: Yes

Interview is by invitation: Yes

RESIDENCY

In-state/in-province versus out-of-state/out-of-province

Admissions process distinguishes between in-state/in-province and out-of-state/out-of-province applicants: Yes

Preference given to residents of: None

Reciprocity Admissions Agreement available for legal residents of: None

Generally and over time, percentage of your first-year enrollment that is in-state: 50%

Origin of out-of-state/out-of-province enrollees: CA-2, FL-3, IL-28, MI-5, MN-5, ND-1, NE-1, TX-1, UT-1, WA-2

International

Applications are accepted from international (noncitizens/nonpermanent residents): Yes

Origin of international enrollees: Canada-1

APPLICATION AND ENROLLMENT	NUMBER OF APPLICANTS	ESTIMATED NUMBER INTERVIEWED	ESTIMATED NUMBER ENROLLED
In-state or province applicants/enrollees	187	112	50
Out-of-state or province applicants/enrollees	2,063	220	49
International applicants/enrollees (noncitizens/nonpermanent residents)	146	4	1

DEMOGRAPHIC DESCRIPTIONS OF APPLICANTS: 2014 ENTERING CLASS

	APPLICANTS			ENROLLEES		
	M	W	Gender Unknown or Not Reported	M	W	Gender Unknown or Not Reported
American Indian or Alaska Native	2	3	0	0	0	0
Asian	260	269	9	5	8	0
Black or African American	31	40	1	3	1	0
Hispanic or Latino	66	78	1	3	4	0
Native Hawaiian or Other Pacific Islander	4	2	0	0	0	0
White	810	540	8	34	37	0
Two or more races	25	28	1	2	1	0
Race and ethnicity unknown	36	30	6	1	0	0
International	76	68	2	1	0	0

	MINIMUM	MAXIMUM	MEAN
2014 entering class enrollees by age	20	32	23

CURRICULUM

Marquette University School of Dentistry's competency-based dental curriculum develops the skills and knowledge students need to successfully enter their profession. The curriculum, which also impresses on students an understanding of the responsibility of delivering oral health care in an ethical manner, embraces a patient-centered, comprehensive care model. This model emphasizes active student learning, a mentoring/modeling role for faculty and a clinical environment that closely matches the practice of dentistry in the community. To support this educational model, faculty continuously develop their skills as scholars and educators, leading to recognition as innovators in educational design and instruction.

Student research opportunities: Yes

SPECIAL PROGRAMS AND SERVICES

PREDENTAL
DAT workshops
Other summer enrichment programs
Special affiliations with colleges and universities: Marquette University

DURING DENTAL SCHOOL
Academic counseling and tutoring
Community service opportunities
Internships, externships, or extramural programs
Mentoring
Personal counseling
Professional- and career-development programming
Transfer applicants considered if space is available

ACTIVE STUDENT ORGANIZATIONS
American Association for Dental Research National Student Research Group
American Student Dental Association
Hispanic Dental Association
Student National Dental Association

INTERNATIONAL DENTISTS
Graduates of international dental schools considered for traditional predoctoral program: No
Advanced standing program offered for graduates of international dental schools: Yes
Advanced standing program description: Program based on a space-available basis awarding a dental degree

COMBINED AND ALTERNATE DEGREES

Ph.D.	M.S.	M.P.H.	M.D.	B.A./B.S.	Other
—	—	—	—	✓	—

COSTS: 2014–15 SCHOOL YEAR

	FIRST YEAR	SECOND YEAR	THIRD YEAR	FOURTH YEAR
Tuition, resident	$45,560	$45,560	$45,560	$45,560
Tuition, nonresident	$54,220	$54,220	$54,220	$54,220
Tuition, other				
Fees	NA	NA	NA	NA
Instruments, books, and supplies	$12,480	$6,070	$3,450	$650
Estimated living expenses	$28,288	$28,288	$28,288	$19,270
Total, resident	$86,328	$79,918	$77,298	$65,480
Total, nonresident	$94,988	$88,578	$85,958	$74,140
Total, other				

FINANCIAL AID: 2014 ENTERING CLASS ESTIMATES

FINANCIAL AID AWARDS TO FIRST-YEAR STUDENTS 2014–15

Total number of first-year recipients: 89
Percentage of the first-year class: 89%
Percentage of awards that are grants? 20%
Percentage of awards that are loans? 84%

	AVERAGE AWARDS	RANGE OF AWARDS
Residents	$64,682	$2,100–$86,326
Nonresidents	$66,678	$2,500–$94,986

For more information, please visit: http://www.marquette.edu/dentistry/admissions/FinancialAid.shtml

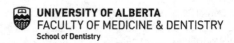

UNIVERSITY OF ALBERTA
FACULTY OF MEDICINE & DENTISTRY
School of Dentistry

UNIVERSITY OF ALBERTA
SCHOOL OF DENTISTRY

Paul W. Major, D.D.S., M.Sc., Chair

The University of Alberta, Canada's second-largest university, is publicly supported, nondenominational and coeducational. The university has developed an international reputation in many fields and excels in medical research and other areas. Faculty members are actively involved in basic, clinical and educational research, as well as in maintaining their personal patient skills. Their research projects often involve students. The School of Dentistry (UAlberta SOD) provides many facilities, such as a complete dental laboratory, instrument sterilization on the premises and computer systems. The proximity of the University of Alberta Hospital affords easy access to varied clinical instruction, and a rotation at the Youville Hospital provides experience with geriatric patients. A rotation to northern Alberta offers senior students extensive experience in operating a practice in an underprivileged area.

MISSION

To prepare physicians, dentists and other health care providers to deliver the highest quality of health services to the people of Alberta and beyond.

Vision: To advance knowledge and skills through fundamental, clinical and applied research.

Core Values: Dedication to the improvement of health through excellence and leadership in health care, medical education and medical research.

Type of institution: Public	Doctoral dental degree offered: D.D.S.
Year opened: 1917	Targeted predoctoral enrollment: 138
Term type: Semester	Targeted entering class size: 32
Time to degree in months: 48	Campus setting: Urban
Start month: August	Campus housing available: Yes

CONTACT INFORMATION

www.dentistry.ualberta.ca
Phone: 780-492-3312
Fax: 780-492-7536

ADMISSIONS

5th floor, Edmonton Clinic Health Academy
11405 - 87 Ave NW
Edmonton, AB T6G 1C9
Phone: 780-492-1319

SCHOLARSHIPS AND AWARDS

120 Admin Building
Edmonton, AB T6G 2M7
Phone: 780-492-3221

STUDENT AFFAIRS

Dr. Steve Patterson
Phone: 780-492-7383

INDIGENOUS HEALTH INITIATIVES PROGRAM

Mr. Kenton Boutillier
Administrator
2-115 Edmonton Clinic Health Academy
Edmonton, AB T6G 1C9
Phone: 780-492-9526

RESIDENCE AND OTHER HOUSING

44 Lister Hall
Edmonton, AB T6G 2N8
Phone: 780-492-4281

INTERNATIONAL ADMISSIONS

Phone: 780-492-1100

PREPARATION

Formal minimum preparation in semester/quarter hours: Semester: 60   Quarter: 90
Baccalaureate degree preferred: No
Number of first-year, first-time enrollees whose highest degree is:
   Baccalaureate: 12
   Master's degree and beyond: 0
Of first-year, first-time enrollees without baccalaureates, the number with:
   Equivalent of 60 undergraduate credit hours or less: 9
   Equivalent of 61–90 undergraduate credit hours: 4
   Equivalent of 91 or more undergraduate credit hours: 19

PREREQUISITE COURSE	REQUIRED	RECOMMENDED	LAB REQUIRED	CREDITS (SEMESTER/QUARTER)
BCP (biology-chemistry-physics) sciences				
Biology	✓		✓	2
Chemistry, general/inorganic	✓		✓	2
Chemistry, organic	✓		✓	2
Physics	✓		✓	2
Additional biological sciences				
Anatomy				
Biochemistry	✓			1
Cell biology				
Histology				
Immunology				
Microbiology		✓		

PREPARATION (CONTINUED)

PREREQUISITE COURSE	REQUIRED	RECOMMENDED	LAB REQUIRED	CREDITS (SEMESTER/QUARTER)
Molecular biology/genetics				
Physiology				
Zoology				
Other				
Statistics	✓			1
English	✓			2

Community college coursework accepted for prerequisites: Yes
Community college coursework accepted for electives: Yes
Limits on community college credit hours: No
Maximum number of community college credit hours: None
Advanced placement (AP) credit accepted for prerequisites: Yes
Advanced placement (AP) credit accepted for electives: Yes
Job shadowing: Recommended

DAT

Mandatory: Yes
Latest DAT for consideration of application: 11/01/2015
Oldest DAT considered: 11/01/2010
When more than one DAT score is reported: Highest score is considered
U.S. DAT accepted: No
Application considered before DAT scores are submitted: Yes

CANADIAN DAT: 2014 ENTERING CLASS

ENROLLEE DAT SCORES	MEAN	RANGE
Academic Average	NA	NA
Manual Dexterity	24.4	15–29
Perceptual Ability	21.6	17–28
Total Science	NA	NA

GPA: 2014 ENTERING CLASS

ENROLLEE GPA SCORES	UNDERGRAD. MEAN	GRADUATE MEAN	UNDERGRAD. RANGE	GRADUATE RANGE
Science GPA	NR	NR	NR	NR
Total GPA	3.90	NR	3.69–4.00	NR

APPLICATION AND SELECTION

TIMETABLE

Earliest filing date: 07/04/2015
Latest filing date: 11/01/2015
Earliest date for acceptance offers: 05/15/2016
Maximum time in days for applicant's response to acceptance offer: 14 days after receipt of the offer
Requests for deferred entrance considered: No
Fee for application: Yes, submitted only when requested
Amount of fee for application:
    In province: $115   Out of province: $115   International: $115
Fee waiver available: No

	FIRST DEPOSIT	SECOND DEPOSIT	THIRD DEPOSIT
Required to hold place	Yes	No	No
Resident amount	$1,000		
Nonresident amount	$1,000		
Deposit due	As indicated in admission offer		
Applied to tuition	Yes		
Refundable	No		

Note: Deposits are in Canadian dollars.

APPLICATION PROCESS

Participates in Associated American Dental Schools Application Service (AADSAS): No
Accepts direct applicants: Yes
Secondary or supplemental application required: No
Interview is mandatory: Yes
Interview is by invitation: Yes

RESIDENCY

In-state/in-province versus out-of-state/out-of-province
Admissions process distinguishes between in-state/in-province and out-of-state/out-of-province applicants: Yes
Preference given to residents of: Alberta
Reciprocity Admissions Agreement available for legal residents of: None
Generally and over time, percentage of your first-year enrollment that is in-state: 90%
Origin of out-of-state/out-of-province enrollees: NR

International
Applications are accepted from international (noncitizens/nonpermanent residents): Yes
Origin of international enrollees: NA

APPLICATION AND ENROLLMENT	NUMBER OF APPLICANTS	ESTIMATED NUMBER INTERVIEWED	ESTIMATED NUMBER ENROLLED
In-state or province applicants/enrollees	271	85	29
Out-of-state or province applicants/enrollees	155	20	3
International applicants/enrollees (noncitizens/nonpermanent residents)	5	1	0

DEMOGRAPHIC DESCRIPTIONS OF APPLICANTS: 2014 ENTERING CLASS

	APPLICANTS			ENROLLEES		
	M	W	Gender Unknown or Not Reported	M	W	Gender Unknown or Not Reported
American Indian or Alaska Native						
Asian						
Black or African American			Not applicable			
Hispanic or Latino						
Native Hawaiian or Other Pacific Islander						
White						
Two or more races						
Race and ethnicity unknown	212	214	0	20	12	
International	4	1	0			

	MINIMUM	MAXIMUM	MEAN
2014 entering class enrollees by age	20	26	23

CURRICULUM

The School of Medicine and Dentistry offers a four-year D.D.S. program, a two-year Advanced Placement Program for dentistry graduates of nonaccredited dental programs, a Dental Hygiene Diploma program, a Bachelor of Science (Dental Hygiene Specialization) degree and a Master of Science in Orthodontics (two-year program). The first and second years of the dental program are combined with the M.D. program. The curriculum is taught in blocks and covers such areas as infection; immunity and inflammation; endocrine system; cardiovascular, pulmonary and renal systems; gastroenterology and nutrition; musculoskeletal system; neurosciences; and oncology. In addition to bedside and operating instruction in medicine and surgery, junior and senior students are assigned to School of Dentistry dental clinic and University of Alberta Hospital.

Student research opportunities: Yes

SPECIAL PROGRAMS AND SERVICES

PREDENTAL
DAT workshops
Postbaccalaureate programs

DURING DENTAL SCHOOL
Academic counseling and tutoring
Community service opportunities
Internships, externships, or extramural programs
Mentoring
Personal counseling
Professional- and career-development programming
Training for those interested in academic careers

ACTIVE STUDENT ORGANIZATIONS
American Dental Education Association

INTERNATIONAL DENTISTS
Graduates of international dental schools considered for traditional predoctoral program: Yes
Advanced standing program offered for graduates of international dental schools: Yes

COMBINED AND ALTERNATE DEGREES

Ph.D.	M.S.	M.P.H.	M.D.	B.A./B.S.	Other
—	—	—	—	—	—

COSTS: 2014–15 SCHOOL YEAR

	FIRST YEAR	SECOND YEAR	THIRD YEAR	FOURTH YEAR
Tuition, resident	$21,781	$21,781	$21,781	$18,990
Tuition, nonresident	$21,781	$21,781	$21,781	$18,990
Tuition, other	$42,500	$42,500	$42,500	$37,500
Fees				
Instruments, books, and supplies	$8,882	$8,485	$11,035	$11,041
Estimated living expenses	$15,000	$15,000	$15,000	$15,000
Total, resident	$45,663	$45,266	$47,816	$45,031
Total, nonresident	$45,663	$45,266	$47,816	$45,031
Total, other	$66,382	$65,985	$68,535	$63,541

Note: All costs are in Canadian dollars.

FINANCIAL AID

For more information, please visit: https://www.su.ualberta.ca/services/financialaidoffice/

Faculty of Dentistry
The University of British Columbia
www.dentistry.ubc.ca

UNIVERSITY OF BRITISH COLUMBIA
FACULTY OF DENTISTRY

Charles F. Shuler, D.M.D., Ph.D., Dean

GENERAL INFORMATION

The University of British Columbia Faculty of Dentistry (UBC Dentistry) is an integral part of the Health Sciences Centre, which includes the faculties of Medicine and Pharmaceutical Sciences and the schools of Nursing, Rehabilitation, Medicine, Clinical Psychology, Family and Nutritional Sciences, and Social Work. Located on a 1,000-acre site on Point Grey Peninsula in western Vancouver, the university has an enrollment of 35,000 undergraduate students and 8,000 graduate students plus several thousand part-time, evening and continuing education students. UBC Dentistry offers a program leading to a D.M.D. Graduate programs in dental science at the master's and doctorate levels can be arranged, as well as clinical specialty programs in Endodontics, Orthodontics, Pediatric Dentistry, Periodontics, and Prosthodontics. A Bachelor of Dental Science in dental hygiene is offered.

MISSION
To advance oral health through outstanding education, research, and community service.

Type of institution: Public
Year opened: 1964
Term type: Semester
Time to degree in months: 40
Start month: August

Doctoral dental degree offered: D.M.D.
Targeted predoctoral enrollment: 48
Targeted entering class size: NR
Campus setting: Urban
Campus housing available: Yes

PREPARATION

Formal minimum preparation in semester/quarter hours: Semester: 90
Baccalaureate degree preferred: No
Number of first-year, first-time enrollees whose highest degree is:
    Baccalaureate: 46
    Master's degree and beyond: 1
Of first-year, first-time enrollees without baccalaureates, the number with:
    Equivalent of 60 undergraduate credit hours or less: NA
    Equivalent of 61–90 undergraduate credit hours: 1
    Equivalent of 91 or more undergraduate credit hours: 0

PREREQUISITE COURSE	REQUIRED	RECOMMENDED	LAB REQUIRED	CREDITS (SEMESTER/QUARTER)
BCP (biology-chemistry-physics) sciences				
Biology	✓		✓	6/10
Chemistry, general/inorganic	✓		✓	6/10
Chemistry, organic	✓		✓	6/10
Physics				
Additional biological sciences				
Anatomy				
Biochemistry	✓			6/10
Cell biology				
Histology				
Immunology				
Microbiology				
Molecular biology/genetics				
Physiology		✓		
Zoology				

CONTACT INFORMATION
www.dentistry.ubc.ca
Phone: 604-822-8063

ADMISSIONS
Ms. Vicki Koulouris
Manager, Admissions
2199 Wesbrook Mall
Vancouver, BC V6T 1Z3

AWARDS AND FINANCIAL AID OFFICE
1036-1874 East Mall Brock Hall
Vancouver, BC V6T 1Z1
Phone: 604-822-5111
www.students.ubc.ca/finance

STUDENT AFFAIRS
Mr. Brendan Farrell
Manager, Student Services
2199 Wesbrook Mall
Vancouver, BC V6T 1Z3

STUDENT HOUSING OFFICE
1874 East Mall Brock Hall
Vancouver, BC V6T 1Z1
Phone: 604-822-2811
www.housing.ubc.ca

INTERNATIONAL STUDENTS
www.dentistry.ubc.ca

PREPARATION (CONTINUED)

Community college coursework accepted for prerequisites: Yes
Community college coursework accepted for electives: Yes
Limits on community college credit hours: No
Maximum number of community college credit hours: 0
Advanced placement (AP) credit accepted for prerequisites: Yes
Advanced placement (AP) credit accepted for electives: Yes
Comments regarding AP credit: An AP transcript must be submitted
Job shadowing: Recommended
Other factors considered in admission: Multiple interviews and
   Problem-Based Learning (PBL) session

DAT

Mandatory: Yes
Latest DAT for consideration of application: 11/02/2013
Oldest DAT considered: 02/01/2009
When more than one DAT score is reported: Highest overall score is
   considered
U.S. DAT accepted: Yes
Application considered before DAT scores are submitted: Yes

CANADIAN DAT: 2014 ENTERING CLASS

ENROLLEE DAT SCORES	MEAN	RANGE
Academic Average	22.2	20–26
Manual Dexterity		
Perceptual Ability	22.2	19–27
Total Science	NA	NA

GPA: 2014 ENTERING CLASS

ENROLLEE GPA SCORES	MEAN	RANGE
Science GPA	NA	NA
Total GPA	4.00	3.70–4.33

APPLICATION AND SELECTION

TIMETABLE

Earliest filing date: 09/05/2013
Latest filing date: 10/18/2013
Earliest date for acceptance offers: 03/15/2014
Maximum time in days for applicant's response to acceptance offer: 15
Requests for deferred entrance considered: In exceptional
   circumstances only
Fee for application: Yes.
Amount of fee for application:
   In state/province: $208   Out of state/province: $208
   International: NR   Phase 2 Fee: $180
Fee waiver available: No

	FIRST DEPOSIT	SECOND DEPOSIT	THIRD DEPOSIT
Required to hold place	Yes	No	No
Resident amount	20% of total first-year fees		
Nonresident amount	NR		
Deposit due	As indicated in admission offer		
Applied to tuition	No		
Refundable	No		

Note: Nonrefundable deposit applied to first-year clinical fees

APPLICATION PROCESS

Participates in Associated American Dental Schools Application Service
   (AADSAS): No
Accepts direct applicants: Yes
Secondary or supplemental application required: Yes
Secondary or supplemental application website: www.dentistry.ubc.ca
Multiple interviews are mandatory: Yes
Multiple interviews are by invitation: Yes
PBL session is mandatory: Yes
PBL session is by invitation: Yes
Open House is mandatory: Yes
Open House is by invitation: Yes

RESIDENCY

In-state/in-province versus out-of-state/out-of-province
Admissions process distinguishes between in-state/in-province and
   out-of-state/out-of-province applicants: Yes
Preference given to residents of: British Columbia
Reciprocity Admissions Agreement available for legal residents of: None
Generally and over time, percentage of your first-year enrollment that is
   in-state: 90%
Origin of out-of-state/out-of-province enrollees: AL-1, ON-3

International
Applications are accepted from international (noncitizens/
   nonpermanent residents): No
Origin of international enrollees: NA

APPLICATION AND ENROLLMENT	NUMBER OF APPLICANTS	ESTIMATED NUMBER INTERVIEWED	ESTIMATED NUMBER ENROLLED
In-state or province applicants/ enrollees	NR	NR	NR
Out-of-state or province applicants/enrollees	NR	NR	NR
International applicants/enrollees (noncitizens/nonpermanent residents)	NR	NR	NR

DEMOGRAPHIC DESCRIPTIONS OF APPLICANTS: 2013 ENTERING CLASS

	APPLICANTS			ENROLLEES		
	M	W	Gender Unknown or Not Reported	M	W	Gender Unknown or Not Reported
American Indian or Alaska Native						
Asian						
Black or African American						
Hispanic or Latino						
Native Hawaiian or Other Pacific Islander			Not applicable			
White						
Two or more races						
Race and ethnicity unknown						
International						

	MINIMUM	MAXIMUM	MEAN
2014 entering class enrollees by age	NR	NR	NR

CURRICULUM

The objective of the academic program is to prepare dentists who are able to practice their profession with a high degree of technical skill and competence, based on a sound understanding of the fundamental principles of basic biological sciences that underlie the practice of dentistry, and who have acquired a deep insight into their social, professional and ethical responsibilities to the community at large. Students are given clinic exposure early in the program, and actual clinical instruction begins during the second half of the second year. The first two years are taken with students in the Faculty of Medicine and include a course—exclusively for dental students—that correlates biomedical sciences to clinical practice. Clinical and patient-management skills are developed through participation in integrated group practices of third- and fourth-year students managed by a faculty member.

Student research opportunities: Yes

SPECIAL PROGRAMS AND SERVICES

DURING DENTAL SCHOOL
Academic counseling and tutoring
Community service opportunities
Mentoring
Personal counseling
Professional- and career-development programming
Training for those interested in academic careers

INTERNATIONAL DENTISTS
Graduates of international dental schools considered for traditional predoctoral program: NR
Advanced standing program offered for graduates of international dental schools: Yes
Advanced standing program description: Program awarding a dental degree: Successful candidates are admitted via the International Dental Degree Completion Program (IDDCP) and receive the D.M.D. degree upon successful completion.

COMBINED AND ALTERNATE DEGREES

Ph.D.	M.S.	M.P.H.	M.D.	B.A./B.S.	Other
—	—	—	—	—	—

COSTS: 2014–15 SCHOOL YEAR

	FIRST YEAR	SECOND YEAR	THIRD YEAR	FOURTH YEAR
Tuition, resident	$17,066	$17,407	$17,755	$18,111
Tuition, nonresident	$17,066	$17,407	$17,755	$18,111
Tuition, other				
Fees	$32,503	$33,133	$34,308	$36,360
Instruments, books, and supplies	$6,643	$6,428	$3,482	$3,255
Estimated living expenses	$20,000	$20,000	$20,000	$20,000
Total, resident	$76,212	$76,968	$75,545	$77,726
Total, nonresident	$76,212	$76,968	$75,545	$77,726
Total, other				

Comments: Costs are in Canadian dollars.

FINANCIAL AID

Information on awards and financial aid may be obtained from Financial Assistance Enrolment Services Professionals:

Enrolment Services
2016-1874 East Mall
Vancouver, BC, V6T 1Z1
Email: es.medsupport@ubc.ca

http://www.dentistry.ubc.ca/dmd/dmd-financial-info/

UNIVERSITY OF MANITOBA
COLLEGE OF DENTISTRY

Anthony M. Iacopino, D.M.D., Ph.D., Dean

CONTACT INFORMATION

www.umanitoba.ca/dentistry
D113-780 Bannatyne Avenue
Winnipeg, MB R3E 0W2
Phone: 204-789-3631

ADMISSIONS OFFICE

424 University Centre
Winnipeg, MB R3T 2N2
Phone: 204-474-8825

FINANCIAL AID AND AWARDS

422 University Centre
Winnipeg, MB R3T 2N2
Phone: 204-474-8197
http://umanitoba.ca/student/fin_awards

STUDENT AFFAIRS

Ms. Susan Petras
Student Affairs Coordinator
D113 - 780 Bannatyne Avenue
Winnipeg, MB R3E 0W2
Phone: 204-789-3484

HOUSING AND STUDENT LIFE

106 Arthur V. Mauro Residence
Winnipeg, MB R3T 2N2
Phone: 204-474-7662
http://umanitoba.ca/student/housing

INTERNATIONAL DENTIST DEGREE PROGRAM/
ADMISSIONS AND RECRUITMENT

Ms. Jean Lyon
IDDP Coordinator/Admissions & Recruitment
D113 - 780 Bannatyne Avenue
Winnipeg, MB R3E 0W2
Phone: 204-977-5611
www.umanitoba.ca/faculties/dentistry/iddp

GENERAL INFORMATION

The College of Dentistry is dedicated to educating dental, dental hygiene and graduate students in a progressive learning environment; conducting research in oral health; and serving the community and the oral health professions as a source of knowledge and expertise. The faculty serves as a bridge between the profession's fundamental scientific foundation and its translation into health care for the public. Because dentists enhance and promote patients' total health through oral health management, our curriculum ensures that our students graduate as competent dentists prepared to meet the oral health care needs of their patients. It provides the knowledge of basic biomedical, behavioral and clinical sciences, and biomaterials; the cognitive and behavioral skills; and professional and ethical values necessary for practice as a dental professional.

Type of institution: Public
Year opened: 1958
Term type: Semester
Time to degree in months: 48
Start month: August

Doctoral dental degree offered: D.M.D.
Targeted predoctoral enrollment: 128
Targeted entering class size: 29
Campus setting: Urban
Campus housing available: No

PREPARATION

Formal minimum preparation in semester/quarter hours: Semester: 60   Quarter: 90
Baccalaureate degree preferred: No
Number of first-year, first-time enrollees whose highest degree is:
    Baccalaureate: 8
    Master's degree and beyond: NR
Of first-year, first-time enrollees without baccalaureates, the number with:
    Equivalent of 60 undergraduate credit hours or less: NR
    Equivalent of 61–90 undergraduate credit hours: NR
    Equivalent of 91 or more undergraduate credit hours: NR

PREREQUISITE COURSE	REQUIRED	RECOMMENDED	LAB REQUIRED	CREDITS (SEMESTER/QUARTER)
BCP (biology-chemistry-physics) sciences				
Biology	✓		✓	6/10
Chemistry, general/inorganic	✓		✓	6/10
Chemistry, organic	✓		✓	6/10
Physics	✓		✓	6/10
Additional biological sciences				
Anatomy				
Biochemistry	✓			6/10
Cell biology				
Histology				
Immunology				
Microbiology				
Molecular biology/genetics				
Physiology				
Zoology				
Other				
English	✓			
Humanities/Social sciences	✓			

PREPARATION (CONTINUED)

Community college coursework accepted for prerequisites: No
Community college coursework accepted for electives: No
Limits on community college credit hours: NA
Maximum number of community college credit hours: NA
Advanced placement (AP) credit accepted for prerequisites: Yes
Advanced placement (AP) credit accepted for electives: Yes
Comments regarding AP credit: Upon written submission at time of application, Advanced Placement/International Baccalaureate (AP/IB) courses can be used to fulfill core course requirements. However, AP/IB courses shall not be used to fulfill the minimum new credit hour requirement. (see III A.2 of Applicant Information Bulletin).
Job shadowing: Recommended

DAT

Mandatory: Yes
Latest DAT for consideration of application: November 2015
Oldest DAT considered: February 2013
When more than one DAT score is reported: Highest score is considered
U.S. DAT accepted: No
Application considered before DAT scores are submitted: No

CANADIAN DAT: 2014 ENTERING CLASS

ENROLLEE DAT SCORES	MEAN	RANGE
Academic Average	19.8	18–22
Manual Dexterity	26.3	21–29
Perceptual Ability	21.2	21–29
Total Science	19.8	18–22

GPA: 2014 ENTERING CLASS

ENROLLEE GPA SCORES	UNDERGRAD. MEAN	GRADUATE MEAN	UNDERGRAD. RANGE	GRADUATE RANGE
Science GPA	3.93	NR	3.60–4.35	NR
Total GPA	4.09	NR	3.88–4.41	NR

APPLICATION AND SELECTION

TIMETABLE

Earliest filing date: 11/15/2015
Latest filing date: 01/20/2016
Earliest date for acceptance offers: 06/30/2016
Maximum time in days for applicant's response to acceptance offer: 10
Requests for deferred entrance considered: In exceptional circumstances only
Fee for application: Yes, submitted with application (no Associated American Dental Schools Application Service [AADSAS]).
Amount of fee for application:
In state/province: $100   Out of state/province: $100
International: NA
Fee waiver available: No

	FIRST DEPOSIT	SECOND DEPOSIT	THIRD DEPOSIT
Required to hold place	Yes	No	No
Resident amount	$1,000		
Nonresident amount	$1,000		
Deposit due	As indicated in admission offer		
Applied to tuition	Yes		
Refundable	No		

Note: Deposits are in Canadian dollars.

APPLICATION PROCESS

Participates in AADSAS: No
Accepts direct applicants: Yes
Secondary or supplemental application required: Yes
Secondary or supplemental application website: www.umanitoba.ca/dentistry
Interview is mandatory: Yes
Interview is by invitation: Yes

RESIDENCY

In-state/in-province versus out-of-state/out-of-province
Admissions process distinguishes between in-state/in-province and out-of-state/out-of-province applicants: Yes
Preference given to residents of: Manitoba
Reciprocity Admissions Agreement available for legal residents of: Manitoba
Generally and over time, percentage of your first-year enrollment that is in-state: 90%
Origin of out-of-state/out-of-province enrollees: NR

International
Applications are accepted from international (noncitizens/nonpermanent residents): No
Origin of international enrollees: NA

APPLICATION AND ENROLLMENT	NUMBER OF APPLICANTS	ESTIMATED NUMBER INTERVIEWED	ESTIMATED NUMBER ENROLLED
In-state or province applicants/enrollees	105	67	28
Out-of-state or province applicants/enrollees	122	6	1
International applicants/enrollees (noncitizens/nonpermanent residents)	0	0	0

DEMOGRAPHIC DESCRIPTIONS OF APPLICANTS: 2014 ENTERING CLASS

	APPLICANTS			ENROLLEES		
	M	W	Gender Unknown or Not Reported	M	W	Gender Unknown or Not Reported
American Indian or Alaska Native						
Asian						
Black or African American						
Hispanic or Latino		Not applicable				
Native Hawaiian or Other Pacific Islander						
White						
Two or more races						
Race and ethnicity unknown						
International						

	MINIMUM	MAXIMUM	MEAN
2014 entering class enrollees by age		Not reported.	

CURRICULUM

The Doctor of Dental Medicine (D.M.D.) program is a fully accredited four-year program. Following a minimum of two years of prerequisite studies, students complete four years of intense study including extensive clinical experience. Upon successful completion of the National Dental Examining Board of Canada examination, graduates can apply for license to practice in all provinces of Canada; however, other jurisdictions, both in Canada and the United States, have additional licensing requirements. The D.M.D. degree provides the foundation for a variety of career pathways, including further training in dental specialties and research. Over the course of the curriculum, emphasis shifts from teaching to learning, from guided to independent performance, from gaining knowledge in the foundation sciences and skills in the labs to treating patients in a simulated-practice setting working with dental hygiene student partners.

Student research opportunities: Yes

SPECIAL PROGRAMS AND SERVICES

DURING DENTAL SCHOOL

Academic counseling and tutoring
Community service opportunities
Internships, externships, or extramural programs
Mentoring
Personal counseling
Professional- and career-development programming

ACTIVE STUDENT ORGANIZATIONS

American Dental Education Association

INTERNATIONAL DENTISTS

Graduates of international dental schools considered for traditional predoctoral program: No
Advanced standing program offered for graduates of international dental schools: Yes
Advanced standing program description: Program awarding a dental degree

COMBINED AND ALTERNATE DEGREES

Ph.D.	M.S.	M.P.H.	M.D.	B.A./B.S.	Other
—	—	—	—	✓	—

COSTS: 2014–15 SCHOOL YEAR

	FIRST YEAR	SECOND YEAR	THIRD YEAR	FOURTH YEAR
Tuition, resident	$19,692	$19,233	$19,233	$19,233
Tuition, nonresident	$19,692	$19,233	$19,233	$19,233
Tuition, other				
Fees	$797	$797	$797	$797
Instruments, books, and supplies	$18,476	$16,346	$7,512	$4,809
Estimated living expenses	$17,000	$17,000	$17,000	$17,000
Total, resident	$55,965	$53,376	$44,542	$41,839
Total, nonresident	$55,965	$53,376	$44,542	$41,839
Total, other				

Note: All costs are noted in Canadian dollars.

FINANCIAL AID

Students may apply for Canada Student Loans and Provincial Loans. Some university bursaries are available to students who have student loans.

For more information, please visit: www.umanitoba.ca/dentistry

DALHOUSIE UNIVERSITY
FACULTY OF DENTISTRY

Ronald A. Bannerman, D.D.S., M.Sc., M.Ed., Acting Dean

GENERAL INFORMATION

Dalhousie University, a comprehensive teaching and research institution, is Atlantic Canada's leading research university, recognized for strengths in health and ocean studies. Affiliated with teaching hospitals throughout the Maritime Provinces, Dalhousie University has a long tradition of excellence providing a solid foundation for a professional career. The Maritime Dental College became the Faculty of Dentistry of Dalhousie University in 1912, offering the Atlantic Provinces' only D.D.S. program. The program is offered in the modern dentistry buildings, which serve as the main clinical, didactic teaching and research facilities. Tuition and mandatory fees include a laptop computer, electronic textbook library and drug databases, related software and technical support, all clinical instruments, sterilization and clinic attire. Graduates are eligible for license in Canada, the United States and Australia.

MISSION

To promote and provide compassionate oral health care, an integral component of overall health, for regional, national and international communities through quality education, research and service.

Vision: To promote integrity, competence and compassion while providing evidence-based, ethical oral health care to all populations in collaboration with other health professions.

Core Values: The faculty must possess the high degree of ethics, idealism, intellectual integrity and enthusiasm. Students will become ethical, compassionate, caring, knowledgeable and skilled practitioners.

Type of institution: Public	Doctoral dental degree offered: D.D.S.
Year opened: 1908	Targeted predoctoral enrollment: 168
Term type: Semester	Targeted entering class size: 38
Time to degree in months: 36	Campus setting: Urban
Start month: August/September	Campus housing available: Yes

PREPARATION

Formal minimum preparation in semester/quarter hours: Semester: 10   Quarter: 0
Baccalaureate degree preferred: Yes
Number of first-year, first-time enrollees whose highest degree is:
    Baccalaureate: 34
    Master's degree and beyond: 0
Of first-year, first-time enrollees without baccalaureates, the number with:
    Equivalent of 60 undergraduate credit hours or less: 1
    Equivalent of 61–90 undergraduate credit hours: 1
    Equivalent of 91 or more undergraduate credit hours: 36

PREREQUISITE COURSE	REQUIRED	RECOMMENDED	LAB REQUIRED	CREDITS (SEMESTER/QUARTER)
BCP (biology-chemistry-physics) sciences				
Biology	✓		✓	8/12
Chemistry, general/inorganic	✓		✓	8/12
Chemistry, organic	✓		✓	8/12
Physics	✓		✓	8/12
Additional biological sciences				
Anatomy				
Biochemistry	✓			4/6
Cell biology				
Histology				

(Prerequisite Courses continued)

CONTACT INFORMATION

www.dentistry.dal.ca
Phone: 902-494-2274
Fax: 902-949-2527

ADMISSIONS

Dr. Ronald A. Bannerman
5981 University Avenue
Halifax, NS B3H 1W2
Phone: 902-494-2274

FINANCIAL AID

Dr. Ferne Kraglund
Assistant Dean
5981 University Avenue
Halifax, NS B3H 1W2
Phone: 902-494-2824

STUDENT AFFAIRS

Dr. Ferne Kraglund
Assistant Dean
5981 University Avenue
Halifax, NS B3H 1W2
Phone: 902-494-2824

MINORITY AFFAIRS/DIVERSITY

Dr. John Lovas
Assistant Dean
5981 University Avenue
Halifax, NS B3H 1W2
Phone: 902-494-2824

INTERNATIONAL STUDENTS

Dr. Ronald Bannerman/Dr. Ferne Kraglund
5981 University Avenue
Halifax, NS B3H 1W2
Phone: 902-494-2824

PREPARATION (CONTINUED)

PREREQUISITE COURSE	REQUIRED	RECOMMENDED	LAB REQUIRED	CREDITS (SEMESTER/QUARTER)
Immunology				
Microbiology	✓			4/6
Molecular biology/genetics				
Physiology	✓			4/6
Zoology				

Community college coursework accepted for prerequisites: No
Community college coursework accepted for electives: No
Limits on community college credit hours: Yes
Advanced placement (AP) credit accepted for prerequisites: Yes
Advanced placement (AP) credit accepted for electives: Yes
Job shadowing: Recommended
Number of hours of job shadowing required or recommended: 3

DAT

Mandatory: Yes
Latest DAT for consideration of application: 02/28/2015
Oldest DAT considered: 01/01/2013
When more than one DAT score is reported: Highest score is considered
U.S. DAT accepted: Yes
Application considered before DAT scores are submitted: Yes

CANADIAN DAT: 2014 ENTERING CLASS

ENROLLEE DAT SCORES	MEAN	RANGE
Academic Average	21.5	NR
Manual Dexterity		
Perceptual Ability	20.0	NR
Total Science	20.0	NR

GPA: 2014 ENTERING CLASS

ENROLLEE GPA SCORES	MEAN	RANGE
Science GPA	4.00	NR
Total GPA	3.80	NR

APPLICATION AND SELECTION

TIMETABLE

Filing dates: 12/01 (application form and fee);
              02/01 (supporting documents)
Earliest date for acceptance offers: 12/01
Maximum time in days for applicant's response to acceptance offer:
    30 days
Requests for deferred entrance considered: In exceptional
    circumstances only
Fee for application: Yes, submitted only when requested
Amount of fee for application:
    In state/province: $70   Out of state/province: $70
    International: $70
Fee waiver available: No

	FIRST DEPOSIT	SECOND DEPOSIT	THIRD DEPOSIT
Required to hold place	Yes	No	No
Resident amount	$200		
Nonresident amount	$2,500		
Deposit due	As indicated in admission offer		
Applied to tuition	Yes		
Refundable	No		

Note: Deposits are in Canadian dollars.

APPLICATION PROCESS

Participates in Associated American Dental Schools Application Service
    (AADSAS): Yes
Accepts direct applicants: Yes
Secondary or supplemental application required: No
Interview is mandatory: Yes
Interview is by invitation: Yes

RESIDENCY

In-state/in-province versus out-of-state/out-of-province
Admissions process distinguishes between in-state/in-province and
    out-of-state/out-of-province applicants: Yes
Preference given to residents of: Atlantic Provinces of Canada
Reciprocity Admissions Agreement available for legal residents of: None
Generally and over time, percentage of your first-year enrollment that is
    in-state: 75%
Origin of out-of-state/out-of-province enrollees: NR

International
Applications are accepted from international (noncitizens/
    nonpermanent residents): Yes
Origin of international enrollees: NR

APPLICATION AND ENROLLMENT	NUMBER OF APPLICANTS	ESTIMATED NUMBER INTERVIEWED	ESTIMATED NUMBER ENROLLED
In-state or province applicants/enrollees			
Out-of-state or province applicants/enrollees		Not reported	
International applicants/enrollees (noncitizens/nonpermanent residents)			

DEMOGRAPHIC DESCRIPTIONS OF APPLICANTS: 2013 ENTERING CLASS

		APPLICANTS			ENROLLEES	
	M	W	Gender Unknown or Not Reported	M	W	Gender Unknown or Not Reported
American Indian or Alaska Native						
Asian						
Black or African American						
Hispanic or Latino		Not applicable				
Native Hawaiian or Other Pacific Islander						
White						
Two or more races						
Race and ethnicity unknown						
International						

	MINIMUM	MAXIMUM	MEAN
2014 entering class enrollees by age	21	32	24

CURRICULUM

The Dalhousie University Faculty of Dentistry program features clinical experiences beginning in the first year of the program with instruction in digital radiography and electronic patient records.

The curriculum integrates the biological, behavioral and dental sciences with introduction to patient treatment starting the first year. This major emphasis on the biological and behavioral sciences as applied to clinical dentistry with basic foundation sciences continues in the third and fourth years at advanced level. Clinical patient treatment receives greater emphasis in the second year, with continued emphasis on integration of the biological and behavioral sciences. Students practice a total patient care philosophy in the third- and fourth-year clinic, within clinical-oriented disciplines. Students are provided with laptop computers in the first year of the program, and all textbooks are included in searchable electronic formats.

Student research opportunities: Yes

SPECIAL PROGRAMS AND SERVICES

DURING DENTAL SCHOOL

Academic counseling and tutoring: Contact Assistant Dean for Student Affairs to coordinate academic counseling and tutoring.
Internships, externships, or extramural programs: Senior electives, externships for senior students
Mentoring
Personal counseling: Available through Counseling Services, coordinated by Assistant Dean for Student Affairs
Training for those interested in academic careers

ACTIVE STUDENT ORGANIZATIONS

Dalhousie Dental Student Society, Dalhousie Student Union

INTERNATIONAL DENTISTS

Graduates of international dental schools considered for traditional predoctoral program: Yes
Advanced standing program offered for graduates of international dental schools: Dalhousie offers a 24-month D.D.S. Qualifying Program for graduates of international dental schools.

COMBINED AND ALTERNATE DEGREES

Ph.D.	M.S.	M.P.H.	M.D.	B.A./B.S.	Other
—	✓	—	✓	—	—

Note: M.S. in Periodontics; M.D./M.Sc. in Oral and Maxillofacial Surgery

COSTS: 2014–15 SCHOOL YEAR

	FIRST YEAR	SECOND YEAR	THIRD YEAR	FOURTH YEAR
Tuition, resident	$19,108	$19,108	$19,108	$19,108
Tuition, nonresident	$45,320	$45,320	$45,320	$45,320
Tuition, other				
Fees	$1,063	$1,063	$1,063	$1,063
Instruments, books, and supplies	$16,753	$13,972	$11,815	$11,410
Estimated living expenses	$12,000	$12,000	$12,000	$12,000
Total, resident	$48,923	$46,143	$43,986	$43,581
Total, nonresident	$75,136	$72,355	$70,198	$69,793
Total, other				

Comments: All monetary values in this profile are in Canadian dollars.

FINANCIAL AID

Students are eligible for government and provincial/state loans. Canadian citizens are eligible for a professional line of credit from major banks. U.S. citizens are eligible to apply for government loans in the same manner as those attending dentistry programs in the United States. The student loans officer at Dalhousie University provides individual counseling, advice and information to students in making loan applications and accessing funds.

Information about Financial Assistance at Dalhousie can be found at:

www.dal.ca/campus_life/student_services/academic-support/accessibility/financial-assistance.html

The Faculty of Dentistry Assistant Dean for Student Affairs is also available to assist students with financial aid concerns.

UNIVERSITY OF TORONTO
FACULTY OF DENTISTRY

Daniel Haas, D.D.S., Ph.D., Dean

GENERAL INFORMATION

The University of Toronto Faculty of Dentistry, the oldest dental school in Canada, is the country's leading research center for dentistry, offering state-of-the-art laboratory, technical and clinical facilities, including a computerized clinic management system, and an extensive dental library, equipped with a full-service information commons that enables the faculty to provide the best possible climate for teaching and research. In addition to a rich undergraduate tradition, the faculty offers comprehensive graduate educational opportunities and broadly based dental research opportunities. It is the only faculty in Canada to provide advanced clinical training in 10 dental specialty disciplines: dental anesthesia, dental public health, endodontics, oral pathology and oral pathology and medicine, oral radiology, orthodontics, oral and maxillofacial surgery and anesthesia, pediatric dentistry, periodontology and prosthodontics.

Type of institution: Public
Year opened: 1875
Term type: Semester
Time to degree in months: 48
Start month: September

Doctoral dental degree offered: D.D.S.
Targeted predoctoral enrollment: 343
Targeted entering class size: 83
Campus setting: Urban
Campus housing available: Yes

CONTACT INFORMATION
www.dentistry.utoronto.ca
124 Edward Street
Toronto, ON M5G 1G6
Phone: 416-979-4901

ADMISSIONS
124 Edward Street
Toronto, ON M5G 1G6
Phone: 416-979-4901
Email: admissions@dentistry.utoronto.ca

FINANCIAL AID
172 St. George Street
Toronto, ON M5R 0A3
Phone: 416-978-2190
http://www.adm.utoronto.ca/adm-awards/html/awards/mainawdpage.htm

STUDENT AFFAIRS
Ms. Margaret Edghill
Faculty Registrar
124 Edward Street
Toronto, ON M5G 1G6
Phone: 416-979-4901

HOUSING
214 College Street
Toronto, ON M5G 1G6
Phone: 416-978-8045
Email: housing.services@utoronto.ca
www.housing.utoronto.ca

PREPARATION

Formal minimum preparation in semester/quarter hours: Semester: 6   Quarter: 10
Baccalaureate degree preferred: No
Number of first-year, first-time enrollees whose highest degree is:
  Baccalaureate: 37
  Master's degree and beyond: 39
Of first-year, first-time enrollees without baccalaureates, the number with:
  Equivalent of 60 undergraduate credit hours or less: 0
  Equivalent of 61–90 undergraduate credit hours: 20
  Equivalent of 91 or more undergraduate credit hours: 0

PREREQUISITE COURSE	REQUIRED	RECOMMENDED	LAB REQUIRED	CREDITS (SEMESTER/QUARTER)
BCP (biology-chemistry-physics) sciences				
Biology	✓		✓	3/5
Chemistry, general/inorganic				
Chemistry, organic				
Physics		✓	✓	3/5
Additional biological sciences				
Anatomy				
Biochemistry	✓			
Cell biology	✓			
Histology				
Immunology				
Microbiology				
Molecular biology/genetics				
Physiology	✓			
Zoology				

Community college coursework accepted for prerequisites: No
Community college coursework accepted for electives: No
Limits on community college credit hours: Yes

PREPARATION (CONTINUED)

Maximum number of community college credit hours: NA
Advanced placement (AP) credit accepted for prerequisites: No
Advanced placement (AP) credit accepted for electives: No
Job shadowing: NA

DAT

Mandatory: Yes
Latest DAT for consideration of application: 11/30/2014
Oldest DAT considered: 01/01/2013
When more than one DAT score is reported: Highest total score is
    considered
U.S. DAT accepted: Yes, only from students living in or pursuing full-time
    studies at a U.S. educational institution
Application considered before DAT scores are submitted: No

CANADIAN DAT: 2014 ENTERING CLASS

ENROLLEE DAT SCORES	MEAN	RANGE
Academic Average	22.0	18–27
Manual Dexterity	NR	NR
Perceptual Ability	21.0	16–29
Total Science	NR	NR

GPA: 2014 ENTERING CLASS

ENROLLEE GPA SCORES	UNDERGRAD. MEAN	GRADUATE MEAN	UNDERGRAD. RANGE	GRADUATE RANGE
Science GPA	NR	NR	NR	NR
Total GPA	3.86	3.76	3.89–4.00	3.58–3.99

APPLICATION AND SELECTION

TIMETABLE

Earliest filing date: 08/01
Latest filing date: 12/01
Earliest date for acceptance offers: 05/01
Maximum time in days for applicant's response to acceptance offer:
    14 days
Requests for deferred entrance considered: In exceptional
    circumstances only
Fee for application: Yes
Amount of fee for application:
    In state/province: $250   Out of state/province: $250
    International: $250
Fee waiver available: No

	FIRST DEPOSIT	SECOND DEPOSIT	THIRD DEPOSIT
Required to hold place	Yes	Yes	No
Resident amount	$2,000	$2,000	
Nonresident amount	$2,000	$2,000	
Deposit due	As indicated in admission offer	As indicated in admission offer	
Applied to tuition	Yes	Yes	
Refundable	No	No	

Note: Deposits are in Canadian dollars.

APPLICATION PROCESS

Participates in Associated American Dental Schools Application Service
    (AADSAS): No
Accepts direct applicants: Yes
Secondary or supplemental application required: No
Interview is mandatory: Yes
Interview is by invitation: Yes

RESIDENCY

In-state/in-province versus out-of-state/out-of-province
Admissions process distinguishes between in-state/in-province and
    out-of-state/out-of-province applicants: Yes
Preference given to residents of: Ontario
Reciprocity Admissions Agreement available for legal residents of: None
Generally and over time, percentage of your first-year enrollment that is
    in-state: 90%
Origin of out-of-state/out-of-province enrollees: AB-4, BC-4, SK-1

International
Applications are accepted from international (noncitizens/
    nonpermanent residents): Yes
Origin of international enrollees: ZZ-1

APPLICATION AND ENROLLMENT	NUMBER OF APPLICANTS	ESTIMATED NUMBER INTERVIEWED	ESTIMATED NUMBER ENROLLED
In-state or province applicants/ enrollees	428	153	86
Out-of-state or province applicants/enrollees	110	19	9
International applicants/enrollees (noncitizens/nonpermanent residents)	2	1	1

DEMOGRAPHIC DESCRIPTIONS OF APPLICANTS: 2014 ENTERING CLASS

	APPLICANTS			ENROLLEES		
	M	W	Gender Unknown or Not Reported	M	W	Gender Unknown or Not Reported
American Indian or Alaska Native						
Asian						
Black or African American						
Hispanic or Latino			Not applicable			
Native Hawaiian or Other Pacific Islander						
White						
Two or more races						
Race and ethnicity unknown						
International						

	MINIMUM	MAXIMUM	MEAN
2014 entering class enrollees by age		Not reported.	

CURRICULUM

Dental education is designed to unify the basic and clinical sciences, as it is believed that scientific and professional development cannot be sharply differentiated but should proceed concurrently throughout the dental program.

Year 1: Basic sciences with introduction to dentally relevant material.

Year 2: Completion of basic sciences and greater emphasis on the study of dental disease and its prevention and treatment.

Year 3: Intensive clinical study of each of the dental disciplines with emphasis on the assessment and management of patients.

Year 4: Further clinical experience and familiarity with more advanced treatment services; emphasis upon integration of the various disciplines and overall management of patient treatment in preparation for general practice; participation in elective programs, clinical conferences and hospital-based experiences.

Student research opportunities: Yes

SPECIAL PROGRAMS AND SERVICES

DURING DENTAL SCHOOL

Internships, externships, or extramural programs
Mentoring
Personal counseling
Transfer applicants considered if space is available

INTERNATIONAL DENTISTS

Graduates of international dental schools considered for traditional predoctoral program: Yes
Advanced standing program offered for graduates of international dental schools: Yes
Advanced standing program description: Two-and-a-half-year program awarding a dental degree.

COMBINED AND ALTERNATE DEGREES

Ph.D.	M.S.	M.P.H.	M.D.	B.A./B.S.	Other
✓	—	—	—	—	✓

Other degree: M.Sc.

COSTS: 2014–15 SCHOOL YEAR

	FIRST YEAR	SECOND YEAR	THIRD YEAR	FOURTH YEAR
Tuition, resident	$33,910	$33,910	$33,270	$32,040
Tuition, nonresident	$68,870	$68,870	$68,870	$68,050
Tuition, other				
Fees	$1,216	$1,216	$1,216	$1,216
Instruments, books, and supplies	$8,077	$6,783	$3,989	$2,448
Estimated living expenses	NA	NA	NA	NA
Total, resident	$43,203	$41,909	$38,475	$35,704
Total, nonresident	$78,163	$76,869	$74,075	$71,714
Total, other				

Note: All costs are in Canadian dollars.

FINANCIAL AID

Funding opportunities are available through the Ontario Student Assistance Program or another Canadian provincial government financial aid program and through the University of Toronto where appropriate. In addition, banks can make a line of credit available to qualified students under the Professional Student Loan program. The University will provide a grant to cover interest on loans borrowed under this plan up to the level of the assessed unmet need. For further information, please contact the Student Services Office of the Faculty of Dentistry or visit the university's Student Financial Support website.

International students are not eligible for University of Toronto or government assistance.

For more information, please visit: http://www.dentistry.utoronto.ca/students/financial-assistance

WESTERN UNIVERSITY
SCHULICH SCHOOL OF MEDICINE & DENTISTRY

Richard Bohay, D.M.D., M.Sc., Interim Director

CONTACT INFORMATION

www.schulich.uwo.ca/dentistry

Dentistry Program
Schulich School of Medicine & Dentistry
London, ON N6A 5C1
Phone: 519-661-3330
Fax: 519-661-3875
Email: schulich.dentistry@schulich.uwo.ca

ADMISSIONS

Ms. Trish Ashbury
Admissions Coordinator
Schulich School of Medicine & Dentistry
Health Sciences Addition, Room H103
Western University
London, ON N6A 5C1
Phone: 519-661-3744
Fax: 519-519-850-2360
Email: admissions.dentistry@schulich.uwo.ca
www.schulich.uwo.ca/dentistry/future_students/
index.html

FINANCIAL AID

Western University
Western Student Services Building
Room 1100
London, ON N6A 5B8
Phone: 519-661-2100
Email: finaid@uwo.ca
www.registrar.uwo.ca/student_finances/index.html

LEARNER EQUITY AND WELLNESS

Schulich School of Medicine & Dentistry
Western University
London, ON N6A 5C1
Phone: 519-661-4234
Email: equitywellness@schulich.uwo.ca

EQUITY SERVICES

Western University
Somerville House
London, ON N6A 3K7
Phone: 519-661-3334

HOUSING

Western University
Division of Housing & Ancillary Services
Room 102, Elgin Hall
London, ON N6A 5B9
Phone: 519-661-3549
www.residenceatwestern.ca/

INTERNATIONALLY TRAINED DENTISTS PROGRAM

Dentistry Program
Schulich School of Medicine & Dentistry
Western University
London, ON N6A 5C1
Phone: 519-661-2111, ext. 89162
Email: ITD.Program@schulich.uwo.ca
www.schulich.uwo.ca/dentistry/future_students/
internationally_trained_dentists_program/index.
html

GENERAL INFORMATION

Schulich Dentistry enrolled its first students in 1966. In 1997 the Faculty of Dentistry merged with the Faculty of Medicine, and in 2005 the new faculty was renamed the Schulich School of Medicine & Dentistry thanks to a generous contribution to the two programs. Western is a publicly supported institution, chartered by the legislature of Ontario in 1878 as the Western University of London, changing its name to the current one in 1923. Western is one of Canada's oldest, largest and most beautiful universities, situated on an all-contained campus of 162 hectares of picturesque, park-like land in the north end of London, a city of 366,000. More than 26,500 students are enrolled in more than 300 programs offered by 17 faculties and professional schools.

MISSION

We will develop In dental professionals the knowledge and skills to provide exemplary care to the diverse communities that we serve.

Vision: We will influence the future of undergraduate and postgraduate dental education through scholarly inquiry, innovation and research.

Type of institution: Public	Doctoral dental degree offered: D.D.S.
Year opened: 1965	Targeted predoctoral enrollment: 264
Term type: Semester	Targeted entering class size: 56
Time to degree in months: 48	Campus setting: Urban
Start month: September	Campus housing available: Yes

PREPARATION

Formal minimum preparation in semester/quarter hours: Semester: 8
Baccalaureate degree required by all incoming students as of September 2012: Yes
Number of first-year, first-time enrollees whose highest degree is:
   Baccalaureate: 48
   Master's degree and beyond: 6
Of first-year, first-time enrollees without baccalaureates, the number with:
   Equivalent of 60 undergraduate credit hours or less: 0
   Equivalent of 61–90 undergraduate credit hours: 0
   Equivalent of 91 or more undergraduate credit hours: 0

PREREQUISITE COURSE	REQUIRED	RECOMMENDED	LAB REQUIRED	CREDITS (SEMESTER/QUARTER)
BCP (biology-chemistry-physics) sciences				
Biology		✓		
Chemistry, general/inorganic		✓		
Chemistry, organic	✓		✓	Minimum 1 semester
Physics		✓		
Additional biological sciences				
Anatomy				
Biochemistry	✓			Minimum 1 semester
Cell biology				
Histology				
Immunology				
Microbiology				
Molecular biology/genetics				

(Prerequisite Courses continued)

PREPARATION (CONTINUED)

PREREQUISITE COURSE	REQUIRED	RECOMMENDED	LAB REQUIRED	CREDITS (SEMESTER/QUARTER)
Physiology	✓			2 semesters
Zoology				

Community college coursework accepted for prerequisites: No
Community college coursework accepted for electives: No
Limits on community college credit hours: NA
Maximum number of community college credit hours: 0
Advanced placement (AP) credit accepted for prerequisites: Yes
Advanced placement (AP) credit accepted for electives: No
Comments regarding AP credit: AP credits are not assessed a grade, but if the material covered in the course is equivalent to an approved prerequisite course, the requirement is considered fulfilled. We do not have requirements for electives.
Job shadowing: Recommended
Number of hours of job shadowing required or recommended: 0

DAT

Mandatory: Yes
Latest DAT for consideration of application: 11/07/2015 (Canadian DAT)
Oldest DAT considered: 01/01/2014
When more than one DAT score is reported: Most recent score only is considered.
U.S. DAT accepted: Yes, only for internationals and Canadians living outside of Canada.
Application considered before DAT scores are submitted: No

CANADIAN DAT: 2014 ENTERING CLASS

ENROLLEE DAT SCORES	MEAN	RANGE
Academic Average	21.5	18–24
Manual Dexterity	NR	NR
Perceptual Ability	NR	NR
Reading Comprehension	22.0	18–26
Total Science	NR	NR

GPA: 2014 ENTERING CLASS

ENROLLEE GPA SCORES	UNDERGRAD. MEAN	GRADUATE MEAN	UNDERGRAD. RANGE	GRADUATE RANGE
Science GPA	NR	NR	NR	NR
Total GPA	89.50	NR	80.04–95.34	NR

APPLICATION AND SELECTION

TIMETABLE

Earliest filing date: 10/01/2015
Latest filing date: 12/01/2015
Earliest date for acceptance offers: 05/30/2016
Maximum time in days for applicant's response to acceptance offer: 10 business days after offer made
Requests for deferred entrance considered: In exceptional circumstances only
Fee for application: Yes, submitted only when requested
Amount of fee for application:
   In state/province: $250   Out of state/province: $250
   International: $250
Fee waiver available: No

	FIRST DEPOSIT	SECOND DEPOSIT	THIRD DEPOSIT
Required to hold place	Yes	No	No
Resident amount	$1,000		
Nonresident amount	$1,000		
Deposit due	As indicated in admission offer		
Applied to tuition	Yes		
Refundable	Portion		

Note: Deposits are in Canadian dollars.

APPLICATION PROCESS

Participates in Associated American Dental Schools Application Service (AADSAS): No
Accepts direct applicants: Yes
Secondary or supplemental application required: No
Interview is mandatory: Yes
Interview is by invitation: Yes

RESIDENCY

In-state/in-province versus out-of-state/out-of-province
Admissions process distinguishes between in-state/in-province and out-of-state/out-of-province applicants: No
Preference given to residents of: NA
Reciprocity Admissions Agreement available for legal residents of: None
Generally and over time, percentage of your first-year enrollment that is in-state: 92%
Origin of out-of-state/out-of-province enrollees: AB-1, BC-2, QC-1, SK-1

International
Applications are accepted from international (noncitizens/nonpermanent residents): Yes
Origin of international enrollees: Taiwan-1, United States-1

APPLICATION AND ENROLLMENT	NUMBER OF APPLICANTS	ESTIMATED NUMBER INTERVIEWED	ESTIMATED NUMBER ENROLLED
In-state or province applicants/enrollees	442	167	47
Out-of-state or province applicants/enrollees	136	26	5
International applicants/enrollees (noncitizens/nonpermanent residents)	7	3	2

DEMOGRAPHIC DESCRIPTIONS OF APPLICANTS: 2014 ENTERING CLASS

	APPLICANTS			ENROLLEES		
	M	W	Gender Unknown or Not Reported	M	W	Gender Unknown or Not Reported
American Indian or Alaska Native						
Asian						
Black or African American						
Hispanic or Latino			Not applicable			
Native Hawaiian or Other Pacific Islander						
White						
Two or more races						
Race and ethnicity unknown						
International						

	MINIMUM	MAXIMUM	MEAN
2014 entering class enrollees by age	23	38	24

CURRICULUM

The four-year D.D.S. program is designed to graduate dentists who possess the knowledge and skill to conduct a superior general practice and also sufficient knowledge of basic and applied science to permit and stimulate professional and intellectual growth. Rapid advances in science, medicine and technology; an accelerated pace in the delivery of information; and the importance of knowledge in meeting today's health care needs continue to change how Western approaches dental education.

Year 1: Basic medical/dental sciences with introduction to clinical situations.

Year 2: Basic medical/dental sciences plus courses that are clinically focused in preparation for third year in the dental clinic and in hospital electives; start of delivery of dental services to selected patients.

Years 3 and 4: Basic dental sciences together with lectures and rotations in clinical disciplines; delivery of comprehensive dental care to patients in a clinical setting.

Student research opportunities: Yes

SPECIAL PROGRAMS AND SERVICES

PREDENTAL
Postbaccalaureate programs

DURING DENTAL SCHOOL
Academic counseling and tutoring
Community service opportunities
Internships, externships, or extramural programs
Mentoring
Personal counseling
Professional- and career-development programming
Training for those interested in academic careers
Transfer applicants, into second year, considered if space is available

ACTIVE STUDENT ORGANIZATIONS

Canadian Dental Association
Ontario Dental Association
University of Western Ontario Dental Students Society

INTERNATIONAL DENTISTS

Graduates of international dental schools considered for traditional predoctoral program: Yes
Advanced standing program offered for graduates of international dental schools: Yes
Advanced standing program description: Program awarding a dental degree

COMBINED AND ALTERNATE DEGREES

Ph.D.	M.S.	M.P.H.	M.D.	B.A./B.S.	Other
—	✓	—	✓	—	✓

Other degree: Oral and Maxillofacial Surgery degree program, which when completed, allows the candidate to have both an M.Sc. and an M.D. degree.

COSTS: 2014–15 SCHOOL YEAR

	FIRST YEAR	SECOND YEAR	THIRD YEAR	FOURTH YEAR
Tuition, Canadian resident	$32,308	$32,308	$31,696	$30,521
Tuition, international	$60,337	$58,103	$55,951	$53,879
Fees, resident	$12,847	$13,297	$3,922	$1,922
Fees, international	$13,495	$13,945	$4,570	$2,570
Instruments, books, and supplies	$1,700	$1,700	$1,700	$1,700
Estimated living expenses	$16,000	$16,000	$16,000	$16,000
Total, Canadian resident	$62,855	$63,305	$53,318	$50,143
Total, international	$91,532	$89,748	$78,221	$74,149

Note: All costs are in Canadian dollars.

FINANCIAL AID

FINANCIAL AID AWARDS TO FIRST-YEAR STUDENTS 2014–15

Total number of first-year recipients: 9
Percentage of the first-year class: 17%
Percentage of awards that are grants? 9%
Percentage of awards that are loans? 0%

	AVERAGE AWARDS	RANGE OF AWARDS
Residents	$5,100	$600–$10,000
Nonresidents	Not applicable	

Note: Numbers based on scholarships (bursaries excluded).

For more information, please visit: www.registrar.uwo.ca

CONTACT INFORMATION

www.mcgill.ca/dentistry

2001 McGill College Avenue, Suite 500
Montreal, QC H3A 1G1
Phone: 514-398-7203
Fax: 514-398-8900

ADMISSIONS

2001 McGill College Avenue, Room 545B
Montreal, QC H3A 1G1
Phone: 514-398-7203 ext. 00063
www.mcgill.ca/dentistry/prospective

FINANCIAL AID

3600 McTavish Street, Suite 3200
Montreal, QC H3A 0G3
Phone: 514-398-6015
www.mcgill.ca/studentaid

STUDENT AFFAIRS

Student Affairs Office
Phone: 514-398-7203

HOUSING

3473 University Street
Montreal, QC H3A 2A8
Phone: 514-398-6368
www.mcgill.ca/students/housing

McGILL UNIVERSITY
FACULTY OF DENTISTRY

Paul J. Allison, B.D.S., Ph.D., Dean

GENERAL INFORMATION

The Faculty of Dentistry at McGill University is committed to taking a leadership role in preparing Canada's future dentists to care for the oral health of all segments of society. For the first time in the Faculty's history, all preclinical and clinical training, as well as clinical and community-based research will be brought together under one roof. Working within the latest modern clinical facilities and learning spaces, students and researchers will have the opportunity to collaborate even more closely. During the first 18 months of the program, basic and applied sciences are taught in conjunction with the Faculty of Medicine. Students then complete seven months of intense preclinical training followed by two years of clinical training in the Undergraduate Teaching Clinic.

MISSION

Commitment to the promotion of oral health and quality of life in the whole population, with emphasis on the needs of underserved communities and individuals.

Vision: The Faculty of Dentistry, McGill University, envisions a healthy and equitable society.

Core Values: Commitment to:

- Patients and community
- Excellence and innovation
- Educating and nurturing
- Increased knowledge
- Service and outreach
- Improved well-being
- Leadership in education, research and policy

Type of institution: Public	Doctoral dental degree offered: D.M.D.
Year opened: 1821	Targeted predoctoral enrollment: 145
Term type: Semester	Targeted entering class size: 38
Time to degree in months: 48	Campus setting: Urban
Start month: August	Campus housing available: Yes

PREPARATION

Formal minimum preparation in semester/quarter hours: Semester: 8   Quarter: 8
Baccalaureate degree preferred: No
Number of first-year, first-time enrollees whose highest degree is:
  Baccalaureate: 24
  Master's degree and beyond: 4
Of first-year, first-time enrollees without baccalaureates, the number with:
  Equivalent of 60 undergraduate credit hours or less: 10
  Equivalent of 61–90 undergraduate credit hours: 0
  Equivalent of 91 or more undergraduate credit hours: 0

PREREQUISITE COURSE	REQUIRED	RECOMMENDED	LAB REQUIRED	CREDITS (SEMESTER/QUARTER)
BCP (biology-chemistry-physics) sciences				
Biology	✓		✓	
Chemistry, general/inorganic	✓		✓	
Chemistry, organic	✓		✓	
Physics	✓		✓	
Additional biological sciences				
Anatomy		✓		
Biochemistry		✓		
Cell biology		✓		

PREPARATION (CONTINUED)

PREREQUISITE COURSE	REQUIRED	RECOMMENDED	LAB REQUIRED	CREDITS (SEMESTER/QUARTER)
Histology		✓		
Immunology		✓		
Microbiology		✓		
Molecular biology/genetics		✓		
Physiology		✓		
Zoology		✓		
Other				
Genetics		✓		
Statistics		✓		

Community college coursework accepted for prerequisites: No
Community college coursework accepted for electives: Yes
Limits on community college credit hours: Yes
Maximum number of community college credit hours: 60
Advanced placement (AP) credit accepted for prerequisites: Yes
Advanced placement (AP) credit accepted for electives: No
Comments regarding AP credit: Required scores of 5 (extremely well-qualified) or 4 (well-qualified)
Job shadowing: Recommended
Number of hours of job shadowing required or recommended: None specified

DAT

Mandatory: No longer required
Latest DAT for consideration of application: NA
Oldest DAT considered: NA
When more than one DAT score is reported: NA
U.S. DAT accepted: NA
Application considered before DAT scores are submitted: NA

CANADIAN DAT: 2014 ENTERING CLASS

ENROLLEE DAT SCORES	MEAN	RANGE
Academic Average	NR	NR
Manual Dexterity	NR	NR
Perceptual Ability	NR	NR
Total Science	NR	NR

GPA: 2014 ENTERING CLASS

ENROLLEE GPA SCORES	UNDERGRAD. MEAN	GRADUATE MEAN	UNDERGRAD. RANGE	GRADUATE RANGE
Science GPA	NR	NR	NR	NR
Total GPA	3.82	NR	3.63–4.00	NR

APPLICATION AND SELECTION

TIMETABLE

Earliest filing date: 09/01/2015
Latest filing date: 11/01/2015
Earliest date for acceptance offers: 04/01/2015
Maximum time in days for applicant's response to acceptance offer: 14
Requests for deferred entrance considered: In exceptional circumstances only
Fee for application: Yes, submitted at same time as Associated American Dental Schools Application Service (AADSAS) application

Amount of fee for application:
In state/province: $102.20   Out of state/province: $102.20
International: $102.20
Fee waiver available: No

	FIRST DEPOSIT	SECOND DEPOSIT	THIRD DEPOSIT
Required to hold place	Yes	No	No
Resident amount	$500		
Nonresident amount	$500		
Deposit due	As indicated in admission offer		
Applied to tuition	Yes		
Refundable	Yes		
Refundable by	50% refundable up to 6/15		

Note: Deposits are in Canadian dollars.

APPLICATION PROCESS

Participates in Associated American Dental Schools Application Service (AADSAS): No
Accepts direct applicants: No
Secondary or supplemental application required: No
Interview is mandatory: Yes
Interview is by invitation: Yes

RESIDENCY

In-state/in-province versus out-of-state/out-of-province
Admissions process distinguishes between in-state/in-province and out-of-state/out-of-province applicants: Yes
Preference given to residents of: Quebec
Reciprocity Admissions Agreement available for legal residents of: None
Generally and over time, percentage of your first-year enrollment that is in-state: 70%
Origin of out-of-state/out-of-province enrollees: BC-1, ON-6

International
Applications are accepted from international (noncitizens/ nonpermanent residents): Yes
Origin of international enrollees: NA

APPLICATION AND ENROLLMENT	NUMBER OF APPLICANTS	ESTIMATED NUMBER INTERVIEWED	ESTIMATED NUMBER ENROLLED
In-state or province applicants/enrollees	144	42	31
Out-of-state or province applicants/enrollees	223	30	7
International applicants/enrollees (noncitizens/nonpermanent residents)	46	0	0

DEMOGRAPHIC DESCRIPTIONS OF APPLICANTS: 2014 ENTERING CLASS

	APPLICANTS			ENROLLEES		
	M	W	Gender Unknown or Not Reported	M	W	Gender Unknown or Not Reported
American Indian or Alaska Native	0	0	1	0	0	0
Asian						
Black or African American						
Hispanic or Latino			Not applicable			
Native Hawaiian or Other Pacific Islander						
White						
Two or more races						
Race and ethnicity unknown	0	0	366	10	28	0
International	0	0	46	0	0	0

	MINIMUM	MAXIMUM	MEAN
2014 entering class enrollees by age	20	35	23

CURRICULUM

The Faculty of Dentistry is dedicated to the concept that graduates from a dental school should have reasonable competence to begin practice as general practitioners, regardless of what their future aspirations may be. They should develop the understanding and competence both to cope with the dental diseases they will encounter and to apply the preventive and treatment measures of the present and those predicted for the future. Basic sciences in the dental curriculum are taught in the Faculty of Medicine. Introduction to clinical experience begins in the first year, and the integration of basic sciences into clinical dentistry, in the second year. Students are evaluated on the basis of daily progress and end-of-term examinations.

Student research opportunities: Yes

SPECIAL PROGRAMS AND SERVICES

PREDENTAL
Postbaccalaureate programs

DURING DENTAL SCHOOL
Academic counseling and tutoring
Community service opportunities
Internships, externships, or extramural programs
Mentoring
Personal counseling
Professional- and career-development programming
Transfer applicants considered if space is available

ACTIVE STUDENT ORGANIZATIONS
American Dental Education Association

INTERNATIONAL DENTISTS
Graduates of international dental schools considered for traditional predoctoral program: Yes
Advanced standing program offered for graduates of international dental schools: Yes
Advanced standing program description: Program awarding a dental degree

COMBINED AND ALTERNATE DEGREES

Ph.D.	M.S.	M.P.H.	M.D.	B.A./B.S.	Other
—	—	—	—	—	—

COSTS: 2014–15 SCHOOL YEAR

	FIRST YEAR	SECOND YEAR	THIRD YEAR	FOURTH YEAR
Tuition, resident	$4,849	$4,433	$4,016	$2,803
Tuition, nonresident	$14,167	$12,950	$11,732	$8,190
Tuition, other	$37,688	$34,267	$31,125	$21,985
Fees	$6,627	$6,627	$6,587	$6,587
Instruments, books, and supplies	$399	$18,908	$5,939	$4,744
Estimated living expenses	$15,000	$15,000	$15,000	$15,000
Total, resident	$26,875	$44,968	$31,542	$29,134
Total, nonresident	$36,193	$53,485	$39,258	$34,521
Total, other	$59,714	$74,802	$58,651	$48,316

Comments: Costs are indicated in Canadian dollars.

FINANCIAL AID

For more information, please visit: http://www.mcgill.ca/studentaid/scholarships-aid/future-undergrads

UNIVERSITÉ DE MONTRÉAL
FACULTÉ DE MÉDECINE DENTAIRE

Gilles Lavigne, D.M.D., M.Sc., Ph.D., Dean

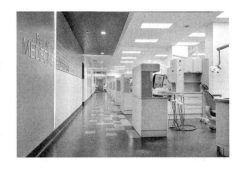

CONTACT INFORMATION

www.medent.umontreal.ca
C.P. 6128, succursale Centre-ville
Montréal, QC H3C 3J7
Phone: 514-343-6111, ext. 3437
Fax: 514-343-2233

ADMISSIONS

M. Claude-André Dupras
C.P. 6128, succursale Centre-ville
Montréal, QC H3C 3J7
Phone: 514-343-7076
Email: claude-andre.dupras@umontreal.ca
www.futursetudiants.umontreal.ca/admission/
demande

FINANCIAL AID

Mme Sylviane Latour
Aide financière
2332 Edouard-Montpetit
Montréal, QC H3C 3J7
Phone: 514-343-3399
Email: sylviane.latour@umontreal.ca
www.baf.umontreal.ca

STUDENT AFFAIRS

Dr. Annie St-Georges
Associate Dean for Undergraduate Studies and Students Affairs
C.P. 6128, succursale Centre-ville
Montréal, QC H3C 3J7
Phone: 514-343-5761
www.medent.umontreal.ca

HOUSING

Mme Lyne Mckay
2350 Edouard-Montpetit
Montréal, QC H3C 3J7
Phone: 514-343-7697

GENERAL INFORMATION

The Faculté de Médecine Dentaire of the Université de Montréal (UdeM FMD) was founded in 1904. UdeM FMD, one of the two francophone dental schools in North America, is publicly funded by the Province of Québec. The faculty is located in the main building of the university and occupies the first, second and fifth floors of the east wing. The teaching facilities allow up to 90 students to be admitted. Graduate programs include orthodontics, pediatric dentistry, dental sciences and a one-year multidisciplinary residency program. We also have a one-year multidisciplinary residency program. There are joint postgraduate programs in biomedical sciences (M.Sc. and Ph.D.) with the Faculté de Médecine.

MISSION

To contribute to the development of knowledge and best practices in dentistry and to promote the oral health of populations in Quebec and elsewhere.

Core Values: Commitment to following the highest national and international standards.

Type of institution: Public	Doctoral dental degree offered: D.M.D.
Year opened: 1904	Targeted predoctoral enrollment: 90
Term type: Trimester (yearly promotion)	Targeted entering class size: 89
Time to degree in months: 58	Campus setting: Urban
Start month: August	Campus housing available: Yes

PREPARATION

Formal minimum preparation: Candidates must have completed CEGEP (college degree) or equivalent.
Baccalaureate degree preferred: No
Number of first-year, first-time enrollees whose highest degree is:
  Baccalaureate: 48
  Master's degree and beyond: 0
Of first-year, first-time enrollees without baccalaureates, the number with:
  Equivalent of 60 undergraduate credit hours or less: 41
  Equivalent of 61–90 undergraduate credit hours: 0
  Equivalent of 91 or more undergraduate credit hours: 0

PREREQUISITE COURSE	REQUIRED	RECOMMENDED	LAB REQUIRED	CREDITS (SEMESTER/QUARTER)
BCP (biology-chemistry-physics) sciences				
Biology	301 and 401		✓	6
Chemistry, general/inorganic	101		✓	3
Chemistry, organic	201 and 202		✓	6
Physics	101, 201, and 301		✓	9
Additional biological sciences				
Anatomy				
Biochemistry				
Cell biology				
Histology				
Immunology				
Microbiology				
Molecular biology/genetics				
Physiology				

(Prerequisite Courses continued)

PREPARATION (CONTINUED)

PREREQUISITE COURSE	REQUIRED	RECOMMENDED	LAB REQUIRED	CREDITS (SEMESTER/QUARTER)
Zoology				
Other				
Mathematics	103 and 203			

Community college coursework accepted for prerequisites: Yes
Community college coursework accepted for electives: No
Limits on community college credit hours: No
Maximum number of community college credit hours: No
Advanced placement (AP) credit accepted for prerequisites: No
Advanced placement (AP) credit accepted for electives: No
Comments regarding AP credit: No
Job shadowing: No
Number of hours of job shadowing required or recommended: None
Other factors considered in admission: Motivation letter and Canadian DAT

DAT

Mandatory: Yes
Latest DAT for consideration of application: 01/15/2015
Oldest DAT considered: If the candidate obtains satisfactory marks, s/he does not have to retake the test. When more than one DAT mark is reported, the highest mark will apply.
U.S. DAT accepted: No
Application considered before DAT scores are submitted: No

CANADIAN DAT: 2014 ENTERING CLASS

ENROLLEE DAT SCORES	MEAN	RANGE
Academic Average	NR	NR
Manual Dexterity	NR	NR
Perceptual Ability	NR	NR
Total Science	NR	NR

GPA: 2014 ENTERING CLASS

ENROLLEE GPA SCORES	UNDERGRAD. MEAN	GRADUATE MEAN	UNDERGRAD. RANGE	GRADUATE RANGE
Science GPA	NR	NR	NR	NR
Total GPA	NR	NR	NR	NR

APPLICATION AND SELECTION

TIMETABLE

Earliest filing date: 12/01/2014
Latest filing date: 03/01/2015 for college applicants only; 02/01/2015 for all other categories of applicants
Earliest date for acceptance offers: 05/01/2015
Maximum time in days for applicant's response to acceptance offer: 30
Requests for deferred entrance considered: No
Fee for application: Yes, submitted only when requested
Amount of fee for application:
    In state/province: $85 Out of state/province: $85 International: NA
Fee waiver available: NR

	FIRST DEPOSIT	SECOND DEPOSIT	THIRD DEPOSIT
Required to hold place	Yes	No	No
Resident amount	$200		
Nonresident amount	NA		
Deposit due	As indicated in admission offer		
Applied to tuition	Yes, if the candidate enters a program at UdeM		
Refundable	No		

Note: Costs are in Canadian dollars

APPLICATION PROCESS

Participates in Associated American Dental Schools Application Service (AADSAS): No
Accepts direct applicants: Yes
Secondary or supplemental application required: No
Interview is mandatory: No
Interview is by invitation: Yes

RESIDENCY

In-state/in-province versus out-of-state/out-of-province
Admissions process distinguishes between in-state/in-province and out-of-state/out-of-province applicants: Yes
Preference given to residents of: Quebec
Reciprocity Admissions Agreement available for legal residents of: None
Generally and over time, percentage of your first-year enrollment that is in-state: 94%
Origin of out-of-state/out-of-province enrollees: NB-4, ON-1

International
Applications are accepted from international (noncitizens/nonpermanent residents): Yes for graduate studies only
Origin of international enrollees: NA

APPLICATION AND ENROLLMENT	NUMBER OF APPLICANTS	ESTIMATED NUMBER INTERVIEWED	ESTIMATED NUMBER ENROLLED
In-state or province applicants/enrollees	711	NR	84
Out-of-state or province applicants/enrollees	51	NR	5
International applicants/enrollees (noncitizens/nonpermanent residents)	0	0	0

DEMOGRAPHIC DESCRIPTIONS OF APPLICANTS: 2014 ENTERING CLASS

	APPLICANTS			ENROLLEES		
	M	W	Gender Unknown or Not Reported	M	W	Gender Unknown or Not Reported
Total	290	472	0	26	63	0
American Indian or Alaska Native						
Asian						
Black or African American						
Hispanic or Latino			Not applicable			
Native Hawaiian or Other Pacific Islander						
White						
Two or more races						
Race and ethnicity unknown						
International						

	MINIMUM	MAXIMUM	MEAN
2014 entering class enrollees by age	18	26	21

CURRICULUM

Training in the basic sciences and preclinical disciplines is emphasized in the first two years of the program. Clinical training starts during the second semester of the second year. Optional clinical courses are offered during the last year of the program. In addition to traditional clinical training such as implantology, periodontics/endodontics and constructive dentistry, off-campus activities in student exchange programs, clinical activities in international cooperation humanitarian projects and off-campus clinics are available. Student performance is evaluated qualitatively and quantitatively throughout the entire clinical program.

Student research opportunities: Yes

SPECIAL PROGRAMS AND SERVICES

PREDENTAL
Summer enrichment programs

DURING DENTAL SCHOOL
Academic counseling and tutoring
Community service opportunities
Personal counseling
Training for those interested in academic careers

ACTIVE STUDENT ORGANIZATIONS
Association des étudiants en médecine dentaire de l'Université de Montréal (AEMDUM)
Canadian Student Dental Association

INTERNATIONAL DENTISTS
Graduates of international dental schools considered for traditional predoctoral program: No (they can be admitted during the second year of the D.M.D. program)
Advanced standing program offered for graduates of international dental schools: No

COMBINED AND ALTERNATE DEGREES

Ph.D.	M.S.	M.P.H.	M.D.	B.A./B.S.	Other
—	—	—	—	—	✓

Other degrees:
M.Sc. in dentistry (Pediatric Dentistry or Orthodontics) combined with a postgraduate clinical program In Pediatric Dentistry or Orthodontics.
M.Sc. in dental sciences, and a one-year multidisciplinary residency program.

COSTS: 2014–15 SCHOOL YEAR

	FIRST YEAR	SECOND YEAR	THIRD YEAR	FOURTH YEAR
Tuition, resident (from Quebec)	$2,955	$3,069	$4,622	$3,107
Tuition, nonresident (from other Canadian provinces)	$8,621	$8,953	$13,485	$9,064
Tuition, other				
Fees	$1,447	$1,447	$4,388	$3,999
Instruments, books, and supplies	$12,380	$8,439	$3,822	$700
Estimated living expenses	$17,000	$15,000	$15,000	$15,000
Total, resident (from Quebec)	$33,782	$27,955	$27,832	$22,806
Total, nonresident (from other Canadian provinces)	$39,448	$33,839	$36,695	$28763

Note: Costs are in Canadian dollars.

FINANCIAL AID

For more information, please visit: www.fmd.umontreal.ca

UNIVERSITÉ LAVAL
FACULTÉ DE MÉDECINE DENTAIRE

André Fournier, D.M.D., Dean

www.fmd.ulaval.ca

fmd@fmd.ulaval.ca
Pavillon de Médecine dentaire
2420, rue de la Terrasse, bureau 1615
Québec, QC, Canada G1V 0A6
Phone: 418-656-7532
Fax: 418-656-2720

ADMISSIONS

Dr. Denis Robert
Chairman, Admission Committee
Pavillon de Médecine dentaire
2420, rue de la Terrasse
Québec, QC, Canada G1V 0A6
Phone: 418-656-2095
denis.robert@fmd.ulaval.ca
www.reg.ulaval.ca

FINANCIAL AID

Pavillon Alphonse-Desjardins
2325, rue de l'Université, bureau 2546
Québec, QC, Canada G1V 0A6
Phone: 418-656-3332
www.bbaf.ulaval.ca

STUDENT AFFAIRS

Dr. Cathia Bergeron
Vice Dean, Academic Affairs
Pavillon de Médecine dentaire
2420, rue de la Terrasse
Québec, QC, Canada G1V 0A6
Phone: 418-656-2131, ext. 2741
cathia.bergeron@fmd.ulaval.ca
www.aide.ulaval.ca

MINORITY AFFAIRS/DIVERSITY

Pavillon Alphonse-Desjardins
Bureau 2344
Québec, QC, Canada G1V 0A6
Phone: 418-656-2765
www.bve.ulaval.ca

HOUSING

Pavillon Alphonse-Marie Parent
2255, rue de l'Université, bureau 1604
Québec, QC, Canada G1V 0A7
Phone: 418-656-2921
www.residences.ulaval.ca

INTERNATIONAL STUDENTS

Maison Eugène-Roberge
2325, rue des Arts
Québec, QC, Canada, G1V 0A6
Phone: 418-656-3994
www.bi.ulaval.ca

GENERAL INFORMATION

The Faculty of Dental Medicine was founded in 1969 and accepted its first students in 1971. All teaching is done in the French language. The faculty occupies permanent quarters suitable for the training of 48 students for each of the four years of the program. A maximum of 54 students per year can be accommodated with the present facilities. The faculty also offers advanced dental education programs: master's degrees in Dental Sciences, Oral and Maxillofacial Surgery, Periodontics, Geriatric Dentistry and a one-year residency program in general dentistry.

MISSION

To educate highly skilled dentists with social awareness, to contribute to knowledge development by articulating fundamental and clinical research, and to actively promote oral health.

Vision: To be a model in educating dentists recognized for their professional and social consciousness through unique integration of research, teaching and service to the community.

Core Values: Excellence, Respect, Integrity, Professionalism, Compassion

Type of institution: State-related	Doctoral dental degree offered: D.M.D.
Year opened: 1971	Targeted predoctoral enrollment: 192
Term type: Trimester	Targeted entering class size: 48
Time to degree in months: 48	Campus setting: Urban
Start month: September	Campus housing available: Yes

PREPARATION

Formal minimum preparation in semester/quarter hours: Semester: 4
Baccalaureate degree preferred: No
Number of first-year, first-time enrollees whose highest degree is:
    Baccalaureate: 1
    Master's degree and beyond: 0
Of first-year, first-time enrollees without baccalaureates, the number with:
    Equivalent of 60 undergraduate credit hours or less: 18
    Equivalent of 61–90 undergraduate credit hours: 19
    Equivalent of 91 or more undergraduate credit hours: 10

PREREQUISITE COURSE	REQUIRED	RECOMMENDED	LAB REQUIRED	CREDITS (SEMESTER/QUARTER)
BCP (biology-chemistry-physics) sciences				
Biology	✓		✓	6
Chemistry, general/inorganic	✓		✓	6
Chemistry, organic	✓			3
Physics	✓		✓	9
Additional biological sciences				
Anatomy				
Biochemistry				
Cell biology				
Histology				
Immunology				
Microbiology				
Molecular biology/genetics				
Physiology		✓		
Zoology				

PREPARATION (CONTINUED)

Community college coursework accepted for prerequisites: Yes
Community college coursework accepted for electives: Yes, dental hygiene
Limits on community college credit hours: Yes
Maximum number of community college credit hours: 1
Advanced placement (AP) credit accepted for prerequisites: No
Advanced placement (AP) credit accepted for electives: No
Comments regarding AP credit: Not available in Québec
Job shadowing: Not required
Number of hours of job shadowing required or recommended: Not required

DAT

Mandatory: Yes
Latest DAT for consideration of application: February 2016
Oldest DAT considered: February 2011
When more than one DAT score is reported: Latest score is considered
U.S. DAT accepted: No
Application considered before DAT scores are submitted: No

CANADIAN DAT: 2014 ENTERING CLASS

ENROLLEE DAT SCORES	MEAN	RANGE
Academic Average	NR	NR
Manual Dexterity	NR	NR
Perceptual Ability	18.5	NR
Total Science	NR	NR

GPA: 2014 ENTERING CLASS

ENROLLEE GPA SCORES	UNDERGRAD. MEAN	GRADUATE MEAN	UNDERGRAD. RANGE	GRADUATE RANGE
Science GPA	NR	NR	NR	NR
Total GPA	NR	NR	NR	NR

APPLICATION AND SELECTION

TIMETABLE

Filing date: 03/01/2016
Earliest date for acceptance offers: NR
Maximum time in days for applicant's response to acceptance offer: 10 working days
Requests for deferred entrance considered: No
Fee for application: Yes, submitted only when requested.
Amount of fee for application:
In state/province: $78.50 Out of state/province: $78.50
International: NR
Fee waiver available: No

	FIRST DEPOSIT	SECOND DEPOSIT	THIRD DEPOSIT
Required to hold place	No	No	No
Resident amount	NA		
Nonresident amount	NA		
Deposit due	As indicated in admission offer		
Applied to tuition	Yes		
Refundable	No		

APPLICATION PROCESS

Participates in Associated American Dental Schools Application Service (AADSAS): No
Accepts direct applicants: Yes
Secondary or supplemental application required: No
Interview is mandatory: Yes
Interview is by invitation: Yes

RESIDENCY

In-state/in-province versus out-of-state/out-of-province
Admissions process distinguishes between in-state/in-province and out-of-state/out-of-province applicants: Yes
Preference given to residents of: New Brunswick, Ontario, Quebec
Reciprocity Admissions Agreement available for legal residents of: NR
Generally and over time, percentage of your first-year enrollment that is in-state: 98%
Origin of out-of-state/out-of-province enrollees: NA

International
Applications are accepted from international (noncitizens/nonpermanent residents): No
Origin of international enrollees: NA

APPLICATION AND ENROLLMENT	NUMBER OF APPLICANTS	ESTIMATED NUMBER INTERVIEWED	ESTIMATED NUMBER ENROLLED
In-state or province applicants/enrollees	600	207	48
Out-of-state or province applicants/enrollees	26	2	0
International applicants/enrollees (noncitizens/nonpermanent residents)	15	0	0

DEMOGRAPHIC DESCRIPTIONS OF APPLICANTS: 2014 ENTERING CLASS

	APPLICANTS			ENROLLEES		
	M	W	Gender Unknown or Not Reported	M	W	Gender Unknown or Not Reported
American Indian or Alaska Native						
Asian						
Black or African American						
Hispanic or Latino			Not applicable			
Native Hawaiian or Other Pacific Islander						
White						
Two or more races						
Race and ethnicity unknown						
International						

	MINIMUM	MAXIMUM	MEAN
2014 entering class enrollees by age	18	30	21

CURRICULUM

The program is designed to give its graduates a thorough grounding in the basic sciences and broad clinical experience. Basic health sciences are taught in an integrated health science complex. Preclinical and clinical subjects are under the direct control of dental school personnel. The first two years of the program are devoted to the basic and preclinical sciences. The last two years are devoted almost entirely to clinical work.

Student research opportunities: Yes

SPECIAL PROGRAMS AND SERVICES

ACTIVE STUDENT ORGANIZATIONS

American Association for Dental Research National Student Research Group
American Dental Education Association

INTERNATIONAL DENTISTS

Graduates of international dental schools considered for traditional predoctoral program: No
Advanced standing program offered for graduates of international dental schools: No
Advanced standing program description: Certificate and dental degree programs, and continuing education courses

COMBINED AND ALTERNATE DEGREES

Ph.D.	M.S.	M.P.H.	M.D.	B.A./B.S.	Other
—	✓	—	—	—	—

COSTS: 2014–15 SCHOOL YEAR

	FIRST YEAR	SECOND YEAR	THIRD YEAR	FOURTH YEAR
Tuition, resident	$3,258	$3,258	$3,713	$3,334
Tuition, nonresident	$6,247	$6,247	$7,119	$6,393
Tuition, other				
Fees (included in tuition)	$602	$602	$602	$602
Instruments, books, and supplies	$9,277	$8,456	$4,300	$285
Estimated living expenses	NR	NR	NR	NR
Total, resident	$13,137	$12,316	$8,615	$4,221
Total, nonresident	$16,127	$15,306	$12,021	$7,280
Total, other				

Note: All amounts are in Canadian dollars.

FINANCIAL AID

The school does not have a financial aid program, but students may apply for financial assistance from the Quebec government.

For more information, please visit: http://www2.ulaval.ca/en/future-students/education-costs-and-financing.html

UNIVERSITY OF SASKATCHEWAN
COLLEGE OF DENTISTRY

Gerry Uswak, D.M.D., M.P.H., Dean

GENERAL INFORMATION

The University of Saskatchewan College of Dentistry (U of S COD) is a dynamic college with a reputation for excellence in both teaching and research. By providing students with a well-balanced dental education, we produce graduates who are adaptable to rapid change and competitive with their peers around the world. The university enrolls more than 19,000 students; U of S COD currently enrolls 112. We value the diversity of our university community, the people, their points of view and the contributions they make to our scholarly endeavors. Our preclinical teaching area includes a state-of-the-art clinical simulation facility where students learn basic procedures in a clinical setting with current techniques in infection control, fiber optic technology and intraoral television.

MISSION

To educate dentists to provide high-quality oral health care to the people of Saskatchewan and to advance clinical and scientific knowledge through research.

Type of institution: Public
Year opened: 1965
Term type: Semester
Time to degree in months: 35
Start month: August

Doctoral dental degree offered: D.M.D.
Targeted predoctoral enrollment: 112
Targeted entering class size: 28
Campus setting: Urban
Campus housing available: Yes

PREPARATION

Formal minimum preparation in semester/quarter hours: Semester: 90   Quarter: NR
Baccalaureate degree preferred: Not required
Number of first-year, first-time enrollees whose highest degree is:
   Baccalaureate: 11
   Master's degree and beyond: 0
Of first-year, first-time enrollees without baccalaureates, the number with:
   Equivalent of 60 undergraduate credit hours or less: 4
   Equivalent of 61–90 undergraduate credit hours: 5
   Equivalent of 91 or more undergraduate credit hours: 9

PREREQUISITE COURSE	REQUIRED	RECOMMENDED	LAB REQUIRED	CREDITS (SEMESTER/QUARTER)
BCP (biology-chemistry-physics) sciences				
Biology	✓		✓	6
Chemistry, general/inorganic	✓		✓	3
Chemistry, organic	✓		✓	3
Physics	✓		✓	6
Additional biological sciences				
Anatomy				
Biochemistry	✓			6
Cell biology				
Histology				
Immunology				
Microbiology				
Molecular biology/genetics				
Physiology	✓			6
Zoology				

(Prerequisite Courses continued)

CONTACT INFORMATION

www.usask.ca/dentistry
Room 331, Dental Clinic
105 Wiggins Road
Saskatoon, SK S7N 5E4
Phone: 306-966-5121
Fax: 306-966-5132

OFFICE OF STUDENT SERVICES

Ms. Kelly Mulligan
Director of Academic and Student Affairs
Room 310, Dental Clinic
105 Wiggins Road
Saskatoon, SK S7N5E4
Phone: 306-966-2760

HOUSING

Phone: 306-966-6775
http://explore.usask.ca/housing

PREPARATION (CONTINUED)

PREREQUISITE COURSE	REQUIRED	RECOMMENDED	LAB REQUIRED	CREDITS (SEMESTER/QUARTER)
Other				
Social Science/Humanities	✓			6

Community college coursework accepted for prerequisites: Yes
Community college coursework accepted for electives: Yes
Limits on community college credit hours: Yes
Maximum number of community college credit hours: 30
Advanced placement (AP) credit accepted for prerequisites: Yes
Advanced placement (AP) credit accepted for electives: No
Job shadowing: We do not require or recommend job shadowing.

DAT

Mandatory: Yes
Latest DAT for consideration of application: 11/2014
Oldest DAT considered: 02/2012
When more than one DAT score is reported: Highest score is considered
U.S. DAT accepted: Yes, but students must write the Canadian DAT by November of the year in which they are accepted.
Application considered before DAT scores are submitted: Yes

CANADIAN DAT: 2014 ENTERING CLASS

ENROLLEE DAT SCORES	MEAN	RANGE
Academic Average	19.9	17–26
Manual Dexterity	NA	NA
Perceptual Ability	19.6	15–26
Total Science	NA	NA

GPA: 2014 ENTERING CLASS

ENROLLEE GPA SCORES	UNDERGRAD. MEAN	GRADUATE MEAN	UNDERGRAD. RANGE	GRADUATE RANGE
Science GPA	NR	NR	NR	NR
Total GPA	90.66	NR	82.30–96.25	NR

APPLICATION AND SELECTION

TIMETABLE

Earliest filing date: 08/01/2014
Latest filing date: 12/01/2014
Earliest date for acceptance offers: 03/23/2015
Maximum time in days for applicant's response to acceptance offer: Five (5) working days
Requests for deferred entrance considered: Yes
Fee for application: Yes, submitted with online application
Amount of fee for application:
    In state: $170   Out of state: $170   International: $170
Fee waiver available: No

	FIRST DEPOSIT	SECOND DEPOSIT	THIRD DEPOSIT
Required to hold place	Yes	No	No
Resident amount	$4,944*		
Nonresident amount	$4,944*		
Deposit due	As indicated in admission offer		
Applied to tuition	Yes		
Refundable	No		

*15% of tuition

APPLICATION PROCESS

Participates in Associated American Dental Schools Application Service (AADSAS): No
Accepts direct applicants: Yes
Secondary or supplemental application required: No
Interview is mandatory: Yes
Interview is by invitation: Yes

RESIDENCY

In-state/in-province versus out-of-state/out-of-province
Admissions process distinguishes between in-state/in-province and out-of-state/out-of-province applicants: Yes
Preference given to residents of: Saskatchewan
Reciprocity Admissions Agreement available for legal residents of: None
Generally and over time, percentage of your first-year enrollment that is in-state: 79%
Origin of out-of-state/out-of-province enrollees: AB-4, BC-1, ON-3

International
Applications are accepted from international (noncitizens/nonpermanent residents): Yes
Origin of international enrollees: NA

APPLICATION AND ENROLLMENT	NUMBER OF APPLICANTS	ESTIMATED NUMBER INTERVIEWED	ESTIMATED NUMBER ENROLLED
In-state or province applicants/enrollees	113	56	21
Out-of-state or province applicants/enrollees	287	23	8
International applicants/enrollees (noncitizens/nonpermanent residents)	0	0	0

DEMOGRAPHIC DESCRIPTIONS OF APPLICANTS: 2014 ENTERING CLASS

	APPLICANTS			ENROLLEES		
	M	W	Gender Unknown or Not Reported	M	W	Gender Unknown or Not Reported
American Indian or Alaska Native						
Asian						
Black or African American						
Hispanic or Latino		Not applicable				
Native Hawaiian or Other Pacific Islander						
White						
Two or more races						
Race and ethnicity unknown						
International						

	MINIMUM	MAXIMUM	MEAN
2014 entering class enrollees by age	19	32	23

CURRICULUM

The program (August to May) is four years in length. There are no course/ program offerings during the summer session. The curriculum is structured on a diagonal pattern: The earlier years are heavily weighted with the basic sciences, but some dental sciences are taken in each year. The balance gradually shifts to the dental sciences so that the program is devoted almost entirely to the dental sciences after the end of the second year. Positive efforts are made at all levels to closely integrate the basic and dental sciences and the theoretical and applied aspects of the dental curriculum.

Student research opportunities: Yes

SPECIAL PROGRAMS AND SERVICES

PREDENTAL
Postbaccalaureate programs: Advanced Dental Education Clinical 1-year (Hospital Dental)

DURING DENTAL SCHOOL
Community service opportunities: Outreach opportunities

ACTIVE STUDENT ORGANIZATIONS
Saskatchewan Dental Students' Society

INTERNATIONAL DENTISTS
Graduates of international dental schools considered for traditional predoctoral program: Yes
Advanced standing program offered for graduates of international dental schools: No

COMBINED AND ALTERNATE DEGREES

Ph.D.	M.S.	M.P.H.	M.D.	B.A./B.S.	Other
—	—	—	—	—	—

COSTS: 2014–15 SCHOOL YEAR

	FIRST YEAR	SECOND YEAR	THIRD YEAR	FOURTH YEAR
Tuition, resident	$32,960	$32,960	$32,960	$32,960
Tuition, nonresident	$32,960	$32,960	$32,960	$32,960
Tuition, other				
Fees	$896	$896	$896	$896
Instruments, books, and supplies	$8,752	$7,391	$2,240	$1,095
Estimated living expenses	$7,200	$7,200	$7,200	$7,200
Total, resident	$49,808	$48,447	$43,296	$42,151
Total, nonresident	$49,808	$48,447	$43,296	$42,151
Total, other				

Note: All costs are in Canadian dollars.

FINANCIAL AID

For scholarship information, please visit http://students.usask.ca/money/ scholarships.php.

FINANCIAL AID AWARDS TO FIRST-YEAR STUDENTS 2014–15

Total number of first-year recipients: 2
Percentage of the first-year class: 6%
Percentage of awards that are grants? 100%
Percentage of awards that are loans? 0%

	AVERAGE AWARDS	RANGE OF AWARDS
Residents	$750	$500–$1,000
Nonresidents	$750	$500–$1,000

For more information, please visit: http://www.usask.ca/dentistry/

1 University

6 colleges

Kirksville College of Osteopathic Medicine

School of Osteopathic Medicine in Arizona

Arizona School of Health Sciences

College of Graduate Health Studies

Arizona School of Dentistry & Oral Health

Missouri School of Dentistry & Oral Health

atsu.edu/learn

First in whole person healthcare

Our idea of night life.

At the end of the day, a fulfilling and rewarding career encompasses more than providing dental services. Indian Health Service (IHS) Division of Oral Health (DOH) dental health professionals deliver comprehensive care to an appreciative patient population within culturally diverse American Indian and Alaska Native communities nationwide.

IHS dentists enjoy an integrated, interdisciplinary team environment working within a collegial atmosphere. Combined with opportunities to be part of a rich, cultural tradition, you'll also enjoy a structured, but flexible work schedule and have ample opportunity for recreational pursuits, all while living and working within some of the most beautiful areas of the country.

Professionally fulfilling and personally enriching — explore a world of opportunities in Indian health dental careers at **www.ihs.gov/dentistry**.

Opportunity. Adventure. Purpose.

 IHS DIVISION OF ORAL HEALTH

 Indian Health Service
Dental Careers